Administering Internet Information Server 4

Mitch Tulloch, MCI, MCSE

McGraw-Hill
New York San Francisco Washington, D.C
Auckland Bogotá Caracas Lisbon London
Madrid Mexico City Milan Montreal New Delhi
San Juan Singapore Sydney Tokyo Toronto

Library of Congress Cataloging-in-Publication Data

Tulloch, Mitch.
Administering IIS 4 / Mitch Tulloch.
p. 2 cm.
Includes index.
ISBN 0-07-065536-7
1. Internet (Computer network)—Computer programs. 2. Microsoft
I. Title.
TK5105.875.I57T85 1998
005.7'13769—dc21 98—3868
CIP

McGraw-Hill
A Division of The ***McGraw-Hill*** *Companies*

2 3 4 5 6 7 8 9 0 DOC/DOC 9 0 3 2 1 0 9 8

ISBN 0-07-065536-7

The sponsoring editor for this book was Michael Sprague, the editing supervisor was Ruth Mannino, and the production supervisor was Claire Stanley. It was set in Vendome ICG by Don Feldman of McGraw-Hill's Desktop Publishing Unit in cooperation with Spring Point Publishing Services.

Printed and bound by R. R. Donnelley & Sons Company.

This book is printed on recycled, acid-free paper containing a minimum of 50% recycled, de-inked fiber.

Information contained in this work has been obtained by The McGraw-Hill Companies, Inc.("McGraw-Hill") from sources believed to be reliable. While the author has made every attempt to be accurate in covering the details of administering Internet Information Server 4.0 and related products mentioned in this book, neither McGraw-Hill nor the author assumes liability or responsibility for any loss or damage arising from the information presented in this book. In other words, the information provided in this book is presented on an "as is" basis.

Additionally, administrators contemplating upgrading to IIS 4.0 should be aware that the initial release of any software product nowadays inevitably contains bugs and problems. Before upgrading your servers to IIS 4.0, make sure that you familiarize yourself completely with the product, perform a test upgrade, and back up all important files and site content. Be sure to check the Microsoft Web site, Microsoft public newsgroups, and TechNet on an on-going basis for information about service packs, patches, bug-fixes, and upgrades.

Finally, any similarity between the fictitious company names (e.g., NewCorp Inc., MyCorp Inc., BigCorp Inc., etc.) and their associated domain names (e.g., newcorpinc.com) with real companies is purely coincidental and is not intended to promote, endorse, or refer to such existing companies.

Dedicated to my wife Ingrid.

CONTENTS

PREFACE

In December of 1997 Microsoft released the *Windows NT 4.0 Option Pack,* a set of tools and enhancements primarily intended for Microsoft's Windows NT 4.0 Server operating system. Included in the Option Pack is version 4.0 of Microsoft's award-winning WWW server, *Internet Information Server 4.0* (*IIS 4.0*). Packed with enhancements, new services, and a completely new administration interface, IIS 4.0 is the platform of choice for system and network administrators planning on implementing corporate intranets and extranets, for Internet Service Providers hosting commercial web services, and for programmers developing complex Web-based applications.

Who Should Read This Book?

IIS 4 is intended for network and system administrators who need to learn quickly how to install, configure, and administer IIS 4.0 in their networking environment. In today's fast-paced corporate world with consolidation and downsizing taking place everywhere, administrators are often expected to do more with less, work longer hours, and take on new responsibilities. They have less time to become familiar with the array of new products and upgrades flooding the market; yet learning is an essential part of their job as administrative duties expand to include developing and maintaining intranets, extranets, and various forms of Internet connectivity.

Although you try to keep abreast of Internet developments by learning HTML, PERL, and SSL, your job is made even harder by the fact that the Internet itself keeps evolving, making it necessary for you to acquire new skills such as writing Active Server Pages (ASPs), VBScript and JavaScript, Dynamic HTML, ActiveX and Java, ODBC database connectivity, channels, streaming audio and video, and Internet telephony and fax gateways.

Who can keep up with such a rapid pace of development?—certainly not the overworked network administrator! Web servers, which started out as a welcome diversion from the mundane tasks of network tuning and maintenance, server upgrades and desktop support, have now turned into what some believe is the "next great thing," which others believe is a sinkhole of time, energy, money, and network bandwidth. Two years ago, setting up and maintaining a Web server was fun; now it's often overwhelming because of the high expectations of management.

This book is intended to bring some relief to your daily pressures. Rather than trying to cover everything for everyone, the focus is primarily on how to *quickly* get IIS 4.0 and related tools installed, configured, and running on your network—in other words, how to *manage* and *administer* IIS 4.0 servers within your organization. A *task-oriented* approach is used, with numerous *walkthroughs* emphasizing a *hands-on* approach for learning necessary skills. No previous familiarity with Web servers or earlier versions of IIS is assumed, although this is certainly helpful.

Administering IIS 4 will also be of use to anyone who needs or wants to learn how to configure and use IIS 4.0. MIS managers, Internet Service Providers, network consultants and system integrators, hobbyists, and M.C.S.E.-track students will all benefit from this book's approach. Whether you have set up an IIS server before or not, this book will provide you with the skills and knowledge essential to set up an IIS-based intranet or extranet, administer clients and content-development tools, impart essential skills and knowledge to users, and generally get things up and running as quickly and as painlessly as possible.

An audience for which this book is *not* primarily intended is developers of advanced Web-based applications. Active Server Pages and Microsoft Transaction Server demand a book all to themselves, for the field of Web-application development is rapidly becoming a separate discipline, requiring a knowledge of Windows architecture, ODBC, ActiveX, and high-level programming languages such as C++. Network and system administrators usually do not have the time for such things; their primary concern is supporting and maintaining the essential network infrastructure that supports all network applications (and putting out fires). Writing scripts to perform basic administrative tasks is one thing; high-level programming and distributed application development is another thing entirely.

Thus, information on advanced Web-based application development using tools like Active Server Pages and Microsoft Transaction Server is discussed in Chap. 15 of this book but only briefly and at an introductory level. Knowledge of these tools is not required for performing most basic administrative tasks on IS 4.0, but the information is included to provide an introduction to these tools and what they can do. Serious

Web-application developers will need to consult other sources for more information on using these advanced tools.

What Does This Book Cover?

This book covers three basic areas of system and network administration as it relates to implementing intranets, extranets, and Internet connectivity:

1. *Administering servers.* Covered in detail in this book are the core components relating to Internet Information Server 4.0 that are included in the Windows NT 4.0 Option Pack:

- Components of Internet Information Server 4.0: WWW service, FTP service, SMTP service, and NNTP service
- Microsoft Index Server 2.0
- Microsoft Certificate Server 1.0
- Microsoft Site Server Express 2.0

Microsoft Transaction Server is covered but only briefly. Essential TCP/IP and DNS concepts are covered in the appendices.

2. *Administering clients.* Administering Internet Explorer 4.01 using the Internet Explorer Administration Kit (IEAK) is covered. This tool is not included in the Windows NT 4.0 Option Pack but can be downloaded from the Microsoft Web site, and is a valuable tool for network administrators planning on installing or upgrading client machines to Internet Explorer 4.0.

3. *Administering content developers.* Microsoft FrontPage 98 is covered as a standard tool for introductory- and intermediate-level content developers to use for building Intranet and Web sites. Various methods for publishing Web content is explored, including the Microsoft Web Posting Acceptor and the Microsoft Web Publishing Wizard included with Site Server Express.

Analyzing Web site integrity and reporting on site usage using Site Server Express are covered for administrators who need a fast way of generating the paperwork that management often requires.

Simple Web-database connectivity is briefly covered using Access 97 to create an Active Server Pages Web application for dynamically publishing a database to a Web site. For many purposes this will be sufficient, but advanced Web-based application developers will want to consider such other tools as Microsoft Visual InterDev and Microsoft SQL Server which are not covered in this book.

Developing Web applications with Active Server Pages is introduced briefly using examples. Devleopers who want to learn more about ASPs will need to consult other reference materials.

Features of This Book

Some of the features that make this book useful for administrators, both as a guide for setting up and configuring Internet Information Server 4.0 and as a reference guide for administering and troubleshooting purposes, are:

- *Walkthroughs.* Many of the book's chapters include step-by-step walkthroughs that readers can use as a starting point for gaining hands-on experience with the product. These walkthroughs can easily be customized for your particular network configuration.
- *Task-based section titles.* Section titles usually indicate the administrative task which the section covers, e.g., *configuring WWW logging, creating virtual servers, forcing a scan on a virtual directory, installing Site Server Express, etc.*
- *Screen shots.* Numerous screen shots complement the text, making the book useful for learning both at the console and away from it.
- *For more info.* At the end of each chapter sources of additional information are suggested, including the Microsoft Web site, newsgroups, list servers, magazine articles, and TechNet.

Overview of Chapters

Chapter 1 looks at the various components included in the Windows NT 4.0 Option Pack; the system requirements for installation; installation modes; clean, upgrade, and unattended installations; and a walkthrough of a clean installation on a fresh system. Also included is a checklist for administrators planning on implementing IIS 4.0 in a corporate environment.

Chapter 2 provides an overview of the new Microsoft Management Console (MMC), a Windows NT administrative tool that provides the core framework for managing Internet Information Server, Index Server, and other related BackOffice services. The MMC will be an integral part of the Windows NT 5.0 administrative management system. Also covered in this chapter are HTML-based administration of IIS, and the Windows Scripting Host.

Chapter 3 examines the WWW service configuration options available to administrators; accessing these options through property sheets; and configuring settings at the Master, site, directory and file level. Also included is a basic introduction to the HyperText Transfer Protocol, including both HTTP is 1.0 and the new HTTP 1.1 supported by IIS 4.0.

Chapter 4 looks at the various ways a Web site can be secured, including excluding IP addresses and domains, configuring authentication methods, setting IIS and NTFS permissions, disabling unnecessary services, auditing, security policies, and so on. SSL security is covered in Chap. 12.

Chapter 5 covers creating configuring and deleting virtual servers; creating and configuring virtual directories for local and remote content; and understanding host headers.

Chapter 6 examines establishing policies and procedures for developing Web site content; selecting tools for Web content development; administering and using FrontPage 98 and Microsoft Office 97 for Web content development; and publishing dynamic Web content from an Access database using Access 97.

Chapter 7 looks at implementing Internet Explorer 4.01 as client software; configuring IE 4.01 security options; and using the Internet Explorer Administration Kit to create custom installation packages for administration-based installations of IE 4.01.

Chapter 8 examines managing site indexing using Index Server 2.0; remote administration of Index Server using Web browsers; understanding how Index Server works; creating query pages; and a walkthrough of indexing a virtual server.

Chapter 9 explains the FTP session, configuration of FTP settings using property sheets, and FTP security issues; and gives a walkthrough of creating and connecting to an FTP site.

Chapter 10 looks at monitoring IIS performance using Windows NT Performance Monitor and other Windows NT administrative tools; and techniques for tuning and optimizing performance of IIS servers.

Chapter 11 covers visualizing site integrity with Content Analyzer; importing IIS log files using Usage Import; generating site usage reports using Report Writer; and publishing Web content using Posting Acceptor and the Web Publishing Wizard.

Chapter 12 looks at how the Secure Sockets Layer (SSL) protocol enables secure HTTP sessions; installing and configuring Certificate Server; generating and installing certificate requests using Key Manager; submitting a certificate request to a Certificate Authority; and a walkthrough of enabling SSL on a site.

Chapter 13 describes the mechanism of SMTP service installation of the SMTP service; configuration of the SMTP service settings using property sheets; and use of the SMTP service.

Chapter 14 covers installing and configuring the NNTP service using property sheets, understanding the NNTP service; creating newsgroups on IIS, setting newsgroup expiration policies, posting to newsgroups using Outlook Express, and a walkthrough of creating and posting to a newsgroup.

Chapter 15 covers the basic concepts of creating Web-based applications using Active Server Pages and understanding Microsoft Transaction Server. A number of examples of simple applications using Active Server Pages are demonstrated.

Chapter 16 covers various tips and techniques for troubleshooting problems with Internet Information Server 4.0 and other Windows NT 4.0 Option Pack components. Many of these tips are drawn from real-life situations experienced by administrators of IIS 4.0 servers.

Appendix A covers basic concepts of configuring TCP/IP for networks using Windows NT 4.0, including subnetting concepts necessary for excluding IP addresses.

Appendix B includes an explanation of the Domain Name System (DNS) and a walkthrough of setting up and configuring DNS on a network using Windows NT 4.0.

ADMINISTERING IIS 4

CHAPTER 1

Installing IIS 4.0

Introduction

Microsoft Internet Information Server 4.0 is included in the new Windows NT 4.0 Option Pack, which is available from Microsoft Value-Added Resellers (VARs) everywhere. Installation of IIS 4.0 is relatively straightforward and can be performed in about 20 minutes, depending on the mode of installation selected. After completing this chapter, you will have a basic understanding of

- Components included with the NT 4.0 Option Pack
- System requirements for installing IIS 4.0
- Installation issues of IIS 4.0
- Installing IIS 4.0 on a fresh system
- Upgrading from previous versions of IIS
- Adding and removing components of IIS 4.0 and the Option Pack
- Uninstalling and reinstalling IIS 4.0 and the Option Pack
- Performing unattended installations of IIS 4.0
- Accessing release notes and online documentation

What Is the Windows NT 4.0 Option Pack?

Internet Information Server 4.0 is a part of Microsoft's new Windows NT 4.0 Option Pack. The Option Pack includes the following BackOffice software:

- *Microsoft Internet Information Server 4.0 (IIS 4.0)*, a full-featured Internet server with WWW, FTP, SMTP, and NNTP services; support for Active Server Pages; two administrative tools: an Internet Service Manager snap-in for the Microsoft Management Console, and Internet Service Manager (HTML) for administration by Web browsers; and a sample Web site to show off the capabilities of the product.
- *Microsoft Management Console 1.0 (MMC 1.0)*, a standard software framework within which administrative tools called snap-ins

can run. Snap-ins can be used to administer IIS 4.0, IS 2.0, and MTS. The MMC will be a standard feature on all future BackOffice products and upgrades, including Windows NT 5.0, to provide a standard interface for administration of these products.

- *Microsoft Index Server 2.0 (IS 2.0),* a powerful, automatic, full-text indexing engine with content filters for Microsoft Word and Excel, multilingual support, and sample query forms.
- *Microsoft Certificate Server,* a customizable certificate server capable of issuing standard X.509 digital certificates for enabling Secure Sockets Layer (SSL) encryption on IIS.
- *Microsoft Transaction Server 2.0 (MTS 2.0),* a transaction-processing system for creating distributed Active Server Pages applications through which components can be packaged together so that they must either all succeed or all fail together.
- *Microsoft Site Server Express 2.0,* a site-analysis and reporting tool that can enable administrators to visualize site structure and integrity, and to generate Web site usage reports in various formats.
- *Microsoft Message Queue Server 1.0 (MSMQ 1.0),* a tool for developers that enables applications to asynchronously communicate with each other.
- *Microsoft Internet Connections Services for RAS 1.0,* an upgrade for Windows NT 4.0 RAS services that provides secure communications through the Internet.
- *Microsoft Data Access Components 1.5,* which provides ActiveX Data Objects (ADO) and ODBC services for creating distributed Web-based applications for IIS.
- *FrontPage98 Server Extensions,* which provides interfacing capability between clients running FrontPage98 and Web sites on IIS.
- *Windows Scripting Host (WHS),* a controller of ActiveX scripting engines that allows administrators to run scripts written in VBScript and JScript either from the command line or directly from the desktop.
- *Microsoft Script Debugger 1.0,* which allows administrators to debug Active Server Pages applications containing scripts written in VBScript or JScript.

Source Files for the NT 4.0 Option Pack

There are two ways you can obtain the source files for IIS 4.0 and the Option Pack:

- Order a copy of the NT 4.0 Option pack from a Microsoft-authorized VAR. The Option Pack is also included as a second CD with new copies of Windows NT 4.0 Server.
- Install the full Option Pack (or portions of it) directly from the *Microsoft Web Site* by visiting the following URL:

```
www.microsoft.com/iis/
```

When you install the Option Pack from the Microsoft Web Site, you have the option of either installing it directly on your system or downloading the source files to your system for later installation. It is suggested that you download the files for later installation, since a full download of the Option Pack is about 80 MB—you wouldn't want to have to download it twice! The downloaded source files can then be copied to a file server and used for network installs of IIS 4.0.

System Requirements for Installing IIS 4.0

Listed in this section are the *minimum* and *recommended* hardware and software requirements for systems to run IIS 4.0 or other Option Pack components. Actual system requirements will depend upon factors such as

- The intended use for the server
- The server traffic load expected
- Other applications being run on the server
- Whether clustering is being used

To determine actual system requirements it is recommended that administrators perform a test installation using recommended hardware and software requirements, then monitor server performance using Performance Monitor under real or simulated loads to determine what elements of hardware (processor, memory, disk, network) to upgrade. See Chap. 10 for information about load-testing IIS using the Web Capacity Analysis Tool (WCAT).

Hardware Requirements

The *minimum* hardware requirements for installing IIS 4.0 or other components of the Option Pack, as stated by Microsoft, are as follows:

Processor	486 DX2/66
Memory	32 MB
HD space available	50 MB
Monitor	VGA

In addition, a CD-ROM drive will be required if the installation is performed from CD.

The *recommended* hardware requirements for installing IIS 4.0 and other components of the Option Pack, as stated by Microsoft, are as follows:

Processor	Pentium 90
Memory	64 MB
HD space available	200 MB
Monitor	SVGA

Here are some notes on these hardware requirements:

- Use the recommended requirements as your minimum or starting requirements; performance with 32 MB of RAM is unbearably slow, so start with 64 MB of RAM and work upward.
- In addition, the stated HD space requirements should be at least doubled if a *custom* install is performed and most components are selected.
- The SVGA monitor is important for viewing Web content only.
- In general, production Web servers running IIS 4.0 probably want to have at least Pentium II 200 processors with 128 MB RAM and 100 MB Ethernet cards in most medium- and large-scale corporate intranet environments.

Software Requirements

Following are the software prerequisites for installing IIS 4.0 or Option Pack components:

- Windows NT 4.0 Server operating system or later
- Windows NT Service Pack 3 or later
- Internet Explorer 4.01 or later (*required* for installing IIS 4.0)
- TCP/IP protocol
- NTFS for all IIS drives (recommended for security reasons)

In addition, you should remove any third-party Web server software from your system prior to installing IIS 4.0.

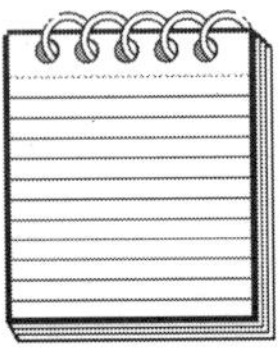

NOTE: *IIS 4.0 may also be installed on Windows NT 4.0 Workstation or Windows 95, but it installs on these platforms as the Microsoft Personal Web Server 4.0 (PWS 4.0) and is missing some of the essential features it has when installed on NT Server, such as the ability to*

- *Host multiple Web sites on one machine*
- *Log to an ODBC compliant database*
- *Restrict access by IP addresses*
- *Perform indexing*
- *Isolate processes*

Essentially, PWS 4.0 is not intended to be a production Web server but may rather be used for

- *Publishing workgroup Web content within a LAN*
- *Performing remote administration of IIS on NT server*

In addition, PWS 4.0 on Windows 95 lacks the NTFS security features available with Windows NT Workstation.

Software Recommendations

The following software is recommended if you plan to use IIS 4.0 in a medium- or large-scale corporate intranet production environment:

- *Name resolution services.* Either a WINS server or a DNS server (DNS recommended).

- *Client browser software.* Microsoft Internet Explorer 4.01
- *Content development tools.* Microsoft FrontPage 98
- *Application development tools.* Microsoft Visual InterDev
- *Relational database management systems.* Microsoft SQL Server 6.5 or Access

Installation Issues for IIS 4.0

The following sections describe some issues that you should be aware of before and after performing an installation of IIS 4.0 on your system.

Operating System Issues

- IIS 4.0 can be installed on Windows NT 4.0 Server or Windows NT 4.0 Workstation.
- IIS 4.0 *cannot* be installed on any version of Windows NT 5.0.

Compatibility Issues

Proxy Server

- IIS 4.0 is incompatible with Proxy Server 1.0.
- If you already have Proxy Server 2.0 installed on your system, you will need to rerun Setup for Proxy Server 2.0 after you install IIS 4.0.

Certificate Server

- If you already have Certificate Server installed on your system, stop the associated service before installing IIS 4.0. You can do this by opening the SETTINGS program in CONTROL PANEL, selecting the CERTIFICATE AUTHORITY service, and clicking the STOP button. Be sure to restart this service after IIS 4.0 is installed.

IIS 4.0 Beta 3.0

- IIS 4.0 servers *cannot* be administered from IIS 4.0 beta 3.0 servers, and vice versa. You should upgrade all IIS 4.0 beta 3.0 servers to IIS 4.0.

Internet Service Manager for IIS 3.0

- Internet Service Manager for IIS 3.0 will *not* be able to manage IIS 4.0 servers.

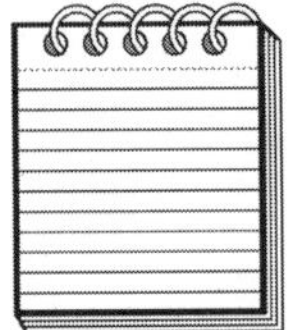

NOTE: *If you plan a staged migration of IIS 3.0 servers to IIS 4.0, be sure to leave Internet Service Manager 3.0 on some systems for managing your IIS 3.0 servers until the migration is complete.*

Server Type Issues

Installing on a BDC

- If installing IIS 4.0 on a Windows NT 4.0 BDC, Microsoft recommends you select the Custom installation mode and deselect the following components:
  Index Server and its subcomponents
  World Wide Web Samples
- These components can be added later by running Setup in *Maintenance mode* (see the Adding and Removing Components section below)

Installing on a Member Server

- If installing IIS 4.0 on a Windows NT 4.0 member server, note that the IUSR_SERVERNAME Internet anonymous user account is created in the *local* SAM database of the member server, not on the global SAM database of the PDC.

Preinstallation Issues

Closing All Applications

- Be sure to close all desktop applications before installing IIS 4.0.

Stopping Unnecessary Background Services

- It is good practice to stop all unnecessary background services running on the server such as Exchange Server services and SQL Server services.

- In particular, all system services using ODBC *must* be stopped prior to installation.
- However, the Browser and Netlogon services *must* be running for installation to succeed.

Postinstallation Issues

Restarting Stopped Background Services

- Be sure to restart any background services that were stopped during installation.

Checking Event Viewer

- Be sure to check the System and Security logs on Event Viewer for errors and problems during installation.

Reinstalling Windows NT 4.0 Service Pack 3

- If you need to reinstall Service Pack 3 after installing IIS 4.0 or Option Pack components on your system, be sure you select *not* to overwrite the newer files that Option Pack Setup installed.

Applying Post-Service Pack 3 Hotfixes

- To resolve newly discovered problems, Microsoft releases Hotfixes to the most recent service pack. If you encounter a problem running IIS 4.0 or Option Pack components, a search of the Microsoft Knowledge Base on Technet or online at

  ```
  www.microsoft.com/support
  ```

  may indicate that you need to apply a Hotfix to Service Pack 3. These Hotfixes may also be found at the Microsoft FTP site:

  ```
  ftp.microsoft.com/bussys/winnt/winnt-public/fixes/usa/NT40/
  hotfixes-postSP3/
  ```

Installing IIS 4.0 on a Fresh System

Doing a clean install of IIS 4.0 on a fresh system presents the fewest potential difficulties. Windows NT 4.0 Option Pack offers three setup modes for installation:

- Minimum install
- Typical install (recommended)
- Custom install

This section describes these above setup modes, presents a walkthrough of a *Typical* mode installation, and examines the changes to the system as a result of such an installation.

Minimum Install

The Minimum mode of NT 4.0 Option Pack setup installs only those components that are required to get IIS 4.0 up and running on your system. Table 1-1 shows which components are installed when MINIMUM is selected during setup.

Typical Install (Recommended)

The Typical mode of NT 4.0 Option Pack setup installs all the components included in the Minimum install, plus further documentation and server functionality. Table 1-2 shows which *additional* components are installed when TYPICAL is selected during setup.

Table 1-1

Minimum Install of NT 4.0 Option Pack

Main Component	Subcomponents Included
Internet Information Server (IIS)	WWW Service
	FTP Service
	Internet Service Manager
	Internet Service Manager (HTML)
Microsoft Transaction Server (MTS)	Documentation
Microsoft Data Access Components (MDAC)	ADO, ODBC, and OLE DB
	Jet/Access, SQL Server Data Sources
NT Option Pack Common Files	None

Table 1-2

Additional Components for Typical Install of NT 4.0 Option Pack

Main Component	Subcomponents Included
Internet Information Server (IIS)	Active Server Pages
	Documentation
	SMTP Service
Microsoft Data Access Components (MDAC)	Documentation
	Remote Data Service (RDS)
Microsoft Index Server (IS)	Documentation
	Sample Files
	Support for U.S. English Language
Microsoft Management Console (MMC)	All components
Microsoft Script Debugger (MSD)	All components
Windows Scripting Host (WSH)	All components
FrontPage 98 Server Extensions	All components

Custom Install

The Custom mode of NT 4.0 Option Pack setup allows administrators to select which components to install, with all Minimum and Typical options preselected. Table 1-3 shows which *additional* components can be installed when CUSTOM is selected during setup.

Dependencies of Components

Administrators choosing to perform a Custom install should be aware of the various dependencies that exist among components of NT 4.0 Option Pack. For information on these dependencies, refer to the section of the Online Documentation entitled "Installing the Option Pack." Generally, if you elect to perform a Custom install and do not *deselect* any of the preselected components (representing the Typical install), but simply select additional components, you avoid many of the problems associated with component dependencies.

Table 1-3

Additional Components Available for Custom Install of NT 4.0 Option Pack

Main Component	Subcomponents Included
Internet Information Server (IIS)	NNTP Service
	WWW Samples
	Streaming Multimedia Support
	Software Development Kit (SDK)
Microsoft Index Server (IS)	Other Language Resources
Microsoft Transaction Server (MTS)	Development Tools
Microsoft Message Queue (MMQ)	All components
Microsoft Site Server Express	All components
Internet Connection Services for RAS	All components
Certificate Server	All components
Visual InterDev RAD Remote Deployment Support	All components

Walkthrough: Performing a Typical Install of IIS 4.0

Installation begins by placing the Windows NT 4.0 Option Pack CD in the CD-ROM drive. If Autorun is enabled, Setup will begin automatically. Otherwise click START, RUN and type

```
<CD_drive_letter>:\setupcd\winnt.srv\default.htm
```

Click OK, and Setup begins to initialize.

If you downloaded the Windows NT 4.0 Option Pack installation files from the Microsoft Web site, simply run `Setup.exe` to start the installation. In a few seconds the Microsoft Windows NT 4.0 Option Pack Setup screen appears (Fig. 1-1). Click NEXT and read over the End User License Agreement (EULA) (Fig. 1-2). If after reading it you agree with all the terms and conditions specified, click ACCEPT. If you do not agree, click DECLINE and Setup will exit.

Note especially that additional Client Access Licenses (CALs) are required for using

- Microsoft Transaction Server
- Microsoft Message Queue Server
- Internet Connection Services for RAS

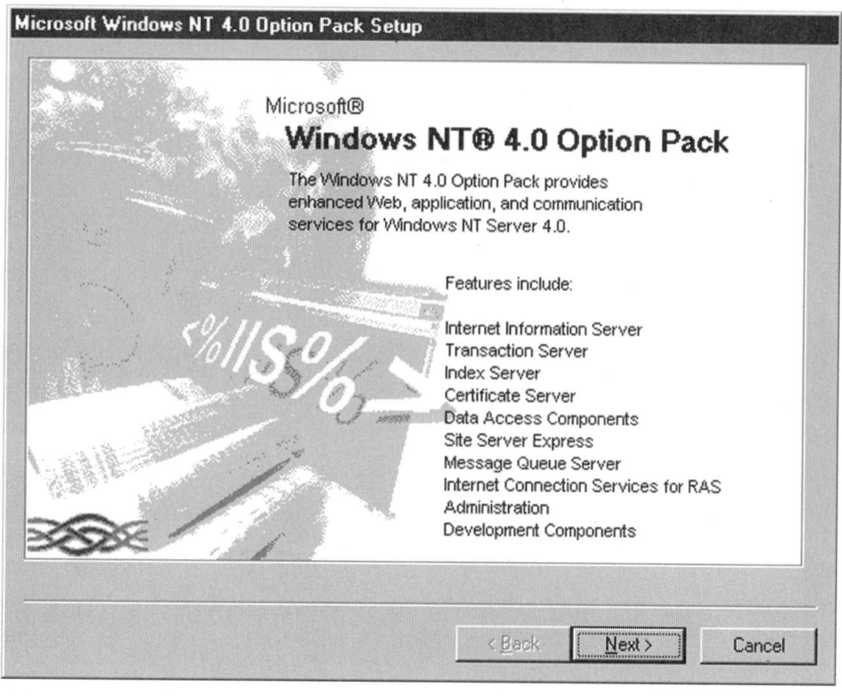

Figure 1-1 Microsoft Windows NT 4.0 Option Pack Setup screen.

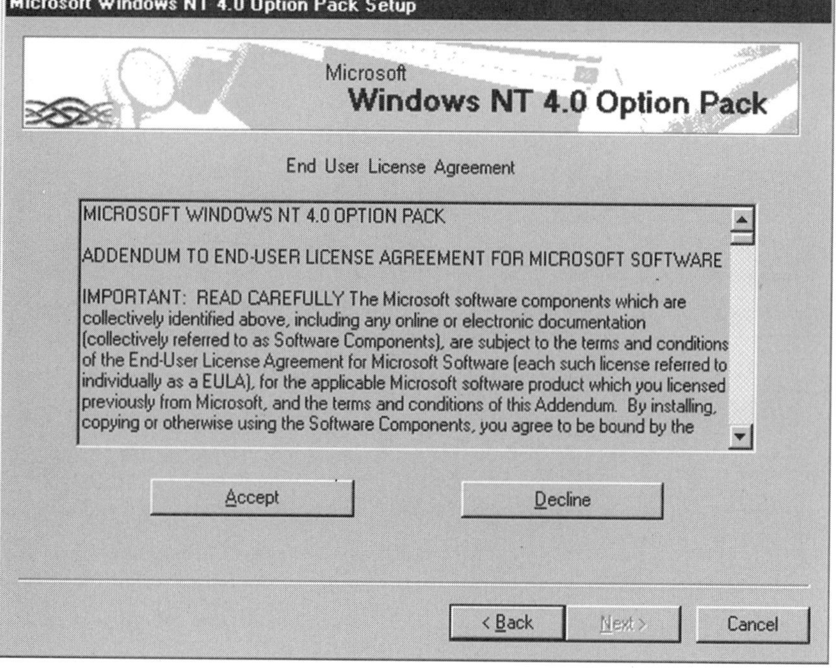

Figure 1-2 Read the End User License Agreement before proceeding further!

The EULA specifies that the NT 4.0 Option Pack components must be installed on a single computer and not separated on several computers. However, the Site Server Express component may be installed on any number of computers.

Anyway, be sure to read the EULA before proceeding further!

The next screen allows you to choose the Setup mode (Fig. 1-3). Choose from the following options:

- *Minimum.* This installs essential components necessary to operate IIS.
- *Typical (recommended).* This installs additional components and documentation.
- *Custom.* You select which components you want to install.

We will select *Typical* and click NEXT.

The next screen allows you to specify the following installation target directories (Fig. 1-4):

- The default home directory for the WWW publishing service. The default location is

```
C:\Inetpub\wwwroot
```

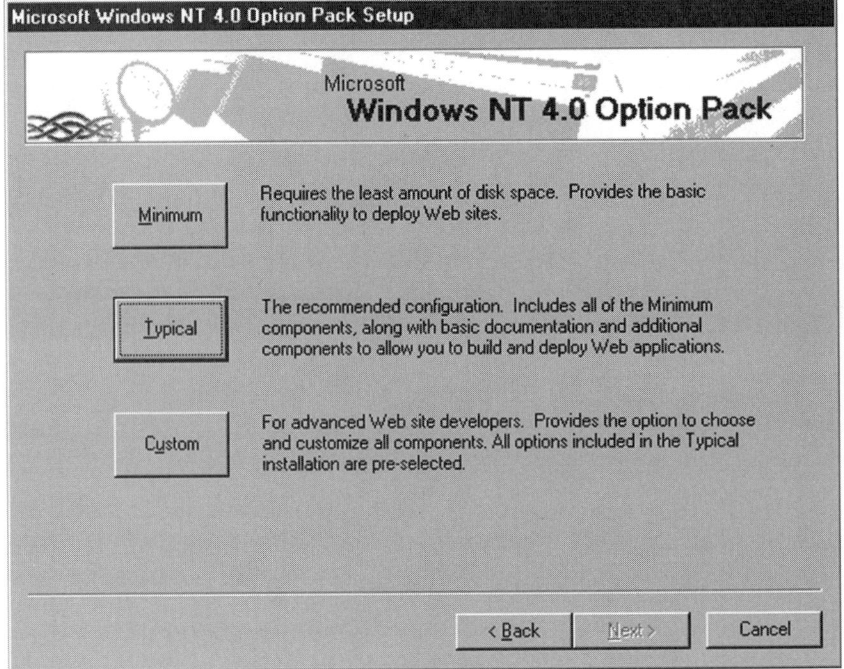

Figure 1-3 Choose your Setup mode.

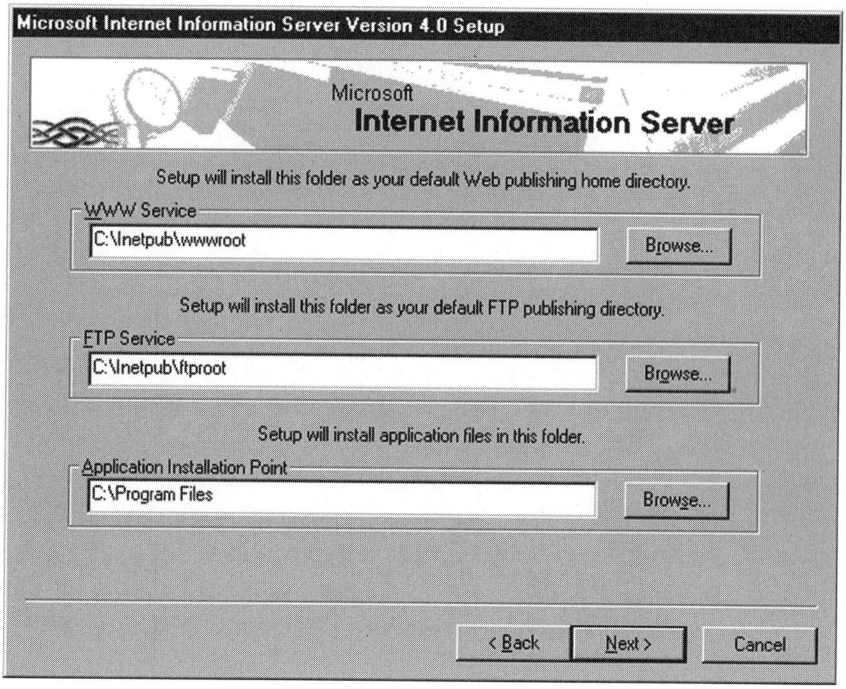

Figure 1-4
Specify default publishing locations.

- The default directory for the FTP publishing service. The default location is

```
C:\Inetpub\ftproot
```

- The location for installing application files. The default location is

```
C:\Program Files
```

Accept the default locations or browse or create new ones, and click NEXT.

The next screen allows you to specify the following target directory (Fig. 1-5):

- The Mailroot directory for the SMTP service. The default location is

```
C:\Inetpub\Mailroot
```

Accept the default location or browse or create a new one, and click NEXT.

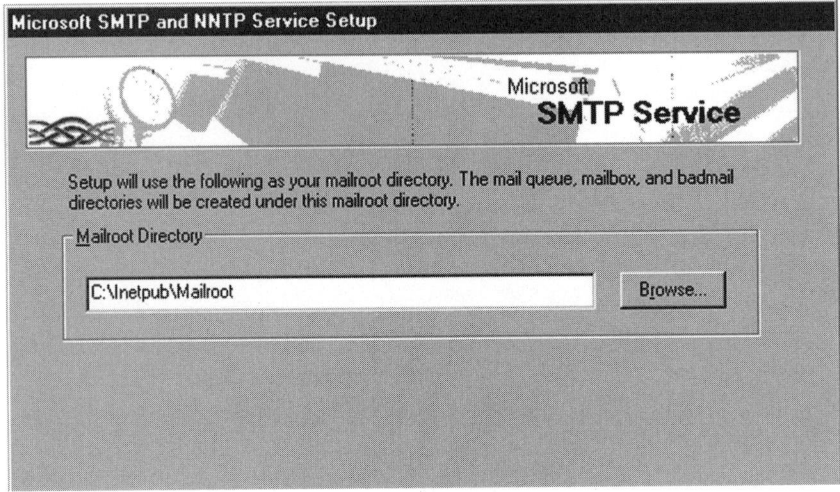

Figure 1-5
Specify the location of the Mailroot directory.

At this point, Setup will begin copying files (Fig. 1-6). This can take from 10 to 30 minutes, depending on the Setup mode chosen (typically about 20 minutes). After files are copied, the various services are configured and initialized.

And that's it! Click FINISH on the next screen to complete the installation (Fig. 1-7), and restart your machine to finalize the settings.

Installation of IIS 4.0 is now complete!

Results of a Typical Install

Once your machine has restarted, click START, PROGRAMS and view the various new start menu shortcuts available under the WINDOWS NT 4.0 OPTION PACK heading (Fig. 1-8). These new shortcuts include the following:

Microsoft Index Server

- Index Server Manager, for administering Index Server from the Microsoft Management Console
- Index Server Manager (HTML), for administering Index Server from a browser
- Index Server Sample Query Form, which demonstrates the capabilities of Index Server

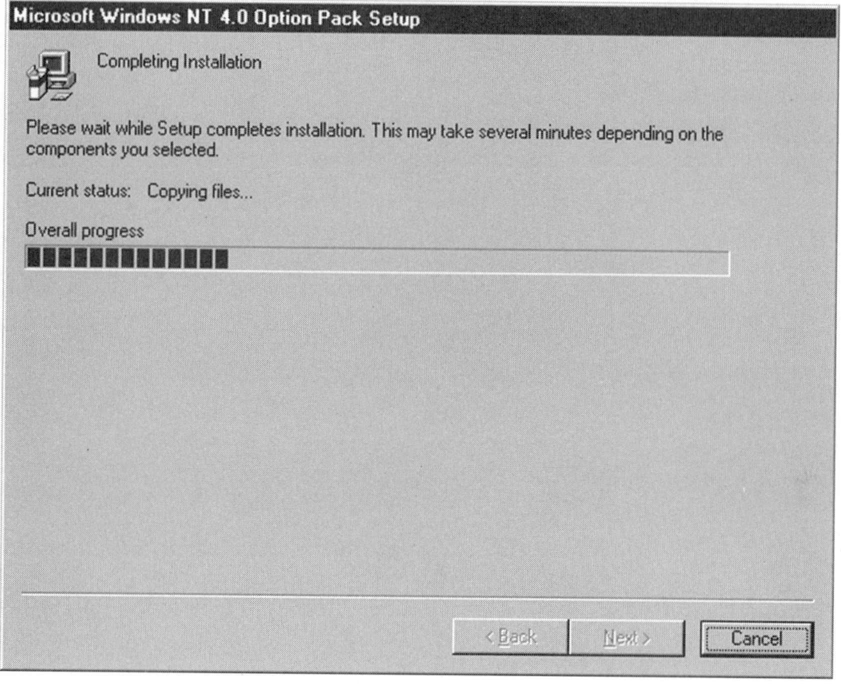

Figure 1-6
Copying files may take from 10 to 30 minutes.

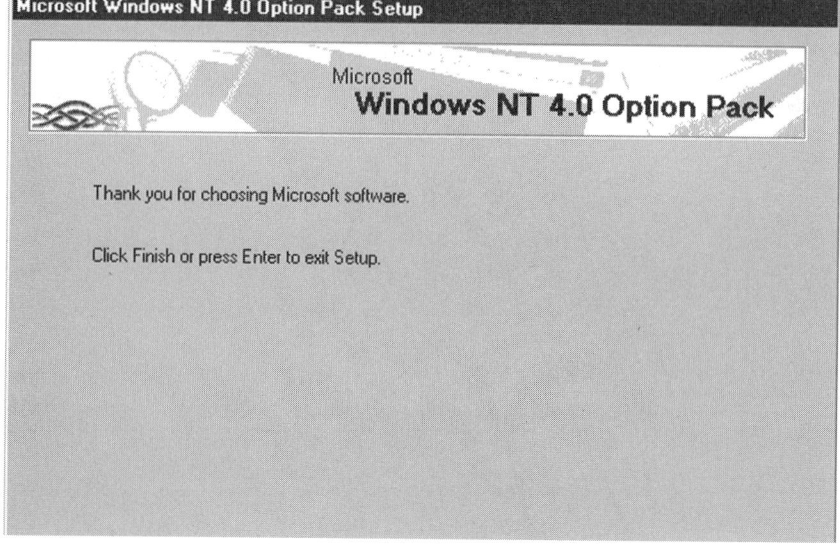

Figure 1-7
Finishing installation.

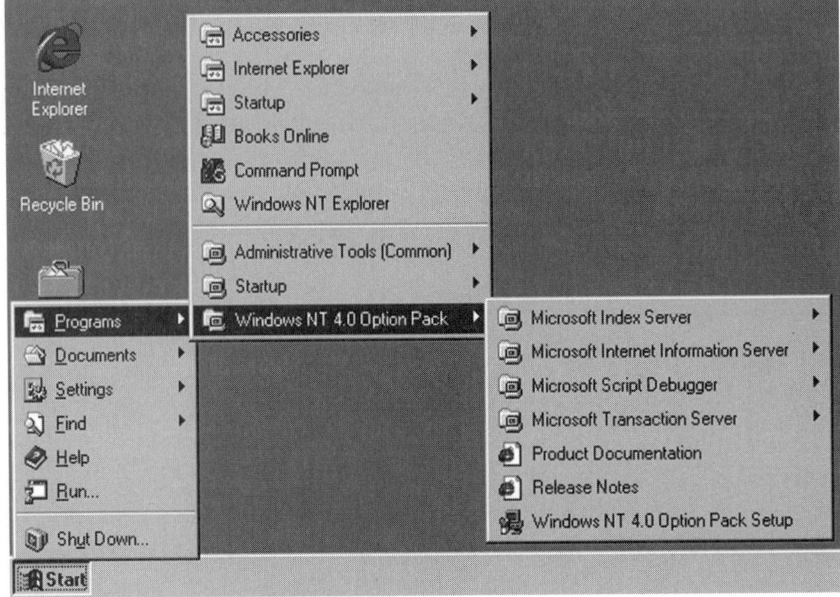

Figure 1-8
New start menu shortcuts installed by Option Pack Setup.

Microsoft Internet Information Server

- Internet Service Manager, for administering IIS from the Microsoft Management Console
- Internet Service Manager (HTML), for administering IIS from a browser
- FrontPage Server Administrator, for configuring FrontPage server extensions

Microsoft SMTP Service

- SMTP Service Manager (HTML), for administering the SMTP service
- SMTP Service Readme and Documentation

Microsoft Script Debugger

- Microsoft Script Debugger, for debugging Active Server Pages
- Microsoft Script Debugger Readme

Microsoft Transaction Server

- Transaction Server Explorer, for administering Microsoft Transaction Server from the Microsoft Management Console
- Transaction Server Readme and Help

Product Documentation for Windows NT 4.0 Option Pack

Release Notes for each component of the Option Pack

Windows NT 4.0 Option Pack Setup, for adding or removing components of the Option Pack and for uninstalling the Option Pack

Using Windows NT Explorer, you can examine some of the new directories installed on the machine, including the various subdirectories of the default content parent directory (Fig. 1-9):

```
C:\Inetpub\
```

This assumes that the defaults were selected during setup. Content subdirectories under `Inetpub` include

`Catalog.wci`	Used by Index Server to store its catalog
`ftproot`	The default directory for the FTP publishing service
`iissamples`	Sample files to show off the capabilities of IIS
`Mail`	Contains files for SMTP administration
`Mailroot`	Contains directories for sending and receiving mail
`scripts`	Location for scripts belonging to the Default Web site
`wwwroot`	The default home directory for the WWW publishing service

New application files are located under

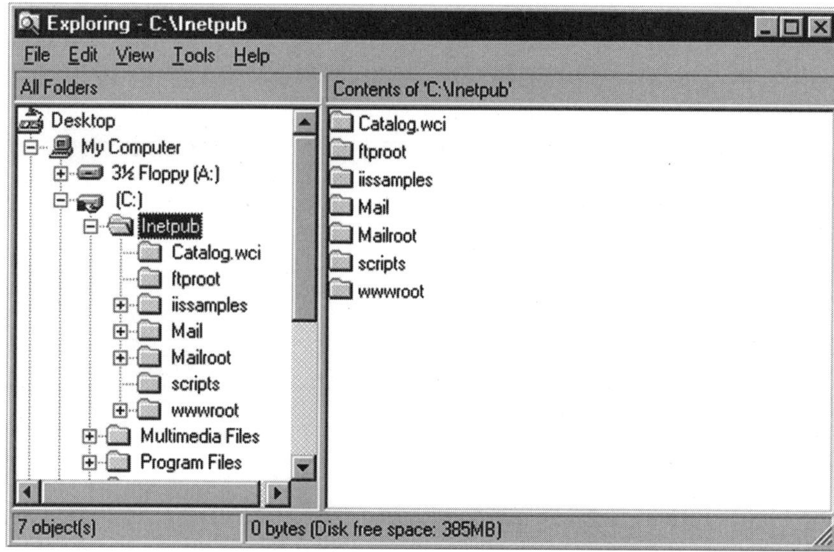

Figure 1-9 Viewing the content subdirectories under `Inetpub`.

```
C:\Program Files\
```

Files for the Internet Service Manager (HTML) are located under

```
C:\winnt\system32\inetsrv\
```

Other files are also scattered in various places by Setup and are discussed later in this book.

Installation also creates two new user accounts (Fig. 1-10). These new accounts are located in the

- *Local* Security Accounts Manager (SAM) database if IIS is installed on a Windows NT 4.0 Server *member server*
- *Domain* Security Accounts Manager (SAM) database if IIS is installed on a Windows NT 4.0 Server *domain controller (PDC or BDC)*

The new accounts are

- `IUSR_SERVERNAME` (or `IUSR_DOMAINNAME`) where `SERVERNAME` is the name of the member server (or `DOMAINNAME` is the name of the domain). This account is called the *Internet Guest Account* and is used by IIS to enable users to connect to the WWW service using Anonymous Access as their authentication method. The account is a member of the *Guests* local group.

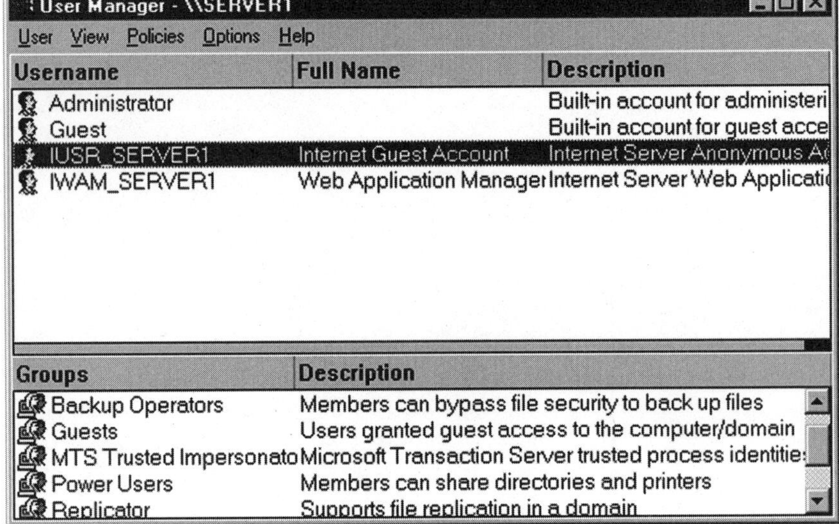

Figure 1-10
New user and group accounts created by Option Pack Setup.

- IWAM_SERVERNAME (or IWAM_DOMAINNAME) where SERVERNAME is the name of the member server (or DOMAINNAME is the name of the domain). This account is called the *Web Application Manager Account* and is used by Microsoft Transaction Server to run secure IIS applications with process isolation. The account is a member of the *Microsoft Transaction Server Trusted Process Identities* local group, which is also created by Option Pack Setup.

Upgrading IIS 4.0

Although installing IIS 4.0 on a clean system is simplest, administrators instead often have to upgrade existing servers with previous versions of IIS installed. In addition, these servers may host Web content, both static and dynamic. This section covers some of the issues involved in upgrading to version 4.0 from earlier versions of IIS.

Upgrading IIS 4.0 Beta Versions

If you have IIS 4.0 Alpha, Beta 1, or Beta 2 installed on your system, you must remove them before installing the final release of IIS 4.0.

To remove an earlier release of IIS 4.0, click START, PROGRAMS, MICROSOFT INTERNET INFORMATION SERVER (COMMON), INTERNET INFORMATION SERVER SETUP. Select NEXT and then choose REMOVE ALL to uninstall the earlier version.

Note that uninstalling IIS does *not* delete the Inetpub content parent directory or any of its subdirectories or files.

Upgrading from IIS 3.0 and IIS 2.0

If you have the Default Web site installed on IIS 3.0 and you plan to upgrade to IIS 4.0, delete the Default Web site home page Default.asp first. Otherwise, Option Pack Setup will *not* overwrite this page with the newer version, and the result may be that you will be unable to view the Default Web site home page from your browser.

Make sure also that the Browser service and Netlogon service are running when you perform your upgrade.

Occasionally upgrades have failed when the initial paging file was set to the amount of RAM in the machine (the default). Increase the initial paging file to RAM + 12 to avoid this issue, using the SYSTEM icon in CONTROL PANEL.

Apart from these few issues, there are no other major issues relating to upgrading to IIS 4.0 from earlier versions of IIS. *Just make sure you do a full backup before performing the upgrade!*

Unattended Installation

To perform an unattended installation of IIS 4.0, first copy the file `unattend.txt` from the Option Pack CD to a folder on the target computer. This file is located on the Option Pack CD at

```
\i386\inetsrv\
```

The `unattend.txt` file may be customized to allow IIS to be installed without user intervention by providing answers to prompts that occur during setup. Instructions on how to modify the file are included in the file itself.

To perform an unattended installation, open a COMMAND PROMPT, change to the directory on the Option Pack CD that contains the file `setup.exe`, and type

```
setup.exe  /u:<full_path_to_unattend.txt_on_local_machine>
```

Note that `unattend.txt` may also be used to perform *Maintenance* installations (that is, adding and removing option pack components).

If errors occur during unattended installation of the Option Pack, these errors are written to a location in the Windows NT Registry specified by the following:

```
HKEY_LOCAL_MACHINE\
    Software\
        Microsoft\
            Windows\
                Setup\
                    Ocmanage\
                        Errors
```

Adding and Removing Components

Running Option Pack Setup in Maintenance mode allows administrators to add and remove selected components of Windows NT 4.0 Option Pack.

To run Setup in Maintenance mode, click START, PROGRAMS, MICROSOFT WINDOWS NT 4.0 OPTION PACK, WINDOWS NT 4.0 OPTION PACK SETUP to open the Microsoft Windows NT 4.0 Option Pack Setup screen (Fig. 1-11).

Selecting ADD/REMOVE opens the SELECT COMPONENTS dialog box, which allows you to choose which components of Option Pack to install or remove (Fig. 1-12).

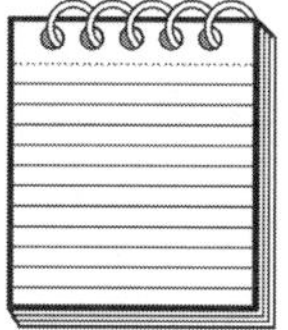

NOTE: *Administrators running Option Pack Setup in Maintenance mode should be aware of the various dependencies that exist between components of NT 4.0 Option Pack. For information on these dependencies, refer to the section of the Online Documentation entitled "Installing the Option Pack."*

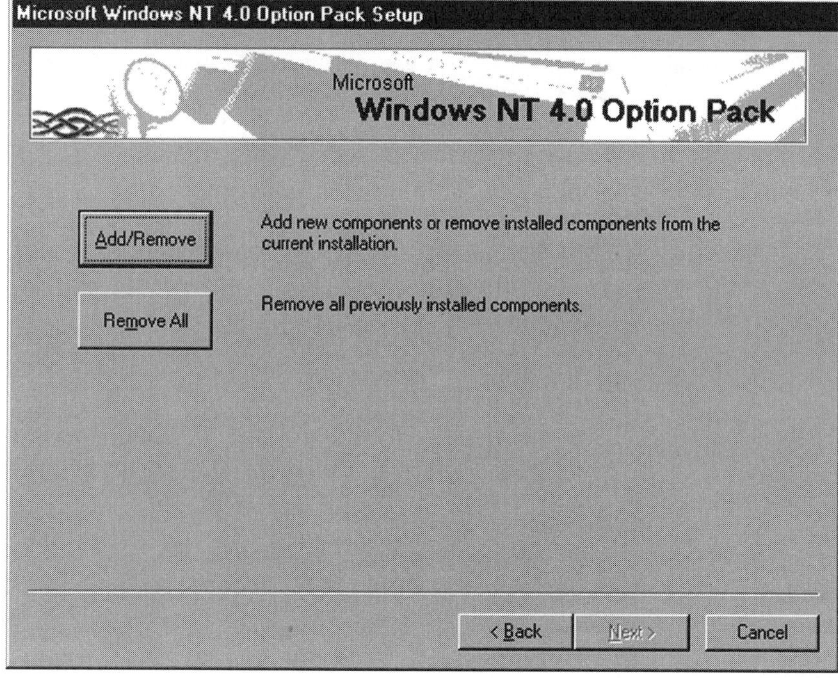

Figure 1-11 Running Option Pack Setup in Maintenance mode.

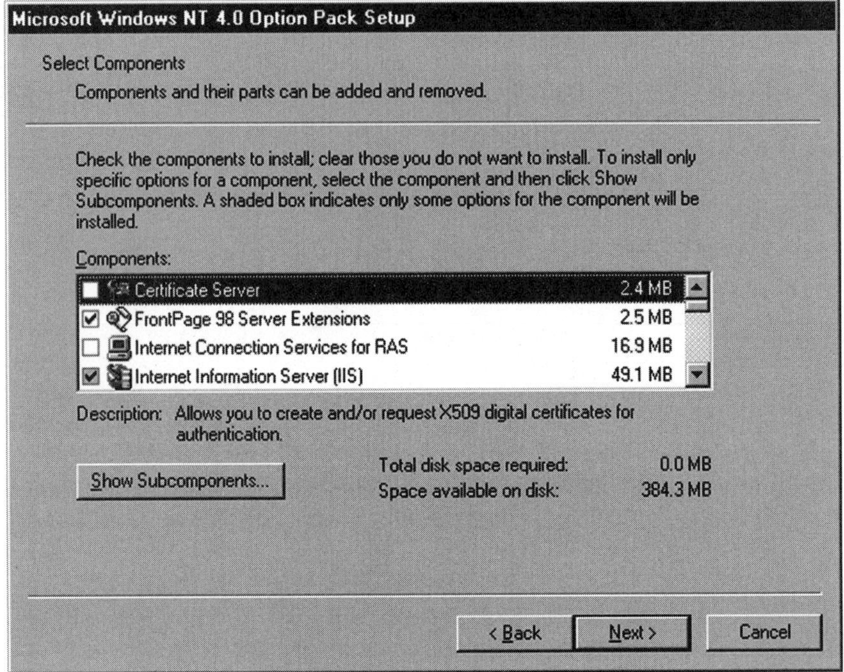

Figure 1-12 Adding or removing components of NT 4.0 Option Pack.

Uninstalling IIS 4.0

To uninstall the Windows NT 4.0 Option Pack including IIS 4.0, click START, PROGRAMS, MICROSOFT WINDOWS NT 4.0 OPTION PACK, WINDOWS NT 4.0 OPTION PACK SETUP to open the Microsoft Windows NT 4.0 Option Pack Setup screen (Fig. 1-11) and click REMOVE ALL. This completely removes Windows NT 4.0 Option Pack from the system.

However, certain directories and files remain on the system after uninstalling the Option Pack. They are listed below. These files may be safely removed from the system (unless they contain Web content you have developed!). Note that some of these directories and files may not be present, depending on the type of setup performed.

IIS content directories:

```
\Inetpub\wwwroot\
\Inetpub\ftproot\
\Inetpub\Iissamples\
\Winnt\System32\inetsrv\iisfecnv.dll
```

NNTP directories:

```
\Inetpub\news\*.*
\Inetpub\nntpfile\*.*
\Winnt\Help\news\
```

SMTP directories:

```
\Inetpub\Mail\
\Inetpub\Mailroot\
```

Microsoft Transaction Server directories:

```
\Program Files\Mts
```

Microsoft Certificate Server directories:

```
\Winnt\System32\certsrc\*.*
\Winnt\System32\CertLog\certsrv.mdb
```

Microsoft Data Access components:

```
\Program Files\Common Files\System\Ado\
\Program Files\Common Files\System\Msadc\
```

Accessing Release Notes

If problems occur during the installation and use of IIS 4.0 or other components of the Windows NT 4.0 Option Pack, you may want to view the *release notes* on these components. Release notes for installing NT 4.0 Option Pack can be obtained prior to installation by starting Internet Explorer 4.01 on the target server and browsing the Option Pack CD for the following file:

```
iirnlink.htm
```

From this file a series of links will allow you to read release notes for the various components of the Option Pack, which are stored on the CD as `.htm` files.

Alternatively, you may want to browse Microsoft's Web site at

```
www.microsoft.com/iis/
```

to find a more up-to-date version of the release notes for IIS.

Accessing Online Documentation

Online documentation for the NT 4.0 Option Pack is installed on the server as Web content, to be read using Internet Explorer 4.01 (Fig. 1-13). Thus, in order to read the documentation, IIS 4.0 must be successfully installed and the WWW service must start properly.

Online documentation may be accessed from remote browsers by using the URL

```
http://<server_name>/iisHelp/
```

where <server_name> is the NetBIOS name, Fully-Qualified Domain Name, or IP Address of the IIS server.

Online documentation contains a facility for printing out entire sections of the documentation if desired.

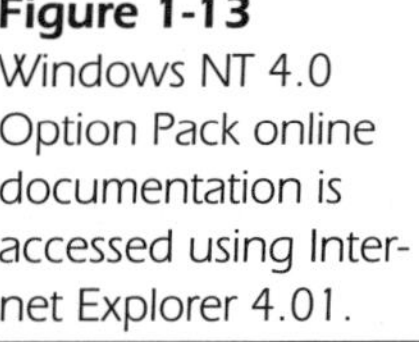

Figure 1-13 Windows NT 4.0 Option Pack online documentation is accessed using Internet Explorer 4.01.

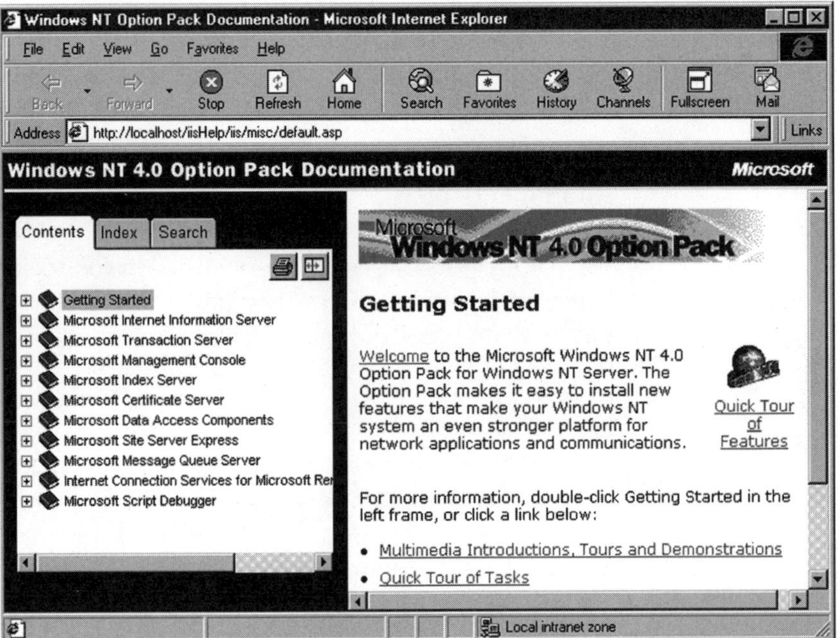

Postscript: Checklist for Implementing IIS 4.0

Some final comments on implementing IIS 4.0 in your networking environment (to help you keep your sanity!). Implementing IIS 4.0 in a corporate environment as an intranet or Internet server is not a job that you as a network administrator should take lightly. Only a few years ago, the situation was much simpler and probably looked something like this:

- As network administrator, you installed and configured a basic Web server for Internet or intranet use, plus any associated tools needed such as a DNS server.
- As network administrator, you registered your company's domain name with Internic.
- As network administrator, you learned enough HTML to create the company Web site, which was probably 10–25 pages in size. You probably stole (borrowed) some graphics from other sites to make it look half decent. You also had the responsibility of updating the site as needed.
- As network administrator, you learned enough Perl to write scripts for enabling forms on your site, and possibly created a simple discussion group as well. But when your boss asked if you could connect your Web site to the company database, you balked and said the tools were just not there yet for doing that.
- As network administrator, your email address was on your home page as Webmaster. You got all the accolades and all the flack from the people who visited your site.

Well, things are *much* different now. The Internet is big business, database connectivity is the norm, commerce systems are the future, Web servers have given way to web farms, HTML has given way to RAD tools, legal issues abound, and expectations have gone through the roof. So before you implement your next web server, it's time to face facts: *you can't do it all anymore.* No single IT professional has the expertise or the time to become familiar with all the myriad aspects of Internet/intranet development these days. You would have to be manager, consultant, network administrator, database programmer, VB expert, graphic designer, trainer, and customer support all rolled up in one to be able to do it all. I don't know about you, but I'd rather die instead.

So where do you begin? To help you implement IIS 4.0 in your network environment, here is a *12-step methodology* that is useful for implementing any significant server upgrades or rollouts in a corporate environment:

1. Assess
2. Propose
3. Recruit
4. Train
5. Procure
6. Test
7. Deploy
8. Document
9. Monitor
10. Evaluate
11. Forecast
12. Maintain

This 12-step methodology is cast below as a series of questions you should ask yourself and tasks you should perform as you progress through the stages of planning, designing, and implementing IIS 4.0 in your corporate network. As you read through it, ask yourself each question and visualize to yourself how each task will be performed. Check off each point as you consider it. Write down additional questions and tasks of your own as they occur to you in the space provided.

1. Assess (Do You Need IIS 4.0?)

- ❑ Are you familiar with aspects of your company's current network configuration as they relate to implementing IIS 4.0?
- ❑ Do you have existing IIS 3.0 servers that will need to be upgraded?
- ❑ Do you have existing Internet Explorer 3.0 browsers that will need to be upgraded to IE 4.0? Will end-user systems require additional memory to run IE 4.0?
- ❑ Have you any concerns regarding the additional network traffic that will result from implementing IIS 4.0 for your intranet or the Internet?
- ❑ Has your company any security policies in place regarding deploying Web servers?

- ❑ Have you familiarized yourself with the features that are new in IIS 4.0? If necessary, visit Microsoft's Web site to review these new features by pointing your browser to

  ```
  www.microsoft.com/iis
  ```

- ❑ Have you reflected on why you want to upgrade your existing Web servers to IIS 4.0? Are the driving reasons valid concerns or pet cows? Which of the following groups are pushing for the deployment? Are any of them resisting it? Why?
  - ❑ Management
  - ❑ IT department
  - ❑ End users
- ❑ Have you the necessary resources at this time to consider implementing IIS 4.0?
  - ❑ Hardware (servers and peripherals)
  - ❑ Hardware (network infrastructure)
  - ❑ Software (rollout, site development, and maintenance)
  - ❑ Training (you and others)
  - ❑ Budget
  - ❑ Time
  - ❑ People (IT, programmers, Web developers)
- ❑ List any additional questions, concerns, or thoughts you may have regarding *assessing* your company's need for IIS 4.0 at this time:

  ____

  ____

  ____

2. Propose (Why? What? How? When? Who? How Much?)

- ❑ List three reasons right now *why* your company needs to upgrade its existing intranet/Internet structure to IIS 4.0. If you can't do this, don't proceed any further.

___

___

___

- ❑ Describe briefly *what* will need to be purchased, upgraded, or reallocated to enable IIS 4.0 to be implemented on your network. Consider such things as
  - ❑ Servers
  - ❑ Peripherals
  - ❑ Networking components
  - ❑ Firewalls
  - ❑ Software (administrative and end-user)
  - ❑ Licenses (per-server and per-seat)
  - ❑ Resource materials (administrative and end-user)
  - ❑ Training courses (administrative and end-user)
  - ❑ Other ___
- ❑ Describe *how* and *when* you plan to implement IIS 4.0 on the network. Outline your plan as a series of steps with a target timeline, leaving yourself room for unforeseen circumstances.
- ❑ Outline *who* has responsibility for what in your plan. Specifically, you should be able at this time to suggest names for each of the functions in Table 1-4, even though you may not plan immediately to use all the features and functionality of IIS 4.0. Some names may appear in more than one place in the table—just make sure your name doesn't appear in every line!
- ❑ Estimate *how much* should be budgeted in order to implement your project. Provide a cost breakdown according to what you need and when you need it.
- ❑ List any additional questions, concerns, or thoughts you may have regarding *writing a proposal* and *preparing a presentation* on implementing IIS 4.0 in your corporate network at this time:

___

___

___

Table 1-4

Implementation Responsibilities

Function/Responsibility	Name(s)
Project leader (chief technical person, mastermind, and planner)	You—that's why you're reading this book! :-)
Project leader's management counterpart (responsible for determining corporate needs, helping to procure funding, establishing policies regarding content and usage, etc.)	
Technical team (from your IT department; people you can delegate technical implementation tasks to)	
Database developer(s) (if you plan to implement database connectivity in your Web site)	
Vbscript/Jscript developer(s) and programmer(s) (may be required for custom site development)	
Person(s) responsible for recruiting, training, and overseeing the Web site development team that will actually create the site content	
Graphic design company(s) for outsourcing of your Web site graphics needs (worth the money!)	
Training company(s) for outsourcing your technical and end-user training needs (also worth the money!)	
Person(s) responsible for ongoing technical support to Web site development team (from your IT department)	

3. Recruit (Think Teamwork and Delegate!)

- ❑ Having had your proposal approved by management, begin by notifying both users and management of the following:
  - ❑ Purpose of deployment of IIS 4.0 in the company
  - ❑ Planned deployment date(s)
  - ❑ How deployment will affect users
  - ❑ Persons and groups responsible for specific functions or tasks
  - ❑ Whom to contact if problems are encountered

- ❑ Create a brief written description of goals and functions for each individual or group that will be involved in the project, including management contacts and end users.
- ❑ Meet with these individuals and groups to review their roles and responsibilities. Schedule regular meetings as appropriate and outline your expectations to them in advance of how they should document and report progress to you.
- ❑ List any additional questions, concerns, or thoughts you may have regarding *recruiting a team* for implementing IIS 4.0 in your corporate network at this time:

____

____

____

4. Train (Know Your Stuff!)

- ❑ Have you read through the online documentation of IIS 4.0?
- ❑ Do you feel a need for yourself to take any additional training before implementing IIS 4.0 in your corporate network? If so, you may want to check out the listing of Microsoft Official Curriculum (MOC) courses on Microsoft's Web site or contact your local Microsoft Authorized Technical Education Center (ATEC) for a schedule of current courses. MOC courses are listed at

  `www.microsoft.com/train_cert`

- ❑ Will the people developing Web site content in your company require any training? You might want to sit down with management or department heads and assess training needs for end users and content developers at this time.
- ❑ Will end users migrating from IE 3.0 to IE 4.0 require training to enable them to make efficient use of the new browser's capabilities and potential?
- ❑ List any additional questions, concerns, or thoughts you may have regarding *training* individuals and groups for successful implementation and use of IIS 4.0 in your corporate network at this time:

____

____

____

5. Procure (Buy It, Beg It, Borrow It, But Please Don't Pirate It!)

- ❑ Go ahead and make your shopping wish list for implementing IIS 4.0 and try to get the invoice approved by management (good luck!).
- ❑ List any additional questions, concerns, or thoughts you may have regarding *procuring* necessary hardware and software to allow a successful implementation of IIS 4.0 in your corporate network at this time:

____

____

____

6. Test (Look Before You Leap!)

- ❑ Perform a testbed installation and fully familiarize yourself with the product. The test machine should be identical in hardware to your final production servers, and it should be either a fresh installation on a new or wiped machine or an upgrade onto a disk-image copy of an existing IIS 3.0 Web server complete with existing company intranet Web site content (if any).
- ❑ Perform a test installation of IE 4.0 on a machine similar to the average end-user machine. Apply any user restrictions you have decided to add by using Microsoft's Internet Explorer Administration Kit. Test these restrictions out.
- ❑ Try accessing all aspects of the migrated content to see if all the Web site functions still work (forms, active server pages, database connectivity, etc.).

- ❑ Have you read the release notes on IIS 4.0? Check www.microsoft.com/iis for the latest release notes regarding problems, patches, and workarounds to installation problems.
- ❑ Have you installed any patches and workarounds you found on Microsoft's Web site? Have you tested them out?
- ❑ Have you browsed the TechNet knowledge base concerning IIS 4.0 to see what other problems you might encounter?
- ❑ Have you posted to the Microsoft public newsgroups any problems you have encountered or any questions you might have? (It is cheaper than dialing Microsoft's support line!) You can find these newsgroups by pointing your news reader to the following NNTP server:

```
msnews.microsoft.com
```

- ❑ List any additional questions, concerns, or thoughts you may have regarding *testing* your hardware and software to allow a successful implementation of IIS 4.0 in your corporate network at this time:

____

____

____

7. Deploy (Roll It Out, But Don't Roll It over Anybody!)

- ❑ Begin by notifying both users and management of the planned date for deployment of your new IIS 4.0 servers. Do this approximately one to two weeks in advance, and again two days before deployment. Ask them to notify you on or after that date if any network problems occur that might relate to the deployment.
- ❑ *Backup your existing IIS servers before upgrading them to IIS 4.0! Backup your Web and FTP content directories, scripts, and applications as well!*
- ❑ Having acquired the necessary hardware, software, and expertise, go ahead and install IIS 4.0 on your new production systems or upgrade your existing IIS 3.0 servers to IIS 4.0. Also apply any service packs, fixes, or patches that are available for this product at this time.

- ❑ Deploy or upgrade end-user systems to Internet Explorer 4.0, making sure you apply any service packs, fixes, or patches available for this product. Use the Internet Explorer Administration Kit to customize end-user browsers for your company's needs.
- ❑ Are you doing all the technical work yourself at this point? Just checking! :-)
- ❑ After completing installation, check Windows NT *Event Viewer* to make sure that there were no unforeseen problems with the installation.
- ❑ While your new servers are still off-line, perform a few basic standalone tests on them, including running each of the administrative tools and connecting to the WWW and FTP services using Internet Explorer 4.0.
- ❑ Configure the security settings on your new servers according to your company's network security policy. Consider all aspects of security, including
  - ❑ Administrative rights
  - ❑ Content-development rights
  - ❑ Browsing and access rights
  - ❑ IP address filtering
  - ❑ Firewall configuration
  - ❑ Remote-access methods
  - ❑ Authentication methods
  - ❑ Directory permissions
- ❑ Install the IIS 4.0 administrative tools on your administrator consoles or install Internet Explorer 4.0 on them for remote administration capabilities.
- ❑ Deploy the new server(s) on the network, and monitor for any abrupt changes in network traffic patterns or user complaints.
- ❑ Test remote administration of your new servers from your administrator consoles.
- ❑ Test access from end-user stations that have browsing rights. Inform end users to contact you if they have problems accessing the new servers.

- ❑ Test creation of content from end-user stations that have content-creation rights. Inform persons responsible for content creation to contact you if they have problems performing their duties.
- ❑ Iron out any other bugs that appear during deployment.
- ❑ List any additional questions, concerns, or thoughts you may have regarding *deployment* of IIS 4.0 in your corporate network at this time:

____

____

____

8. Document (Find the Time to Do This!)

- ❑ Document all problems and issues that appear during testing and deployment.
- ❑ Document all security settings (users, groups, IP, authentication methods, directory permissions) implemented on your new servers. Indicate the order in which these settings were made.
- ❑ Document responsibilities and functions of individuals and groups involved in both deployment and usage.
- ❑ Document any user complaints that occur during the two weeks after deployment, even if they don't seem at the time to be directly related to the IIS 4.0 deployment.
- ❑ List any additional questions, concerns, or thoughts you may have regarding *documentation* of your IIS 4.0 deployment at this time:

____

____

____

9. Monitor (How Does It Perform?)

- ❑ Use Windows NT Performance Monitor to monitor selected objects and counters related to IIS 4.0 performance.

- ❑ Run Performance Monitor as a service (use the perfmon service from the Windows NT 4.0 Resource Kit) and create log files for server analysis and optimization. Be sure you have sufficient disk space for logging.
- ❑ Set alerts for objects and counters that critically affect performance and usability.
- ❑ Use log files to create a baseline for both low- and high-usage periods of your IIS 4.0 servers. To allow for performance to settle as users become familiar with the new servers, wait one or two weeks after deployment before creating your baseline logs from an additional two weeks of logging server activity.
- ❑ Continue logging to create a database of information for server analysis and optimization.
- ❑ Identify any bottlenecks in server performance and try to correct them by implementing hardware upgrades, such as
  - ❑ Adding additional memory
  - ❑ Upgrading processors or adding additional processors
  - ❑ Upgrading disk controllers and hard drives
  - ❑ Upgrading network adapter cards
- ❑ Tune server performance by changing configuration options on property sheets for WWW and FTP services. Monitor the effect of making these changes and try to optimize settings for best performance.
- ❑ Tune performance of your proxy server, if you are using a proxy intermediary to run IIS 4.0 as an Extranet server.
- ❑ Develop a schedule and assign responsibility for long-term ongoing performance monitoring of your IIS 4.0 servers.
- ❑ List any additional questions, concerns, or thoughts you may have regarding *monitoring and optimization* of your IIS 4.0 performance at this time:

____

____

____

10. Evaluate (Have We Met Our Goals?)

- ❑ Approximately two to three months after deployment, meet with your implementation team and end-user contacts and evaluate the success of the project. Specifically address issues such as these:
  - ❑ Are content developers comfortable working with the new platform?
  - ❑ Are developers making use of the new features of IIS 4.0?
  - ❑ Does any group feel that it needs more training to enable it to make full use of the potentialities of IIS 4.0?
  - ❑ Are end users happy with the speed, accessibility, and functionality of the intranet/extranet?
  - ❑ Are end users comfortable with any restrictions on IE 4.0 you have added using the Internet Explorer Administration Kit? Are they aware of the reasons for such customization?
  - ❑ Are current security policies working? Any suggestions for modification?
  - ❑ Has the time, energy, and money spent on the implementation been worthwhile?
  - ❑ Have they any further thoughts, suggestions, or concerns they would like to express at this time?
- ❑ Prepare a brief report for management summarizing developer and end-user satisfaction now that implementation is complete.
- ❑ List any additional questions, concerns, or thoughts you may have regarding *evaluation* of your IIS 4.0 deployment at this time:

  ____

  ____

  ____

11. Forecast (Be Proactive!)

- ❑ Consider your evaluation meeting with content developers and end users and your ongoing performance monitoring, and discuss with your technical team how and when your current IIS 4.0 implementation might require further upgrading. Consider such issues as
  - ❑ Adding additional servers to accommodate user traffic

- ❑ Repositioning servers to handle traffic more efficiently
- ❑ Increasing network capacity (available bandwidth)
- ❑ Adding new development platforms like Microsoft Visual InterDev
- ❑ Adding new server functionality (e.g., other BackOffice products)

❑ Prepare a brief report for management outlining how and when such upgrades might need to be performed, depending on evolution of company and user needs.

❑ List any additional questions, concerns, or thoughts you may have regarding *forecasting future growth* of your IIS 4.0 deployment at this time:

____

____

____

12. Maintain (Keep on Top of Things!)

❑ Visit the Microsoft IIS Web site regularly for any news regarding

- ❑ New or updated versions of IIS 4.0
- ❑ Service packs, fixes, and patches for IIS 4.0
- ❑ New add-ons, controls, and tools to extend IIS 4.0 functionality
- ❑ New or updated versions of IE 4.0
- ❑ Service packs, fixes, and patches for IE 4.0
- ❑ Conferences, events, newsletters, and newsgroups relating to IIS 4.0 and intranet development

❑ Train and establish a technical support group for IIS-4.0-related troubleshooting issues. Require monthly reports from this group concerning the most frequently encountered problems and how they were resolved.

❑ Continue to monitor server performance and evaluate developer and end-user satisfaction on a regular basis. Make reports to management on a regular basis forecasting future requirements and assessing future needs.

- ❑ List any additional questions, concerns, or thoughts you may have regarding *maintaining* your IIS 4.0 deployment at this time:

  ____

  ____

  ____

- ❑ Collect your paycheck—you deserve it! :-)

SUMMARY

Installation of IIS 4.0 and other components of the Windows NT 4.0 Option Pack can be done in three modes: Minimum, Typical, and Custom installs. Administrators should be aware of all issues that need to be addressed before installing IIS 4.0 in a production environment. This chapter has dealt with some of these issues; refer to the current release notes located on the Microsoft Web Site for further issues regarding each component of the Windows NT 4.0 Option Pack.

FOR MORE INFORMATION

The following are a few suggested sources for getting additional information on installing IIS 4.0.

Microsoft Web Site For general information regarding IIS 4.0 and to download the Windows NT 4.0 Option Pack, visit the IIS section of the Microsoft Web Site, located at

```
www.microsoft.com/iis
```

Prior to installing IIS 4.0, make sure you read the latest Release Notes, located at

```
backoffice.microsoft.com/downtrial/moreinfo/ntop_relnotes.asp
```

To download Internet Explorer 4.01, which must be installed first on systems you are upgrading to IIS 4.0, visit the site

```
www.microsoft.com/ie/download/
```

Microsoft Public Newsgroups For general newsgroups relating to IIS 4.0 issues, connect to the news server msnews.microsoft.com and subscribe to the following groups:

```
microsoft.public.inetserver.iis
microsoft.public.inetserver.misc
```

Microsoft TechNet Consult the latest edition of Microsoft TechNet CD for information under the following category:

Internet | Server | MS Internet Information Server

List Servers 15seconds.com maintains a mailing list on IIS 4.0. To subscribe, send email to LISTSERV@PEACH.EASE.LSOFT.COM with this message text (no subject):

```
SUBSCRIBE IIS40 Your Name
```

Reply to the confirmation message you receive by following the instructions in that message, and you will be subscribed to the list.

For more information visit

```
www.15seconds.com
```

Windows NT Magazine Volume 4, issue 1 (January 1998), of *Windows NT Magazine* has a feature article titled "The NT 4.0 Option Pack" that provides a useful overview of the Option Pack components.

You can also visit the *Windows NT Magazine* Web site at

```
www.winntmag.com
```

CHAPTER 2

Tools for Administration

Introduction

A core component of any Web server is the administrative tool used to manage its services, resources, and performance. Microsoft Internet Information Server 4.0 comes with a complete set of administrative tools for both local and remote administration. After completing this chapter, you will have a basic understanding of the functionality and capabilities of the following administrative tools:

- The Microsoft Management Console (MMC), which allows administrators to manage IIS 4.0 servers from any computer on which the MMC and its snap-ins are installed.
- The HTML version of the Internet Service Manager, which allows administrators to remotely administer IIS 4.0 servers from any computer with a browser that supports frames and JScript.
- The Windows Scripting Host (WSH), which enables administrative scripts written in VBScript or JScript to run directly on any desktop or from a command line.

Understanding the Microsoft Management Console

The Microsoft Management Console (MMC) is a common management environment that provides a framework for specially designed network and server administration tools to run on. These specially designed tools are called *snap-ins*, and they provide the administrator the capability for managing a wide variety of network and server resources and services.

A snap-in is the smallest element of network management capability. Unless snap-ins are added to the MMC environment, the MMC is useless, as it has no inherent management functionality. A collection of snap-ins saved as an `.msc` file is known as a *tool*.

In future versions of Windows NT and other BackOffice products, all the standard NT administrative tools (e.g., User Manager, Server Manager, Event Viewer) will run as snap-ins within the Management Console (it will eventually be a requirement for a product bearing the BackOffice logo to be administered using an MMC snap-in). In addition, third-party developers will produce snap-ins for their BackOffice-compatible networking products. The MMC will run on Windows NT 4.0 and higher, and it will also run on Windows 95, allowing administrators to remotely manage network resources and servers even from a Windows 95 workstation.

The advantages of MMC-based administration include

- The ability to create custom management consoles that are *task-based.* Instead of being confronted with a bewildering array of separate tools, an administrator can create one management console specifically for Web server administration that has just those tools needed for administering Web servers, another console for remote access administration, and so on. Administration is simplified by reducing the clutter of unnecessary tools and providing only what is needed for the task at hand.
- The ability to *delegate* limited management tasks to others. A senior administrator can create a console for a junior administrator that allows limited functionality like backup and performance monitoring. The management console is saved as a simple `.msc` file that can be delivered by email or read from a network share.
- The existence of a *standardized framework* providing a single, integrated interface for snap-ins to run on. All snap-ins must conform to the look and feel of the MMC, easing administration and speeding up the learning curve for new administrative tools.

Microsoft Management Console version 1.0 is included with the Windows NT 4.0 Option Pack. This entry-level version of the MMC includes snap-ins to manage the following BackOffice products, which are included in the Option Pack:

- Internet Information Server 4.0
- Index Server 2.0
- Microsoft Transaction Server
- Simple Mail Transfer Protocol (SNMP) service
- Network News Transfer Protocol (NNTP) service

Version 1.0 of the MMC is limited in functionality but is capable of fully administering the above products. Version 1.1 has a target release date of mid-1998 and will include snap-ins to administer Microsoft SQL Server, Systems Management Server, and the beta versions of Windows NT 5.0. Some of the planned features for version 1.1 include

- Wizards for configuring MMC tools

- User mode console files
- Taskpads (task-based user interface tools based on HTML)
- Dynamic extensions
- Policy integration

Using the Microsoft Management Console

Starting the MMC

When IIS 4.0 is installed on a system, the Microsoft Management Console is automatically installed to provide tools for administering IIS. This Microsoft Management Console on an IIS server can be started in two ways:

Method 1 To start the Microsoft Management Console from the Internet Service Manager shortcut on the Start menu, choose START, PROGRAMS, WINDOWS NT 4.0 OPTION PACK, INTERNET SERVICE MANAGER. This opens an MMC console window with the IIS 4.0 snap-in loaded (and possibly other snap-ins as well, depending on what portions of the Windows NT 4.0 Option Pack you chose to install). The Start Menu shortcut is mapped to a Microsoft Management Console configuration file, or *tool* (saved as an `.msc` file), which contains the saved MMC window configuration and layout settings. This configuration file is located by the following path on a Windows NT server:

```
C:\winnt\system32\inetsrv\iis.msc
```

Tools (`.msc` files) are small files that can be copied or emailed to workstations of administrators or server operators who have specific management tasks delegated to them, such as administering the SNMP service on an IIS server. As long as a senior administrator has the MMC installed on his or her machine, along with the snap-in files being present, the senior administrator can create a tailor-made tool and send it to junior administrator or operator, who will be able to start the console simply by clicking on the tool (`.msc` file).

Method 2 To start the MMC with no snap-ins installed (functionality to the empty console can be added by loading snap-ins), click START, RUN and enter the following path:

```
C:\winnt\system32\mmc.exe
```

Snap-ins will need to be loaded into the console to enable it to perform administrative tasks. See the section "Adding a Snap-in to the MMC" for more information on how to do this.

If method 1 is chosen, a console window opens showing the Internet Information Server node under the Console Root node (see Fig. 2-1). There may be other nodes in the window as well (in the figure there is also a node for Microsoft Transaction Server), depending on the way the setup of Windows NT 4.0 Option pack was performed.

The MMC Layout

The layout of the console window is similar to the familiar Windows Explorer format and consists of two panes: the *scope pane* and the *results pane.*

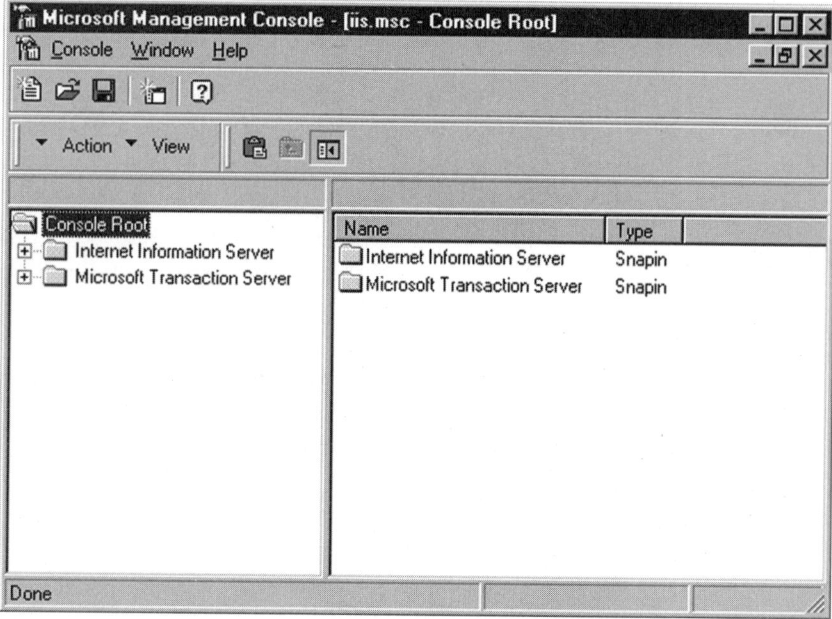

Figure 2-1 The Microsoft Management Console main window, when started from the Start Menu shortcut of Internet Service Manager.

The scope pane (left pane) provides a hierarchical view of all the network elements that can be managed using the MMC. These network elements are called *nodes*, and include servers, network services, directories, files, ActiveX controls, and so on. This collection of all manageable nodes is called the *namespace*.

The results pane (right pane) shows the manageable properties of whatever node is selected in the scope pane. In Fig. 2-2 the Default Web Site node under the IIS server called server1 is selected in the scope pane (namespace), while the results pane shows all the manageable nodes that exist in the namespace hierarchy under the server1 node, including virtual directories and even files.

The MMC is a *Multiple Document Interface (MDI) application*. That is, you can create multiple child windows within the same console parent window. Figure 2-2 shows the console with only one child window open; other windows can be added showing different views of the same namespace, and these windows can then be tiled, cascaded, maximized, or minimized as in any MDI application.

Other elements of the console window include the *menu bar*, the *main toolbar*, and the *rebar*. The menu bar (at the top) is used for the following functions:

- Create a *new* tool (`.msc` file)

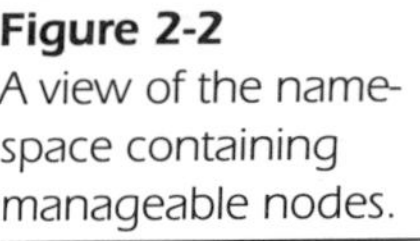

Figure 2-2
A view of the namespace containing manageable nodes.

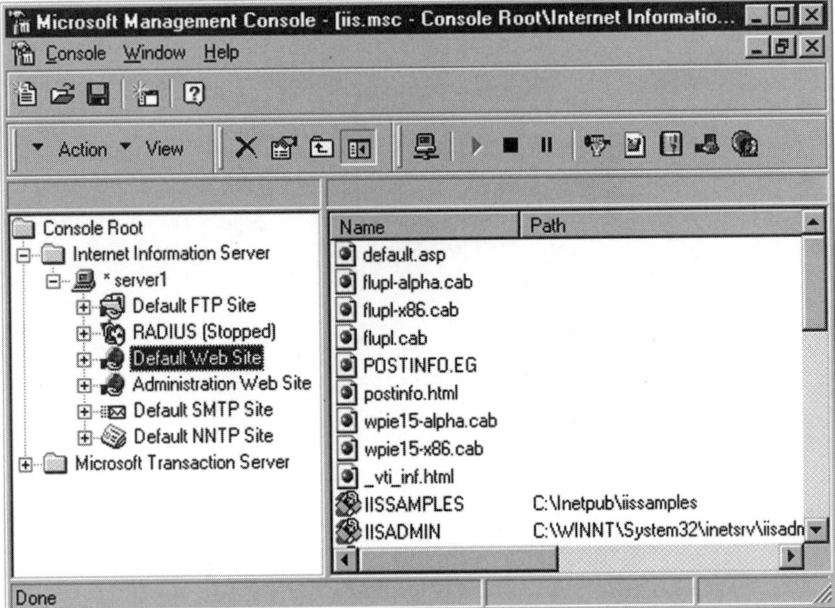

- *Open* an existing tool
- *Save* a tool configuration
- *Add* (or *remove*) a snap-in to the console
- *Customize* the appearance of the MMC
- *Access* the MMC help files

The main toolbar (below the menu bar) serves essentially the same function as the menu bar. Contained on it are the following five buttons:

- *Create* a new console button
- *Open* an existing console button
- *Save* the current console button
- *New* window button
- *About* button

The rebar (below the main toolbar—see Fig. 2-3), a customizable toolbar whose context-sensitive appearance depends on the currently selected node in the scope pane. A comparison between Figs. 2-1 and 2-2 shows the varying appearance of the rebar.

For example, when the Default Web Site (or any other node in the IIS section of the MMC namespace) is selected, the rebar shows the following buttons:

- *Action* button: clicking this button generates a drop-down menu that has essentially the same functionality as the shortcut menu that is accessed by right-clicking on a node in the namespace.
- *View* button: clicking this button generates a drop-down menu that allows you to change the view of icons in the results pane (just as in Windows Explorer).
- *Delete* a node button.
- *Show properties* of a node button.
- *Up one level* button.

Figure 2-3 Typical appearance of the rebar (varies with node being administered).

- *Show/Hide* the scope pane button.
- *Add a computer* to the list button.
- *Start* node button to start a Web site.
- *Stop* node button to stop a Web site.
- *Pause* node button to pause a Web site.

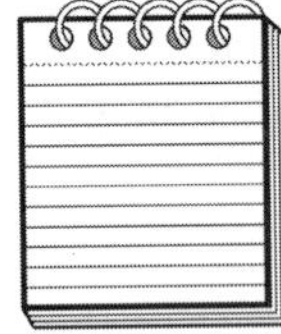

NOTE: *In previous versions of IIS administrators had three ways of stopping the WWW service on IIS, thus shutting down all Web sites on the server:*

1. *Select the WWW Service in Internet Service Manager and click the* STOP *button.*
2. *Open a command prompt and type* `net stop w3svc` *to terminate the* `inetinfo.exe` *process.*
3. *Open Services in Control Panel and stop the World Wide Web Publishing service.*

Because IIS 4.0 has a different architecture for supporting multiple Web sites, stopping and starting the WWW service is accomplished differently on IIS 4.0:

1. *Selecting a Web site (virtual server) node in the MMC and clicking the* STOP *button only stops that site, not the WWW service itself.*
2. *Using* `net stop w3svc` *at the command prompt or stopping the WWW Publishing service from Control Panel, Services stops the W3SVC service but leaves a second service IISADMIN still running so that* `inetinfo.exe` *is still running.*

If you need to unload and reload `inetinfo.exe` *completely for some reason, perform the following steps:*

1. *Open a command prompt.*
2. *Type*

   ```
   net stop iisadmin
   ```

3. *Type*

   ```
   net start w3svc
   ```

The remaining five buttons present on the rebar when an IIS node is selected launch key Windows NT administration tools, namely,

- *Key Manager* button
- *Performance Monitor* button
- *Event Viewer* button
- *Server Manager* button
- *User Manager for Domains* button

The status bar (bottom of console) shows details concerning the currently selected node (not functioning in MMC 1.0).

Creating a New MMC Console

To create a new (empty) console window:

From the menu bar, choose FILE, NEW.

or

Click the CREATE A NEW CONSOLE button on the main toolbar.

You will be prompted whether to save the current console settings (Fig. 2-4). Clicking YES will allow you to save the current console settings as an `.msc` file. Choosing NO will leave the currently opened console unmodified. Choose NO for now.

An empty console window will appear (Fig. 2-5). Notice the single child window within the parent console window. The only node in the console is the top-level node called Console Root.

The console window will have no management capability until we add snap-ins to it.

Figure 2-4 Choose whether to save your current console when creating a new one.

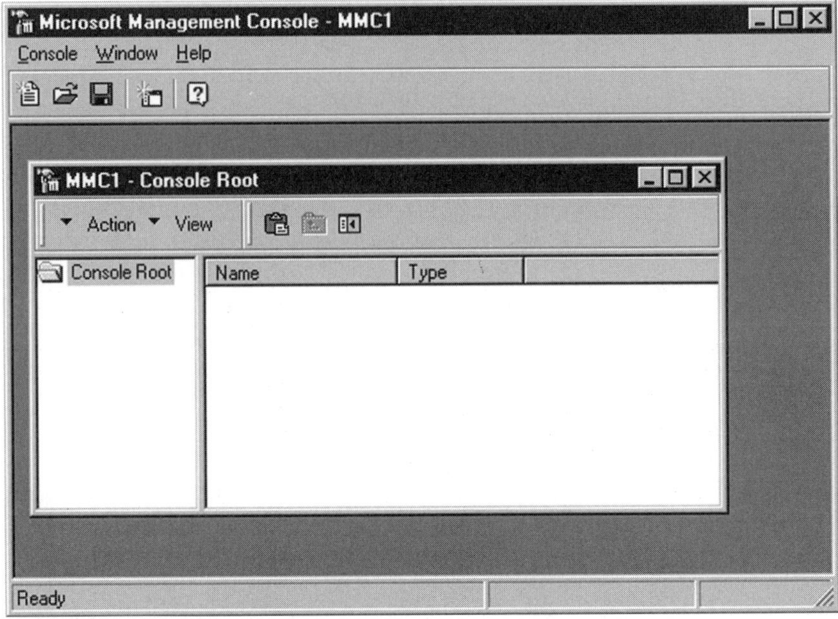

Figure 2-5
A new (empty) console showing only the Console Root node.

Adding a Snap-in to the MMC

Next we will add a standalone snap-in for Internet Service Manager to the console window. There are two basic types of snap-ins for the MMC:

- *Standalone snap-ins* (or just *snap-ins*) supply management capability for selected BackOffice products. An example would be the Internet Information Server snap-in, which provides the functionality of the Internet Service Manager.
- *Snap-in extensions* (or just *extensions*) supply additional functionality by extending the management capabilities of existing snap-ins. An example would be the Mail-SMTP extension for the Internet Information Server snap-in.

As the MMC evolves, Microsoft anticipates that third-party vendors will develop a variety of extensions that will add to the functionality of the MMC by supplying new menus, toolbars, wizards, and so on. Check the Microsoft Web site for these developments.

To add a new snap-in to the MMC, from the menu bar select CONSOLE, ADD/REMOVE SNAP-IN....The Add/Remove Snap-in dialog box appears (Fig. 2-6).

To add a standalone snap-in, select the Standalone tab and click ADD. The Add Standalone Snap-in box appears (Fig. 2-7). Select Internet Information Server (for example) and click OK. Internet Information Server is now listed as a console snap-in in the Add/Remove Snap-in dialog box. The Internet Information Server snap-in provides the full functionality of the Internet Service Manager for configuring your IIS 4.0 server.

In addition to adding standalone snap-ins to your console namespace, the Add Standalone Snap-in dialog box also allows you to add

- *Folders,* which are virtual folders that can be used to organize your MMC namespace. Note that the Root Console and Internet Information Server nodes also appear as folder icons in the MMC namespace.

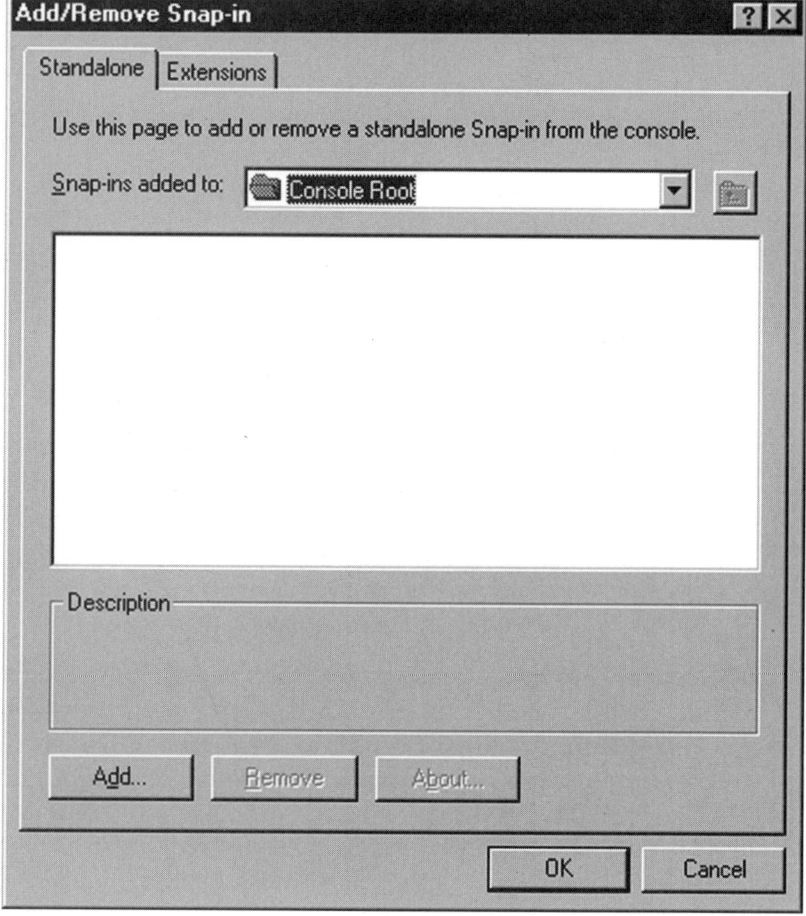

Figure 2-6
The Add/Remove Snap-in box.

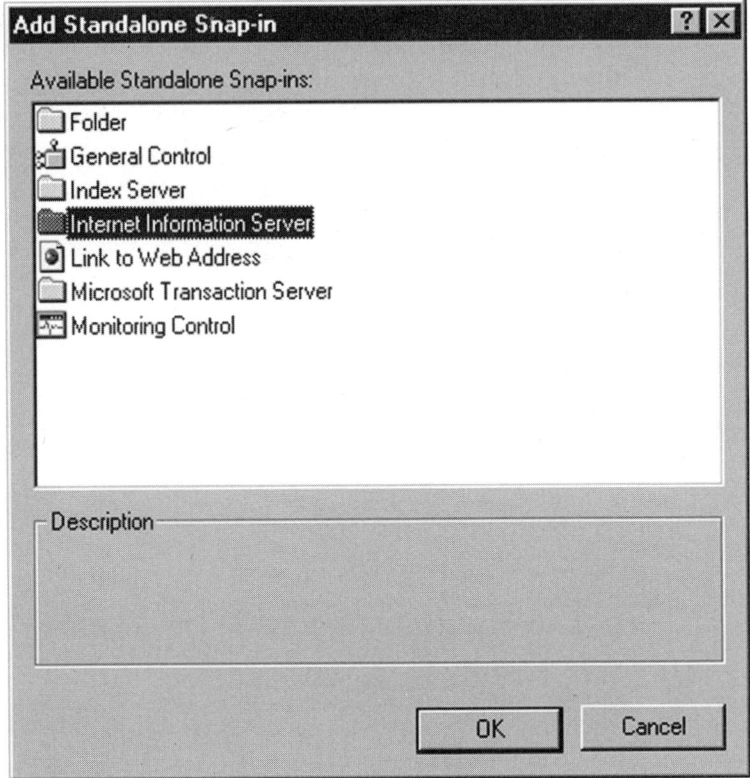

Figure 2-7
Choosing to install the Internet Service Manager standalone snap-in.

- *Links to Web addresses,* which are hyperlink URL nodes that will appear in the results pane when they are selected. An example appears below in the section "Adding a Node to the MMC."
- *General controls* and *monitoring controls,* which are ActiveX controls that may be embedded in the namespace as the results node for the node you are currently installing (this functionality is provided as a framework for developers, and will be further extended in later releases of the MMC).

To add a snap-in extension, select the Extensions tab on the Add/Remove Snap-in box (Fig. 2-8). Select the snap-in you wish to extend from the drop-down list to get a series of checkboxes showing the extensions you can add. Select the desired extensions (for example, the Mail-SMTP extension) and click OK to return to the MMC console window. The Internet Information Server snap-in with the Mail-SMTP extension has now been added to the console window (Fig. 2-9).

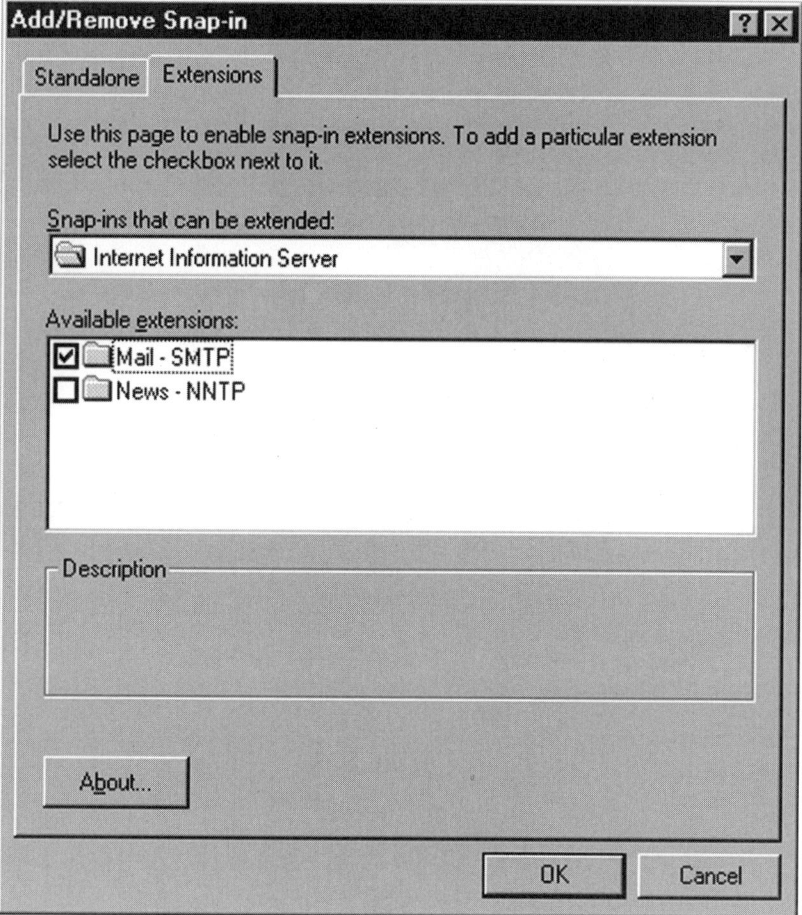

Figure 2-8
Adding the Mail-SMTP extension to the Internet Information Server snap-in.

Customizing an MMC Console

Shown in Fig. 2-9 is the new console created in the previous section. Notice that this console has one child window, titled *MMC1—Console Root.*

Our newly created console can be customized in a variety of ways. For example, you may want to create a new child window whose function is to allow administration of a single IIS 4.0 server. To do this, select the Internet Information Server node in the scope pane to show the IIS 4.0 servers that can currently be managed in the results pane. If the server you wish to administer doesn't appear in the results pane, you will need to connect to it first by right-clicking on the Internet Information Server

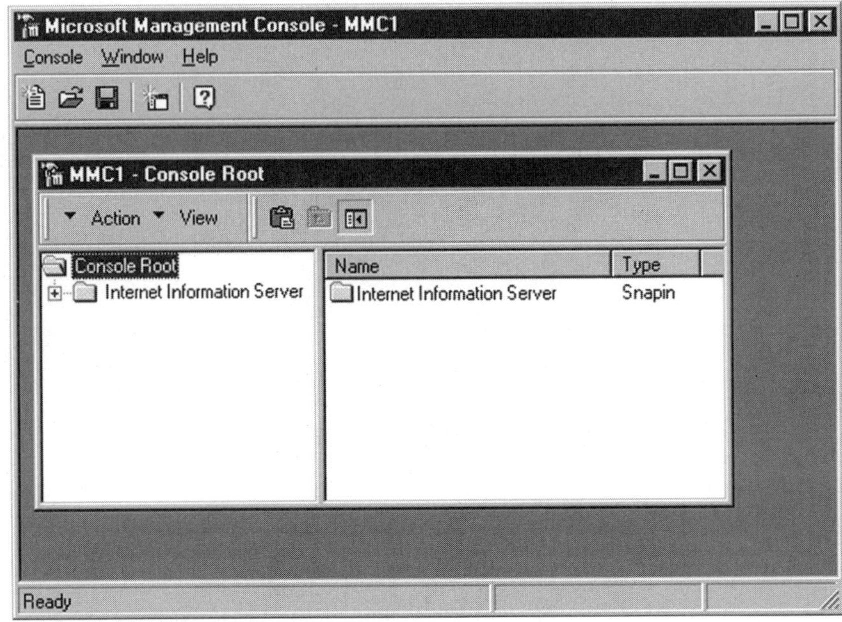

Figure 2-9 A newly created console with the Internet Information Server snap-in installed.

node in the scope pane, selecting CONNECT from the shortcut menu, and entering in the name of the IIS 4.0 server you wish to connect to.

In the results pane, select the IIS 4.0 server you wish to create a MMC child window for and

Right-click on the server node and select NEW WINDOW FROM HERE from the shortcut menu.

or

Click the ACTION button on the rebar and select NEW WINDOW FROM HERE from the drop-down menu.

Either of these actions retitles the original child window as MMC 1:1 and creates a second child window titled MMC 1:2 (see Fig. 2-10). The second child window has the IIS 4.0 server you selected in the above steps as the top of its namespace.

Note that although the two windows have different root nodes, they both give views of the *same* namespace. An MMC console can show only one namespace at a time.

These two child windows can be resized, tiled, or cascaded as in any MDI application. For example, select the new MMC 1:2 window, maxi-

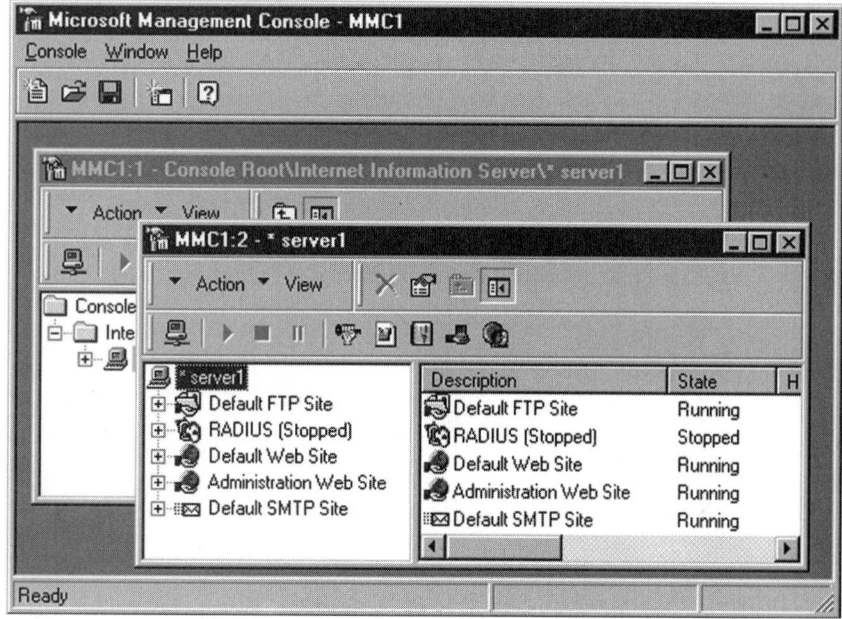

Figure 2-10
A console with two child windows.

mize it, and then change the view in the results pane by clicking the VIEW button on the rebar and selecting LARGE from the drop-down list as the icon size in the results pane. The result is shown in Fig. 2-11.

After creating the second child window, you could close the original child window, which contains the Console Root node. If you do this, the top of your MMC namespace for your currently open console becomes a single IIS 4.0 server (server1 in Figs. 2-10 and 2-11). The console settings can then be saved as an `.msc` configuration file, set to read-only mode, and delivered to a designated administrator or operator whose task is only to administer the single server called server1.

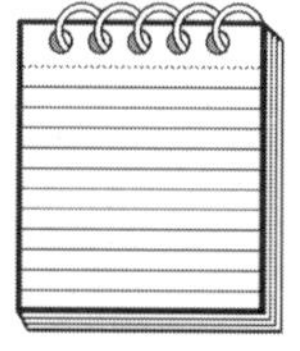

NOTE: *Read-only mode is not implemented in this release of the MMC. Furthermore, a bug in version 1.0 of the MMC may cause the program to shut down due to an illegal operation being performed if you try to close the original console child window. This happens, for example, if you create a new child window starting from the default Web site and then try to close the previous child window for the server hosting the default Web site. This bug will probably be fixed by the time this book appears.*

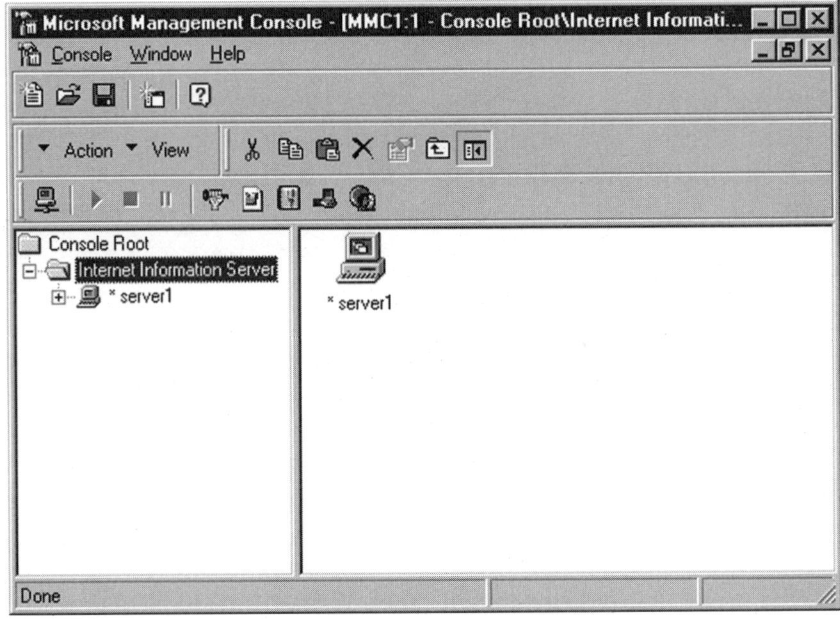

Figure 2-11 A new view of a customized MMC console.

Adding a Node to the MMC

As mentioned earlier, several types of nodes may be added to the console, including virtual folders, links to Web addresses, and ActiveX controls. Here we give an example of adding a node to the console that functions as a link to the IIS server's home page on its default Web site. This node will be placed immediately beneath the Internet Information Server node in the namespace.

To add a new node to the MMC:

Select the Internet Information Server node in the scope pane and choose CONSOLE, ADD-REMOVE SNAP-IN from the menu to open the Add/Remove Snap-in box. Click the ADD button to open the Add Standalone Snap-in box, select LINK TO WEB ADDRESS (for example), and click OK.

or

Simply right-click on the Internet Information Server node in the scope pane, and select NEW, LINK TO WEB ADDRESS from the shortcut menu.

Either method will open the Link to Web Address wizard. Type in the URL:

```
http://<server_name>
```

where <server_name> is the name (NetBIOS or fully-qualified domain name) of the IIS 4.0 server for which you wish to create a link to its home page on its default Web site (Fig. 2-12).

Click NEXT and enter a friendly name (description) for this new node (we have chosen the friendly name *Home Page for Default Web* in this example). Then click FINISH to create the new node. Notice that a Web page icon appears in the results pane when the Internet Information Server node is selected in the scope pane (Fig. 2-13).

Your console window can be further customized by using the fact that nodes that have folder icons (e.g., virtual folders and snap-ins), links to Web addresses, and ActiveX controls can be cut, copied, and pasted into different arrangements using the ACTION button on the rebar or using the shortcut menus that appear when you right-click on these nodes.

Finally, click on the new Home Page for Default Web icon in the scope pane (or double-click on its node in the results pane), and the Web page will open up in the results pane, as shown in Fig. 2-14.

Note that when a Web page is open in the results pane, additional Web navigation buttons are available on the rebar (see Fig. 2-14).

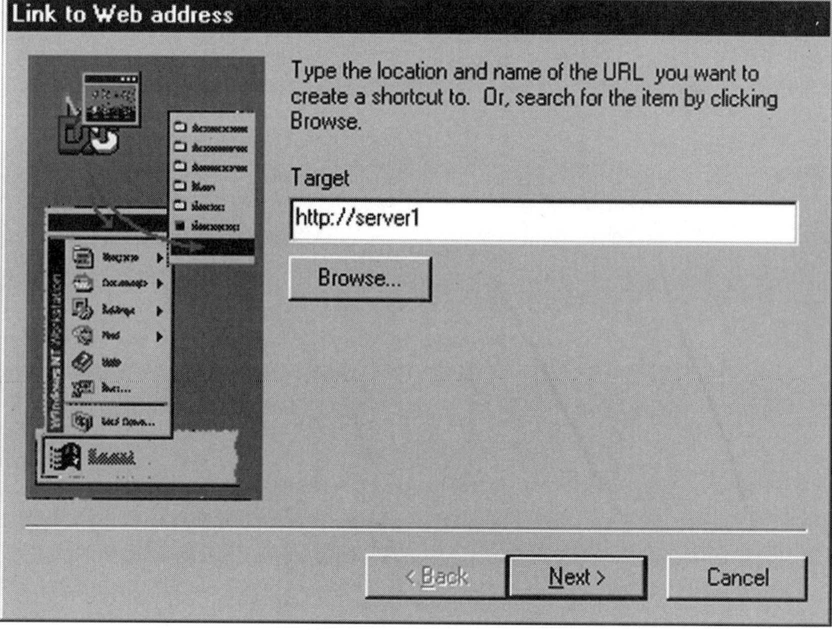

Figure 2-12 Adding a node linking to an IIS 4.0 server's default home page.

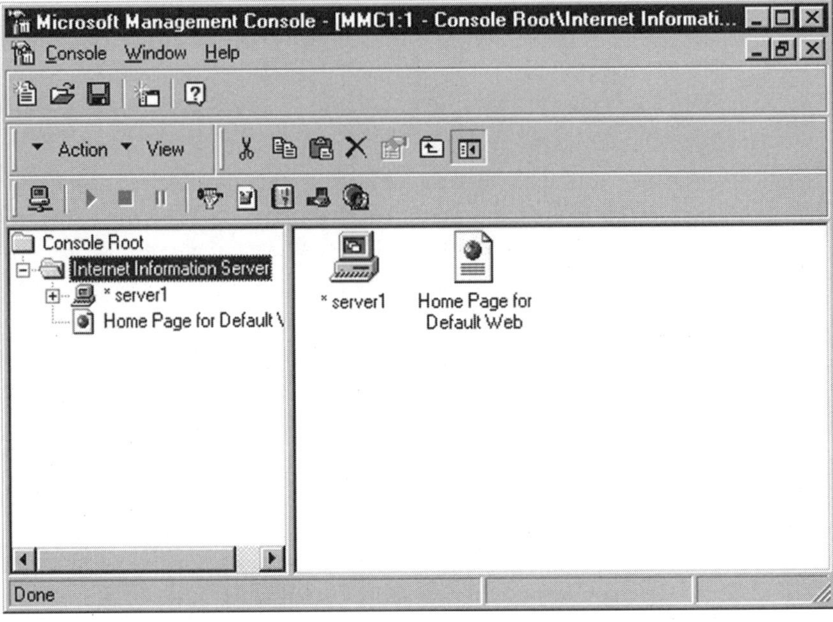

Figure 2-13 A new Link to Web Address node has been created under the IIS node.

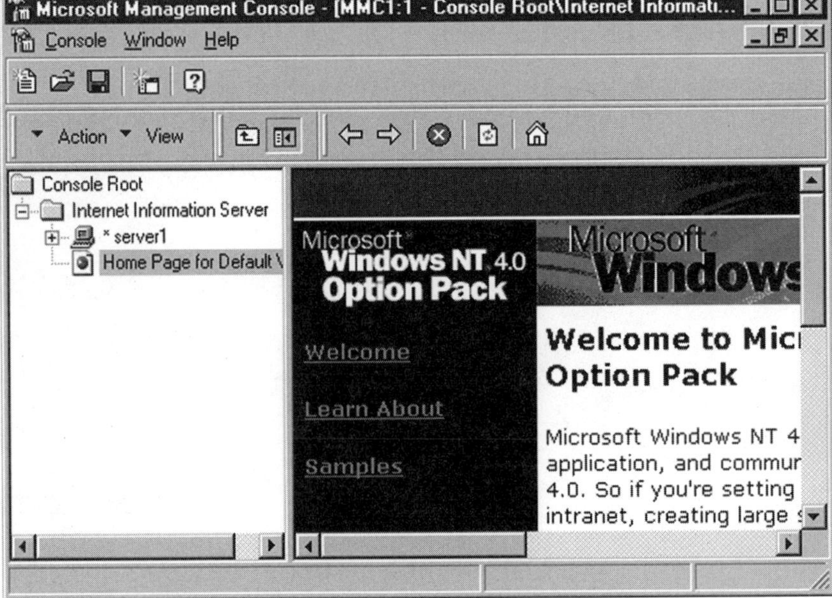

Figure 2-14 A Web page as the results view of a selected node in the scope pane.

Remember that the appearance of the rebar changes in a context-sensitive manner depending on which node is currently selected.

Saving an MMC Console

To save your newly configured console:

Choose CONSOLE, SAVE or SAVE AS from the menu.

or

Click the SAVE button on the main toolbar.

The Save As dialog box appears. Type a filename for your new console and save it with the default extension of `.msc` in the location you specify. The `.msc` file you create is called a *tool.*

Possible locations for saving a tool include the following:

- The folder My Administrative Tools (the default location for saving `.msc` files), which appears in the Programs folder on the Start menu and is stored within your currently open user profile (see Fig. 2-15). For example, if you are currently logged on as the user `administrator`, you will be prompted to save the `.msc` file in the location

```
C:\winnt\profiles\administrator\Start Menu\Programs\My Administrative Tools\
```

Figure 2-15 Saving MMC console settings as a file called `TestConsole.msc`.

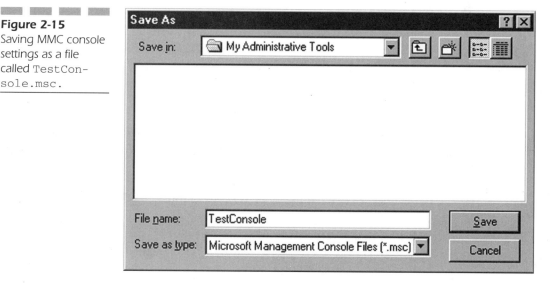

- A network share on an NTFS volume accessible to other administrators and server operators. For example, if you create a custom console with only certain nodes added, you may want to set the `.msc` file to read-only mode so that the administrator or operator you delegate the console to cannot permanently modify the file.
- Attached to an email message mailed to a designated administrator operator.

NOTE: *The designated administrator or operator who uses the* `.msc` *file you created must have the MMC locally installed on his or her machine with the necessary snap-ins added in order to be able to use the* `.msc` *file. The* `.msc` *file contains configuration information only and has no intrinsic management capability.*

Further Examples of Using the MMC

Look back for a moment to Fig. 2-2, which shows the default Web site selected in the scope pane on the IIS 4.0 server called server1. The results pane shows the contents (Web pages and files) that make up this Web site. But where are the contents actually located? In other words, what is the location (local or network) of the home directory for the default Web site?

To answer this question, in the screen of Fig. 2-2 simply right-click on the Default Web Site node in the MMC and select EXPLORE to open Windows Explorer (Fig. 2-16). This action will open up Windows Explorer at the home directory for the default Web site, in this case

```
C:\winnt\inetpub\wwwroot\
```

Configuring settings for a Web site is easy using the MMC. In the screen of Fig. 2-2 simply right-click on the Administration Web Site node and select PROPERTIES to access the Administration Web Site Properties box (see Fig. 2-17).

In Chap. 3 we will see how to use these property sheets to configure a wide variety of settings for servers, Web and FTP sites, and even individual directories and files.

Settings that are made on these property sheets are stored in the *Metabase.* This is a hierarchical memory-resident database where IIS 4.0 settings and properties are stored. Many of these settings were stored in

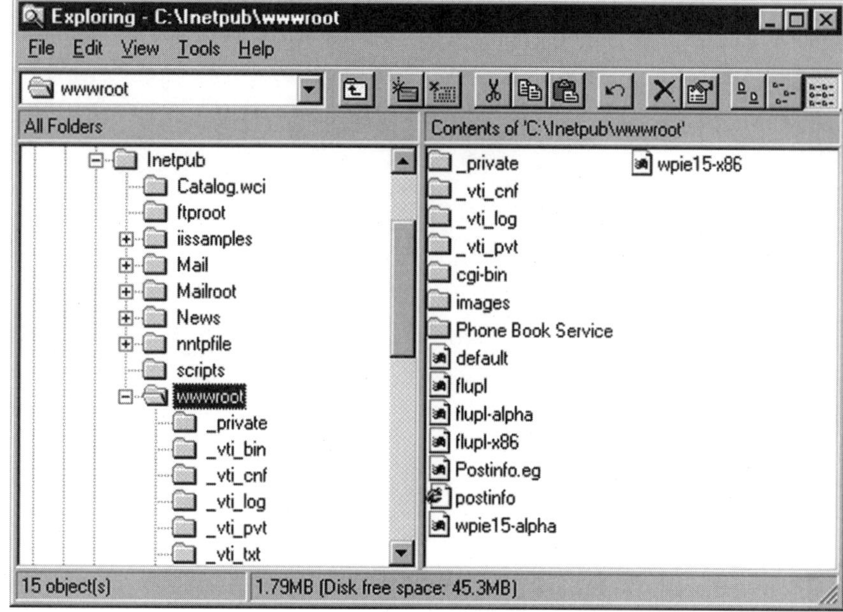

Figure 2-16 Locating a web site's home directory in Windows Explorer.

the Registry in previous versions of IIS, but these settings have now been migrated to the Metabase because it is more flexible and faster to access than the Registry. However, some IIS registry keys remain to provide backward compatibility with earlier versions of IIS.

Currently there is no specific tool for going in and tweaking the Metabase the way you can do to the Registry using `regedt32.exe` or something similar. Instead, Metabase settings may be changed using scripts written in VBScript and run from within Web pages or using the Windows Scripting Host, described below.

Just as with the Registry, configuring settings in the Metabase incorrectly may render your IIS 4.0 server inoperable, and should only be done with utmost care. For information on VBScript APIs for editing the Metabase, refer to the IIS online documentation.

Walkthrough: Using the MMC to Enable Internet Service Manager (HTML) for Remote Administration

You can use the MMC to configure Web and FTP sites you have created on your IIS server. For example, in Fig. 2-2 simply right-click on the

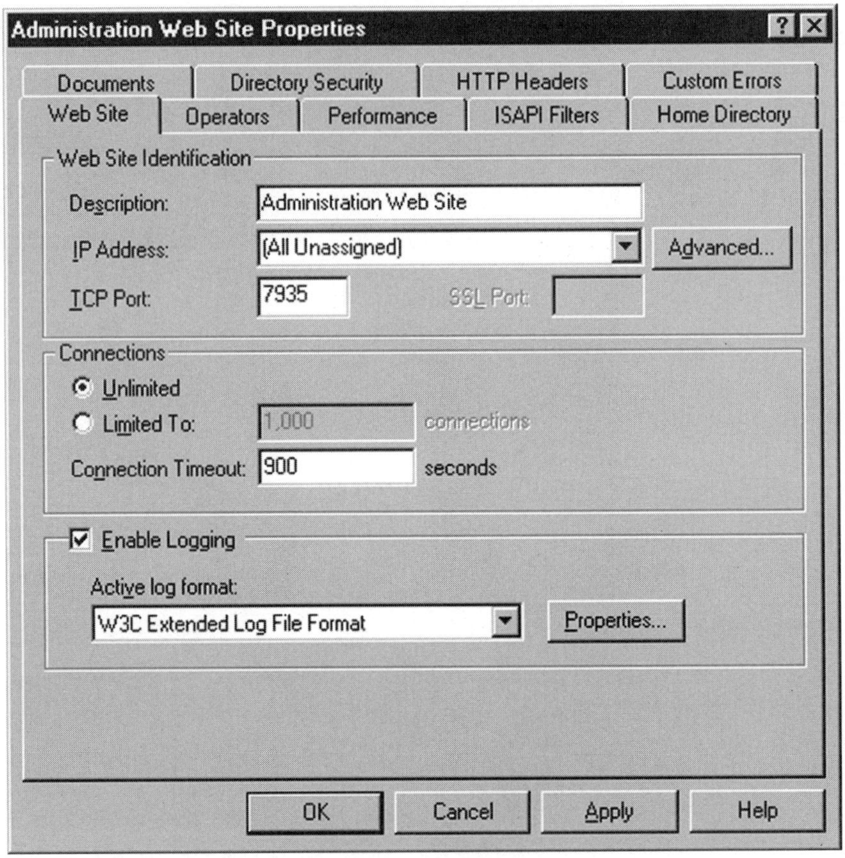

Figure 2-17 Configuring properties for the Administration Web.

Administration Web Site node and select OPEN or BROWSE from the shortcut menu. This opens the home page of the administration Web site, used to remotely administer IIS 4.0 servers using only a browser. The administration Web site is also known as the *Internet Service Manager HTML* and is a tool for remotely administering IIS servers using a standard Web browser. The Internet Service Manager (HTML) is covered in the next section of this chapter.

Notice in Fig. 2-18 that what actually opens up if we try the above procedure is an *HTTP Error 403* page. This is because after a default installation of IIS 4.0 the security settings will need to be modified to enable remote administration of IIS 4.0 servers by accessing the administration Web site from a browser. The default settings for the administration Web site when IIS 4.0 is installed include an IP address restriction that allows the site only to be accessed by the following URLs:

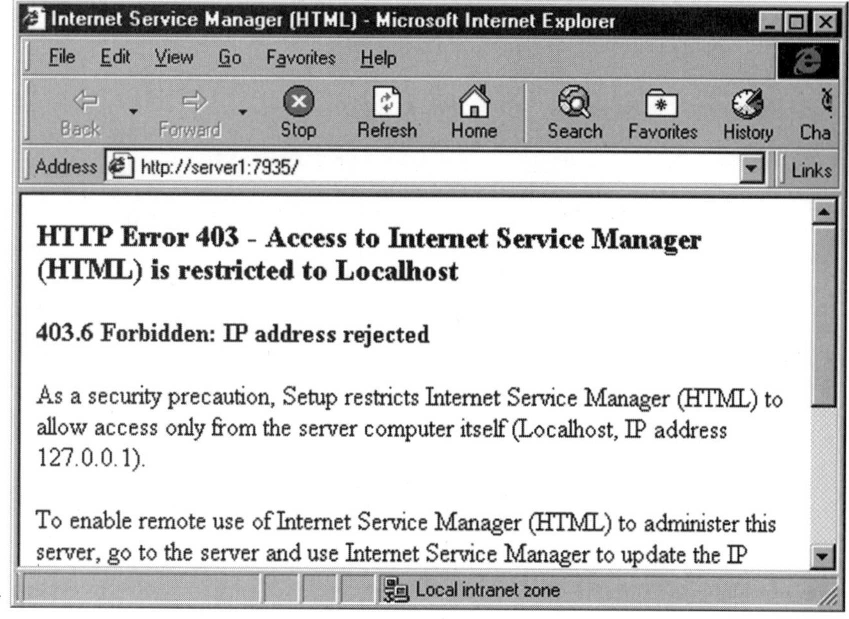

Figure 2-18 Trying to browse the administration Web site from the MMC.

```
http://localhost:<tcp_port_number>
```

or

```
http://127.0.0.1:<tcp_port_number>
```

where <tcp_port_number> is the port number for the administration Web site. This can be found from the Web site tab of the Administration Web Site Properties sheet. In Fig. 2-17 this port number is 7935, so the administration Web site can be accessed from the URL

```
http://localhost:7935
```

or

```
http://127.0.0.1:7935
```

However, the two URLs above work only if the browser is installed on the server itself. Furthermore, if you right-click on the administration Web site node in the MMC and select BROWSE, the browser tries to open up the site

```
http://<server_name>:<tcp_port_number>
```

or in this case

```
http://server1:7935
```

which fails to work locally and remotely because of the IP address restriction in place.

This default IP address restriction essentially means that when you install IIS 4.0 you can only use the Internet Service Manager (HTML) to manage the server from a browser that is installed locally on the IIS server, and you have to access it through localhost or the loopback address, not the server's NetBIOS name or fully qualified domain name. So if we want to enable administrators to use browsers on remote computers to administer their IIS servers, we need to reconfigure the default security settings.

To remove this IP address restriction, access the Administration Web Site Properties sheet (Fig. 2-17), select the Directory Security tab, and click the EDIT button for IP Address and Domain Name Restrictions. This brings up the IP Address and Domain Name Restrictions dialog box as shown in Fig. 2-19.

Note the default setting for this Web site, namely, that all IP addresses are to be denied access except the *loopback* address 127.0.0.1 is granted access to the site.

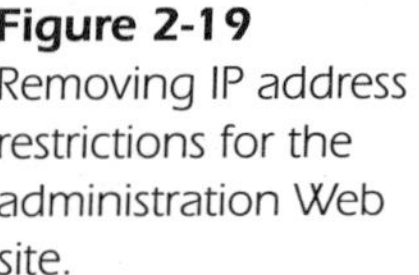

Figure 2-19 Removing IP address restrictions for the administration Web site.

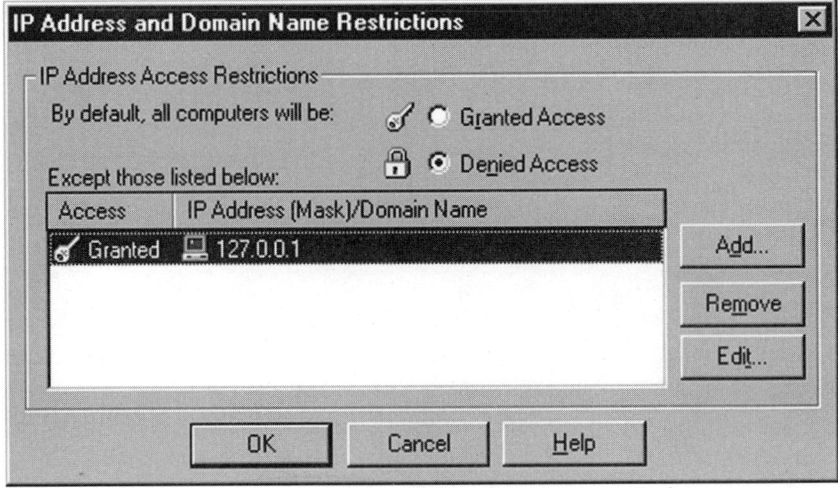

Select the radio button GRANTED ACCESS to grant all computers access to this Web site. This way an administrator will be able to administer the IIS server using the administration Web site from any computer regardless of its IP address, as long as that computer has a suitable browser installed on it.

Of course, granting all computers access to the administration Web site creates a security hole: anyone who knows which port the administration Web site is running on can connect to the site and perform administrative tasks.

We need to close this hole, so on the Administration Web Site Properties sheet, select the Directory Security tab again and deselect ALLOW ANONYMOUS ACCESS (if it is selected), making sure that only Windows NT Challenge/Response authentication is enabled. By doing this, you add to the site the further security restriction that to administer the site you will need to have a valid Windows NT domain user account.

Next, select the Operators tab and make sure that the only group that has been granted operator privileges on the administration Web site is the Administrators local group. This renders the site secure because only members of the Administrators local group have permission to access it. The Administrators local group on the IIS server should of course contain the Domain Admins global group.

Finally, to safeguard security, make sure that the Everyone group is removed from all files and subdirectories in the directory containing the Internet Service Manager (HTML) files, namely

```
C:\winnt\system32\inetsrv\
```

You should now be able to securely connect to the administration Web site locally or remotely by using the following URL from a suitable browser on any computer in the domain where you are logged on as administrator:

```
http://<server_name>:<tcp_port_number>
```

or in this case

```
http://server1:7935
```

When you use this URL in Internet Explorer 4.0, the result is as shown in Fig. 2-20.

Using the MMC to configure IIS 4.0 server property sheets for Web and FTP sites will be covered in more detail in Chaps. 3 and 10.

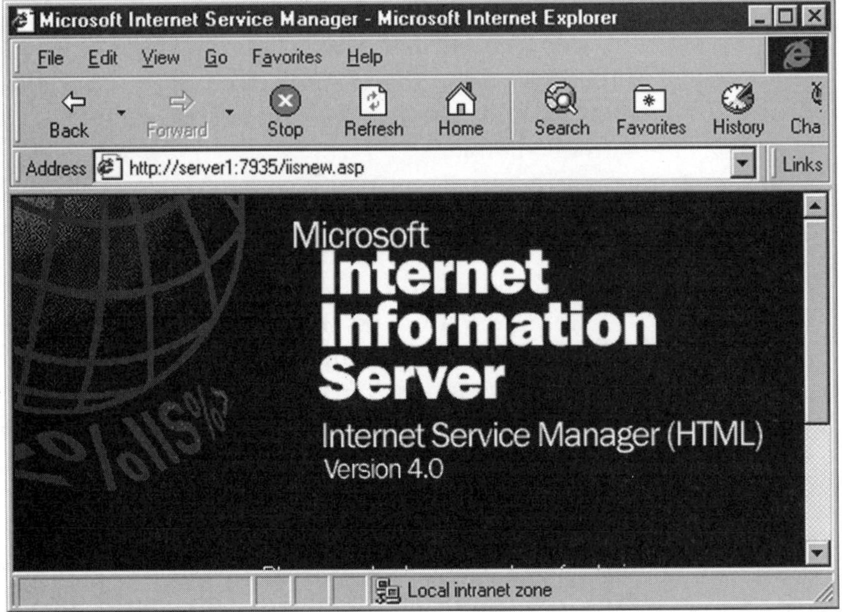

Figure 2-20 Connecting to the administration Web site to use the ISM (HTML).

Understanding the Internet Service Manager (HTML)

As mentioned above, included with IIS 4.0 is a browser-based version of the Internet Service Manager called *Internet Service Manager (HTML)*. The ISM (HTML) allows administrators to remotely administer IIS 4.0 servers from browsers over an intranet or the Internet. The previous section dealt with using the MMC to modify IIS security settings, in order to enable remote administration with the ISM (HTML).

In order to use the ISM (HTML), the administrator needs to know what TCP port the administration Web site is configured to use. This is because when IIS 4.0 is installed on a machine, it randomly assigns a port number between 2000 and 9999 to the administration Web site. However, the administration Web site will respond to all of the domain names configured on the IIS server, as long as the port number is appended to the request.

The ISM (HTML) will run from any browser that supports JScript and frames. Internet Explorer 3.02 or higher is supported.

The ISM (HTML) allows administrators to perform most of the management functions that the MMC provides. However, certain functions that can be performed on the MMC cannot be performed from the ISM (HTML), such as configuring the administration Web site itself.

Using the Internet Service Manager (HTML)

Starting the Internet Service Manager (HTML)

To start the ISM (HTML) from the IIS server itself,

Click START, PROGRAMS, WINDOWS NT 4.0 OPTION PACK, MICROSOFT INTERNET INFORMATION SERVER, INTERNET SERVICE MANAGER (HTML).

or

Access the URL

```
http://<host>:<admin_port_number>
```

where <host> is either the IP address, NetBIOS name, or fully qualified domain name of the server and <admin_port_number> is the TCP port number assigned to the administration Web site.

The result is shown in the screenshot of Fig. 2-20. Scroll down the screen, and click on LARGE or SMALL for font size. The result is the main ISM (HTML) page shown in Fig. 2-21.

To access the ISM (HTML) from a remote machine, access the URL

```
http://<hostname>:<admin_port_number>
```

or

```
http://<hostname>/iisadmin:<admin_port_number>
```

Members of the Administrators group may use either method above; other Web site operators must use the second method only.

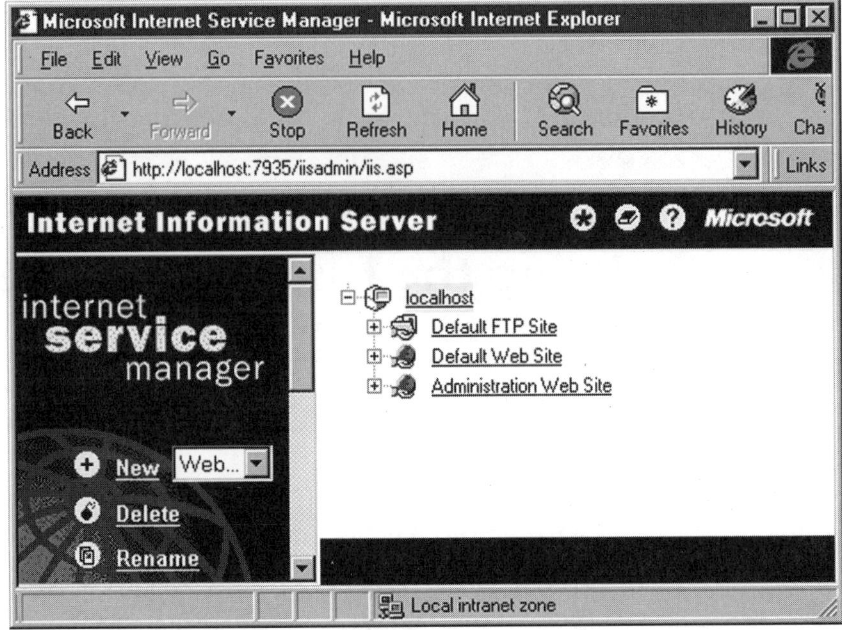

Figure 2-21 The main screen of the Internet Service Manager (HTML).

Configuring Site Properties with the Internet Service Manager (HTML)

Chapter 3 fully discusses the various options for configuring IIS 4.0. Chapter 3 deals only with using the MMC to administer IIS, but using the ISM (HTML) is essentially the same, except that instead of using tabbed property sheets, the ISM (HTML) uses hyperlinks to access different configuration pages. After learning how to administer IIS with the MMC, it is only a small step further to administering it with the ISM (HTML).

Nevertheless, here is one small example of using the ISM (HTML) to configure IIS. To configure the MYCORP\IIS Operators global group as Web site operators for the default Web site, perform the following steps using the ISM (HTML):

Select the Default Web Site icon in the right-hand frame in Fig. 2-21 and click the Properties hyperlink in the left-hand frame.

or

Click on the Default Web Site hyperlink in the right-hand frame in Fig. 2-21.

Either method causes a new page to load in the browser, which looks like Fig. 2-22.

To grant operator privileges for the default Web site to a global group called IIS Operators on the MYCORP domain controller, click the ADD button in Fig. 2-22. The Explorer User Prompt dialog box appears, prompting you to enter in the name of the user or group you want to grant operator privileges to (see Fig. 2-23). The group must be specified in the form

```
<domain_name>\<group>
```

For our example, you would enter

```
MYCORP\IIS Operators
```

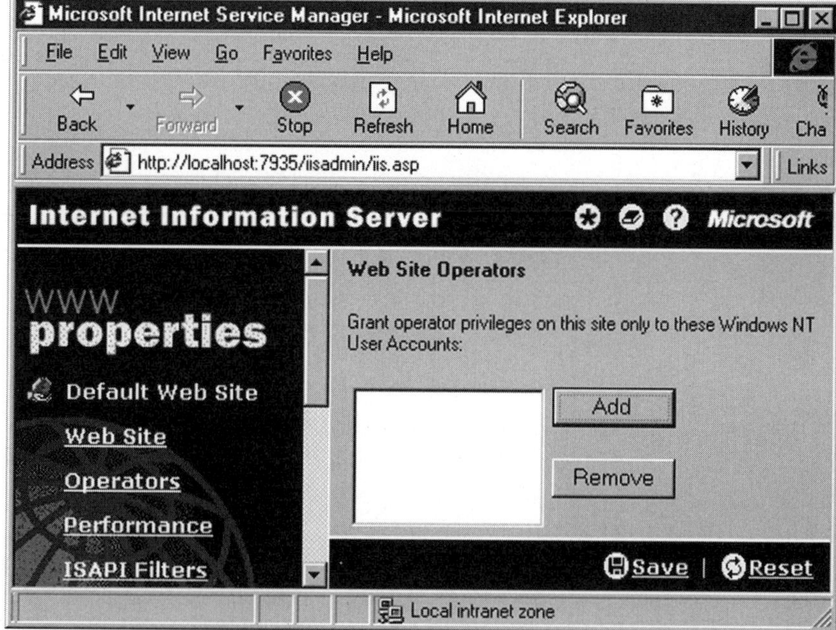

Figure 2-22 Accessing the Web Site Operators settings using the (ISM) HTML.

Explorer User Prompt

JavaScript Prompt:

Enter a domain and user name.

OK

Cancel

DOMAIN\username

Figure 2-23 Specify the group to be added to the list of Web site operators.

Click OK to close the dialog box. To apply the settings, click the SAVE icon at the bottom of the ISM (HTML) page.

To check your work, open the MMC on the server and access the Property sheet for the default Web site. Select the Operators tab and verify that `MYCORP\IIS Operators` has been added to the list of operators.

Understanding the Windows Scripting Host

The third and last management tool included with IIS 4.0 in the Windows NT 4.0 Option Pack is the *Windows Scripting Host (WSH).* This tool functions as a controller of ActiveX scripting engines, allowing administrative scripts to be run either from the command line or directly from shortcuts on the desktop.

Microsoft now has three products that run scripting languages:

- Internet Information Server runs Active Server Pages, which are server-side scripts that run on Web servers.
- Internet Explorer can run client-side scripts on the browser.
- The Windows Scripting Host can run scripts directly on administrator consoles.

The usual scripting languages for the Windows Scripting Host are VBScript (Visual Basic Scripting language) and Jscript (JavaScript), but other scripting engines like Perl can be registered on the system and mapped to the WSH. Refer to the NT 4.0 Option Pack online documentation in the section entitled "Windows Scripting Host Programmer's Reference" for more information on how to register a new scripting engine for WSH.

The main advantage of using the WSH is that scripts written in VBScript and Jscript are far more powerful than those written with the standard scripting language of MS-DOS command batch files. Using VBScript or Jscript, the administrator can write either interactive or batch (i.e., noninteractive) scripts that perform administrative tasks such as

- Creating users and groups
- Configuring environment variables

- Configuring registry and metabase keys
- Mapping network drives
- Performing additional user authentication

The WSH will run on Windows NT 4.0 Server, Windows NT 4.0 Workstation, and Windows 95. It will be an integral part of both Windows NT 5.0 and Windows 98 when they are released.

You can download the WSH separately and install it on your machine by visiting the following URL at the Microsoft Web site:

```
www.microsoft.com/management/WSH.htm
```

Sample scripts are included with the installation of the WSH from the NT 4.0 Option Pack. These sample scripts are located in

```
C:\winnt\samples\WSH\
```

Included are the samples listed in Table 2-1.

The scripts of Table 2-1 and other sample scripts are also available from the Microsoft Web site as a self-extracting file. To download these samples, open the URL

```
www.microsoft.com/management/WSH.htm
```

Table 2-1

Sample Scripts Included with the Installation of the WSH from the NT 4.0 Option Pack

Script	What It Does
Chart.vbs	Demonstrates how to access Microsoft Excel using the WSH.
Chart.js	
Excel.vbs	Displays the properties of WSH in Microsoft Excel.
Excel.js	
Network.vbs	Displays user and computer names, lists network drives, and maps new ones.
Network.js	
Registry.vbs	Writes keys to the registry and then deletes them.
Registry.js	
Shortcut.vbs	Creates a shortcut to Notepad on the desktop.
Shortcut.js	
Showvar.vbs	Lists server environment variables.

Using the Windows Scripting Host

This section deals with configuring and running scripts using the WSH. Developing and testing scripts in VBScripts and Jscript requires knowledge of these scripting languages and is beyond the scope of this book.

Running Scripts from the Command Line Using the WSH

Scripts written in either VBScript or Jscript can be run from the command line using the command-line-only version of the WSH. This *command-line version of WSH* is called `cscript.exe` and is located in the path

```
C:\winnt\system32\cscript.exe
```

although it can be installed anywhere in the main system path.

To run the `showvar.vbs` sample script from the command line, open a Command Prompt window and type

```
cscript showvar.vbs
```

The result will be a series of dialog boxes displaying the currently defined environment variables on the IIS server.

Command-Line Options for the WSH

The full syntax for running scripts with the command-line version of WSH is as follows:

```
cscript <script_filename> <host_options> <script_options>
```

where

- <script_filename> is the path to the script (unless it is located in the current directory).
- <host_options> are options preceded by two forward slashes (//) that enable or disable certain aspects of WSH.

- <script_options> are parameters preceded by one forward slash (/) that are passed to the script for it to execute properly (depending on the script).

Table 2-2 explains the host options available with the command-line version of WSH.

Running Scripts from the Desktop Using the WSH

Scripts written in VBScript or Jscript can be run from the desktop using the *Windows version of the WSH.* This version of WSH is called `wscript.exe` and is located in the path

```
C:\winnt\system32\wscript.exe
```

although it can be installed anywhere in the main system path.

Table 2-2

Host Options Available with the Command-line Version of WSH

Host Option	What It Does
`//I`	Runs the script in interactive mode—i.e., the user is presented with the results of running the script and has to follow the prompts at various points.
`//B`	Runs the script in batch mode—i.e., the script offers no visible user output and requires no user response. This mode is suitable for scripts like logon scripts that have to run automatically at logon.
`//logo`	Displays information about the version of WSH being run when the script is executed.
`//nologo`	Suppresses the information about the version of WSH being run when the script is executed.
`//T:nn`	Runs the script for a time of `nn` seconds. If not finished by that time, the script is terminated. This is important so that runaway scripts don't cause the system to be brought down.
`//S`	Saves the currently defined options for the user currently using the WSH.
`//H:Wscript` or `//H:Cscript`	Switches the default application for executing scripts from Cscript to Wscript or vice versa.
`//?`	Lists the various options available for configuring the WSH.

To run the `showvar.vbs` sample script from the desktop, do one of the following:

- Double-click on the icon for `showvar.vbs` in Windows Explorer, My Computer, the Find box, or on the desktop. The WSH makes use of the file extensions `.vbs` and `.js` for executing scripts.
- Click START, RUN, type the path to the script, and click OK.
- Go to the command line and type

```
wscript showvar.vbs
```

Again, the result will be a series of dialog boxes displaying the currently defined environment variables on the IIS server.

Configuring .WSH Files for Windows-Based WSH Scripts

Just as DOS programs running on the old Windows 3.1 platform needed a PIF file to configure the environment in which they ran, similarly scripts that are run with the Windows-based version of the WSH can make use of a configuration file, called a `.wsh` file.

Settings can be configured at the per-script level by creating a `.wsh` file for each script. Scripts may have multiple `.wsh` files, allowing an administrator to create multiple configurations for running scripts and then assign different configurations to different people on the system.

To create a `.wsh` file for a script (for example, `showvar.vbs`), locate the script in Windows Explorer or My Computer, right-click on the script, and select PROPERTIES. Select the Scripts tab of the property sheet, and select the runtime configuration options as desired for this particular script.

When you close the Properties box, a file called `showvar.wsh` is created in the same directory as the script. This file can be opened in any text editor and looks something like this, depending on what options were selected:

```
[ScriptFile]
Path = C:\winnt\Samples\wsh\showvar.vbs

[Options]
Timeout = 10
DisplayLogo = 1
BatchMode = 0
```

While `.wsh` files set options for specific scripts, it is also possible to set global options for all scripts being executed by the WSH. To set global options for all scripts executed by the WSH, locate the file `wscript.exe` in the System32 directory and double-click on it to open the Windows Scripting Host box. Under the General tab, select the run-time options you desire as defaults for all scripts run on your machine. The options currently available with version 1.0 of the WSH are

- Stop scripts after specified number of seconds.
- Display logo when scripts are executed in command mode.

Because the available options are more limited, the Windows-based version of WSH is more suited to interactive scripts than batch scripts.

To run a script while making use of its `.wsh` file, double-click on the `.wsh` file to execute the script. If you double-click the script itself, it will ignore the `.wsh` file.

NOTE: *Be sure to keep the* `.wsh` *file in the same directory as the script. If you move the* `.wsh` *file to a different directory, you should edit the file and modify the* `Path` *statement inside it.*

SUMMARY

IIS 4.0 when installed from Windows NT 4.0 Option Pack comes with three management tools: the Microsoft Management Console for local administration of IIS 4.0 servers, the HTML version of Internet Service Manager for remote administration using a browser, and the Windows Scripting Host for batch and interactive scripting of administrative commands, which is run either from the desktop or from the command line. You can select the tool most suited to the administrative tasks that need to be performed. Administrators should also regularly visit Microsoft's Web site for updates to these management tools.

FOR MORE INFORMATION

Microsoft Web Site For general information regarding Microsoft Management tools visit the Microsoft Web site at

```
www.microsoft.com/management
```

Latest information on the Microsoft Management Console (MMC) can be found at

```
http://www.microsoft.com/management/mmc/helpmenu_productnews.htm
```

Latest information on the Windows Scripting Host (WSH) can be found at

```
http://www.microsoft.com/management/WSH.htm
```

Microsoft Public Newsgroups For newsgroups relating to the MMC, connect to the news server *msnews.microsoft.com* and subscribe to the following:

```
microsoft.public.management.mmc
```

Microsoft TechNet To see where Microsoft is headed with the MMC, read the following technical article in Microsoft TechNet:

```
MS BackOffice and Enterprise Systems | MS BackOffice | MS Windows
NT Server |Technical Notes | "Microsoft Management Console—
Overview"
```

WINDOWS NT MAGAZINE

Volume 3, issue 12 (December 1997), has a feature article titled "Managing IIS 4.0 with the Microsoft Management Console" that provides a useful overview of the MMC.

Volume 4, issue 2 (February 1998), has a feature article titled "Windows Scripting Host in Action" that provides an overview of the WSH.

You can also visit the *Windows NT Magazine* Web site at *www.winntmag.com.*

CHAPTER 3

Administering the WWW Service

Introduction

The World Wide Web (WWW) Publishing Service is the core component of Internet Information Server 4.0, enabling the publishing of both static and dynamic Web content and enabling remote administration of IIS 4.0 through the Internet Explorer 4.0 Web browser. After completing this chapter, you will be able to

- Understand the HyperText Transfer Protocol (HTTP), which underlies the WWW service, including the differences between HTTP 1.0 and the new HTTP 1.1 protocol implemented in IIS 4.0.
- Configure the WWW service on IIS 4.0.
- Configure the Master, Site, Directory, and File properties for WWW sites.
- Back up IIS 4.0 configuration settings.

Understanding the HyperText Transfer Protocol

The WWW Publishing Service is the server portion of the HTTP client/server protocol. HTTP is the application-layer protocol that underlies communication between WWW clients (called browsers) and WWW servers (or Web servers). Browsers make HTTP requests to Web servers, and the server responds with HTTP responses.

Until recently, most WWW servers supported version 1.0 of HTTP. Because of certain deficiencies in version 1.0, a new version, called HTTP 1.1, has been proposed by the World Wide Web Consortium (W3C) and the Internet Engineering Task Force (IETF) HTTP Working Group. HTTP 1.1 is being implemented in the latest generation of Web servers (including IIS 4.0) and browser clients (including Internet Explorer 4.0).

Understanding HTTP 1.0

HTTP 1.0 is a *stateless* protocol. In other words, a WWW client forms a connection with a WWW server, the server transfers the requested file to the client, and the connection is then terminated, with the server

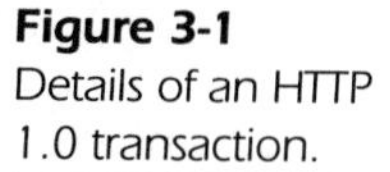

Figure 3-1
Details of an HTTP 1.0 transaction.

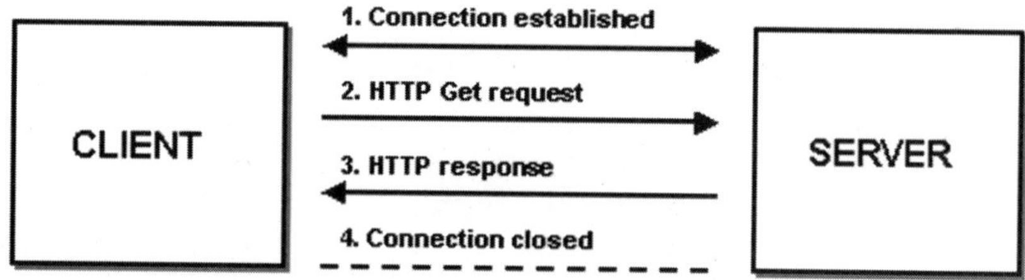

retaining no memory of the transaction. Here is the HTTP 1.0 transaction process in more detail (see Fig. 3-1):

1. A WWW client (such as Internet Explorer) uses a transport-level protocol (usually TCP) to establish a connection, usually on port 80, with the WWW service running on the WWW server (such as Internet Information Server).
2. Once the connection is established, the client sends a request to the server, usually an HTTP Get request message, requesting a file from the server (the first file requested is the text of the Web page itself). The HTTP Get request includes a number of request headers that contain information about the type of transaction method requested, the capabilities of the WWW client (browser) that is making the request, and other data.
3. The WWW service on the server responds to the request by transferring the requested file (an error code is returned if the requested file is unavailable).
4. The server then closes the TCP connection, and the process begins again at step 1. A new connection is established, another file associated with the Web page (such as an image on the page) is requested and transferred, the connection is closed, and the process continues until all the elements of the Web page have been downloaded and displayed by the client.

One problem with HTTP 1.0 is that each time a file is transferred from server to client, a transport-level connection must be established and then terminated. Unfortunately, Web pages today usually contain a large number of auxiliary files such as graphic images, video clips, and Java applets. Thus the transfer of a single Web page consisting of text, 12 images, and two applets would lead to a total of 15 connections being established and terminated. The result is wasted time in forming connections, additional network traffic due to a high number of small TCP control packets, and sluggish transfer of Web pages.

One way to get around the limitations of HTTP 1.0 is to allow browsers to establish multiple concurrent (simultaneous) TCP connections with WWW servers. Typically, a browser such as Internet Explorer 3.0 or Netscape Navigator 3.0 will establish up to four concurrent connections, allowing four requests to be pending and four files to be simultaneously downloaded. Then the connections are closed and new ones are formed to download additional files.

Understanding HTTP 1.1

To overcome the deficiencies of the original HTTP protocol, the W3C and IETF have proposed a new version of HTTP called HTTP 1.1 (see Fig. 3-2). This new version includes the following features:

- *Persistent connections,* the ability of the server to keep TCP connections open once they are established. This speeds the transfer of the files that make up Web pages by reducing the need to establish repeated or multiple connections. In other words, a TCP session is established, a file is requested and transferred, and the session remains open to allow further files to be requested. HTTP 1.1 persistent connections are a variation of the HTTP 1.0 Keep-Alive extension.
- *Pipelining,* a process where the client sends multiple IP packets to the server without waiting for responses from the server. In HTTP 1.0 when a client sends an IP packet containing an HTTP Get request to the server, the client must wait for a response from the server before sending the next request packet. Pipelining results in fewer delays and faster file transfers.
- *Buffering,* a process whereby several HTTP Get requests are collected together (buffered) and then sent to a server as a single packet. This results in fewer, larger packets being sent to the server and speeds up the transfer process.

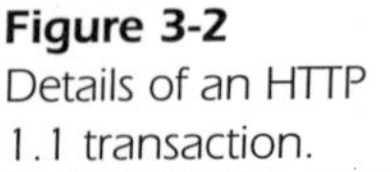

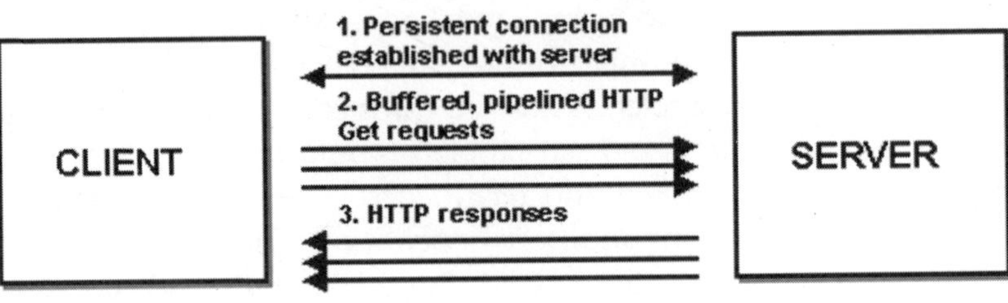

Figure 3-2 Details of an HTTP 1.1 transaction.

In order for HTTP 1.1 to function properly, both the client (browser) and the Web server must implement its features. Tests suggest that full implementation of HTTP 1.1 results in at least a twofold reduction in the number of packets transmitted (which is good for the network) and an increase in overall transfer speed of up to 40 percent (which is good for frustrated surfers!). Implementing other features such as the new HTML Cascading Style Sheets and the new PNG graphics format, can increase WWW performance even further.

A Sample HTTP Session

Using a tool such as Microsoft's Network Monitor allows you to view the contents of HTTP packets directly and gain an understanding of what happens when a browser makes an HTTP request to a WWW server. Let's consider an example where Internet Explorer 4.0 is the client and Internet Information Server 4.0 is the server.

1. The user viewing a Web page in the browser clicks on a hyperlink that points to the URL

   ```
   Server1.anycorp.com/resumes/janet.htm
   ```

2. Clicking on this link causes the browser to send the following HTTP Get request message to the server:

   ```
   GET /resumes/janet.htm HTTP/1.1

   Accept: image/gif, image/x-xbitmap, image/jpeg, image/pjpeg,
     application/msword, application/vnd.ms-powerpoint, */*

   Accept-Language: en-us

   Accept-Encoding: gzip, deflate

   User-Agent: Mozilla/4.0 (compatible; MSIE 4.0; Windows NT)

   Host: server1
   Connection: Keep-Alive
   ```

   From the client's request headers we can observe that

   - The name of the WWW server computer is server1.
   - The client (IE4.0) is an HTTP 1.1–compliant browser.
   - The client requests the file `/resumes/janet.htm` starting from the server's root.

3. The server receives the request and replies with a series of HTTP packets, the first of which contains response headers and the beginning portion of the requested file:

```
HTTP/1.1 200 OK

Server: Microsoft-IIS/4.0

Connection: Keep-Alive

Date: Sat, 08 Nov 1997 19:00:36 GMT

Content-Type: text/html

Accept-Ranges: bytes

Last-Modified: Fri, 07 Nov 1997 17:45:28 GM

ETtag: "d0293c63743cbc1:df3"

Content-Length: 3097
<HTML><HEAD><TITLE>Resume of Janet
Smith</TITLE></HEAD><BODY><H1>Janet Smith,
M.C.S.E.</H1><P><HR><P>My name is Janet Smith, and I am
currently a consultant with…
```

From the server's response headers we can observe that

- The server (IIS 4.0) is an HTTP 1.1–compliant WWW server.
- The content-type being returned to the client is text/html.
- The length of the file being returned is 3097 bytes.

Understanding the WWW Service

IIS 4.0 has an HTTP 1.1–compliant WWW service with a wide range of settings that can be configured for optimal use as an intranet, extranet, or Internet server. The main tool for administering and configuring the WWW service on IIS 4.0 is the Internet Service Manager (ISM) snap-in for the Microsoft Management Console (MMC). Using the ISM snap-in for the MMC, an administrator can manage any number of IIS 4.0 servers on a local network. This differs from earlier versions of IIS (3.0 and earlier servers), in which a standalone version of the ISM was used to administer the WWW and FTP (and defunct Gopher) services.

For remote management of IIS 4.0 using a Web browser, the Internet Service Manager (HTML) provides most of the same functionality as the MMC. Because of the similarity in function of the two tools, only the ISM snap-in for the MMC will be covered in this chapter, since it is the primary tool for server administration.

To start Internet Service Manager, choose START, PROGRAMS, WINDOWS NT 4.0 OPTION PACK, MICROSOFT INTERNET INFORMATION SERVER, INTERNET SERVICE MANAGER. This will open the Microsoft Management Console, from which you can expand the Internet Information Server node in the scope pane (left side) and select the locally installed IIS server—in this case server1. The results pane (right side) shows the configurable nodes of IIS running on server1 (see Fig. 3-3).

The WWW service running on the selected server (server1 in our example) is primarily managed by using *property sheets.* Each node in the server's namespace (which includes the IIS server itself, the default Web site, other virtual servers and virtual directories, and even individual Web pages and files) is a node in the MMC that has its own set of *properties.* These properties are accessed by

- Selecting the node and clicking the PROPERTIES button on the rebar
- Selecting the node, clicking the ACTION button on the rebar, and choosing PROPERTIES from the drop-down menu
- Right-clicking on the node and choosing PROPERTIES from the shortcut menu

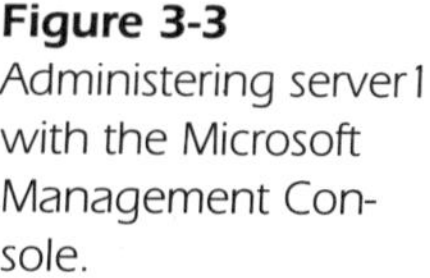

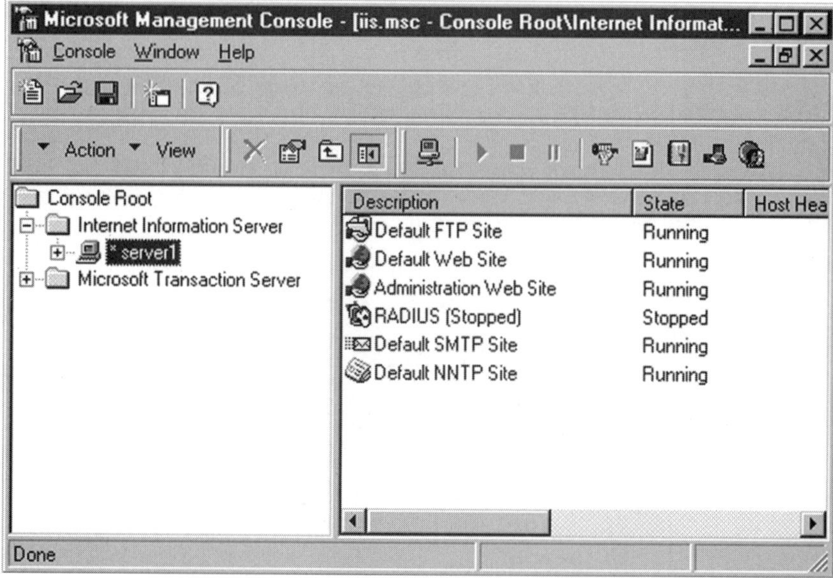

Figure 3-3 Administering server1 with the Microsoft Management Console.

IIS 4.0 can be configured to have an unlimited number of Web sites running on it simultaneously, each responding to its own unique IP address and fully qualified domain name (FQDN). Each of these *virtual servers* (or Web sites) acts and behaves as if it were an entirely distinct machine, as if you had multiple IIS 4.0 machines on your network. Each can be configured separately and can be stopped, started, and paused independently. The creation of virtual servers (Web sites) will be covered in more detail in Chap. 5.

Understanding Types of WWW Property Sheets

The property sheets for the WWW service on IIS 4.0 can be configured at four different levels:

Master property sheets

Site property sheets

Directory property sheets

File property sheets

Following is an explanation of the four levels of IIS property sheets for the WWW service, along with instructions on how you can access and configure property settings for each level.

1. *Master properties.* Master properties can be configured for all Web sites running on the IIS server. To access Master properties, right-click on the IIS server node in the Microsoft Management Console and select PROPERTIES from the shortcut menu.
2. *Site properties.* Site properties (or virtual server properties) can be configured individually for each Web site running on the IIS server, including the default Web site that is created when IIS is installed. To access Site properties, right-click on the Web site node in the MMC and select PROPERTIES from the shortcut menu.
3. *Directory properties.* Directory properties (or virtual directory properties) can be configured individually for each virtual directory defined within a Web site on the server. All files will inherit the property settings of the virtual directory that contains them. To access Directory properties, right-click on the virtual directory within the Web site and select PROPERTIES from the shortcut menu.

4. *File properties.* File properties can be configured individually for each Web page within a virtual directory or Web site. To access File properties, right-click on the selected Web page and choose PROPERTIES from the shortcut menu.

Settings made to any of the WWW property sheets are stored in the *metabase*, a database structure that replaces some of the functions of the Windows NT registry for IIS 4.0.

The following sections describe how to access and configure the four types of property sheets, using as an example the default Web site created when IIS 4.0 is installed.

Accessing the WWW Service Master Properties Sheet

Right-click on the server node (server1 in Fig. 3-3) and select PROPERTIES from the shortcut menu to bring up the Server Properties sheet (see Fig. 3-4). From this sheet select WWW SERVICE and click EDIT to bring up the WWW Service Master Properties sheet.

Any settings made to the Master Properties sheet are automatically inherited by the default (root) Web site and by all *new* virtual Web sites that are created afterward. However, if the Master Properties are later changed, existing virtual Web sites do *not* inherit these changes unless they are specified to do so; only new virtual Web sites will automatically inherit them.

Accessing the WWW Site Properties Sheet

Right-click on the Default Web Site node (see Fig. 3-3) and select PROPERTIES from the shortcut menu to bring up the WWW Site Properties sheet (in this case the Default WWW Site Properties sheet). Any settings made to this property sheet affect only the selected Web site and override any settings made in the WWW Master Properties sheet.

The Default Web site in Fig. 3-3 can be accessed by a browser through the URL

```
http://server1/
```

Note that the WWW Site Properties sheet has the same tabs as the WWW Master Properties sheet, except for the absence of the IIS 3.0 Admin tab.

Accessing the WWW Directory Properties Sheet

Right-click on any virtual directory (such as the IISSAMPLES node under the default Web site) and select PROPERTIES from the shortcut menu to bring up the Virtual Directory Properties sheet (in this case the IISSAMPLES Properties sheet). Any settings made to this property sheet affect only the selected virtual directory and override any previously made settings in the WWW Master Properties and WWW Site Properties sheets.

The IISSAMPLES virtual directory under the Default Web site in Fig. 3-3 can be accessed by a browser through the URL

```
http://server1/IISSAMPLES/
```

Accessing the WWW File Properties sheet

Right-click on any file node (Web page, image file, script file, etc.) and select PROPERTIES from the context menu to bring up the File Properties sheet. Any settings made to this property sheet affect the selected file only.

For the rest of this chapter the diagrams will be taken from the WWW Master Properties and Default WWW Site Properties sheets since these two property sheets have the most options to configure. Most of what is said, however, applies to the WWW Directory Properties and WWW File Properties sheets as well.

Understanding Inheritance Overrides

To see how setting the properties of a node on the server namespace can affect the properties of child nodes beneath it, try the following exercise:

Access the WWW Service Master Properties sheet for your installed IIS 4.0 server. Change the Connection Timeout from the default value of 900 seconds to a new value of 450 seconds and click OK twice.

Next access the Default WWW Site Properties sheet and note that the Connection Timeout is now 450 seconds. Change this value to 1800 seconds and click OK.

Again access the WWW Service Master Properties sheet. Change the Connection Timeout from 450 seconds back to 900 seconds and click OK. A dialog box called Inheritance Overrides will appear, indicating that the Default WWW Site Properties child node has overridden the Connection Timeout value you have just set, and asking you whether you want to select this child node to have its Connection Timeout value revert to the new default value. Select DEFAULT WWW SERVICE and click OK twice.

Check that *both* the WWW Service Master Properties and the Default WWW Site Properties sheets now have a timeout of 900 seconds.

The way it all works is like this:

- When a *new* Web site is created, it automatically inherits the Master property settings of the IIS server on which it is created.
- When a *new* Web virtual directory is created, it automatically inherits the Site property settings of the Web site on which it is created.
- When a *new* Web page or subdirectory is created in a virtual directory or Web site, it automatically inherits the properties of the virtual directory or Web site that contains it.

However,

- When a Master property setting is changed, you are given the option of passing this change along to all *existing* Web sites on the IIS server.
- When a Site property setting is changed, you are given the option of passing this change along to all *existing* virtual directories on the Web site.
- *But* when a property on a virtual directory is changed, the changes are *automatically* passed along to all Web pages and subdirectories in the virtual directory.

Configuring WWW Property Sheets

The four different types of WWW property sheets have different options (tabs) available depending upon whether they configure options at the Master, Site, Directory, or File level. Here are the property sheet tabs available for each level:

- *Web Site* tab (Master, Site, and Directory levels): configure site identification, IP address, TCP port, limit connections, enable and configure logging
- *Operators* tab (Master and Site levels): grant operator privileges
- *Performance* tab (Master and Site levels): tune server caching performance, throttle bandwidth for site, enable HTTP Keep-Alives
- *ISAPI Filters* tab (Master and Site levels): set options for ISAPI filters
- *Home Directory* tab (Master, Site, Directory, and File levels): configure content location, access permissions, enable indexing, create FrontPage Web, allow directory browsing, enable logging, configure application settings, set execution permissions (at the Directory properties level this is called the *Virtual Directory* tab, and at the File properties level it is called the *File* tab)
- *Documents* tab (Master, Site, and Directory levels): specify default documents, enable footers
- *Directory Security* tab (Master, Site, Directory, and File levels): configure authentication methods, configure SSL, grant or deny access to IP addresses and domain names
- *HTTP Headers* tab (Master, Site, Directory, and File levels): configure content expiration, specify custom HTTP headers, configure content ratings, modify MIME mappings
- *Custom Errors* tab (Master, Site, Directory, and File levels): configure custom HTTP error messages
- *IIS 3.0 Admin* tab (Master level only): designate which Web site can be administered by the older IIS 3.0 Internet Service Manager

In addition to these, the IIS Server Properties sheet can be used to globally throttle WWW bandwidth and configure the global MIME mappings.

Configuring Default Properties for IIS

To configure the default properties for an IIS server, select a server node (e.g., server1) under the Internet Information Server hierarchy in the scope pane of the MMC and click the PROPERTIES button on the rebar to access the Server Properties sheet (where "Server" is replaced by the

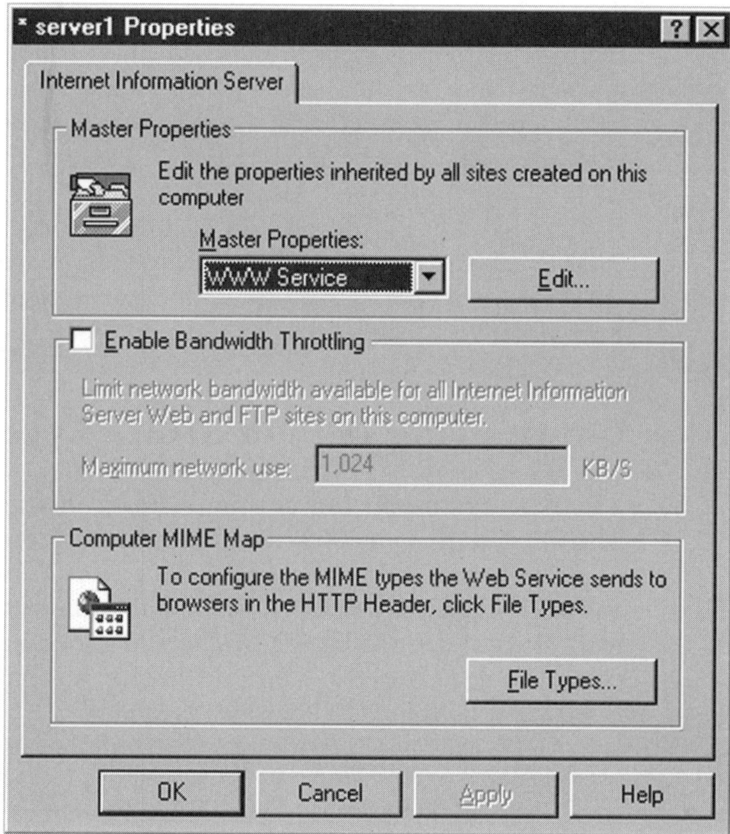

Figure 3-4 Property sheet for server1.

actual name of the server, in this case server1 (see Fig. 3-4). From this property sheet you can set default or global properties for all Web and FTP sites on the selected server. These properties include the maximum bandwidth used by the WWW and FTP services and the default MIME types recognized.

Configuring Default Bandwidth Throttling for IIS

To limit the amount of network bandwidth that the WWW and FTP services use, check ENABLE BANDWIDTH THROTTLING on this property sheet and enter a value for maximum network use in kilobytes per second (kB/s). The default value is 1024 MB/s or 1 megabyte per second (MB/s). Bandwidth throttling is useful if your IIS server fulfills multiple roles on your network, such as functioning as a domain controller or mail server.

A rule of thumb suggested by Microsoft is that you initially throttle the bandwidth at 50 percent and then adjust it upward or downward as necessary and monitor server performance. For a standard 100-Mbps backbone PCI Ethernet card, a good starting value for maximum network use would thus be 50 Mbps (6100 kB/s).

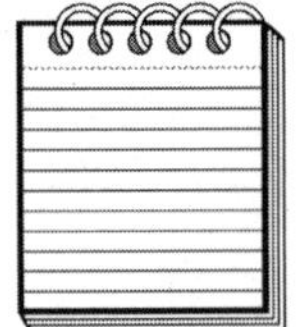

NOTE: *Bandwidth throttling of the WWW service applies only to the delivery of static Web pages (HTML) and not to dynamic pages such as Active Server Pages (ASPs).*

Configuring Default MIME Types for IIS

Another option you can configure from this property sheet is the MIME types that the WWW service sends to browsers in the HTTP response header. MIME stands for *Multipurpose Internet Mail Extensions* and was originally developed as an extension to the original Internet mail protocol defined by RFC 822 to allow the transmission of nontext content to be packaged and encoded within text-only email messages.

MIME is used in HTTP sessions as follows:

1. A browser client contacts a WWW server requesting a document, which could be text, HTML, images, audio, or some other format. For example, say the client requests a sound file from the server given by the URL

   ```
   server1.anycorp.com/sounds/bullfrog.au
   ```

2. The server looks up the file extension `.au` in its table of MIME mappings (a table that matches file extensions with MIME types) and then determines that the MIME type for the requested file is

   ```
   audio/basic
   ```

3. The server returns the requested file, preceded by a series of response headers. One of the response headers indicates the MIME type of the document being returned, in the form of a content-type header:

   ```
   Content-type: audio/basic
   ```

4. The client looks up this content type in its own table of MIME mappings to determine what to do with the file, that is, whether to
   - Display the document in the browser window
   - Invoke a helper application to render the document
   - Ask for user intervention (i.e., a dialog box appears requesting whether the user wants to save or open the file; if OPEN is selected, the user must then specify which application to use to open the file, as the client is unfamiliar with the MIME type returned)

To view a list of MIME mappings for the WWW service, click the FILE TYPES button on the Server Property sheet to get the File Types property sheet (Fig. 3-5):

To configure a new MIME mapping, click NEW TYPE and enter the MIME content type and the file association to be mapped to this type. To edit an existing type, select the type and click EDIT.

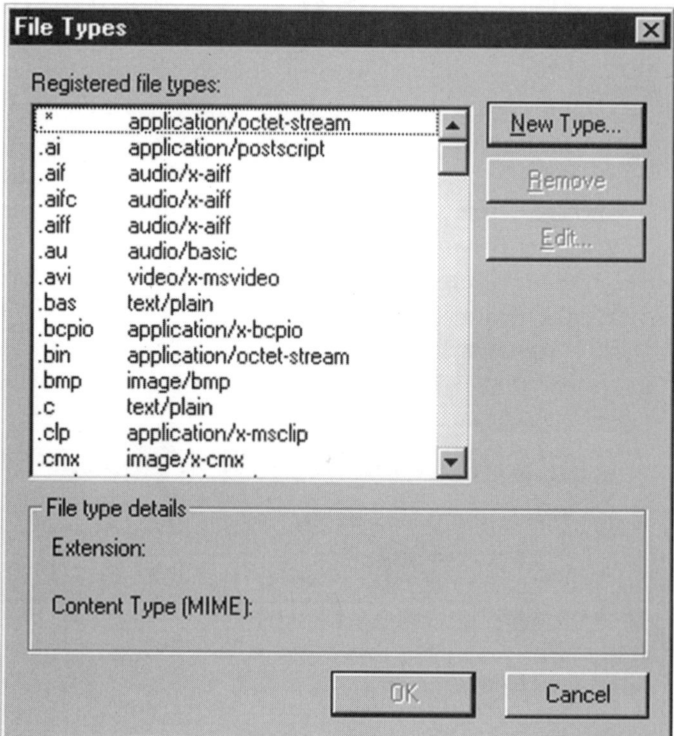

Figure 3-5
Table of MIME mappings for the WWW Service.

Why might you want to create your own MIME mapping? Say that you have a collection of Perl scripts that you want to make available as plain text files for browsing to users in your Developer global group. Perl scripts usually have the extension `.pl` yet are saved in plain text format. What you can do is register a new MIME type for your WWW service by clicking NEW TYPE and entering the file extension and MIME type, as shown in Fig. 3-6. Now when a browser tries to access a URL such as

```
server1.anycorp.com/scripts/sample.pl
```

the server will return the file with a header indicating that the file is of type text/plain, and the browser will display the file as unformatted text within the browser window. Of course, you should make sure that the Perl scripts reside on an NTFS volume so that only the Developer global group can be assigned permission to read the directory containing the scripts.

Configuring WWW Server Master Properties

In addition to configuring default bandwidth throttling and default MIME types, the Server Properties sheet allows you to access and edit the server's Master properties. These Master properties settings will be inherited as defaults by all Web sites created afterward on the server (though these settings can be overridden by setting properties for the Web sites themselves).

To configure the WWW Master properties, select WWW SERVICE in the Master Properties drop-down box on the Server Properties sheet and click the EDIT button. The WWW Service Master Properties sheet will appear (Fig. 3-7). The ten tabs on this property sheet allow full cus-

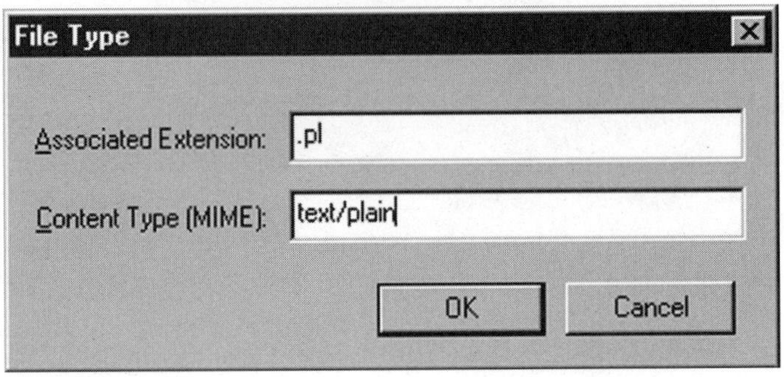

Figure 3-6 Creating a MIME mapping for Perl scripts.

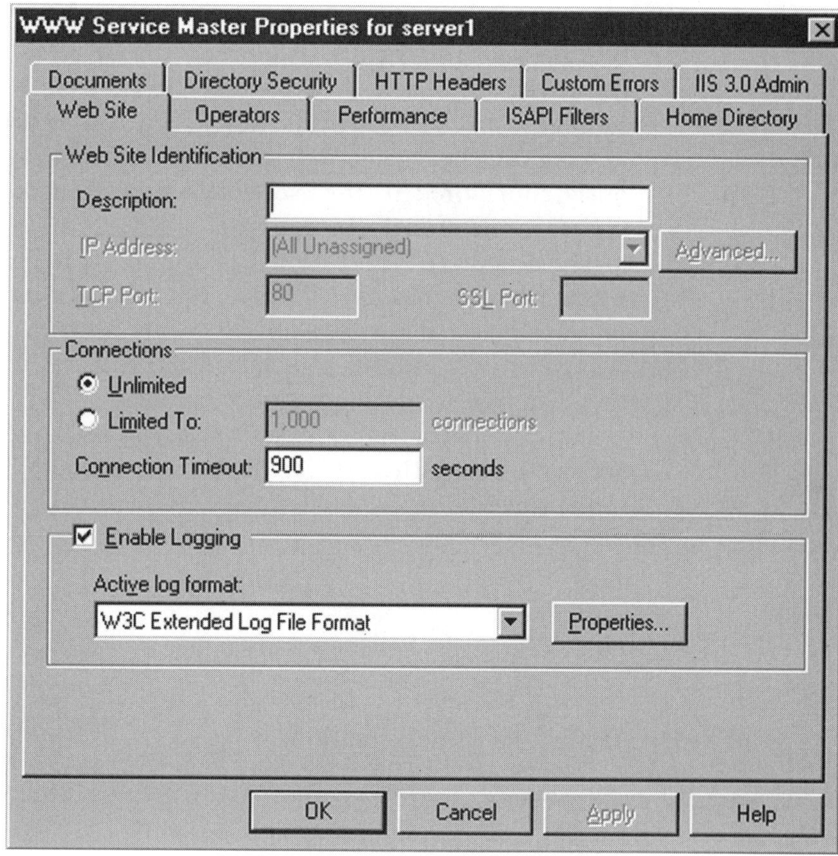

Figure 3-7 The WWW Service Master Properties sheet for server1 showing the Web Site tab.

tomization of the default properties for all Web sites created afterward on the selected IIS server. The following sections give details on many of the settings that can be configured using this property sheet, although the settings operate in essentially the same way whether they are configured at the Master, Site, Directory, or File level.

Configuring WWW Site Identification Enter a friendly description in the Description textbox for the Web site selected. This description will appear attached to the Web site node in the MMC.

Certain settings on this WWW Service Master Properties sheet are grayed out in Fig. 3-7 because a server has been selected to be configured rather than a specific Web site. The IP Address, TCP Port, and Advanced properties can be configured only from the WWW Site Properties sheet, not from the WWW Service Master Properties sheet. SSL Port can be configured only if the Web site is set up to use SSL.

On the WWW Site Properties sheet, use the IP Address drop-down box to assign a particular IP address to the selected Web site. If you leave the setting here at ALL UNASSIGNED, the Web site will respond to all IP addresses that are not specifically assigned to other Web sites, in effect making this the default Web site. Only IP addresses that have been previously configured in the Network application of Control Panel will appear in the drop-down box here.

The default TCP port for HTTP is port 80. To change this value, enter a new number into the TCP Port box. *Note that the IIS server will need to be rebooted for the new port number to come into effect.* Notify users of the change in port numbers, because when they try to access this FTP site, they will have to include the port number.

For example, if the port is changed to 6800 and users are trying to access the site with Internet Explorer, they must browse with an URL something like

```
http://139.53.5.118:6800
```

or

```
http://super.mycorpinc.com:6800
```

(using DNS name resolution) or

```
http://super:6800
```

(using NetBIOS name resolution).

NOTE: *Do not use any of the Well-Known Port Numbers other than port 80 for the HTTP port number. Otherwise conflicts may occur with other TCP services. Well-Known Port Numbers are discussed in Chap. 9.*

The SSL Port box will be covered in Chap. 12.

The ADVANCED button is used to configure additional identities for the Web site. It allows you to configure Host Header Names, a feature of IIS 4.0 that allows multiple Web sites to each have their own fully qualified domain name but be mapped to the same IP address and TCP port number. This is covered in Chap. 5.

Configuring WWW Connection Limits and Timeouts Select either

- UNLIMITED, to allow an unlimited number of simultaneous connections to the server
- LIMITED TO, to specify the maximum number of simultaneous connections allowed to the server. The default value is 1000 connections.

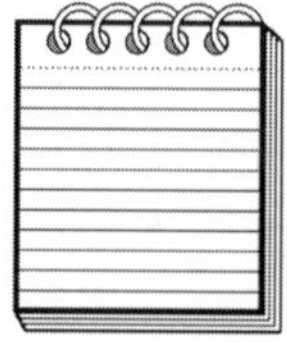

NOTE: *To temporarily deny access to your Web server, you might set the* LIMITED TO *field to zero. Then when a client tries to access a page on the server, the server will return a status code 403 message that will produce the following display in the browser window:*

HTTP Error 403

403.9 Access Forbidden: Too many users are connected

This error can be caused if the Web server is busy and cannot process your request due to heavy traffic. Please try to connect again later.

Please contact the Web server's administrator if the problem persists.

HTTP status codes will be dealt with later in this chapter.

Set the CONNECTION TIMEOUT Interval to the length of time, in seconds, until the server disconnects from an inactive user. The default value is 900 seconds (15 minutes). If HTTP Keep-Alive is enabled on the Performance tab, a client will request a page from the server, a connection is formed, the server delivers the page to the client, and the connection remains open in case the client requests another page (speeding up the process by eliminating the need for the client to establish a fresh connection). But if the client does not require an additional page, this timeout feature causes the connection to eventually be closed by the server, freeing up TCP ports for other uses.

Configuring WWW Logging Select ENABLE LOGGING to turn on the WWW Service logging features. Logging is enabled by default so that administrators can keep track of which sites are being accessed by which users, how often these sites are being accessed, whether or not the server's responses have been successful, and so on.

Select an Active log format from the drop-down list. Microsoft IIS 4.0 offers logging in four possible formats:

- Microsoft IIS Log File Format
- NCSA Common Log File Format

- W3C Extended Log File Format (the default format)
- ODBC Logging

The first three formats produce simple ASCII text logs. These can be viewed in a simple text editor such as Notepad, imported into a database, or imported into and analyzed with Microsoft Site Server Express, which is included with the NT 4.0 Option Pack. Site Server Express is covered in Chap. 11.

In addition, the W3C Extended Log File Format is customizable, allowing administrators to select which parameters to include in the log. The default format for IIS logging is the W3C Extended Log File Format.

To set the logging options for these three formats, select the desired format and click the PROPERTIES button to access the Microsoft Logging Properties sheet. Then use this sheet to select

- The logging time period, for example:
  - Create new logs on a daily, weekly, or monthly basis.
  - Allow the log file to grow to an unlimited size.
  - Create a new log file when the old one reaches a specified fixed limit.
- The location of the log files, which by default are in the directory

  ```
  C:\winnt\system32\logfile\
  ```

- Which parameters to include in the log (for W3C Extended Log File Format only)

Understanding the Microsoft IIS Log File Format This format is a comma-delimited fixed-field ASCII text file. A typical name for such a log file might be

`in971109.log` created on November 9, 1997

`inetsv23.log` the twenty-third limited-size log file created

Typical output from such a log might be as follows:

```
10.107.3.201, -, 11/9/97, 11:02:22, W3SVC1, SERVER1,
10.107.3.200, 53998, 275, 5585, 200, 0, GET, /Default.asp, -,

10.107.3.201, -, 11/9/97, 11:02:28, W3SVC1, SERVER1,
10.107.3.200, 2354, 395, 2167, 200, 0, GET,
/iissamples/default/nav2.gif, -,

10.107.3.201, -, 11/9/97, 11:02:28, W3SVC1, SERVER1, 10.107.3.200,
2634, 395, 644, 200, 0, GET,
/iissamples/default/MSFT.GIF, -,
```

To help in interpreting the Microsoft IIS Log File Format, Table 3-1 lists the fields contained in the last entry of the preceding log and their meaning.

Understanding the NCSA Common Log File Format The NCSA Common Log File Format is a space-delimited fixed-field ASCII text file. A typical name for such a log file might be:

`nc971109.log` created on November 9, 1997

`ncsa23.log` the twenty-third limited-size log file created

Typical output from such a log might be as follows:

```
10.107.3.201 - - [09/Nov/1997:11:06:39 -0600] "GET
/iissamples/default/iis3.GIF HTTP/1.0" 200 3558

10.107.3.201 - - [09/Nov/1997:11:06:42 -0600] "GET /default.asp
HTTP/1.0" 200 5518

10.107.3.201 - - [09/Nov/1997:11:06:46 -0600] "GET
/iissamples/default/IE.GIF HTTP/1.0" 200 8866
```

Table 3-1

Sample Fields in Microsoft IIS Log File Format

Data Element	Typical Value
Client's IP address	10.107.3.201
Client's username (- if anonymous)	-
Date of request	11/9/97
Time of request	11:02:28
Service requested (W3SVC1 is the WWW service)	W3SVC1
Server's name	SERVER1
Server's IP address	10.107.3.200
Elapsed server processing time (msec)	2634
Bytes sent by client's request	395
Bytes returned by server's response	644
Status code returned by WWW service	200
Windows NT status code	0
Request method	GET
Document requested	/iissamples/default/MSFT.GIF

Table 3-2
Sample Fields in NCSA Common Log File Format

Data Element	Typical Value
Client's IP address	`0.107.3.201`
Client's domain\username	[blank]
Date and time of request	`09/Nov/1997:11:06:46`
GMT offset	`-0600`
HTTP request	`"GET /iissamples/default/IE.GIF HTTP/1.0"`
HTTP status code	`200`
Bytes returned by server	`8866`

To help in interpreting the NCSA Common Log File Format, Table 3-2 lists the fields contained in the last entry of the preceding log and their meaning.

Understanding the W3C Extended Log File Format The W3C Extended Log File Format is a space-delimited variable-field ASCII text file with headers. A typical name for such a log file might be:

`ex971109.log` created on November 9, 1997

`extend23.log` the twenty-third limited-size log file created

Typical output from such a log might be as follows when all extended logging options are selected:

```
#Software: Microsoft Internet Information Server 4.0

#Version: 1.0

#Date: 1997-11-10 01:02:54

#Fields: date time c-ip cs-username s-sitename s-computername s-
ip cs-method cs-uri-stem cs-uri-query sc-status sc-win32-status sc-
bytes cs-bytes time-taken s-port cs(User-Agent) cs(Cookie)
cs(Referer)

1997-11-10 01:02:54 10.107.3.201 - W3SVC1 SERVER1 10.107.3.200
GET /Default.asp - 200 0 5585 275 4697 80
Mozilla/2.0+(compatible;+MSIE + 3.0;+Windows + 95) - -

1997-11-10 01:02:56 10.107.3.201 - W3SVC1 SERVER1 10.107.3.200
GET /iissamples/default/IISTitle.gif - 200 0 21576 399 761 80
Mozilla/2.0+(compatible;+MSIE + 3.0;+Windows + 95)
ASPSESSIONIDGQGGGGYP = HILJEGPCGGLNFFKEKHEBCGHM http://server1/

1997-11-10 01:02:56 10.107.3.201 - W3SVC1 SERVER1 10.107.3.200
GET /iissamples/default/nav2.gif - 200 0 2167 395 1282 80
```

```
Mozilla/2.0+(compatible;+MSIE + 3.0;+Windows + 95)
ASPSESSIONIDGQGGGGYP = HILJEGPCGGLNFFKEKHEBCGHM http://server1/
```

To help in interpreting the W3C Extended Log File Format, Table 3-3 lists the fields contained in the last entry of the preceding log and their meaning.

Understanding ODBC Logging The fourth log format is ODBC Logging, which is specific to IIS and allows administrators to log WWW transactions directly to an ODBC-compliant database such as Microsoft SQL

Table 3-3

Sample fields in W3C Extended Log File Format

Data Element	Typical Value
Date of request	`1997-11-10`
Time of request	`01:02:56`
Client's IP address	`10.107.3.201`
Client's username (- if anonymous)	-
Service requested (`W3SVC1` is the WWW service)	`W3SVC1`
Server's name	`SERVER1`
Server's IP address	`10.107.3.200`
Request method	`GET`
Document requested	`/iissamples/default/nav2.gif`
Search query (if any)	-
HTTP status code returned	`200`
Win32 status code returned	`0`
Bytes returned by server's response	`2167`
Bytes sent by client's request	`395`
Server's elapsed processor time (ms)	`1282`
Server's TCP port	`80`
Type of client (a.k.a. user agent)	`Mozilla/2.0+(compatible;+MSIE + 3.0;+Windows + 95)`
Cookie (if any)	`ASPSESSIONIDGQGGGGYP = HILJEGPCGGLNFFKEKHEBCGHM`
Referrer (the site containing the link that the user clicked to get to this page)	`http://server1/`

Server or Microsoft Access. The steps involved in logging to a database are as follows:

1. Create a database and define a table within it. Give the table a name (the default suggested name is InternetLog).
2. Create the following fields within the table to hold the logged data:

Field	Data Type
ClientHost	varchar(255)
Username	varchar(255)
LogTime	datetime
Service	varchar(255)
Machine	varchar(255)
ServerIP	varchar(50)
ProcessingTime	int
BytesRecvd	int
BytesSent	int
ServiceStatus	int
Win32Status	int
Operation	varchar(255)
Target	varchar(255)
Parameters	varchar(255)

3. Use the System DSN property sheet of the ODBC option in Control Panel and give the database a system DSN (data source name). This is necessary so that ODBC can reference the table. The default suggested DSN is HTTPLOG.
4. Select ODBC LOGGING as the Active log format on the Web Site tab of the WWW Service Master Properties sheet. Click the PROPERTIES button to access the ODBC Logging Properties sheet (Fig. 3-8).
5. Enter the system DSN, table name, and the username and password, if these are necessary to connect with the database, and click OK to begin logging.

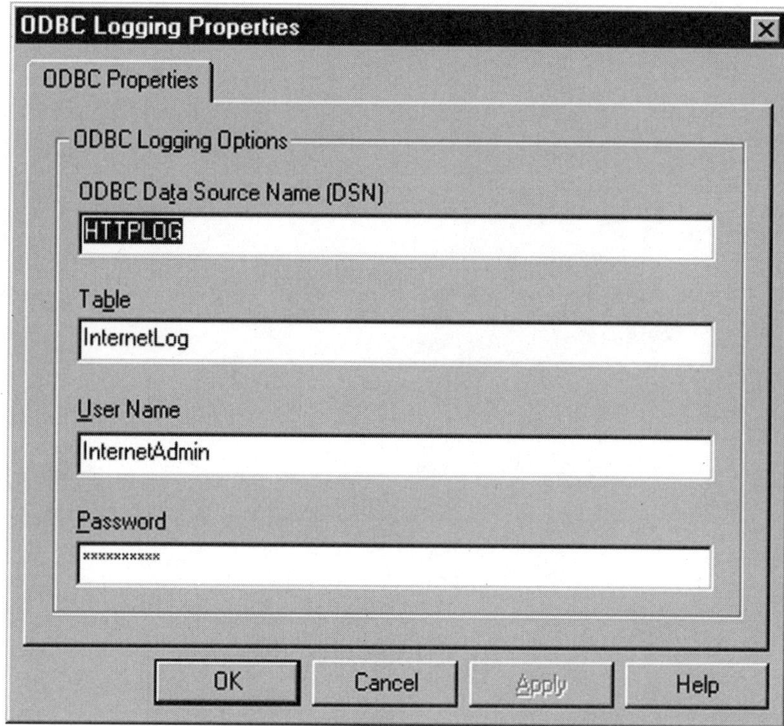

Figure 3-8 The ODBC Logging Properties sheet.

Configuring WWW Site Operators The Operators tab on the WWW Service Master Properties sheet is used to specify which Windows NT user accounts will have operator privileges for all Web sites on the IIS server (Fig. 3-9). The Operators tab on a WWW Site Properties sheet can be used to specify which Windows NT user accounts will have operator privileges for a particular Web site selected. By default, the Administrators local group is assigned operator privileges on all Web sites on the IIS server. But Web site operators do *not* have to be members of the Administrators local group.

To add a user or group to the operators list, click ADD and select the user or group from the Add Users and Groups property sheet.

Web site operators have the right to perform simple administrative tasks on the Web sites to which they are assigned. These tasks include:

- Setting access permissions
- Enabling and configuring logging
- Enabling and configuring content expiration
- Enabling and configuring content ratings

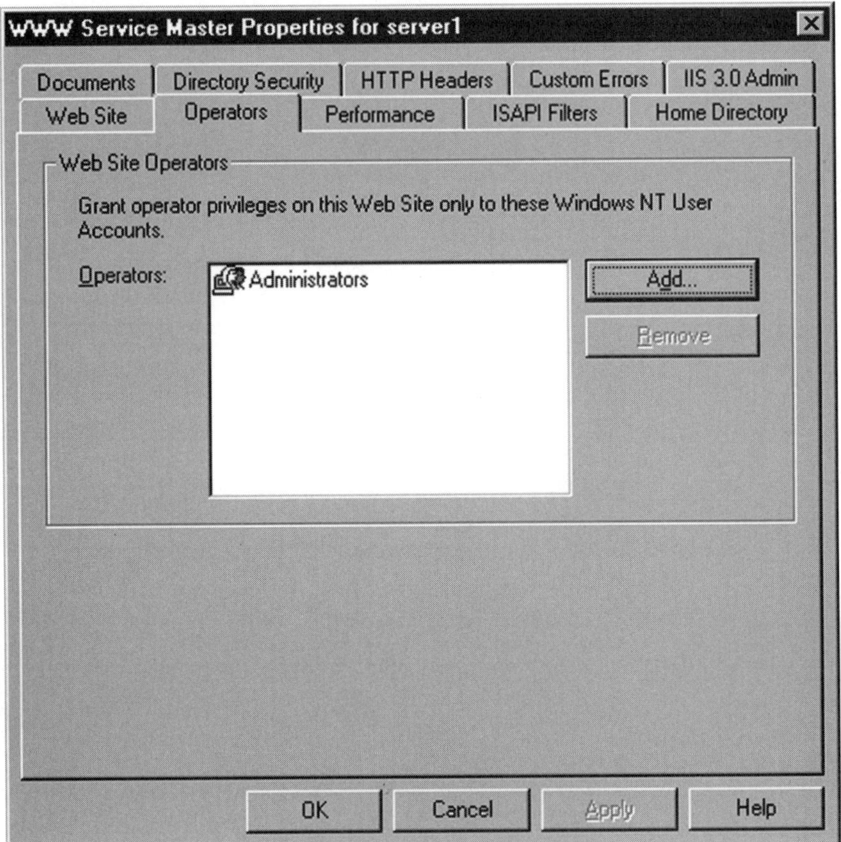

Figure 3-9 Adding new WWW Service Operators.

- Defining default documents
- Adding footers to Web pages

Operators *cannot* perform the following tasks unless they are also members of the Administrators local group:

- Configuring IP address and port number
- Throttling bandwidth
- Changing the anonymous user account
- Creating and mapping virtual directories
- Configuring application settings

Typically, Web site operators include the Administrators local group and the company or departmental person responsible for managing the particular Web site. An administrator generally creates a *read-only mode*

.msc file representing an MMC window with only one node in the scope pane, namely, the Web site to be administered. The Web site operator is then allowed to use this .msc file to open an MMC window to administer the Web site.

Configuring WWW Performance Tuning The sliding control featured in the Performance tab (Fig. 3-10) allows you to tune the performance of your server based on the expected number of hits per day. If the number selected is slightly greater than the actual number of hits, the server will perform well. But if the number selected is much greater than the actual number of hits, too much server memory will be used for caching server hits, and the result will be a decrease in overall performance of the server. Use the IIS logging capabilities to determine the number of hits per day on your server, and adjust the setting here accordingly.

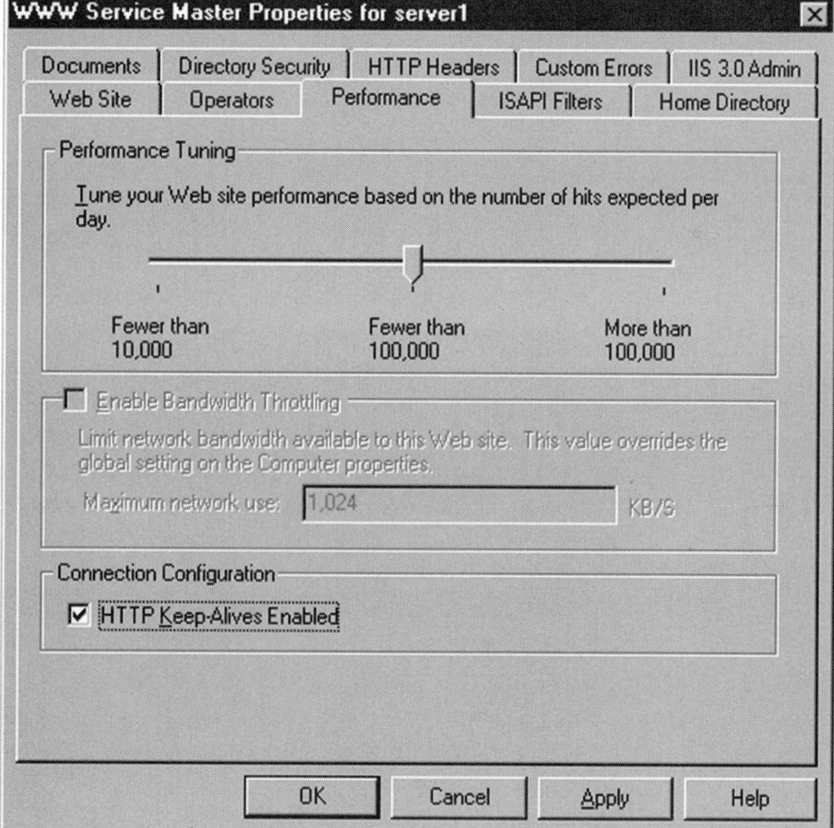

Figure 3-10 Configuring performance tuning, bandwidth throttling, and HTTP Keep-Alives.

Configuring WWW Bandwidth Throttling As Fig. 3-10 illustrates, this option is grayed out for the WWW Service Master Properties sheet, since it is configured globally on the Server Properties sheet (see Fig. 3-4). On the WWW Site Properties sheet the value selected here will always override the default value set on the Server Properties sheet, even if the value selected is greater than the value on the Server Properties sheet.

Configuring HTTP Keep-Alive Check the checkbox shown in Fig. 3-10 to enable or disable HTTP Keep-Alives on the server. When the box is checked, the server will keep a connection open with a client instead of opening and closing a new connection every time an HTTP Get request is made by the client. HTTP Keep-Alive is an enhanced form of HTTP 1.1 Persistent Connections and is enabled by default.

Configuring ISAPI Filters IIS 4.0 supports a variety of ways of extending the functionality of the WWW service, including

- Active Server Pages (ASPs)
- Internet Server Application Programming Interface (ISAPI)
- Common Gateway Interface (CGI)
- Internet Database Connector (IDC)

Prior to the introduction of IIS, most WWW servers supported only Common Gateway Interface (CGI) applications. CGI is an early standard allowing WWW servers to communicate with server-side gateway applications. Typically, a webmaster would write a CGI script in a scripting language such as Perl, and then save the script in the cgi-bin/ subdirectory of the Web site being developed. This CGI program might be a simple script to process the results of a submission from an HTML form. The basic problem is that each time a CGI program is called, a new process is started on the server. Thus, when CGI programs are called frequently, the added overhead due to multiple instances of the same CGI program running simultaneously on the server can easily cause the server's performance to decline noticeably.

Microsoft developed ISAPI as an alternative to CGI. Like CGI, ISAPI applications provide a way to extend the capabilities of a WWW server. Calling an ISAPI application does not create a new instance of the application, whereas invoking a CGI script always generates a new process, even if a similar process is already running on the server. ISAPI applications are multithreaded and can run within the same process space as IIS, thus making more efficient use of system resources and improving server performance considerably. ISAPI applications are usually written and compiled in C++ and provide much better performance than interpreted scripting engines such as Perl. Writing and developing ISAPI applications requires knowledge of a high-level programming language such as C++ and is beyond the scope of this book.

ISAPI applications fall into two categories:

- *ISAPI extensions* are loaded on demand to provide additional functionality for specific Web sites running on the server. An example is a DLL that handles a form submission on a Web page. In general, ISAPI extensions are DLLs that process data received from an HTTP request, for example:

  ```
  http://scripts/extension.dll?var1 + var2 + var…
  ```

- *ISAPI filters* are loaded when the WWW service initializes and remain in memory until the IIS server is shut down. They are triggered when some system event occurs on the IIS server and provide additional functionality to all Web sites running on the server. Examples include DLLs that provide a custom authentication method, perform data encryption, generate custom logs, and perform traffic analysis.

Use the ISAPI Filters tab on the WWW Service Master Properties sheet (Fig. 3-11) or WWW Site Properties sheet to add, remove, edit, or change the order of ISAPI filters on the server or site. Click ADD to add a new ISAPI filter by mapping a friendly name for the filter to the local or network path of the filter's executable file. Filters can be added, removed or deleted, and assigned a priority rating and an order of execution.

The Details box shows the current status (loaded into memory, unloaded from memory, or disabled) of each ISAPI filter, its friendly name and executable file, and its priority.

Creating ISAPI filters involves high-level programming and is beyond the scope of this book. Refer to the Windows NT 4.0 Option Pack Online Documentation for more information about creating ISAPI applications. IIS 4.0 comes with some sample ISAPI applications that can be compiled with a C++ compiler and tested on IIS 4.0. You'll find more information on these samples in the online documentation, if you're interested.

Configuring WWW Content Location The Home Directory of a Web site is the location where its home page and other related content is stored. This setting is grayed out on the WWW Service Master Properties sheet (see Fig. 3-12) but is available on the WWW Site Properties sheet.

When you install IIS, it creates a default Web site with a home directory located at

```
C:\inetpub\wwwroot
```

If you create a new Web site on the server, you have the option of specifying the location of the new site's home directory. Using the radio buttons on this property sheet, you can choose one of three possible settings:

- A *local directory* on this computer

  Enter the path or browse to the new home directory located on this server, for example:

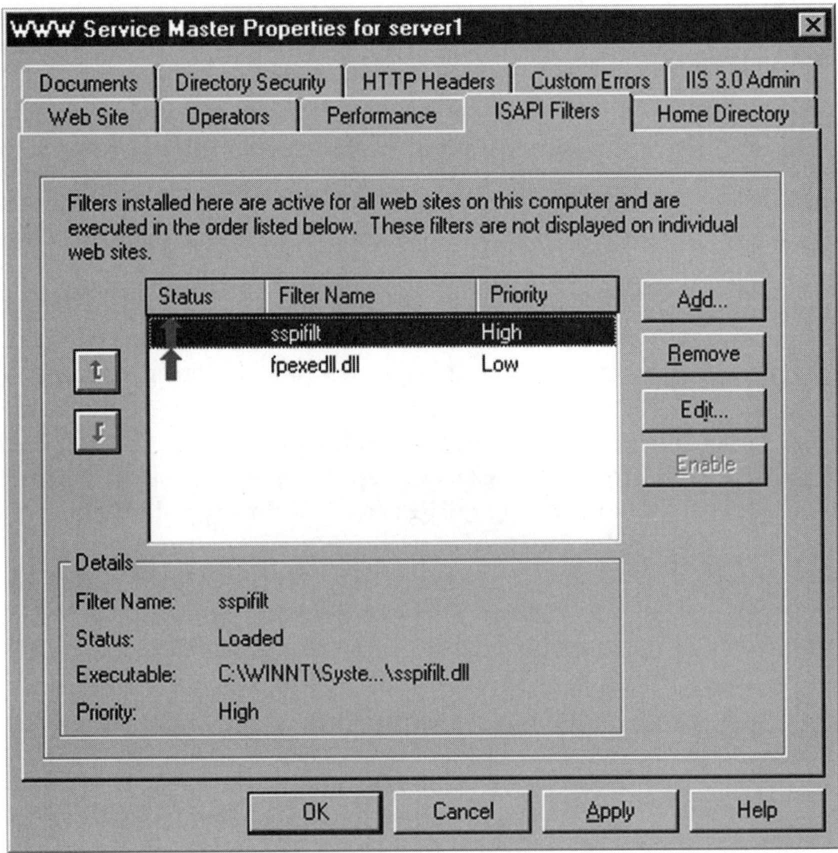

Figure 3-11 Configuring ISAPI filters.

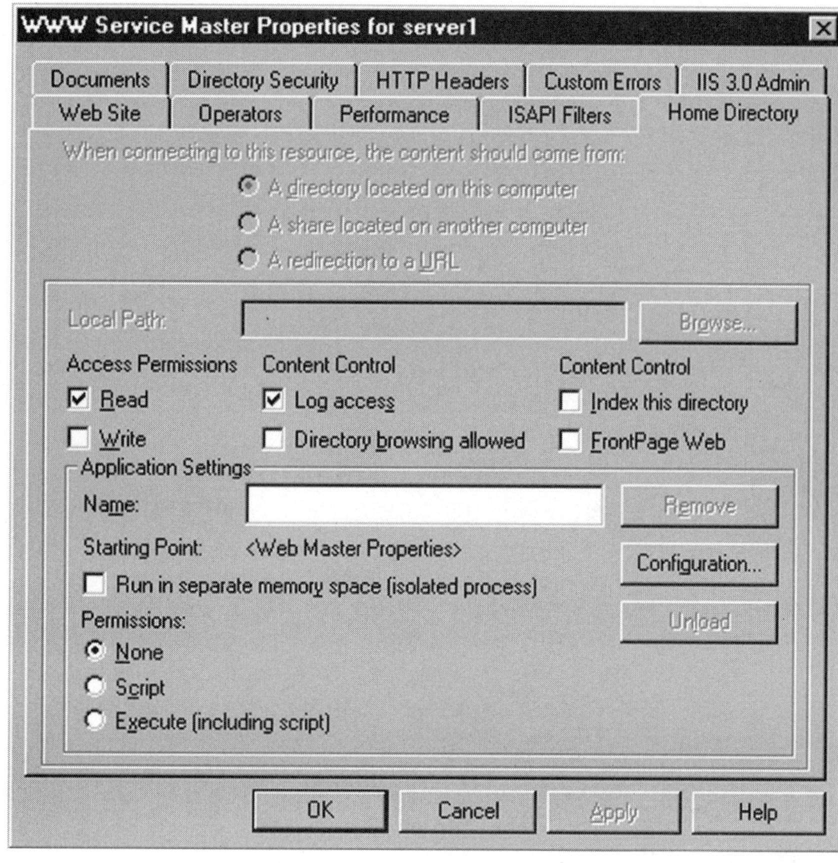

Figure 3-12 Setting the Home Directory options.

```
C:\webstuff\newhome
```

- A *network share* located on another computer

  Enter the UNC path to the share on the selected server, for example:

  ```
  \\webcontent\newhome
  ```

  Click CONNECT AS and enter the username and password of the security credentials that will be used to allow users to access the contents of the network share. Do not use an Administrator account here, which could pose a possible security risk.

- A *redirection* to a URL

  Redirection tells the client to look elsewhere for the document it seeks. You can redirect client requests for the home directory by entering a fully qualified URL in the textbox, such as

```
http://webserver2/newhome
```

Creating new Web sites and configuring their home directories is covered in more detail in Chap. 5.

Configuring WWW Access Permissions If the home directory of a Web site is mapped to a local directory or a share on the network (options 1 and 2 in the preceding list), the following IIS access permissions can be enabled for that directory (see Fig. 3-12):

- Enable READ access if you want users to be able to browse the contents of the home or a selected directory. Normally directories containing HTML files (Web pages) should be assigned READ access so that users can view them; directories containing files you don't want users to be able to read (e.g., CGI scripts and ISAPI applications) should have READ access disabled.
- Enable WRITE access if you want clients to be able to upload content or edit files in the directory.

Note that the Web access permissions assigned to directories in this way must be combined with the NTFS permissions if the directory is on an NTFS volume. This is covered in more detail in Chap. 4.

NOTE: *To temporarily deny access to a Web site so that you can make changes to it, select the WWW Site Properties sheet, select the Home Directory tab, and clear the* READ checkbox.

Configuring WWW Content Control As illustrated in Fig. 3-12, select LOG ACCESS if you want to have client visits to the home or selected directory logged. Note that logging must *first* be enabled on the Web Site tab of the properties sheet. This setting allows logging to be selectively enabled on different Web sites on the server and on different virtual directories within a site.

Select DIRECTORY BROWSING ALLOWED if you want to allow users to browse your Web site's directory structure. Normally, directory browsing is disabled by leaving this option cleared. This is because allowing a user access to information about your Web site's directory structure could help them gain unauthorized access to content on your site.

If your home or selected directory lacks a default document (`default.htm` or `default.asp` or `index.htm`) and directory browsing is disabled, then a browser trying to access your directory will receive an HTTP status code 403 message:

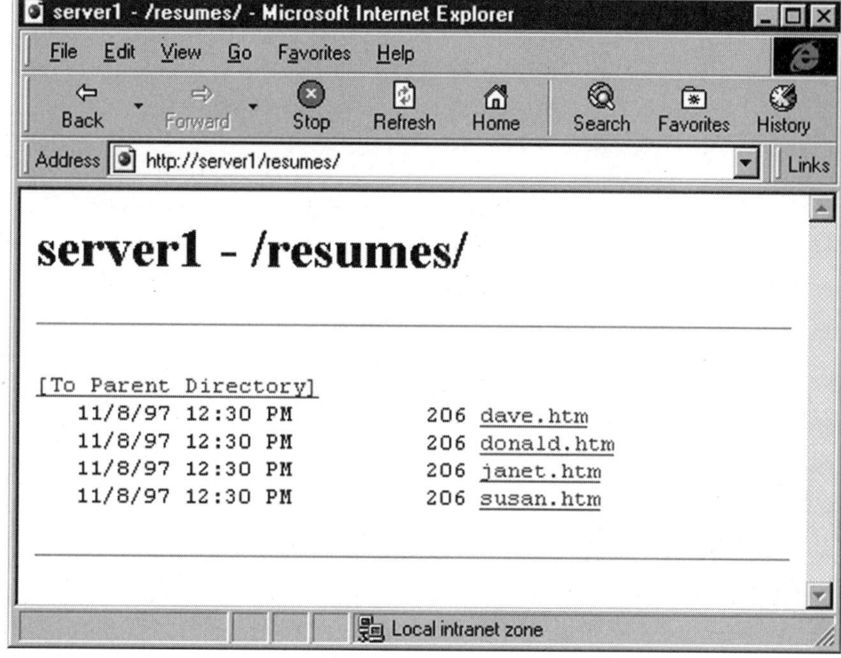

Figure 3-13 View of a directory when directory browsing is enabled on the server.

HTTP/1.1 403 Access Forbidden

If your home or selected directory lacks a default document but directory browsing is enabled, then a browser accessing your directory will display a UNIX-style directory structure. Figure 3-13 illustrates a browser trying to access the /resumes directory on server1:

NOTE: *Virtual directories do not appear in directory listings. In order to browse the directory of a virtual directory, you must enter the full URL for the virtual directory in the browser.*

Select INDEX THIS DIRECTORY to have Microsoft Index Server include the home or selected directory for full-text indexing of your Web site. This will be covered in more detail in Chap. 8.

Select FRONTPAGE WEB to create a FrontPage Web for the home or selected directory. This will be covered in more detail in Chap. 6.

Configuring WWW Application Settings Applications include all the directories and files in a directory that are specified as an application starting point, until another starting point is encountered. Configuring the home directory of a Web site ensures that all directories under the home directory, and all virtual directories within the site, are part of the same application. Application settings are particularly relevant for sites containing Active Server Pages (ASP) scripts.

Click the REMOVE button in the WWW Service Master Properties sheet (Fig. 3-12) to remove an existing application from the site. The REMOVE button now becomes a CREATE button. To create a new application for your site, click the CREATE button and enter a friendly name for your application in the Name textbox. Click the CONFIGURATION button to configure your application using the Application Configuration property sheet (see Fig. 3-14).

The App Mappings tab on the Application Configuration property sheet can be used to map interpreters and script engines to certain file-name extensions. For example, if a browser tries to access the URL

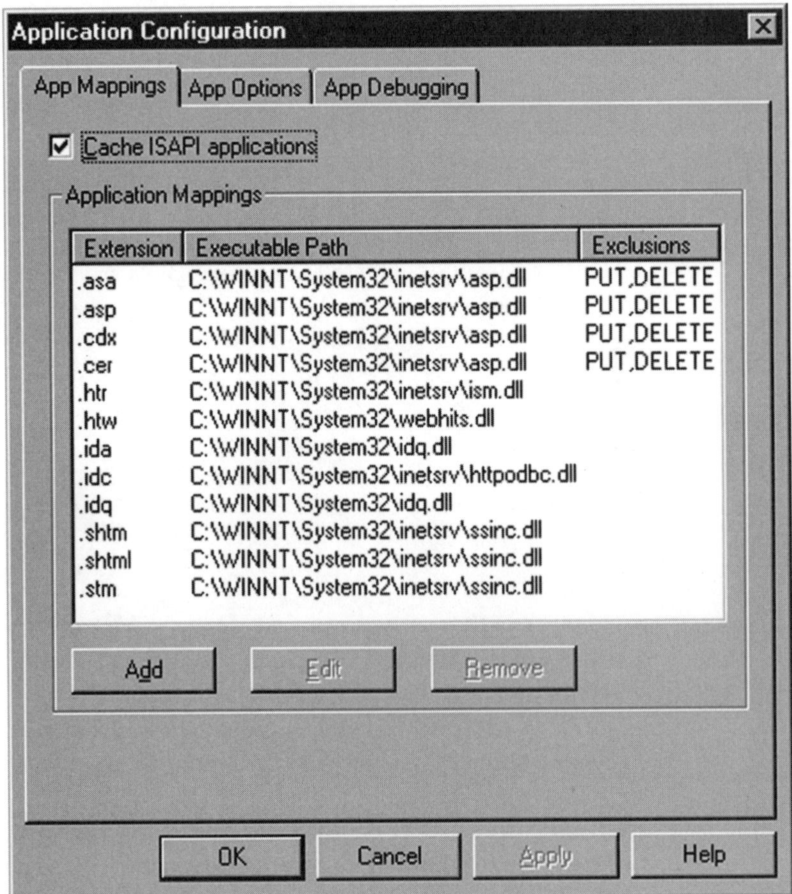

Figure 3-14 Configuring a WWW application.

```
http://server1/default.asp
```

the application mappings settings determine that if a user tries to access the site's home directory, the server notices the file mapping `*.asp` and looks up which application deals with this type, namely,

```
C:\inetpub\wwwroot\system32\inetsrv\asp.dll
```

Selecting CACHE ISAPI APPLICATIONS allows ISAPI DLLs to be loaded and then cached, which speeds up operation of the server.

The App Options tab on the Application Configuration property sheet provides the following options:

- ENABLE SESSION STATE. Selecting this checkbox will enable ASP applications to create a new session for each user and allow the user to be tracked across multiple ASP pages.
- ENABLE BUFFERING. Selecting this checkbox will cause the server to collect ASP output and buffer it before sending it to the client.
- ENABLE PARENT PATHS. Selecting this checkbox allows ASPs to use relative paths to parent directories by using `../` to go one level up. If this is enabled, do not give the home directory execute permission; a security breach might occur if the user can browse up to the home directory and execute a binary within this directory.
- DEFAULT ASP LANGUAGE, The default ASP language is VBScript. This may be changed here (e.g., to Jscript).
- ASP SCRIPT TIMEOUT. This setting determines how long `asp.dll` will allow an ASP script to run.

The App Debugging tab on the Application Configuration property sheet can be used to

- Enable ASP server-side script debugging.
- Enable ASP client-side script debugging.
- Cause detailed ASP error messages to be sent to the client when an error occurs. Included with the error message is the file and the line number in the script that caused the error.
- Cause a text message to be sent to the client when an error occurs.

By returning to the Home Directory tab on the WWW Site Properties sheet, you can configure the ASP application to run in a separate memory space, different from the memory space within which IIS 4.0 itself runs. This is useful because if an application is running in its own memory space and crashes, it won't bring down the server.

Finally, permissions must be assigned for the application to run.

- Script permission allows the execution of scripts mapped to a script engine.
- Execute permission allows any binary executable to run in the directory.

NOTE: *Script permission is generally safer than execute permission and should always be used when a site contains scripts mapped to a script engine running on IIS 4.0.*

Configuring WWW Default Documents Under the Documents tab, select ENABLE DEFAULT DOCUMENT (see Fig. 3-15) to define that file is returned when a request from a browser contains a directory (e.g., `asdf`) but not a specific file. If this setting is enabled, then the requested URL

```
http://server1/asdf/
```

will return one of the following files:

```
http://server1/asdf/default.htm
```

or

```
http://server1/asdf/default.asp
```

If both types of files exist in the home directory, the first one in the listbox (`default.htm`) will be returned to the browser. The order in the listbox can be modified by using the up and down arrow buttons.

Other default file types can be defined. A common one to define is *index.htm,* which can be either an index page or a home page. If no default document is found, the server will either return a status code 403 (Access Forbidden) message or provide a listing of files and subdirectories in the directory, depending on whether the server is configured to allow directory browsing.

Configuring WWW Document Footers Select ENABLE DOCUMENT FOOTER (see Fig. 3-15) to have an HTML segment automatically appended

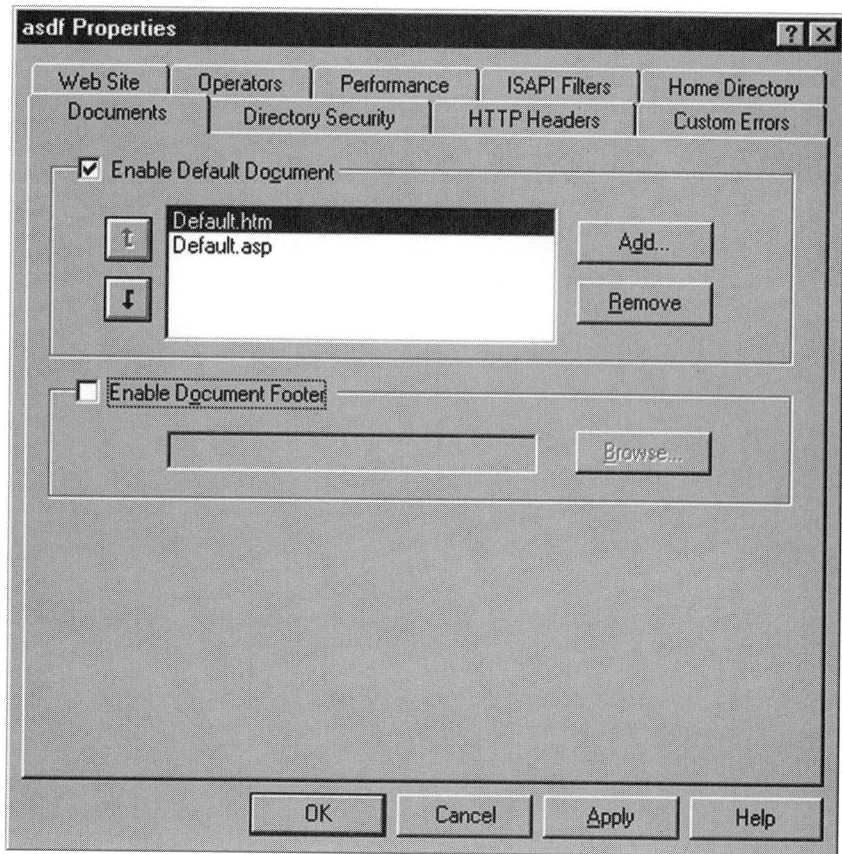

Figure 3-15 Configuring default documents and footers.

to every document retrieved from the server. Specify the full local path to the footer segment.

Configuring WWW Anonymous Access and Authentication Control Use the Directory Security tab in the property sheet (see Fig. 3-16) to configure the kind of logon authentication to be used by browsers trying to access your Web site. These settings will be considered in detail in Chap. 4.

Configuring WWW Secure Communications The Directory Security tab in the property sheet can also be used to help configure SSL settings for your Web site (see Fig. 3-16). These settings will be considered in detail in Chap. 12.

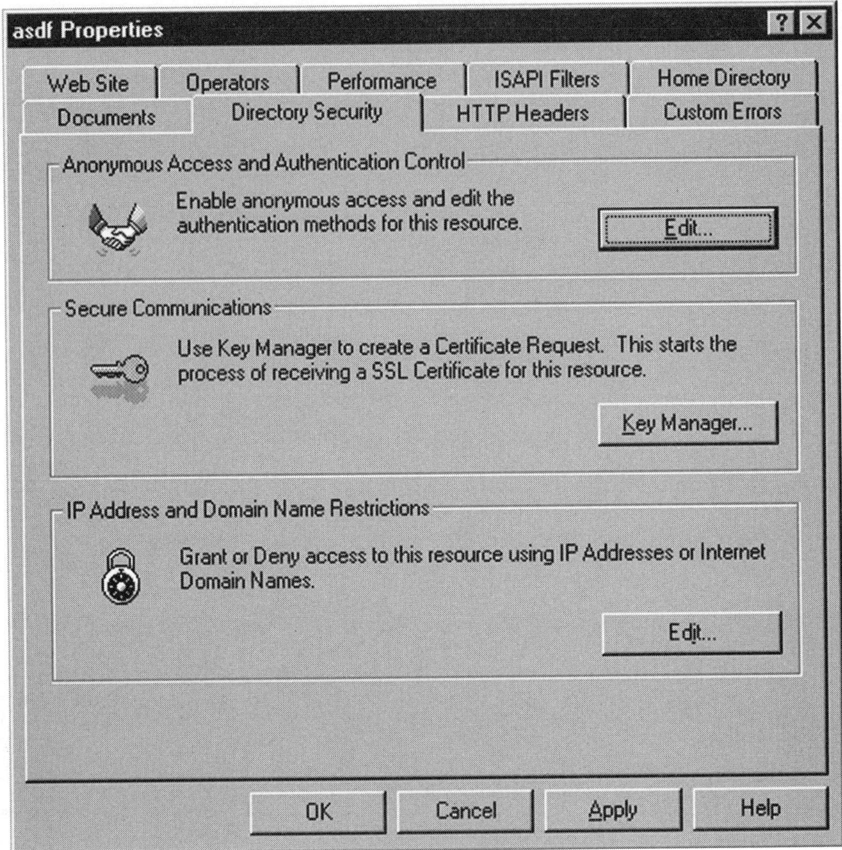

Figure 3-16 Configuring WWW security settings.

Configuring WWW IP Address and Domain Name Restrictions The Directory Security tab of the property sheet can also be used to set your server's security properties (see Fig. 3-16). These settings will be considered in detail in Chap. 4.

Configuring WWW Content Expiration In the HTTP Headers tab, select ENABLE CONTENT EXPIRATION (see Fig. 3-17) to allow your server to return content expiration information in the response headers to an HTTP request. Use these settings for Web pages that regularly or frequently change their content (e.g., announcement pages) and to speed up the browsing process.

If content expiration is enabled, the next time a browser accesses a page it will use the response header information to determine if the content on the page is considered to have expired or not. If the content has expired, the browser will request a new copy of the page with the

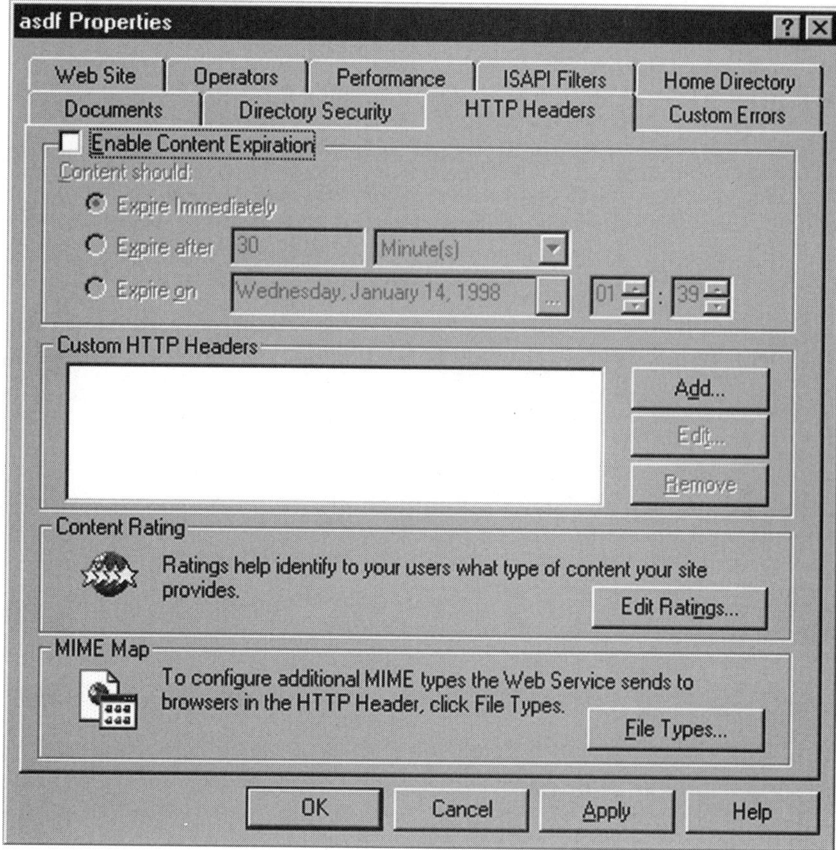

Figure 3-17
Configuring content expiration, custom HTTP headers, content ratings, and MIME map.

expectation that the page has been updated since the original was received. If the content has not expired, the browser assumes that the current content is still valid and will try to retrieve the page from its client-side cache, which speeds up the browsing process.

The content expiration settings include

- EXPIRE IMMEDIATELY. A new copy of the page will be downloaded the next time the page is requested; the page will never load from the client-side cache.
- EXPIRE AFTER *<minutes/hours/days>*. The content will expire after the specified time interval. Until this interval passes, the client will try to retrieve the page from cache, which will speed up the browsing process.
- EXPIRE ON *<date/time>*. The content will expire on the specified date and time. Until that time has passed, the client will try

to retrieve the page from cache, speeding up the browsing process.

Configuring WWW Custom HTTP Headers As shown in Fig. 3-17, click ADD to create custom HTTP response headers (name/value pairs) to be returned to clients making HTTP requests to the home or selected directory. These headers can contain control information that invokes specialized responses from suitably configured browser clients, firewalls, and proxy servers.

Configuring WWW Content Rating As shown in Fig. 3-17, select EDIT RATINGS to establish content ratings for the home or selected directory. These content ratings have been developed by the Recreational Software Advisory Council (RSAC) and can be used by browsers such as Internet Explorer 3.0 and higher versions to determine whether the client has the privileges to view the site. For more information on RSAC, visit their Web site at

`www.rsac.org.`

Content ratings can be established in four areas (see Fig. 3-18):

- Violence
- Sex
- Nudity
- Language

To test the Content Ratings system, try the following exercise:

Check the ENABLE RATINGS FOR THIS RESOURCE box, select the LANGUAGE category, and move the slider to level 2 (moderate expletives). Enter your email address as the person rating the content of your server, and set the expiration date for a week from today. Click APPLY to configure the ratings for your server. This indicates that your site contains moderate expletives and should be viewed only by those with the corresponding privileges.

Now start a content ratings–enabled browser such as Internet Explorer 4.0, and choose INTERNET OPTIONS from the View menu on the browser. Select the Content tab on the Internet Options property sheet. Note that Content Advisor has a button labeled ENABLE; this indicates that Content Advisor has not yet been enabled on your

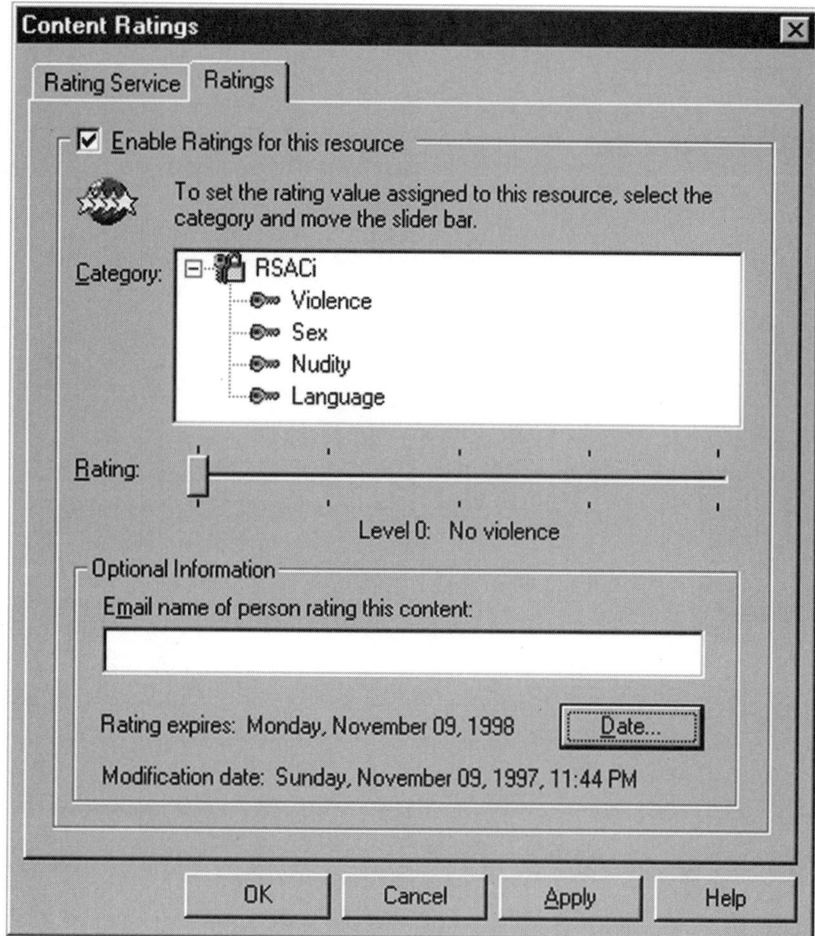

Figure 3-18 The Content Ratings property sheet with content ratings enabled.

browser. Try to access your server's default Web site using the browser; you should have no difficulty doing so.

Enable Content Advisor on your browser by clicking the ENABLE button on the Content tab of the Internet Options property sheet. You are requested to enter a supervisor password, which is used to prevent unauthorized personnel (such as your children) from altering the ratings you are about to set. Type `password` as your supervisor password, and retype it for confirmation.

The Content Advisor property sheet now appears, which is similar in appearance to the Content Ratings property sheet of IIS 4.0 shown in Fig. 3-18. Select the LANGUAGE category, and verify that the slider is set

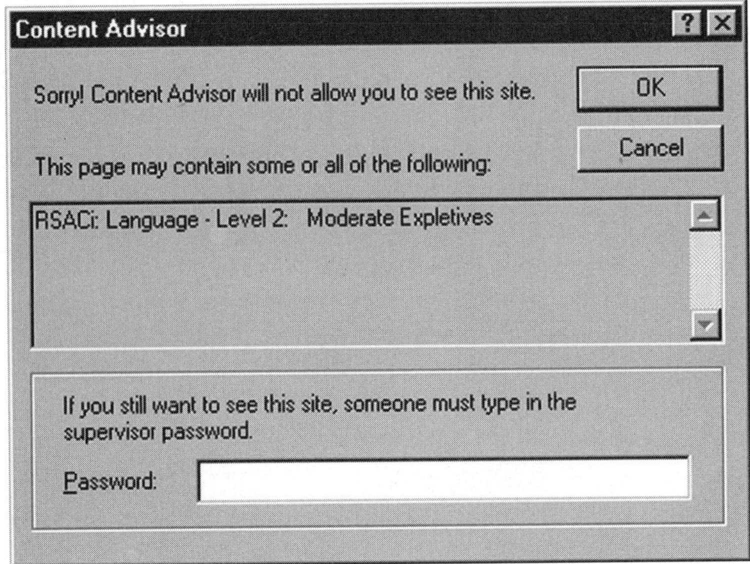

Figure 3-19 Trying to access a site configured with content ratings enabled.

at level zero (inoffensive slang). This indicates that sites specified as having a level 0 language rating are acceptable to the browser and will be displayed, but any sites with a higher-level language rating will be inaccessible. Click OK twice, and then close your browser; the Content Advisor will not take effect until the browser restarts.

Now test your site's rating by restarting your browser and trying to access your server's default Web site again. This time you should receive a message box like the one in Fig. 3-19.

Notice that your browser will not allow you to access the site unless you enter the supervisor password. Enter `password` and view the site. Now configure your browser's Content Advisor to allow you to view sites with level 2 language ratings. Shut down and restart your browser, and try to access the site; this time you should succeed.

Finally, disable the Content Advisor feature on Internet Explorer 4.0, and disable content ratings on your server to return everything to the state you began with.

The Content Advisor property sheet for Internet Explorer 4.0 has a General tab with two important configuration options:

- Select USERS CAN SEE SITES THAT HAVE NO RATING if you are using your browser to view sites on the Internet. The vast majority of sites on the Internet are not rated under this system, so leaving this option unchecked will mean that you will be able to access practically nothing at all on the Internet. Content Advisor is effective only if it is widely implemented on browsers such as Internet Explorer and on servers such as Internet Information Server.

- Select SUPERVISOR CAN TYPE A PASSWORD TO ALLOW USERS TO VIEW RESTRICTED CONTENT if you want the option of viewing restricted content when you browse a site.

Configuring WWW Additional MIME Types You can configure other MIME types in addition to the ones already defined in the section "Configuring Default MIME Types for IIS." If MIME types are configured here for the home or selected directory and then the Master MIME types are changed, the Master MIME types overwrite the changes made to the home or selected directory; the changes are not merged.

Configuring HTTP Error Messages When a client (browser) makes an HTTP request to a server, the server responds by sending a series of response headers followed by the requested file or files. If the transaction is successful, the first request header sent by the server typically looks like this:

```
HTTP/1.1 200 OK
```

(Refer back to the section "A Sample HTTP Session" in this chapter if you need more information on HTTP request/response headers.) The number 200 in the response header is an HTTP status code signifying that the transaction was successful. HTTP status codes generally fall into one of three categories:

- 200 through 299 signify the transaction was *successful.*
- 300 through 399 signify that *redirection* has occurred.
- 400 through 599 signify that some sort of *error* has occurred.

IIS 4.0 allows the administrator to customize HTTP status code messages from the third category. To customize an HTTP status code, first select it on the property sheet (see Fig. 3-20) and then

Click SET TO DEFAULT if you want the server to return the default (standard) status message.

or

Click EDIT PROPERTIES to access the Error Mapping Properties box

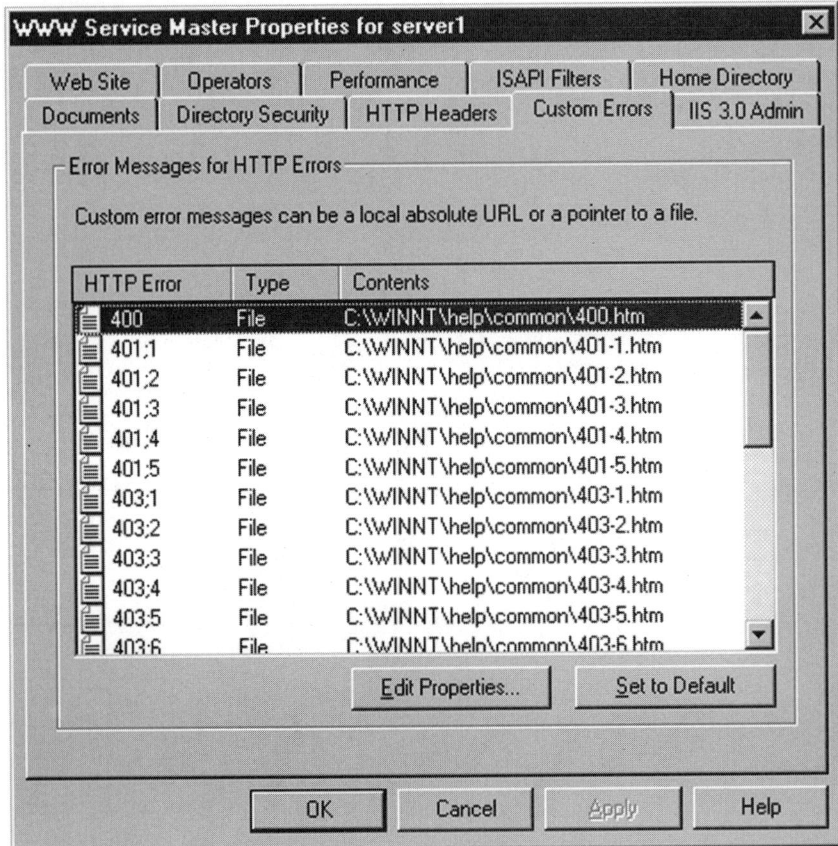

Figure 3-20 Configuring custom HTTP error codes.

Accessing the Error Mapping Properties box allows you to customize an HTTP status code in three possible ways, by selecting the message type as either:

- DEFAULT, to have the server display the default (standard) status message. These messages are defined by the HTTP specifications and are quite brief and sometimes uninformative (e.g., "400 Bad Request").
- FILE, to have the server display a custom error page stored locally on the server or on a network drive. Microsoft supplies a set of customized error pages that are more informative than the default error messages (see Table 3-4). As an administrator you may want to further customize these pages by adding the com-

Table 3-4

Custom HTTP Status Code Messages

Status Code	Default Message	IIS 4.0 Custom Message
400	Bad Request	The request could not be understood by the server due to malformed syntax. The client should not repeat the request without modifications.
401.1	Unauthorized: Logon Failed	This error indicates that the credentials passed to the server do not match the credentials that are allowed to log on to the server. This is usually caused because the credentials sent from the client have been refused by the server. Please contact the Web server's administrator to verify if you have access to the resource requested.
401.2	Unauthorized: Logon Failed due to server configuration	This error indicates that the credentials passed to the server do not match the credentials that are allowed to log on to the server. This is usually caused by not sending the proper WWW-Authenticate header field. Please contact the Web server's administrator to verify if you have access to the resource requested.
401.3	Unauthorized: Unauthorized due to ACL on resource	This error indicates that the credentials passed by the client do not have access to the particular resource on the server. This resource could be either the page or file listed in the address line of the client, or it could be another file on the server that is needed to process the file listed on the address line of the client. Please make a note of the entire address you were trying to access and then contact the Web server's administrator to verify if you have access to the resource requested.
401.4	Unauthorized: Authorization failed by filter	This error indicates that the Web server has a filter program installed to verify users connecting to the server. The authentication used to connect to the server was denied access by this filter program. Please make a note of the entire address you were trying to access and then contact the Web server's administrator to verify if you have access to the resource requested.

Table 3-4

Custom HTTP Status Code Messages (*Continued*)

Status Code	Default Message	IIS 4.0 Custom Message
401.5	Unauthorized: Authorization failed by ISAPI/CGI app	This error indicates that the address on the Web erver you attempted to use has an ISAPI or CGI program installed that verifies user credentials before proceeding. The authentication used to connect to the server was denied access by this program. Please make a note of the entire address you were trying to access and then contact the Web server's administrator to verify if you have access to the resource requested.
403.1	Forbidden: Execute Access Forbidden	This error can be caused if you try to execute a CGI/ISAPI or other executable program from a directory that does not allow programs to be executed. Please contact the Web server's administrator if the problem persists.
403.2	Forbidden: Read Access Forbidden	This error can be caused if there is no default page available to display and directory browsing has not been enabled for the directory, or if you are trying to display an HTML page that resides in a directory marked for Execute or Script permissions only. Please contact the Web server's administrator if the problem persists.
403.3	Forbidden: Write Access Forbidden	This error can be caused if you attempt to upload or modify a file into a directory that does not allow Write access. Please contact the Web server's administrator if the problem persists.
403.4	Forbidden: SSL required	This error indicates that the page you are trying to access is secured with SSL. In order to view it, you need to enable SSL by typing "https://" at the beginning of the address you are attempting to reach. Please contact the Web server's administrator if the problem persists
403.5	Forbidden: SSL 128 required	This error message indicates that the resource you are trying to access is secured with a 128-bit version of Secure Sockets Layer (SSL). In order to view this resource, you need a browser that supports this level of SSL. Please confirm that your browser supports 128-bit SSL security. If it does, then contact the Web server's administrator and report the problem.

Table 3-4

Custom HTTP Status Code Messages (*Continued*)

Status Code	Default Message	IIS 4.0 Custom Message
403.6	Forbidden: IP address rejected	This error is caused when the server has a list of IP addresses that are not allowed to access the site and the IP address you are using is in this list. Please contact the Web server's administrator if the problem persists.
403.7	Forbidden: Client certificate required	This error occurs when the resource you are attempting to access requires your browser to have a client SSL certificate that the server recognizes. This is used for authenticating you as a valid user of the resource. Please contact the Web server's administrator to obtain a valid client certificate.
403.8	Forbidden: Site access denied	This error can be caused if the Web server is not servicing requests, or if you do not have permission to connect to the site. Please contact the Web server's administrator.
403.9	Access Forbidden: Tool many users are connected	This error can be caused if the Web server is busy and cannot process your request due to heavy traffic. Please try to connect again later. Please contact the Web server's administrator if the problem persists.
403.10	Access Forbidden: Invalid Configuration	There is a configuration problem on the Web server at this time. Please contact the Web server's administrator if the problem persists.
403.11	Access Forbidden: Password Change	This error can be caused if the user has entered the wrong password during authentication. Please refresh the page and try again. Please contact the Web server's administrator if the problem persists.
403.12	Access Forbidden: Mapper Denied Access	Your client certificate map has been denied access to this Web site. Please contact the site administrator to establish client certificate permissions. You can also change your client certificate and retry, if appropriate.
404	File Not Found	The file you have requested may not have been installed during setup. To install this file, please run Setup again and choose the appropriate documentation option. This documentation may not be available on some operating systems.

Table 3-4

Custom HTTP Status Code Messages (*Continued*)

Status Code	Default Message	IIS 4.0 Custom Message
405	Method Not Allowed	The method specified in the Request Line is not allowed for the resource identified by the request. Please ensure that you have the proper MIME type set up for the resource you are requesting. Please contact the server's administrator if this problem persists.
406	Not Acceptable	The resource identified by the request is only capable of generating response entities which have content characteristics not acceptable according to the accept headers sent in the request. Please contact the server's administrator if this problem persists.
407	Proxy Authentication Required	You must authenticate with a proxy server before this request can be serviced. Please log on to your proxy server, and then try again. Please contact the Web server's administrator if this problem persists.
412	Preconditon Failed	The precondition given in one or more of the request-header fields evaluated to FALSE when it was tested on the server. This response code allows the client to place preconditions on the current resource meta-information (header field data) and thus prevent the requested method from being applied to a resource other than the one intended. Please contact the Web server's administrator if the problem persists.
414	Request-URI Too Long	The server is refusing to service the request because the Request-URI is longer than the server is willing to interpret. This rare condition is only likely to occur when a client has improperly converted a POST request to a GET request with long query information, when the client has encountered a redirection problem (for example, a redirected URL prefix that points to a suffix of itself), or when the server is under attack by a client attempting to exploit security holes present in some servers using fixed-length buffers for reading or manipulating the Request-URI. Please contact the Web server's administrator if this problem persists.
500	Internal Server Error	The Web server is incapable of performing the request. Please try your request again later. Please contact the Web server's administrator if this problem persists.

Table 3-4

Custom HTTP Status Code Messages (*Continued*)

Status Code	Default Message	IIS 4.0 Custom Message
501	Not Implemented	The Web server does not support the functionality required to fulfill the request. Please check your URL for errors, and contact the Web server's administrator if the problem persists.
502	Bad Gateway	The server, while acting as a gateway or proxy, received an invalid response from the upstream server it accessed in attempting to fulfill the request.

pany logo, a mailto link to the site administrator, a feedback form, advertising, and so on. These custom error pages are located on your server in the directory

```
C:\winnt\help\common
```

- URL, to have the server redirect the client to a URL, which must be an URL on a local server. This URL could point to a custom page or to a script or executable program that handles the error condition. The only requirement is that the URL must exist; otherwise the server will return a "200 Request Successful" message to the client.

Configuring the Default IIS 3.0 Web Site For each IIS 4.0 installation, one (and only one) Web site on the server can be selected for administration by a previous version of Internet Service Manager (version 3.0 or earlier). Choose which site (if any) you want to administer this way from the drop-down box in the IIS 3.0 Admin tab (see Fig. 3-21). This tab appears *only* on the WWW Service Master Properties sheet.

FOR MORE INFORMATION

Following are some additional sources of information concerning the HyperText Transfer Protocol (HTTP).

Microsoft Windows NT Server 4.0 Resource Kit The *Internet Guide* volume of the Resource Kit contains some basic information about HTTP in

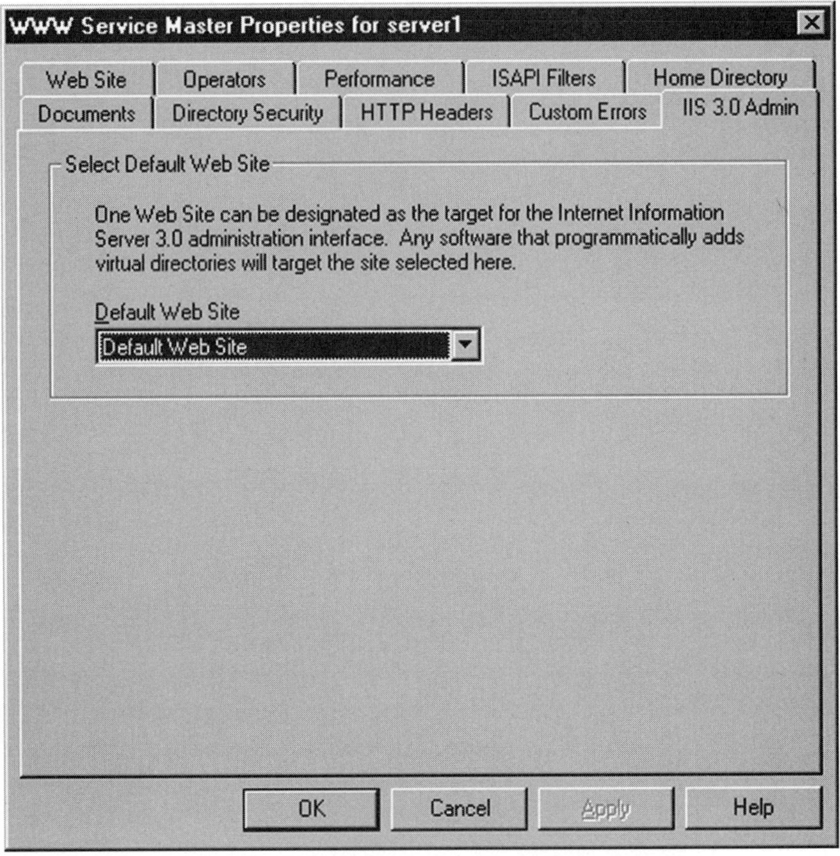

Figure 3-21 Configuring the Default IIS 3.0 Web site.

Chapter 1, "Internet Information Server Architecture" (the system architecture information is, of course, outdated as far as it relates to version 4.0 of IIS).

The World Wide Web Consortium (W3C) The World Wide Web Consortium is a group of international, vendor-neutral organizations whose goal is to promote the development of protocol standards for the World Wide Web. For information about the current status of HTTP, visit the W3C Web site at

```
www.w3.org
```

The W3C also publishes a magazine called the *World Wide Web Journal.* There is an online version of this magazine at

```
www.w3j.com
```

To participate in technical discussions regarding the development of HTTP and related software, you can subscribe to the mailing list at

```
www-talk@w3.org
```

by sending an email message to `www-talk-request@w3.org` with the subject SUBSCRIBE and nothing in the body of the message. There are literally dozens of mailing lists available from the W3C, but this one is probably the one of most general interest.

To post more general and less technical questions regarding HTTP, try posting to the newsgroup

```
comp.infosystems.www
```

or one of the other relevant comp.infosystems newsgroups.

The Internet Engineering Task Force (IETF) The IETF is another organization concerned with developing the underlying architecture of the Internet protocols to increase the overall performance of the Internet. The IETF consists of individuals organized into working groups devoted to specific tasks, communicating mainly through mailing lists. The HTTP Working Group is one example. For more information about the IETF, visit their Web site at

```
www.ietf.org
```

CHAPTER 4

Administering Security

Introduction

Security is a prime concern for network administrators, and Internet Information Server 4.0 running on Windows NT 4.0 forms a reliable, scalable environment for securely hosting Internet, intranet, and extranet Web sites. After completing this chapter, you will be able to

- Describe the various security methods available for Web sites hosted by IIS 4.0 running on Windows NT 4.0.
- Configure IIS to grant and deny access to users based on their client IP addresses or Internet domain names.
- Understand and configure IIS authentication security, including anonymous access, basic authentication, and NT challenge/response authentication.
- Understand and configure IIS permissions for Web sites and individual pages.
- Understand and configure NTFS permissions for Web sites and individual pages.
- Understand how to combine IIS and NTFS permissions.
- Understand other methods of increasing security of IIS servers, including disabling unnecessary protocols and services, monitoring effectiveness of security settings by implementing NTFS auditing and IIS logging, and applying service packs and hotfixes to close security holes as they are discovered.

Additional security for IIS can be realized by implementing Secure Sockets Layer (SSL) in combination with X.509 client certificates. This is covered in Chap. 12.

Understanding IIS Security

Administrators can control access to Web content hosted on IIS 4.0 running on Windows NT 4.0 servers in four main ways:

- *IP address and domain name security.* IIS allows administrators to control access by clients to Web sites, virtual directories, and individual files based upon the IP address or domain name of the client or group attempting to access the resource. IP address and domain name security applies to all users who try to access the resource, regardless of which groups they belong to.

- *IIS authentication security.* IIS allows administrators to control access by clients to Web sites, virtual directories, and individual files based on the kind of user authentication methods configured for the resource. IIS authentication security applies to all users who try to access the resource, regardless of which groups they belong to.
- *IIS permissions.* IIS allows administrators to control access by clients to Web sites, virtual directories, and individual files based on Web access permissions for the resource. IIS permissions apply to all users who try to access the resource, regardless of which groups they belong to.
- *NTFS permissions.* Windows NT allows administrators to control access by clients to physical directories and files based on NTFS access permissions for the resource. Unlike the other three methods, NTFS permissions provide granularity by allowing different permissions to be assigned to different users and groups.

Of these four alternatives, the most fundamental method of securing access to Web sites is the Windows NT File System (NTFS). Prior to configuring any other form of security, make sure that the NTFS permissions for the content being published are set correctly. IIS is only as secure as the file system on which it runs.

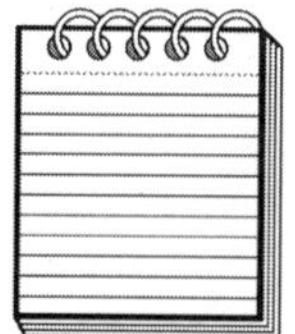

NOTE: *The File Allocation Table (FAT) file system is not recommended for hosting Web content, since it does not provide any directory- or file-level security. If you have Web content stored on a FAT partition, use the Windows NT utility* `convert.exe` *to change the file system to NTFS. The syntax for using this command is:*

```
Convert C:/fs:ntfs
```

Figure 4-1 shows the process by which the four security methods are applied when IIS receives a request to access a resource. Based on this figure, each of the security schemes will be examined in detail in the order in which they are applied.

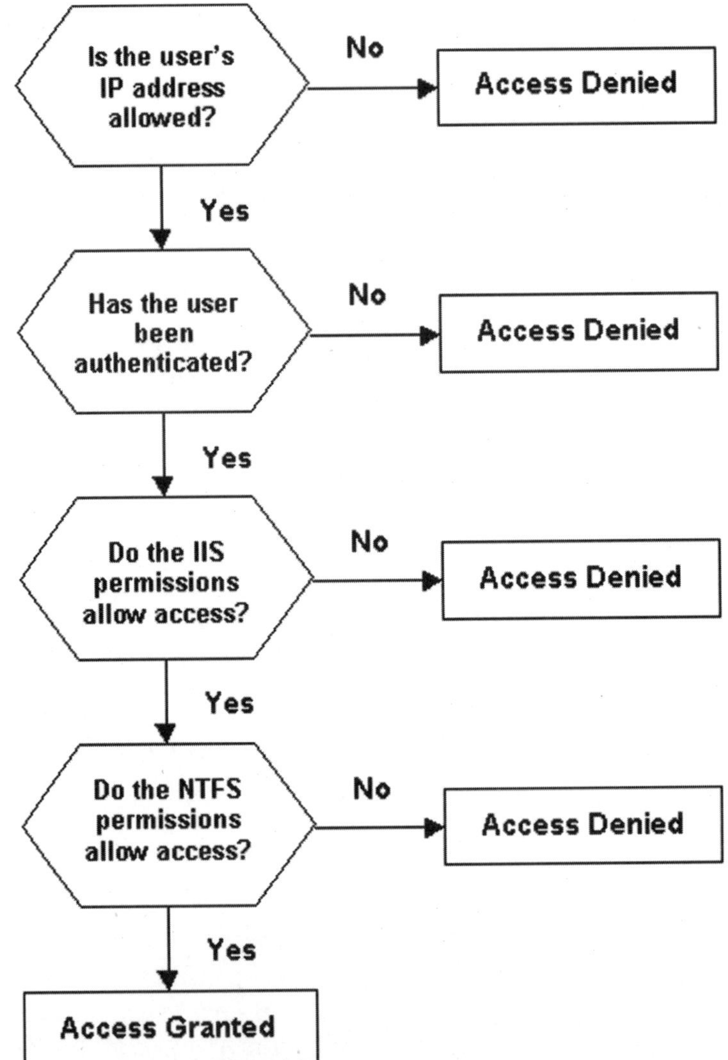

Figure 4-1 Applying the four security methods when a user tries to access IIS.

Understanding IP Address and Domain Name Security

IIS can be configured to grant or deny access to Web sites, virtual directories, or individual files depending upon the IP address or Internet domain name of the client. This is done by configuring IP address and domain name restrictions for the resource. The clients may be either individual hosts or all computers in a particular subnet. This is a global security setting for each resource, and is independent of the particular group that the user accessing the resource belongs to.

Configuring IP Address and Domain Name Restrictions

- To configure IP address and domain name restrictions for virtual servers (Web sites), virtual directories, and any physical subdirectories of a virtual server, right-click on the resource's node in the Microsoft Management Console (MMC), select PROPERTIES from the Context menu, choose the Directory Security tab on the property sheet, and click EDIT under IP Address and Domain Name Restrictions.
- To configure IP address and domain name restrictions for any file in a virtual directory or server, right-click on the file's node in the MMC, select PROPERTIES from the Context menu, choose the File Security tab on the property sheet, and click EDIT under IP Address and Domain Name Restrictions.

The IP Address and Domain Name Restrictions box allows administrators to grant or deny access to servers, sites, and pages based on IP addresses and Internet domain names (see Fig. 4-2). Before configuring IP address and domain name security you must decide whether to

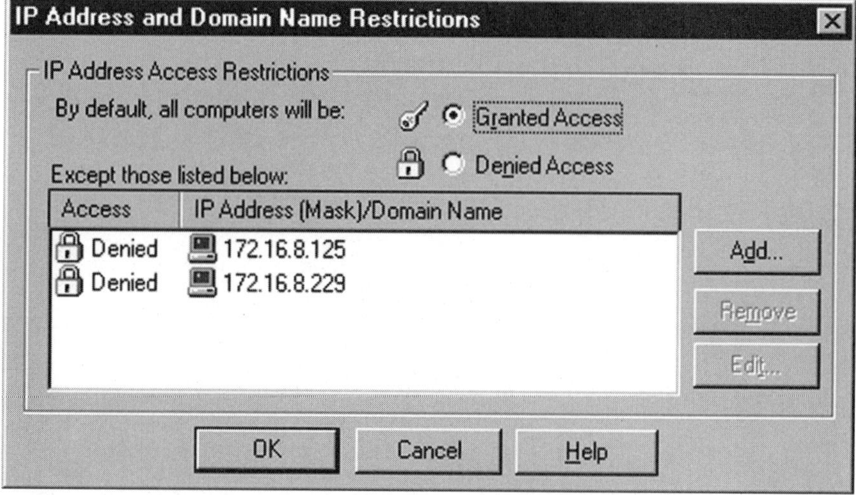

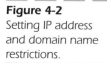

Figure 4-2 Setting IP address and domain name restrictions.

Grant access to all hosts *except* for those specified

or

Deny access to all hosts *except* for those specified

To grant or deny access to hosts, click ADD to bring up the Grant (or Deny) Access On box, and then choose one of the following options:

- *Single computer.* Enter the IP address of the individual host you want to grant or deny access to. If your network supports DNS, you can also click DNS LOOKUP, enter the fully qualified domain name (FQDN) of the host you want to grant or deny access to, and have your DNS server resolve the FQDN into an IP address.
- *Group of computers.* Enter the IP network address and subnet mask of the network you want to grant or deny access to (see Fig. 4-3).
- *Domain name.* Enter the domain name of the Internet domain you want to grant or deny access to. A dialog box may appear warning you that this option requires DNS Reverse Lookup and may impact the performance of your server.

Strategies for Using IP Address and Domain Name Security

- If your Web server provides an extranet connection to another company, you might want to deny access to all computers except for the IP network addresses of the other company.

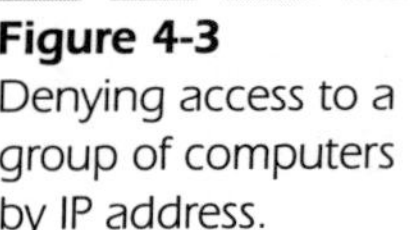

Figure 4-3
Denying access to a group of computers by IP address.

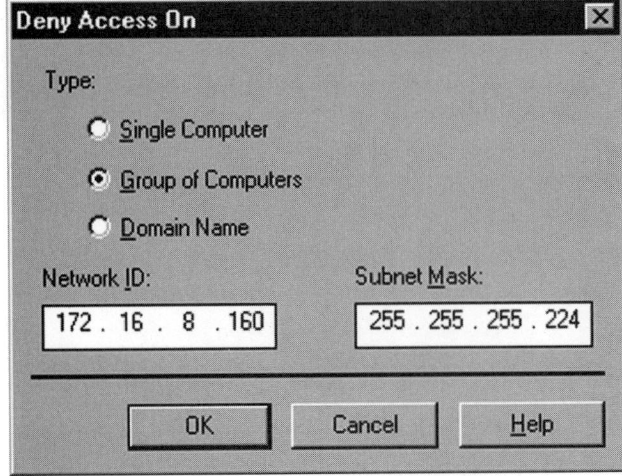

- If an attempt to hack into your network has come from 207.166.52.4, you might want to deny access to that IP address or to the entire 207.166.52.0 network.
- If your IIS server provides intranet services to your LAN and your LAN is also connected to the Internet outside, you might want to grant access to your own network numbers while denying access to everyone else.

Understanding IIS Authentication Security

IIS can be configured to control access to Web sites, virtual directories, or individual files depending on the logon authentication method used by the client. This is done by configuring IIS authentication security for the resource. This is a global security setting for each resource, and is independent of the particular group the user accessing the resource belongs to.

The three IIS authentication schemes available are

- *Anonymous access.* Everyone can access the Web site, virtual directory, or individual file configured with this setting.
- *Basic authentication.* Users must enter a valid Windows NT user account and password in response to a logon dialog box in order to access the Web site, virtual directory, or individual file configured with this setting.
- *NT challenge/response.* Users already logged on to their machines with a valid Windows NT user account are automatically authenticated and allowed to access the Web site, virtual directory, or individual file configured with this setting.

These three authentication schemes may be configured to control access to

- All Web content hosted on your IIS server
- Individual Web sites hosted on your IIS server
- Individual virtual directories in a Web site
- Individual physical subdirectories in a Web site
- Individual Web pages or other files in a Web site

To configure IIS authentication security as the default setting for *all Web sites* hosted on your IIS server, start the Microsoft Management Console (MMC), open the WWW Service Master Properties sheet for your IIS server, and select the Directory Security tab (Fig. 4-4). Next click EDIT to open the Authentication Methods dialog box (Fig. 4-5). Select any combination of the three authentication methods available, and click OK to close the Authentication Methods property sheet.

Now click APPLY on the WWW Service Master Properties sheet. If the default settings you have chosen differ from the settings of any child nodes on the server, *and* these child node settings have changed since the default settings were previously set, then the Inheritance Overrides box will open, allowing you to select which child nodes should inherit the default settings you have selected for the parent node (see Fig. 4-6). By default, *all* child nodes automatically inherit any settings made using the WWW Service Master Properties sheet.

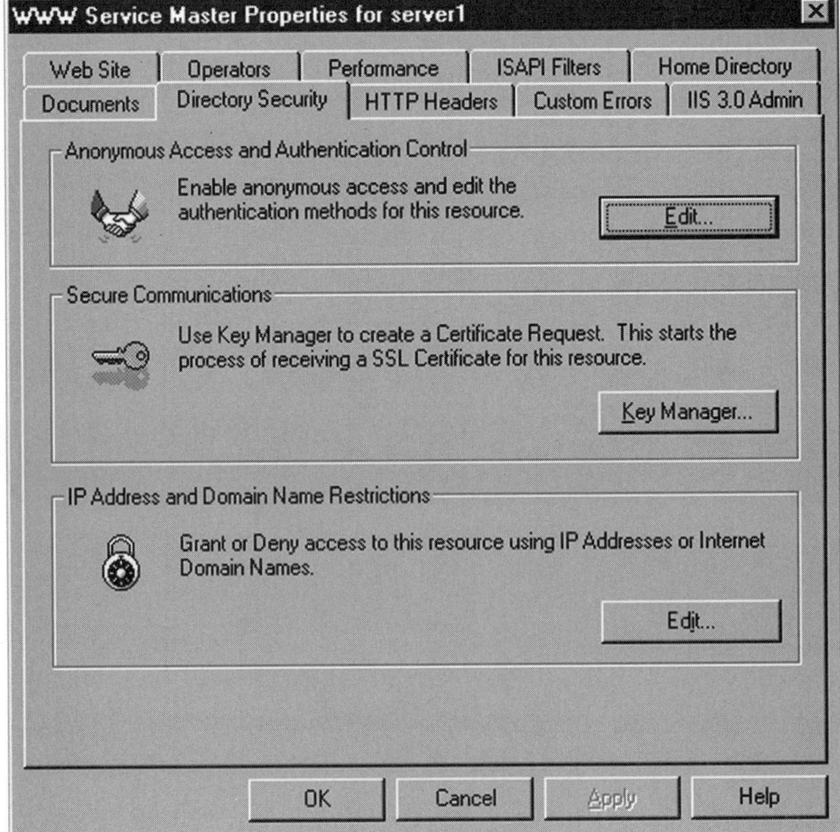

Figure 4-4
The Directory Security tab of the WWW Service Master Properties sheet.

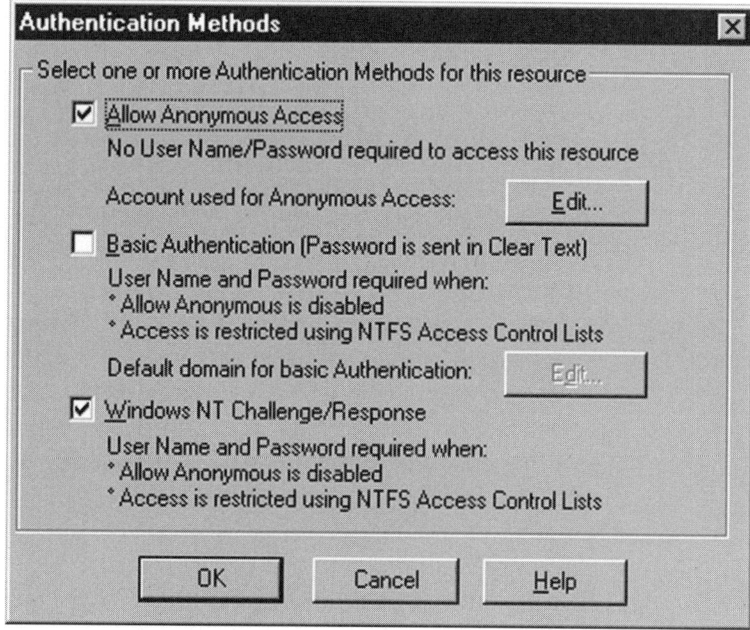

Figure 4-5 Selecting authentication methods.

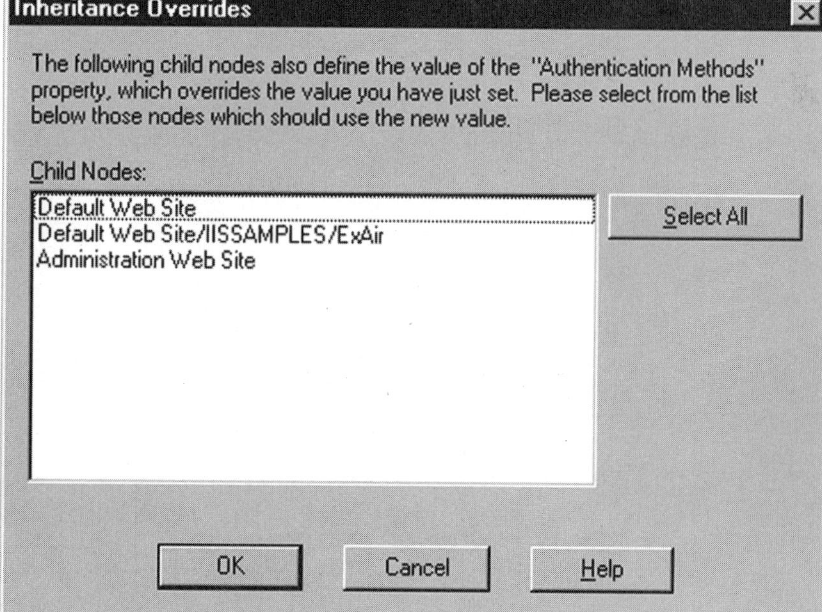

Figure 4-6 The Inheritance Overrides box.

To configure IIS authentication security for a *specific* Web site, virtual directory, or physical directory hosted on your IIS server, use the MMC and right-click on the node representing the resource you want to restrict access to and select PROPERTIES to open the <resource_name> Properties sheet for your resource.

Next choose the Directory Security tab and click EDIT to open the Authentication Methods property sheet. Select any combination of the three authentication methods available, and click OK to close the Authentication Methods property sheet.

Now click APPLY on the <resource_name> Properties sheet. If the settings you have chosen for this Web site differ from the settings of any child nodes under this site, *and* these child node settings have changed since the default settings were previously set, then the Inheritance Overrides box will open, allowing you to specify which child nodes should inherit the settings you have selected.

Finally, to configure IIS authentication security for a specific *file* within a virtual server or directory, use the MMC, right-click on the node representing the file you want to restrict access to, and select PROPERTIES to open the <resource_name> Properties sheet for this page. Choose the File Security tab and click EDIT to open the Authentication Methods property sheet. Select any combination of the three authentication methods available, and click OK.

Configuring Anonymous Access

The first IIS authentication scheme we examine is called *anonymous access.* When IIS is installed, the setup program creates a special user account called the *Internet Guest Account.* Using User Manager (if IIS is installed on a member server, or User Manager for Domains if IIS is installed on a domain controller), we can see that this account has the following properties:

- The username is IUSR_SERVERNAME, where SERVERNAME is the name of the server on which IIS is installed.
- The user cannot change the password.
- The password never expires.
- The user is a member of the Guests local group.

In addition, by using User Manager and selecting USER RIGHTS from the Policies menu, we can see that the Internet Guest Account has only one

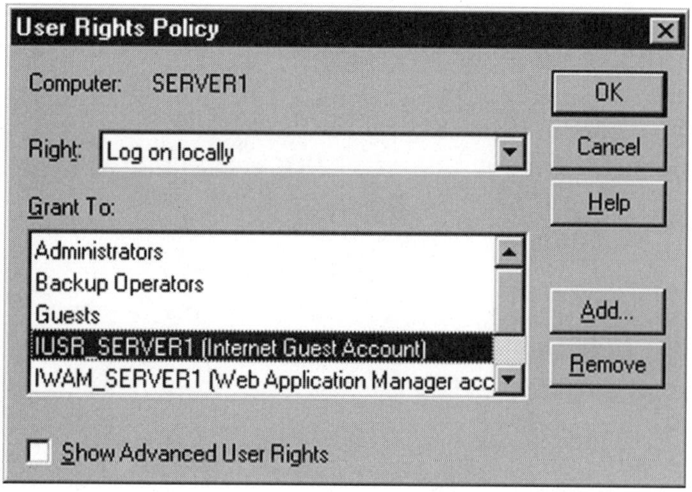

Figure 4-7
IUSR_SERVER1 must have only the right to log on locally.

right: the right to *log on locally* to the machine on which IIS is installed (see Fig. 4-7).

By default, ALLOW ANONYMOUS ACCESS is enabled on the Authentication Methods property sheet for your IIS server (see Fig. 4-5). This means that all users, whether they have valid Windows NT user accounts or not, are allowed access to Web content on your IIS server. In other words, the IUSR_SERVERNAME account allows guest access to all users who access your server, without requiring a specific user account and password.

If necessary, the account used to allow anonymous access can be changed by selecting EDIT on the Authentication Methods property sheet. This opens the Anonymous User Account box (see Fig. 4-8). You might use this option in one of the following situations:

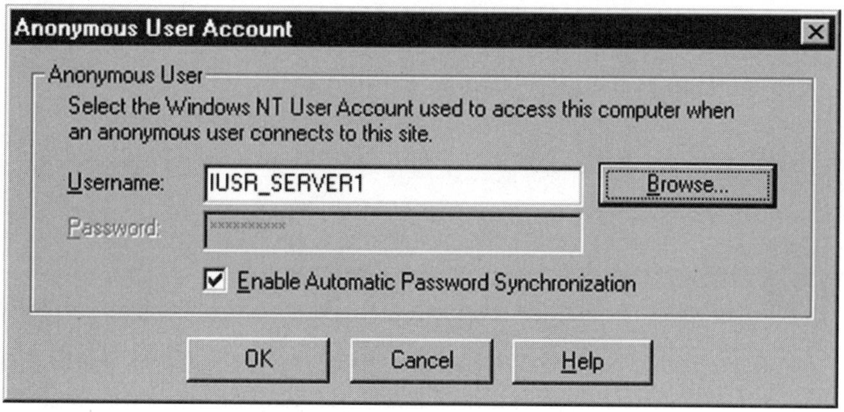

Figure 4-8
Configuring Anonymous User Account.

- You accidentally deleted the existing IUSR_SERVERNAME account and you need to create a new account for anonymous access.
- You wish to rename the IUSR_SERVERNAME account to prevent any security breach that might occur if someone changes the rights and permissions of the Guests group. Someone might try to hack the IUSR_SERVERNAME account on the chance that the settings for the Guests group are incorrect.
- If your IIS server is installed on a Windows NT *member server,* and IIS needs to provide anonymous access to Web content stored on other servers in your domain, you may need to replace the default IUSR_SERVERNAME, which is a local account on the member server, with a domain-wide account that can be assigned permissions on other servers in the domain. If IIS is installed on a *domain controller,* this is not an issue.
- If you have several IIS servers installed on Windows NT member servers, and you want to harmonize their various IUSR_SERVERNAME accounts so that you have only one Internet Guest Account, you can create a new IUSR account on a domain controller and replace the existing local IUSR accounts with the new global IUSR account. This will simplify setting up ACLs for resources containing Web content on NTFS volumes.

Before you use this option, you need to create a new account for anonymous access using User Manager or User Manager for Domains. Be sure to assign it the same right as IUSR_SERVERNAME has, namely, the right to log on locally to the IIS server(s) it applies to. Then use the Anonymous User Account box to assign a new user account for anonymous access to your IIS server. Leave the ENABLE AUTOMATIC PASSWORD SYNCHRONIZATION checkbox selected so that Windows NT will automatically synchronize the IIS settings with the password defined in User Manager.

Strategies for Using Anonymous Access

When should anonymous access be used? Some possible situations are as follows:

- Where security needs are low and the site is intended to be generally available to the public through the Internet
- On a corporate intranet with no connection to the Internet

- Where security needs are high and users must not be allowed to accidentally pass their credentials over WAN links to access the corporate Web site

NOTE: If you have modified the rights and permissions of the Guests local group, then the Internet Guest Account will inherit these new rights and permissions as well since it is a member of the Guests group. Always check what rights and permissions the Guests group has on your system before allowing anonymous access to your IIS Web server!

Configuring Basic Authentication

The second IIS authentication scheme we cover is called *basic authentication.* Basic authentication is the standard HTTP method of user authentication and is supported by most Web browsers.

If BASIC AUTHENTICATION is selected on the Authentication Methods property sheet for a resource (see Fig. 4-5), then a client trying to access a virtual server, virtual directory, or individual file will be presented with an Enter Network Password dialog box (Fig. 4-9). The user must then enter a valid Windows NT user account and password to be allowed to access the page they are trying to view. If an invalid account is successively entered three times into this box, the server will return the following message to the client browser:

```
HTTP Error 401.1 Unauthorized Logon Failed
```

Figure 4-9
The Enter Network Password dialog box for basic authentication.

Basic authentication is not a secure authentication scheme and should be used only in low-security environments. In basic authentication, the username and password are encoded into a string of ASCII characters using a process known as *uuencoding.* (The Authentication Methods dialog box says that basic authentication sends the username and password as *clear text,* but this is not actually the case.) This uuencoded string, which is easily decipherable using a simple mathematical algorithm, is then included in the HTTP Get Request packet as an HTTP Request Header, such as

```
Authentication: Basic ZG9uYWxkOnBhc3N3b3Jk
```

Figure 4-10 shows a Network Monitor capture of a basic authentication request. Anyone with sufficient access to your network to capture such packets can easily decode the authentication string and then use the username and password to hack into your Windows NT network. So don't use basic authentication unless it is necessary on one of the following grounds:

- To provide a basic level of authentication in a low-security environment

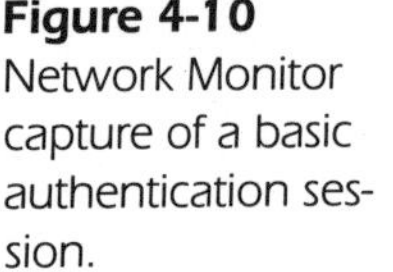

Figure 4-10 Network Monitor capture of a basic authentication session.

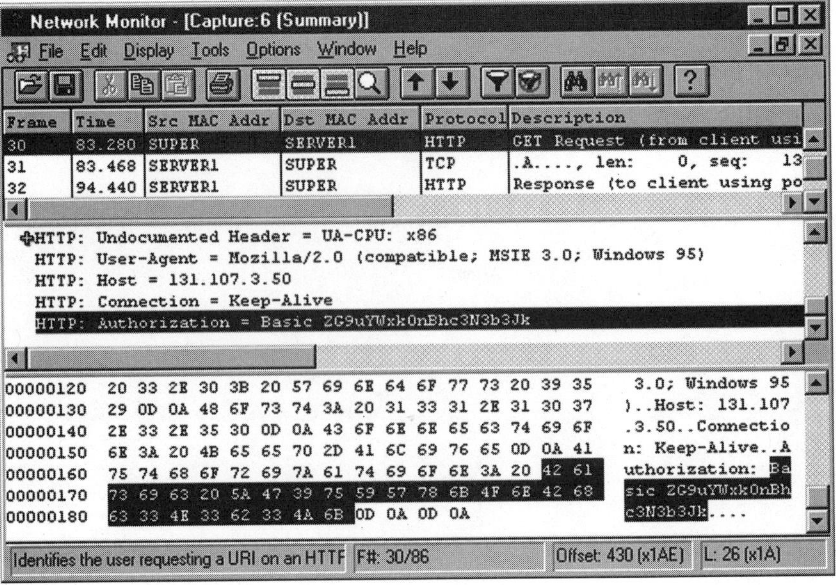

- To provide authentication for non-Microsoft clients in a *heterogeneous network* (i.e., a network that also includes UNIX workstations, Macintosh clients, etc.)

Basic authentication can be combined with Secure Sockets Layer (SSL) encryption to provide a secure authentication scheme in heterogeneous environments. This ensures that not just user authentication but *all* client/server traffic, including data transfer, is strongly encrypted. SSL encryption provides a greater degree of security but negatively impacts server performance. SSL is covered in Chap. 12.

You can configure IIS to forward a request for basic authentication to a domain other than the server's domain. To do this, select BASIC AUTHENTICATION on the Authentication Methods property sheet and click EDIT to bring up the Basic Authentication Domain box. Browse to or enter the name of the domain to be used for authentication and click OK (see Fig. 4-11).

Strategies for Using Basic Authentication

When should basic authentication be used? Some possible situations are as follows:

- In a heterogeneous networking environment where security is low and authentication by non–Windows NT systems is required.

Figure 4-11 Configuring Basic Authentication Domain.

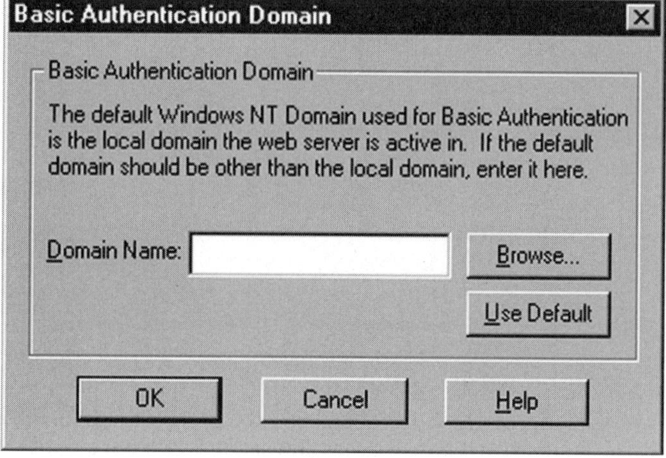
Basic Authentication Domain
Basic Authentication Domain
The default Windows NT Domain used for Basic Authentication is the local domain the web server is active in. If the default domain should be other than the local domain, enter it here.
Domain Name:
Browse...
Use Default
OK
Cancel
Help

- In a low-security environment where some users use browsers such as Netscape Navigator that cannot use NT challenge/response authentication.
- In a medium-security environment where companies need to provide extranet access to content that is not sensitive (e.g., providing distributors with access to online catalogs). A single account is created by the supplier and is used by distributors to log on to the supplier's Web server. This account is changed on a regular basis.
- In a high-security environment combined with SSL to allow sensitive information to be securely transmitted via extranet connections between companies.

Configuring NT Challenge/Response

The third and last IIS authentication method is called *Windows NT challenge/response* authentication. In challenge/response, the server authenticates the client through an interchange of encrypted packets, none of which contain the password in any form. This is the most secure of the three IIS authentication schemes from a network perspective, and it takes place in different ways, depending on the network configuration.

- If the user is logged on to a Windows NT system using a valid domain user account, then the challenge/response security process is transparent to the user. The user simply tries to access the desired resource, a series of HTTP packets automatically authenticate the user based on his or her current logon credentials, and the user accesses the page. No logon box appears for the user to deal with. However, a domain controller must be accessible for NT challenge/response authentication to succeed.
- If the user is logged on to a Windows 95 system participating in a workgroup, he or she is confronted with an Enter Network Logon dialog box and must enter a valid Windows NT username and password to access the resource. Again, a domain controller must be accessible for the challenge/response method to succeed.

Windows NT challenge/response authentication is supported by the client software Microsoft Explorer 2.0 and higher. It is not currently supported by any version of Netscape Navigator.

As in any password authentication scheme, simple guidelines must be followed to ensure that security is not breached. Administrators need to plan and enforce the proper account policy to ensure that passwords are not stolen or guessed. Using User Manager for Domains, select ACCOUNT from the Policies menu to bring up the Account Policy dialog box (Fig. 4-12).

Use the Account Policy box to establish password policies such as

- Setting a minimum password length
- Establishing a maximum password age before expiration
- Ensuring password uniqueness by keeping password history
- Enabling account lockout after a few bad logon attempts
- Forcing users to log on before they can change a password

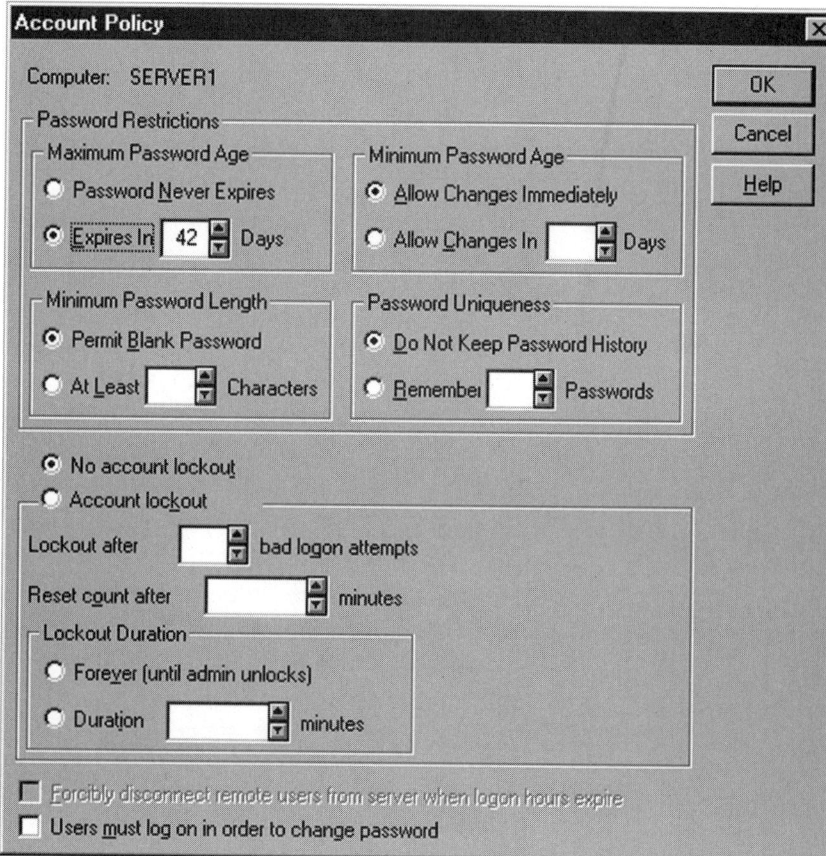

Figure 4-12 The Account Policy dialog box.

In addition to the preceding measures, make sure that you have a written network security policy in place, with clear guidelines for users on how to choose a secure password, how to protect a password, and the consequences of violating the company security policy.

Strategies for Using NT Challenge/Response Authentication

When should NT challenge/response authentication be used? Some possible situations are as follows:

- Where the security needs are high and only domain users are to be allowed access to the site
- In a corporate intranet composed of Windows NT and Windows 95 workstations, to provide security and eliminate the need for users to enter logon information each time they access the intranet

Combining IIS Authentication Methods

Any two or all three of the authentication methods may be enabled on the same resource. The general rules for combining these methods are as follows:

- If anonymous access and another authentication method (basic authentication or NT challenge/response) are both enabled on the same resource, anonymous access is attempted first. If this fails (for example, if the NTFS permission on the resource has access explicitly denied to IUSR_SERVERNAME), the other method is attempted.
- If basic authentication and NT challenge/response are both enabled on the same resource, NT challenge/response has precedence and will be attempted first by the client browser.

Understanding IIS Permissions

IIS can be configured to control access to Web sites, virtual or physical directories, or individual files based on Web access permissions assigned to the resource. This is done by configuring IIS permissions for the resource. This is a global security setting for each resource, and is independent of the particular group that the user accessing the resource belongs to.

Configuring IIS Permissions

- To configure IIS permissions for a virtual server, right-click on its node in the MMC, select PROPERTIES from the Context menu, and choose the Home Directory tab on the property sheet for the node.
- To configure IIS permissions for a virtual directory, right-click on its node in the MMC, select PROPERTIES from the Context menu, and choose the Virtual Directory tab on the property sheet for the node.
- To configure IIS permissions for a physical directory, right-click on its node in the MMC, select PROPERTIES from the Context menu, and choose the Directory tab on the property sheet for the node.
- To configure IIS permissions for an individual file, right-click on its node in the MMC, select PROPERTIES from the Context menu, and choose the File tab on the property sheet for the node.

Figure 4-13 shows the Virtual Directory tab for the IISSAMPLES property sheet as an example. Note that the *read* and *script* permissions are enabled on the virtual directory and its contents.

IIS offers two kinds of *access permissions* to restrict access to virtual directories, folders, and files (see Fig. 4-13). Either or both of these may be selected for any resource.

- *Read.* Select this checkbox to allow clients to display the contents of your virtual directory or folder, or to allow them to display your file.
- *Write.* Select this checkbox to allow clients to write to the contents of your virtual directory or folder, or to allow them to overwrite an existing file.

In addition to access permissions, if your directory contains executable files or scripts, you can configure *application settings* for these files by choosing one of the following:

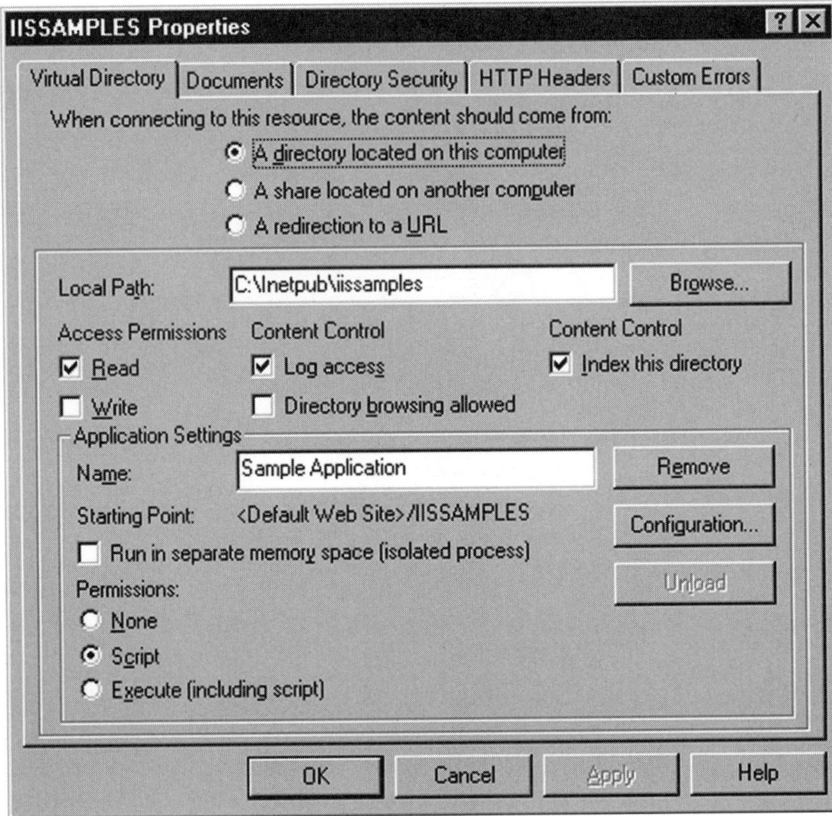

Figure 4-13 Configuring IIS permissions for a virtual directory.

- *None.* No executables are allowed to run in this directory.
- *Script.* Scripts that are mapped to a script engine are allowed to run in this directory. This includes Active Server Pages, IDC scripts, CGI scripts, and so on.
- *Execute.* Both scripts and executable binaries are allowed to run in this directory.

Strategies for Securing Your Site with IIS Permissions

IIS permissions are assigned depending on the kind of resource being accessed. Typical IIS permissions for various resources are listed in Table 4-1.

Table 4-1

Suggested IIS Permissions

Type of Web Content	Suggested IIS Permissions
Static Web content	Read and none
Active Server Pages	Read and script
Other scripts	Read and script
Executable programs	Read and execute
Database content	Read, write, and none

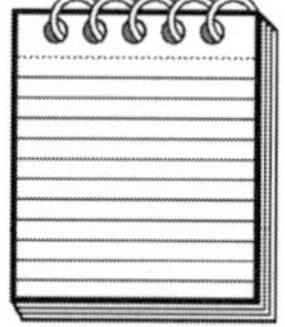

NOTE: *Be careful about assigning both write and execute permission to a folder. This may allow users to upload and run binary executables on your server. This level of permission should be assigned only to trusted developers. Wherever possible, use script instead of execute permission.*

Understanding NTFS Permissions

Windows NT can be configured to control access to physical directories and files based on NTFS permissions assigned to the resource. Unlike the other three methods described, NTFS permissions provide granularity by allowing different permissions to be assigned to different users and groups. For NTFS permissions to be used, volumes hosting Web content must be formatted with the Windows NT File System (NTFS).

There are six basic NTFS permissions:

1. Read (R)
2. Write (W)
3. Execute (X)
4. Delete (D)
5. Change permissions (P)
6. Take ownership (O)

These six permissions are rarely used individually, but are grouped to form what are called *NTFS standard permissions.* There are two different sets of NTFS standard permissions: those applying to folders (directories) and those applying to individual files. Tables 4-2 and 4-3 summarize these two types. In addition to these standard permissions, administrators can create *special access* permissions consisting of any grouping of the NTFS basic permissions RWXDP and O.

Table 4-2

NTFS Standard Permissions for Folders

Type of Access	NTFS Standard Permission	
	Folders	Files in the Folders
No access	None	None
Read	RX	RX
Change	RWXD	RWXD
Add	WX	Unspecified
Add and read	RWX	RX
List	RX	Unspecified
Full control	RWXDPO	RWXDPO

Table 4-3

NTFS Standard Permissions for Files

Type of Access	NTFS Standard Permission
No access	None
Read	RX
Change	RWXD
Full control	RWXDPO

When a volume is formatted with NTFS, all resources (files and folders) on the volume have *access control lists (ACLs)* created for them. The ACL for a resource specifies which users and groups have which kind of access to the resource. Figure 4-14 shows the ACL for the folder `C:\intepub\wwwroot` on a typical IIS server. Note that by default administrators have *full control* of resources on NTFS volumes (good!) while the Everyone group has *change* access to resources (bad!). The Everyone group will be discussed later.

Configuring NTFS Permissions

A user's access to a resource on an NTFS volume is determined by the ACL of the resource and the user's membership in Windows NT groups. For example, if the user has *full control* permission and a group the user belongs to has only *read* permission on the resource, then the user has *full control* permission on the resource. In other words, when NTFS permissions are combined, the effective permission is the *least restrictive* permission:

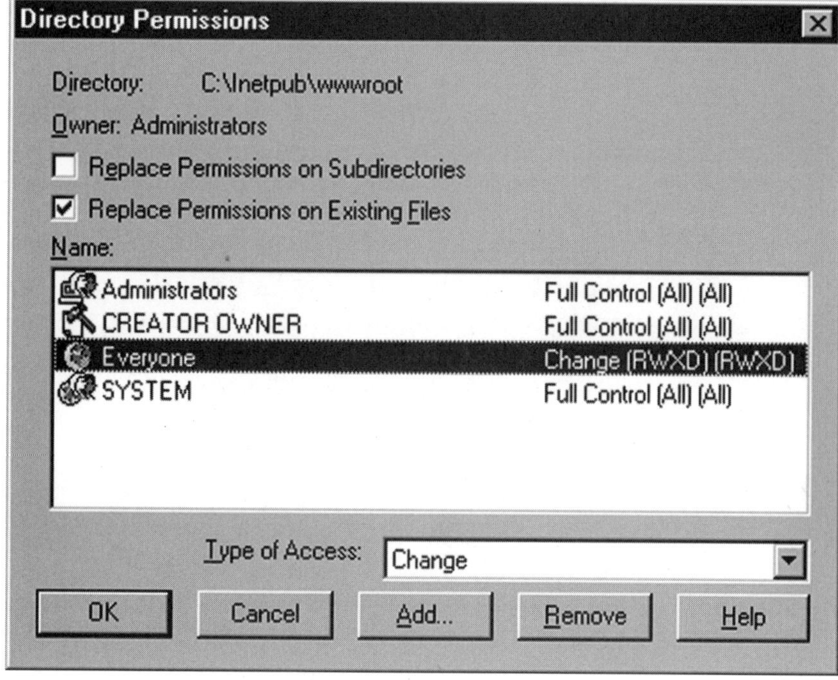

Figure 4-14 Remove the Everyone group from the access control list.

Full control + Read = Full control

The exception to this rule is that when *no access* permission combines with any other NTFS standard permission, the result is always *no access:*

No access + Any NTFS permission = No access

When the ACL of a folder is modified, all files within that folder normally inherit the new settings. This can be toggled off by deselecting the REPLACE PERMISSIONS ON EXISTING FILES checkbox in the Directory Permissions dialog box (see Fig. 4-14). This feature can also be applied recursively by checking the REPLACE PERMISSIONS ON SUBDIRECTORIES checkbox.

Strategies for Securing Your Site with NTFS Permissions

Configuring NTFS permissions should be your primary concern in securing access to a Web site. The first step in configuring NTFS security on an IIS server should be the removal of the Everyone group from the

ACL for the virtual directory or Web page. The Everyone group means for exactly what it says—*everyone!* This includes the Internet Guest Account, the built-in Windows NT Guest Account, the Guests group, and so on. Removing the Everyone group eliminates the possibility of a security breach based on forms of guest account access.

If basic or NT challenge/response authentication is used, the simplest strategy is to assign the built-in Users group *read (RX)* permission to allow all valid Windows NT domain users read access to your Web sites. This might be the best strategy if your IIS server hosts Web content for employee access on the company intranet. Access could then be restricted for individuals or departments by individually assigning them *no access* permission on the resource, which overrides the previously assigned *read* permission. Access could be broadened for content developers, for example, by assigning them *change (RWXD)* permission.

Another issue to consider is that the NTFS permissions assigned to a resource depend on the kind of resource being accessed. Similar to IIS permissions discussed earlier, typical NTFS permissions for various resources are listed in Table 4-4.

Combining NTFS and IIS Permissions

The most secure scheme is to employ both IIS and NTFS permissions. The simple rule for such a combination is that permissions that explicitly deny access take precedence over permissions that explicitly grant access. For intranets, a general strategy for planning combinations of IIS and NTFS permissions might include the following guidelines:

- Assign IIS read permission to the directory to allow browsing.

Table 4-4

Suggested NTFS Permissions

Type of Web Content	Suggested NTFS Permission
Static Web content	Read(RX)
Active Server Pages	Read (RX)
Other scripts	Read (RX) or special access (X)
Executable programs	Read (RX) or special access (X)
Database content	Change (RWXD)

- Assign IIS script permission for directories containing Active Server Pages or other scripts.
- Assign NTFS read permission to the Users local group.
- Assign NTFS change permission to the group responsible for creating content in the directory.
- Assign NTFS full control permission to the Administrators local group and to any other group responsible for administering the server on which the directory resides.
- Assign NTFS no access permission to any group or user who should not be allowed to browse the contents of the directory.
- Remove the Everyone group from the ACL.

NOTE: *Do not change the NTFS permissions on system files, such as your* `C:\winnt` *directory and its various subdirectories, as this may cause your system to crash or operate improperly.*

Other Methods of Securing IIS Servers

This section discusses some additional actions that administrators can perform to enhance the security of IIS servers.

Securing IIS by Disabling Unnecessary Services, Protocols, and Bindings

Disabling unnecessary services on your IIS server has several advantages:

- Performance will improve due to the decreased demand on system resources.
- Fewer administrative errors will occur because there are fewer options to configure.
- Fewer system weaknesses exist to be exploited by malicious hackers.

Services can be disabled using the Services icon in Control Panel. Double-click on the Services icon in Control Panel to open the Services dialog box (Fig. 4-15). Select the service you want to disable, and click STARTUP to bring up the Service dialog box (Fig. 4-16). Choose DISABLED and click OK.

One service you may want to disable on your IIS server is the Server service. The reason for doing so is that when the Server service is running, any shares that are created on the server will appear when users browse the network. These shares could form a potential point of entry to your server. For example, on an NTFS volume Windows NT automatically shares the root as a hidden share for administrative purposes (e.g., as \\SERVERNAME\C$). With the Server service disabled, hackers are prevented from attempting to connect to such shares.

An alternative is to install a second network card onto your IIS server, and connect one card to the LAN and the other to the Internet. The network card bindings can then be configured using Network in Control Panel so that the Server service is bound only to the LAN-side network card.

Be aware that if the Server service is allowed to function over the Internet, not only may it serve as a possible security leak, but also you may no longer be fulfilling Microsoft licensing requirements! This is because IIS uses HTTP while the Server service uses the Server Message Block (SMB) protocol, and Microsoft's licensing requirements apply to SMB but not to HTTP. Therefore, any SMB connections to your Server service from over the Internet will require a client license to comply with Microsoft's licensing requirements for Windows NT Server.

Figure 4-15
The Services dialog box.

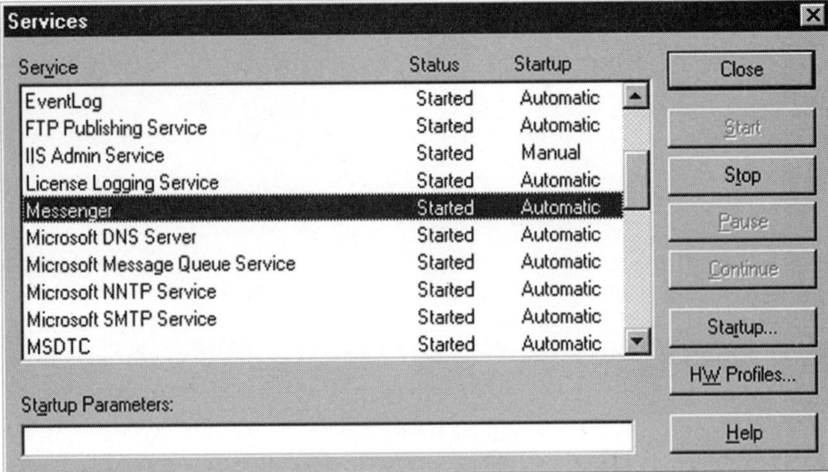

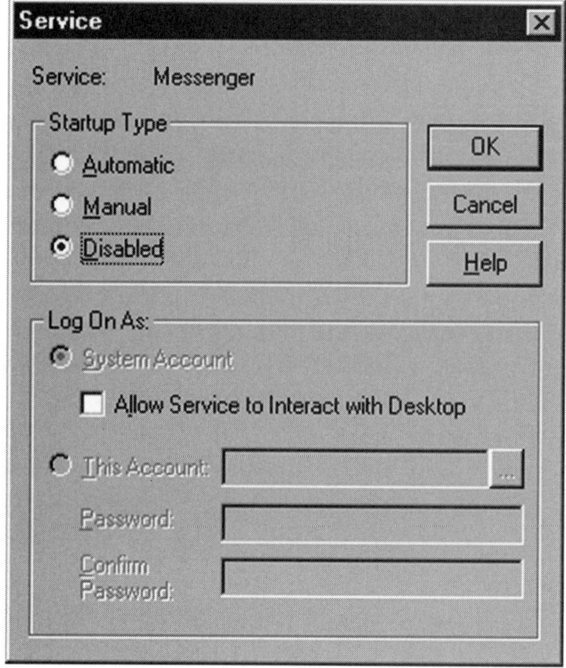

Figure 4-16 Disabling unnecessary services.

In addition, it is a good idea to remove or unbind unnecessary protocols, for the obvious reason that the simpler your system is, the easier it is to configure and the less likely it is that something important will be overlooked or misconfigured.

NOTE: *Stopping the Server service also stops the Computer Browser service and Microsoft Message Queue service. Be sure you understand the consequences of stopping services on your system; otherwise you may experience unexpected results.*

Securing IIS by Disabling Directory Browsing

It was mentioned in the previous chapter that directory browsing should normally be disabled so that users cannot see and navigate around your server's directory structure, looking for weak points to probe. To disable directory browsing on a virtual server, virtual directory, or folder, access the node's Property sheet and select the Home Directory, Virtual Directory, or Directory tab, respectively. Make sure that DIRECTORY BROWSING ALLOWED is deselected.

Securing IIS by Logging

Logging the HTTP activity on your server is another way of securing your site. Logging allows you to look for unusual patterns of server access that could indicate hacking attempts. For example, a log might indicate that a single client IP address attempted to log on to a particular site 600 times in a single day, which could indicate an attempt to break into the system.

Logging can also reveal other unusual client behavior patterns. For example, you may discover that clients are frequently visiting a relatively unimportant part of your Web site. You should probably check that section yourself in case the activity is associated with a security leak in that section of the site.

The important thing is to review your logs on a regular basis to detect possible security breaches. A good way to do this is to import your IIS log files into Site Server Express and use this to generate usage reports for your site. This is covered in Chap. 11.

Securing IIS by NTFS Auditing

NTFS volumes provide another form of logging called auditing. Together, IIS logging and NTFS auditing provide important information concerning the security performance of your IIS server.

To enable auditing on a file, folder, or drive, start User Manager (or User Manager for Domains) and choose AUDIT from the Options menu. This will open the Audit Policy box (Fig. 4-17). To enable auditing of the resource, choose the AUDIT THESE EVENTS option. Select which kind of activity you want to track on your server, and click OK. Events will be written to your Security log and can be viewed using Event Viewer.

Strategies for Auditing Web Content Here are a few strategies concerning auditing:

- Check SUCCESS for Logon and Logoff to get statistics on the number of users connecting successfully to your IIS server.
- Check FAILURE for Logon and Logoff to detect possible attempts to hack your server.
- Check FAILURE for File and Object Access to track attempts to connect to content that is not intended to be generally available to everyone.

Figure 4-17 Establishing an audit policy.

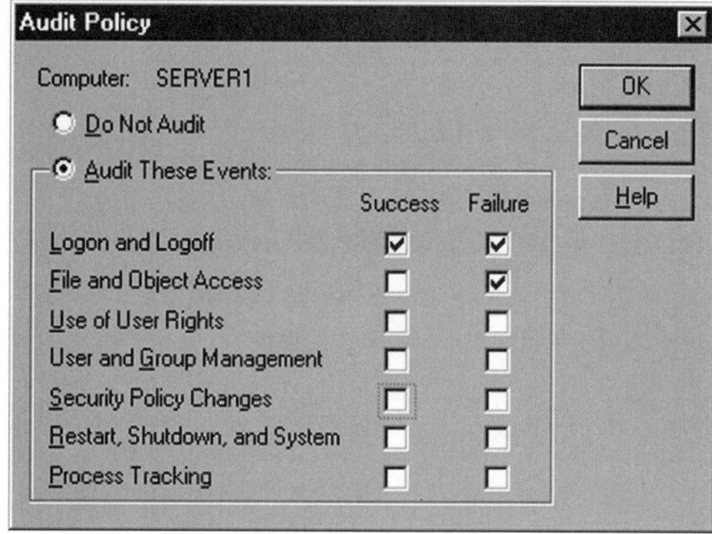

Once auditing has been enabled on your system, you can access the Property sheet for any object, select the AUDITING button on the Security tab, and click ADD to add users and groups to be audited. Usually the only group added to the audit list is the Everyone group, and you should audit all basic NTFS permissions to provide the widest scope of audited data (see Fig. 4-18).

Securing IIS by Applying Service Packs and Hotfixes

You should always apply the latest service packs, hotfixes, and upgrades to IIS 4.0 and Windows NT 4.0 to close any security holes that have been discovered in these products. No product is completely secure, and your continued vigilance as an administrator is critical to maintaining a secure, functioning Web server (and possibly to keeping your job as well!).

Securing IIS by Writing and Publishing a Corporate Security Policy

In corporate networks it is critical that you not only configure security settings but also establish a written company security policy. A good

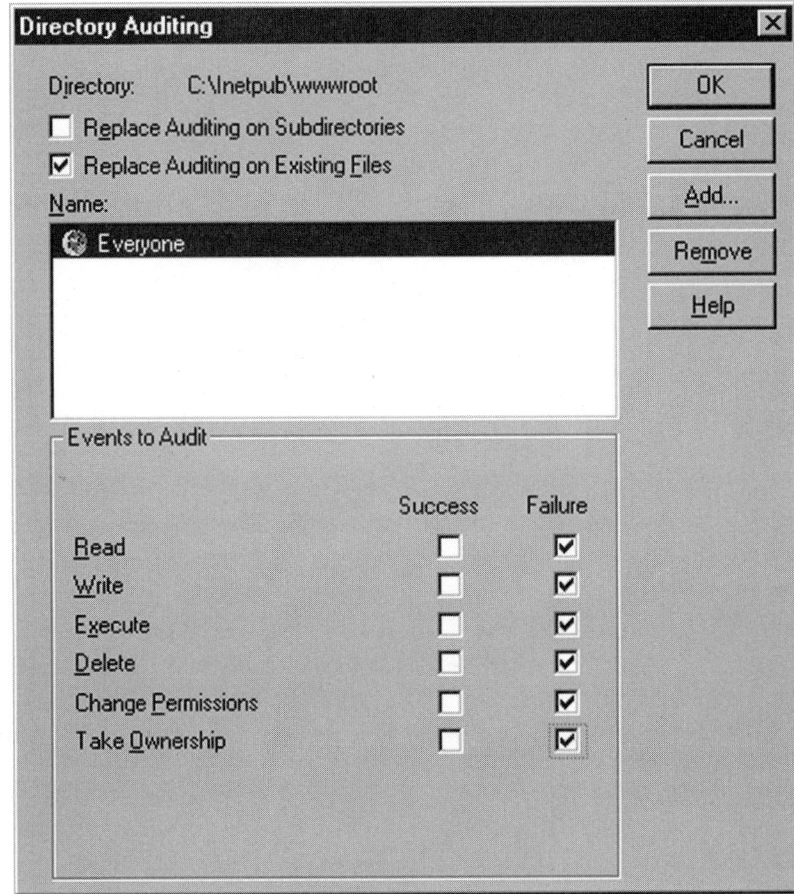

Figure 4-18 Configuring NTFS auditing for a directory.

portion of network security breaches come not from outside hackers but from disgruntled employees, and a clearly communicated security policy outlining unacceptable conduct and its possible consequences can serve as an effective deterrent to employee sabotage of your servers.

SUMMARY

IIS 4.0 provides a number of mechanisms for securing access to your server, whether it is employed as an Internet, intranet, or extranet server. These include IIS authentication, IIS permissions, NTFS permissions, IP address and domain name restrictions, disabling and unbinding unnecessary services and protocols, logging and auditing access to your site, applying service packs and hotfixes, and establishing and communicating a company security policy. This chapter has outlined strategies for using these approaches in securing your server against unauthorized access.

FOR MORE INFORMATION

Microsoft Web Site For an excellent source of information on security issues regarding IIS and Windows NT, visit the Microsoft Security Advisor Web site at

```
www.microsoft.com/security
```

The site has white papers, case studies, information on security standards and technologies, and separate sections dealing with security issues for various Microsoft products.

Microsoft Public Newsgroups Client-side security is discussed in the newsgroup

```
microsoft.public.inetexplorer.ie4.security
```

General IIS issues including security are discussed in the newsgroups

```
microsoft.public.inetserver.iis
microsoft.public.inetserver.misc
```

Microsoft Windows NT 4.0 Server Resource Kit The *Internet Guide* component of the NT 4.0 Server Resource Kit has useful information on security issues in chapter 3, "Server Security on the Internet," though some of the material will have to be updated for version 4 of IIS. More useful information can be found in Supplement 1 to the Resource Kit, in chapter 1, "Securing Your Web Site."

Microsoft IIS Resource Kit The IIS Resource Kit for Internet Information Server 4.0 should be released by the time this book is in print. Chapter 8, "IIS Security," should have useful information about securing IIS servers.

Microsoft TechNet TechNet has some useful papers on Internet security located in Technologies | Internet.

CHAPTER 5

Administering Virtual Directories and Servers

Introduction

Organizing your Web content is an important issue for corporate intranets spanning multiple departments, and for Internet servers hosting content for more than one company. Internet Information Server 4.0 allows administrators to organize Web content in two ways: by using virtual directories and using virtual servers. After completing this chapter, you will be able to

- Understand what virtual directories are and what they are used for
- Create, configure, and delete virtual directories for content stored both locally and on remote servers
- Understand what virtual servers are and what they are used for
- Create, configure, and delete virtual servers for content stored both locally and on remote servers
- Understand host headers and how they are used to configure virtual servers

Understanding Virtual Directories

Virtual directories are a mechanism that allows Web content to be stored in locations other than the default directory,

```
C:\inetpub\wwwroot
```

which is the home directory for the default Web site that is created on the local machine on which IIS is installed. This is accomplished by defining an *alias* for the virtual directory and mapping this alias to the physical location of the Web content. The actual Web content may be located in

- A directory on the local machine (hence a *local virtual directory*)
- A share on a remote server (hence a *remote virtual directory*)

Local Virtual Directories

For an example of a local virtual directory, consider the mapping

```
marketing↔D:\MarketingDept\Webstuff
```

which assigns the alias `marketing` to the Web content stored in the directory

```
D:\MarketingDept\Webstuff
```

which is on the local machine (i.e., the machine on which IIS is installed). If the local machine is an intranet server called server1, then the Marketing Department Web site would be accessed by the following URL:

```
http://server1/marketing
```

The example above illustrates why the term *virtual directory* is used: the user attempts to access the subdirectory `marketing`, which *appears* to be a subdirectory of the home directory of the default Web site on the IIS server. In other words, the path for the Marketing directory appears to be

```
C:\inetpub\wwwroot\marketing
```

But this subdirectory doesn't actually exist. Instead, it is an alias representing the real directory:

```
D:\MarketingDept\Webstuff
```

So we could say that virtual directories are *mappings of URL space onto directory space.*

Remote Virtual Directories

For an example of a *remote virtual directory,* consider the mapping

```
sales↔\\Fileserv4\SalesWeb
```

which assigns the alias `sales` to the Web content stored in the share `SalesWeb`, which is on the remote machine `Fileserv4`.

Note that remote virtual directories are mapped to UNC network shares. Again, if IIS is installed on a machine called server1, then the Sales Department Web site would be accessed by the following URL:

```
http://server1/sales
```

Why Use Virtual Directories?

Virtual directories, especially remote ones, are useful for several reasons:

- It's *easier* to allow existing content to be left on existing file servers instead of being moved to a new IIS server. Moving content from one server to another involves several administrative tasks: capacity planning and upgrading for the new server, establishing new drive mappings for non-Web access to the content, educating users concerning the change in location of content, and so on. A key rule of thumb for administrators is, If it works OK, don't change it!
- Performing *backups* of content is simpler if the content is left on existing file servers. Your network has a backup scheme in place for its existing file servers; using remote virtual directories means you don't have to modify your existing backup scheme.
- *Upgrading* the capacity of servers storing the content for your intranet can be performed without shutting down the Web servers themselves, minimizing Web server downtime.
- *Security* is enhanced by allowing those who create content access only to servers hosting content, not the Web servers themselves. No shares need to be created on the Web servers, making the Web servers more impervious to attack from hackers.
- Content can be *segregated* between departments by using virtual directories. Each department can access its own Web content through a unique URL (`http://<server>/<dept_alias>`) that maps to a unique directory on a server. Departments can work independently on their sites, and only need to have their home pages linked to the default home page of the company Web site (`http://<server>/default.htm`) in order for them to be located and viewed on the intranet.
- *Load balancing* can take place by storing content for different departments on different file servers.
- Content can be stored on the network in locations where it is *easily accessed and updated.* Web servers can be installed in locations where they are easily accessed by administrators (although the HTML version of Internet Service Manager allows most IIS management functions to be performed remotely from anywhere in the network).

Disadvantages of Virtual Directories

The main disadvantage of using virtual directories is the slight drop in performance that occurs when content stored on remote servers is accessed over the network. This can be minimized by

- Upgrading network cards in servers
- Locating Web servers physically close to stored content

Walkthrough: Creating a Virtual Directory

Virtual directories can be created and managed using any of the following tools:

- The Internet Service Manager (ISM) snap-in of the Microsoft Management Console (MMC)
- The HTML version of the Internet Service Manager
- The Windows Scripting Host

In this walkthrough we will use the MMC with ISM snap-in to create and configure a virtual directory on the default Web site.

First create and store the Web content that needs to be published in either a local directory on your IIS server or on a remote network share. Assign appropriate NTFS permissions for controlling access to the folder containing your content.

From the Microsoft Management Console, right-click on the Web site (here the Default Web Site) to which you wish to add a virtual directory. From the shortcut menu that appears select NEW, VIRTUAL DIRECTORY, and the New Virtual Directory Wizard will appear. Enter the alias to be used to access the virtual directory and click NEXT (Fig. 5-1).

Next you will need to specify either the path to the content directory on the *local* machine if you are creating a *local* virtual directory (Fig. 5-2) or the UNC path to the network share containing the Web content if you are creating a *remote* virtual directory (Fig. 5-3). In either case, you can either type in the path or select BROWSE to locate it.

If you specify content stored on a remote server, the next step will be to enter credentials sufficient to allow access to the remote folder (Fig. 5-4). This can be a guest account, a specially defined domain user

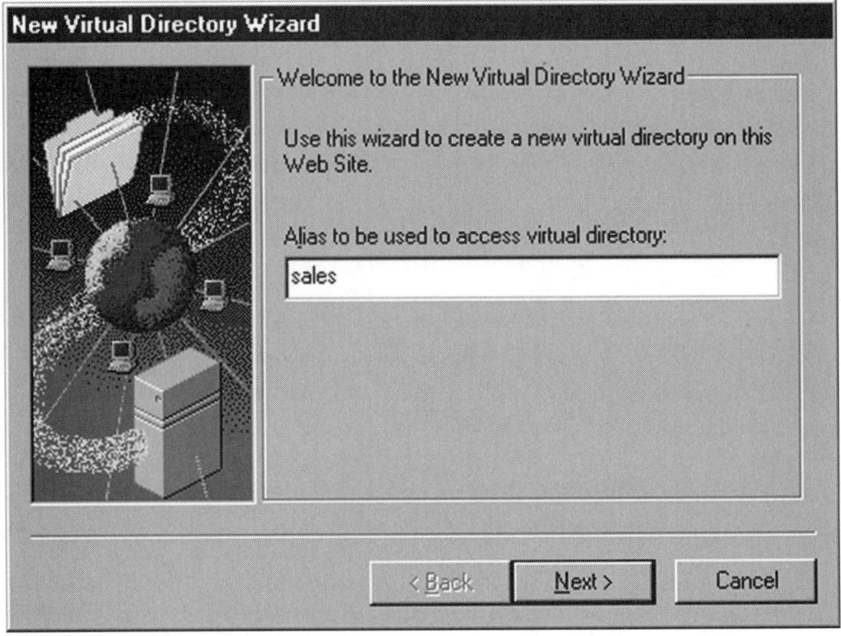

Figure 5-1 The New Virtual Directory Wizard.

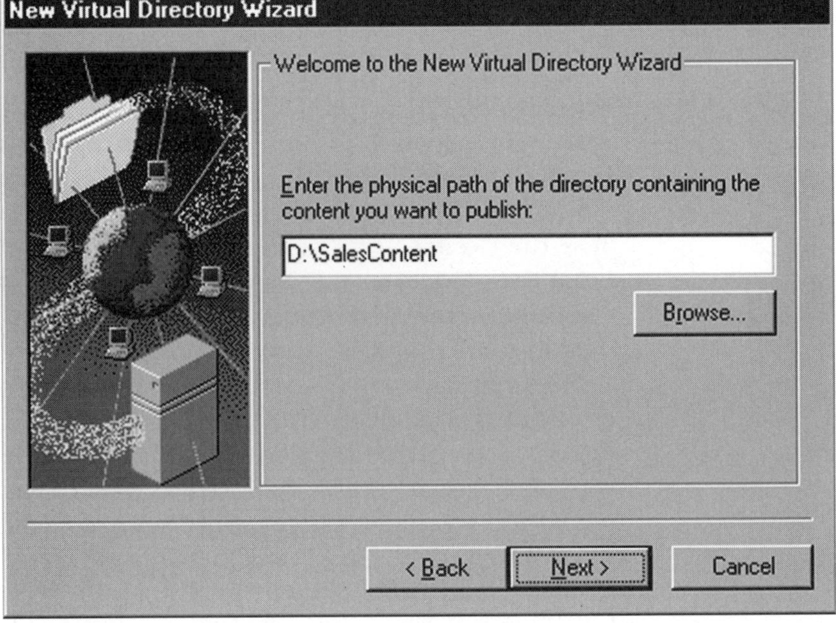

Figure 5-2 Specifying the path to locally stored content.

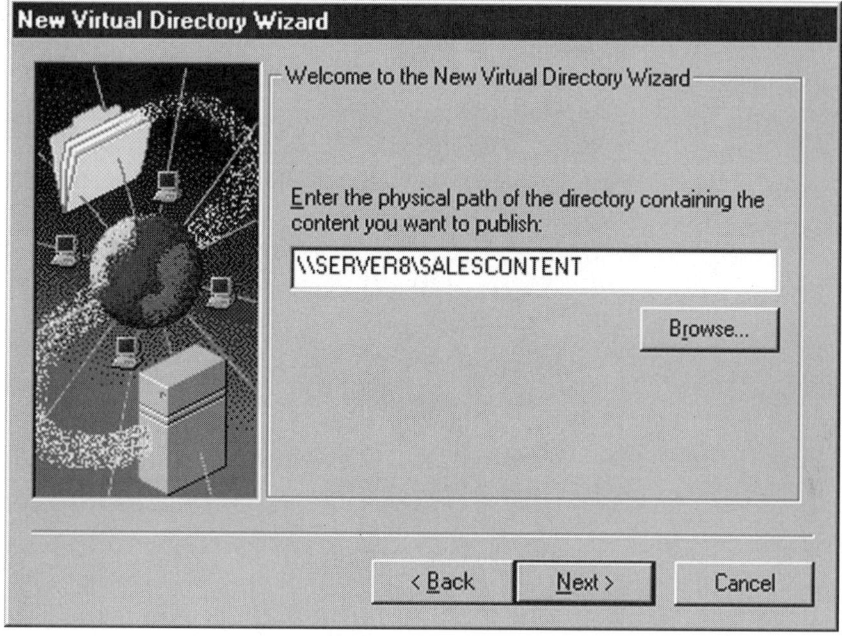

Figure 5-3 Specifying the UNC path to remotely stored content.

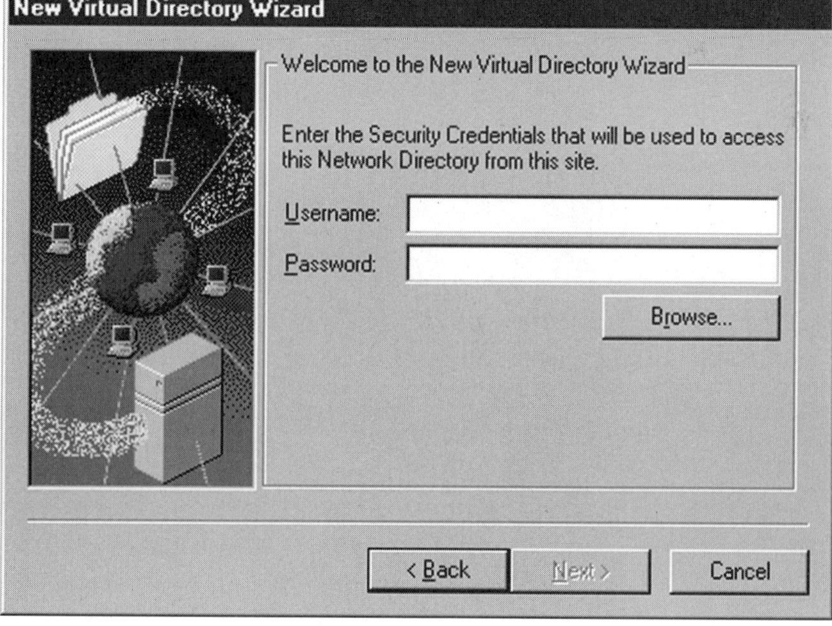

Figure 5-4 Specifying credentials to access remote content.

account, or an account belonging to the group that will have sole access to the virtual directory. Be careful to use an account with the minimum permissions necessary to provide access to the content. *Never use an administrator account to provide access to a virtual directory.*

Finally, specify the IIS access permissions you want for the virtual directory (Fig. 5-5). These include whether or not to allow

- Read access
- Write access
- Script access
- Execute access
- Directory browsing access

By default, read and script access permissions are enabled.

Configuring Virtual Directories

When a virtual directory is created, it inherits the settings established in the Web Site Property sheet for the Web site to which the virtual directory belongs, which itself inherits the settings established in the

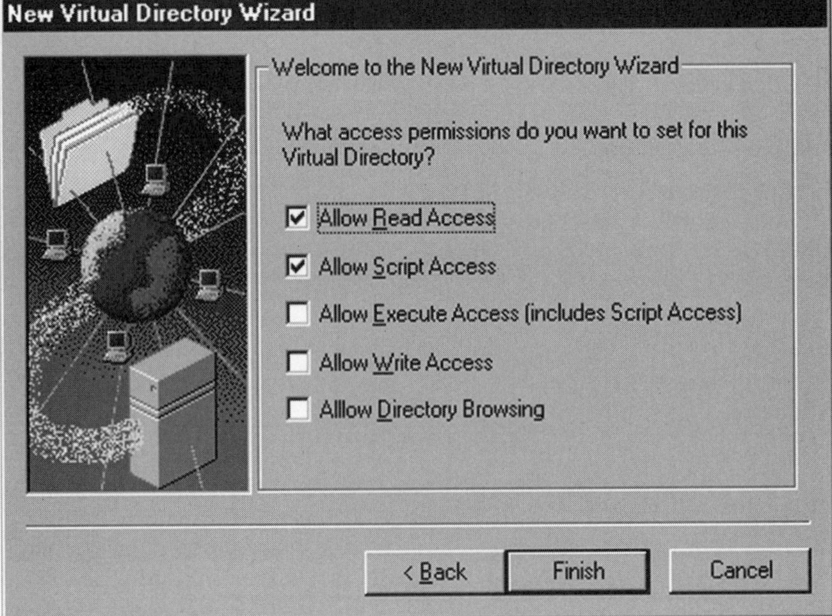

Figure 5-5 Specifying access permissions for the virtual directory.

Master Property sheet for the IIS server. To modify these settings for the virtual directory, right-click on the virtual directory in the MMC and select PROPERTIES from the shortcut menu. This will open the Virtual Directory Property sheet (Fig. 5-6), which has five tabs that allow you to configure settings as follows:

- *Virtual Directory* tab: location of mapped folder, access permissions, application settings
- *Documents* tab: default documents, footers
- *Directory Security* tab: authentication types, IP restrictions, SSL
- *HTTP Headers* tab: content expiration, custom headers, content ratings, MIME mappings
- *Custom Errors* tab: map to HTTP status code pages

For more information on configuring any of these settings, refer to Chap. 3.

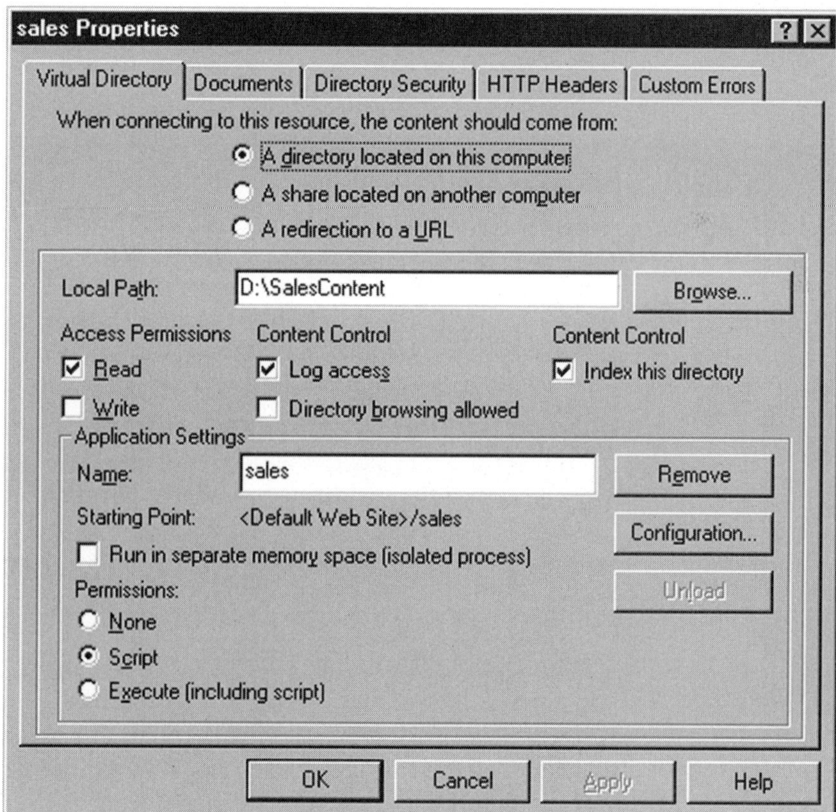

Figure 5-6 Virtual Directory Property sheet for the Sales virtual directory.

Deleting Virtual Directories

To delete a virtual directory, right-click on the virtual directory node in the Microsoft Management Console and select DELETE from the shortcut menu and confirm the deletion. You can also delete the virtual directory by selecting the node and pressing the Delete key on the keyboard, or choosing the Delete icon from the rebar, or selecting DELETE from the Action drop-down menu on the rebar.

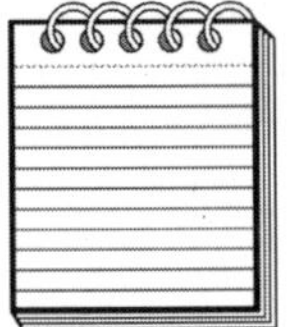

NOTE: *Deleting a virtual directory does* not *delete the Web content stored in the folder or share to which the home directory alias is mapped. It only deletes the mapping between the alias and the content folder.*

Using Virtual Directories

The following scenario illustrates the usefulness of using virtual directories in your intranet deployment.

Scenario

The network administrator for BuildCorp Ltd. is assigned by management the task of developing a corporate intranet. This intranet will contain content created by the following divisions: Planning, Records, and Design. Each division will be responsible for developing its own content. These divisions also have extensive legacy content (Word, Excel, and PowerPoint documents) stored on a fileserver called `file2.buildcorp.com`, which is working at near capacity. The network administrator is asked to employ minimal resources for building the intranet. Users currently have Office 95 and Netscape Navigator 2 on their desktops. The problem is how to proceed.

Possible Solution

Instruct content developers to store their Web content in their division's folder on `file2.buildcorp.com`. Provide them with HTML creation tools and enough training to get them going. This might be a good time to upgrade to Office 97, which provides users with basic HTML creation capability. Or you can download the Internet Assistants for Word 95, Excel 95, and Powerpoint 95 from Microsoft's Web site, which add HTML functionality to Office 95.

Install Internet Information Server on an existing server that is not being utilized near full capacity. As an example choose `bdc3.buildcorp.com`.

Create three virtual directories called *planning*, *records*, and *design* within the default Web site on the IIS server. Map these aliases to the appropriate shared folders on the remote fileserver to allow access through URLs such as

- `http://bdc3.buildcorp.com/planning`
- `http://bdc3.buildcorp.com/records`
- `http://bdc3.buildcorp.com/design`

Leave the NTFS permissions as currently set on `file2.buildcorp.com`, and modify IIS security settings as seems appropriate, given the security needs of the company and the nature of the content being published.

Create a home page for the default Web site that identifies this as the company intranet, establishes policies and rules of use, and provides links to each division's home page in its own virtual directory.

Standardize on Internet Explorer 4.0 as the browser client to be used throughout the company. Download the Word, Excel, and PowerPoint viewer plug-ins if users do not have Office 97 installed on their desktops. Either way will provide the capability of viewing legacy documents from within Internet Explorer without necessitating the conversion of large quantities of legacy documents into HTML format first.

Understanding Virtual Servers

Virtual servers are different from virtual directories. On IIS, virtual servers are a mechanism by which several Web sites can be hosted on a single IIS 4.0 server. In effect, the IIS server behaves as if it were actually multiple IIS servers, each with its own properties, content, and assigned Web site operators. IIS 4.0 allows an unlimited number of virtual servers to be created. Virtual servers, in turn, may have one or more virtual directories contained in them. A virtual directory is always created within a virtual server or on the default Web site.

Virtual servers are created by defining a new Web site and mapping this site to the home directory of the Web content for the site. The home directory for the virtual server may be mapped to

- A directory on the local machine
- A share on a remote server

Virtual servers make it possible for multiple host or domain names to refer to the same physical IIS server. For example, the URLs

- `http://mis`
- `http://marketing`
- `http://sales`

could all refer to the same physical intranet server. As another example, the URLs

- `http://hq.mycorp.com`
- `http://www.bigcorp.com`
- `http://snowball.dynamo.com`

could likewise refer to the same physical Internet server In this case, each Web site or virtual server belongs to a separate company.

NOTE: *Another name for a virtual server is a* Web site. *These two terms will be used interchangeably in this book.*

What Characterizes a Virtual Server?

Virtual servers (that is, Web sites) are uniquely identified by the following three parameters:

- IP address
- TCP port number
- Host header name

As long as two virtual servers differ in one of these parameters, they can both exist and run on the same IIS server. For example, on an IIS server with only one IP address assigned and only one hostname defined on the DNS server, you can still host multiple Web sites by assigning them each a unique port number. These would be individually identified by

URLs, such as

- `http://server6`
- `http://server6:7200`
- `http://server6:25803`

In the first URL above, the port number is not specified, causing the server to respond to the default HTTP port, which is port 80. In the other two URLs, a port number has been randomly chosen from the numbers 1023 to 65535, excluding the well-known port numbers defined in the text file

```
C:\winnt\system32\drivers\etc\services
```

Similarly, multiple Web sites could be created on IIS 4 each with a different IP address but the same (default) TCP port number (port 80).

The feature of Windows NT Server 4.0 that makes virtual servers possible is the assignment of multiple IP addresses to a single server, a process known as *multihoming*. In order to host multiple domain names on a single IIS server, you can assign as many IP addresses to your server as you have Web sites to host, and when you create each Web site you assign it one of the IP addresses bound to your IIS server. To see how to add additional IP addresses to your NT 4.0 server, see App. A.

Multiple Web sites can also have the same IP address and TCP port number by using a feature called *host header names*, which is explained later in this chapter.

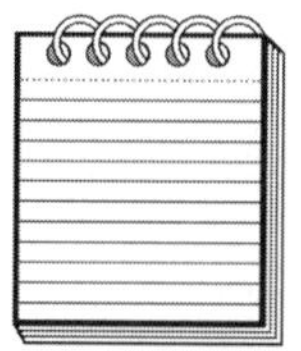

NOTE: *When you have multiple IP addresses assigned to an IIS server, each time you create a new virtual server you must assign it an IP address. If you do not assign the virtual server an IP address but instead leave the IP address as "all unassigned" on the virtual server's property sheet, the virtual server responds to any IP addresses that are bound to the server but are not assigned to any other virtual server, making this virtual server the default Web site.*

Why Use Virtual Servers?

- Virtual servers are useful for many of the same reasons that virtual directories are: security, easy backups and upgrades, content segregation and administration, and so on. However, virtual servers offer even more features than virtual directories do.

- Virtual servers are *completely configurable.* Each virtual server behaves as if it is a separate IIS server, and all the configuration options for the default Web site are available for any other Web site.
- Virtual servers may be *stopped, started,* and *paused* just like a real IIS server. For example, you may want to stop a virtual server while updating it with new content or changing its access permissions.
- Virtual servers may be assigned separate *Web site operators.* Each department could have its own virtual server and assign users who can fully administer its site. *Note:* From an administrator's point of view, this is probably the main benefit of using virtual servers—you can *delegate* administration of virtual servers to their Web site operators!
- *Bandwidth throttling* and *performance tuning* settings may be established for each virtual server.
- Virtual servers may contain any number of virtual directories. For example, the Marketing Web site could contain a home directory and several subdirectories whose content can be located in noncontiguous locations on various servers in the network, such as
  - `http://marketing.mycorp.com/`
  - `http://marketing.mycorp.com/proposals/`
  - `http://marketing.mycorp.com/contacts/`

Walkthrough: Creating a Virtual Server

Virtual servers can be created and managed using the same tools used for creating and managing virtual directories, namely:

- The Internet Service Manager (ISM) snap-in of the Microsoft Management Console (MMC)
- The HTML version of the Internet Service Manager
- The Windows Scripting Host

In this walkthrough we will use the MMC to create and configure a virtual server (Web site) on an IIS 4 machine.

First create and store your primary Web content (the home page and pages of similar importance) that needs to be published in either a local directory on your IIS server or on a remote network share. Assign appropriate NTFS permissions for controlling access to the folder containing your content.

To create a virtual server using the Microsoft Management Console, right-click on the physical IIS server (the icon looks like a small computer) to which you wish to add a virtual server. From the shortcut menu that appears select NEW, WEB SITE, and the New Web Site Wizard will appear. Enter a friendly name to describe the Web site (this name will appear beside the virtual server's node in the MMC) and click NEXT (Fig. 5-7).

Use the drop-down box to select an available IP address from the IP addresses bound to your server or select ALL UNASSIGNED if you wish this virtual server to be your new default Web site (Fig. 5-8).

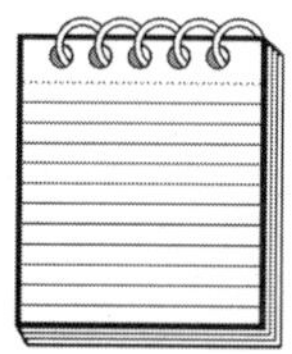

NOTE: *Be sure to select an IP address not already used by another virtual server or by your default Web site. If you select an IP address that is already in use, the New Web Site Wizard will not indicate any error at this point, but when you try to start the virtual server afterward, a dialog box will appear with the message, "A duplicate name exists on the network," and you will be unable to start the virtual server.*

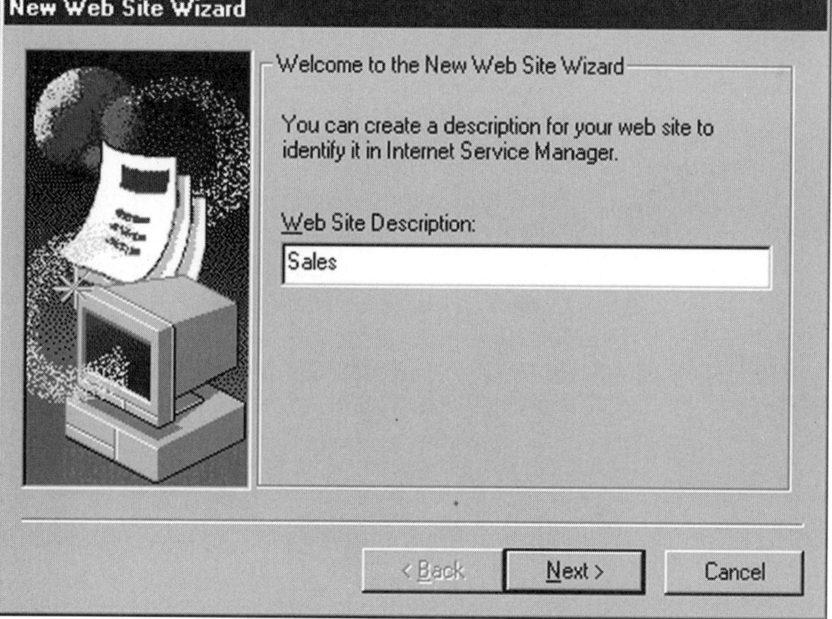

Figure 5-7 The New Web Site Wizard for creating a new virtual server.

Figure 5-8 Assigning IP address and port number to the virtual server.

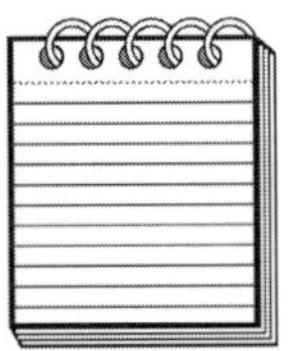

Similarly, if the existing default Web site has "All Unassigned" as its IP address (see the Web Site tab on the Default Web Site Properties sheet), and you try to assign the same value "All Unassigned" as the IP address for your new virtual server, you will receive an error message when you try to start your virtual server: "The service could not be started because it is not correctly configured. Make sure that its server bindings do not conflict with other sites running on the same machine."

You can also configure which TCP *port* your virtual server is to be accessed from (the default port is 80).

If SSL is enabled, you can also configure which SSL port the virtual server should use (the default is 443).

Next, specify the location of the *home directory,* which is your virtual server's main content directory and contains your Web site's home page. This can be either a folder on the local server (Fig. 5-9) or a UNC path to a share on a remote server (Fig. 5-10). In either case, you can also choose at this point to allow anonymous access to your Web site by checking the checkbox.

If you choose to map the virtual server's home directory to a network share, you will need to specify credentials that allow the proper level of

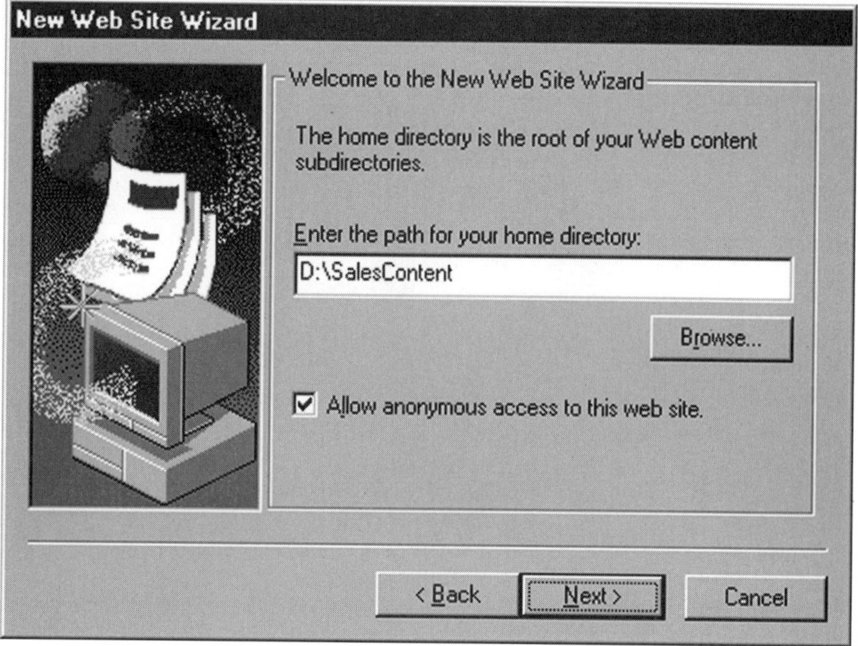

Figure 5-9 Mapping a virtual server's home directory to a local folder.

Figure 5-10 Mapping a virtual server's home directory to a network share.

Figure 5-11 Specifying credentials for access to remote folder.

access to the remote folder (Fig. 5-11). Do not assign an administrator account to a virtual server.

Finally, specify the IIS access permissions you want for the virtual server (Fig. 5-12). These include whether or not to allow

- Read access
- Write access
- Script access
- Execute access
- Directory browsing access

By default, read and script access permissions are enabled.

Your virtual server (Web site) is now created, but it is in a *stopped* condition. To start your virtual server, right-click on its node in the MMC and select START from the shortcut menu.

Configuring Virtual Servers

When a virtual server is created, it inherits the settings established in the Master Property sheet for the IIS server on which it is created. To

Figure 5-12 Assigning access permissions to the virtual server.

modify these settings for the virtual directory, right-click on the virtual server in the MMC and select PROPERTIES from the shortcut menu. This will open the Web Site Property sheet (Fig. 5-13), which has the same nine tabs that the Default Web Site Property sheet has, allowing you to fully configure the settings for your Web site. For more information on any of these settings, refer to Chap. 3.

Deleting Virtual Servers

To delete a virtual server, right-click on its node in the Microsoft Management Console and select DELETE from the shortcut menu to confirm the deletion.

NOTE: *Deleting a virtual server does* not *delete the Web content in its home directory; it only deletes the mapping from the virtual server to the home directory.*

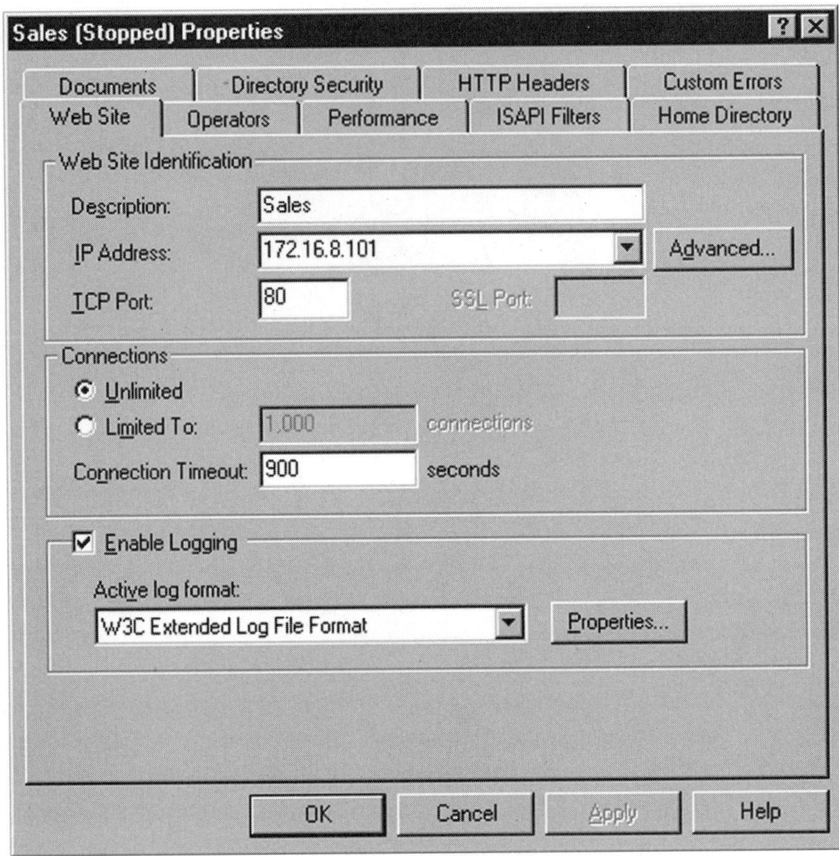

Figure 5-13 Web site properties for a virtual server in a stopped condition.

Using Virtual Servers

Below we revisit the scenario given earlier in this chapter to illustrate the usefulness of using virtual servers in your intranet deployment.

Scenario

Management assigns the network administrator for BuildCorp Ltd. the task of developing a corporate intranet. This intranet will contain content created and managed by the following divisions: Planning, Records, and Design. Each division will be responsible for developing its own content and managing access to it. These divisions also have extensive legacy content (Word, Excel, and PowerPoint documents) stored in various folders on several fileservers. Minimal resources are to be employed for building the intranet. What is the best way to proceed?

Possible Solution

Create a home directory for each division on a fileserver that has available space to house the home directories. Instruct content developers to store their home pages and other relevant pages in their home directories. Provide them with HTML creation tools and enough training to get them going.

Install Internet Information Server on an existing server that has sufficient free resources. Say, for sake of argument, that this server is called `www.buildcorp.com`. Create three virtual servers on the IIS server. Call these servers

```
planning.buildcorp.com
records.buildcorp.com
design.buildcorp.com
```

Map these virtual servers to their respective home directories.

Assign Web site operators for each virtual server, specifically the person responsible in each division for administering and managing its virtual server. Give these individuals training on how to modify their Web site settings, how to create virtual directories, how to manage access to their sites, and so on. The operators will need to create virtual directories to allow access to legacy content without necessitating conversion of the content to HTML. For example, the Planning division might create a virtual directory accessed by the URL

```
http://planning.buildcorp.com/ppt
```

which maps to a folder containing PowerPoint files of planning session presentations.

Create a home page for the default Web site `www.buildcorp.com` that identifies this as the company intranet, establishes policies and rules of use, and provides links to each division's home page on its own Web site.

Standardize on Internet Explorer 4.0 as the browser client to be used throughout the company. Download the Word, Excel, and PowerPoint viewer plug-ins if users do not have Office 97 installed on their desktops.

Understanding Host Header Names

IIS 4.0 allows multiple domain names to be mapped to a single IP address and TCP port number using a mechanism called *host header names.* This mechanism is a new feature of IIS 4.0 not available in previous versions of IIS, and is a new feature of the HTTP 1.1 specification. To use host headers on an intranet or the Internet, the following must be configured:

- Multiple host names must be mapped to a single IP address using either a DNS server or a HOSTS file so that the host names can be resolved to the IP address. For information on configuring Windows NT Server's DNS server, see App. B.
- HTTP 1.1–compliant browsers must be used (MS Internet Explorer 3.0 or later, or Netscape Navigator 2.0 or later). (Microsoft does suggest a way for older browsers to support host headers. See the topic "Supporting Host Header Names in Older Browsers" in the online documentation for details.)
- Multiple host header names must be configured on the Web Site Property sheet for each virtual server.

Configuring Multiple Identities for a Virtual Server

To configure multiple identities for a virtual server, right-click on the selected virtual server in the MMC and select PROPERTIES from the shortcut menu to open the Web Site Properties sheet. Select the Web Site tab and click the ADVANCED button to open the Advanced Multiple Web Site Configuration sheet (Fig. 5-14). This sheet is used to add, remove, and edit identities for your Web site.

To specify an additional identity for your Web site, click the ADD button and specify the IP address, port, and host header name (Fig. 5-15). IIS 4.0 allows you to specify multiple host header names for the same IP/port combination.

Why Use Host Header Names?

Suppose your company MyCorp Ltd. has an IIS server with a Web site accessed by the URL

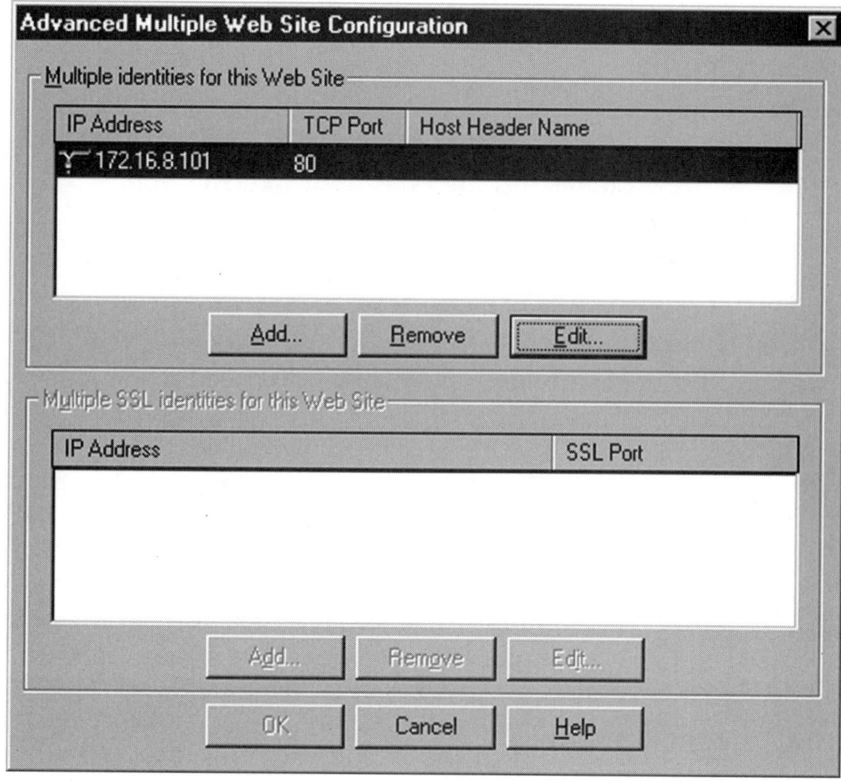

Figure 5-14
The Advanced Multiple Web Site Properties sheet.

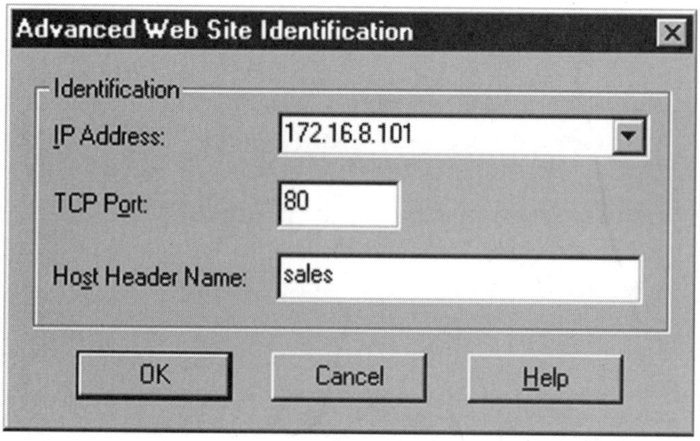

Advanced Web Site Identification

Identification

IP Address: 172.16.8.101

TCP Port: 80

Host Header Name: sales

OK Cancel Help

Figure 5-15
Specifying a Web site identity.

```
http://www.mycorp.com
```

A merger takes place with another company, and for a period of time your company has a dual identity, MyCorp Ltd. and BigNewCorp Ltd. You register the new domain name `bignew.com` using the same IP address because you want to access your MyCorp Web site with the alternative URL

```
http://www.bignew.com
```

To complete the process, you configure your Web server to respond to the additional identity as described in the previous section and access the site using an HTTP 1.1–compliant browser.

As another example, suppose you are an Internet service provider hosting several hundred Web sites each having its own domain name, but you only have a limited number of available IP addresses. To overcome this limitation, you could use host header names and assign all of the domain names to a single IP address. In this situation, you would need to enable users with older browsers that do not support host header names to be able to reach the correct site. Refer to the IIS 4.0 online documentation for the topic "Supporting Host Header Names in Older Browsers" for more information on how to configure this.

SUMMARY

IIS 4.0 provides two mechanisms for mapping local and remote content to URLs: virtual servers (or Web sites) and virtual directories. By combining these two features, administrators can delegate management of Web sites to departmental Web site operators on intranets, or to Web site owners on a public Internet site, thus making their own job easier. These virtual servers and directories can be created and deleted without affecting the content on which they are based.

FOR MORE INFORMATION

Microsoft TechNet TechNet has some useful information on virtual servers and virtual directories, although it refers to previous versions of

IIS. Look in the following location for "Planning Your Content Directories and Virtual Servers:"

```
Internet | Server | MS Internet Information Server | Technical
Notes | Installation and Planning Guide | Chapter 6
```

CHAPTER 6

Administering Content

Introduction

Creating and maintaining the content of your Web sites should not be the job of the administrator, but the responsibility of Web page developers, database developers, and programmers. The job of the administrator is to provide technical expertise, guidance, and support to these groups, and to establish rules, procedures, and mechanisms to facilitate the development and maintenance of Web sites. This chapter will cover issues relating to Web site development that are of importance to administrators, including

- Establishing policies and procedures for developing Web site content
- Selecting appropriate tools for Web content development
- Administering and utilizing Microsoft FrontPage for Web content development
- Administering and utilizing Microsoft Office for Web content development
- Publishing an Access database to the Web using Active Server Pages

What Does It Mean to "Administer Content"?

Administering content is not the same as developing content, but it does include a basic understanding of the tools, procedures, and mechanisms for content development. In today's rapidly changing IT environment, as companies adjust to changes and reallocating resources to remain competitive, management often attempts to delegate to the overworked network or system administrator the additional task of planning, developing, and maintaining company Internet or intranet Web sites.

Resist their attempt to delegate this task to you!

The reason for doing this is that the essence of Web site development is not formatting documents with HTML or writing scripts or programs. These are merely the underlying structure that support what Web sites really are, namely:

- Vehicles for communicating company goals, policies, products, and services to employees, business partners, and the world.

- Tools for enabling collaborative business functions between departments and between clients and services.
- A reflection of management's understanding of where the company is coming from and where it is headed.

As a network or system administrator, you would normally not expect management to ask you to perform tasks like

- Designing a new company logo
- Producing a newsletter for customers
- Writing a company annual report or business plan
- Producing a TV commercial to market a service
- Writing a policy not directly relating to IT issues
- Deciding which company documents should be published and which shouldn't
- Designing a standard template for employee resumes
- Determining who should be allowed access to certain company files

Yet what those in management often do not understand is that by asking you as network administrator to create the company Web site or intranet site, they are in fact asking you to perform the kinds of tasks and make the kinds of decisions listed above, tasks and decisions that really belong to the domain of executive and departmental management and are normally performed by clerical and middle-management staff.

As administrator, it is important that you point these things out to management, not just to release yourself from extra duties to perform but because you should not assume responsibility for tasks and decisions that rightly belong to others who are trained to do them—or else you will find yourself treading on other people's toes, often with painful results!

Establishing Content Development Policies and Procedures

Your response to management asking you to develop the company's Internet or intranet site should involve the following:

1. Meet with management to determine the overall goals of the site, what the intended objectives are, and how to evaluate whether those objectives have been met—in other words, choose a project leadership team. Representatives of executive management, marketing, and IT should usually be involved in this.
2. Determine which people will be responsible for making decisions about what specifically should be included in the site and what should not. Usually this means assigning leadership to sections of the site to departmental middle managers.
3. Determine which people will be responsible for soliciting and creating content, developing applications, and custom programming. Usually this involves teams of secretarial and clerical staff, applications developers, and IT support staff.
4. Establish a written policy indicating who is responsible for what regarding site development. For more information on this aspect, see the last section of Chap. 1.
5. Determine what resources will be required to complete the project, including hardware, software, and training for individuals. Develop a proposal that includes a cost analysis showing that it is cheaper to train and use existing people and to outsource programming needs than to utilize the costly time of an administrator or provide him or her with additional technical training. For example, training five secretarial people to use FrontPage and having them perform 100 hours of site development will be faster and cheaper than having a high-paid network administrator perform 500 hours of site development. Or as another example, outsourcing database development or other programming needs for $5000 will be considerably easier, cheaper, and faster than having an administrator take several weeks of advanced technical training courses in programming or database development.
6. Familiarize yourself with the basic tools that will be used to create the company Internet or intranet site. This way you can assist content developers by making recommendations on designing site structure and navigation, giving advice on making use of advanced features of these tools, and providing other technical advice and support. If possible, try to have management budget for you or your IT staff to take Microsoft Official Curriculum courses for tools such as Internet Information Server 4.0, Internet Explorer 4.0, FrontPage, Visual InterDev, SQL Server, and so on.

7. Finally, develop procedures for content developers and programmers so that they will know exactly how to

   - Add, edit, and remove content on their portion of the site
   - Create, test, and debug scripts, programs, and applications
   - Conform to standards of style and navigation structure to give the whole Internet or intranet site a consistent look and feel
   - Perform the limited administrative tasks assigned to Web site operators
   - Request technical assistance from the IT department's Web site support people

Tools for Content Development

The decision on what tools will be used to build your company Internet or intranet site is one that you should not make yourself, but rather decide in close conjunction with management. The final decision on which tools to employ will depend upon a number of factors:

- Available software purchasing funds
- Available training funds
- Licensing requirements (another cost issue)
- Server and client capacity issues (e.g., mcmory and IID requirements)
- Legacy document conversion issues
- Graphic design and layout costs
- Scripting and programming requirements
- Security restrictions and requirements

As an example, I've seen large companies with thousands of employees develop a functional intranet with Notepad as their main content development tool. Graphics were downloaded from the Internet, and scanned images were processed using shareware image editing tools. The IT department and management worked together to establish policies to determine who would be responsible for what section of the intranet, and then handed out a few pages of instructions on basic HTML and some pointers to find more information on the Internet. And it was amazing how much they accomplished with such a limited outlay of resources!

Then again, I've seen small companies use tools like Microsoft FrontPage, Access 97, and SQL Server to set up Web sites to enhance their business functionality. With a few days of technical training and a lot of wizards, these companies have set up online order systems, published interactive catalogs, established secure extranets, and so on.

In this book we're obviously not going to consider how to use Notepad as a Web content development tool—although there are still real reasons for having content developers learn HTML. One reason is that most Web development tools are to a certain extent "buggy," and this isn't principally due to negligence on the part of the company that developed the tool but is more a result of the incredible pace at which HTML and the Internet are evolving in general. So when you use a tool such as Word 97 to create an HTML document, then edit the document by moving sections around, changing and recharging the format, and so on, occasionally you find things like margins that won't reset properly, tables that fail to display correctly, and other artifacts produced by too much editing of the document (what usually happens is that one of a pair of HTML tags has not been deleted, resulting in unusual formatting that can only be corrected by either deleting and recreating the entire section at fault, or if you know HTML by going directly into the source code and deleting the offending tag).

What we will consider in the rest of this chapter is how to implement, administer, and use two of the more popular and useful Microsoft Web publishing tools, namely Microsoft FrontPage 98 and Microsoft Office 97. As an administrator, you will need to know enough about the functionality of such tools to properly install them, assign appropriate permissions, and give technical advice to content developers on how to use them to create new Web content, convert legacy content to HTML, create connectivity to database content, and so on.

For despite everything that was said above about delegating content development to appropriate clerical and middle-management staff, the fact is that at first you will probably be responsible for designing the structure of the site, building a draft home page, and perhaps creating a demonstration Web-database application for test or pilot purposes. So it is to your advantage as an administrator that you know enough about content development to get started—just don't let them make you do the whole thing!

Creating Web Content with Microsoft FrontPage

FrontPage is Microsoft's highly popular Web content creation tool. It actually consists of several integrated tools, and includes facilities for both development and management of Web sites. The current version is FrontPage 98, which sports some significant improvements over earlier versions and is well worth the modest upgrade price.

Here are some of the features of FrontPage 98:

- A full-featured WYSIWYG Web page editor called FrontPage Editor
- A hierarchical Web site management environment called FrontPage Explorer that includes multiple views and link management capability
- Drag-and-drop frameset creation and management
- Wizards for easy creation of various types of Web sites
- Templates for Web page creation
- Themes for customizing the layout and graphic design of sites
- Automatic generation of navigation bars
- FrontPage components (formerly WebBots) for automating tasks like indexing a site, adding search capability, activating forms, and scheduling includes
- Support for Dynamic HTML, Cascading Style Sheets, ActiveX controls, Java applets, JavaScript, and Visual Basic scripts
- Active Server Pages support and ODBC database connectivity wizards
- Integration with Microsoft Office for spell checking and thesaurus

End users who use FrontPage as their primary content development tool will need guidance and support to use FrontPage effectively. Typical FrontPage training courses will provide them with the skills necessary to produce simple FrontPage Webs and to design and edit Web pages, but either you, the administrator, or a member of your IT support team will need to be familiar enough with FrontPage so that you can give technical advice on issues like

- Creating and managing document templates

- Using includes for document headers and footers
- Designing pages that will load quickly and not waste bandwidth
- Incorporating ActiveX components or Java applets into their sites
- Importing Web content created with other tools into FrontPage Webs
- Generating logs and reports of site usage
- Incorporating Index Server for full text search capability
- Assigning FrontPage browsing, authoring, and administering permissions to users and groups
- Installing and configuring FrontPage extensions using FrontPage Server Administrator

Walkthrough: Creating a FrontPage Web

The following section takes you on a walkthrough on how to create and add content to a FrontPage Web on an IIS 4.0 server. Microsoft FrontPage uses the term *Web* to refer to a Web site or virtual server.

Before you implement FrontPage as a content development tool, some consideration has to be given to where and how to install FrontPage on the network. Typically, one of three scenarios are chosen (see Fig. 6-1):

1. Install FrontPage on client machines (95 or NT Workstation) *without* installing the Personal Web Server on the client machines. Have developers create and edit content *directly* on production servers running IIS. This is the simplest method and is suitable for low- to medium-security environments.
2. Install FrontPage on client machines along *with* the Personal Web Server. Have developers create and edit content on their client machines, and then publish the content to the production servers running IIS (or have an administrator copy the content to the production server). This method is suitable when Web sites do not involve complex scripts or applications that are beyond the capability of being developed on Microsoft's Personal Web Server.
3. Install FrontPage on client machines *without* installing the Personal Web Server on the client machines. Have developers create and edit content on an intermediate staging server running IIS. Have administrators copy the content from the staging servers

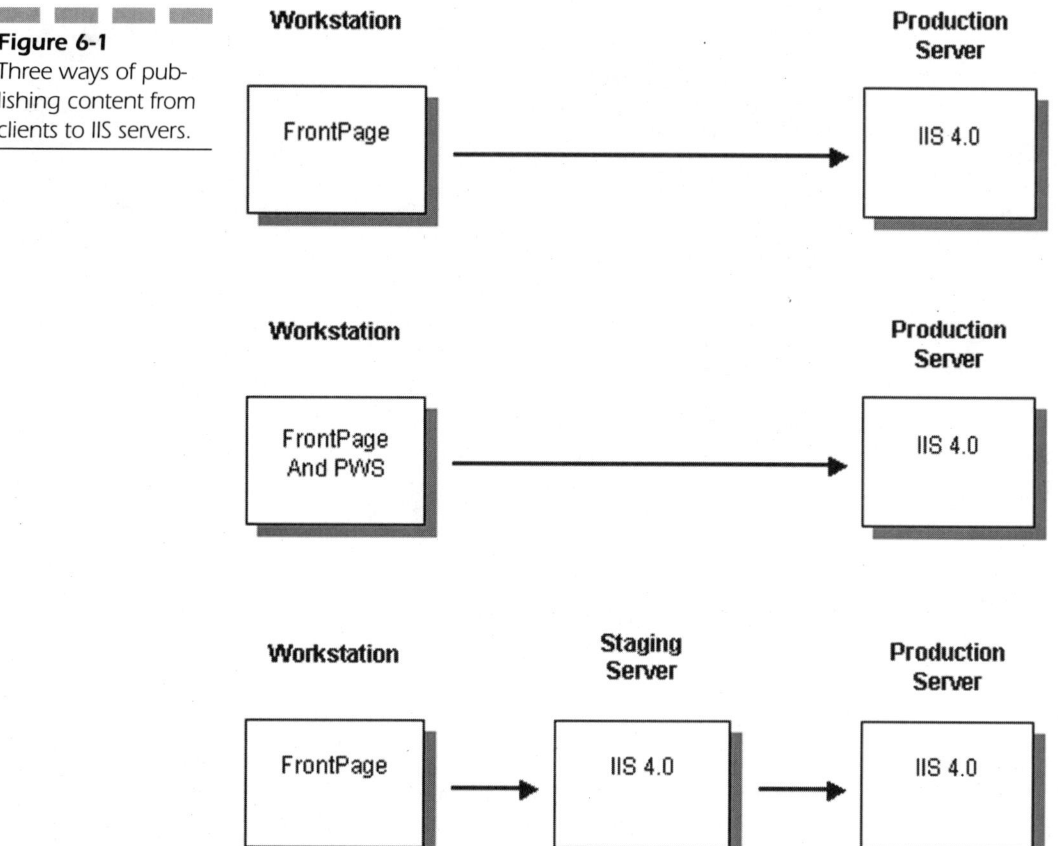

Figure 6-1
Three ways of publishing content from clients to IIS servers.

to the production servers. This method is suitable for medium- to high-security environments, but it requires more administrative overhead.

Let's assume the first scenario above, and install only the Web development portions of FrontPage 98 on a client workstation, omitting the Personal Web Server and other administrative components. Log on to the client workstation as Administrator and install FrontPage 98, choosing not to select the Personal Web Server or FrontPage Server Extensions (Fig. 6-2).

An alternative would be to install FrontPage 98 on the server itself, and log on to the server as Administrator to perform the steps below. The advantage of doing it this way is that you can create Webs and assign authoring permissions without having to go to the client machine to do so. This is the procedure we follow below.

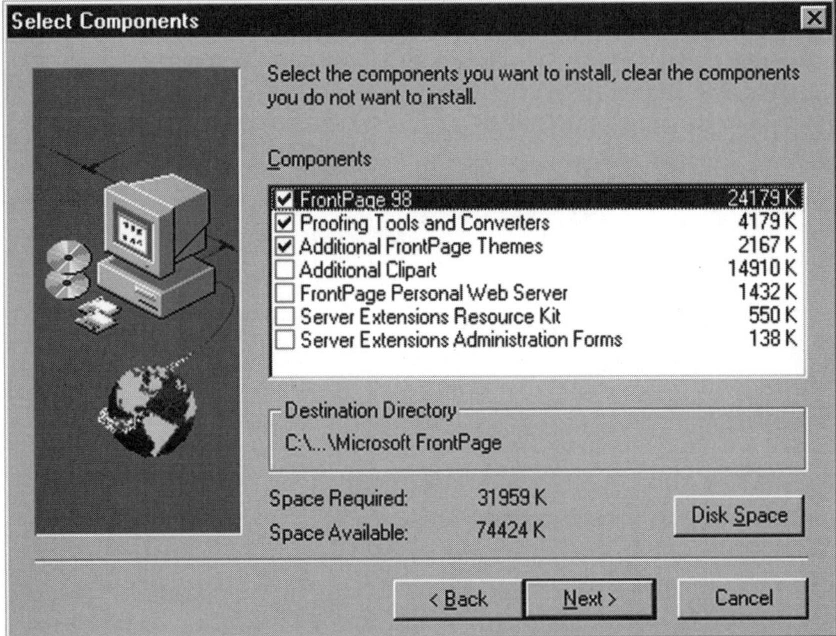

Figure 6-2
Installing FrontPage 98.

In either case, when you install FrontPage 98 either on the server or on client machines, *do not install* the FrontPage server extensions from the FrontPage 98 CD. Instead, when as administrator you have created a new virtual server (Web site), install the FrontPage server extensions on that virtual server (Web site) at the time you create it and using the extensions installed by the Windows NT 4.0 Option Pack, as these are a newer set of extensions than the ones on the FrontPage 98 CD.

If you are working with FrontPage in your networking environment, it is a good idea to visit the Microsoft Web site regularly and download and install the most current version of FrontPage server extensions, not only to eliminate bugs in earlier versions but to take advantage of exciting new features for Web developers.

After installing FrontPage, our next task will be to create a new virtual server (Web site) on the IIS server to contain the content created using FrontPage.

Using the Microsoft Management Console, connect to the IIS server, right-click on the server icon, and select NEW, WEB SITE from the shortcut menu to open the New Web Site Wizard. Complete the steps of the wizard to create a new Web site by

- Assigning it a friendly name (in this case MyCorp)

- Assigning it a fixed IP address (here 172.16.8.102)
- Entering the path to the home directory for the site (here `C:\MyCorpHome`)
- Assigning appropriate permissions (leave READ and SCRIPT selected)

Note that the newly created Web site is in a stopped state and has no content yet, since the site's home directory, `C:\MyCorpHome`, is currently empty (Fig. 6-3).

At this point, if the home directory, `C:\MyCorpHome`, is on an NTFS volume, you may want to check the permissions on the directory and make sure that those who will have the responsibility of creating and editing Web site content have the necessary permissions (e.g., change or RWXD).

Now that we have created a new Web site, our next job will be to prepare it for receiving content from FrontPage. Open the MyCorp Property sheet by right-clicking on the MyCorp node and selecting PROPERTIES from the shortcut menu. Select the Home Directory tab and check the FRONTPAGE WEB checkbox under the label Content Control (Fig. 6-4).

Checking this checkbox and clicking APPLY or OK installs the *FrontPage Server Extensions* on the MyCorp virtual server. This action creates a

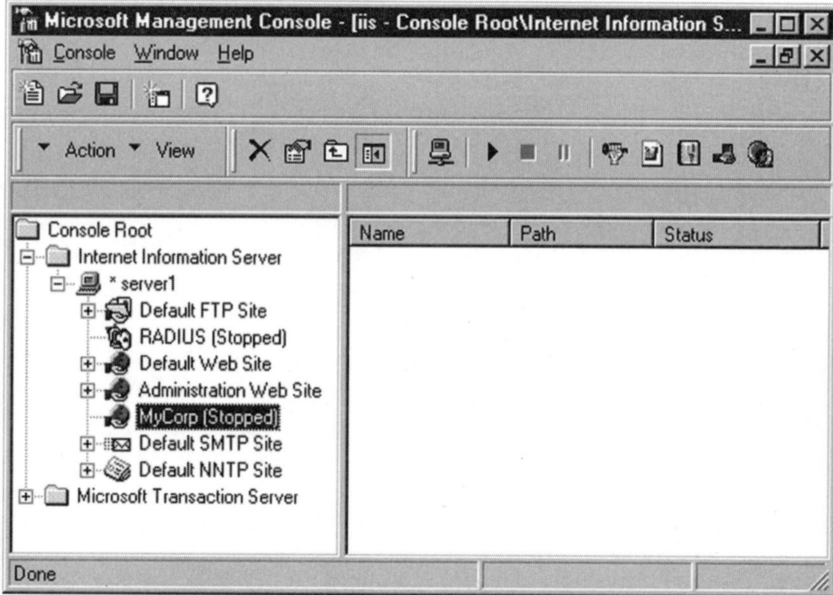

Figure 6-3
A newly created empty Web site called MyCorp, still in a stopped state.

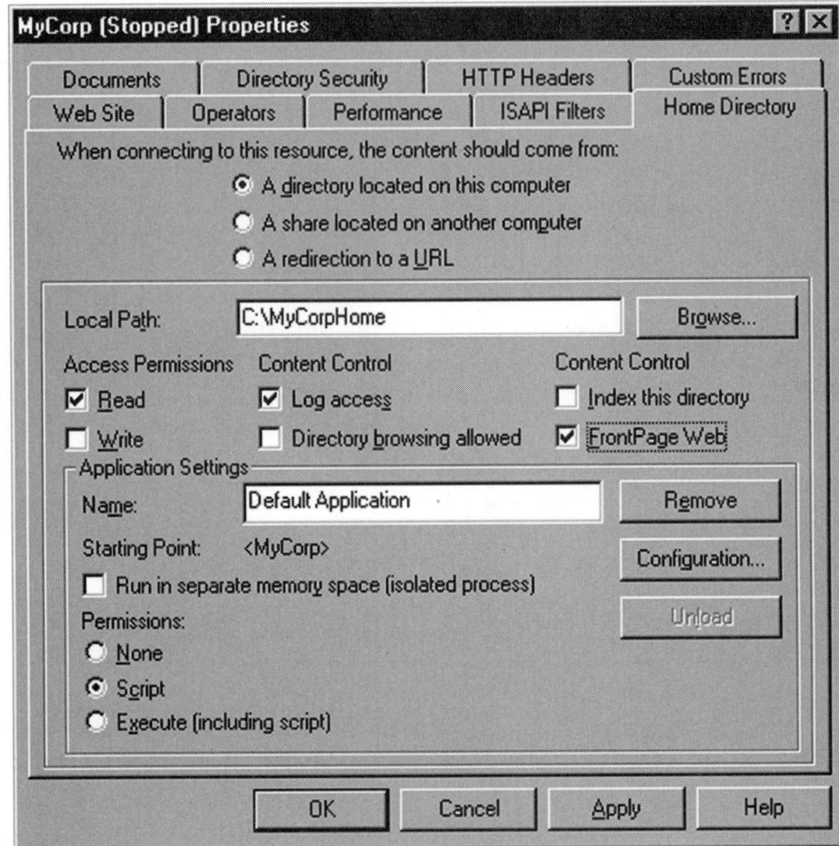

Figure 6-4 Checking the FrontPage Web checkbox to enable FrontPage server extensions on the virtual server.

series of virtual directories used by FrontPage for creating content and places executable files (FrontPage components) in some of the folders.

Essentially, what has happened is that a new FrontPage root Web has been formed on the virtual server MyCorp. To see these virtual directories under MyCorp by using the MMC, you may need to click the ACTION button and select REFRESH from the drop-down menu (Fig. 6-5). These virtual directories map to real subdirectories of the site's home directory, `C:\MyCorpHome`. Many of these subdirectories are hidden and will not show up in Windows Explorer unless SHOW ALL FILES is enabled on the Options property sheet opened by VIEW, OPTIONS in Windows Explorer.

Some of these virtual directories are important for administrators, so here is a brief explanation of what they are used for (refer to books on FrontPage for more information regarding these virtual directories):

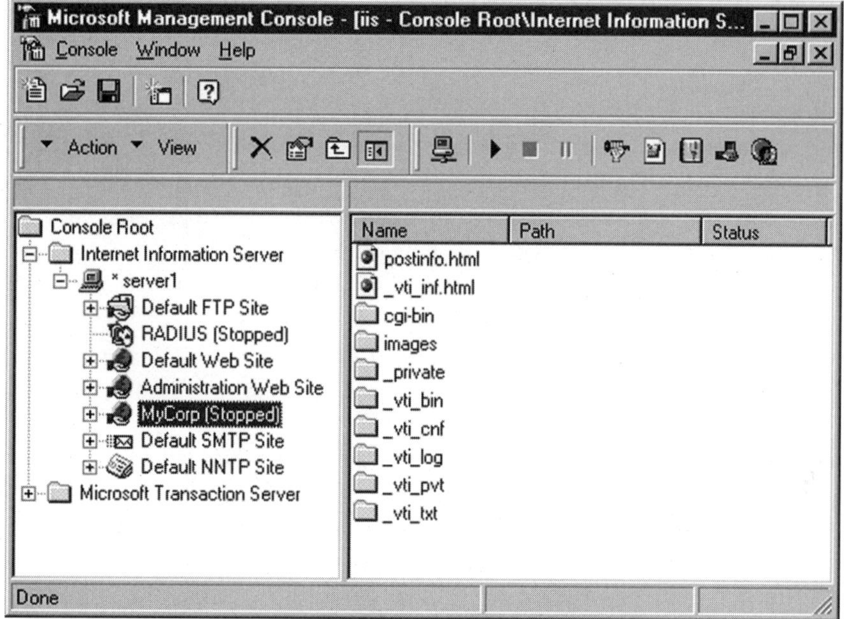

Figure 6-5 Virtual directories of the FrontPage root Web on the virtual server MyCorp.

`_private/` Used for pages that should not be visible in browsers or indexed by search engines (e.g., templates, headers, footers, includes).

`_vti_cnf/` Looks as if it contains a duplicate of every page in the Web site. Actually, the duplicate pages only have the same name as the original, and contain instead a series of name/value pairs specifying things like the date page was last modified, who modified, and so on.

`_vti_bin/` Contains executables (DLLs) used by FrontPage for administration and authoring purposes.

`_vti_txt/` Contains text indexes for the FrontPage Search WebBot component.

`_vti_pvt/` Contains other FrontPage information, such as the list of dependencies and child Webs.

`images/` You can store all your images for your site in this directory if you like.

`cgi-bin/` Used for storing traditional cgi scripts (e.g., Perl scripts).

Finally, as administrator you need to specify who has permission to create content for your new Web site (here MyCorp). To do so, start

FrontPage on the server by clicking START, PROGRAMS, MICROSOFT FRONTPAGE to open FrontPage Explorer. If this is the first time you have used FrontPage on the machine, the Getting Started box appears.

Click the MORE WEBS button to open the Open FrontPage Webs dialog box (Fig. 6-6). Note that since we have assigned the new virtual server the IP address of `172.16.8.102`, we must type this into the textbox and click the LIST WEBS button to show the root Web for this server. Click OK to open the root Web for MyCorp.

Continue by selecting TOOLS, PERMISSIONS to open the Permissions <Root Web> dialog box (Fig. 6-7). Select the Users tab and click ADD, and add the users who will be developing Web content and assign them permission to AUTHOR AND BROWSE this Web (we added the user Mitch to this group). Click OK.

Now that the administrator has created a new virtual server with a FrontPage root Web on the IIS server, we use the MMC to START the virtual server, and then we can go to the client machine with FrontPage installed and connect to this new FrontPage Web we have created and update it with new content.

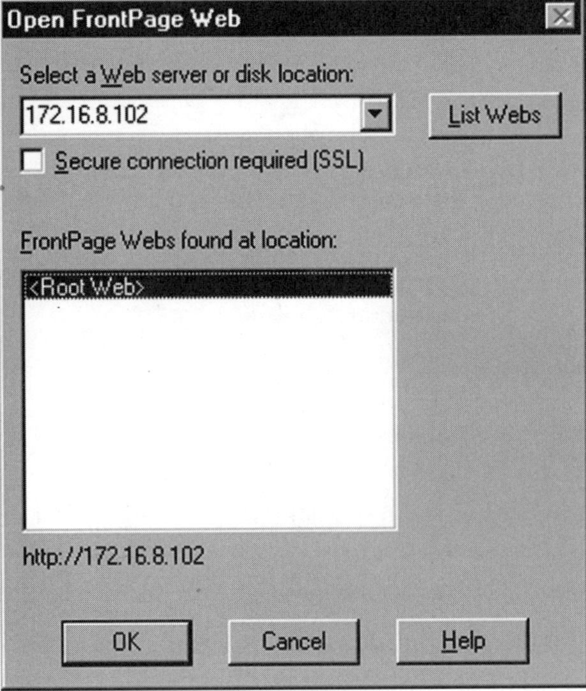

Figure 6-6 Opening the root Web of MyCorp (172.16.8.102).

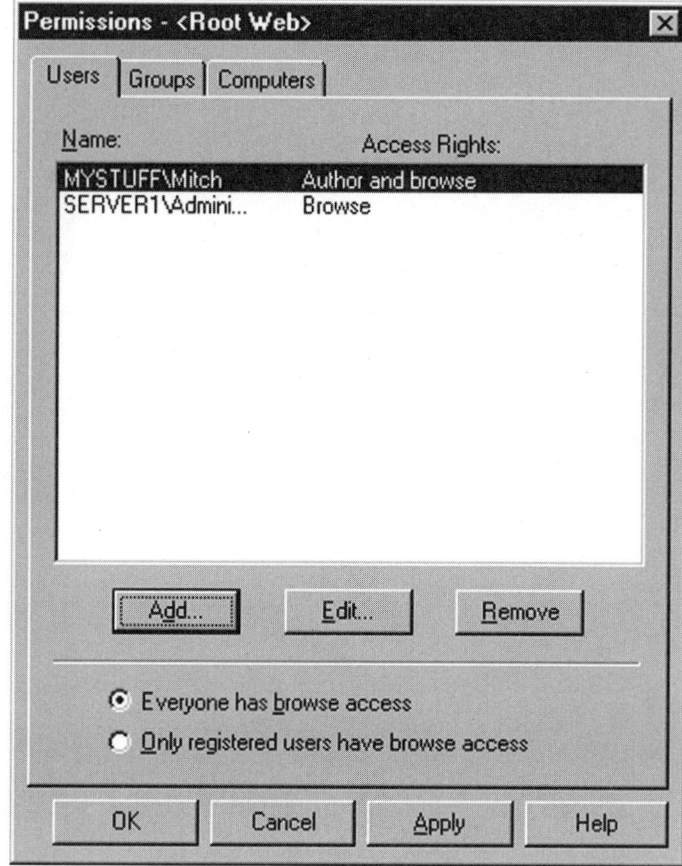

Figure 6-7 *Assigning author and browse permission to a content developer.*

Log on to the client machine as a user with author and browse permission and start FrontPage. In the Getting Started dialog box, select OPEN AN EXISTING FRONTPAGE WEB and click the MORE WEBS button.

In the Open FrontPage Web dialog box, type or select the IP address (or domain name if DNS is enabled) of the virtual server you want to connect to (in this case `172.16.8.102` for MyCorp) and click LIST WEBS to get a list of FrontPage Webs on this server. You should only see <Root Web> in the list box (Fig. 6-8). Click OK to open the root Web for MyCorp. FrontPage Explorer should now show the <Root Web> for the selected virtual server (Fig. 6-9).

To create some content for this Web site, we will create a new Web using a wizard and add the resulting content to the existing <Root Web>. Select FILE, NEW, FRONTPAGE WEB to open the New FrontPage Web

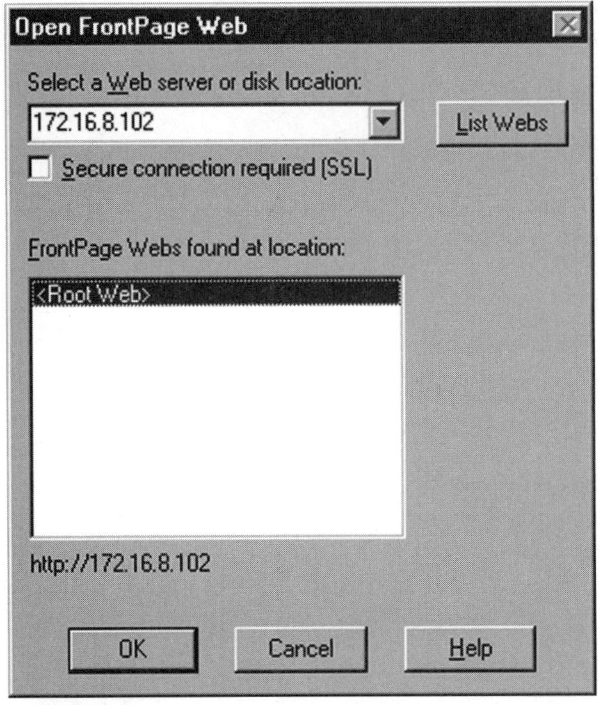

Figure 6-8
List of Webs for the selected virtual server at the client machine.

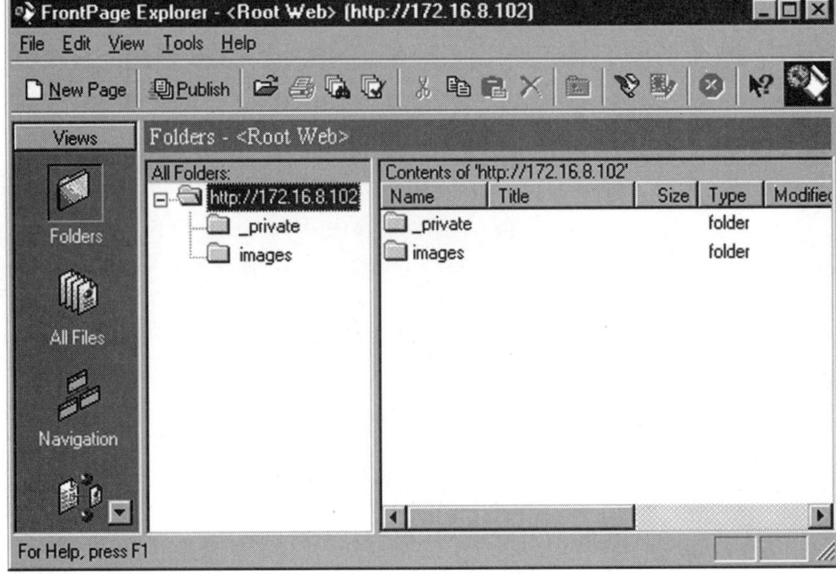

Figure 6-9
<Root Web> for http://172.16.8.102 is shown in Folder View in FrontPage Explorer.

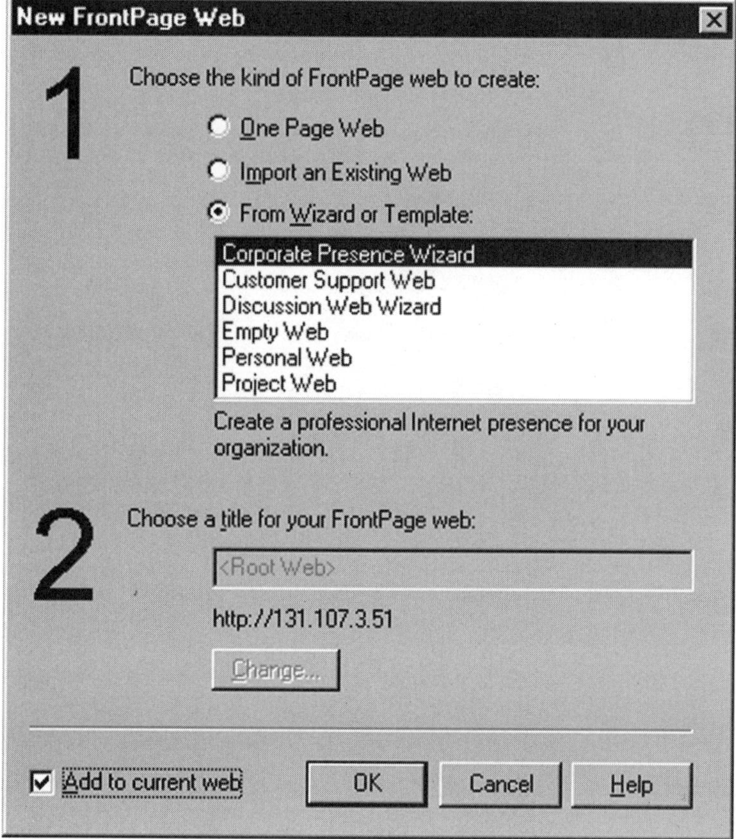

Figure 6-10 Adding content to an existing Web by using a wizard.

dialog box (Fig. 6-10). Select FROM A WIZARD OR TEMPLATE, highlight the Corporate Presence Wizard, check the ADD TO CURRENT WEB checkbox, and click OK to start the Corporate Presence Web Wizard (Fig. 6-11). Follow through the steps of the wizard, making selections to customize the site as desired, and click FINISH in the last step, and FrontPage will automatically create a basic corporate Web site.

FrontPage Explorer now shows the various pages that make up your newly created Web site. Explore the various views for your site by using the Views bar on the left. Figure 6-12 shows the site in Folder view, but other views allow you to examine the site's navigation structure, view the status of its hyperlinks, fix any broken links, and so on.

At this point you may want to add graphics to your Web site by selecting and applying one of the available *themes*. These themes are design templates that specify the layout and graphic look of all pages in

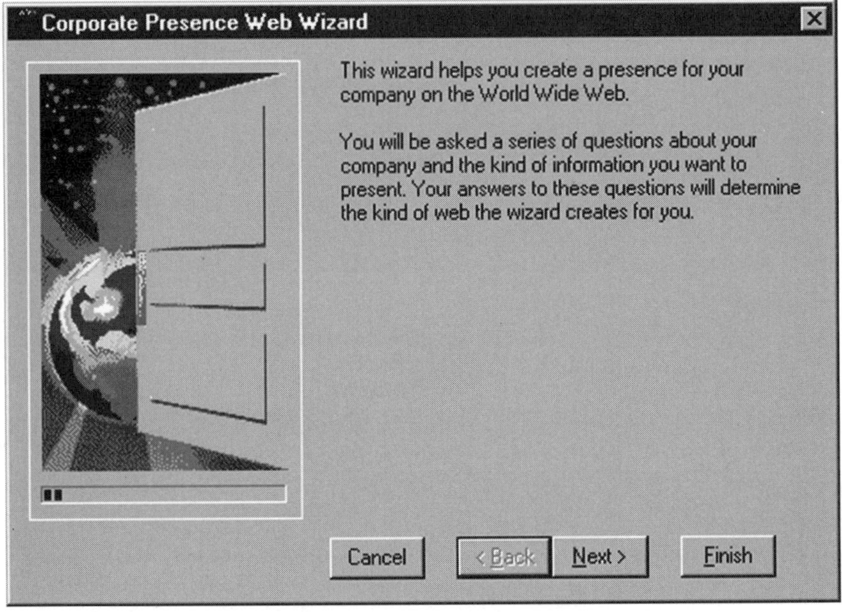

Figure 6-11 The Corporate Presence Web Wizard helps you build a professional-looking Web site.

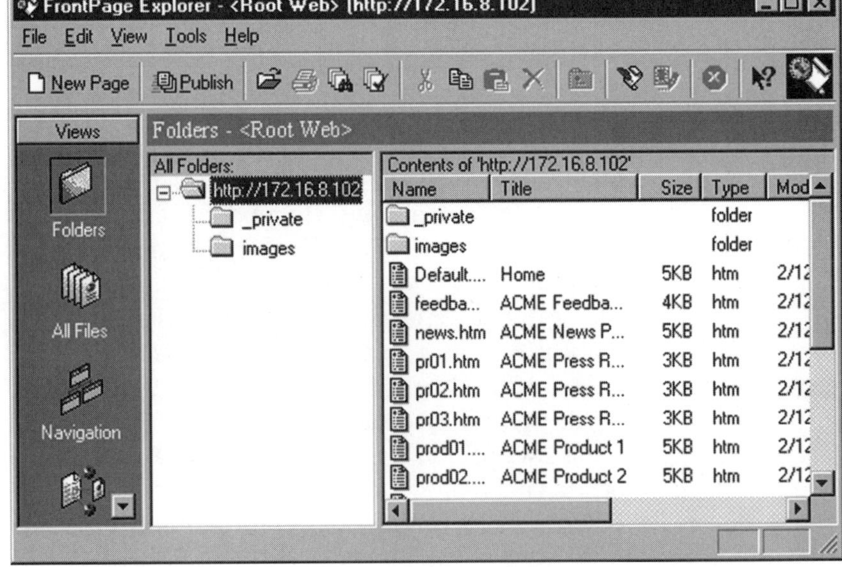

Figure 6-12 The MyCorp Web site created using FrontPage 98.

your site. A theme can be changed at any time with a few clicks of the mouse, so that your Web site need never look old and boring but may be updated any time.

In the Views bar on the left side of FrontPage Explorer, select THEMES to open the site in Themes View. Choose the USE SELECTED THEME button and highlight the theme you want to use. Select whether you want to use vivid colors, add active graphics, or add a background image, and click APPLY (Fig. 6-13).

As a final step, view your new Web site using a browser like Internet Explorer (Fig. 6-14). If the site is for intranet use, view its appearance in the browser you have chosen as a standard for your company. If it is an Internet Web site, view it in both Internet Explorer and Netscape Navigator, using both current and older versions of the software. This will ensure that whoever looks at your site sees what you expect them to see.

Creating Web Content with Microsoft Office

Microsoft Office is also a powerful content development platform for Web sites. Office 97 comes with built-in HTML functionality, allowing

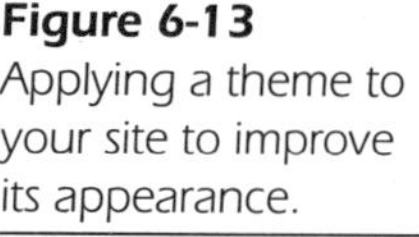

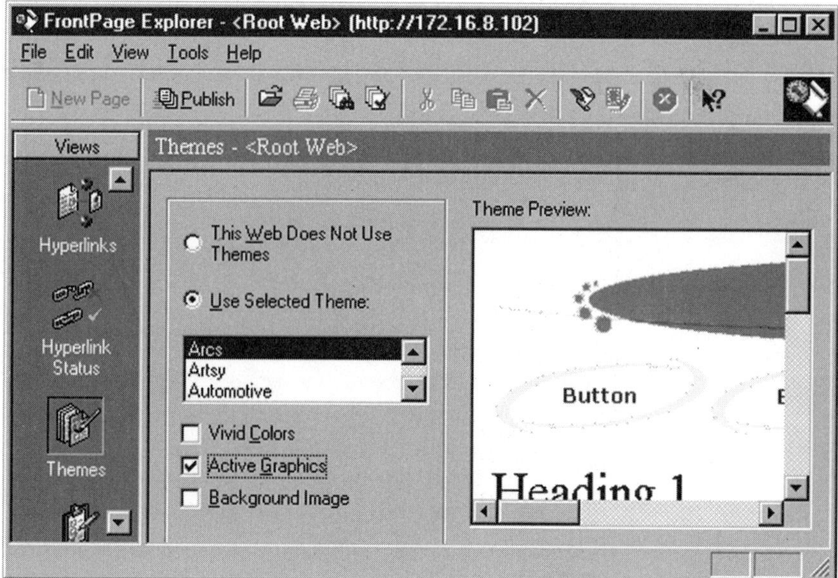

Figure 6-13
Applying a theme to your site to improve its appearance.

Figure 6-14 The final Web site for MyCorp. All it needs is for real content to be added!

you both to create new Web pages easily and to convert legacy documents to HTML for universal access. Office 95 has no built-in HTML functionality, but by downloading free Internet Assistants for Word 95, Excel 95, Access 95, and PowerPoint 95, this functionality can be easily added.

Web pages represent a kind of universal document format, because a Web page created on one machine can be viewed from any other machine equipped with a browser. Browsers are available for all platforms, and hence constitute a kind of *universal client software.*

Office suites such as Microsoft Office, on the other hand, constitute a kind of legacy publishing system. In order to view a Word or Excel document produced on one machine, the client machine must either have

- Full versions of Microsoft Word or Excel installed

or

- Special read-only Word or Excel viewers installed

If your Web site will contain quantities of legacy documents (Word, Excel, or PowerPoint documents), you have two options for displaying them:

1. Convert the legacy documents to HTML using Office 97 or using Office 95 with Internet Assistant software added to it.
2. Ensure that client machines that need to browse your site have either Microsoft Office installed on them or at least the read-only Office viewers installed.

If you cannot control what software your client machines will have installed on them (which is the usual case with Internet sites), the first option may be the only viable one for you to follow. Unfortunately, converting legacy documents to HTML can have unexpected results, because HTML was not designed to give the precise formatting control that modern word processing or desktop publishing programs do.

As an example, consider Fig. 6-15, which shows a simple newsletter page called `test.doc` that was created using Microsoft Word 97. Conversion to HTML using Office 97 is almost trivially simple: select FILE, SAVE AS, and in the Save as type drop-down box select HTML DOCUMENT. This will convert the document to HTML format and save it with the file extension `.html` in the specified destination directory. The result of converting the document shown in Fig. 6-15 is the Web page

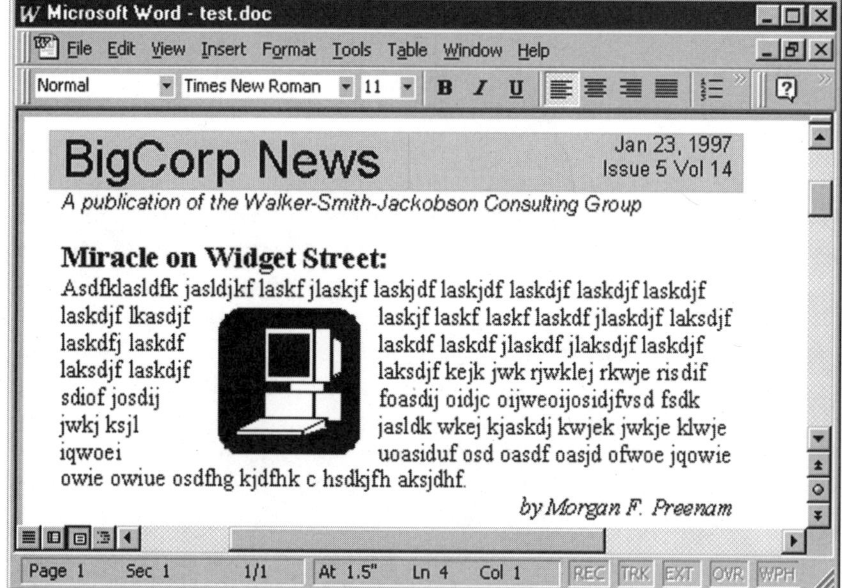

Figure 6-15 A document created using Microsoft Word 97.

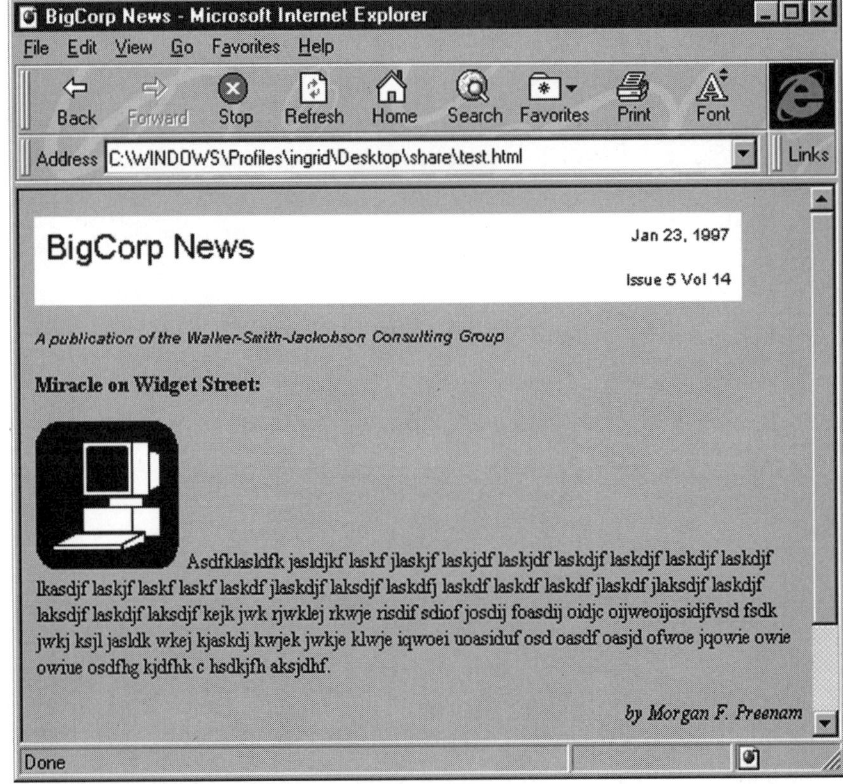

Figure 6-16 The Word document after being converted to HTML and viewed in IE 3.02.

`test.html`, which is shown as viewed by Internet Explorer 3.02 in Fig. 6-16. Notice the unexpected changes in formatting: a gray background instead of white, no text wrap around the clip art image, loss of the shading in the title.

Now some of these formatting problems can be fixed, but the point is that if you have thousands of legacy documents that need conversion to HTML, this may take time, especially if the final HTML documents have to be tweaked to closely resemble the original legacy documents in layout and appearance.

A better solution, where possible, is to ensure that all client machines are equipped with either Microsoft Office or at least the read-only Word, Excel, and PowerPoint viewers. For intranet sites, such standards can be enforced companywide. For Internet sites, your best bet might be to have a page that contains links to the viewer programs and instructions on how users can download and install them in order to view legacy document content on the site.

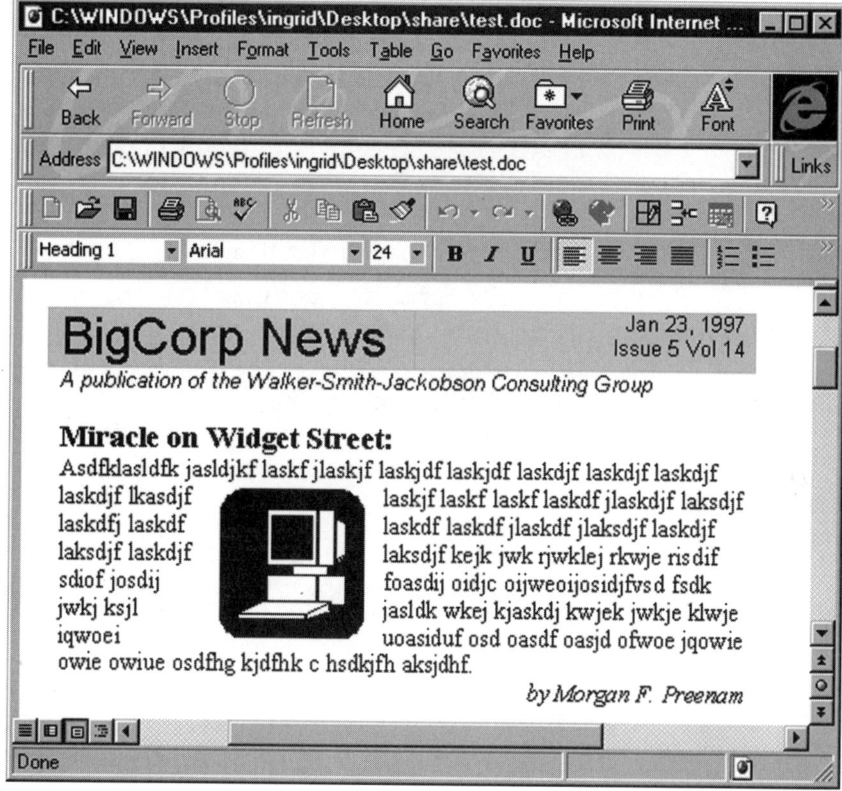

Figure 6-17 Viewing a Word document using IE 3.02 on a machine with Office 97 installed.

Figure 6-17 shows the result of browsing the document `test.doc` using Internet Explorer 3.02 when the client machine also has Office 97 installed on it. The result is that the Word application opens within the browser window, allowing users with appropriate permissions not only to read the documents but also to edit them, all while staying within the confines of their browser window. Microsoft truly has positioned the browser as the Universal Client!

Publishing to a Web Site from a Database

As another example of the power of Microsoft tools for creating Web content, the following walkthrough illustrates how easy it is to use Microsoft Access 97 to create Active Server Pages that connect to and display content from an Access database.

Integrating relational databases into your Web site can be done in two basic ways:

1. The *push method* has the database engine automatically generate static HTML pages on a periodic basis or every time a certain amount of information in the database is updated. The push method is useful for databases that change infrequently. The static HTML pages generated can represent data in tables, results of queries, and so on. A good example of this method is the SQL Server Web Assistant, which is a tool for publishing static HTML content from an SQL database.
2. The *pull method* involves using Active Server Pages or some other mechanism for dynamically generating database content each time the page is accessed. This method is most useful when the database information frequently changes or it is necessary to always access the most current information. An example of the pull model is creating Active server Pages to query an Access database by using the Access 97 Publish to the Web Wizard.

Both of these methods make use of the *Open Database Connectivity (ODBC)* mechanism, which can be used to access data from almost any commercial relational database.

Walkthrough: Publishing an Access 97 Database Using Active Server Pages

The following walkthrough shows how to use Access 97 to create dynamic Active Server Pages that publish information from an Access database to the previously created virtual server MyCorp. Access is suitable for the workgroup level when only a few dozen users are querying the database, while SQL Server is suitable for enterprise-level Web-database applications. Access 97 allows you to publish using either the push or the pull method. We will examine the pull method.

Start Microsoft Access 97 and either use an existing database or create a new one using the New Database Wizard. The database shown in Fig. 6-18 was created using the Membership template in the New Database Wizard; it was populated with sample data created by the wizard. This database is called `Membership1.mdb` and is located in the home directory of the MyCorp Web site on the IIS server, that is, in the `C:\MyCorpHome` directory, which is shared on the network as `\\SERVER1\MyCorpHome`.

From the File menu select SAVE AS HTML to open the Publish to the Web Wizard (Fig. 6-19). From the opening box of the wizard, select NEXT

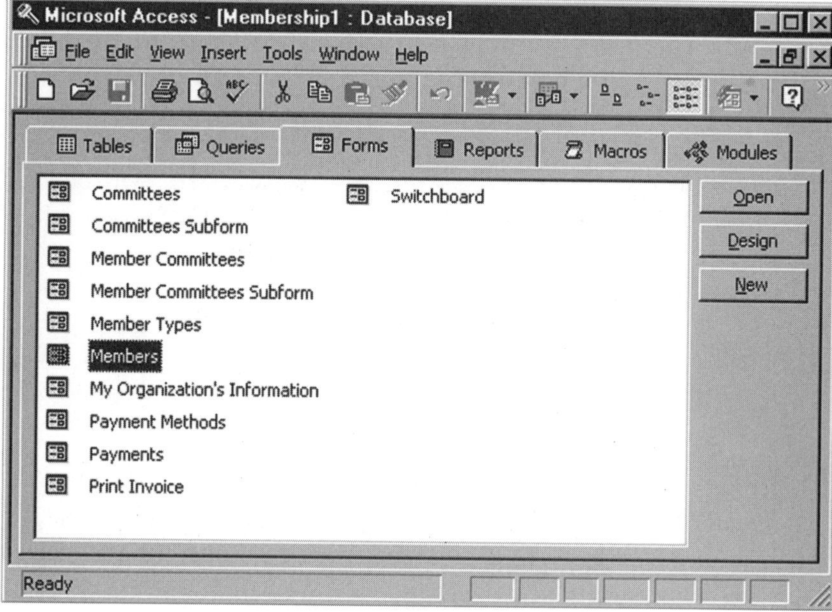

Figure 6-18 A database called `Membership1.mdb` created using Access 97.

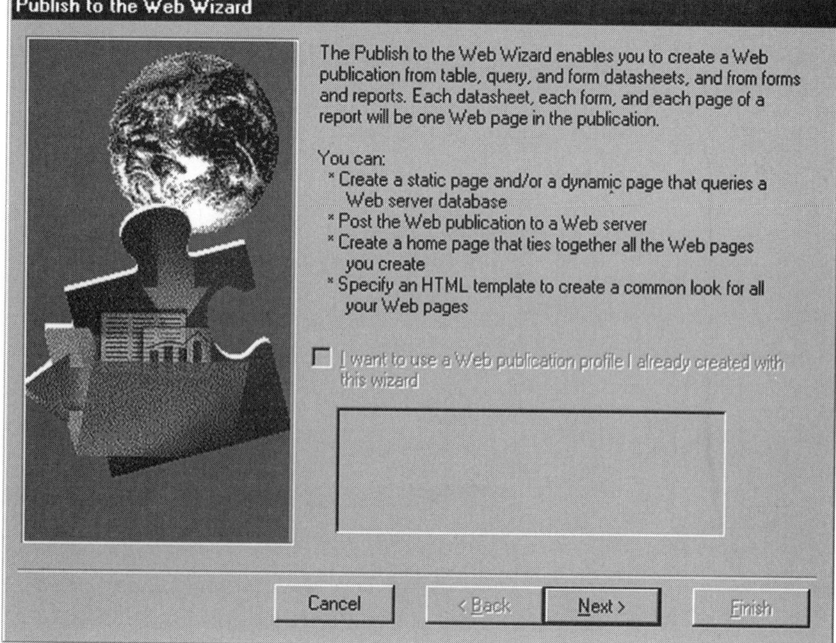

Figure 6-19 Access 97 Publish to the Web Wizard.

and choose which tables, queries, forms, and reports you wish to publish on your Web site. The table Payments has been selected to be published in Fig. 6-20. Note that publishing all objects in your database to the Web can take some time, especially if your tables have a large number of fields and records.

Next you can select a template that will be applied to your dynamically generated Web pages to add formatting and improve their appearance (Fig. 6-21). Access 97 comes with a set of Web templates, but you can also customize your own so that the pages have a look uniform with the rest of your Web site.

Note that if you decide to choose a template, you should first copy the template to the location where your database is going to be located (i.e., copy the template to your Web site's home directory on the IIS server if this is the location where the database will reside). In this walkthrough, no template is specified.

Next select the default publishing format you wish to use. You can select either

- Static HTML
- Dynamic HTML using HTX/IDC

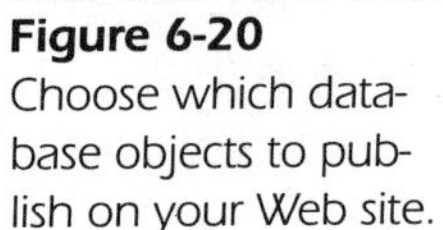

Figure 6-20
Choose which database objects to publish on your Web site.

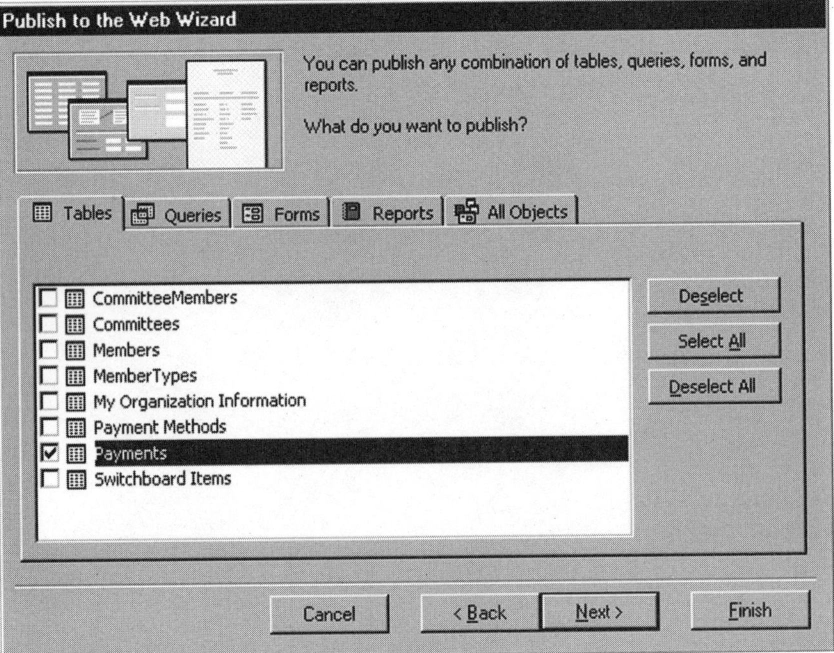

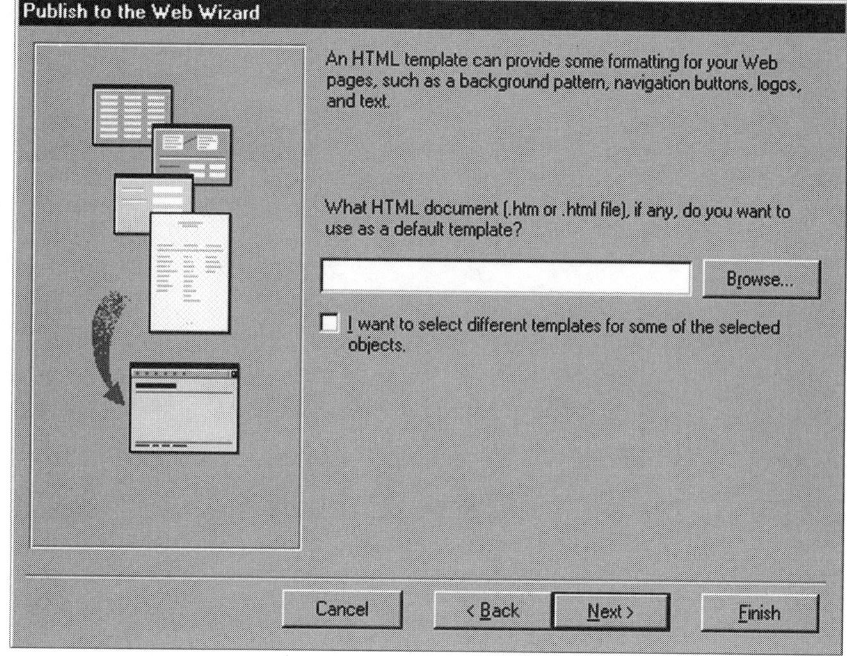

Figure 6-21 Select a template to format your dynamically generated pages.

- Dynamic HTML using Active Server Pages

Static HTML is an example of the push method. Dynamic HTML may use either HTX/IDC or Active Server Pages (ASPs) to publish the database to the Web:

- *HTX/IDC* involves the creation of two files, an Internet database connectivity (IDC) file that specifies how to connect to and query the database, and an HTML extension (HTX) file that formats the result set of the query.
- *Active Server Pages* involves scripts that run on the server to dynamically generate both query pages and their result sets in real time.

In Fig. 6-22 we have selected dynamic ASP as our default publishing format.

In order for your IIS server to connect with the Access database you wish to publish, you will need to specify a *data source name (DSN)* for Open Database Connectivity (ODBC).

In this example, the database is called `Membership1.mdb` and the data source name selected to represent it on the network is `member` (see Fig. 6-23). The simplest option is to establish this as a System DSN (a user

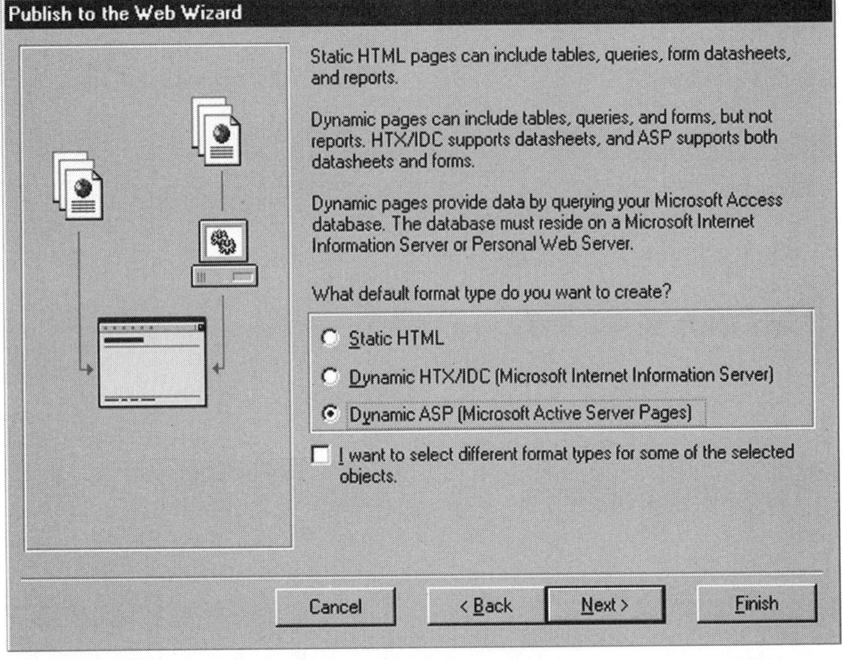

Publish to the Web Wizard
Static HTML pages can include tables, queries, form datasheets, and reports.
Dynamic pages can include tables, queries, and forms, but not reports. HTX/IDC supports datasheets, and ASP supports both datasheets and forms.
Dynamic pages provide data by querying your Microsoft Access database. The database must reside on a Microsoft Internet Information Server or Personal Web Server.
What default format type do you want to create?
Static HTML
Dynamic HTX/IDC (Microsoft Internet Information Server)
Dynamic ASP (Microsoft Active Server Pages)
I want to select different format types for some of the selected objects.
Cancel
< Back
Next >
Finish

Figure 6-22 Choose dynamic HTML using Active Server Pages for the widest level of functionality in publishing your Access database to the Web.

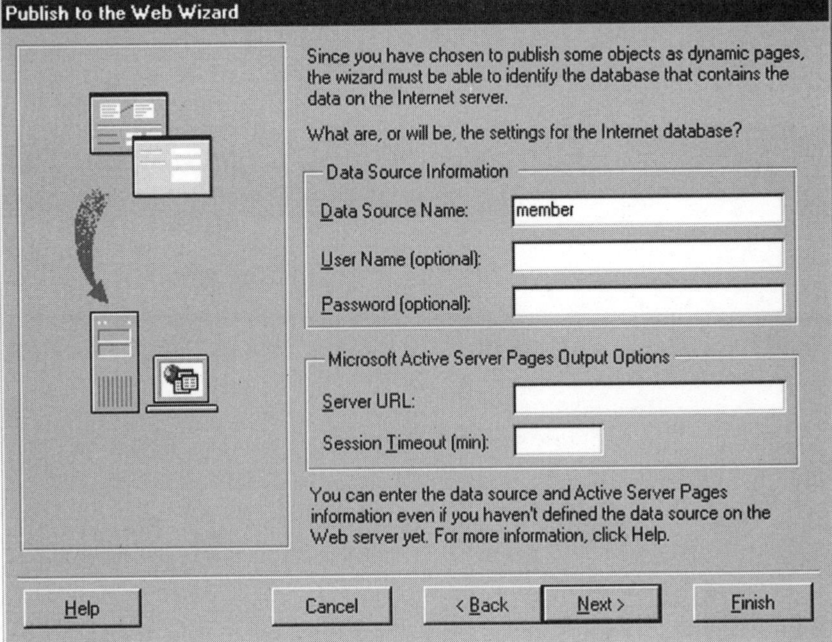

Publish to the Web Wizard
Since you have chosen to publish some objects as dynamic pages, the wizard must be able to identify the database that contains the data on the Internet server.
What are, or will be, the settings for the Internet database?
Data Source Information
Data Source Name:
member
User Name (optional):
Password (optional):
Microsoft Active Server Pages Output Options
Server URL:
Session Timeout (min):
You can enter the data source and Active Server Pages information even if you haven't defined the data source on the Web server yet. For more information, click Help.
Help
Cancel
< Back
Next >
Finish

Figure 6-23 Specify the data source name for ODBC connectivity.

account and password may be required) so that the data source will be visible to all users on the machine where the data source is defined This will be done later using the ODBC32 program in Control Panel.

Next we need to specify where we want to publish the database to, that is, which local directory or network share we want the generated Active Server Pages to be placed in. In this example, shown in Fig. 6-24, we have chosen to publish the pages to the directory where the database itself is located, namely, the MyCorp Web site home directory located on the IIS server at `C:\MyCorpHome`, which is shared on the network as `\\SERVER1\MyCorpHome`.

The next step in the wizard (Fig. 6-25) allows us to automatically create a home page that will contain links to all the dynamic pages generated by the wizard. This would be useful if we decide to publish the database information to its own virtual directory on the Web site. Since we have chosen to publish only a single table called Payments, it is easier to create a link to this page from our existing home page.

The final option in the wizard allows us to save all of our publishing options in a Web publication profile (Fig. 6-26). This will make it easy

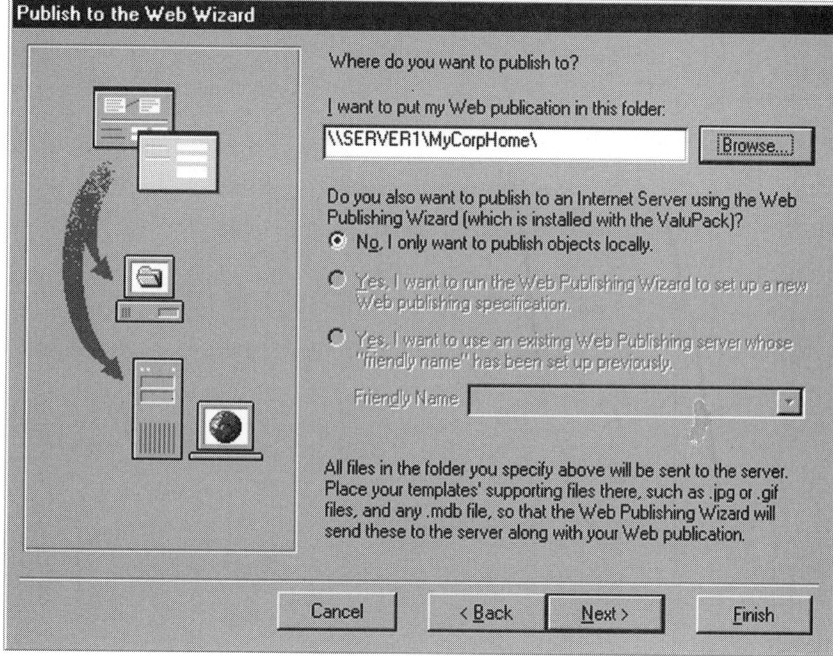

Publish to the Web Wizard
Where do you want to publish to?
I want to put my Web publication in this folder:
\\SERVER1\MyCorpHome\
Browse...
Do you also want to publish to an Internet Server using the Web Publishing Wizard (which is installed with the ValuPack)?
No, I only want to publish objects locally.
Yes, I want to run the Web Publishing Wizard to set up a new Web publishing specification.
Yes, I want to use an existing Web Publishing server whose "friendly name" has been set up previously.
Friendly Name
All files in the folder you specify above will be sent to the server. Place your templates' supporting files there, such as .jpg or .gif files, and any .mdb file, so that the Web Publishing Wizard will send these to the server along with your Web publication.
Cancel
< Back
Next >
Finish

Figure 6-24
Select a destination directory where the dynamic content will be published to.

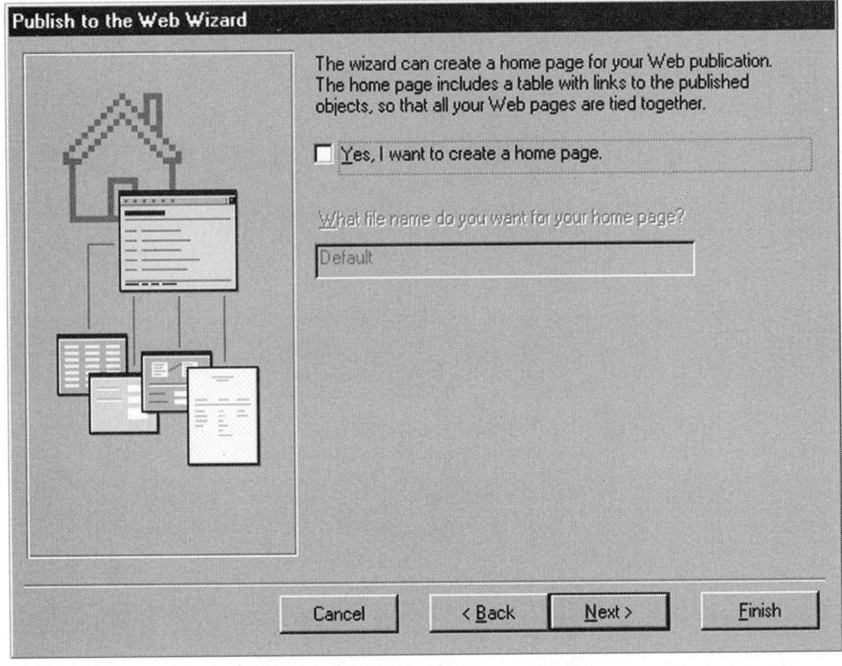

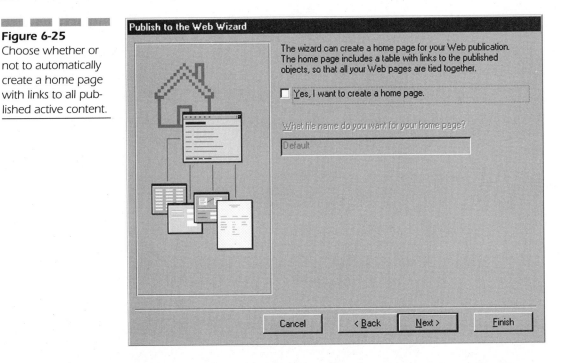

Figure 6-25 Choose whether or not to automatically create a home page with links to all published active content.

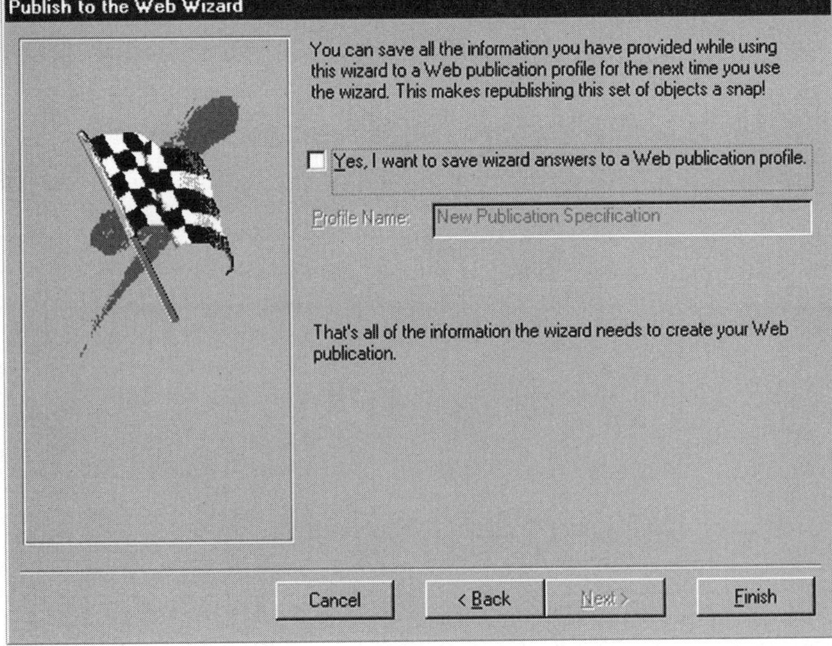

Figure 6-26 Saving your settings as a Web publication profile.

should we decide later to republish objects from our database to the same Web site. We will leave this option unchecked.

Figure 6-27 now shows the contents of the MyCorp Web site in the Microsoft Management Console (you may have to select REFRESH from the drop-down Action menu to get this view). Notice the following files:

- `Membership1.mdb` (the database itself—the file `Membership1.ldb` is an artifact of the database file being open under Access 97)
- `Payments_1.asp` (the Active Server Page that generates a Web page containing the current contents of the Payments table)

Before we can actually browse the Active Server Page, we must first define the System DSN for the database in ODBC. Launch the Control Panel and start the ODBC32 program to open the ODBC Data Source Administrator property sheets. Select the System DSN tab and click ADD (Fig. 6-28). The Create New Data Source box appears. Select the Microsoft Access Driver as the database driver to be used to connect to your database and click FINISH (Fig. 6-29). The ODBC Microsoft Access 97 Setup dialog box appears. Enter `member` as the Data Source Name (see Fig. 6-30).

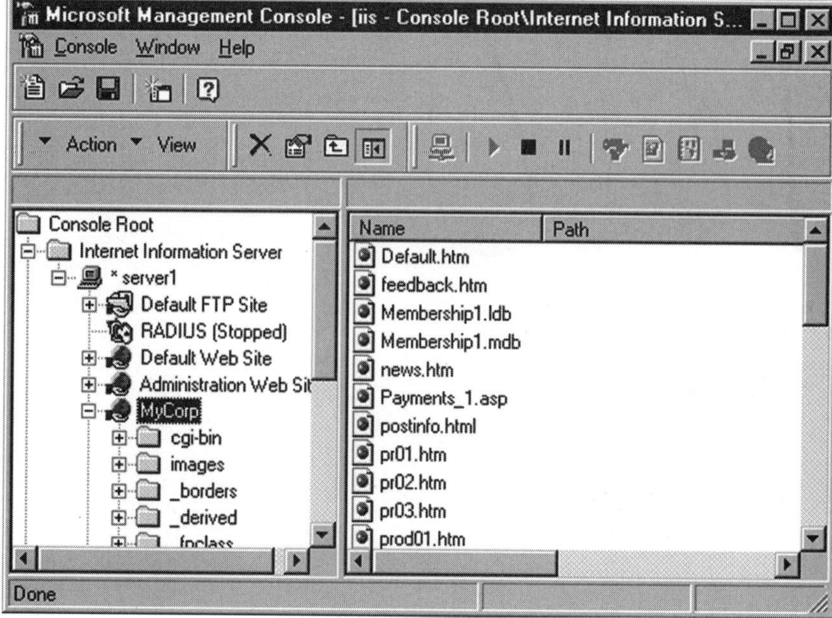

Figure 6-27
An Active Server Page has been added to the MyCorp Web site.

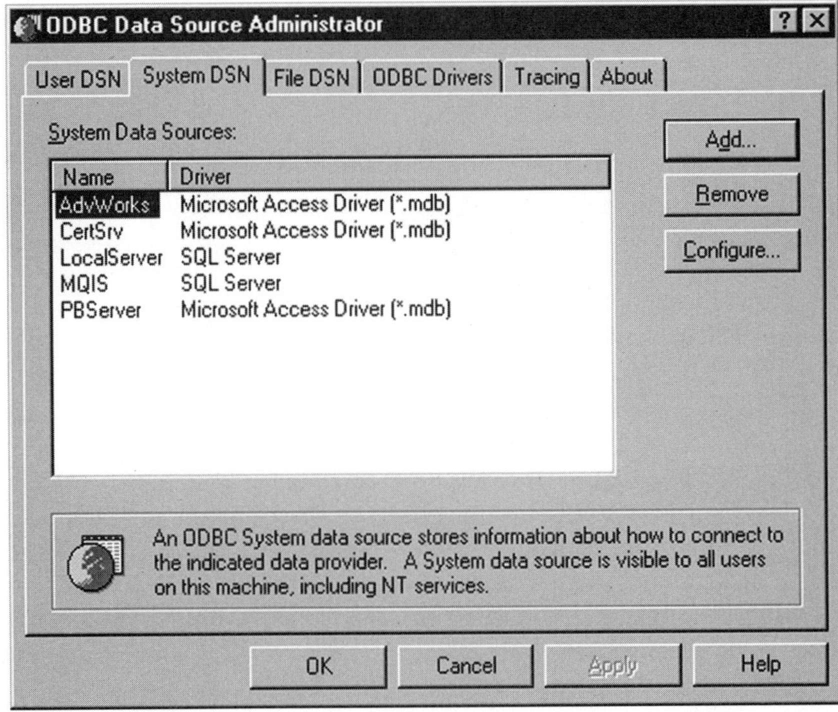

Figure 6-28
The System DSN tab in ODBC32.

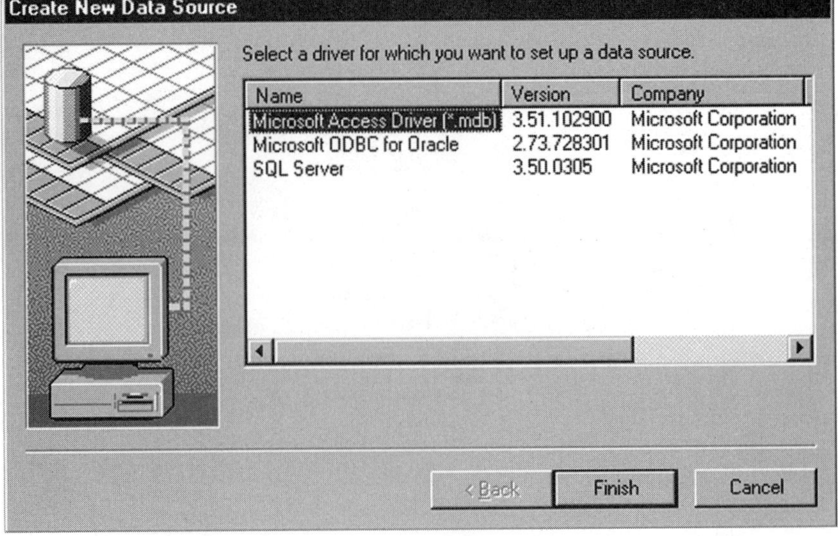

Figure 6-29
Select the Microsoft Access Driver.

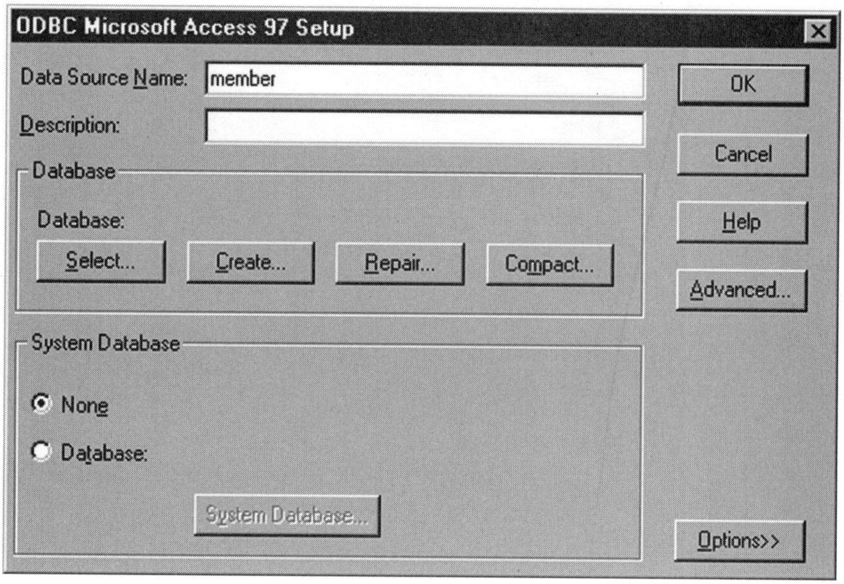

Figure 6-30
Assign a data source name to your database.

ODBC Microsoft Access 97 Setup

Data Source Name: member
Description:
Database
Database:
Select... Create... Repair... Compact...
System Database
None
Database:
System Database...
OK
Cancel
Help
Advanced...
Options>>

Then click SELECT and browse to locate the `Membership1.mdb` database in the home directory `C:\MyCorpHome`.

You can also create a new database at this point, or compact or repair an existing one. For explanation of other options see the ODBC help file.

When browsing to select your database, you can also specify the following options by checking the appropriate checkbox:

- Read-only mode
- Exclusive mode

Select the Membership1.mdb database and click OK to finish (Fig. 6-31).

You are finally ready to test the Active Server Page to see if it dynamically queries the database for its information. Make sure that the MyCorp home directory has both read and script permissions in IIS (check the MyCorp property sheet in the MMC), as these permissions are required for Active Server Pages to execute properly.

In the MMC right-click on the file `Payments_1.asp` and select BROWSE from the shortcut menu. This will launch Internet Explorer and execute the script on the page, causing it to return the current contents of the Payments table to the Web browser (Fig. 6-32).

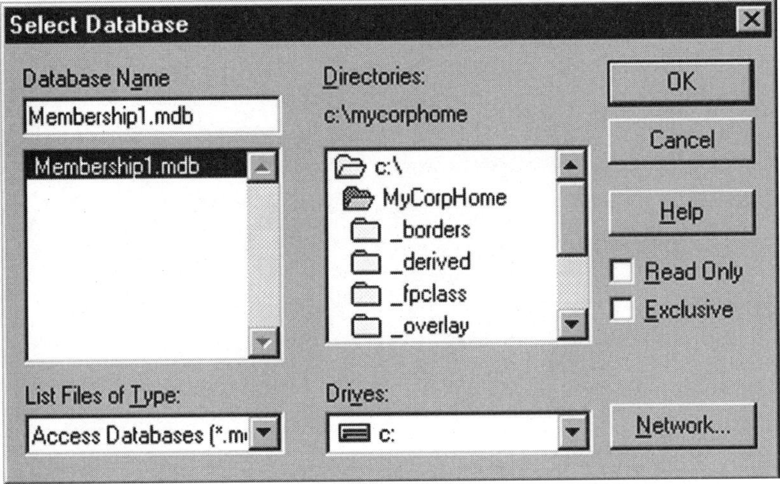

Figure 6-31
Map the database file to the System DSN.

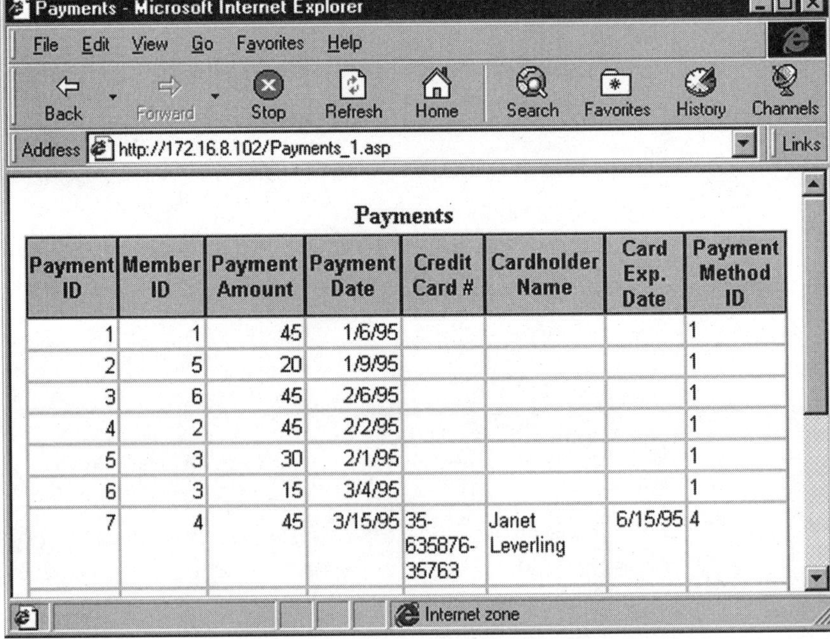

Payments

Payment ID	Member ID	Payment Amount	Payment Date	Credit Card #	Cardholder Name	Card Exp. Date	Payment Method ID
1	1	45	1/6/95				1
2	5	20	1/9/95				1
3	6	45	2/6/95				1
4	2	45	2/2/95				1
5	3	30	2/1/95				1
6	3	15	3/4/95				1
7	4	45	3/15/95	35-635876-35763	Janet Leverling	6/15/95	4

Figure 6-32
Results of executing `Payments_1.asp.`

FOR MORE INFORMATION

Microsoft Web Site For an excellent source of information on all aspects of FrontPage 98, visit

```
www.microsoft.com/frontpage
```

The site has general information, new themes and templates, information on site hosting, and information for Web administrators.

For a guide to the Publish to the Web Wizard of Access 97, visit the site

```
www.microsoft.com/access
```

and select the appropriate link.

Microsoft Public Newsgroups Microsoft FrontPage issues are discussed in the newsgroups

```
microsoft.public.frontpage.client
microsoft.public.frontpage.extensions.windowsnt
microsoft.public.frontpage.frontpage98.eval
```

Microsoft Access has a large number of different newsgroups to browse:

```
Microsoft.public.access.*
```

Microsoft TechNet TechNet has FrontPage 98 manuals located at

```
MS Office and Desktop Applications | MS FrontPage | FrontPage Manu-
als
```

Also included is the FrontPage 98 Server Extensions Resource Kit at

```
MS Office and Desktop Applications | MS FrontPage | Resource Kit
```

CHAPTER 7

Administering Clients

Introduction

Administering Internet Information Server 4.0 is only half the battle for the network administrator; the other half is administering the end-user client software. In Chap. 6 we considered administering end-user content creation tools; in this chapter we look at administering the client browser software itself. After completing this chapter, you will have a basic understanding of how to install, configure, and manage Microsoft Internet Explorer 4.0 (IE 4.0) using the Internet Explorer Administration Kit (IEAK). In particular, we will look at

- The basic features and functionality of Internet Explorer 4.0
- Configuring IE 4.0 security options
- The IE 4.0 Active Setup process
- Using the IEAK to create custom packages
- Distributing IEAK custom packages to clients

What Is Internet Explorer 4.0?

Internet Explorer 4.0 is Microsoft's newest version of its award-winning Internet browser client software. New features introduced with this version include:

- *Active desktop,* which provides the capability of embedding Web content directly onto the desktop
- *The Explorer bar,* which enables new toolbars to enhance search, history, favorites, and channels features
- *Subscriptions,* which subscribe to Web sites to download Web content on a scheduled basis
- *Channels,* a new Web content distribution format for automatic browsing of subscribed pages
- *Dynamic HTML,* which supports DHTML styles, content, object binding, and object positioning features
- *HTTP 1.1,* which supports version 1.1 of the Hyper-Text Transfer Protocol
- *Microsoft Java Virtual Machine,* which extends basic Java functionality with Win32 API capability

IE 4.0 also includes a number of add-on components to further extend client functionality in both Internet and intranet environments:

- Communication add-ons: NetMeeting, Outlook Express, Chat 2.0
- Multimedia add-ons: NetShow, VRML 2.0 Viewer, RealPlayer, and more
- Authoring add-ons: FrontPage Express, Web Publishing Wizard
- Additional enhancements: Microsoft Wallet, Task Scheduler, Web Fonts
- Multiple language support

Why Use Internet Explorer 4.0?

Version 4.01 of Internet Explorer is required on any server on which you plan to install Internet Information Server 4.0. In addition, to take full advantage of IIS 4.0 capabilities (e.g., HTTP 1.1), client machines should have Internet Explorer 4.0 installed on them.

In a corporate network, it is fairly straightforward to standardize on IE 4.0 for client machines. Administration of client machines is further simplified by using the Microsoft Internet Explorer Administration Kit, described later in this chapter.

In a public Internet environment, users should be directed to upgrade to IE 4.0 to enhance their browsing experience and take full advantage of IIS 4.0 hosted sites.

Understanding and Configuring Internet Explorer 4.0 Security

In order to use Internet Explorer 4.0 within a corporate environment (and to use it effectively in an Internet environment), it is essential to understand Internet Explorer security. Internet Explorer 4.0 security can be controlled through

- Security zones
- Site certificates
- Security options settings

We will consider security zones and options settings in this chapter; site certificates are considered in Chap. 12.

Configuring IE 4.0 Security Zones

Internet Explorer 4.0 allows you to assign particular Web sites to specific zones. A *zone* is a security setting that controls access to a specific group of Web sites. When Internet Explorer 4.0 is installed, it creates four different security zones:

- *Local intranet zone*, which contains all Web sites on your company's intranet (LAN) and any specific sites you wish to add. Or from another angle, it contains all Web sites that don't require a proxy server to access them. Using the Internet Explorer Administration Kit, which is described later in this chapter, an administrator can define which sites are to be included in this zone.
- *Trusted sites zone*, which contains any specific sites you trust that you wish to add.
- *Internet zone*, which contains all Internet sites, i.e., anything not on the local machine, not on the local network, and not assigned to any other zone.
- *Restricted sites zone*, which contains any specific sites you don't trust that you wish to add.

These four zones can each be configured to one of the following security levels:

- *High security.* All content that might damage the client system is excluded.
- *Medium security.* The user is warned before content that might damage the client system is run.
- *Low security.* All content is run without warning or notification to the user.
- *Custom security.* The security setting for each form of active content is configured as prompt, disable, or enable.

The default security settings for the four zones when Internet Explorer 4.0 is installed are as follows:

Local intranet zone	Medium security
Trusted sites zone	Low security

Internet zone	Medium security
Restricted sites zone	High security

NOTE: *The previous version, 3.02, of Internet Explorer also had high, medium, and low security settings. However, the new security settings have different meanings from the old ones. If you upgrade from IE 3.02 to IE 4.01, you should examine the security settings and adjust them as necessary.*

To configure security zones for IE 4.0, go to Control Panel, click INTERNET, and select the Security tab on the Internet Options property sheet that appears (see Fig. 7-1). From this property sheet you can add specific

Figure 7-1
Accessing the IE 4.0 security zone configuration

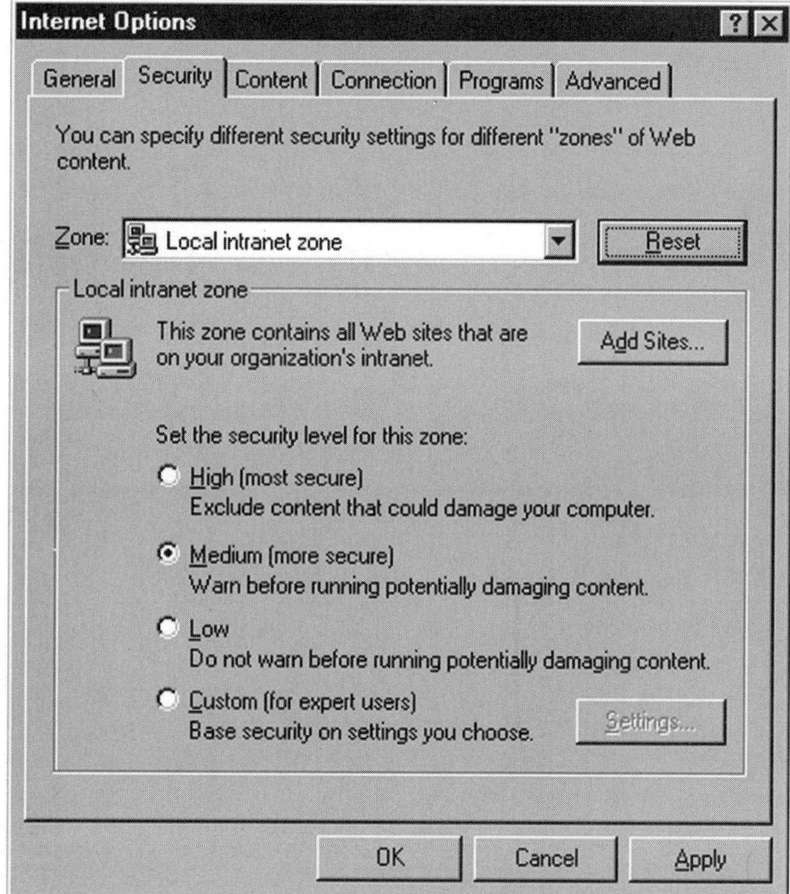

Web sites to any of the four zones except the Internet zone (which cannot be configured).

For example, let us add a new site to the local intranet zone (possibly an external site with the proxy server disabled for this site). On the Security tab, select LOCAL INTRANET ZONE and click on ADD SITES. The Local intranet zone dialog box appears, asking whether you want to include in this zone the following:

- All local intranet sites not listed in other zones
- All sites that bypass the proxy server
- All network paths (using UNC paths)

By default, each of the above three items is checked (see Fig. 7-2).

Click ADVANCED to open another Local intranet zone dialog box (see Fig. 7-3). In this new box you can

- Specify which Web sites will be added to the local intranet zone
- Specify whether or not to require connection to sites in this zone using HTTPS

Enter the Web sites you want to consider as part of the local intranet zone and click OK. Other zones are configured similarly.

Configuring IE 4.0 Security Options Settings

The custom security setting described above allows you to enable, disable, or prompt regarding a number of security issues. To access these

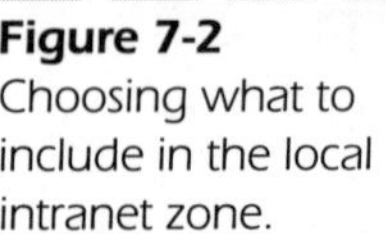

Figure 7-2 Choosing what to include in the local intranet zone.

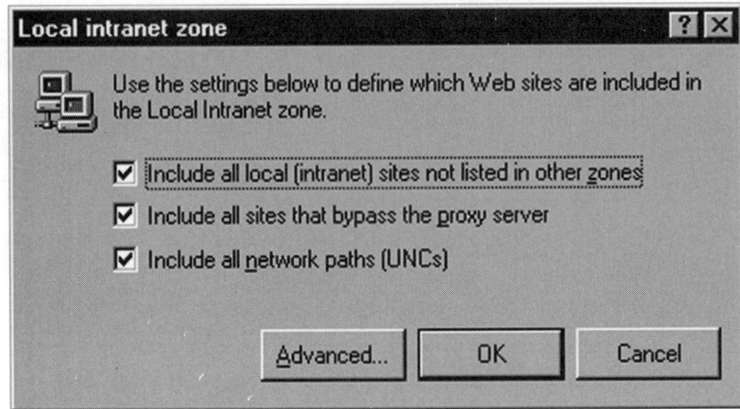

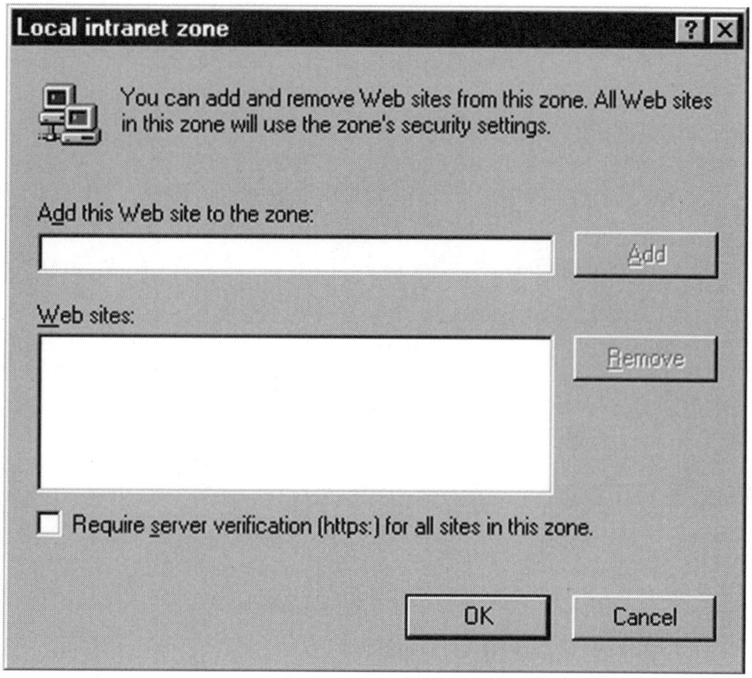

Figure 7-3
Adding a specific Web site to the local intranet zone.

security options, go to Control Panel and open the Internet icon, select the Security tab, select CUSTOM, and click the SETTINGS button.

The following security options can be configured:

ActiveX controls and plug-ins settings:

- Download unsigned ActiveX controls
- Script ActiveX controls marked safe for scripting
- Initialize and script ActiveX controls not marked as safe
- Download signed ActiveX controls
- Run ActiveX controls and plug-ins

User authentication settings (choose one of the following):

- Anonymous logon (disables HTTP authentication and uses guest account)
- Prompt for username and password
- Automatic logon in intranet zone (prompts for username and password in other zones)
- Automatic logon with current username and password (Windows NT Challenge / Response)

Download settings:

- File downloads
- Font downloads

Java settings:

- Java permissions: high, medium, low, disabled, or custom

Miscellaneous settings:

- Software channel permissions
- Launching applications and files in an IFRAME
- Installation of desktop items
- Submit nonencrypted form data
- Drag and drop or copy and paste files

Scripting settings:

- Scripting of Java applets
- Active scripting

Still other security options may be configured by using the Advanced tab on the Internet Options property sheet (Fig. 7-4).

Understanding Internet Explorer 4.0 Active Setup

In order to administer Internet Explorer 4.0, we require a basic understanding of the Active Setup process. Internet Explorer 4.0 setup uses ActiveX technology running on the client computer to provide a faster, more efficient, modular setup process. Active Setup includes features such as the ability for setup to reconnect to the distribution source and resume setup where it was interrupted, and it provides detailed progress information about setup including the estimated time to completion.

IE 4.0 Active Setup is initiated by running the self-extracting file `IE4setup.exe`. This file is 407 kB in size, and can be downloaded from the Internet, copied from a distribution server, supplied on an installation CD, or even distributed on a floppy.

`IE4setup.exe` gathers necessary information from the client, and then it downloads or copies to the local drive only those `.cab` files that are necessary to install or upgrade the selected components. When the

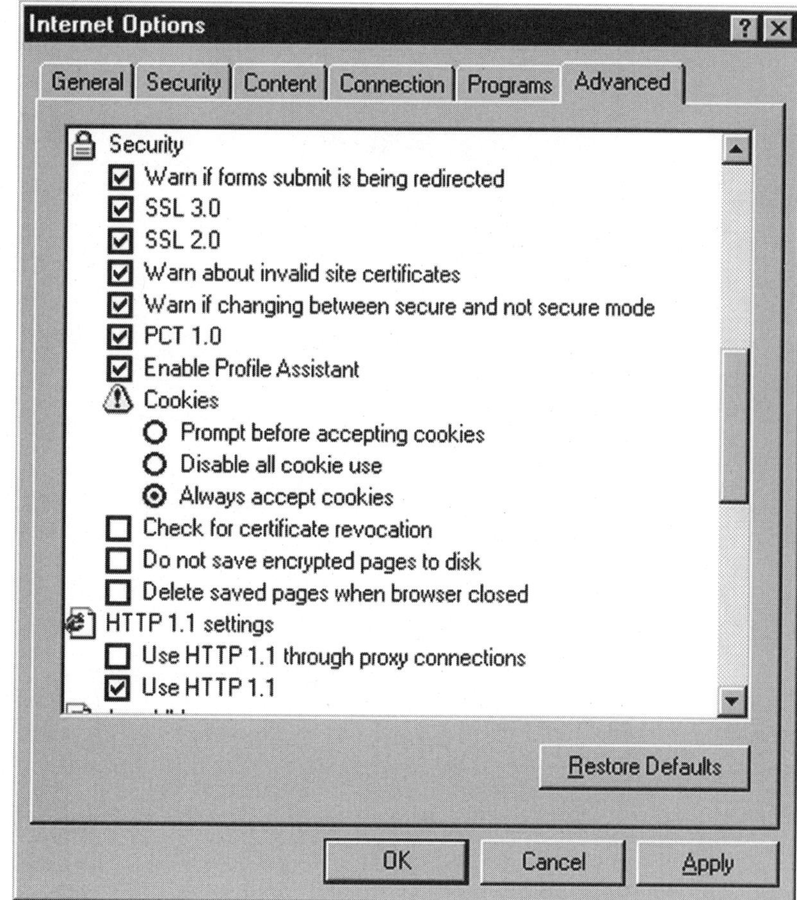

Figure 7-4 Other security settings on the Advanced tab of the Internet Options property sheet.

necessary `.cab` files have been downloaded, Active Setup ends and the traditional ACME setup engine takes over.

Administering IE 4.0 Clients Using the Internet Explorer Administration Kit

The Internet Explorer Administration Kit (IEAK) is a tool for helping administrators deploy and support custom configurations of Internet Explorer 4.0. The IEAK is not included as a part of Windows NT 4.0

Option Pack, but it is an essential tool for administrators rolling out IE 4.0 on corporate intranets, or ISPs wanting to provide customers with customized, preconfigured browser clients. In this section we will examine how to plan, prepare for, create, and distribute customized IE 4.0 packages using the IEAK.

What Is the Internet Explorer Administration Kit?

The IEAK includes the following tools:

- *IEAK Wizard* allows administrators to create customized packages for IE 4.0 installations.
- *IEAK Profile Manager* allows administrators to maintain IE 4.0 clients by configuring user options from a centralized place.
- *IEAK Help* provides instructions on how to use IEAK effectively.

Uses of the Internet Explorer Administration Kit

The IEAK can be used in different ways, depending on whether you are a corporate intranet administrator, an Internet content provider, or an Internet service provider.

Corporate Intranet Administrators Corporate intranet administrators can use the IEAK to perform hands-free installations of IE 4.0, customized to meet the particular needs of their companies. Administrators can

- Roll out IE 4.0 browsers with customized Search, Favorites, Start Page, title bar, and logo
- Preconfigure IE 4.0 security settings including security zones, content ratings, proxy settings, and certificates
- Customize setup to include optional components including third-party custom components
- Configure multiple distribution servers for load-balancing
- Perform silent (unattended) installations
- Apply system policies and other restrictions during installation

Internet Service Providers Internet service providers (ISPs) can use the IEAK to create custom IE 4.0 installation packages for Internet clients. ISPs can

- Create installation packages that include bundled third-party software components
- Designate which language version of IE 4.0 to install
- Customize IE 4.0 with Search, Start, Favorites, support pages, logo, and title
- Create sign-up packages for new customers and upgrade packages for existing customers
- Use the IE 4.0 logo on their packaging materials, in accordance with the license agreement

Internet Content Providers Internet content providers (ICPs) can use the IEAK to create custom IE 4.0 installations packages similar to Internet service providers. In addition, ICPs can

- Perform automatic software distribution via the Internet

Obtaining and Installing the IEAK

The IEAK can be downloaded from the secure Web site

```
http://ieak.microsoft.com
```

The process for obtaining the IEAK from this site involves the following steps:

1. Register your name and company in the IEAK database. Click on the Get the IEAK image on the left-hand side of the page, select NEW REGISTRATION, and complete the registration form. Include your email address. When you complete your registration, a site password will be emailed to you within a few hours.
2. When you receive your site password, enter your email address and site password in the logon box. When you are admitted to the site, you will need to select one of the following options describing how you plan to distribute IE 4.0:
    - To customers outside your organization
    - To company employees within your organization

- To meet special requirements (128-bit browser, dial-up networking)

Select your distribution option and click NEXT to read your licensing agreement.

3. Read the licensing agreement carefully, and if you agree click on the link SIGN A LICENSE AND DISTRIBUTION AGREEMENT. When you click the link, email will be automatically sent to you containing another password, called a customization keycode. This keycode validates you as an authorized IEAK user, and you will need it in order to run your copy of IEAK, so make sure you print it out and store it in a safe place. You should also print out and keep a copy of your licensing agreement.
4. Download the language version of IEAK of your choice by clicking the link GET INTERNET EXPLORER ADMINISTRATION KIT. You can also order it on CD at a nominal cost.
5. As per your licensing agreement, you must make quarterly reports to Microsoft of the licenses you distribute to customers.

Preparing to Use the IEAK in a Corporate Environment

Begin by being aware of the hardware and software requirements for installing the IEAK:

- 486 DX2/66 processor or higher
- Windows NT 4.0 Server or Windows NT 4.0 Workstation with 16-MB RAM; or Windows 95 with 8-MB RAM minimum
- Disk space varying from 43 to 59 MB, depending on type of installation selected (standard, enhanced, or full)
- Additional disk space if third-party components are to be bundled with the installation package
- Internet Explorer 4.0 installed on the system to download the IEAK

In addition, you should gather all necessary information and additional custom files before running the IEAK. This should include the following:

- Create any custom bitmaps you wish to use to customize the browser, and place them in a folder on the distribution server.
- Plan your distribution method for the IEAK custom package (from the Internet, from a distribution server, on a CD, or on a floppy).
- Obtain a digital certificate from a Certificate Authority and sign your cabinet files and custom files, if necessary because of browser security settings.
- Collect URLs for users' Start Page, Favorites, and support pages.
- Plan out what kind of security settings you want implemented on the browsers.
- Plan how you want to configure the Windows Desktop Upgrade.

Walkthrough: Using the IEAK to Create a Package

The following walkthrough leads you through using the IEAK Wizard to create custom packages for the purposes of distributing and installing IE 4.0 on a corporate intranet environment. For use in an Internet service provider environment, consult the IEAK online documentation.

The IEAK Wizard runs through a series of five stages, each stage consisting of several steps. To start the IEAK Wizard, click on START, PROGRAMS, MICROSOFT IEAK, IEAK WIZARD.

Stage 1: Gathering Information Stage 1 of the IEAK Wizard is called *Gathering Information* (Fig. 7-5). In stage 1 you will be prompted by the IEAK Wizard to enter the following information (Fig. 7-6):

- Your company's name
- Your customization code (obtained during the IEAK registration process)

You will also need to provide the role you selected in your licensing agreement for using the IEAK:

- Content Provider/Developer
- Service Provider
- Corporate Administrator (we selected this option)

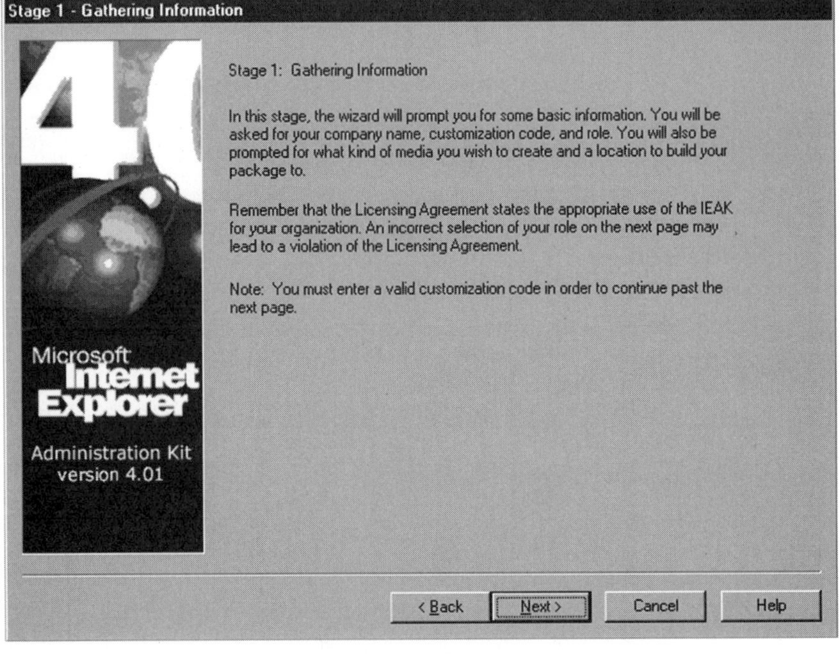

Figure 7-5 Stage 1 of the IEAK Wizard is called *Gathering Information.*

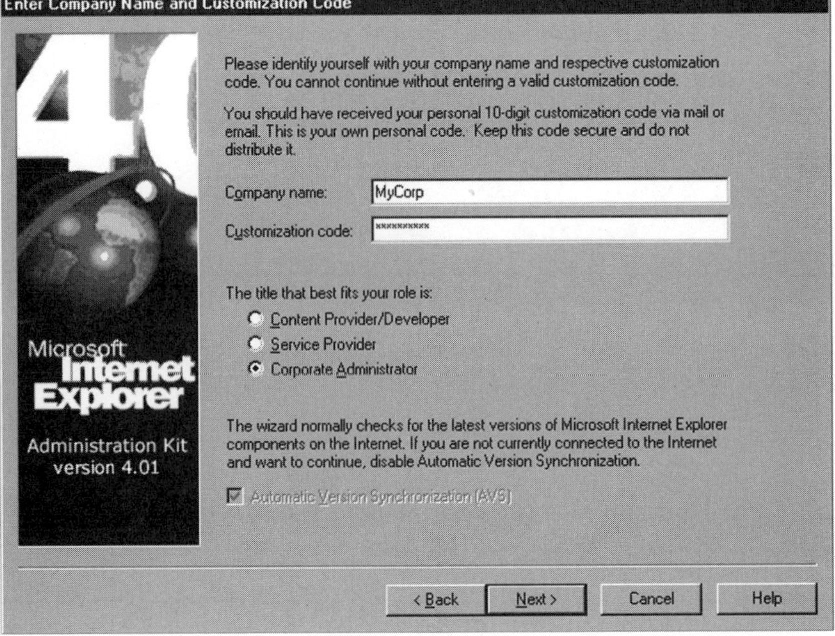

Figure 7-6 Enter your customization code in order to proceed with the Wizard.

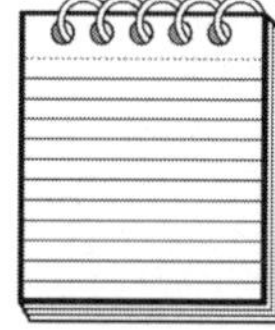

NOTE: *It is important that the selection you make on the screen shown in Fig. 7-6 matches the selection you made when accepting your licensing agreement. If the two are different, you may be violating your licensing agreement.*

Next select the language you want for the IE 4.0 package you are creating. Run the IEAK Wizard once for each language version you want to create.

Next select or create the folder where your customized IE 4.0 packages will be placed when the wizard is finished (Fig. 7-7). Your IE 4.0 installations will be performed from this download directory. In our example we have chosen the directory `C:\ieaktest`. Select at this point any other installation media you wish to use for deploying IE 4.0 on your intranet, such as CD or floppies. This completes stage 1, Gathering Information.

Stage 2: Specifying Active Setup Parameters Stage 2 of the IEAK Wizard is called *Specifying Active Setup Parameters* (Fig. 7-8). In stage 2 you will need to connect with a Microsoft download site and download the IE 4.0 components you will use to create your custom installation

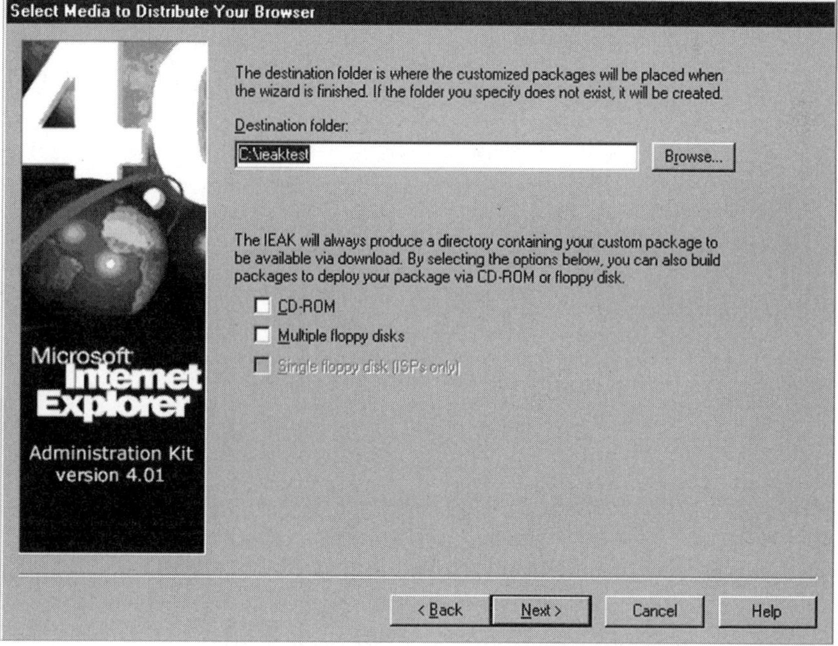

Figure 7-7
Choose a download destination directory and optional additional installation media.

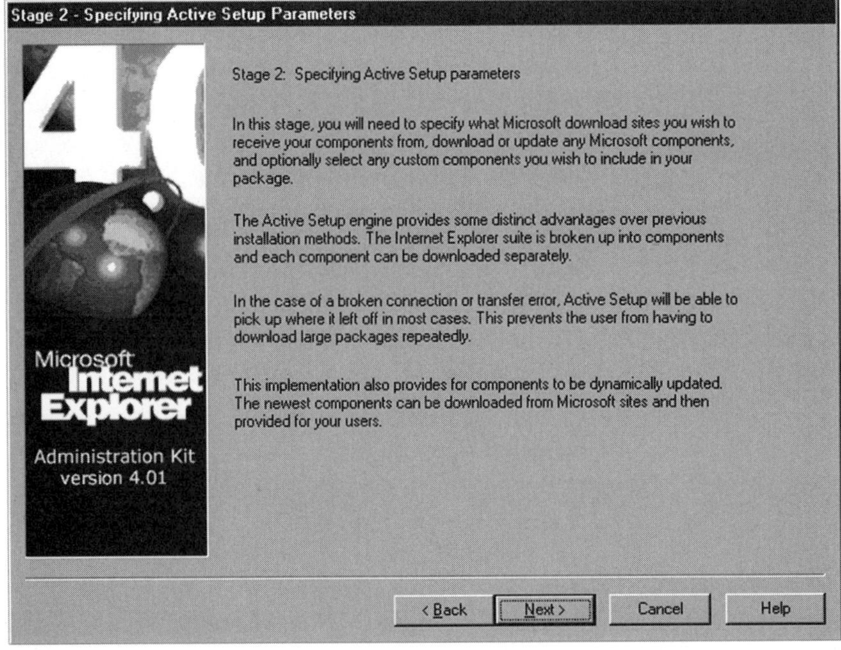

Stage 2 - Specifying Active Setup Parameters
Microsoft Internet Explorer
Administration Kit version 4.01
Stage 2: Specifying Active Setup parameters
In this stage, you will need to specify what Microsoft download sites you wish to receive your components from, download or update any Microsoft components, and optionally select any custom components you wish to include in your package.
The Active Setup engine provides some distinct advantages over previous installation methods. The Internet Explorer suite is broken up into components and each component can be downloaded separately.
In the case of a broken connection or transfer error, Active Setup will be able to pick up where it left off in most cases. This prevents the user from having to download large packages repeatedly.
This implementation also provides for components to be dynamically updated. The newest components can be downloaded from Microsoft sites and then provided for your users.
< Back
Next >
Cancel
Help

Figure 7-8 Stage 2 of the IEAK Wizard is called *Specifying Active Setup Parameters.*

packages, plus supply any additional third-party components that you want to bundle into your package.

First you will be asked to select a Microsoft download site from which to download the newest versions of Internet Explorer 4.0 and its optional components.

Next, select which components you wish to download from the Automatic Version Synchronization (AVS) screen (Fig. 7-9). This screen graphically shows you which components you have and don't have, and whether your components are up to date. The files that will be downloaded will be used to create the custom installation packages.

Select the components you wish to download and click on SYNCHRONIZE, or click on SYNCHRONIZE ALL to download all the components. Note: Only Internet Explorer 4.0 *must* be downloaded; all other components are optional.

Next you will be given the opportunity to select up to 10 custom or third-party components to incorporate into your installation packages. These components should be in the form of self-extracting `.exe` files or cabinet (`.cab`) files.

Next select the trusted publisher you will be using to sign your installation package. Any third-party custom components must be signed. This completes stage 2, Specifying Active Setup Parameters.

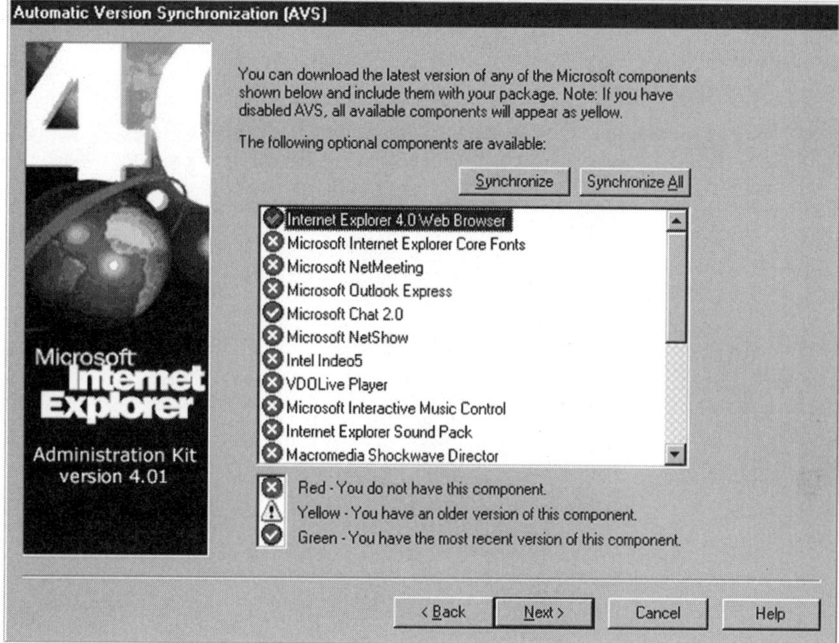

Figure 7-9 Select which components to download for creating custom IE 4.0 installation packages.

Stage 3: Customizing Active Setup In stage 3 of the IEAK Wizard you customize the Active Setup program that will be used to install your custom packages (Fig. 7-10). Customization includes title bar, bitmap, user download sites, and more.

Begin this stage by choosing whether you want to customize the title bar and bitmap of the Active Setup screen for your customized package. If you chose to create a CD installation package, you can also customize the CD Autorun screen.

Next decide whether you want to perform a *silent install* of your custom package. A silent install requires no input from the user whose machine IE 4.0 is being installed on, and the user will not even be aware that the installation is taking place (other than the increase in CPU and drive activity). Silent installations have the following limitations:

- You may specify only 1 (not 10) installation option for different types of installs.
- You may specify only 1 (not 10) download site for downloading your package.
- You must decide whether to include the Active Desktop upgrade or not.

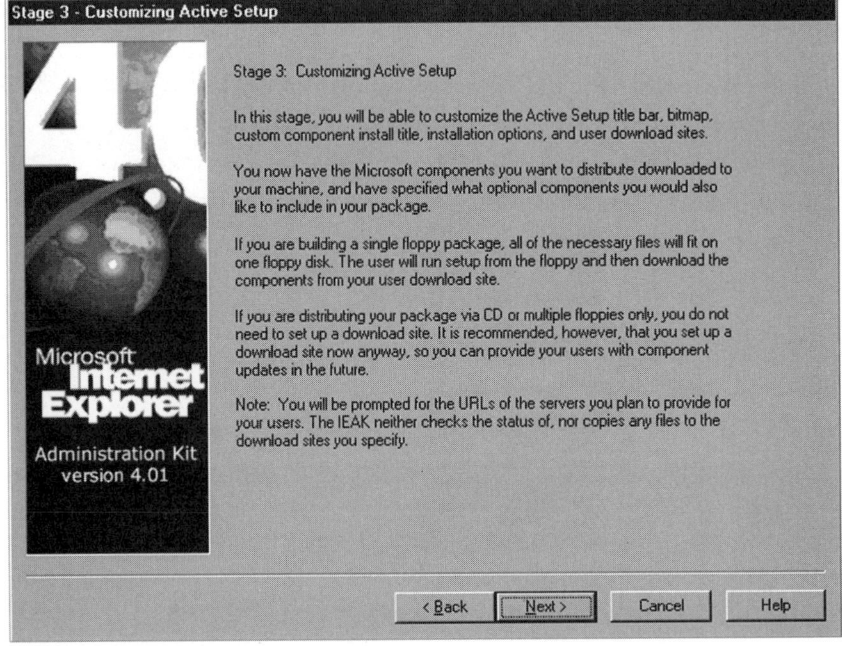

Figure 7-10 Stage 3 of the IEAK Wizard is called *Customizing Active Setup.*

In Fig. 7-11 we have selected to perform a silent install.

Next create an installation option or configure an existing option and select which components to install when this option is selected. Note that with silent install, you can only configure one installation option (Fig. 7-12).

Next specify the download sites from which your custom package will be installed (Fig. 7-13). For each download site you must specify

- The site name
- The site URL
- The site region

Note that the URL specified here is *not checked* by the IEAK Wizard. You may specify up to 10 download sites. If you are performing a silent install, however, you may only specify one download site.

Next you need to specify a unique version number for your custom packages, to ensure that later versions are updated properly. You can also specify the URL to which the Internet Explorer *Add a component* option points. *Add a component* is accessed from the Internet icon in Control Panel.

Figure 7-11
Choose whether or not to perform a silent install.

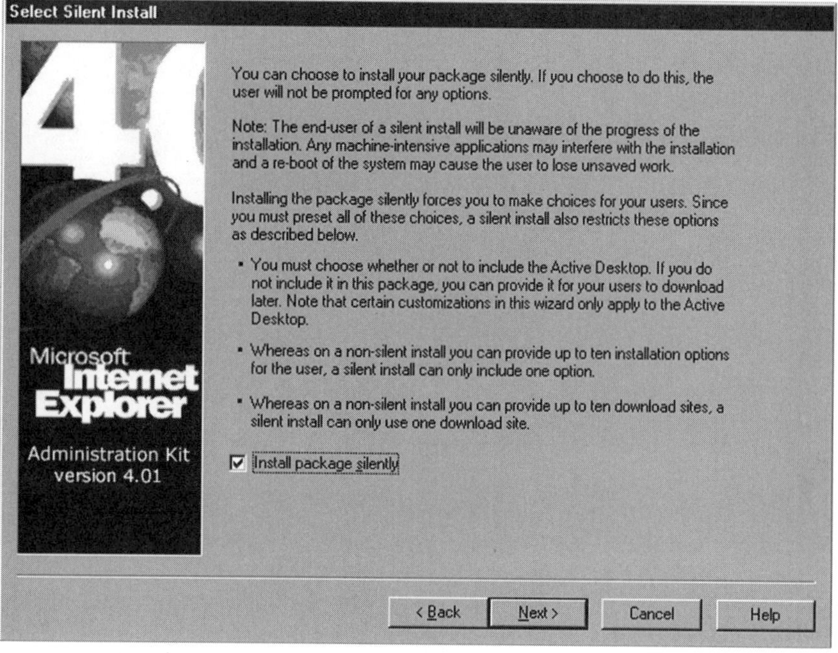

Figure 7-12
Create installation options.

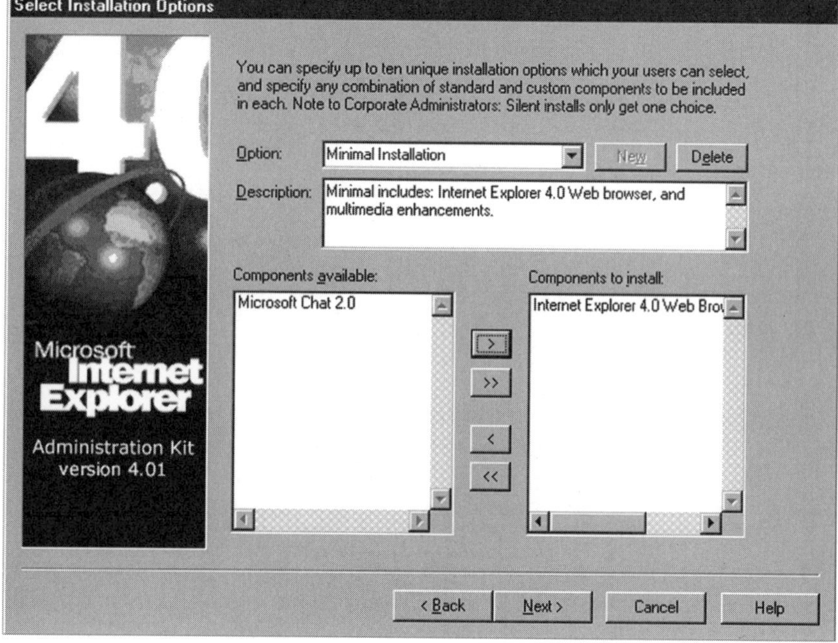

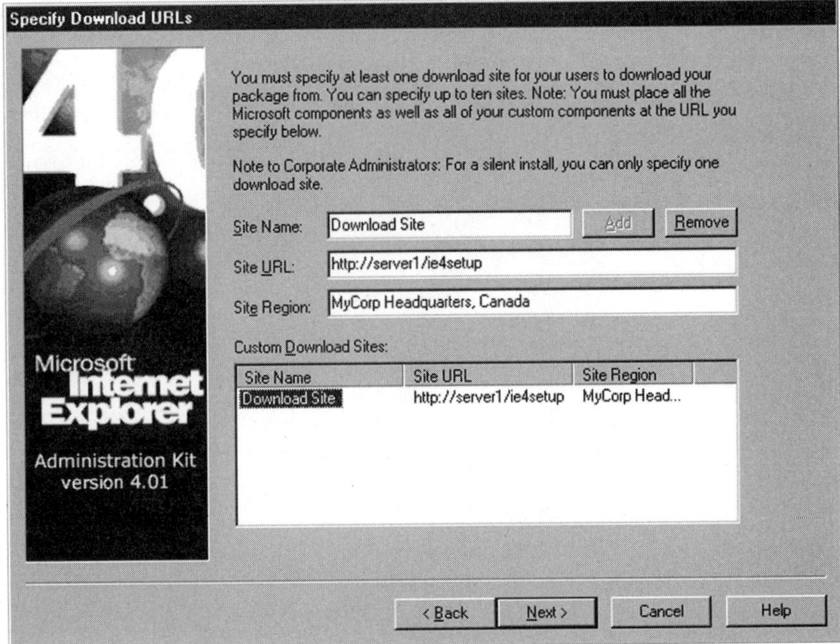

Figure 7-13 Specify download sites for performing custom installations.

Next specify the target directory on the client computers on which the Internet Explorer program will be installed. You can specify

- A subdirectory in the Windows directory
- A subdirectory in the Program Files directory
- The complete path for the destination directory

Next specify whether or not the Windows Desktop Update should be installed along with IE 4.0 (Fig. 7-14). You can also allow the user to make this choice (unless you are performing a silent install). This completes stage 3, Customizing Active Setup.

Stage 4: Customizing the Browser In stage 4 of the IEAK Wizard you will customize the IE 4.0 browser that will be installed on client machines (Fig. 7-15). Customization options include title bar, bitmap, start page, search page, favorites, security zones, and more.

Begin by choosing whether to customize the title bar and the toolbar background bitmap of Internet Explorer 4.0.

Next specify the following custom pages (Fig. 7-16):

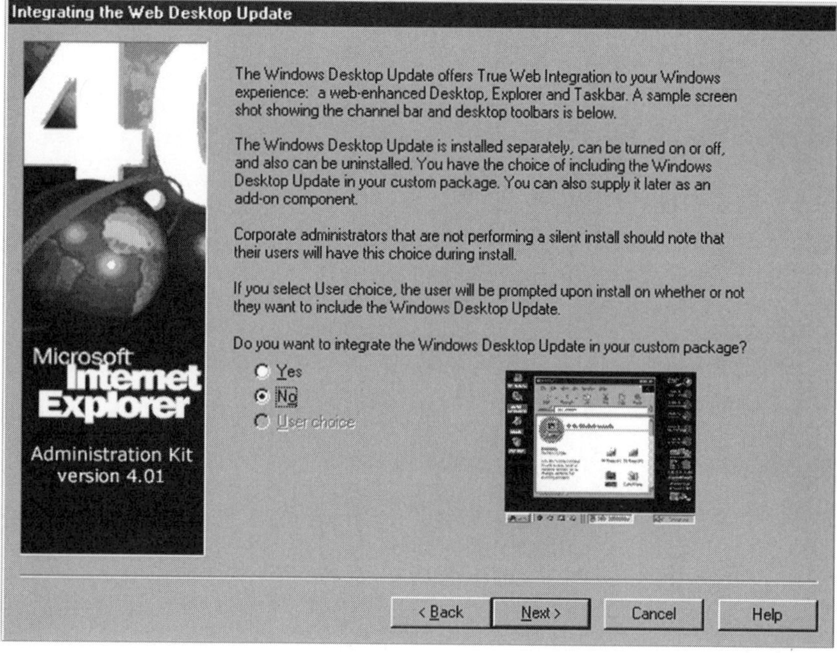

Figure 7-14 Specify whether or not to install the Windows Desktop Update.

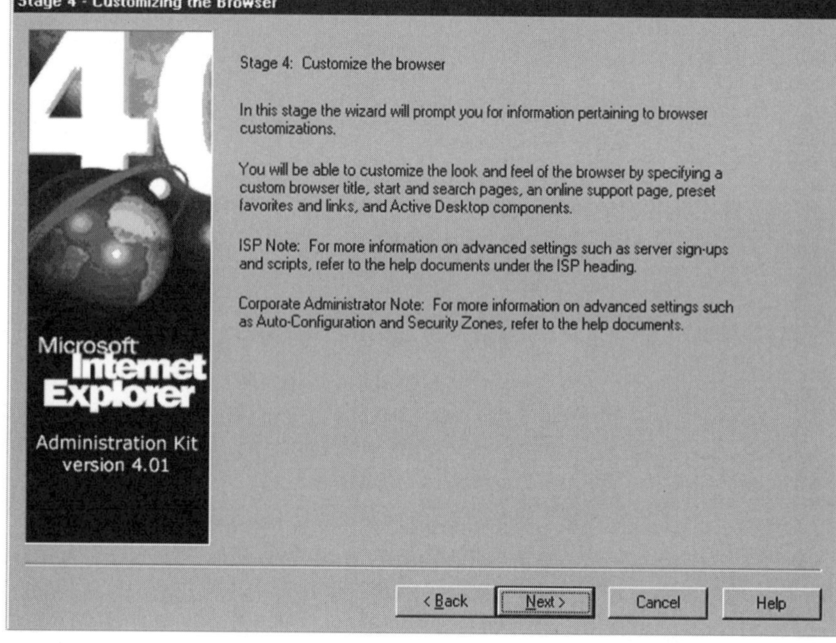

Figure 7-15 Stage 4 of the IEAK Wizard is called *Customizing the Browser.*

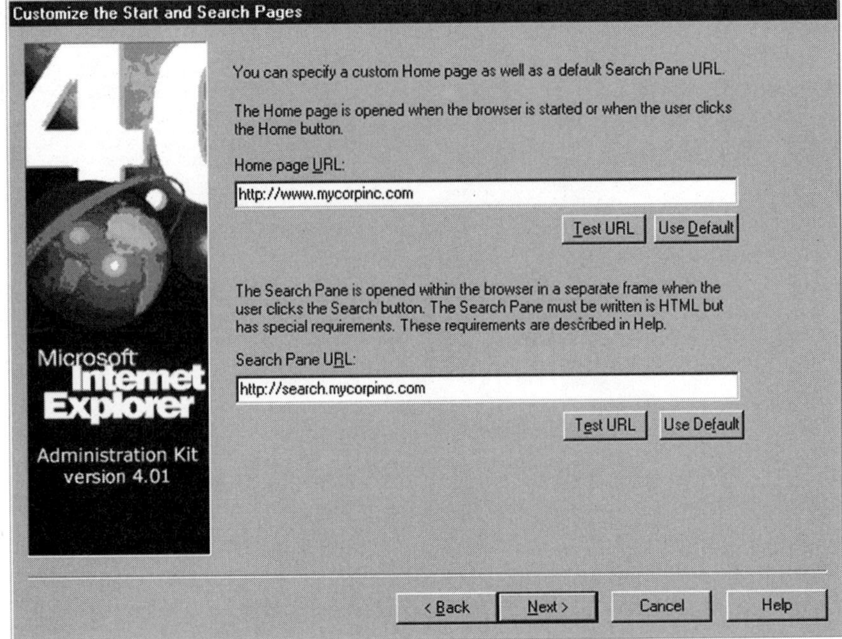

Figure 7-16 Select your custom start and search pages.

- Custom home page
- Custom search page

You can also click TEST URL to verify your choices above.

Next supply the URL of a support page where users can go to get online support for Internet Explorer 4.0 and optional components.

Next create a custom favorites list with URLs and folders to organize them (Fig. 7-17). Click ADD FOLDER to create a folder to organize your favorites, and click ADD URL to specify a favorite. You can also click IMPORT to load an existing favorites list into your installation package.

Next choose whether or not to display the Microsoft Internet Explorer welcome page the first time the browser is started (Fig. 7-18). You can also create a custom welcome page suitable for your corporate intranet.

The first two times a user logs on after Internet Explorer 4.0 is installed on the user's machine, the Internet Explorer welcome window will be displayed, asking whether the user wants to take a quick tour of IE 4.0 features, explore channels, or register their browser online. To disable this feature, check the checkbox on this screen.

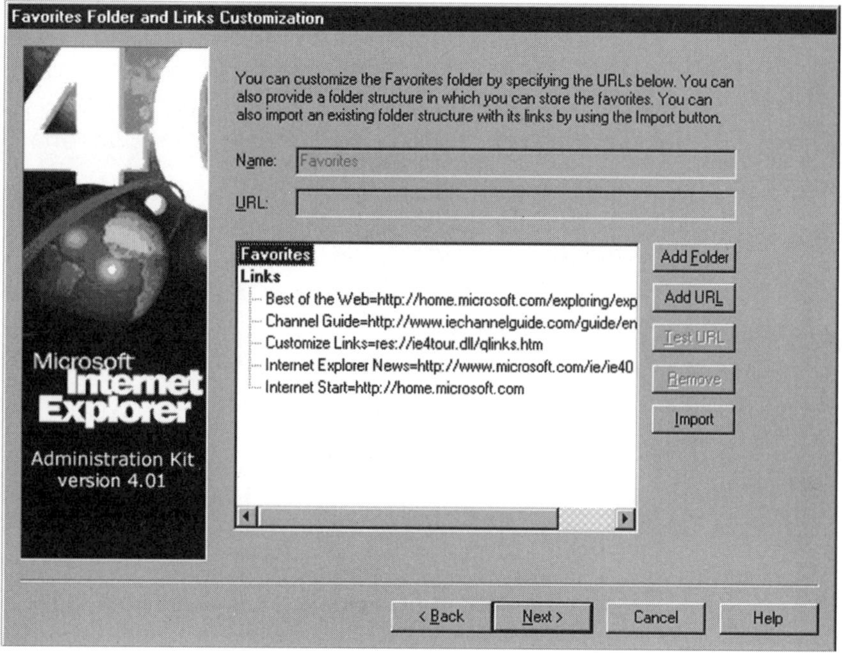

Figure 7-17
Create a custom favorites list.

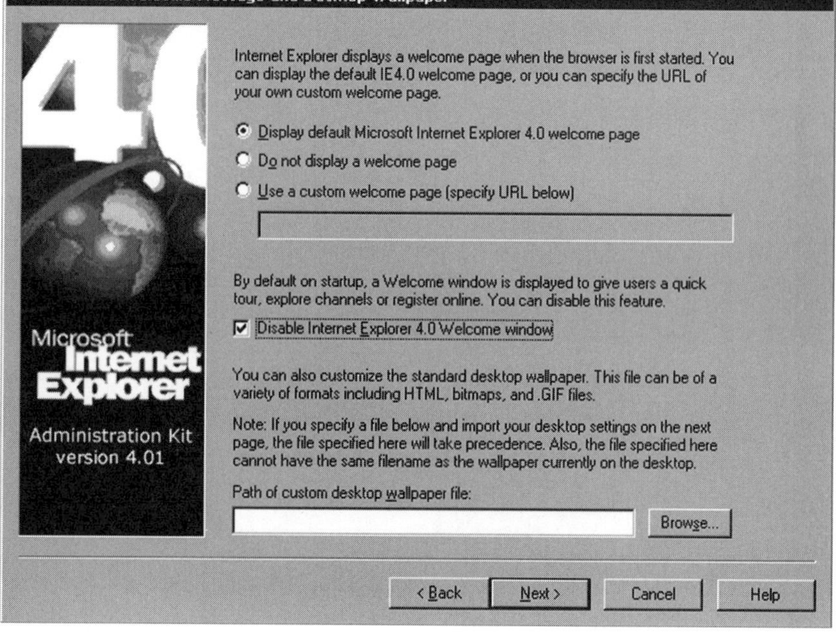

Figure 7-18
Select the welcome page and enable or disable the welcome window.

NOTE: *You probably want to disable the IE 4.0 welcome window, as it considerably slows down user logon the first two times the user logs on after IE 4.0 has been installed. Also, depending upon your firewall setup, some of the features offered by the IE 4.0 welcome window may be unavailable anyway.*

Next you can customize the Active Desktop items, if you decided to install the Windows Desktop Upgrade.

Next you can customize which channels should be shown in the channel bar.

Next you can select whether or not to use software distribution channels. Software distribution channels use channel technology (a.k.a. Webcasting) to enable automatic upgrading of IE 4.0 on users' machines.

Next you can specify a custom user-agent string to be appended to the default user-agent string that the browser sends to the Web server during an HTTP request.

Next supply a path to the directory that contains the `.ins` file that automatically configures your browser (Fig. 7-19). The `.ins` file can be modified and configured using the IEAK Profile Manager, and is discussed later in this section.

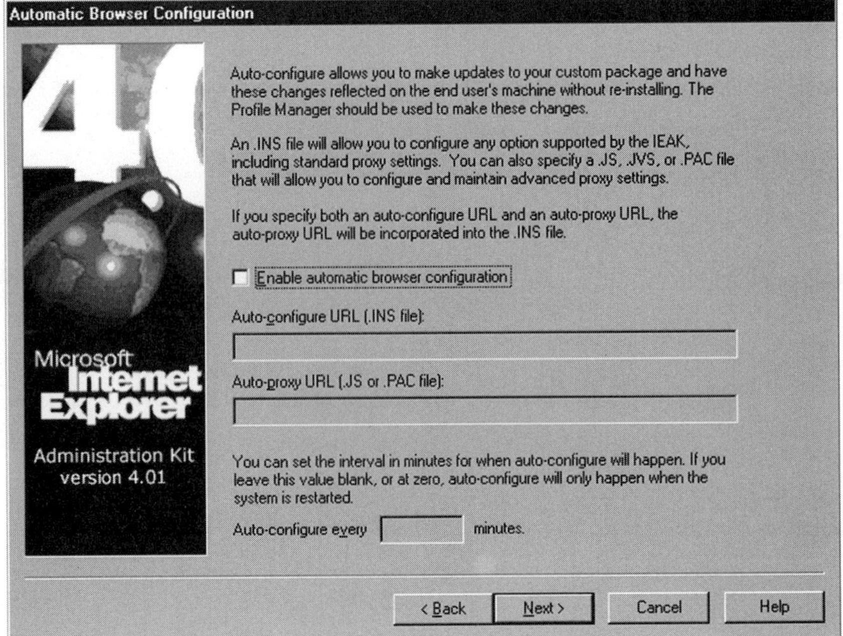

Figure 7-19 Enable automatic browser configuration using an `.ins` file

Next you can configure your proxy settings for each of the Internet protocols (HTTP, FTP, etc.) and select whether or not to use the proxy settings for the local intranet (the default is NO).

Next you can configure security for your IE 4.0 browser. Configuration options here include choosing to

- Import and modify Certificate Authorities (CAs) from the local machine
- Add a new root certificate
- Import and modify authenticode settings
- Customize security zone settings
- Customize content ratings settings

See Fig. 7-20 for an example of the last two options. This completes stage 4, Customizing the Browser.

Stage 5: Customizing Components In stage 5 of the IEAK Wizard you can customize available options for optional components and third-party components you have chosen to bundle with your installation package (Fig. 7-21). Administrators can also configure system policies and various settings for users' machines.

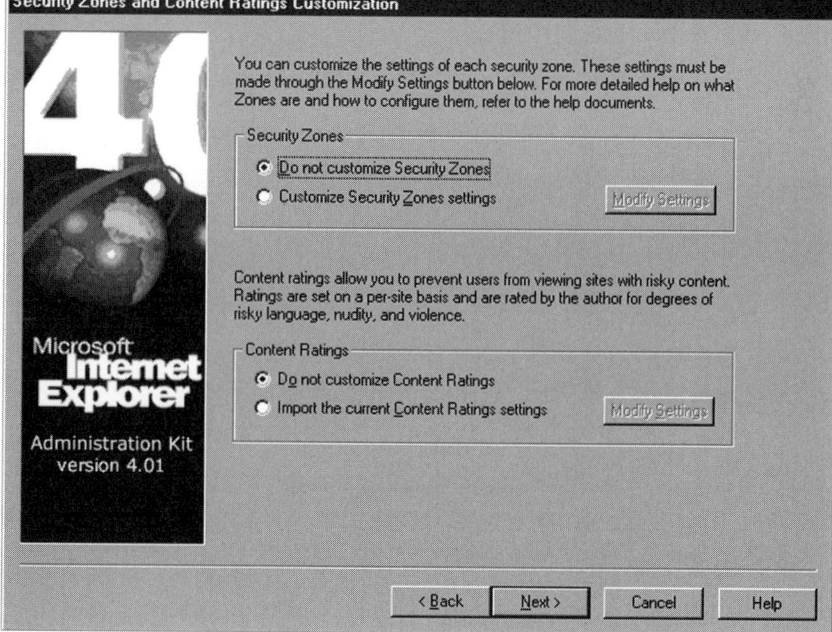

Figure 7-20 Security settings for security zones and content ratings.

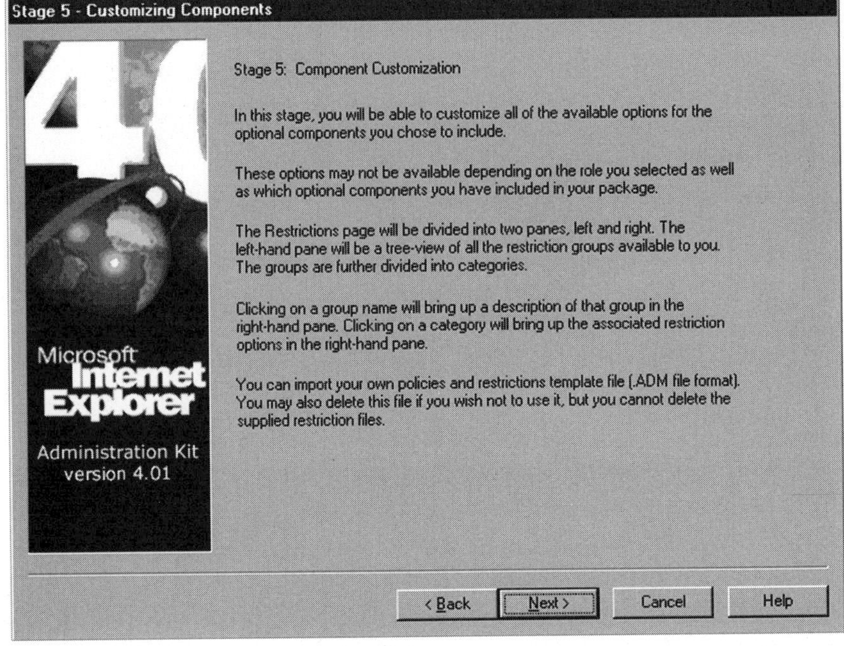

Figure 7-21 Stage 5 of the IEAK Wizard is called *Customizing Components.*

First the System Policies and Restrictions screen allows administrators to configure settings and apply system policies for various applications and categories (Fig. 7-22). These include

- Microsoft NetMeeting settings
- Web Desktop settings (includes system policies)
- Internet settings (e.g., LDAP settings)
- Outlook Express settings (e.g., which mail and news servers to use)
- Subscriptions
- Internet restrictions
- Microsoft Chat settings

Administrators can also import existing policy files at this point.

Finally, click FINISH to close the IEAK Wizard. The Internet Explorer Administration Kit Wizard now has all the information it requires to create your custom installation package.

The IEAK Wizard then completes the following tasks (Fig. 7-23):

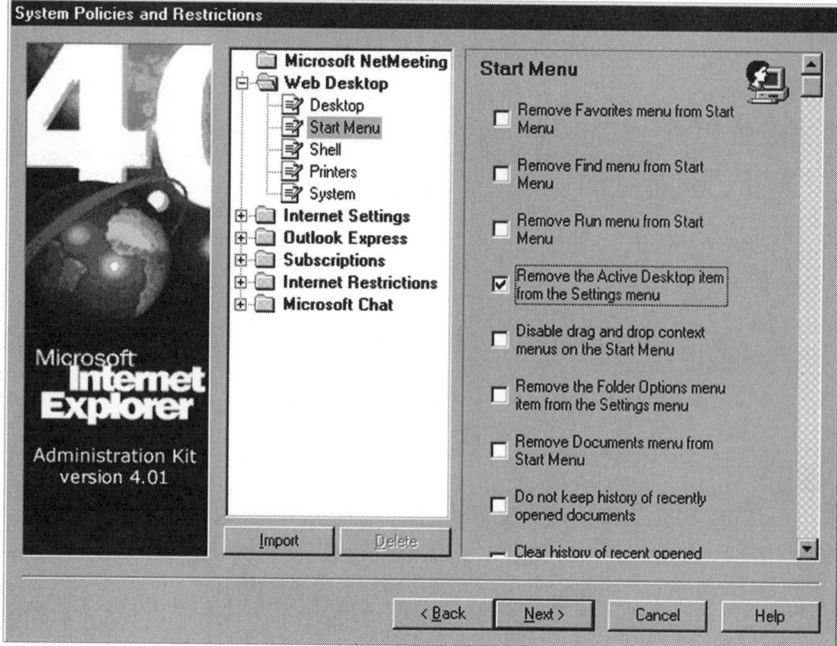

Figure 7-22 Customize settings and system policies.

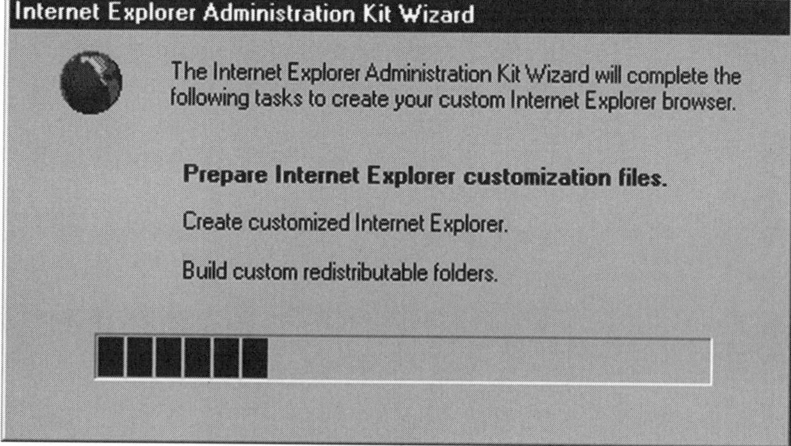

Figure 7-23 Completion of the IEAK Wizard.

- Preparing IE 4.0 customization files
- Creating the customized IE 4.0
- Building the custom redistributable folders

Finally, a message box will appear indicating that the package has been created and is located in the indicated path (Fig. 7-24).

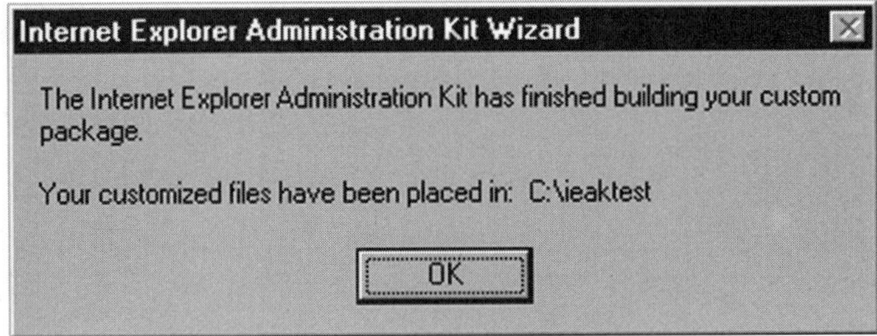

Figure 7-24 The IE 4.0 custom installation package has been successfully created.

Distributing IE 4.0 Using IEAK Packages

To distribute your custom package to your corporate intranet client machines, create a Web site or virtual directory providing information on the download process and containing a link to the Active Setup installation engine file, `IE4setup.exe`. For more information on distributing IEAK packages, refer to the IEAK online documentation.

Maintaining Your IE 4.0 Package Using the IEAK Profile Manager

The IEAK Profile Manager allows administrators to create, edit, and save `.ins` files, which contain the configuration settings for IEAK installation packages.

The default `.ins` file is called `Install.ins` and in our walkthrough is located by the path

```
C:\ieaktest\Install.ins
```

See Fig. 7-25 for the folder structure created in the package installation directory,

```
C:\ieaktest
```

To edit the `Install.ins` file, start the IEAK Profile Manager by clicking START, PROGRAMS, MICROSOFT IEAK, PROFILE MANAGER. The result is shown in Fig. 7-26. Now select FILE, OPEN and browse to open the `Install.ins` file for editing. In the left-hand pane select any item under

- *Wizard Settings* to modify settings selected during the running of the IEAK Wizard

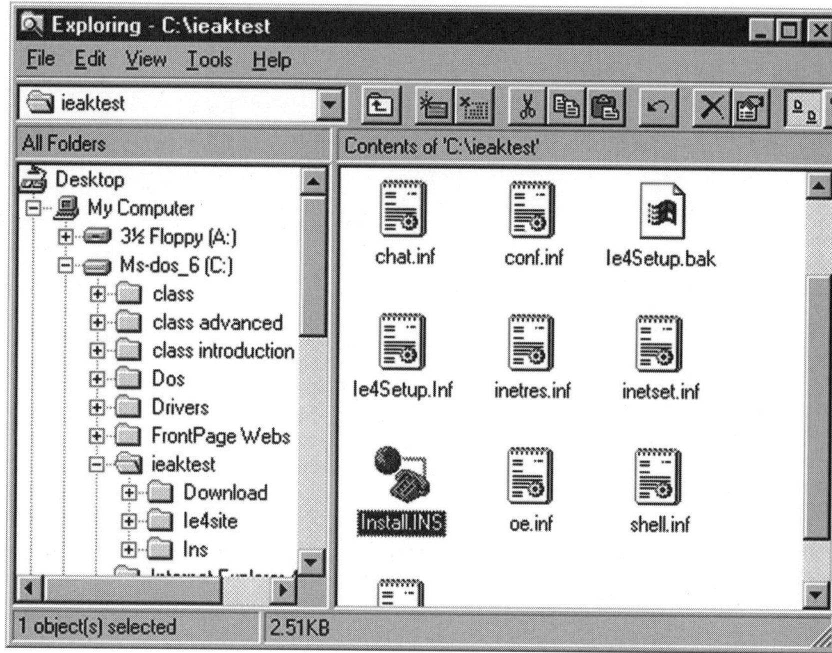

Figure 7-25 The `Install.ins` file.

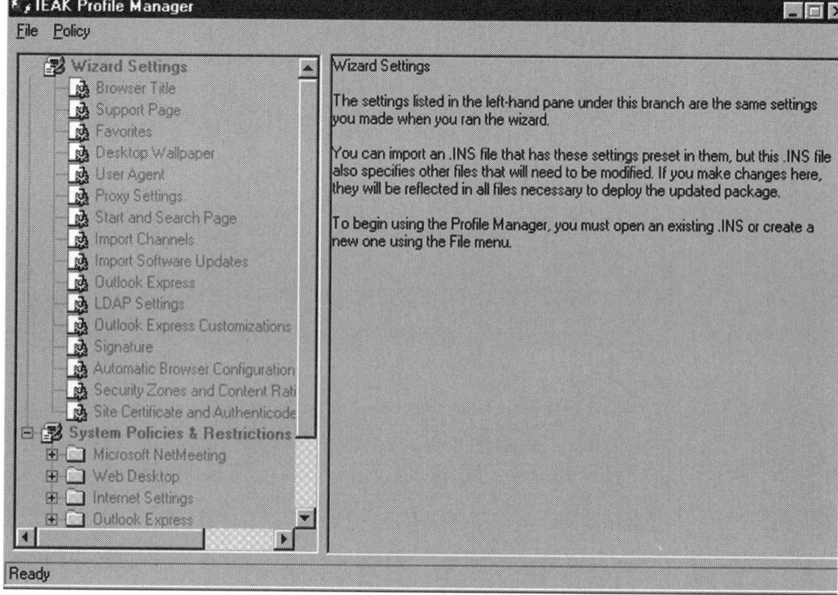

Figure 7-26 Starting the IEAK Profile Manager.

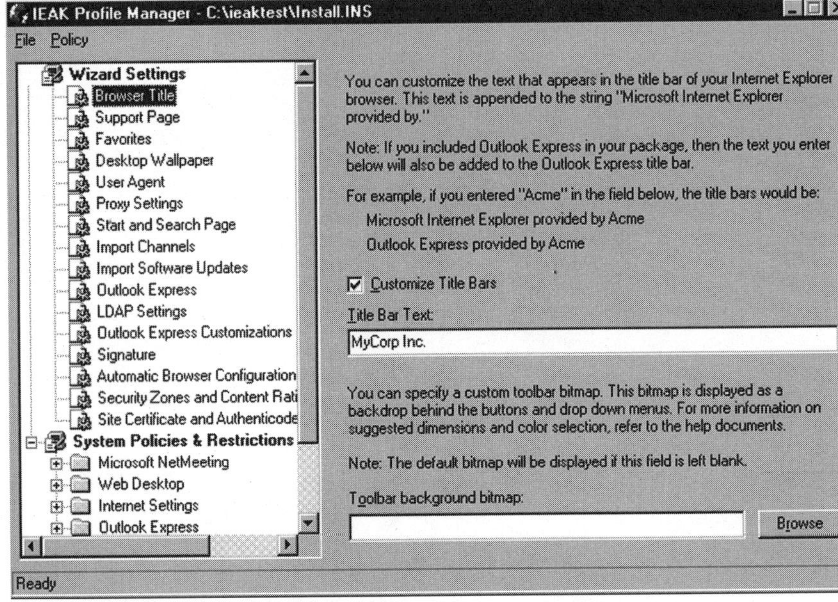

Figure 7-27 Modify settings for an IEAK installation package by editing the `Install.ins` file.

- *System Policies and Restrictions* to modify system policy settings and restrictions

In Fig. 7-27 the item Browser Title is selected under the Wizard Settings heading. In the right-hand pane you can now modify the title bar and bitmap, just as if you had rerun a screen from the IEAK Wizard.

When all desired settings have been modified, choose FILE, SAVE to save the changes to the `.ins` file.

SUMMARY

Microsoft Internet Explorer 4.0 is the ideal browser client to complement Internet Information Server 4.0 in both intranet and Internet environments. To enable corporate administrators and ISPs to manage and configure customized IE 4.0 packages for clients, Microsoft supplies the additional tool, the Microsoft Internet Explorer Administration Kit.

FOR MORE INFORMATION

Microsoft Web Site For the latest information on Internet Explorer 4.0, see the Microsoft Web site at

```
www.microsoft.com/ie
```

To register and download the Internet Explorer Administration Kit, visit the Web site

```
ieak.microsoft.com
```

Microsoft Public Newsgroups Microsoft Internet Explorer 4.0 issues are discussed in the newsgroups

```
microsoft.public.inetexplorer.ie4.*
```

Microsoft Internet Explorer Administration Kit is discussed in the newsgroup

```
microsoft.public.inetexplorer.ieak
```

Microsoft TechNet You can find the Internet Explorer Deployment Guide on TechNet in the location

```
Internet | Client | MS Internet Explorer | Technical Notes |
Deployment Guide
```

CHAPTER 8

Administering Indexing

Introduction

The ability to index a large corpus of documents is an important feature for any Internet or intranet server. Microsoft Internet Information Server 4.0 includes *Index Server 2.0,* a fully integrated indexing engine that can index HTML and legacy-format documents quickly and accurately. After completing this chapter, you will have a basic understanding of the capabilities, functions, and management of Index Server, including

- Basic capabilities of Index Server 2.0
- An understanding of the indexing process
- An understanding of the querying process
- Configuring indexing for various situations
- Managing indexing using the MMC
- Managing indexing using the Index Server Manager (HTML)
- Indexing a virtual server

What Can Index Server Do?

Microsoft Index Server 2.0 is integrated into Internet Information Server 4.0 and affords a means for Web server administrators to develop search tools for their sites. Index Server fully indexes both the content (text) and the properties of a variety of document formats, including

- HTML Web pages (`.htm` or `.html`)
- ASCII text files (`.txt`)
- Microsoft Word 95 and Word 97 documents (`.doc`)
- Microsoft Excel 95 and Excel 97 spreadsheets (`.xls`)
- Microsoft PowerPoint 95 and 97 presentations (`.ppt`)

In addition, Index Server is extensible and can be configured to index other file formats, such as WordPerfect documents or Adobe PDF documents. The administrator simply has to obtain and install third-party *content filters* for the file formats required.

Index Server can index documents on multiple Web sites (virtual servers), multiple physical Web servers, and even file servers running Novell NetWare or any other server that can be accessed by a Universal Naming Convention (UNC) path. Index Server *catalogs* can be restricted in scope to a single virtual directory or a single virtual server or span many virtual or physical directories and servers.

Because catalog information is stored as Unicode characters, Index Server is capable of indexing and querying content in multiple languages, including

- English (U.S.)
- English (International)
- Dutch
- French
- German
- Italian
- Japanese
- Spanish
- Swedish

Although Index Server is self-configuring and runs automatically in the background as a Windows NT service, using system resources when they are available, the administrator also has full control of the indexing process and can force a scan or a merge at any time to bring the index up to date. Index Server requires zero maintenance and is self-correcting when errors occur.

Index Server includes a proprietary scripting language for constructing query engines using `.htm`, `.idq`, and `.htx` files. In addition, Active Server Pages may be used to construct queries, but these are generally slower and less efficient.

Other advanced features of Index Server include hit highlighting, which is the ability to highlight word occurrences in queried documents, and the ability to index USENET news content.

Index Server is fully integrated with IIS 4.0 and supports all Windows NT 4.0 security features. For example, by placing indexed content on an NTFS volume, a client performing a search query will only see returned documents that the client is allowed to read by NTFS permissions; the query will return no information concerning documents the client does not have read permission on, and the client will not even know of the existence of such documents.

NOTE: *Although content to be indexed can be placed on any server, including Windows 95 machines or Novell NetWare servers, it is recommended that content to be indexed be placed on NTFS volumes on Windows NT 4.0 Servers. This*

enables Index Server to make use of Windows NT security features. Furthermore, the Windows NT file system automatically notifies Index Server when content is added, removed, or changed on the server, while Windows 95 or NetWare servers need to be regularly polled for changes.

How Does Index Server Work?

Indexing takes place automatically in the background when Index Server's *Content Index* service is running. As documents are added or changed in the *corpus,* the body of documents to be indexed, the Content Index service incrementally adds these documents to the catalog when system resources are available so that the overall performance of the IIS server will not degrade.

The following section explains the automatic indexing process in detail. Later sections will deal with how to manually administer the Content Index service.

Understanding the Indexing Process

The basic process by which indexing takes place can be broken down into a series of steps:

1. *Scanning:* inventorying virtual directories and servers for new documents to be indexed
2. *Filtering:* using content filters to create word lists from documents scanned
3. *Merging:* combining word lists and previous indexes to create more up-to-date indexes

Scanning takes place in two ways:

- *Full scan.* All documents in a directory are indexed.
- *Incremental scan.* Only documents that were modified are indexed.

Scanning takes place whenever

- A new virtual directory or server is added that needs to be indexed. This triggers a full scan of the newly added directory or server.

- The system is booted and the Content Index service initializes. This triggers an incremental scan of all previously indexed directories to determine if any documents have been added, deleted, or changed and so need to be re-indexed.
- The Windows NT 4.0 file system determines that a document has been added, removed, or changed in a directory that is configured to be indexed. The change notification is sent by the Windows NT file system to Index Server, and an incremental scan of the directory takes place.
- A Windows 95 or Novell NetWare server is polled for changes to documents in an indexed directory. If changes are found, an incremental scan takes place.
- A full scan is forced by the administrator using the Index Server Manager snap-in of the Microsoft Management Console or the Index Service Manager (HTML).

When a scan takes place and a new or changed document is found, its content must be added to the index. Figure 8-1 outlines the content filtering process in detail. Documents in the corpus that have been scanned and require indexing are first sent to a *content filter,* whose main function is to extract text from the document. Content filters are associated with different document formats; for example, there will be one content filter for Microsoft Word, another content filter for Excel, and so on. The content filter mechanism is extensible so that third-party filters may be added to Index Server to enable it to index other document formats.

Figure 8-1
Outline of the filtering process.

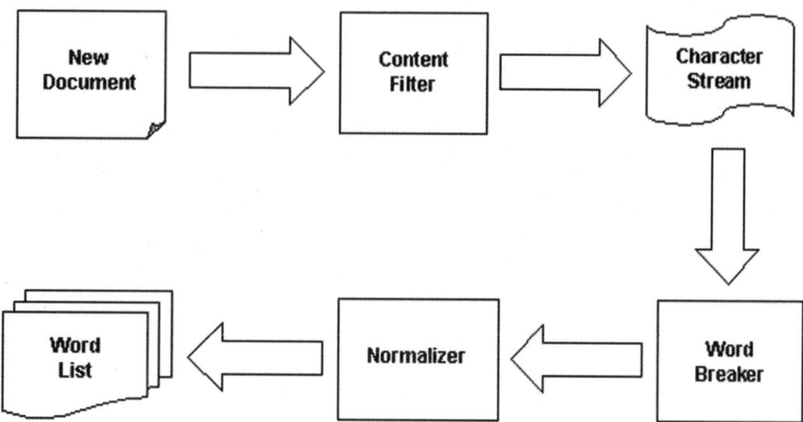

Content filters are also responsible for recognizing when embedded objects occur in documents and activating the appropriate content filter to handle these objects. Finally, content filters handle language shifts in documents, for example from French to English and back again.

The stream of text characters produced by the content filter is then sent to a *word breaker,* a language-specific tool for recognizing words within the character stream. The words that are emitted from the word breaker are next sent to a *normalizer,* which performs a number of tasks including:

- Removing noise words (*and, the, to,* etc.)
- Handling capitalization
- Removing punctuation

The final result produced by the normalizer in the content filtering process is a *word list,* which is a temporary index of the document that remains stored in the server's RAM in an uncompressed state. Word lists are the end result of the scanning and content filtering process and are the simplest kind of index produced by Index Server. They act as a kind of temporary staging ground for the creation of *persistent indexes,* which are compressed multiple-document indexes stored on disk.

The final stage of indexing is the combining together, or *merging,* of word lists and persistent indexes to create a single master index. This merging process takes place in two stages, which are outlined in Figs. 8-2 and 8-3.

Shadow indexes are persistent indexes (indexes stored on disk) that are formed by merging volatile word lists and other shadow indexes. This

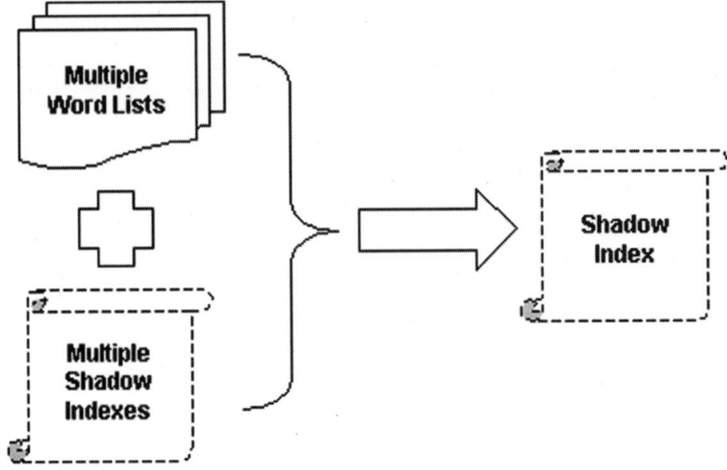

Figure 8-2 Word lists and shadow indexes are combined into a new shadow index by a shadow merge.

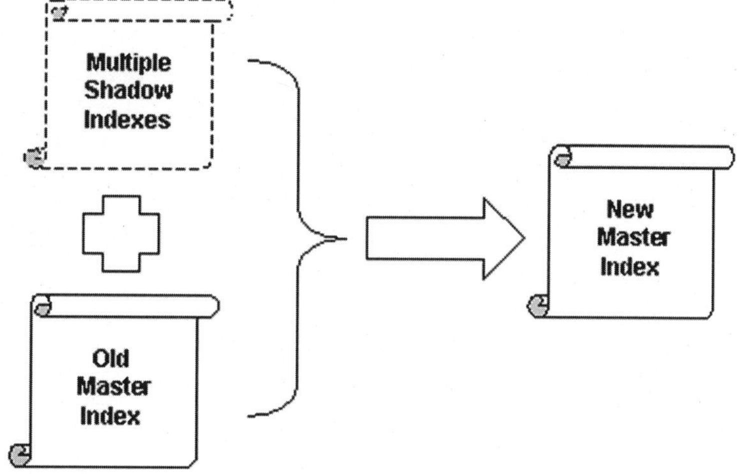

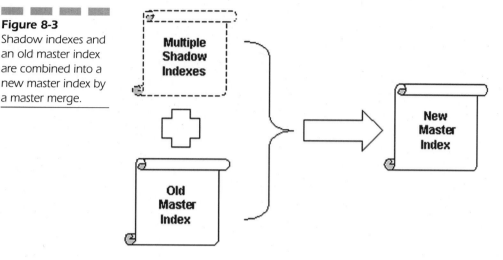

Figure 8-3
Shadow indexes and an old master index are combined into a new master index by a master merge.

process is called a *shadow merge,* and it frees up server memory and speeds up the resolution of queries. The merging process allows redundant data to be eliminated from the catalog, which increases the efficiency of the query process. There can be, and usually are, multiple shadow indexes in the catalog at any given time. Shadow indexes are also distinguished from word lists by the fact that the index data is stored in a compressed format. Shadow merges happen when certain conditions occur; these conditions are specified by settings in the registry, but they can also be forced from the Index Server Manager.

If the system is relatively idle and resources are available, an *annealing merge* occurs. An annealing merge is a kind of shadow merge, and it results in fewer shadow indexes, thus freeing up disk space and speeding up queries.

The *master index* is the end product of the content indexing process. There is only one master index per catalog, and this master index is kept up-to-date by merging it with shadow indexes to create a new master index by a process known as a *master merge,* a process that is very resource-intensive on the server. The master index is a persistent index whose data is stored in a highly compressed format. When indexing is complete for a corpus, there are no word lists or shadow indexes, only a master index, making the querying process even more efficient. Master merges are triggered by conditions specified by settings in the registry, but they can also be forced from the Index Server Manager.

The *catalog* is the top-level organizational structure in Index Server, and contains the index, configuration information identifying the directories and shares being indexed, and other property information. Each catalog is a distinct, separate entity; queries may not cross multiple catalogs but are instead restricted to a single catalog. When a Typical installation of IIS 4.0 is performed, a single *default catalog* is created for the server and the following virtual directories and virtual servers are indexed (assuming that IIS 4.0 is installed on C: drive):

Default Web site	`C:inetpub\wwwroot\`
IIS samples virtual directory	`C:\inetpub\iissamples\`
IIS administration Web site	`C:\winnt\system32\inetsrv\iisadmin\`
IIS documentation	`C:\winnt\help\`
ActiveX data objects directory	`C:\program files\common files\system\ado\`
Remote data service directory	`C:\program files\common files\system\msdac\`
SMTP mail directory	`C:\inetpub\mail\`

The default catalog is stored in the following path:

```
C:\inetpub\catalog.wci\
```

The `Catalog.wci` directory is never indexed by Index Server, even if it is mapped to a virtual directory.

Additional catalogs can be created, and these can be assigned to documents stored in virtual directories, virtual servers, and even multiple physical servers. Catalogs that are created must be contained in locations whose ACLs allow administrators and system to have full control. A walkthrough of this is given later in this chapter.

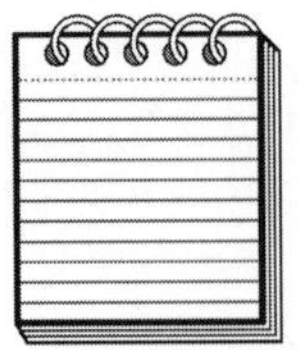

NOTE: *Since queries cannot span multiple catalogs, creating new catalogs means that you will no longer be able to globally search your entire corpus of documents. This may or may not be desirable, depending on the function of your site.*

Understanding the Query Process

Performing a query on an Index Server catalog requires three types of files:

- An HTML *query form,* which the user completes and submits (`.htm` file)

- An *Internet data query file*, which defines the basic parameters for the query, including its scope and restrictions (`.idq` file)
- An *HTML extension file*, which formats the result of the query and is used to generate an HTML response page (`.htx` file).

The `.idq` and `.htx` files must be in a virtual directory with read and script (or read and execute) permissions assigned.

The basic process of issuing a query and receiving a response from Index Server can also be broken down into a series of steps (see Fig. 8-4):

1. The user submitting the query completes and submits the query form (here called `Query.htm`).
2. The submitted query and the `.idq` file (here called `Query.idq`) are passed by IIS to Index Server, where they are processed against the catalog files.
3. Index Server then returns the raw results of the query and formats them using the `.htx` file (here called `Query.htx`).
4. The formatted results are returned to the user as a static HTML page (here called `Result.htm`).

Figure 8-4
The `.idq/.htx` query process.

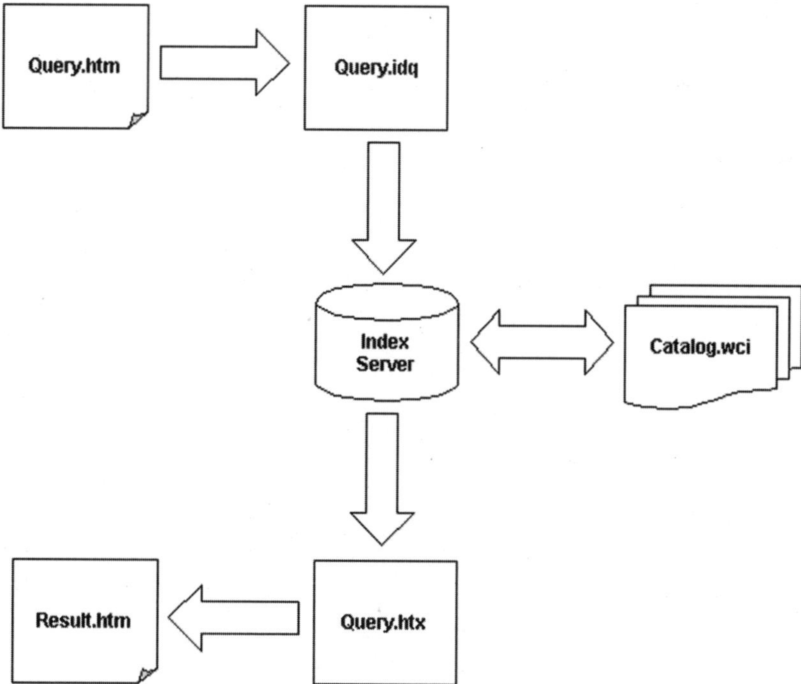

To understand the .idq/.htx query process better, let's work through a simple example. First, here is the .htm file for a simple form that requests that the user enter keywords into the query textbox and press "Submit" to execute the query:

```
<HTML>
<HEAD><TITLE>Simple Query Form</TITLE></HEAD>
<BODY>
<FORM ACTION = "query.idq" METHOD = "GET">
<p>Search for the following:
<INPUT TYPE = "text" NAME = "CiRestriction">
<INPUT TYPE = "submit" VALUE = "Search now!">
<INPUT TYPE = "reset" VALUE = "Erase and start again!">
</FORM>
</BODY>
</HTML>
```

Notice in the above HTML form that

- The file Query.idq takes the place of a regular form handler.
- The form sends its data using the GET method, which appends the query data to the URL of the handler and passes this as a text string to the server.
- The query words typed into the text box are assigned to the variable CiRestriction.

Next assume that the Internet query data (.idq) file has the following structure:

```
[Query]
CiCatalog = c:\iscatalogs
CiRestriction = %CiRestriction%
CiMaxRecordsInResultSet = 50
CiMaxRecordsPerPage = 10
CiScope = /
CiFlags = DEEP
CiTemplate = /Query.htx
```

The above Query.idq file can be explained as follows:

- The catalog to be searched is contained in the directory C:\iscatalogs.
- The query words searched for are contained in the variable %CiRestriction% that is passed from the query form.
- The maximum number of results returned is 50.
- The number of results returned per page is 10.
- The scope of the query begins at the root (/) of the corpus and includes all subdirectories (DEEP).

- The results generated by the query will be formatted by the file `Query.htx`.

Finally, assume that when Index Server processes the query, the results it returns are processed with the following `.htx` file:

```
<HTML>
<HEAD><TITLE>Results of Simple Query</TITLE></HEAD>
<BODY>
<%if CiMatchedRecordCount eq 0%>
No documents for the query "<%CiRestriction%>".
<%else%>
Documents<%CiFirstRecordNumber%>to<%CiLastRecordNumber%>of
   <%if CiMatchedRecordCount eq CiMaxRecordsInResultSet%>
   the first
   <%endif%>
<%CiMatchedRecordCount%>
matching the query"<%CiRestriction%>".
<%endif%>
</BODY>
</HTML>
```

The way the `query.htx` file works is that if the query returns a total of 25 documents, then the following results page will be presented to the user:

```
Documents 1 to 10 of 25 matching the query.
```

For more information on the syntax for creating `.idq` and `.htx` files, refer to the IIS 4.0 online documentation for Index Server. A sample query based on the `.idq/.htx` mechanism that queries the corpus indexed in the default catalog can be accessed by clicking START, PROGRAMS, WINDOWS NT 4.0 OPTION PACK, INDEX SERVER, INDEX SERVER SAMPLE QUERY FORM. The design of this sample query is discussed in detail in the online documentation for Index Server.

NOTE: *You can also create Index Server query forms using Active Server Pages (ASPs), but `.idq/.htx` queries are generally faster and more efficient in use of server resources than ASP queries. See the online documentation for more details.*

Index Server's Automatic Error Correction Features

When an error occurs in the indexing process, Index Server 4.0 is often able to correct the error without any user intervention. Examples include the following:

- *Disconnected paths.* If Index Server is indexing content on a remote network share and that share becomes disconnected, Index Server will repeatedly poll the remote share until the connection returns and the catalog can be updated.
- *Buffer overflows.* If content is stored on a local NTFS volume, the file system normally notifies Index Server when files are modified and need to be re-indexed. If the rate of file change is high, the number of file modification messages will be high and the notification buffer can overflow, resulting in lost messages. Index Server detects this condition and does an incremental scan to correct it.
- *Disk full.* If the volume where the catalog is located is nearly full, indexing stops and an event log message is written to the application log. The administrator should then stop Index Server, correct the problem by extending the volume or moving the catalog to a different volume, and then restart Index Server (the steps for moving the catalog to another volume are outlined in the online documentation).
- *Data corruption.* If catalog data becomes corrupt, Index Server writes an event log message to the application log and automatically performs a recovery, refiltering the entire corpus if necessary. If refiltering is required, no queries are allowed and the administrator should stop and then restart the Content Index service so that the recovery may be initiated.

NOTE: *Many of the events written to the application log by the Content Index (Ci) service are informational only. Administrators should monitor these logs regularly for warnings and stop events.*

Configuring Index Server

Index Server and the indexing process can be managed several ways:

- By using the Index Server Manager snap-in for the Microsoft Management Console
- By using the Index Server Manager (HTML) on the Start menu for remote administration through a browser (for the default catalog only)

- By creating a set of custom `.ida/.htx` files for remote administration through a browser (for user-created catalogs)
- By configuring certain registry settings to manage the automatic scanning and merging processes

Before we implement Index Server, however, certain planning issues should be addressed.

Planning Indexing

The following issues and system requirements should be considered before implementing Index Server (and since Index Server is automatically installed during a Typical install of IIS 4.0, these issues should be addressed before installing IIS 4.0 as well):

- Index Server program files can occupy 3 to 12 MB, depending on language modules installed.
- Recommended RAM depends on the size of the corpus to be indexed. Microsoft's recommendations are as follows:

Number of Documents	RAM Required, MB
Less than 100,000	32
100,000–250,000	64
250,000–500,000	96
More than 500,000	128

- The above RAM values are estimates only. Actual requirements will depend on the rate of queries and the rate of modification of files in the corpus. Monitor the performance of Index Server to determine if more RAM will be required.
- The total size of the corpus to be indexed should be estimated beforehand. Approximately 40 percent of this value will be the disk space required by the `Catalog.wci` files for this corpus, so select a drive for the catalog that will have sufficient free space.

  For example, if the corpus of documents to be indexed occupies 500 MB of space on the hard drive, you will need an *additional* 40% × 500 MB = 200 MB of free space on the hard drive for the Index Server catalog and its associated files.

- The preferred location for your corpus and for the catalog is an NTFS volume on a Windows NT 4.0 Server to take advantage of the security and file change notification features of NTFS volumes.

Administering Index Server Using the MMC

As mentioned earlier, when IIS 4.0 is installed in a Typical install, Index Server 2.0 is also installed, and the default Web site is indexed immediately, creating a default catalog `Catalog.wci` located in:

```
C:\inetpub\
```

To administer the default catalog on Index Server, select START, PROGRAMS, WINDOWS NT 4.0 OPTION PACK, MICROSOFT INDEX SERVER to open the Microsoft Management Console with the Index Server Manager snap-in installed (Fig. 8-5).

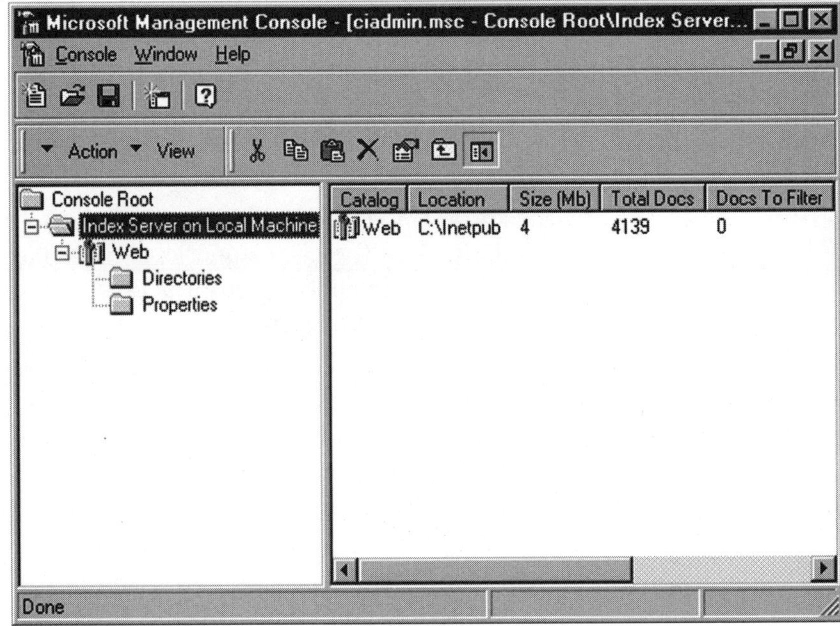

Figure 8-5 Managing Index Server using the MMC.

Checking the Indexing Status

To check the indexing status of each catalog, select the Index Server icon in the scope pane (on the left) and a list of catalogs will appear in the result pane (on the right). In the case of Fig. 8-5, the only catalog is the default catalog, which has been given the friendly name Web.

The columns that appear in the results frame when the Index Server icon is selected in the scope pane are as follows:

- *Catalog:* friendly name for catalog
- *Location:* physical location of `catalog.wci` directory
- *Size:* disk space occupied by persistent indexes
- *Total docs:* size of corpus indexed so far
- *Docs to filter:* amount of corpus that remains to be indexed
- *Wordlists:* number of wordlists currently in RAM
- *Persistent indexes:* number of persistent indexes on the hard drive
- *Status:* status of content indexing process

When *persistent indexes* equals 1 while *Docs to filter* and *Wordlists* equal 0, the corpus is fully indexed and fully optimized for queries.

The status field may take on the following values:

- Shadow merge
- Master merge
- Annealing merge
- Scan required
- Scanning
- Recovering

The only status message that requires the action of the administrator is "Scan required." When you see this message, you should force a scan (how to do this is explained later).

Configuring Index Server Global Properties

To configure global properties for Index Server, right-click on the Index Server icon in the scope pane and select PROPERTIES from the shortcut menu. The <catalog_name> Properties sheet appears, with three tabs (Figs. 8-6 through 8-8).

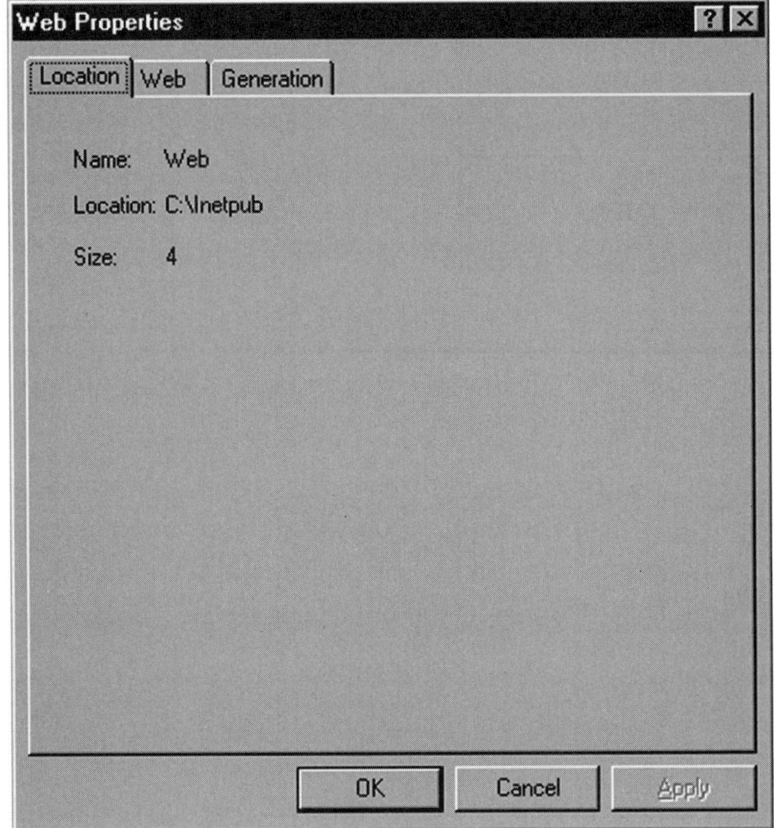

Figure 8-6 The Location tab on the property sheet for the Index Server catalog called Web.

The Location tab (Fig. 8-6) displays

- The friendly name of the catalog (the default catalog is called Web)
- The physical location of the catalog directory
- The current size of the master index in megabytes

The <catalog_name> tab, here called the Web tab (Fig. 8-7), allows you to

- Select whether to allow indexing of virtual directories for the selected catalog
- Select which virtual server (Web site) to associate with your selected catalog
- Select which news server to associate with your selected catalog

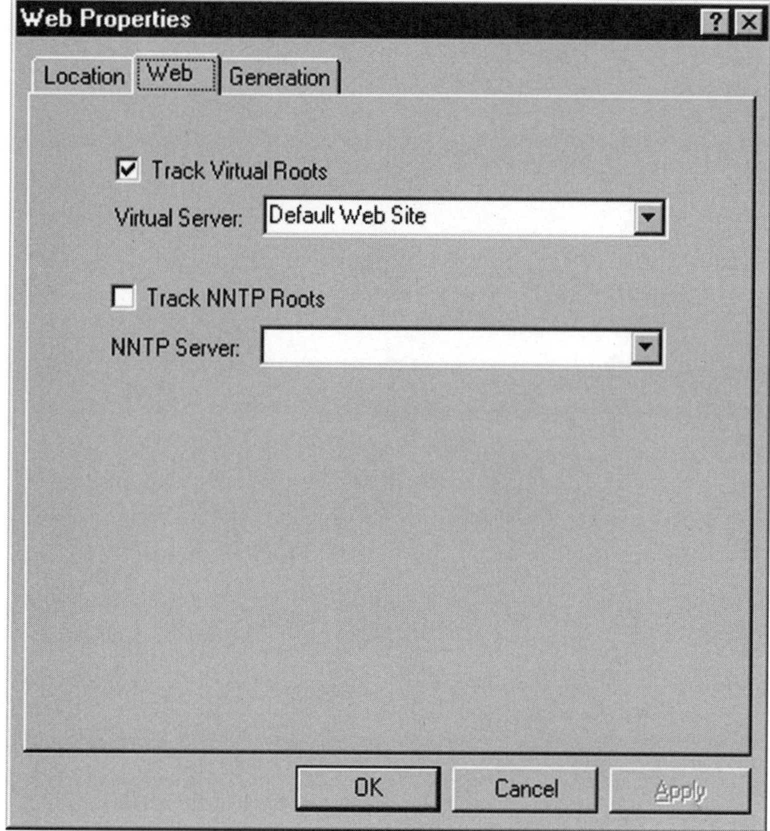

Figure 8-7 The <catalog_name> tab on the property sheet for the Index Server catalog called Web.

The Generation tab (Fig. 8-8) allows you to

- Choose whether files having unregistered file extensions will still be filtered (default is yes)
- Choose whether to have summaries (characterizations) displayed when a query is executed (default is yes)
- Determine the maximum size in bytes of the summaries displayed when a query is executed (default is 320 bytes)

Determining the Directories Currently Being Indexed

To determine which physical directories are currently being indexed, expand the selected catalog node in the scope pane to show the Direc-

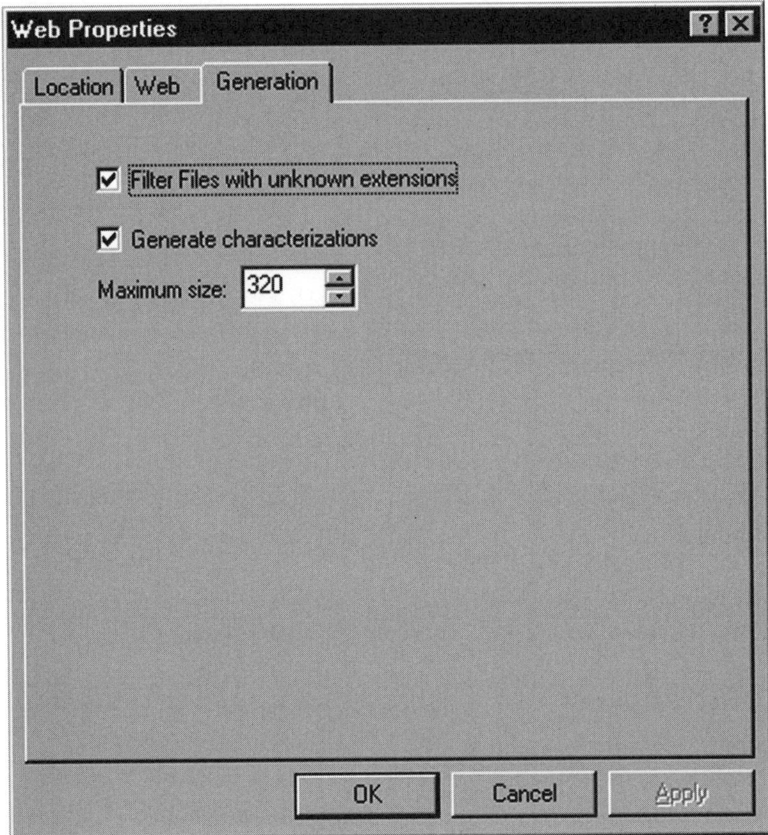

Figure 8-8
The Generation tab on the property sheet for the Index Server catalog called Web.

tories and Properties folder icons beneath it. Click on the Directories folder icon to select it, and view the virtual directories being indexed in this catalog in the results pane (the physical directories mapped to the virtual directories in the site are actually displayed here; see Fig. 8-9).

The columns displayed for each virtual directory being indexed include

- *Root,* which shows the physical path for each root being indexed
- *Alias,* a path that the user adds that is returned when a client submits a query from a remote computer (default is Not Applicable)
- *Exclude,* in which a "Yes" means the directory has been excluded from the scope and is not indexed

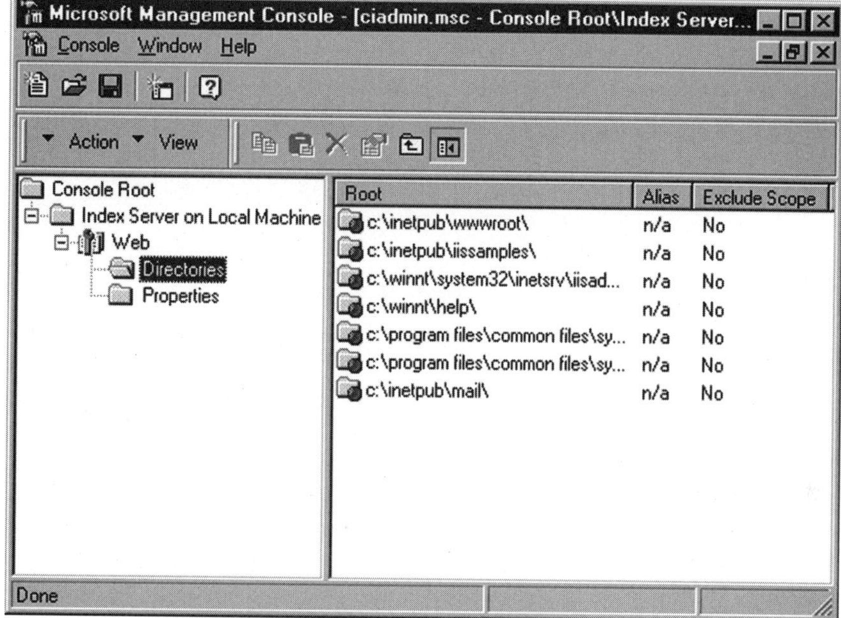

Figure 8-9 A list of virtual directories being indexed for the catalog called Web, shown by their physical paths.

Determining the Properties Cached by a Catalog

To determine the properties cached by a catalog, click on the *Properties* folder icon beneath the icon for the selected catalog in the scope pane, and view the cached properties for the selected catalog in the results pane (Fig. 8-10).

Index Server indexes not only the text of documents but also their properties. Listed in the results pane are the various properties that can be indexed, some of which are described by friendly names. If a selected property has no entry in the Data Type and Cached Size columns, no instances of that property are currently cached. Information on individual properties can also be accessed by right-clicking on a selected property and choosing PROPERTIES from the shortcut menu, which opens the Property sheet for the selected property (Fig. 8-11).

For more information on properties that can be cached, refer to the Index Server online documentation.

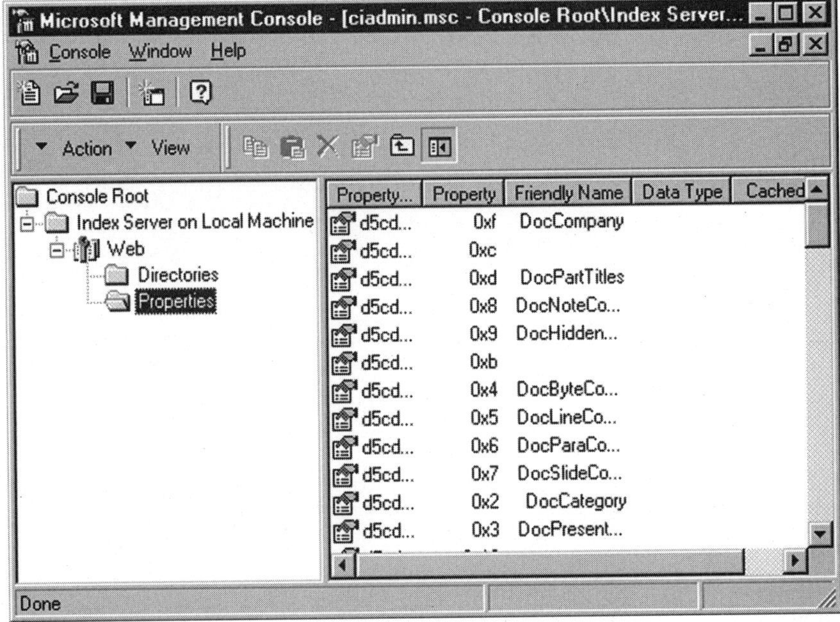

Figure 8-10 Viewing cached properties for a selected catalog.

Forcing a Scan on a Virtual Directory

To force a scan on a virtual directory, expand the selected catalog node in the scope pane to show the Directories and Properties folder icons beneath it (Fig. 8-9). Click on the Directories folder icon to select it, and from the list of virtual directories shown in the results pane, right-click on the virtual directory you want to scan and select RESCAN from the shortcut menu. The Full Rescan dialog box will appear, prompting you to confirm your decision by clicking YES.

A scan should generally be forced when

- You have changed the characterization size on the property sheet for Index Server.
- You have added or removed a new word-breaker or filter (e.g., for another language).
- You have changed the filtering on extensions that are not recognized.

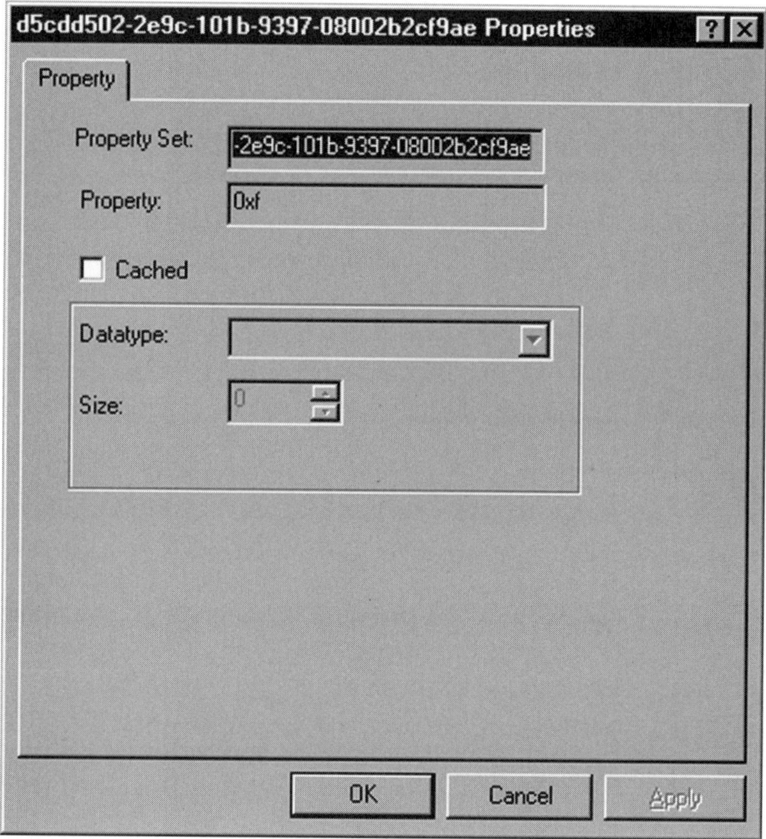

Figure 8-11 Property sheet for a particular property.

Forcing a Merge

To force a merge of all persistent indexes in a catalog, right-click on the catalog node in the scope pane and select MERGE from the shortcut menu. The Merge catalog dialog box will appear, prompting you to confirm your decision by clicking YES.

Merges should generally be forced when

- You add a large number of new documents to the corpus and they need to be queried immediately.
- Queries to your catalog have slowed down due to the large number of persistent indexes. Forcing a merge will create one efficient master index, which will optimize the query process.

Stopping and Starting the Content Index Service

To stop or start the Content Index service, you can use one of two methods:

- In the Index Server Manager (MMC with Index Server snap-in installed), right-click on the Index Server node in the scope pane and select STOP or START from the shortcut menu.
- Open Control Panel, open the Services program, select the Content Index service in the list box, and click on STOP or START (Fig. 8-12).

Enabling Indexing on Virtual Directories

To cause a virtual directory to be indexed, right-click on the virtual directory (or its parent virtual server, if you want to index all virtual directories that belong to a given virtual server) in the Internet Service Manager (MMC with IIS snap-in installed), select PROPERTIES to open the Directory Property sheet, select the Directory tab, and under the label Content Control place a checkmark in the INDEX THIS DIRECTORY checkbox. This will cause Index Server (if it is running) to index your virtual directory.

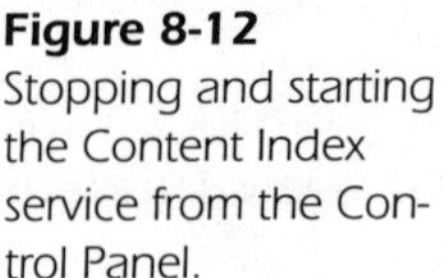

Figure 8-12
Stopping and starting the Content Index service from the Control Panel.

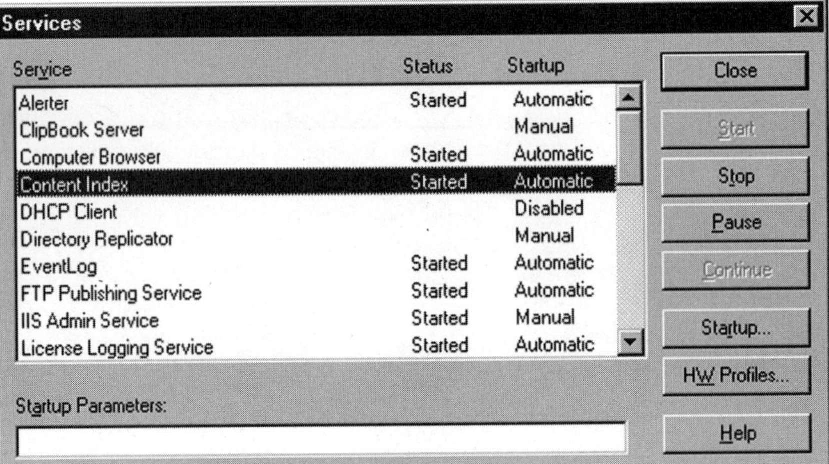

An example of this procedure is shown in the walkthrough later in this chapter.

Enabling Indexing on Nonvirtual (Physical) Directories

To cause a nonvirtual (physical) directory to be indexed, right-click on the catalog in which you want the directory to be indexed in the Index Server Manager (MMC with Index Server snap-in installed), and select CREATE NEW, DIRECTORY from the shortcut menu (note that this does not create a physical directory, but simply makes an existing physical directory available for indexing). The Add Directory dialog box now appears (Fig. 8-13).

Enter the local path to the physical directory you want to index, then type in a UNC alias that will be the path returned to the client when the client queries the directory (typically this is the UNC of the share created on the directory), and click OK.

Administering Index Server Using Index Server Manager (HTML)

Many of the functions of Index Server administration that can be performed using the MMC can also be performed remotely using a Web

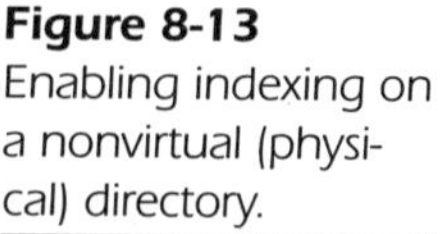

Figure 8-13
Enabling indexing on a nonvirtual (physical) directory.

browser. As an example of this, included in the installation of IIS is a Start menu shortcut to the Index Server Manager (HTML), which is a collection of `.ida` (Internet Data Administration) and `.htx` files that allows the administrator to manage the default catalog `C:\Inetpub\Catalog.wci` remotely.

The `.ida` files are similar in syntax to the `.idq` files discussed earlier in this chapter, except that they are used to administer Index Server properties instead of creating queries. If you create a new catalog and want to administer it using a browser, you can either create your own `.ida/.htx` files for administration or modify the existing Index Server Manager (HTML) to meet your needs. Further information on writing `.ida` files can be found in the online documentation for Index Server.

The rest of this section illustrates the Index Server Manager (HTML), which allows remote administration of the default catalog using a browser like Internet Explorer 4.01.

To start Index Server Manager (HTML), click START, PROGRAMS, WINDOWS NT 4.0 OPTION PACK, INDEX SERVER, INDEX SERVER MANAGER (HTML) on the local machine, or browse the following URL from a remote machine where you are logged on as Administrator:

```
http://<server_name>/iisadmin/isadmin/admin.htm:<admin_tcp_port>
```

The first screen that opens up is Fig. 8-14. The *Index Statistics* page shown in Fig. 8-14 allows the administrator to view the cache and index statistics for the default catalog. The Index Statistics are largely available through the MMC, but the current implementation of the Index Server snap-in for the MMC does not allow viewing of cache statistics for tracking the success or failure of queries.

Also shown is a general status message at the bottom of the browser window indicating that "All filtering is up to date; indexing is complete."

Clicking on the hyperlink on the left side called Unfiltered Documents brings up the *Unfiltered Documents* page (Fig. 8-15). The Unfiltered Documents page indicates which portions of the corpus are not successfully filtered. In the screenshot the status message is, "All documents have been successfully filtered," which indicates there were no problems with the filtering process. Filtering problems can be caused by problems with filter DLLs.

Click the Virtual Root Data hyperlink on the left side to bring up the third and final page of Index Server Manager (HTML) (see Fig. 8-16). The *Virtual Root Data* page allows you to force a rescan of virtual roots asso-

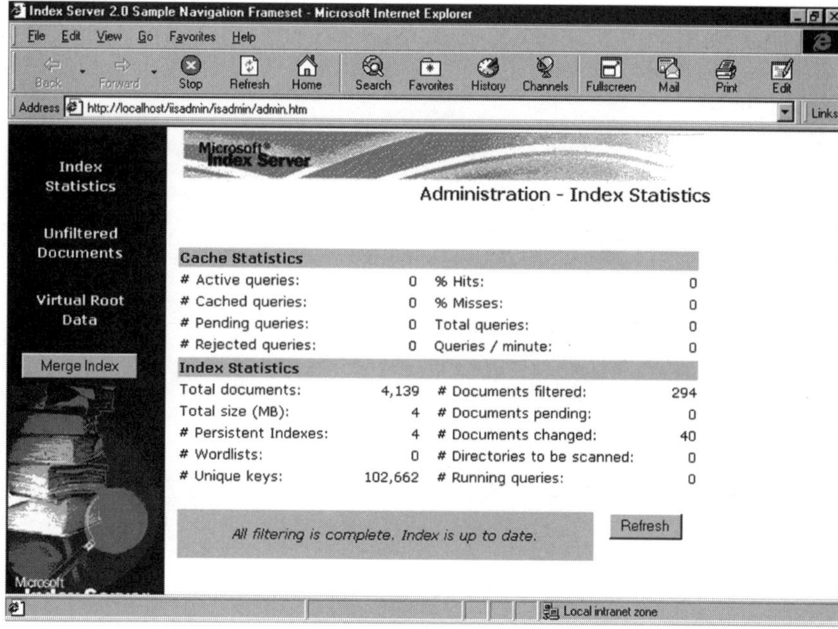

Figure 8-14 Index Server Manager (HTML) showing Index Statistics page.

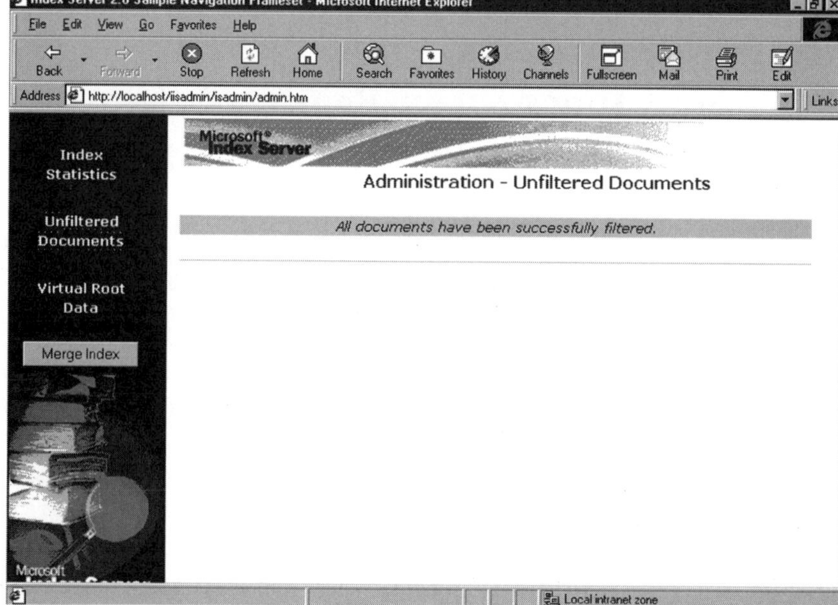

Figure 8-15 Index Server Manager (HTML) showing the Unfiltered Documents page.

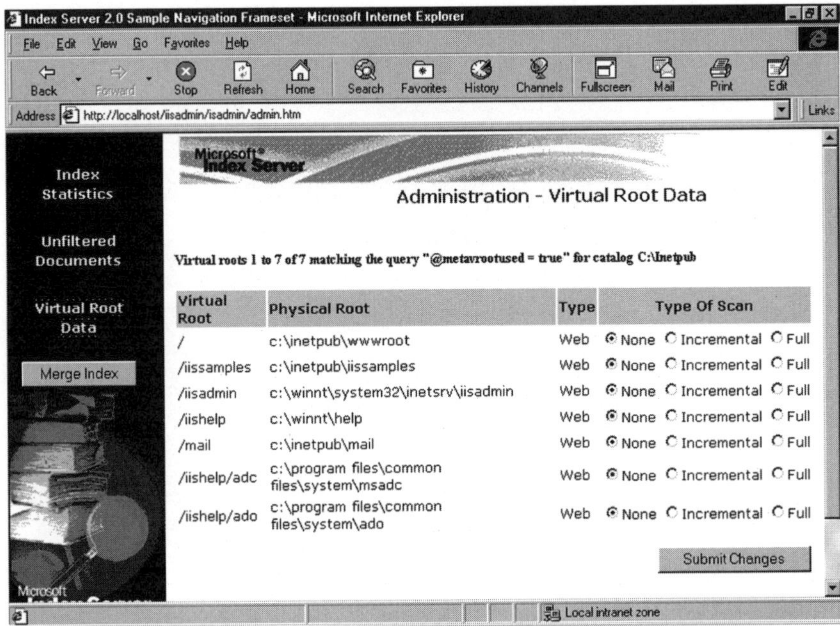

Figure 8-16 Index Server manager (HTML) showing Virtual Root Data page.

ciated with the default catalog. Select which roots to scan, choose the type of scan, and click SUBMIT CHANGES to initiate scanning.

Index Server Registry Settings

Administrators can also configure certain registry settings of Index Server to control how the automatic scanning and merging processes take place. The following is a list of some of the more important registry settings. These registry settings are stored under

```
\HKEY_LOCAL_MACHINE
    System
        CurrentControlSet
            Control
                ContentIndex
```

Registry settings associated with *word lists* and *shadow merges:*

- *MaxWordLists.* The maximum number of word lists that can exist at any time. When this number is exceeded, a shadow merge occurs.
- *MaxWordlistSize.* The maximum amount of memory occupied by a word list in increments of 128 kB.

- *MinWordlistMemory.* The minimum amount of free memory needed to create word lists.
- *MinSizemergeWordlists.* The minimum aggregate size of word lists that forces a shadow merge.

Registry settings associated with *master merges:*

- *MasterMergeTime.* The default time for master merge is nightly at midnight. You can change this to the time when server load is least.
- *MinDiskFreeForceMerge.* A master merge will be initiated if the free disk space is less than this parameter and the aggregate shadow index space is greater than MaxShadowFreeForceMerge.
- *MaxShadowIndexSize.* A master merge will be initiated if the aggregate shadow index space exceeds this value.
- *MaxFreshCount.* If the number of documents modified since the previous master merge exceeds this value, a new master merge is done.

Walkthrough: Indexing a Virtual Server

In the following walkthrough we will use Index Server to index a new virtual server whose Web content resides both on the local machine and on a network share. In the process we will also create a new catalog exclusively for this virtual server and modify an existing set of `.idq/.htx` query files to support a search page for our Web site. You'll need some mixed content (Word and HTML files, for instance) for the new site if you want to follow along.

First we will modify the MMC to allow us to administer both IIS and Index Server. Click START, PROGRAMS, WINDOWS NT 4.0 OPTION PACK, MICROSOFT INTERNET SERVER MANAGER, INTERNET SERVICE MANAGER to open the MMC with the snap-in for IIS installed.

From the MMC menu bar, click CONSOLE, ADD/REMOVE SNAP-IN. In the Add/Remove Snap-in dialog box click ADD, select Index Server, and click OK. At this point the Connect to Computer dialog box appears to ask you if the Index Server you want to manage is local or remote (Fig. 8-17). Select LOCAL COMPUTER and click FINISH, then click OK to return to the MMC.

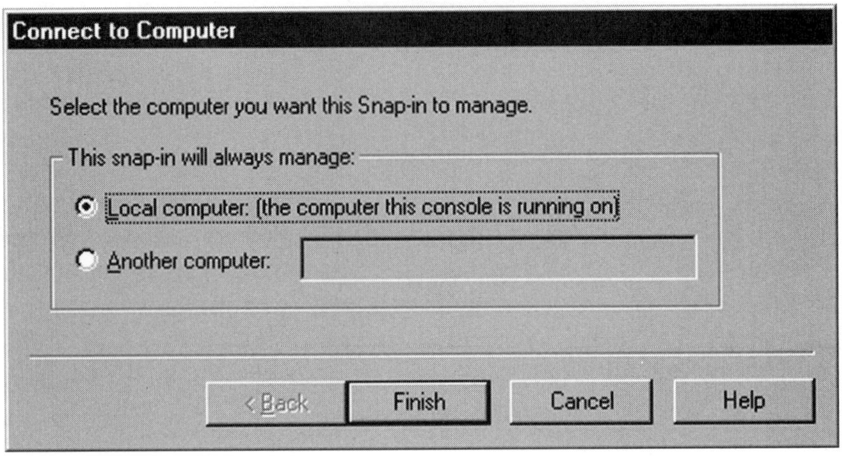

Figure 8-17
Adding Index Server to the MMC.

Connect to Computer

Select the computer you want this Snap-in to manage.

This snap-in will always manage:

Local computer: (the computer this console is running on)

Another computer:

< Back | Finish | Cancel | Help

Next we will create a new Web with a local home directory and two content directories, one local and one remote. But before we do this, we will create the directories needed. We create the following directories and add the content described to them:

- On server1 (local machine):
  Create `D:\litroot.`
  Directory contains `default.htm`.
  Create `D:\lit.`
  Directory contains HTML documents.
- On server2 (remote machine):
  Create `C:\lit2.`
  Share as `MORELIT.`
  Directory contains Word documents.

To create the new virtual server, open the Internet Information Server node in the MMC, select the local server's node (here server1), right-click and select NEW, WEB SITE from the shortcut menu.

The New Web Site Wizard appears. Enter a name for the Web site (for example, MyLitWeb), select an IP address (here 172.16.8.102, which is one of four IP addresses bound to the network adapter card on server1), choose `D:\litroot` as the home directory, accept the remaining defaults, and click FINISH to create the new virtual server.

To create the two virtual directories for content, right-click on the newly created MyLitWeb node and select NEW, VIRTUAL DIRECTORY to run the New Virtual Directory Wizard. Map aliases to physical directories as follows:

Alias: `lit1`

Map to: `D:\lit on SERVER1`

Alias: `lit2`

Map to: `\\SERVER2\MORELIT`

Note than when mapping the second alias to the UNC share, a dialog box appears asking for the security credentials that should be used to access the share from the Web site. We previously created a user called `lituser` on the domain controller and assigned this user read permission to the `MORELIT` share on server2, and this is the user whose credentials are entered into the wizard at this point.

Finally we need to start the new virtual server by right-clicking on the MyLitWeb node and selecting START from the shortcut menu (or select the node and click the START button on the rebar). Figure 8-18 shows the newly created virtual server and its virtual directories.

Now we will create a new Index Server catalog specifically for our new Web site. In the MMC right-click on the Index Server node and select STOP from the shortcut menu to stop the Content Indexing service.

On the local server create a folder to contain the new catalog (for example, `D:\litcat`).

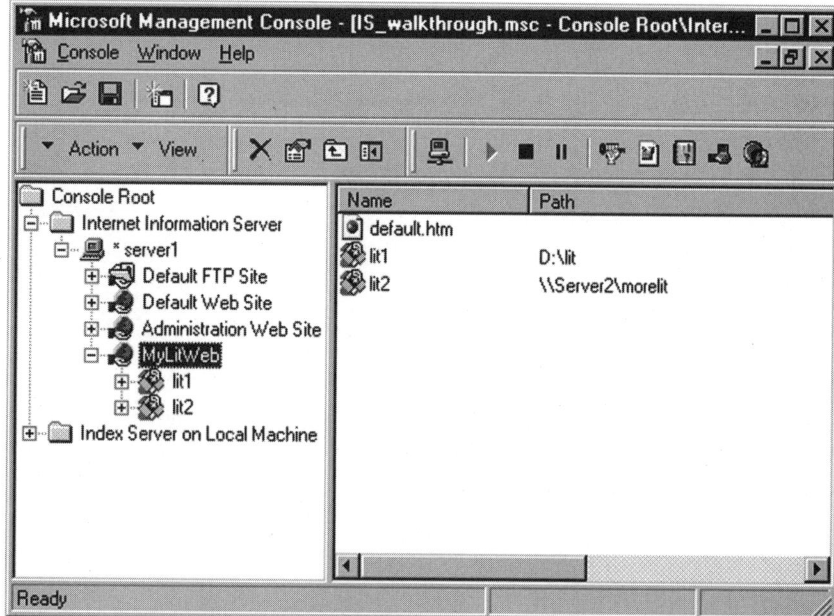

Figure 8-18 The new virtual server MyLitWeb is created.

Right-click on the Index Server node and select NEW, CATALOG from the shortcut menu. The Add Catalog dialog box appears. Give the new catalog a name and enter its location (Fig. 8-19). Click OK. A dialog box warns you that the newly created catalog will remain offline until you restart the Content Index service (Fig. 8-20).

Note that under the Index Server node you now have two child nodes (Fig. 8-21):

- *Web,* which is the default catalog
- *Literature Catalog,* which is the newly created catalog

Fields for catalog size, number of documents, and so on are listed as `n/a` in the MMC results pane. This is because the Content Index service has not yet been restarted.

If you use Windows Explorer to look at the contents of `D:\litcat` at this point, you will see that it now contains a `Catalog.wci` folder within it.

At this point, before we restart Index Server, we will configure the new catalog we have created. Right-click on the Literature Catalog node (or whatever you have called it) and select PROPERTIES from the shortcut menu to bring up the Literature Catalog Properties sheet.

Figure 8-19 Creating a new catalog for the new virtual server.

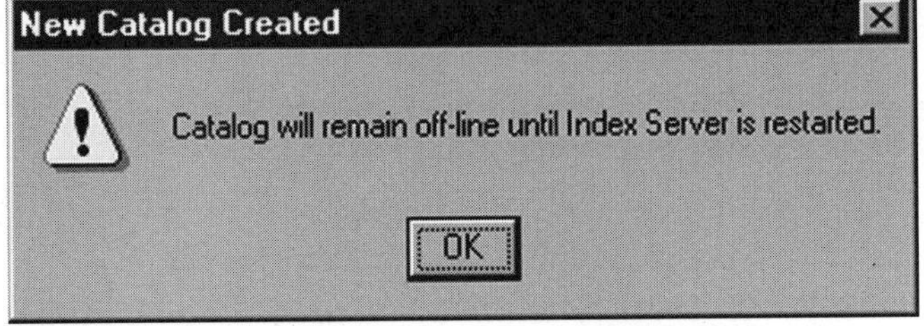

Figure 8-20 The new catalog is offline until the Content Index service is restarted.

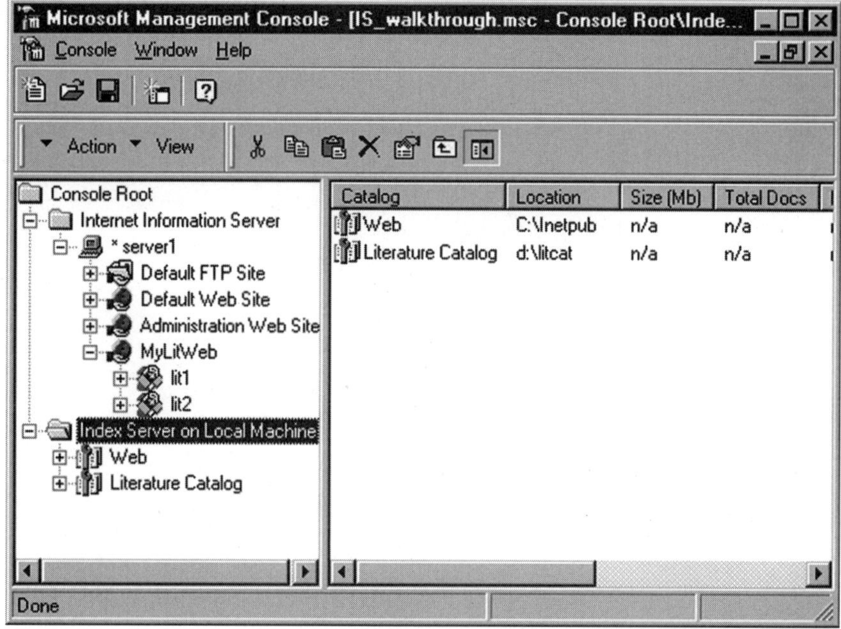

Figure 8-21 A new catalog is created to index the virtual server MyLitWeb.

The Location tab on this property sheet indicates the following information for the new catalog:

- Name of catalog
- Location of catalog
- Size of catalog

The Web tab specifies

- Whether to index virtual directories (the default is checked)
- What virtual server to map to the catalog
- Whether to index news directories and map a news server to the catalog

From the Virtual Server drop-down box select MyLitWeb. This action associates the new catalog with the new virtual server (Fig. 8-22).

The Generation tab specifies

- Whether to index files that have unrecognized extensions (the default is checked)
- Whether to return abstracts or summaries of documents when a query is performed (the default is checked)
- The size in characters of the file abstracts returned by the query

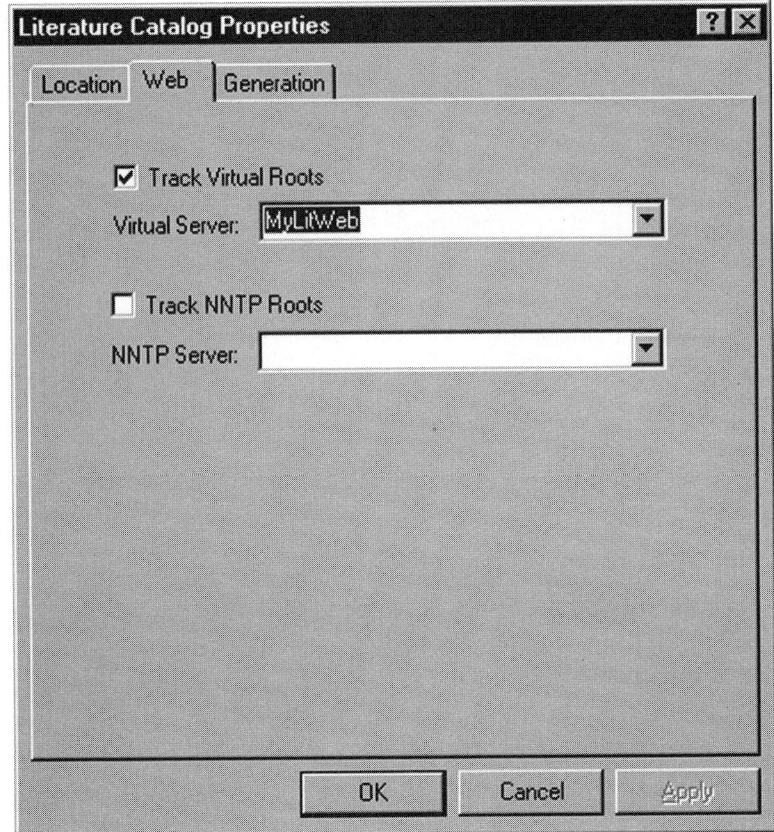

Figure 8-22 Mapping a virtual server to a new catalog.

At this point we should enable our new virtual server for indexing. In the MMC under the Internet Information Server node, right-click on MyLitWeb to bring up its property sheet (Fig. 8-23). Select the Home Directory tab and under Content Control place a checkmark beside *Index the directory* and click OK. The whole site, including both its home directory and any virtual directories, is now enabled for indexing and automatically starts being indexed by Index Server.

Now select the Index Server node in the MMC and click the START button on the rebar to restart Index Server.

NOTE: If you don't want to wait for automatic indexing to begin, you can force a scan of virtual directories to begin the indexing process. If this fails to start the indexing process, reboot the machine to get indexing going again.

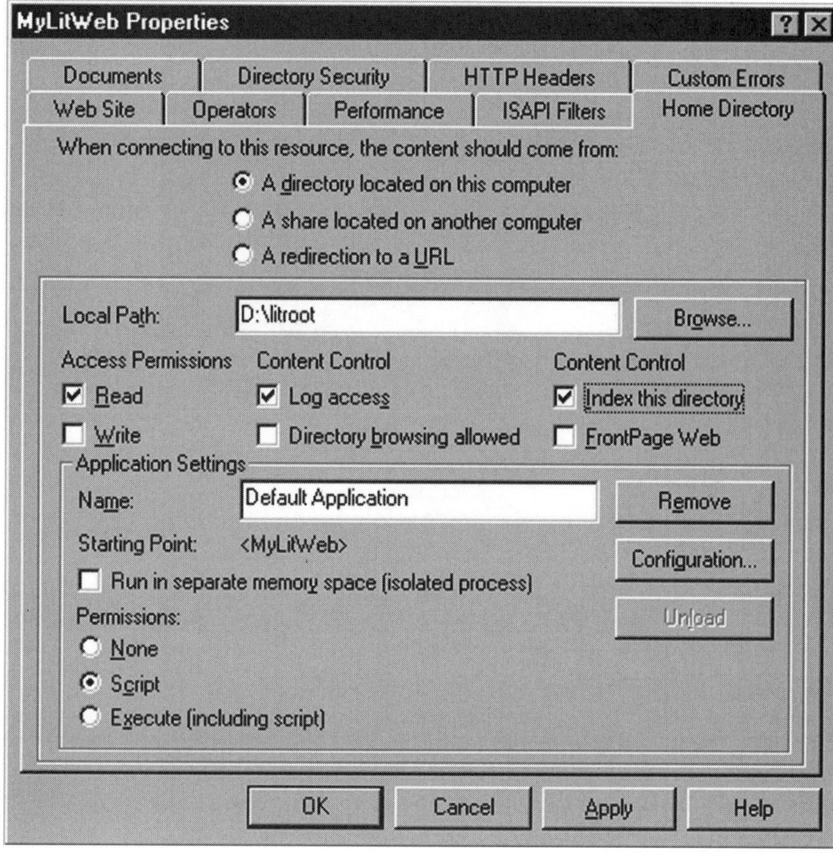

Figure 8-23 Enabling indexing on a virtual server.

The result so far is shown in Fig. 8-24. Notice the following in this figure:

- Under the catalog node (MyLitWeb) are two folders: Directories and Properties.
- Under the Directories node are the home folder and the two virtual directory nodes.

If the corpus to be indexed is sufficiently large, you will be able to watch indexing taking place for the new virtual server. Select the Index Server node in the scope pane of the MMC and then hide the scope pane using the SHOW/HIDE SCOPE button on the rebar. Figure 8-25 shows indexing of MyLitWeb taking place. Virtual roots are being scanned, and at this point there are

- Fourteen of 32 documents remaining to be filtered

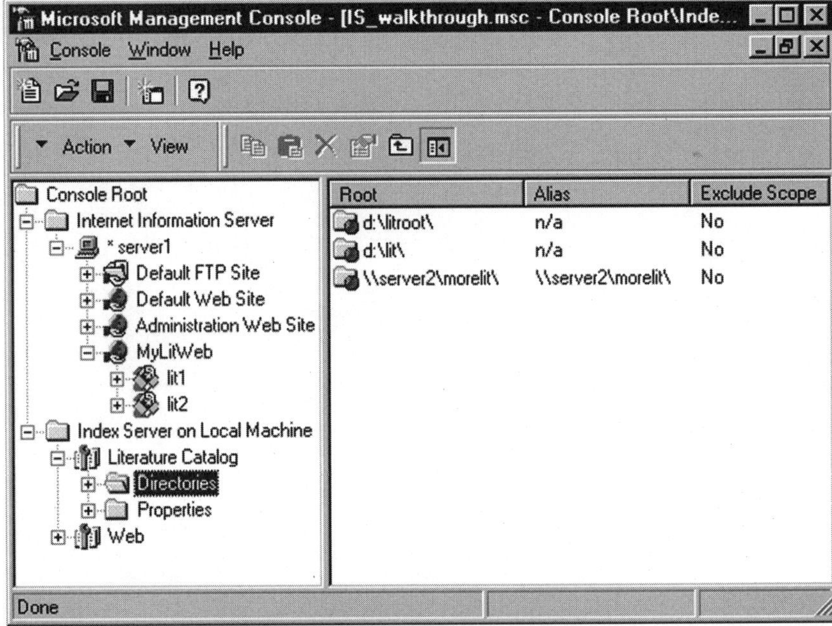

Figure 8-24 New nodes under the new catalog node in the MMC namespace.

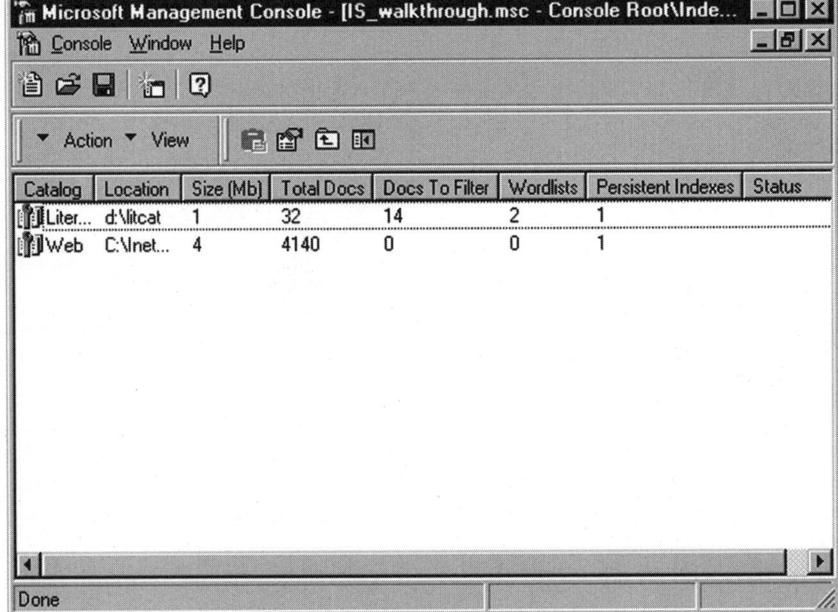

Figure 8-25 Indexing taking place in the Literature Catalog.

- Two wordlists residing in memory
- One persistent (shadow) index on the HD

A short time later scanning (filtering) of documents is complete. Figure 8-26 shows the following:

- All documents have now been filtered.
- Five wordlists reside in memory.
- One persistent (shadow) index resides on the HD.

At this point we can right-click the Literature Catalog node and select MERGE from the shortcut menu. The Merge catalog dialog box appears (Fig. 8-27). Click YES to force a shadow merge and then a master merge. The final result is shown in Fig. 8-28, where we see that there are

- No word lists residing in memory anymore
- One persistent (master) index

Our final job is to make the necessary files to enable us to query the new catalog. To do this, we will copy the existing files,

- `Query.htm`
- `Query.idq`

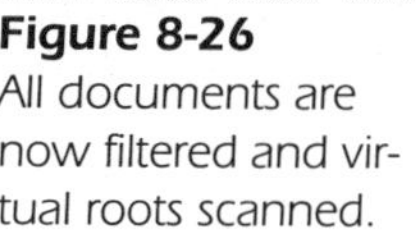

Figure 8-26 All documents are now filtered and virtual roots scanned.

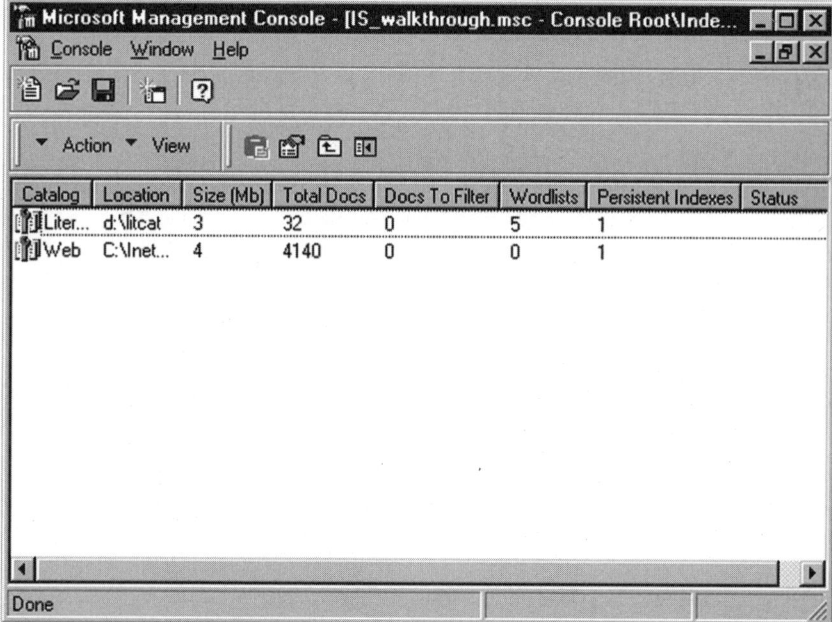

Figure 8-27
The Merge catalog dialog box.

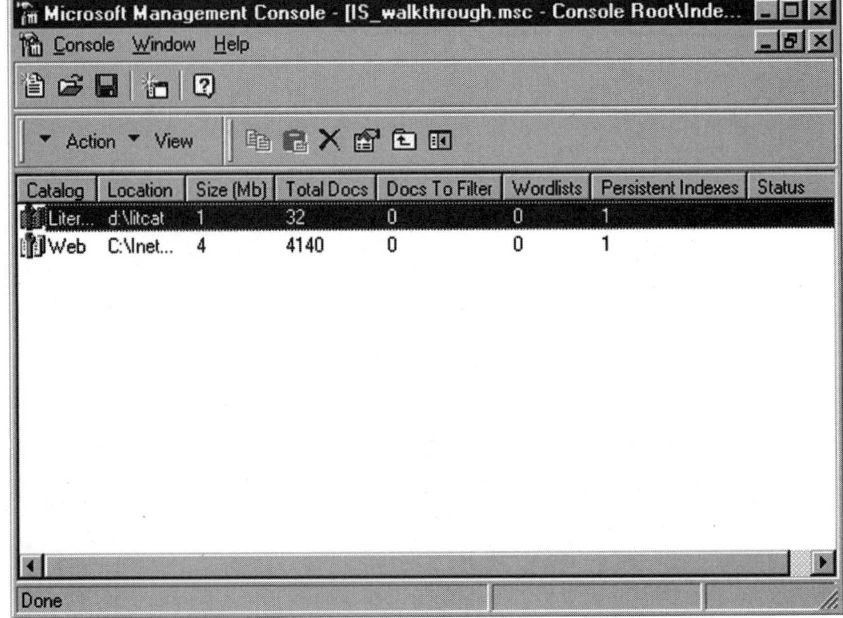

Figure 8-28
The indexing process is now complete.

- `Query.htx`

from the samples directory located in

```
C:\inetpub\iissamples\issamples\
```

to the home directory for our new Web site, namely, `D:\litroot`. Once the files are copied there, make a link to `Query.htm` from the home page `Default.htm`.

The three copied files required have been simplified and modified somewhat in the listings below. These modifications include giving them new titles, cleaning up formatting, removing comments, and making the following changes:

`Query.htm` has been modified as follows:

- All the image links broken because of copying the file to the new directory have been removed.

`Query.idq` has been modified as follows:

- The line starting with

```
#CiCatalog = ...
```

which was commented out by # in the original file has been modified to reflect the location of the new catalog. The new line reads,

```
CiCatalog = d:\litcat
```

- The line starting with

```
CiTemplate = ...
```

has been modified to reflect the new template file's location. It now reads simply,

```
CiTemplate = /%TemplateName%.htx
```

where `%TemplateName%` is a variable that was assigned in the `Query.htm` file and passed as a `Hidden` argument to the `Query.idq` file.

`Query.htx` has been modified as follows:

- The `Include` statement at the end has been removed since its relative URL is now incorrect.

LISTING OF THE FILE `Query.htm`

```
<HTML>
<HEAD><TITLE>Search for Literature</TITLE></HEAD>
<BODY>
<H1>Search for Literature</H1><HR>
<FORM ACTION = "query.idq" METHOD = "GET">
<TABLE WIDTH = 500>
<TR><td>Enter your query below:</td></TR>
<TR><TD><INPUT TYPE = "TEXT" NAME = "CiRestriction" SIZE = "65"
MAXLENGTH = "100" VALUE = ""></TD>
<TD><INPUT TYPE = "SUBMIT" VALUE = "Go"></TD></TR>
</TABLE>
```

```
<INPUT TYPE = "HIDDEN" NAME = "CiScope" VALUE = "/">
<INPUT TYPE = "HIDDEN" NAME = "CiMaxRecordsPerPage" VALUE = "10">
<INPUT TYPE = "HIDDEN" NAME = "TemplateName" VALUE = "query">
<INPUT TYPE = "HIDDEN" NAME = "CiSort" VALUE = "rank[d]">
<INPUT TYPE = "HIDDEN" NAME = "HTMLQueryForm" VALUE = "query.htm">
</FORM>
</BODY>
</HTML>
```

LISTING OF THE FILE `Query.idq`

```
[Query]
CiCatalog = d:\litcat
CiColumns = filename,size,rank,characterization,vpath,DocTitle,write
CiFlags = DEEP
CiRestriction = %if FreeText eq on% $contents "%CiRestriction%"
%else% %CiRestriction% %endif%
CiMaxRecordsInResultSet = 300
CiMaxRecordsPerPage = %CiMaxRecordsPerPage%
CiScope = %CiScope%
CiTemplate = /query.htx
CiSort = %CiSort%
CiForceUseCi = true
```

LISTING OF THE FILE `Query.htx`

```
<HTML>
<HEAD><TITLE>Search Results</TITLE></HEAD>
<BODY>
<H1>Literature Search Results</H1>

<H5>
<%if CiMatchedRecordCount eq 0%>
No documents matched the query "<%CiRestriction%>".
<%else%>
Documents <%CiFirstRecordNumber%> to <%CiLastRecordNumber%> of
<%if CiMatchedRecordCount eq CiMaxRecordsInResultSet%>
the best
<%endif%>
<%CiMatchedRecordCount%> matching the query
"<%CiRestriction%>".
<%endif%>
</H5>

<TABLE WIDTH = 80%>
<TD> <A HREF = "<%HTMLQueryForm%>">New query</A> </TD>
<%if CiContainsFirstRecord eq 0%>
<TD ALIGN = LEFT>
<FORM ACTION = "query.idq" METHOD = "GET">
<INPUT TYPE = "HIDDEN" NAME = "CiBookMark" VALUE = "<%CiBookMark%>" >
<INPUT TYPE = "HIDDEN" NAME = "CiBookmarkSkipCount" VALUE = "-
<%EscapeRAW CiMaxRecordsPerPage%>" >
<INPUT TYPE = "HIDDEN" NAME = "CiMaxRecordsInResultSet" VALUE =
"<%EscapeRAW CiMaxRecordsInResultSet%>" >
<INPUT TYPE = "HIDDEN" NAME = "CiRestriction" VALUE = "<%CiRestric-
tion%>" >
<INPUT TYPE = "HIDDEN" NAME = "CiMaxRecordsPerPage" VALUE = "'
"<%EscapeRAW CiMaxRecordsPerPage%>" >
```

```
<INPUT TYPE = "HIDDEN" NAME = "CiScope" VALUE = "<%CiScope%>" >
<INPUT TYPE = "HIDDEN" NAME = "TemplateName" VALUE =
"<%TemplateName%>" >
<INPUT TYPE = "HIDDEN" NAME = "CiSort" VALUE = "<%CiSort%>" >
<INPUT TYPE = "HIDDEN" NAME = "HTMLQueryForm" VALUE = "<%HTMLQuery-
Form%>" >
<INPUT TYPE = "SUBMIT" VALUE = "Previous <%CiMaxRecordsPerPage%>
documents">
</FORM>
</TD>
<%endif%>

<%if CiContainsLastRecord eq 0%>
<TD ALIGN = RIGHT>
<FORM ACTION = "query.idq" METHOD = "GET">
<INPUT TYPE = "HIDDEN" NAME = "CiBookMark" VALUE = "<%CiBookMark%>" >
<INPUT TYPE = "HIDDEN" NAME = "CiBookmarkSkipCount" VALUE =
"<%EscapeRAW CiMaxRecordsPerPage%>" >
<INPUT TYPE = "HIDDEN" NAME = "CiMaxRecordsInResultSet" VALUE =
"<%EscapeRAW CiMaxRecordsInResultSet%>" >
<INPUT TYPE = "HIDDEN" NAME = "CiRestriction" VALUE = "<%CiRestric-
tion%>" >
<INPUT TYPE = "HIDDEN" NAME = "CiMaxRecordsPerPage" VALUE =
"<%EscapeRAW CiMaxRecordsPerPage%>" >
<INPUT TYPE = "HIDDEN" NAME = "CiScope" VALUE = "<%CiScope%>" >
<INPUT TYPE = "HIDDEN" NAME = "TemplateName" VALUE =
"<%TemplateName%>" >
<INPUT TYPE = "HIDDEN" NAME = "CiSort" VALUE = "<%CiSort%>" >
<INPUT TYPE = "HIDDEN" NAME = "HTMLQueryForm" VALUE = "<%HTMLQuery-
Form%>" >
<INPUT TYPE = "SUBMIT" VALUE = "Next <%CiRecordsNextPage%> docu-
ments">
</FORM>
</TD>
<%endif%>

</TABLE>
<HR>

<%begindetail%>

<table border = 0>
<tr class = "RecordTitle">
<td align = "right" valign = "top" class = "RecordTitle" style =
"background-color:white;">
<%CiCurrentRecordNumber%>.
</td>
<td><b class = "RecordTitle">
<%if DocTitle isempty%>
<a href = "<%EscapeURL vpath%>" class = "RecordTitle"><%file-
name%></a>
<%else%>
<a href = "<%EscapeURL vpath%>" class = "RecordTitle"><%DocTi-
tle%></a>
<%endif%>
</b></td>
</tr>
<tr>
<td></td>
```

```
<td>
<b><i>Abstract: </i></b><%characterization%>
</td>
</tr>
<tr>
<td></td>
<td>
<i class = "RecordStats"><a href = "<%EscapeURL vpath%>"
class = "RecordStats"
style = "color:blue;">http://<%server_name%><%vpath%></a>
<br><%if size eq ""%>(size and time unknown)<%else%>size
<%size%> bytes - <%write%> GMT<%endif%>
</i>
</td>
</tr>
</table>
<br>

<%enddetail%>
</dl>
<P>
<%if CiMatchedRecordCount ne 0%>
<!— Only display a line if there were any hits that matched the
query —>
<HR>
<%endif%>
<TABLE WIDTH = 80%>

<TD> <A HREF = "<%HTMLQueryForm%>">New query</A> </TD>
<%if CiContainsFirstRecord eq 0%>
<TD ALIGN = LEFT>
<FORM ACTION = "query.idq" METHOD = "GET">
<INPUT TYPE = "HIDDEN" NAME = "CiBookMark" VALUE = "<%CiBookMark%>" >
<INPUT TYPE = "HIDDEN" NAME = "CiBookmarkSkipCount" VALUE = "-
<%EscapeRAW CiMaxRecordsPerPage%>" >
<INPUT TYPE = "HIDDEN" NAME = "CiMaxRecordsInResultSet" VALUE =
"<%EscapeRAW CiMaxRecordsInResultSet%>" >
<INPUT TYPE = "HIDDEN" NAME = "CiRestriction" VALUE = "<%CiRestric-
tion%>" >
<INPUT TYPE = "HIDDEN" NAME = "CiMaxRecordsPerPage" VALUE = "-
<%EscapeRAW CiMaxRecordsPerPage%>" >
<INPUT TYPE = "HIDDEN" NAME = "CiScope" VALUE = "<%CiScope%>" >
<INPUT TYPE = "HIDDEN" NAME = "TemplateName" VALUE =
"<%TemplateName%>" >
<INPUT TYPE = "HIDDEN" NAME = "CiSort" VALUE = "<%CiSort%>" >
<INPUT TYPE = "HIDDEN" NAME = "HTMLQueryForm" VALUE = "<%HTMLQuery-
Form%>" >
<INPUT TYPE = "SUBMIT" VALUE = "Previous <%CiMaxRecordsPerPage%>
documents">
</FORM>
</TD>
<%endif%>

<%if CiContainsLastRecord eq 0%>
<TD ALIGN = RIGHT>
<FORM ACTION = "query.idq" METHOD = "GET">
<INPUT TYPE = "HIDDEN" NAME = "CiBookMark" VALUE = "<%CiBookMark%>" >
<INPUT TYPE = "HIDDEN" NAME = "CiBookmarkSkipCount" VALUE =
"<%EscapeRAW CiMaxRecordsPerPage%>" >
```

```
<INPUT TYPE = "HIDDEN" NAME = "CiMaxRecordsInResultSet" VALUE =
"<%EscapeRAW CiMaxRecordsInResultSet%>" >
<INPUT TYPE = "HIDDEN" NAME = "CiRestriction" VALUE = "<%CiRestric-
tion%>" >
<INPUT TYPE = "HIDDEN" NAME = "CiMaxRecordsPerPage" VALUE =
"<%EscapeRAW CiMaxRecordsPerPage%>" >
<INPUT TYPE = "HIDDEN" NAME = "CiScope" VALUE = "<%CiScope%>" >
<INPUT TYPE = "HIDDEN" NAME = "TemplateName" VALUE =
"<%TemplateName%>" >
<INPUT TYPE = "HIDDEN" NAME = "CiSort" VALUE = "<%CiSort%>" >
<INPUT TYPE = "HIDDEN" NAME = "HTMLQueryForm" VALUE = "<%HTMLQuery-
Form%>" >
<INPUT TYPE = "SUBMIT" VALUE = "Next <%CiRecordsNextPage%> docu-
ments">
</FORM>
</TD>
<%endif%>

</TABLE>

<P><BR>
<%if CiOutOfDate eq 0%>
<P><I<<B>The index is up-to-date.</B></I><BR>
<%endif%>
<%if CiQueryIncomplete ne 0%>
<P><I><B>The query is too expensive to complete.</B></I><BR>
<%endif%>

<%if CiQueryTimedOut ne 0%>
<P><I><B>The query took too long to complete.</B></I><BR>
<%endif%>

<%if CiTotalNumberPages gt 0%>
<P>Page <%CiCurrentPageNumber%> of <%CiTotalNumberPages%>
<%endif%>

</BODY>
</HTML>
```

Finally, we will test the query files by opening the `Query.htm` page and issuing a query (Fig. 8-29). The result of our query is shown in Fig. 8-30.

SUMMARY

Index Server 2.0 is integrated into IIS 4.0 and provides administrators with a mechanism for indexing HTML and legacy content on virtual servers. Complex queries may be performed by suitably building `.idq/.htx` files or Active Server Pages. Index Server runs automatically in the background as a Windows NT service, but it can also be manually

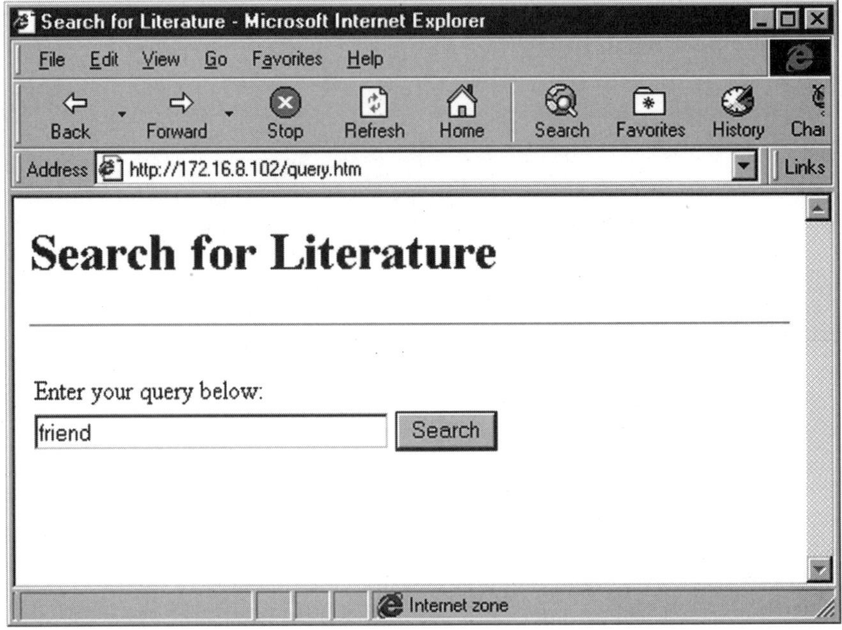

Figure 8-29 Issuing a query on our new catalog.

administered using the Microsoft Management Console or through a Web browser.

FOR MORE INFORMATION

Microsoft Web Site For general information about Index Server, visit the IIS 4.0 Web site at

```
www.microsoft.com/iis
```

Microsoft Newsgroup The following newsgroup is devoted to discussions of Index Server:

```
microsoft.public.inetserver.iis.tripoli
```

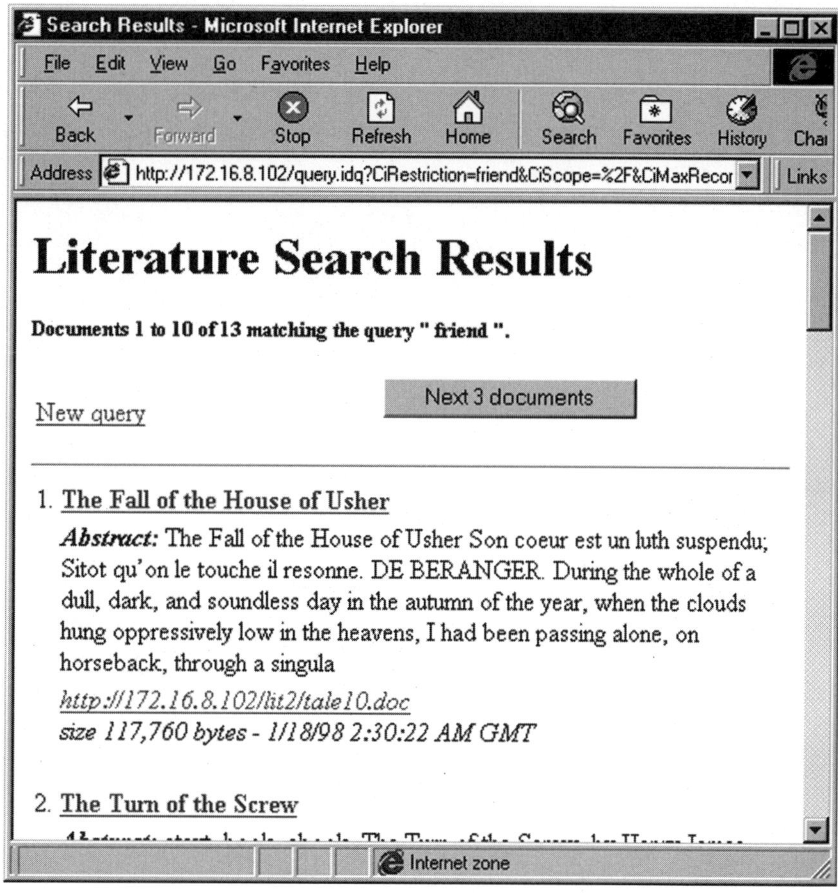

Figure 8-30 Successful query performed on corpus of new virtual server.

CHAPTER 9

Administering the FTP Service

Introduction

The File Transfer Protocol (FTP) Publishing Service is another core component of Internet Information Server 4.0, enabling users to transfer files to and from Internet and intranet sites. After completing this chapter, you will be able to administer the FTP service on IIS 4.0 and be able to

- Explain the underlying mechanism of FTP.
- Understand the security implications of using FTP.
- Configure various property settings for FTP sites.
- Create and manage an FTP site.
- Access an FTP site from both Internet Explorer and the command line.

Understanding the File Transfer Protocol

File Transfer Protocol, or FTP, is one of the oldest Internet protocols and specifies a mechanism whereby files can be transferred from one host to another. Although the HTTP protocol has taken over some of the functions of FTP, FTP continues to be popular for tasks such as:

- Providing high-speed dedicated sites for downloading applications and for software upgrades and patches
- Providing anonymous write-only drop boxes for uploading files to servers
- Enabling file transfers in heterogeneous (mixed) networking configurations (e.g., between Windows NT and UNIX)

One reason for the continued popularity of FTP is its simple administration, about which we will learn more shortly.

FTP is a client-server protocol. In order for files to be transferred between two hosts, one of them must be running FTP *server* software (such as IIS 4.0) and the other must be running FTP *client* software (such as IE 4.0 or the command line FTP utility that is part of Windows 95 and NT). File transfers can be either ASCII or binary and take one of two forms:

- *Uploading* or *putting*—transferring files from the client to the server
- *Downloading* or *getting*—transferring files from the server to the client

How an FTP Session Works

Like HTTP, FTP uses TCP as a transport protocol, which provides for reliable connection-oriented file transfers. When an FTP client connects with an FTP server such as IIS 4.0, a TCP connection is established, and the connection remains open until the session is terminated or until the server issues a timeout.

The following outline explains the basic process of establishing an FTP session and transferring a file (see Fig. 9-1).

1. The FTP client forms a TCP connection with the FTP server using a TCP three-way handshake.
2. In order for a TCP connection to be formed, both the client and the server must open a TCP port. FTP servers have two preassigned port numbers.
   - Port 21 is used for sending and receiving FTP control information. This port is continuously monitored by the FTP

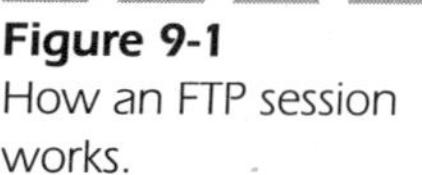

Figure 9-1
How an FTP session works.

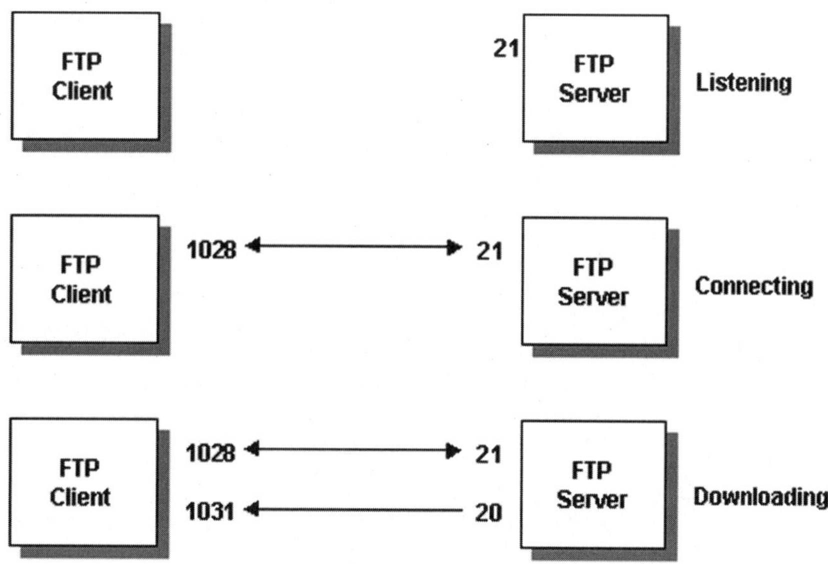

server, which listens for an FTP client that wants to connect to it. Once an FTP session is established, the connection to port 21 remains open for the entire session.
- Port 20 is used for sending and receiving FTP data (ASCII or binary files). The data port is open only when data is being transferred, and is closed when the transfer is complete.

3. FTP clients have their port numbers dynamically assigned when the FTP client service is invoked. These client port numbers are chosen from the range 1024 to 65,535. Ports 0 through 1023 are known as *Well-Known Port Numbers* and have uses preassigned to them by the Internet Assigned Numbers Authority (IANA). For a listing of Well-Known Port Numbers used by Windows NT 4.0, open the text file

```
C:\winnt\system32\drivers\etc\services
```

4. When an FTP session is started, the client opens a control port that connects to port 21 on the server.
5. When data needs to be transferred, the client opens a second port to connect to port 20 on the server. Each time a file is transferred, a new data port is opened by the client and then released.

The `netstat` Utility

The `netstat` command-line utility, available for both Windows NT and Windows 95, may be used to monitor and troubleshoot FTP connections. By typing

```
netstat -p tcp
```

an administrator can view the connection statistics for the TCP protocol on either the client or the server.

As an example of using the netstat utility, the following are the results of running the command `netstat -p tcp` on the server during the various stages of a typical FTP session. The client is a Windows 95 host called SUPER running the command-line FTP utility, and the server is an FTP site on IIS 4.0.

1. Prior to the client establishing an FTP session, there are only local TCP connections.

Active Connections

Protocol	Local Address	Foreign Address	State
TCP	server1:1025	localhost:1026	ESTABLISHED
TCP	server1:1026	localhost:1025	ESTABLISHED
TCP	server1:1027	localhost:1029	ESTABLISHED
TCP	server1:1029	localhost:1027	ESTABLISHED
TCP	server1:1041	localhost:1043	ESTABLISHED
TCP	server1:1043	localhost:1041	ESTABLISHED

2. After an FTP session has been opened from the client by typing `ftp 172.16.8.101` and logging on as `anonymous`, the client machine is dynamically assigned the port number 1040 as its FTP control port connecting to port 21 on the server (port 21 on the server is called port ftp here). Note that from here on the localhost TCP connections are omitted.

Active Connections

Protocol	Local Address	Foreign Address	State
TCP	server1:ftp	SUPER:1040	ESTABLISHED

3. After `dir` is typed on the client to get a directory listing from the FTP server, data port 1047 is assigned to the client to connect to port 20 on the server (port 20 on the server is called port ftp-data here). Once the data has been transferred, the server port goes into a TIME_WAIT state and is unavailable for further use until the server causes the port to time out.

Active Connections

Protocol	Local Address	Foreign Address	State
TCP	server1:ftp-data	SUPER:1047	TIME_WAIT
TCP	server1:ftp	SUPER:1045	ESTABLISHED

4. After `get test.txt` is typed to download a file called test.txt from the server, a second data port (1048) is opened on the client for the new data transfer.

Active Connections

Protocol	Local Address	Foreign Address	State
TCP	server1:ftp-data	SUPER:1047	TIME_WAIT
TCP	server1:ftp-data	SUPER:1048	TIME_WAIT
TCP	server1:ftp	SUPER:1045	ESTABLISHED

5. After the connection with the server is closed by typing `bye`, all the ports opened on the server are placed in the TIME_WAIT state until they time out.

Active Connections

Protocol	Local Address	Foreign Address	State
TCP	server1:ftp-data	SUPER:1047	TIME_WAIT
TCP	server1:ftp-data	SUPER:1048	TIME_WAIT
TCP	server1:ftp	SUPER:1045	TIME_WAIT

Understanding FTP Site Security

FTP sites should generally be accessed using *anonymous access.* With anonymous access, a user trying to connect to an FTP site uses the IUSR_*SERVERNAME* account created when IIS is installed. When anonymous access is enabled,

- Users connecting with the Windows NT or 95 command-line FTP utility will have to actually log on to the FTP site using the username `anonymous` and anything for a password (it is traditional to use your email address for your password, which allows the sitemaster to determine who is logged on to the FTP site at any given time).
- Users connecting with browsers such as Internet Explorer are automatically authenticated using the IUSR_*SERVERNAME* account. No username or password needs to be entered from the browser.

With FTP, the only alternative to anonymous access is for the user to access the site using a valid Windows NT user account. The problem is that with FTP authentication, the username and password are transmitted as clear text (i.e., unencrypted). Anyone running Network Monitor or some other protocol analyzer on your network would be able to trap user credentials, and a security breach could result. For this reason, FTP sites should generally be set for anonymous access, and this should be the *only* authentication scheme allowed. This will prevent users from trying to use their NT domain credentials to try to gain access to the site. The procedure for doing this will be explained later in this chapter.

Additional security methods should be employed when necessary, especially when your FTP site is connected to the Internet. Be sure to consider the following options:

- Denying access to all users except those from certain blocks of IP network numbers or Internet domains
- Checking that NTFS permissions are set properly on home directories, which includes changing the permission on the Everyone group to *change* (RWXD) instead of *full control* (RWXD-PO), or removing the Everyone group and adding the IUSR_*SERVERNAME* account with *change* (RWXD) permission
- Changing the default FTP control port 21 to some other value
- Logging all FTP connections and reviewing them regularly to check for evidence of hacking
- Setting up a proxy server and firewall to filter packets and control FTP access (Microsoft Proxy Server 2 can fulfill this role)

Configuring FTP Site Properties

Like the WWW service, IIS 4.0 can be configured to have an unlimited number of FTP servers running on it simultaneously, each responding to its own unique IP address and fully qualified domain name (FQDN). Each of these *virtual* FTP servers (or FTP sites) behaves as if it were a distinct machine. Each can be configured separately and can be stopped, started, and paused independently.

Also like the WWW service, the property sheets for the FTP service on IIS 4.0 can be configured at several levels: *Master, Site,* and *Directory* levels.

Finally, again like the WWW service, when a new FTP site is created, it automatically inherits the Master FTP property settings of the IIS server on which it is created. Likewise, when a new FTP virtual directory is created, it automatically inherits the Site property settings of the FTP site on which it is created. When a Master FTP property setting is changed, you are given the option of passing this change along to all existing FTP sites on the IIS server. Similarly, when a property setting is changed on an FTP site, you are given the option of passing this change along to all existing virtual directories on the FTP site.

You can access and configure property settings for each of the three levels as follows:

- *Master* properties can be configured for all FTP sites running on the IIS server. To access Master properties, right-click on the IIS server node in the Microsoft Management Console (MMC) and select PROPERTIES from the shortcut menu (or select the IIS server node in the MMC, click the ACTION button on the rebar, and select PROPERTIES from the drop-down menu).
- *Site* properties (or Virtual Server properties) can be configured individually for each FTP site running on the IIS server, including the default FTP site created when IIS is installed. To access Site properties, right-click on the FTP site node in the MMC and select PROPERTIES from the shortcut menu.
- *Directory* properties (or Virtual Directory properties) can be configured individually for each virtual directory defined within an FTP site on the server. All files will inherit the property settings of the virtual directory that contains them. To access Directory properties, right-click on the virtual directory within the FTP site and select PROPERTIES from the shortcut menu.

FTP property sheets have different options available depending on whether they configure Master, Site, or Directory settings. Here are the property sheet tabs available for each level and the function they provide:

- *FTP Site* tab (Master and Site levels): configure site identification, limit connections, enable logging, view current sessions
- *Security Accounts* tab (Master and Site levels): configure anonymous access, grant operator privileges
- *Messages* tab (Master and Site levels): configure welcome, exit, and busy messages

- *Home (or Virtual) Directory* tab (Master, Site, and Directory levels): configure content location, access permissions, choose directory listing style
- *Directory Security* tab (Master, Site, and Directory levels): grant or deny access to hosts
- *IIS 3.0 Admin* tab (Master level only): designate which FTP site is to be administered by IIS 3.0 Internet Service Manager

In addition to these functions, the IIS Server Properties sheet can be used to throttle FTP bandwidth and configure the global MIME mappings. These features are covered in Chap. 3 and function the same for both the WWW and FTP services.

Configuring FTP Site Identification

To give the FTP site a friendly description that will appear beside the node in the MMC, type a name in the Description textbox (see Fig. 9-2).

Use the IP Address drop-down box to assign a particular IP address to the FTP site. If you leave the setting here at ALL UNASSIGNED, the FTP site will respond to all IP addresses that are not specifically assigned to other FTP sites, in effect making this the new default FTP site. Only IP addresses that have been previously configured in the Network application of Control Panel will appear in the drop-down box here.

The default TCP port for FTP control messages is port 21. To change this value, enter a new number in the TCP Port box. *Note that the IIS server will need to be rebooted for the new port number to come into effect.* Users will need to be notified of the change in port numbers, because when they try to access this FTP site they will have to include the port number.

For example, if the port is changed to 1253 and users are using the command-line FTP utility in Windows 95 or NT to connect to an FTP site with the address 164.43.25.8, they will have to type the following at the command prompt to open a session:

```
ftp 164.43.25.8:1253
```

If they try to access the same server using Internet Explorer, they must use the URL

```
ftp://164.43.25.8:1253
```

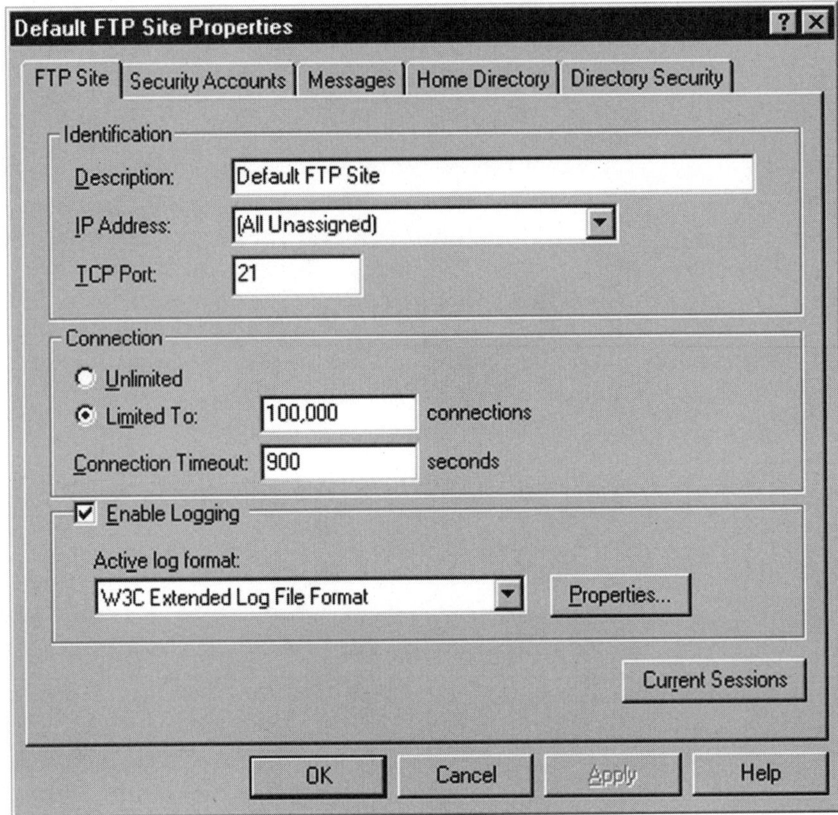

Figure 9-2 Configuring site identification, limiting connections, enabling logging, and viewing connections.

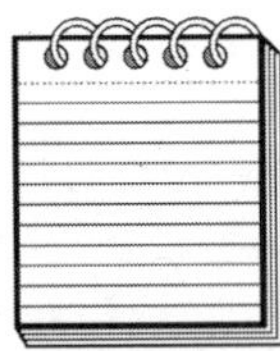

NOTE: *Do not use any of the Well-Known Port Numbers for the FTP control port number, other than port 21. Otherwise conflicts may occur with other TCP services.*

Configuring FTP Connection Limits and Timeouts

Selecting UNLIMITED (see Fig. 9-2) will allow the FTP site to service an unlimited number of connections simultaneously. To limit the number of simultaneous FTP connections allowed to your site (or to the server, if this is a Master property setting), choose LIMITED TO and enter a value in the textbox (the default is 100,000).

To configure the amount of time an FTP connection remains in a TIME_WAIT state before timing out and freeing the port for other use, enter a value in the Connection Timeout textbox (the default is 900 seconds, or 15 minutes).

Configuring FTP Logging

By default, the ENABLE LOGGING checkbox is selected (see Fig. 9-2), and logs are recorded in W3C Extended Log File Format. FTP sites may be logged in one of three formats:

- Microsoft IIS Log File Format
- ODBC Logging
- W3C Extended Log File Format

To configure logging for any of these formats, select the format using the Active log format drop-down box and click the PROPERTIES button. Configuring logging formats is covered in Chap. 3.

Viewing and Terminating FTP User Sessions

To view the currently open FTP sessions, click the CURRENT SESSIONS button on the FTP Site tab of the Site (or Master) property sheet. This opens the FTP User Sessions box (Fig. 9-3), with which you can view three kinds of information concerning connected users:

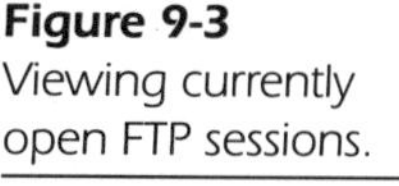

Figure 9-3 Viewing currently open FTP sessions.

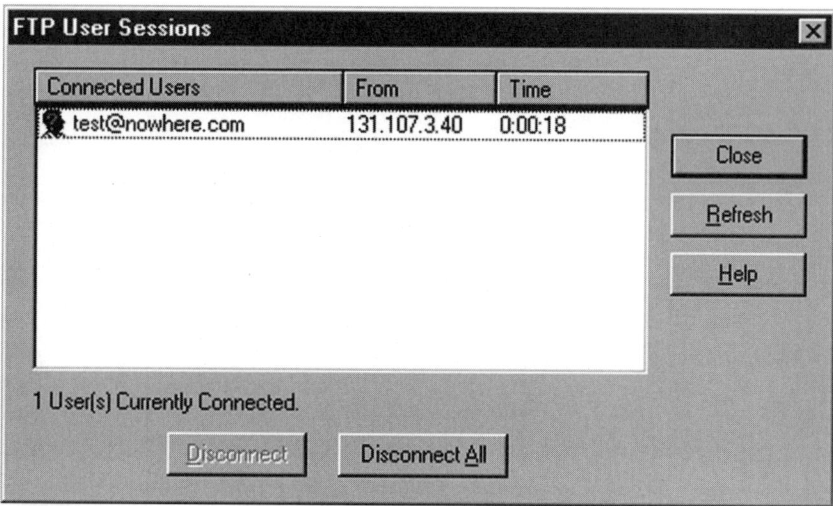

- The password used to log on to the FTP site (with anonymous access, users generally log on with the username `anonymous` and use their email address for a password, although they may use anything for a password)
- The IP address of the user's machine
- The amount of time since the session started

To disconnect a particular user, select the user and click DISCONNECT. To terminate all sessions, click DISCONNECT ALL. Click REFRESH to refresh the list of sessions currently open.

Configuring FTP Authentication Methods

To allow anonymous access to your FTP site, use the Security Accounts tab in the Default FTP Site Properties sheet, and select the ALLOW

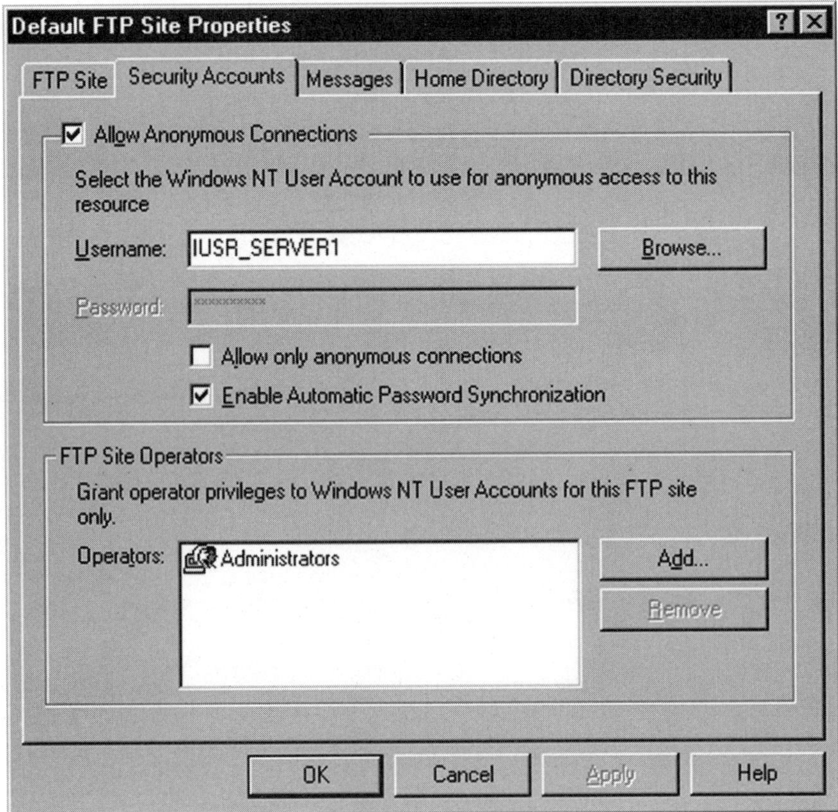

Figure 9-4 Configuring anonymous access and granting operator privileges.

ANONYMOUS CONNECTIONS checkbox (this is selected by default; see Fig. 9-4). To limit access to *only* anonymous connections, select the ALLOW ONLY ANONYMOUS CONNECTIONS checkbox (this is cleared by default). As discussed previously, *both* checkboxes should normally be selected so that users do not try to access the FTP site using their NT domain credentials. Because these credentials would be passed to the server as clear text, they can be viewed by any protocol analyzer connected to the network, creating the risk of a security breach.

Anonymous access to an FTP site makes use of the IUSR_*SERVERNAME* account that is created when IIS is installed. If you want to change this account, create a new user account in User Manager for Domains, and enter the username and password of this account in the Username and Password textboxes on this property sheet (you can also select BROWSE to locate the new account on the domain controller). Make sure this account is assigned the right to log on locally in User Manager for Domains, as anonymous access requires this right. Instead of entering the account password in the Password textbox, you can select the ENABLE AUTOMATIC PASSWORD SYNCHRONIZATION checkbox to synchronize the passwords between this property sheet and User Manager; however, you can do this only if the IUSR_*SERVERNAME* account is an account *local* to the machine on which IIS is installed.

Enabling anonymous access to your FTP site means that users *must* log on with the username `anonymous` but can use anything for a password.

For more on the security implications of enabling or not enabling anonymous access to your FTP site or server, see the section "Understanding FTP Site Security" earlier in this chapter.

Configuring FTP Site Operators

Grant operator privileges for your FTP site or server to Windows NT user accounts and groups by clicking the ADD button (see Fig. 9-4) and browsing the accounts list (a domain controller must be available). By default, the Administrators local group is assigned operator privileges, but FTP site operators do not *have* to be members of the Administrators local group.

FTP site operators have the right to administer *only* the FTP site to which they are assigned. Operators have limited administration rights and are able to perform simple administrative tasks such as

- Setting access permissions

- Enabling and configuring logging
- Limiting connections to the site
- Enabling/disabling anonymous access
- Creating welcome and exit messages
- Configuring IP level security
- Choosing a directory listing style

Operators cannot perform the following tasks unless they are also members of the Administrators local group:

- Configuring a new anonymous account
- Creating new virtual directories
- Viewing connected users and disconnecting them
- Changing the IP address or TCP port number of the site
- Granting operator privileges to users
- Changing the home directory

Typically, FTP site operators will consist of the Administrators local group and the company or departmental person responsible for managing the particular FTP site.

Configuring FTP Messages

Use the Messages tab to configure welcome, exit, and busy messages for your site or server (see Fig. 9-5). *Welcome* messages may include such information as

- The purpose of the FTP site
- Who owns and manages the site and the sitemaster's email address
- A brief description of the top-level directory or the location of an INDEX.TXT file cataloging the site
- Names and locations of mirror sites
- Rules on uploading or downloading files

Exit messages are typically short and sweet. *Maximum connections* messages indicate that the FTP site is currently too busy to respond to the user's request for a session. They may also include a list of mirror sites that may be tried.

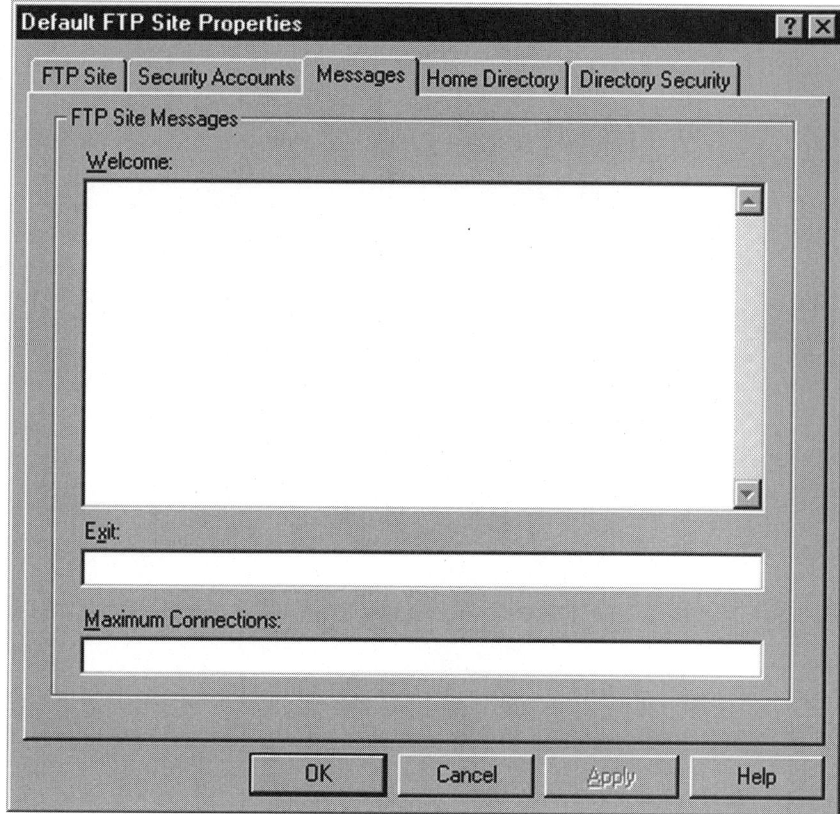

Figure 9-5 Configuring welcome, exit, and busy messages.

Configuring FTP Home Directory Location

The actual content for an FTP site may be a folder in

- The local computer (IIS server)
- A remote network share

The default FTP site created when IIS is installed is located at

```
C:\inetpub\ftproot
```

but this is a purely arbitrary location.

For FTP Site properties, the Home Directory tab (see Fig. 9-6) can be used to configure the location of the home content for the FTP site. For FTP Directory properties, the Virtual Directory tab can be used to configure the location of the content mapped to the virtual directory on the FTP site.

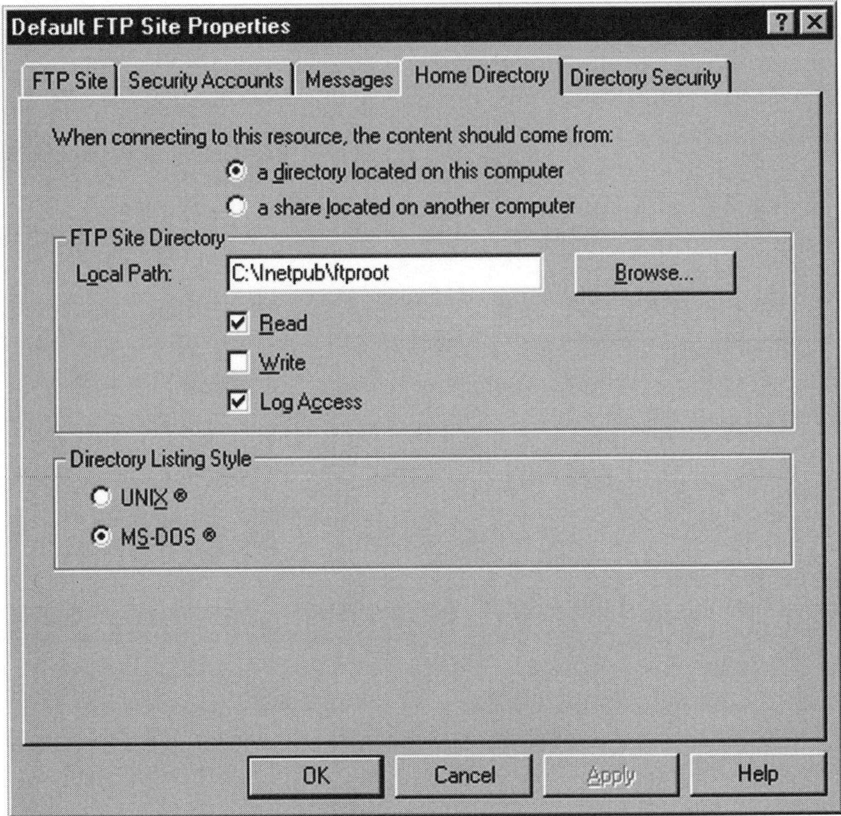

Figure 9-6 Configuring content location, access permissions, and directory listing style.

- To specify *local* content, select A DIRECTORY LOCATED ON THIS COMPUTER, and type the full path to the folder in the Local Path textbox or use the BROWSE button to locate it.
- To specify *remote* content, select A SHARE LOCATED ON ANOTHER COMPUTER, and type the UNC path to the share in the Network Share textbox. You *must* then specify a valid Windows NT account that has access permissions to the network share. Click CONNECT AS and enter an appropriate account in the Network Directory Security Credentials dialog box. If anonymous access is enabled on the FTP site, the anonymous account IUSR_*SERVERNAME* can be assigned NTFS or share-level permissions on the shared folder and can be entered in the Network Directory Security Credentials box.

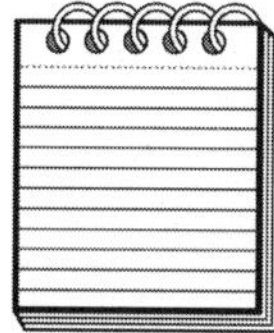

NOTE: Do not enter an Administrator account in this dialog box; this may lead to a security breach.

Configuring FTP Access Permissions

Access permissions to FTP home and virtual directories are best controlled by locating the content folder on an NTFS volume and assigning NTFS permissions. Typical NTFS permissions for FTP content directories are read (RX), add (WX), and change (RWXD). If the volume is also located on a remote host, shared folder permissions will also have to be assigned (usually read or change).

The permissions assigned on this property sheet (see Fig. 9-6) combine with NTFS and shared permissions on the content folder so that those permissions that explicitly deny access take precedence over those that explicitly grant access. Typically you should select

- READ for FTP sites and directories that allow users to download files (e.g., the `download` directory)
- WRITE for FTP sites and directories that allow users to upload files (e.g., the `incoming` directory)

The third checkbox LOG ACCESS, logs all visits to the home or virtual directory in the FTP site.

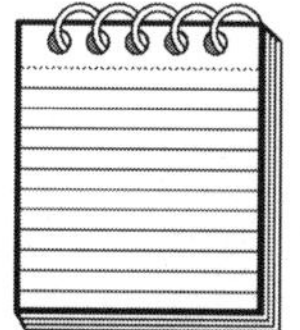

NOTE: LOG ACCESS allows you to selectively log some FTP virtual directories but not others, reducing server overhead due to the cost of logging.

Configuring FTP Directory Listing Style

When a GUI client such as Internet Explorer accesses an FTP site, it is presented with a directory listing. This directory listing can be configured to be either of two styles (see Fig. 9-6):

- MS-DOS style
- UNIX style

Generally, UNIX style is preferred for Internet sites, as some older browsers understand only this format. MS-DOS style is easier to navigate and is preferred for intranet sites that have standardized on Internet Explorer.

Note that this option can be configured only at the FTP site level, and not at the level of individual virtual directories on a site.

Configuring FTP Site IP Level Security

Using the Directory Security tab (Fig. 9-7), you can grant or deny access to your FTP site or virtual directory on a

- *Global* basis (either grant all computers access or deny all computers access)
- *Per-host* basis, according to IP address
- *Per-Network* basis, according to IP network number and subnet mask

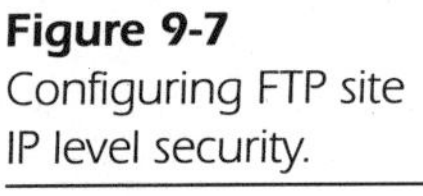

Figure 9-7
Configuring FTP site IP level security.

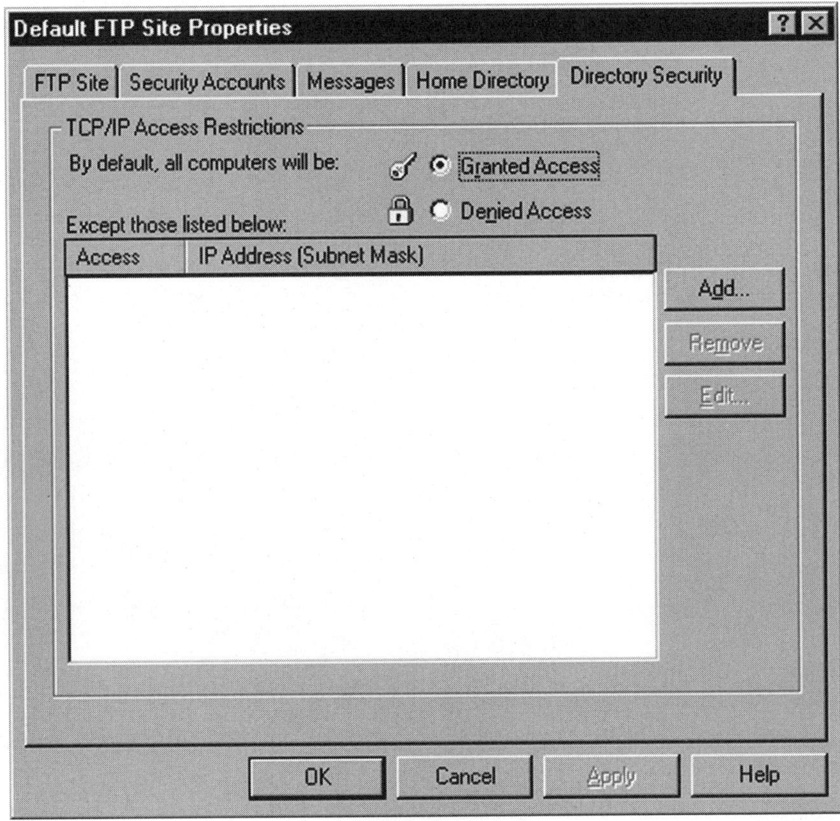

- *Per-fully-qualified-domain-name* basis, using DNS Lookup (if available)

Note that using DNS Lookup may slow down site access because of the extra overhead related to the name resolution process.

Configuring FTP for Administration by IIS 3.0

If your network contains a mix of IIS 4.0 and IIS 3.0 servers, you can configure one and only one FTP site on each IIS 4.0 server to be administered by the IIS 3.0 version of Internet Service Manager by using the IIS 3.0 Admin tab on the FTP Service Master Properties sheet for your server (Fig. 9-8).

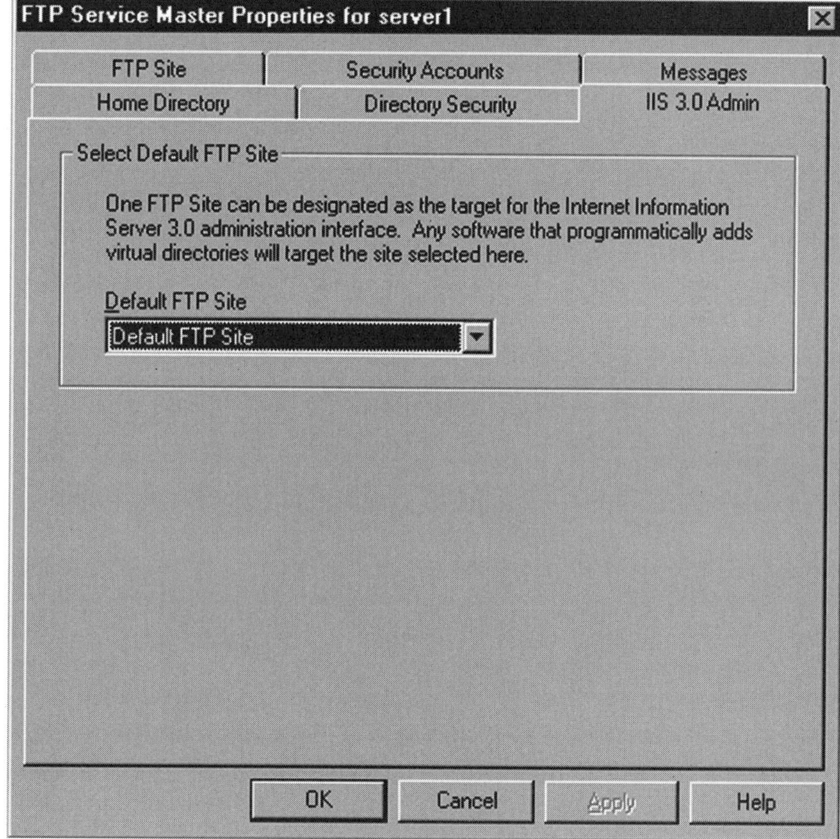

Figure 9-8 Configuring FTP for administration by IIS 3.0.

Walkthrough: Creating an FTP Site

FTP sites can be created and managed on IIS 4.0 using any of the following tools:

- The Internet Service manager (ISM) snap-in of the Microsoft Management Console (MMC)
- The HTML version of the Internet Service Manager
- The Windows Scripting Host

This walkthrough will cover use of the MMC with ISM snap-in to create, configure, and test a new FTP site with virtual directories.

Create the following local folders on your IIS server to host the content for the FTP site:

- `C:\MyFtpHome`
- `C:\MyFtpDownload`
- `C:\MyFtpUpload`

Create a file called `downtest.txt` and place it in the `MyFtpDownload` folder. Create a second file called `uptest.txt` and place it in the root of the machine you are using to connect to the FTP site. If these content folders are on an NTFS volume, make sure they have at least change (RWXD) permission assigned to them for the Everyone group.

From the MMC, right-click on the IIS server node and select NEW, FTP SITE from the shortcut menu. The New FTP Site Wizard appears (Fig. 9-9). Enter a friendly name for your new FTP site (here MyFtpSite has been selected as the name). This name may also be defined in a host record on a DNS server if the site will be accessed through domain names, so avoid spaces and non-alphanumeric characters in your site name.

Next select an IP address and port number for your new FTP site (Fig. 9-10). Typically, the IP address should be unique to the site, and the port should be the default port 21.

Next specify the local or network path to the home directory for the FTP site (Fig. 9-11). Here we have chosen the local folder

```
C:\MyFtpHome
```

as the home directory for the site.

Read access is now assigned to the home directory of the new site (Fig. 9-12). This is a typical choice, as the home directory usually contains

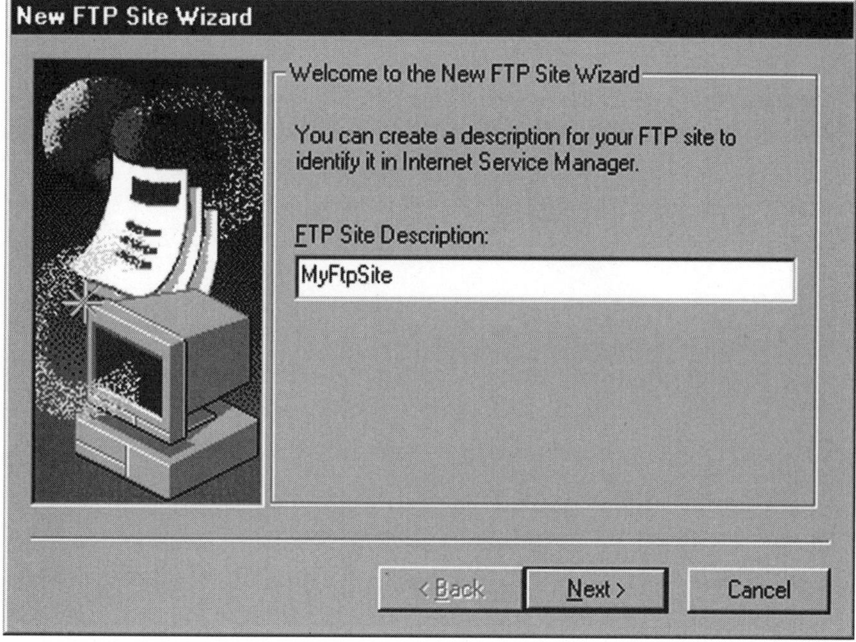

Figure 9-9
The New FTP Site Wizard.

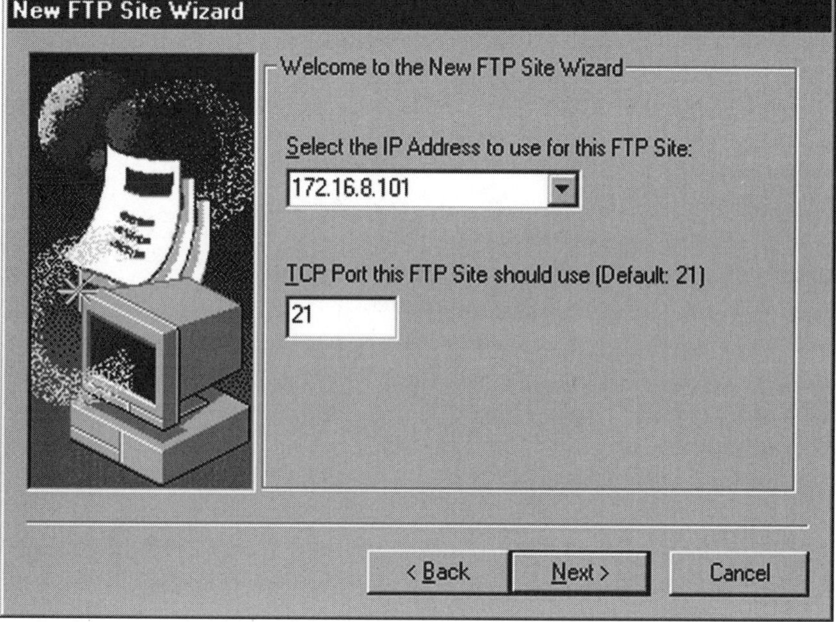

Figure 9-10
Assign an IP address and port number.

Figure 9-11 Specify a home directory for the new site.

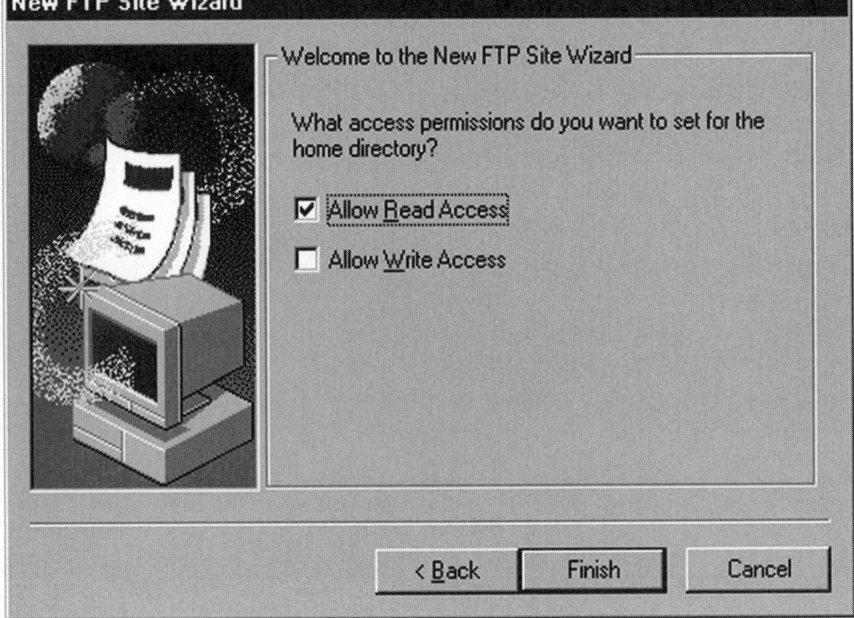

Figure 9-12 Allow read access to the home directory.

only read-only top-level documents such as the site index or list or README.TXT file.

Click FINISH now to create the new FTP site on the server. The newly created site is in a stopped state, so use the START button on the rebar to start the new site.

Now that we have created a new FTP site called MyFtpSite, we will create two new virtual directories within this site:

- `Download` will be used for storing files that users can download.
- `Incoming` will be used as a drop box for users who need to upload files to the site.

Create the `Incoming` virtual directory by right-clicking on the MyFtpSite icon in the MMC and selecting NEW, VIRTUAL DIRECTORY from the shortcut menu. This starts the New Virtual Directory Wizard (Fig. 9-13). Enter the name `incoming` as the alias for the new virtual directory.

Next enter the path to the folder that the incoming virtual directory will be mapped to (Fig. 9-14), namely,

```
C:\MyFtpUpload
```

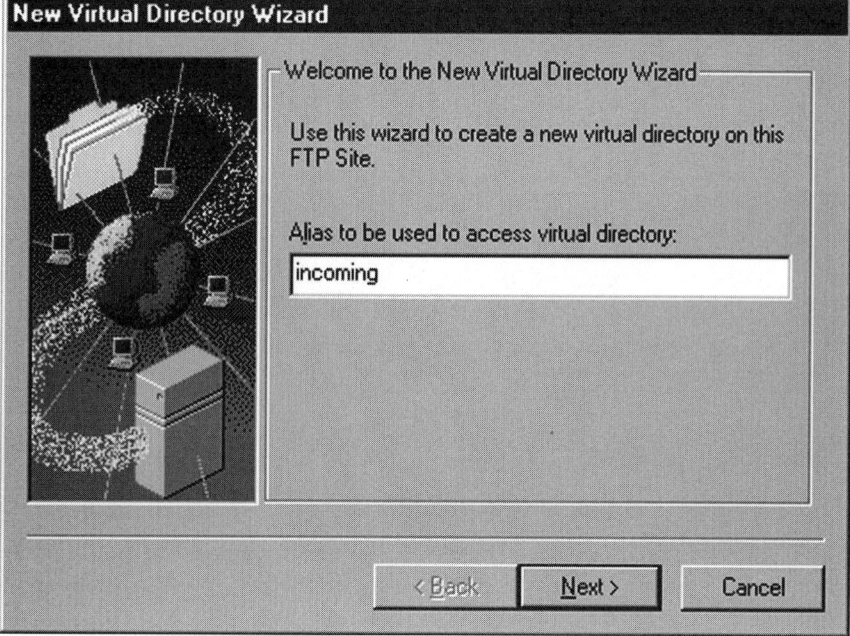

Figure 9-13 The New Virtual Directory Wizard.

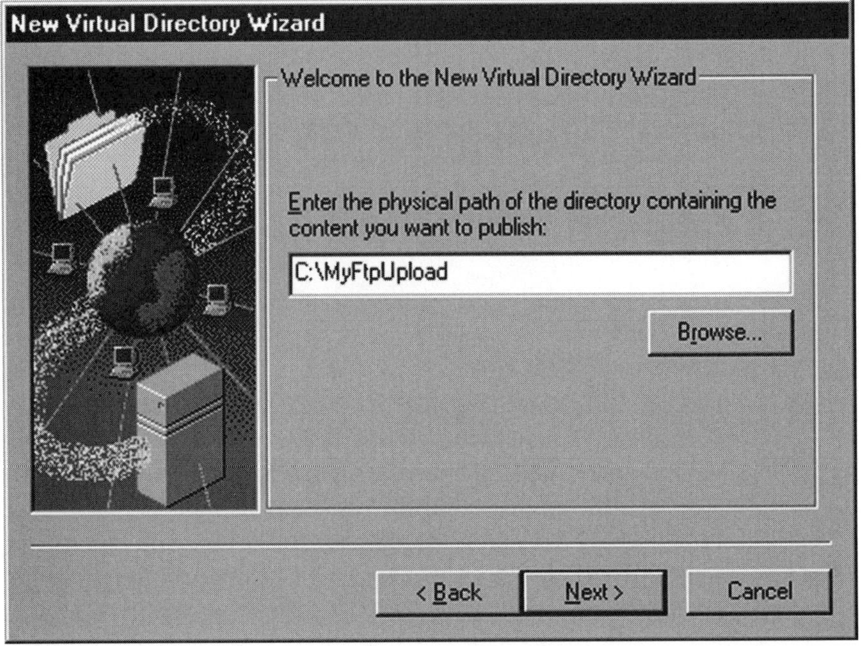

Figure 9-14 Map the new virtual directory to a content folder.

Finally, assign write Access *only* to the new virtual directory (Fig. 9-15). This will allow anonymous users to upload files to the `incoming` directory but will not allow them to see what files other users have uploaded. This is a typical setup, called an *FTP drop box,* which protects the privacy of users uploading their files. This is also called a location for *blind uploads.*

Click FINISH to create the virtual directory. Create the `download` virtual directory similarly, assigning it read Access only.

We can now view the results in the MMC (Fig. 9-16). Note the new icons in the scope pane (left side) for the FTP site and virtual directories. If you want to view the contents of a virtual directory, right-click on the virtual directory and choose OPEN or EXPLORE from the shortcut menu.

We can try connecting to the new site using the command-line FTP utility on a Windows NT or 95 host, either the local host or a remote one. Just open a Command Prompt session, type `ftp` to start the utility, and then type `open` to open the site (Fig. 9-17).

Following is a transcript of a session where we have connected to the new FTP site from a command prompt. In it we download the file `download.txt` from the `/download` directory and upload the file `upload.txt` to the `/incoming` directory.

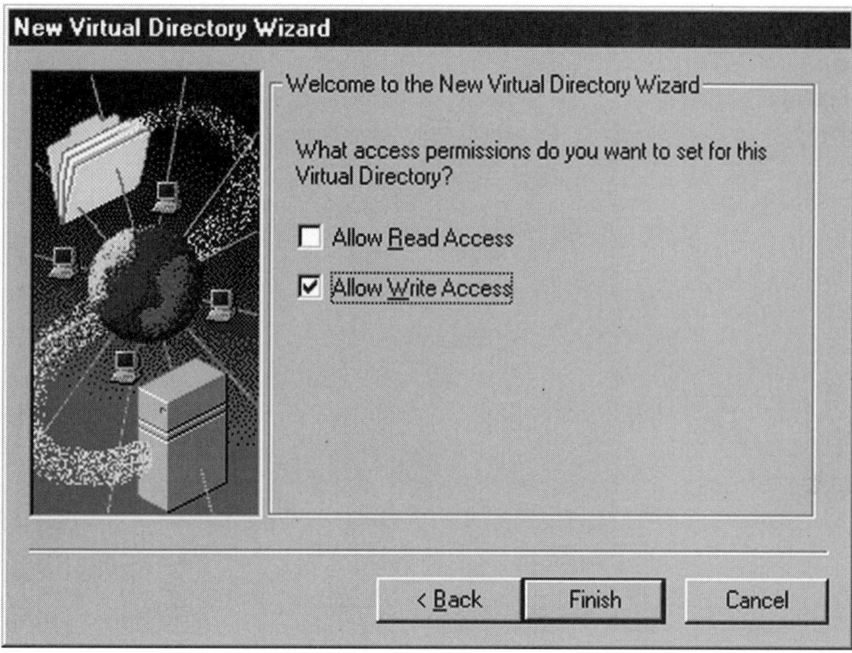

Figure 9-15 Creating an FTP drop box having write access only.

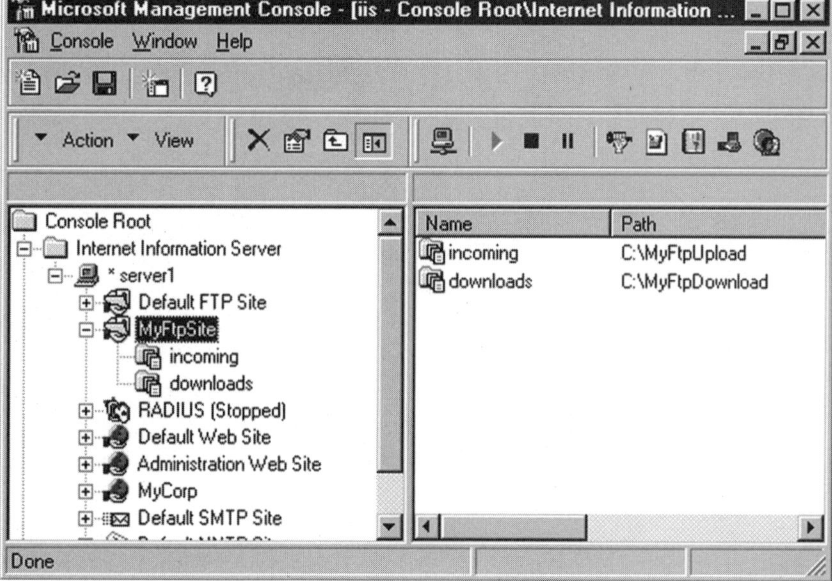

Figure 9-16 Viewing the new FTP site in the MMC.

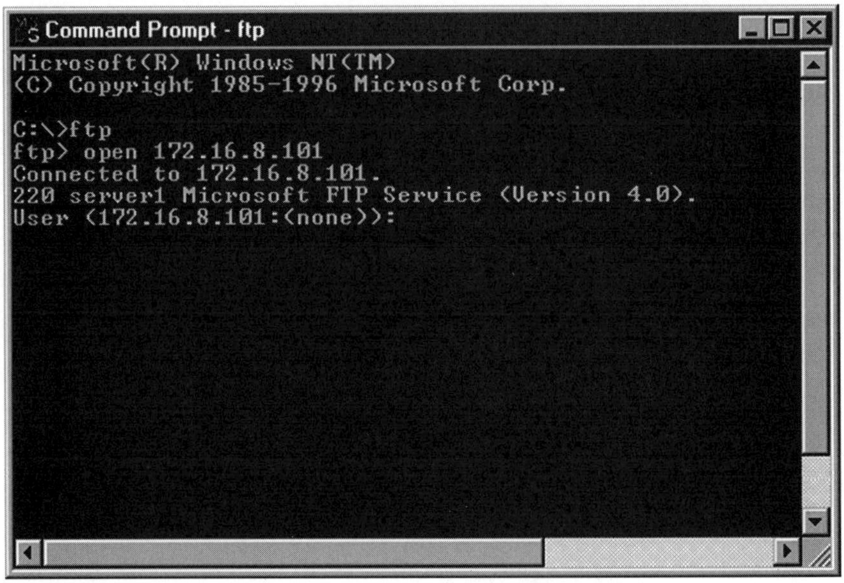

```
Command Prompt - ftp
Microsoft(R) Windows NT(TM)
(C) Copyright 1985-1996 Microsoft Corp.

C:\>ftp
ftp> open 172.16.8.101
Connected to 172.16.8.101.
220 server1 Microsoft FTP Service (Version 4.0).
User (172.16.8.101:(none)):
```

Figure 9-17 Testing the new FTP site from a command prompt.

```
C:\>ftp
ftp> open 172.16.8.101
Connected to 172.16.8.101.
220 server1 Microsoft FTP Service (Version 4.0).
User (172.16.8.101:(none)): anonymous
331 Anonymous access allowed, send identity (e-mail name) as pass-
word.
Password:
230-Welcome to my FTP site!
230-= = = = = = = = = = = = = = = = = = = = = = = = = = = = = = = =
230-put uploads into /incoming
230-get downloads from /download
230-= = = = = = = = = = = = = = = = = = = = = = = = = = = = = = = =
230 Anonymous user logged in.
ftp> cd download
250 CWD command successful.
ftp> dir
200 PORT command successful.
150 Opening ASCII mode data connection for /bin/ls.
-r-xr-xr-x   1 owner   group   87 Jan   2 16:50
downtest.txt
226 Transfer complete.
73 bytes received in 0.02 seconds (3.65 kbps)
ftp> get downtest.txt
200 PORT command successful.
150 Opening ASCII mode data connection for downtest.txt(87 bytes).
226 Transfer complete.
ftp> cd ../incoming
250 CWD command successful.
ftp> dir
200 PORT command successful.
150 Opening ASCII mode data connection for /bin/ls.
550 .: Access is denied.
```

```
ftp> put uptest.txt
200 PORT command successful.
150 Opening ASCII mode data connection for uptest.txt.
226 Transfer complete.
ftp> bye
221 Thanks for visiting!
```

This session listing illustrates how to use basic FTP command-line commands such as `open`, `close`, `get`, and `put`. For a listing of all available FTP command-line commands, type the following at the command prompt:

```
C:\> ftp
fpt> ?
```

A list of all FTP commands will appear. To get a brief explanation about a specific command—for example, the command `put`—simply type:

```
ftp> ? put
put    send one file
```

The three-digit number at the start of each line returned by the FTP server is called an *FTP return code*. For example, the return code 200 always means that the command was successfully executed.

Another way of testing the new FTP site is to use Internet Explorer as an FTP client program. Start Internet Explorer and open the following URL

```
ftp://172.16.8.101/download
```

The result is the directory listing shown in Fig. 9-18. This is an example of the MS-DOS style of directory listing.

With Internet Explorer 4.0, if the browser tries to access an FTP site that is either stopped or has read access disabled, the error message in Fig. 9-19 appears. FTP error messages are not configurable with IIS 4.0.

SUMMARY

IIS 4.0 has a fully configurable FTP service with the capability of hosting multiple FTP sites (virtual servers) on a single machine. Content for FTP sites may be hosted on either the local IIS server or on a remote network share. FTP sites are a useful complement to Web sites, providing a centralized location for downloads and making blind uploads possible.

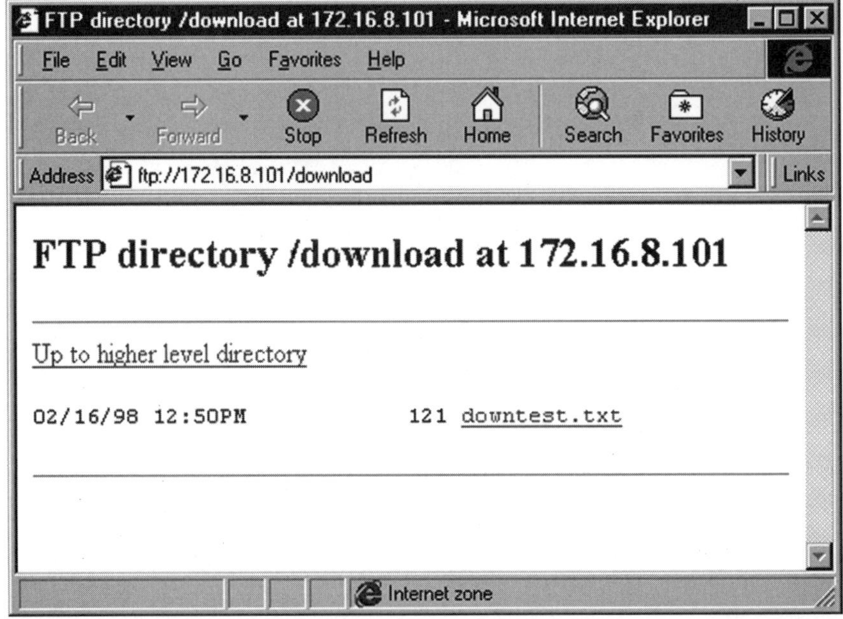

Figure 9-18 Accessing an FTP site using Internet Explorer.

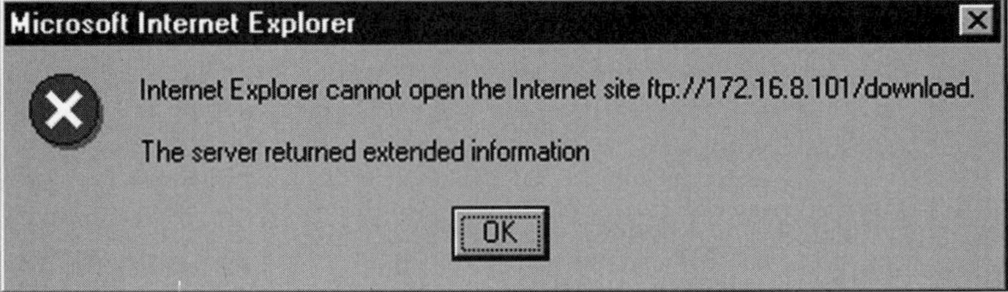

Figure 9-19 Message indicating an inaccessible FTP site.

FOR MORE INFORMATION

Microsoft Web Site Visit a really large FTP site,

```
ftp.microsoft.com
```

and view how it is organized and laid out by opening the site in Internet Explorer.

Microsoft Newsgroups You can post questions about the Microsoft FTP service on IIS 4.0 to the group

```
microsoft.public.inetserver.iis
```

CHAPTER 10

Administering Performance

Introduction

Monitoring and optimizing the performance of servers is an important task for any administrator. Ensuring that Web, FTP, and other Internet servers can handle peak loads effectively is critical for any company using the Internet for business purposes. This chapter looks at Windows NT 4.0 monitoring and diagnostic tools as they apply to Internet Information Server 4.0, including

- Performance Monitor
- Task Manager
- Command-line TCP/IP utilities
- IIS logs
- Event Viewer
- Network Monitor
- IIS Web Capacity Analysis Tool (WCAT)

Also discussed are various techniques for tuning and optimizing the performance of IIS services, including

- Optimizing hardware components
- Relocating resource-consuming applications
- Stopping unnecessary services
- Restricting the use of logging
- Restricting the use of SSL
- Throttling bandwidth
- Limiting the number of connections
- Maximizing processor time for services
- Adjusting cache size to optimize memory usage
- Optimizing content type
- Enabling HTTP Keep-Alives

IIS Performance Monitoring

Monitoring the performance of IIS servers can provide the administrator with information about

- Bottlenecks affecting server performance
- Unbalanced loads resulting from frequently accessed sites
- Inability of users to form connections because of high traffic
- Average and peak resource usage
- Long-term trends in resource usage
- Server errors due to hardware or software failures

This performance information can be used to

- Plan hardware and software upgrades to meet expected capacity.
- Isolate and correct hardware and software problems affecting performance.
- Tune and optimize services to meet average and peak loads.
- Report site access statistics for billing purposes.
- Minimize overspending related to the purchase of unnecessary hardware upgrades.

The tools used to monitor IIS performance are the basic monitoring and troubleshooting tools that come with the Windows NT 4.0 Server operating system, plus additional tools developed specifically for IIS.

Performance Monitor

Windows NT Performance Monitor is the primary tool for monitoring and evaluating IIS performance (Fig. 10-1). With Performance Monitor administrators can

- Monitor various aspects of IIS services in real time.
- Log performance data over time to identify baselines and evaluate trends.
- Create charts and reports to display performance data.
- Set alert conditions to notify administrators when performance criteria are exceeded.
- Identify bottlenecks in processor, memory, disk, and network subsystems.
- Observe how performance changes in response to hardware/software configuration changes.
- Calculate system capacity and forecast future needs.

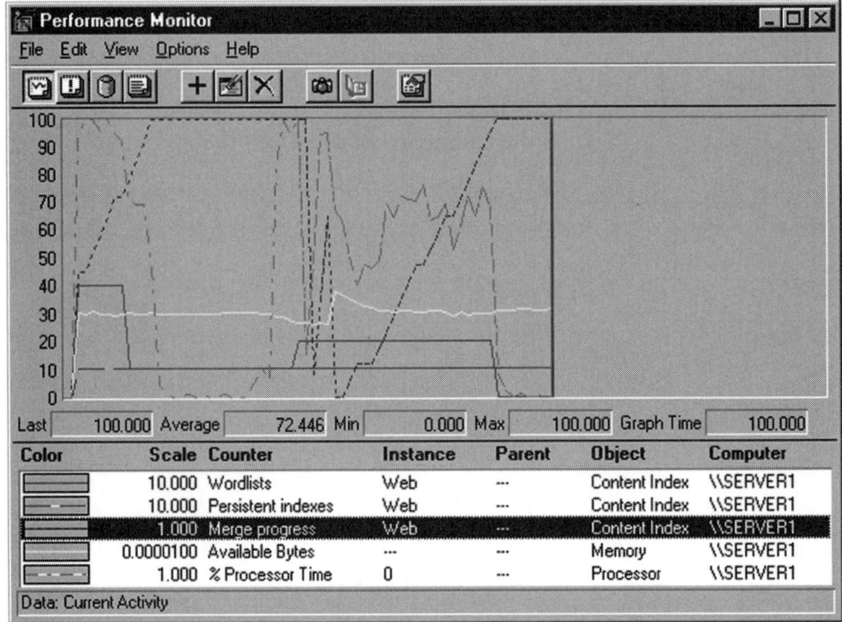

Figure 10-1 Using Performance Monitor to chart server activity.

Performance Monitor can display or log the activity of *instances* of *counters* belonging to various kinds of server *objects. Objects* refer to hardware and software processes that make use of server resources. Examples of objects are

- Memory
- LogicalDisk
- PagingFile
- Redirector

Counters are grouped according to the type of object they belong to and specify the particular form of hardware or software activity to be monitored. Examples of counters for the object LogicalDisk are

- LogicalDisk: % Disk Read Time
- LogicalDisk: % Free Space
- LogicalDisk: Disk Bytes/Transfer
- LogicalDisk: Free Megabytes

When Performance Monitor is monitoring a particular object, it collects all instances of all counters for that object.

Instances are multiple occurrences of particular counters, depending on the hardware and software involved. For example, the LogicalDisk: Free Megabytes counter might have the instances

- 0 = = > C:
- 0 = = > D:
- Total = = > _Total

meaning the instance "Logical Drive C," the instance "Logical Drive D," and the instance "Total of all Logical Drives," respectively.

Figure 10-2 show an Add to Chart dialog box illustrating the preceding example. To see a description of what type of information the selected counter collects, click the EXPLAIN button in the Add to Chart box, and a Counter Definition section will appear at the bottom of the dialog box.

When various components of IIS 4.0 are installed on a system, new Performance Monitor objects are also installed to enable administrators to monitor these services. These new objects, in addition to standard Windows NT Performance Monitor objects, provide administrators with a wide range of tools for monitoring the performance of IIS servers. To review the functions monitored by standard Windows NT Performance Monitor objects, refer to the Windows NT 4.0 Server Resource Kit, the Windows NT 4.0 Workstation Resource Kit, and the Windows NT 4.0 Server Resource Kit Supplements 1 and 2, published by Microsoft Press.

Table 10-1 lists some of the new Performance Monitor objects that are included when an IIS service is installed.

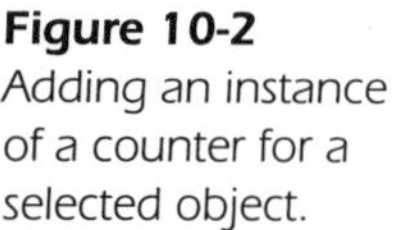

Figure 10-2
Adding an instance of a counter for a selected object.

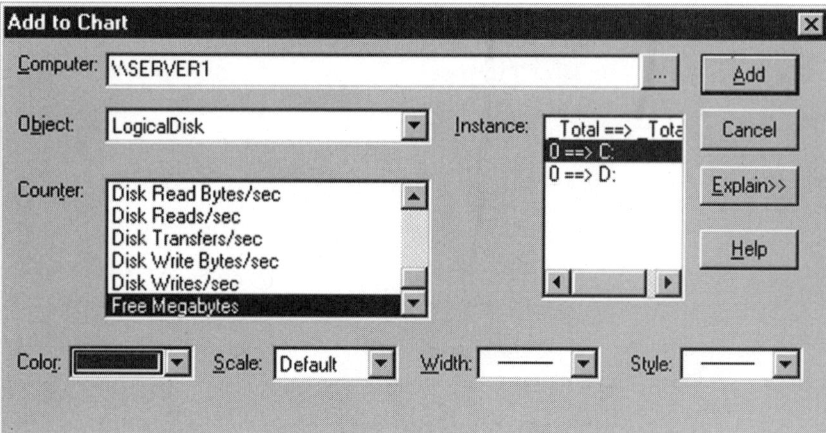

Table 10-1

New Performance Monitor Objects Included with IIS

Service	Object
IIS default (WWW and FTP)	Internet Information Services Global
	Web Service
	FTP Service
	Active Server Pages
SMTP	SMTP Server
NNTP	NNTP Server
	NNTP Commands
Content indexing	Content Index
	Content Index Filter
	HTTP Content Index

We will now list in detail the counters available for the following new objects, along with the counter definitions as viewed by clicking the EXPLAIN button on the Add to Chart dialog box:

- Internet Information Services Global
- Web Service
- FTP Service
- Content Index
- Content Index Filter
- HTTP Content Index

Information about other new objects listed in Table 10-1 may be found in later chapters of this book. Information about Active Server Pages objects can be found in the online documentation.

The counters can be classified into four main categories, depending on how they are collected:

- *Instantaneous* counters give moment-by-moment readings.
- *Average* counters give average values over a recent time interval (usually one minute).
- *Cumulative* counters give total values since the associated service was last started.
- *Maximum* counters give peak values since the associated service was last started.

In addition to monitoring the objects in the following list, administrators should also monitor the basic counters for detecting bottlenecks in processor, memory, disk drive, and network usage, since these are the four basic hardware elements that most affect server performance.

1. Recommended counters for monitoring the *processor* include

   - Processor: % Processor Time (should be less than 75 percent most of the time)
   - System: Processor Queue Length (should be less than 2 most of the time)
   - Processor: Interrupts/sec (a drastic increase here could indicate a device failure)

   Failure to satisfy one or more of these criteria indicates that your processor could be a bottleneck. The solution is to upgrade the processor, add another processor, or offload some of the server load to another machine.

2. Recommended counters for monitoring *memory* include

   - Memory: Available Bytes (should be above 4 MB most of the time)
   - Memory: Committed Bytes (should be less than the amount of physical RAM)
   - Memory: Pages/sec (should be less than 5 most of the time)

   Failure to satisfy one or more of these criteria indicates that your physical memory (RAM) could be a bottleneck. The solution is to add more RAM.

3. Recommended counters for monitoring the *disk subsystem* include

   - PhysicalDisk: % Disk Time (should not be close to 100 percent for frequent, extended periods)
   - PhysicalDisk: Disk Queue Length (should be less than 2 most of the time)
   - The same two counters for the LogicalDisk object

   Failure to satisfy one or more of these criteria indicates that your disk subsystem could be a bottleneck. The solution is to upgrade to a better controller, a faster spindle, or a RAID 0 stripe set.

4. Recommended counters for monitoring the *network subsystem* include

- Network Segment: % Network Utilization (a sustained value of 60 to 80 percent is considered saturated)
- Network Interface: Bytes Total/sec (the higher the value, the better the network card)

Failure to satisfy one or more of these criteria indicates that your network subsystem could be a bottleneck. Upgrade to a faster network card, add another network card, or segment the network to reduce broadcast traffic.

NOTE: *The PhysicalDisk and LogicalDisk objects require enabling to be monitored. To enable these objects from the command prompt, type*

`diskperf -y` (for a regular hard drive)

or

`diskperf -ye` (for a RAID stripe set)

The Network Segment object is available in Performance Monitor only when the Network Monitor Agent service is installed on the server.

The Network Interface object is available in Performance Monitor only when the SNMP service is installed on the server.

Internet Information Services Global Counters Counters for the object Internet Information Services Global provide performance information regarding all IIS services running (i.e., WWW, FTP, NNTP, SMTP, etc.). The following counters may be monitored for this object; the descriptions are taken verbatim from the explanation offered when you click on the EXPLAIN button after selecting a counter to add.

Cache Flushes	The number of times a portion of the memory cache has been expired due to file or directory changes in an Internet Information Services directory tree
Cache Hits	The total number of times a file open, directory listing, or service-specific object request was found in the cache
Cache Hits %	The ratio of cache hits to all cache requests

Cache Misses	The total number of times a file open, directory listing, or service-specific object request was not found in the cache
Cached File Handles	The number of open file handles cached by all of the Internet Information Services
Current Blocked Async I/O Requests	Current requests temporarily blocked due to bandwidth throttling settings
Directory Listings	The number of directory listings cached by all of the Internet Information Services
Measured Async I/O Bandwidth Usage	Measured bandwidth of asynchronous I/O averaged over a minute
Objects (the default counter)	The number of objects cached by all of the Internet Information Services (including file handle tracking objects, directory listing objects, and service-specific objects)
Total Allowed Async I/O Requests	Total requests allowed by bandwidth throttling settings (counted since service startup)
Total Blocked Async I/O Requests	Total requests temporarily blocked due to bandwidth throttling settings (counted since service startup)
Total Rejected Async I/O Requests	Total requests rejected due to bandwidth throttling settings (counted since service startup)

Web Service Counters Counters for the object Web Service provide performance information specifically related to the WWW service on IIS. The following counters may be monitored for this object.

Anonymous Users/sec	The rate at which users are making anonymous connections using the Web service
Bytes Received/sec	The rate at which data bytes are received by the Web service
Bytes Sent/sec	The rate at which data bytes are sent by the Web service
Bytes Total/sec (the default counter)	The sum of Bytes Sent/sec and Bytes Received/sec, i.e., the total rate of bytes transferred by the Web service

CGI Requests/sec	The rate of CGI requests being simultaneously processed by the Web service
Connection Attempts/sec	The rate at which connections using the Web service are being attempted
Current Anonymous Users	The number of users who currently have anonymous connections using the Web service
Current Blocked Async I/O Requests	Current requests temporarily blocked due to bandwidth throttling settings
Current CGI Requests	The current number of CGI requests simultaneously being processed by the Web service
Current Connections	The current number of connections established with the Web service
Current ISAPI Extension Requests	The current number of extension requests simultaneously being processed by the Web service
Current Nonanonymous Users	The number of users who currently have a nonanonymous connection using the Web service
Delete Requests/sec	The rate at which HTTP requests using the Delete method are made (such requests are generally used for file removals)
Files Received/sec	The rate at which files are received by the Web service
Files Sent/sec	The rate at which files are sent by the Web service
Files/sec	The rate at which files are transferred (i.e., sent and received) by the Web service
Get Requests/sec	The rate at which HTTP requests using the Get method are made (such requests are generally used for basic file retrievals or image maps, though they can also be used with forms)
Head Requests/sec	The rate at which HTTP requests using the Head method are made (such requests generally indicate that a client is querying the state of a document to see if it needs to be refreshed)

ISAPI Extension Requests/sec	The rate of ISAPI extension requests that are simultaneously being processed by the Web service
Logon Attempts/sec	The rate at which logons using the Web service are being attempted
Maximum Anonymous Users	The maximum number of users establishing concurrent anonymous connections using the Web service (counted since system startup)
Maximum CGI Requests	The maximum number of CGI requests simultaneously processed by the Web service
Maximum Connections	The maximum number of simultaneous connections established with the Web service
Maximum ISAPI Extension Requests	The maximum number of extension requests simultaneously processed by the Web service
Maximum Nonanonymous Users	The maximum number of users establishing concurrent nonanonymous connections using the Web service (counted since service startup)
Measured Async I/O Bandwidth Usage	The measured bandwidth of asynchronous I/O averaged over a minute
Nonanonymous Users/sec	The rate at which users are making non-anonymous connections using the Web service
Not Found Errors/sec	The rate of errors due to requests that couldn't be satisfied by the server because the requested documents could not be found (generally reported as an HTTP 404 error code to the client)
Other Request Methods/sec	The rate at which HTTP requests are made that do not use the Get, Post, Put, Delete, Trace, or Head method (these may include Link or other methods supported by gateway applications)
Post Requests/sec	The rate at which HTTP requests using the Post method are made (post requests are generally used for forms or gateway requests)
Put Requests/sec	The rate at which HTTP requests using the Put method are made

System Code Resident Bytes	System code resident bytes (!)
Total Allowed Async I/O Requests	Total requests allowed by bandwidth throttling settings (counted since system startup)
Total Anonymous Users	The total number of users establishing an anonymous connection with the Web service (counted since service startup)
Total Blocked Async I/O Requests	Total requests temporarily blocked due to bandwidth throttling settings (counted since service startup)
Total CGI Requests	Total Common Gateway Interface (CGI) requests—custom gateway executables (.exe) that the administrator can install to add forms processing or other dynamic data sources; CGI requests spawn a process on the server that can be a large drain on server resources (counted since service startup)
Total Connection Attempts	The number of connections that have been attempted using the Web service (counted since service startup)
Total Delete Requests	The number of HTTP requests using the Delete method (generally used for file removals; counted since service startup)
Total Files Received	The total number of files received by the Web service (counted since service startup)
Total Files Sent	The total number of files sent by the Web service (counted since service startup)
Total Files Transferred	The sum of Total Files Sent and Total Files Received, the total number of files transferred by the Web service (counted since service startup)
Total Get Requests	The number of HTTP requests using the Get method (generally used for basic file retrievals or image maps, though they can be used with forms, counted since service startup)
Total Head Requests	The number of HTTP requests using the Head method (such requests generally indicate that a client is querying the state of a document to see if it needs to be refreshed; counted since service startup)

Total ISAPI Extension Requests	Total custom gateway dynamic link libraries (.dll) the administrator can install to add forms processing or other dynamic data sources; unlike CGI requests, ISAPI requests are simple calls to a DLL library routine and thus are better suited to high-performance gateway applications (counted since service startup)
Total Logon Attempts	The number of logons that have been attempted using the Web service (counted since service startup)
Total Method Requests	The number of HTTP Get, Post, Put, Delete, Trace, Head, and other method requests (counted since service startup)
Total Method Requests/sec	The rate at which HTTP requests using Get, Post, Put, Delete, Trace, or Head methods are made
Total Nonanonymous Users	The total number of users establishing a nonanonymous connection with the Web service (counted since service startup)
Total Not Found Errors	The number of requests that couldn't be satisfied by the server because the requested document could not be found (generally reported as an HTTP 404 error code to the client; counted since service startup)
Total Other Request Methods	The number of HTTP requests that do not use the Get, Post, Put, Delete, Trace, or Head methods (may include Link or other methods supported by gateway applications; counted since system startup)
Total Post Requests	The number of HTTP requests using the Post method (generally used for forms or gateway requests) (counted since service startup)
Total Put Requests	The number of HTTP requests using the Put method (counted since service startup)
Total Rejected Async I/O Requests	Total requests rejected due to bandwidth throttling settings (counted since service startup)

Total Trace Requests	The number of HTTP requests using the Trace method; such requests allow the client to see what is being received at the end of the request chain and use the information for diagnostic purposes (counted since service startup)

FTP Service Counters Counters for the object FTP Service provide performance information specifically relating to the FTP service on IIS. The following counters may be monitored for this object.

Bytes Received/sec	The rate at which that data bytes are received by the FTP service
Bytes Sent/sec	The rate at which data bytes are sent by the FTP service
Bytes Total/sec (the default counter)	The sum of Bytes Sent/sec and Byte Received/sec, the total rate at which bytes are transferred by the FTP service
Current Anonymous Users	The number of users who currently have an anonymous connection using the FTP service
Current Connections	The current number of connections established with the FTP service
Current Nonanonymous Users	The number of users who currently have a nonanonymous connection with the FTP service
Maximum Anonymous Users	The maximum number of users establishing concurrent anonymous connections with the FTP service (counted since system startup)
Maximum Connections	The maximum number of simultaneous connections established with the FTP service
Maximum Nonanonymous Users	The maximum number of users establishing concurrent nonanonymous connections with the FTP service
Total Anonymous Users	The total number of users establishing an anonymous connection with the FTP service (since service startup)
Total Connection Attempts (all instances)	The number of connections that have been attempted using the FTP service (since service startup), for all instances listed

Total Files Received	The total number of files received by the FTP service
Total Files Sent	The total number of files sent by the FTP service since service startup
Total Files Transferred	The sum of Total Files Sent and Total Files Received, the total number of files transferred by the FTP service since service startup
Total Logon Attempts	The number of logons that have been attempted using the FTP service (since service startup)
Total Nonanonymous Users	The total number of users establishing a nonanonymous connection with the FTP service (since service startup)

Content Index Counters Counters for the object Content Index provide performance information specifically relating to the Content Index (Ci) service for Index Server. The following counters may be monitored for this object:

# documents filtered	The number of documents filtered since the index was mounted
Files to be filtered	Files to be filtered and added to the index
Index size (MB)	Size of the content index in megabytes
Merge progress	Percentage of current merge completed
Persistent indexes	Number of persistent indexes
Running queries	Number of running queries
Total # documents	Total number of documents in the index
Unique keys	Number of unique keys (words, etc.) in the index
Wordlists (the default counter)	Number of wordlists

Content Index Filters Counters Counters for the object Content Index Filters provide additional performance information relating to the Content Index (Ci) service for Index Server. The following counters may be monitored for this object:

Binding time (ms)	Average time spent binding to indexing filters
Filter speed (Mbph)	Speed of filtering contents of files, in megabytes per hour

Total filter speed (Mbph)	Speed of filtering file contents and properties, in megabytes per hour

Http Content Index Counters Counters for the object Http Content Index provide performance information relating to running queries and caching results on the Content Index (Ci) service for Index Server. The following counters may be monitored for this object:

% Cache hits	Percentage of queries found in the query cache
% Cache misses	Percentage of queries not found in the query cache
Active queries	Current number of running queries
Cache items	Number of completed queries in cache
Current requests queued	Current number of query requests queued
Queries per minute	Number of queries per minute
Total queries	Total number of queries run since service startup
Total requests rejected	Total number of query requests rejected

Task Manager

Windows NT Task Manager is a useful tool for monitoring performance and detecting problems with IIS services (Fig. 10-3). With Task Manager, administrators can

- Monitor the instantaneous CPU and memory usage of `inetinfo.exe`, the global IIS process.
- Monitor the instantaneous CPU and memory usage of related services such as `cisrv.exe` and `cidaemon.exe` (Index Server), `certsrv.exe` (Certificate Server), and so on.
- Graphically view the running CPU and memory usage for all processes combined.
- Detect and terminate runaway processes and applications.

Command-Line TCP/IP Utilities

Several TCP/IP command-line utilities are useful to administrators for monitoring and troubleshooting IIS services. These utilities include

- The general TCP/IP troubleshooting utilities `ipconfig` and `ping` (see App. A).

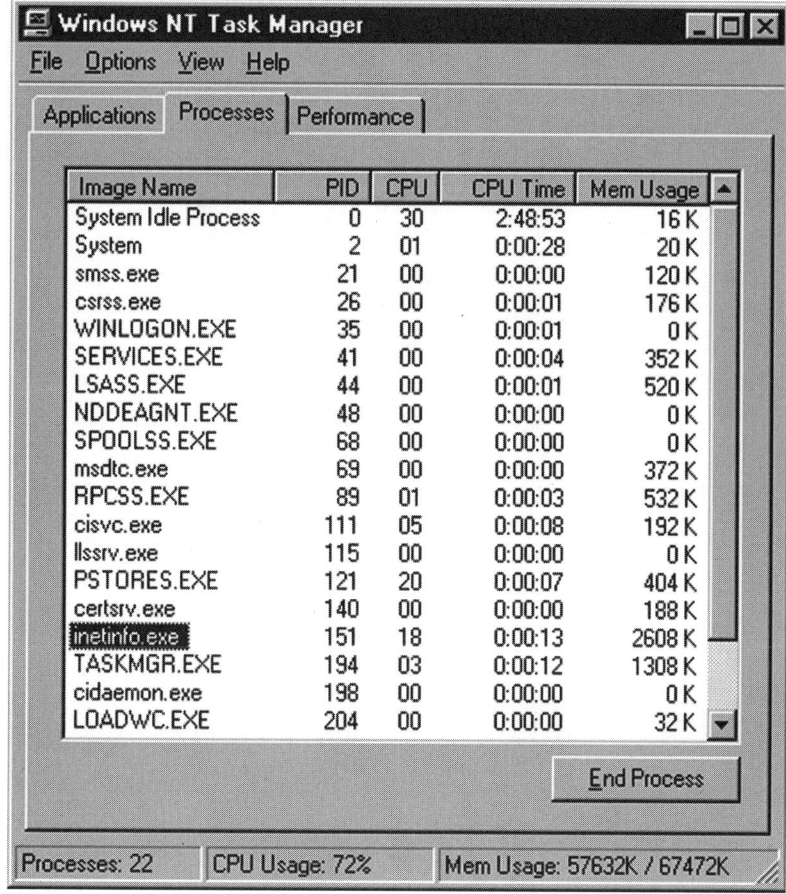

Figure 10-3
Windows NT Task Manager monitoring the `inetinfo.exe` process.

- `telnet`, which allows you to impersonate a client and send commands a line at a time to each IIS service. For example, if you are having problems with NNTP clients connecting to the NNTP service on IIS, try connecting with `telnet` instead by using the default NNTP port 119 on the server (Fig. 10-4). When a connection is made, the NNTP server should return a `200 NNTP` status message. Respond to this message by typing `list` and then pressing ENTER (you must have TERMINAL, PREFERENCES, LOCAL ECHO enabled to be able to see what you type in `telnet`). If `telnet` replies with a list of newsgroups, your news server is probably functioning properly, and the problem likely resides with the news client (Fig. 10-5). To obtain a list of commands understood by the NNTP service, type `help` and press ENTER.

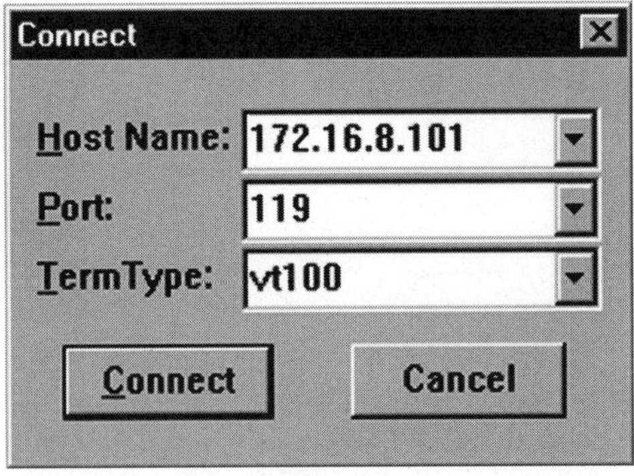

Figure 10-4 Connecting to the NNTP service using `telnet`.

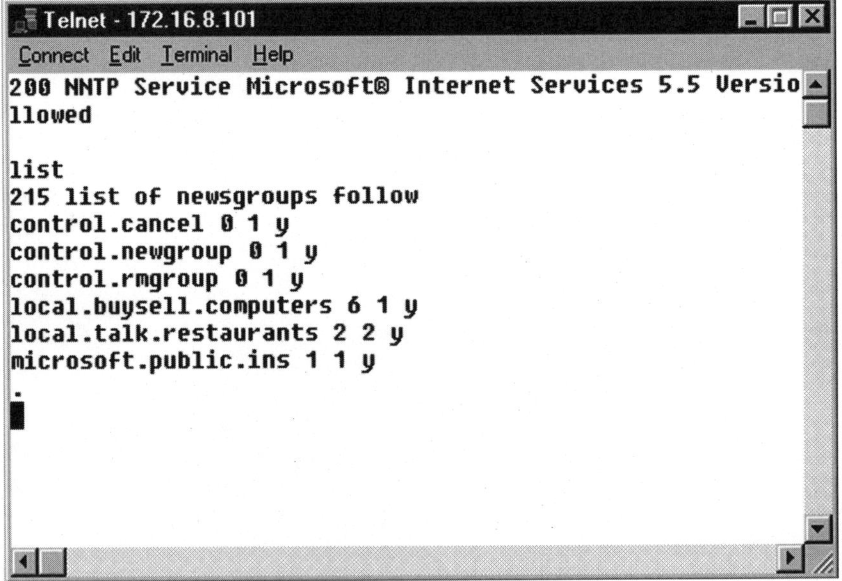

Figure 10-5 Connecting to the NNTP service on IIS using `telnet`.

- `netstat`, which displays the current state of TCP/IP connections and various TCP/IP protocol statistics for the server. Type `netstat /?` at the command prompt for usage information about this command. Some of the more important parameters are as follows:

  ```
  netstat -a
  ```

  displays all connections and listening ports (server-side connections are normally not shown).

  ```
  netstat -n
  ```

displays addresses and port numbers in numerical form.

```
netstat -s
```

displays per-protocol statistics.

```
netstat -p tcp
```

shows connections for the TCP protocol; this may be used with the `-s` option to display per-protocol statistics.

- `nslookup`, a command-line utility for examining records in the DNS server database, generally used to troubleshoot DNS-related problems (see App. B).

IIS Logs

The IIS logging capability allows administrators to determine how many clients are connecting to the server, when they connect, what they are viewing, and so on. This information is useful for

- Determining which sites or services are most popular so that these sites can be tuned for maximum responsiveness
- Determining which sites have problems such as broken links or failed applications

Logged information can be viewed directly in text files, exported from an ODBC-compliant database, or imported into Site Server Express for further analysis and reporting. See Chap. 11 for more information on the last option.

Event Viewer

Event Viewer provides administrators with information regarding system errors, warnings, and significant events related to Windows NT services. Event Viewer records three kinds of logs:

- *System* log: contains events related to Windows NT services and device drivers
- *Security* log: contains the Windows NT audit log
- *Application* log: contains events related to applications running on Windows NT

Events related to IIS and other NT Option Pack services are logged in the System log (Fig. 10-6). The keywords in the *Source* column may be filtered to focus in on particular IIS and related services, such as

- W3SVC: the WWW service
- MSFTPSVC: the FTP service
- SMTPSVC: the SMTP service
- NNTPSVC: the NNTP service

Events related to other NT Option Pack services are logged in the Application log. Keywords in the *Source* column include

- Ci: the Content Indexing service
- CERTSVC: Certificate Server
- MSDTC: Microsoft Transaction Server
- Active Server Pages

Network Monitor

Network Monitor can be used by administrators to capture and analyze network traffic at the packet level. (Figure 10-7 shows a Network Monitor trace of an HTTP Get request.) Network Monitor is more a diagnostic tool than a performance tool, allowing administrators to examine

Figure 10-6 The System log in Event Viewer showing IIS-related events.

Event Viewer - System Log on \\SERVER1

Log View Options Help

Date	Time	Source	Category	Event	Us
2/1/98	10:37:29 AM	EventLog	None	6005	
2/1/98	10:35:31 AM	BROWSER	None	8033	
2/1/98	10:27:55 AM	Srv	None	2013	
2/1/98	10:23:30 AM	SMTPSVC	None	525	
2/1/98	10:23:26 AM	SMTPSVC	None	554	
2/1/98	10:23:26 AM	SMTPSVC	None	423	
2/1/98	10:23:26 AM	W3SVC	None	101	
2/1/98	10:23:26 AM	W3SVC	None	101	
2/1/98	10:23:25 AM	W3SVC	None	101	
2/1/98	10:23:20 AM	W3SVC	None	101	
2/1/98	10:23:20 AM	W3SVC	None	101	
2/1/98	10:23:12 AM	SMTPSVC	None	531	
2/1/98	10:22:53 AM	NETLOGON	None	5719	
2/1/98	10:22:16 AM	EventLog	None	6005	
2/1/98	10:20:30 AM	BROWSER	None	8033	
2/1/98	10:19:56 AM	W3SVC	None	101	

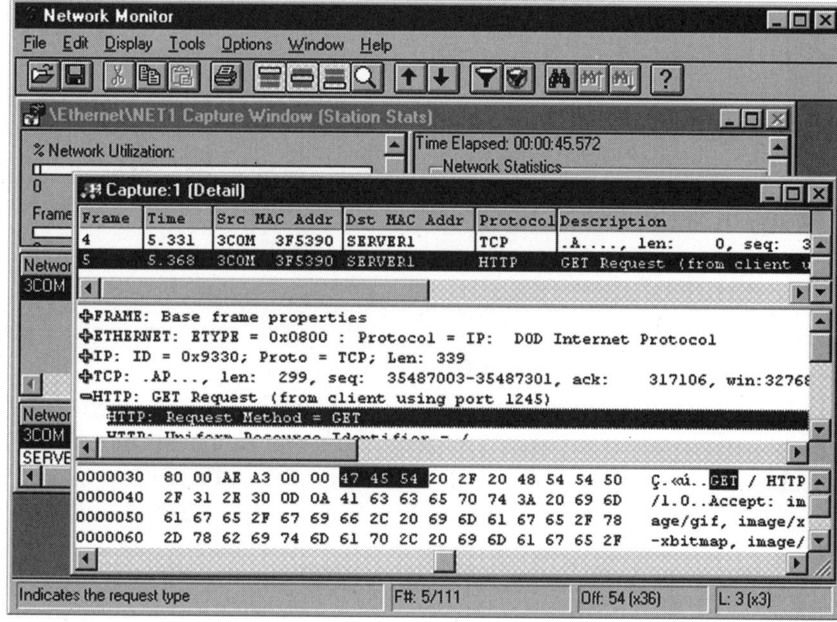

Figure 10-7 Network Monitor trace of an HTTP Get request.

- Packet traffic *from* the server to troubleshoot connection problems, addressing problems, and protocol problems
- Packet traffic *to* the server to detect attempts to hack IIS servers, plus the problems mentioned above

The version of Network Monitor included with Windows NT 4.0 Server is limited to capturing traffic to or from the server on which it is installed, and is limited also in the number and types of protocols it can detect. A full version of Network Monitor is included with Microsoft Systems Management Server (SMS).

IIS Web Capacity Analysis Tool (WCAT)

A new tool in the administrator's arsenal is Microsoft's Web Capacity Analysis Tool (WCAT), which is included with the IIS 4.0 Resource Kit from Microsoft. The WCAT is designed to simulate workloads on IIS servers and test their response to a variety of client requests, including HTTP methods, FTP, SSL, ASP, ISAPI, and CGI. By studying the response of your IIS server under different kinds of simulated loads, you can identify bottlenecks and determine how best to optimize IIS performance through hardware upgrades and software performance tuning.

Microsoft also has WCAT available as a free download from their Site Builder Network. Just point your browser to

```
http://www.microsoft.com/workshop/server/toolbox/webcat.asp
```

Running WCAT requires three machines, all of which have to be running Windows NT 4.0 (Fig. 10-8):

- *The WCAT server.* This is the machine being tested and that has IIS installed on it. Installing the WCAT server components on an IIS server simply adds a number of test files that can later be deleted from the server.
- *The WCAT client.* This machine runs the virtual clients that make connections to and request pages from the WCAT server. Each virtual client is a thread running within a single WCAT process. WCAT supports up to 200 virtual clients per machine, and since most browsers typically use four separate connections for downloading Web content, this translates into simulating up to 50 browser clients. To exceed this limit, you can use several machines as WCAT clients.
- *The WCAT controller.* This machine administers and monitors the WCAT testing procedure, and controls the nature of the test being administered through controller input files. The output of a WCAT test can be a log file or a Performance Monitor file, which allows a variety of methods to be used for analyzing and interpreting the test results.

WCAT comes with over 40 prepackaged tests that administrators can run to determine server performance under different workloads. For each test, the administrator can vary parameters to adjust the load on the server. These parameters include

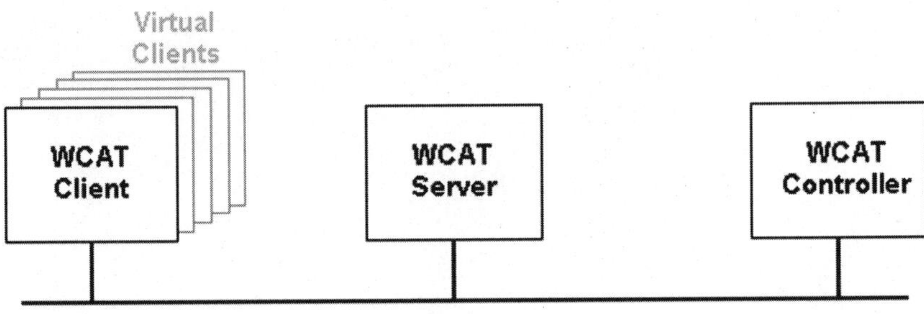

Figure 10-8 Using the Web Capacity Analysis Tool (WCAT).

- Number of clients in the test
- Rate of requests by clients
- Size and type of page requested by clients
- Frequency of requests for each page
- Total length of time of the test

Administrators can also customize server load by writing their own client controller scripts.

For more information on WCAT, refer to the IIS 4.0 Resource Kit or the Web page mentioned earlier.

IIS Performance Tuning

In this section we examine various strategies, tips, and tricks that administrators can use for tuning the performance of IIS servers. These are listed in no special order.

Removing Unnecessary Applications

Running other resource-intensive applications (e.g., Microsoft Exchange Server, File and Print services) on an IIS server will severely impact the resources available to IIS services. It's a good idea to move such applications to a separate server so that IIS has full control of the machine's hardware resources.

Stopping Unnecessary Services

Every service running on Windows NT Server uses valuable system resources. Services that are not necessary to the functioning of your machine should either be stopped and set to start manually, or disabled entirely.

Administrators should be fully aware of service dependencies before they begin to disable unnecessary services. A good practice is to disable services one at a time and monitor the effect on system performance and integrity for a period of time before disabling the next service. To stop or disable a service, use the Services program in Control Panel. To view dependencies between services, start Windows NT Diagnostics, select the Services tab, click the SERVICES button, double-click on the service you are studying, and select the Dependencies tab on the service Property sheet.

The following services are *not required* on a dedicated IIS server.

- Alerter
- ClipBook Server
- DHCP Client
- Messenger
- Net Logon
- Network DDE
- Network DDE DSDM
- Network Monitor Agent
- NWLink NetBIOS
- NWLink IPX/SPX Compatible Transport
- Spooler
- TCP/IP NetBIOS Helper
- UPS

The following services may be required for *specific purposes.*

- RPC Locator (required for remote administration)
- Server (required for use of User Manager)
- Workstation (required if you are using remote UNC virtual roots)

Optimizing Use of IIS Logging

IIS logging slows server performance. It is a good idea to enable logging only on sites, virtual directories, and individual files that need to be logged for billing or performance monitoring purposes.

To disable logging on a site's home directory, a particular virtual directory, or an individual file, access the Property sheet for the object, select the Home Directory, Virtual Directory, or File tab, and clear the LOG ACCESS checkbox under Content Control.

To disable logging entirely for a Web site, access the site Property sheet, select the Web Site tab, and clear the ENABLE LOGGING checkbox.

Optimizing Use of SSL

SSL slows IIS performance significantly. SSL should be enabled only on sites and portions of sites where it is needed. For example, on a shopping site SSL could be enabled only for those Web pages that contain Web forms for users to submit their credit card information, and disabled everywhere else on the site.

To disable SSL on a particular virtual directory or an individual file, access the Property sheet for the object, select the Directory Security or File Security tab, click EDIT under Secure Communications, and clear the REQUIRE SECURE CHANNEL WHEN ACCESSING THIS RESOURCE checkbox (this assumes that SSL has already been enabled on the server).

To disable SSL entirely for a Web site, access the site Property sheet, select the Directory Security tab, click EDIT under Secure Communications, and clear the REQUIRE SECURE CHANNEL WHEN ACCESSING THIS RESOURCE checkbox.

Restricting Use of Bandwidth

If other network-intensive applications must run together with IIS on a single machine, you may need to restrict the total bandwidth used by IIS on the machine's network subsystem. To restrict bandwidth for all IIS services running on a machine, access the server Property sheet and check the ENABLE BANDWIDTH THROTTLING checkbox. Specify the limit for the network bandwidth that should be made available to all IIS Web and FTP sites on the machine.

Another situation that calls for restricted bandwidth is when an IIS server hosts several sites, one of which is extremely popular. To ensure that the other sites can be easily accessed under heavy load, you can restrict the bandwidth available to the popular site. To restrict the bandwidth for a particular site on an IIS server, access the site Property sheet, select the Performance tab, and check the ENABLE BANDWIDTH THROTTLING checkbox. Specify the limit for the network bandwidth that should be made available to the particular site.

If your IIS server is using more than 50 percent of its network bandwidth on a regular basis, you need to upgrade your network subsystem. Consider adding a second network card, upgrading to a faster card, or off-loading some of the server content to another server.

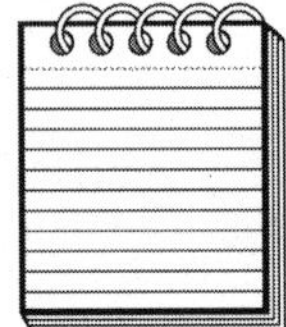

NOTE: *Bandwidth throttling applies only to* static *HTML files, not Active Server Pages or other dynamic content.*

Limiting Connections

Limiting connections to your IIS server is another method of conserving and managing network bandwidth. Limiting connections can be done only at the Web site (virtual server) level, not at the virtual directory or file level. To limit connections to a particular site on an IIS server, access the site Property sheet, select the Web Site tab, and under Connections select LIMITED TO and specify the maximum number of simultaneous connections allowed as well as the Connection Timeout value. Because browsers typically form up to four simultaneous connections with a Web server when they connect to download files, the value specified in the LIMITED TO textbox represents four times the maximum number of client browsers that can simultaneously connect to the server.

If a browser tries to connect to the server and then breaks off in midstream (for example, if the user waits 5 seconds for the connection and then hits the STOP button on the browser—a typical occurrence), the server continues processing the connection request until the timeout occurs. A lower value of Connection Timeout will ensure that these broken connections are terminated more quickly, freeing resources for more connections to occur. Too low a value of Connection Timeout may terminate client connections before the client has completed downloading, resulting in slower response at the client end.

Enabling HTTP Keep-Alives

HTTP Keep-Alives are enabled by default on all sites on an IIS server. This performance-enhancing function of IIS should be left enabled by administrators; only advanced developers might consider temporarily disabling this feature under certain specialized circumstances.

Optimizing Memory Usage against Response Speed

IIS allows administrators to control how IIS uses memory in order to optimize the server's response speed to client requests. To optimize memory usage for response speed for a particular site on an IIS server, access the site Property sheet, select the Performance tab, and under Performance Tuning adjust the slide control so that the setting is *slightly higher* than the observed number of connections per day (see Fig. 10-9). If the slide control is set *much higher* than the observed number of connections per day, the result will be an unnecessary expenditure of the server's memory resources and an overall drop in performance.

Optimizing Content Type

Response speed is dependent on the type of content residing on the Web server. Server performance can be improved by using the following content types *only when necessary:*

- Active Server Pages

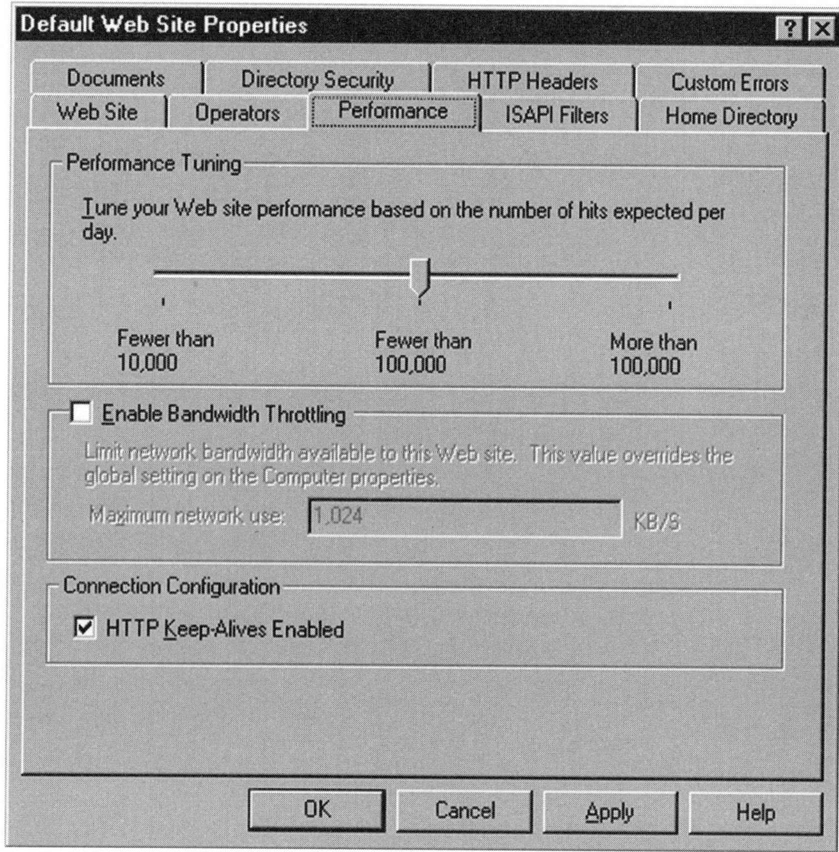

Figure 10-9 Optimizing memory usage against response speed.

- CGI scripts
- ISAPI applications
- Database queries
- Video files
- High-resolution JPEG image files

Don't be fancy for fancy's sake!

Optimizing Processor Usage

IIS services run in the background like other Windows NT services. Windows NT usually gives foreground applications a boost to ensure they receive a large share of processor time so that they will be responsive to the user. IIS performance can be enhanced by disabling this boost.

- To disable the processor boost for foreground applications on Windows NT, access the System program in Control Panel to open the System Properties sheet, select the Performance tab, and move the Boost slider to the NONE position (Fig. 10-10). This setting gives all processes, whether in the foreground or background, equal amounts of processing time.

Maximize Throughput for Network Applications

Because IIS maintains its own cache, separate from the Windows NT file system cache, performance can be enhanced by adjusting the balance between memory committed to applications and memory committed to file system caching.

To adjust the memory balance so that IIS has more memory available for itself, open the Network program in Control Panel, select the Services tab, select the Server service, and click the PROPERTIES button to open the Server dialog box (Fig. 10-11). Select MAXIMIZE THROUGHPUT FOR NETWORK APPLICATIONS and click OK twice.

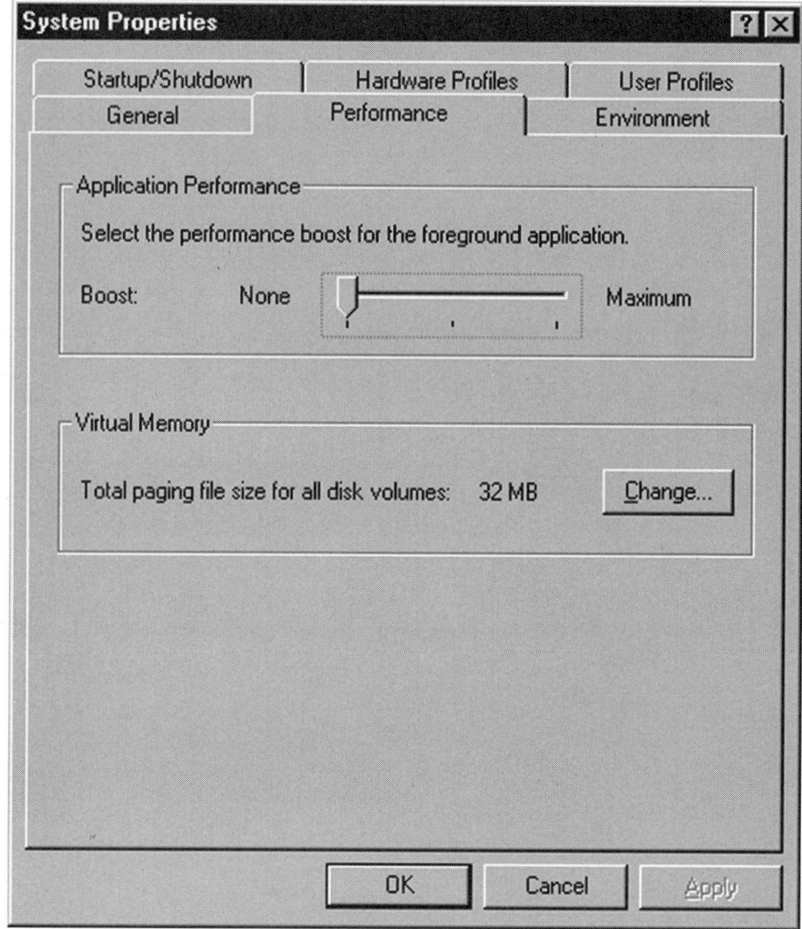

Figure 10-10 Disabling the processor boost for foreground applications.

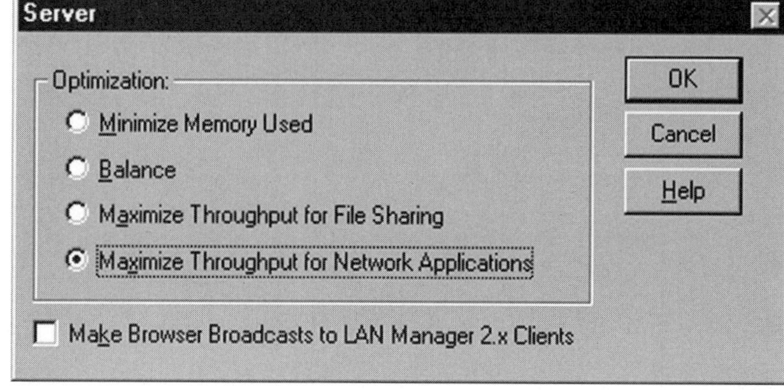

Figure 10-11 Maximizing throughput for network applications.

SUMMARY

The performance of IIS servers can be monitored using a variety of standard Windows NT tools, plus some new ones from Microsoft. A variety of techniques can be used to enhance the performance of IIS servers under various conditions. An important part of the administrator's job is to monitor, maintain, and enhance the operation of IIS servers for both intranet and Internet use.

FOR MORE INFORMATION

Microsoft Web Site Download the Web Capacity Analysis Tool from the site

```
www.microsoft.com/workshop/server/toolbox/webcat.asp
```

Microsoft Newsgroups Newsgroups are a good place to hold discussions about such things as IIS 4.0 performance. Post an article to or lurk around the newsgroup

```
microsoft.public.inetserver.iis
```

CHAPTER 11

Administering Usage with Site Server Express

Introduction

Administrators of Web servers need tools that can provide useful information to developers, site content managers, and site business managers. *Microsoft Site Server Express 2.0* provides administrators with the tools necessary to analyze site structure and content, post new content, and report on site usage and availability. After completing this chapter, you will be able to use the various tools included in the Windows NT 4.0 Option Pack limited version of *Microsoft Site Server,* namely,

- *Content Analyzer,* for visualizing site structure and integrity
- *Usage Import,* for importing IIS log files into the Usage Analyst database
- *Report Writer,* for generating reports of Web site usage in conjunction with Usage Analyst
- *Posting Acceptor,* for allowing developers to upload content to IIS servers
- *Web Publishing Wizard,* for posting content to sites

Installing Site Server Express

Site Server Express is not installed during a *typical* installation of Windows NT 4.0 Option Pack. To install Site Server Express, select START, PROGRAMS, WINDOWS NT 4.0 OPTION PACK, WINDOWS NT 4.0 OPTION PACK SETUP. When the welcome screen appears, click NEXT. Use the ADD/REMOVE button to open the Select Components screen. Check the MICROSOFT SITE SERVER EXPRESS 2.0 checkbox, and click NEXT to begin copying files. When installation is complete, click FINISH to return to the desktop.

In the Select Components screen you can also click SHOW SUB-COMPONENTS to view the four subcomponents that can be installed from Site Server Express, namely,

- Analysis—Content
- Analysis—Usage
- Publishing—Posting Acceptor 1.01
- Publishing—Web Publishing Wizard 1.52

By default, installation of Site Server Express includes all of these subcomponents.

Using Site Server Express: Content Analyzer

The Content Analyzer component of Site Server Express can be used by administrators to

- Graphically view the structure of your Web site.
- Locate broken hyperlinks within your site.
- Examine properties of files within your site.
- Generate a summary report of your site's structure, properties, and integrity.
- Perform various other site management tasks.

When Content Analyzer is used to analyze a site, it creates a special file for the site called a *WebMap*. This WebMap file is a database that contains information about the various objects and links in the Web site. The following walkthrough illustrates how to create, view, and interpret the WebMap for a site.

Walkthrough: Creating a WebMap with Content Analyzer

To start Content Analyzer, select START, PROGRAMS, WINDOWS NT 4.0 OPTION PACK, MICROSOFT SITE SERVER EXPRESS 2.0, CONTENT ANALYZER. This will open the Welcome to Microsoft Site Server Express—Content Analyzer screen (Fig. 11-1). The welcome screen has three options:

- *View User's Guide* opens Internet Explorer and allows you to view the online documentation for Content Analyzer.
- *Open WebMap* allows you to open a previously saved WebMap (there is also a sample WebMap for you to view).
- *New WebMap* allows you to create a WebMap for an existing Web site on your server.

Choose NEW WEBMAP to open the New Map dialog box (Fig. 11-2). This dialog box allows you to create a new WebMap

- Using the URL of the site that you want to map using Content Analyzer
- Using the path and filename of the content that you want to map

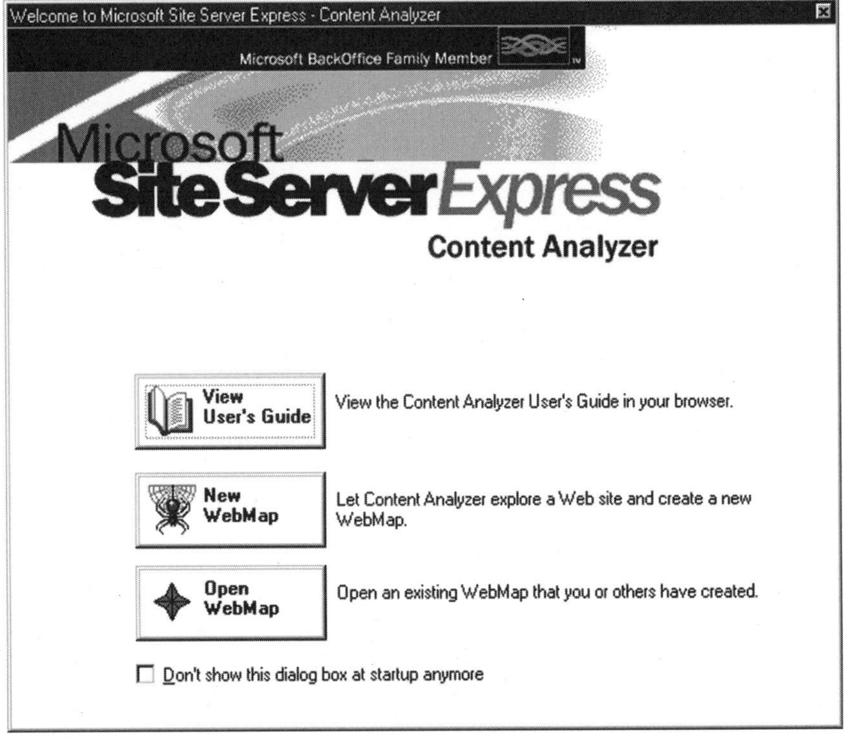

Figure 11-1 The Welcome to Site Server Express—Content Analyzer screen.

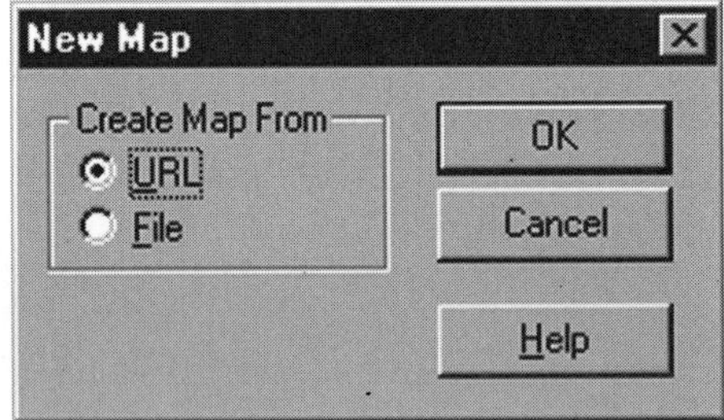

Figure 11-2 The New Map dialog box.

Select the URL option to open the New Map from URL dialog box (Fig. 11-3). Enter the URL for the site you want to map (here we use the URL of the default Web site, which includes the World Wide Web Sample Site, which is installed from the Windows NT 4.0 Option Pack Custom Setup).

Selecting the option EXPLORE ENTIRE SITE will cause Content Analyzer to start mapping at the site's home page and look up every URL in the site, including links to applications and to World Wide Web sites. If this option is cleared, Content Analyzer will explore the selected site to the

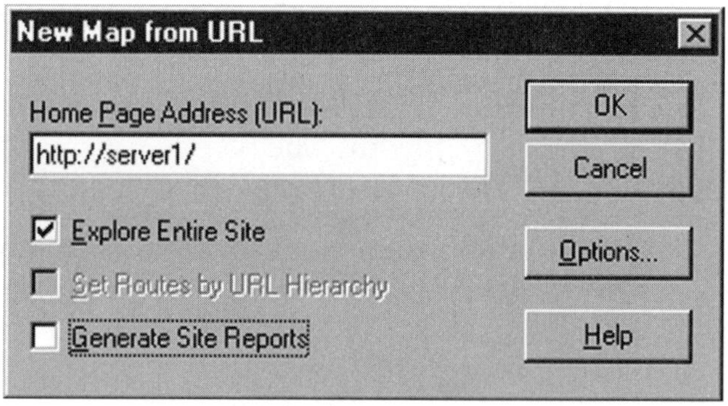

Figure 11-3
The New Map from URL dialog box.

New Map from URL
Home Page Address (URL):
http://server1/
Explore Entire Site
Set Routes by URL Hierarchy
Generate Site Reports
OK
Cancel
Options...
Help

default depth defined in the Content Analyzer options (a maximum of 100 pages and a depth of three levels).

Selecting GENERATE SITE REPORTS will cause Content Analyzer to produce a Summary Report for the site viewable in your browser.

Selecting OPTIONS opens the Mapping from URL Options—New Map property sheet, which includes options for verifying offsite links, respecting the Robots.txt protocol, and so on.

Clear the Generate Site Reports checkbox and click OK to generate the WebMap. A dialog box will indicate the progress of mapping until mapping is complete. When mapping is complete, the new WebMap will be visible in the main Site Server Express window (Fig. 11-4).

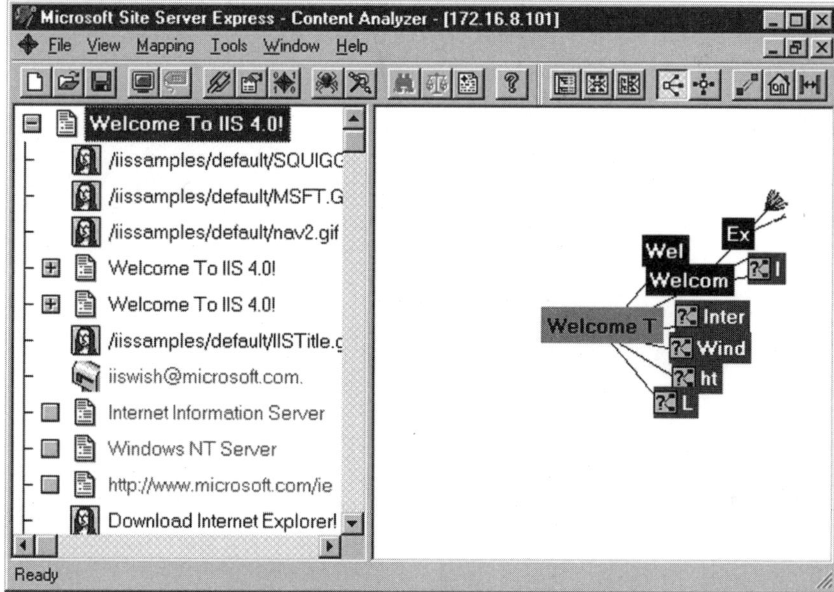

Figure 11-4
The WebMap generated for the default Web site.

Analyzing a WebMap Using Content Analyzer

The main Content Analyzer window is a multiple-document interface (MDI) application allowing you to open many WebMaps in separate child windows. The window for the site mapped contains two panes:

- The left pane contains a hierarchical, linear view of the WebMap known as *Tree View*. Control icons allow the hierarchy of files to be expanded or collapsed at any point where there is a link from one page to another.
- The right pane contains a flexible, nonlinear connected-graph view of the same WebMap known as *Cyperbolic View*.

Both views use icons and labels to identify various files in the map and their status.

Cyperbolic View is the preferred view, enabling you to get a picture of the entire site structure at a glance. Clicking on an icon or label in Cyperbolic View causes the map to reorient itself so that the selected icon has the focus. By clicking on icons or labels in the map, you can easily get a feel for the structure of even large, complex sites. In addition, you can click and drag an icon or label to a new position in the window, causing the map to modify its shape and size accordingly.

In Fig. 11-4 the home page of the site is selected in Tree View, and the right pane shows the focus applied to the same page in Cyperbolic View. Note that the two views are synchronized.

Icons and labels identify *nodes* in the WebMap. These nodes may refer to objects such as

- HTML files
- GIF and JPEG images
- Audio and video files
- Text files
- Gateway scripts
- FTP, Gopher, Mailto, and other URLs
- Java applets

Each of these object types is represented by a unique icon. For an explanation of the various icons used in WebMaps and what they represent, refer to the online documentation for Content Analyzer.

Labels for nodes in Cyperbolic View are color-coded to provide information about the nodes.

- *Purple:* a label only for the currently selected object
- *Light blue:* a label only for the home page of the site
- *Black:* objects that are on main navigation routes
- *Green:* alternative routes to objects
- *Dark Blue:* objects not part of this site (e.g., WWW hyperlinks)
- *Red:* object currently unavailable (e.g., broken link, server down)

The *Cyperbolic toolbar* enables you to control the Cyperbolic view of the WebMap (Fig. 11-5). Many of the toolbar options are available from the menu bar as well.

The first three buttons on the toolbar allow you to switch between

- Tree View only
- Cyperbolic View only (preferred)
- Both views (the default)

The next two buttons allow you to switch between a left-right orientation and a centered orientation of the WebMap.

Selecting the SNAP MODE button allows you to reorient the map instantly by clicking on a different icon in it. Deselecting the SNAP MODE button causes the map to glide to its new orientation when you click an icon in it.

The JUMP TO HOME PAGE button orients the map so that the home page has the focus.

The NODE DISTANCE button brings up the Node Distance dialog box, which allows you to dynamically alter the size of the map and thus the number of icons it can display (Fig. 11-6).

The main toolbar is used for analyzing and configuring WebMaps and for setting Content Analyzer options (Fig. 11-7). Many of these toolbar options are available from the menu bar as well.

The first three toolbar buttons allow you to create new maps, open existing maps, and save maps you have created. By default, maps are saved in the directory

```
C:\Program Files\Content Analyzer\Webmaps
```

with the extension `*.wmp`.

Figure 11-5
The Content Analyzer Cyperbolic toolbar.

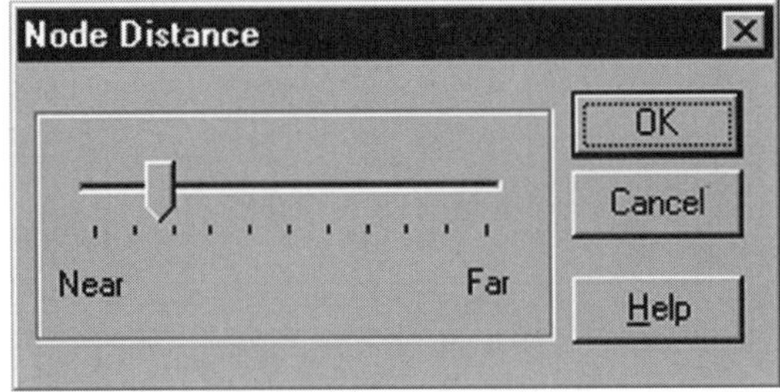

Figure 11-6
The Node Distance dialog box.

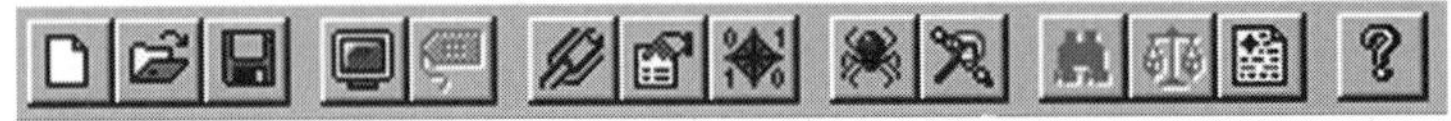

Figure 11-7
The Content Analyzer main toolbar.

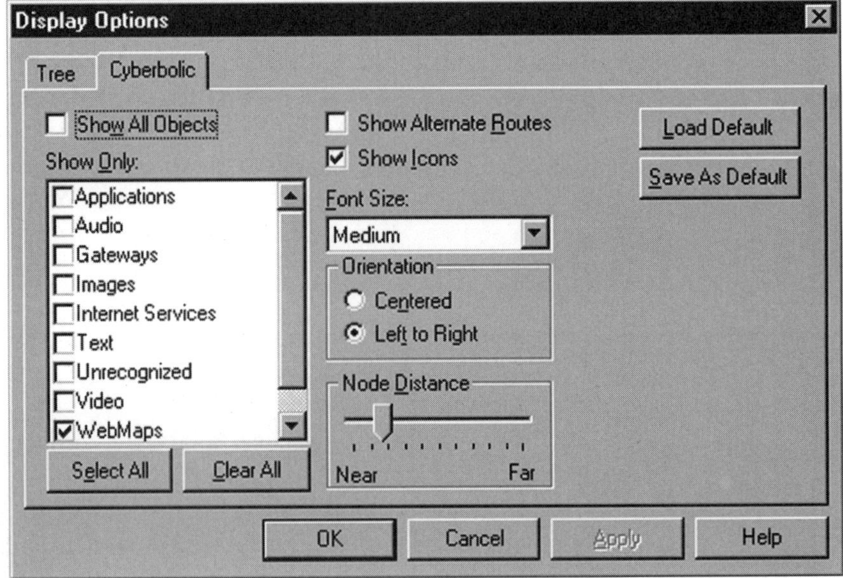

Figure 11-8
The Display Options dialog box.

The DISPLAY OPTIONS button opens the Display Options dialog box (Fig. 11-8). This box allows you to customize both Tree and Cyperbolic view maps by specifying

- Which file objects are to be included on the map (select SHOW ALL OBJECTS to include all listed object types). Pages are always shown by default.

- Whether to show *alternate routes* to objects (objects pointed to by more than one link).
- Whether to represent different types of objects by different icons.
- A default orientation and node distance for the WebMap.

Click SAVE AS DEFAULT to save your settings.

Selecting an object in the WebMap and clicking the OBJECT LINKS button opens the Link Info for dialog box (Fig. 11-9). This dialog box shows the links that are associated with the selected object. Select

- LINKS ON PAGE to show all links on the selected page (for HTML pages only)
- INLINKS to show all links pointing to the selected object that originate on other pages

Color-coding applies here also.

- *Black* links are to objects in the current site.
- *Blue* links are to objects outside the current site.
- *Green* links show alternate routes to an object.
- *Red* links are currently broken.

You can also select a link and click the VIEW button to open the link in the browser. Select FOLLOW to change the focus of the WebMap to the selected object and to view the links of the object that now has the focus. Select BACK to return to the previous view.

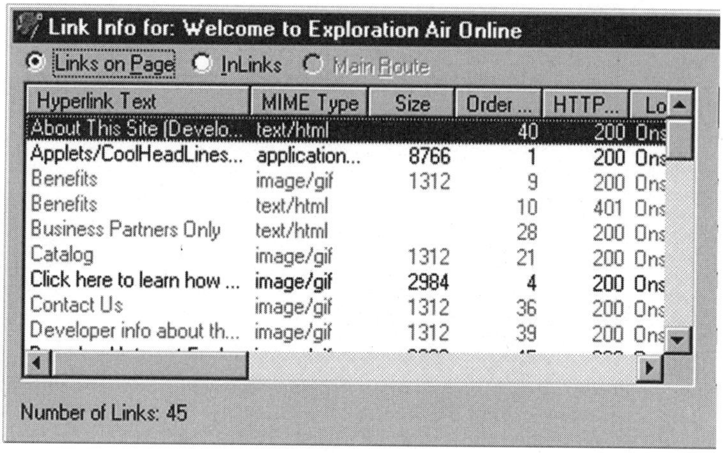

Figure 11-9 The Link Info for dialog box.

Selecting an object in the WebMap and clicking the OBJECT PROPERTIES button opens a Properties sheet for the selected object (Fig. 11-10). The Properties sheet lists various information about the object, such as its URL or local path, MIME type, and HTTP status.

The SITE STATISTICS button opens the Statistics dialog box (Fig. 11-11). This dialog box shows general statistics about the site, including number of pages, links and images, and domain and root path.

The EXPLORE SITE button opens the Explore dialog box (Fig. 11-12). This dialog box allows you to configure the default maximum number of pages analyzed and default site depth analyzed. It also allows you to access the Mapping From URL Options dialog box for the selected WebMap.

The VERIFY LINKS button opens the Verify Links dialog box (Fig. 11-13). This dialog box allows you to verify either all links or broken links only, for links within the site, offsite, or both.

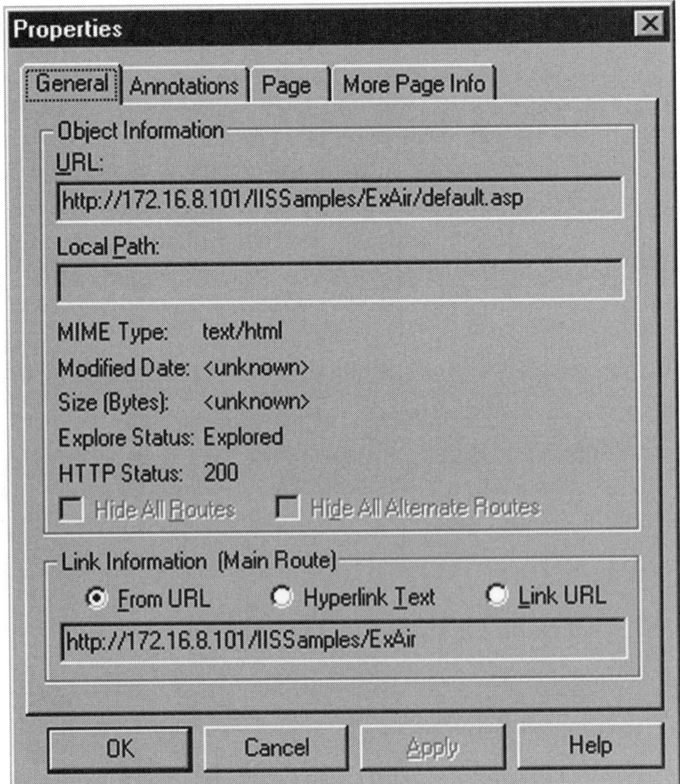

Figure 11-10
The Properties sheet for a selected object in the WebMap.

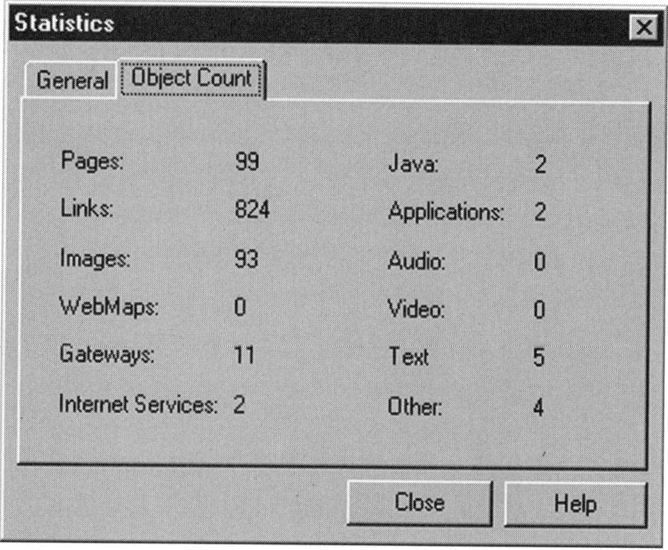

Figure 11-11 The Statistics dialog box.

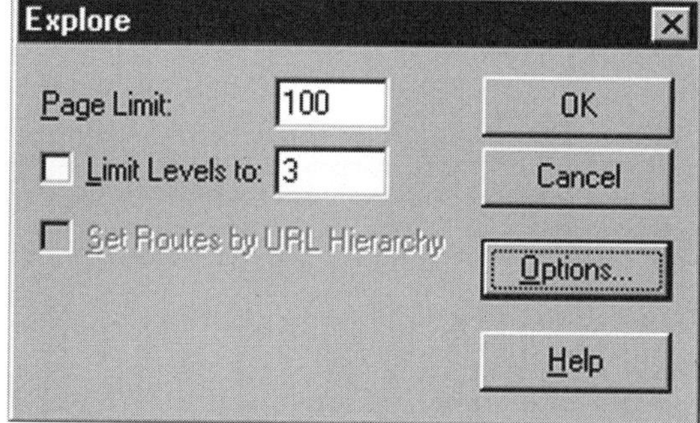

Figure 11-12 The Explore dialog box.

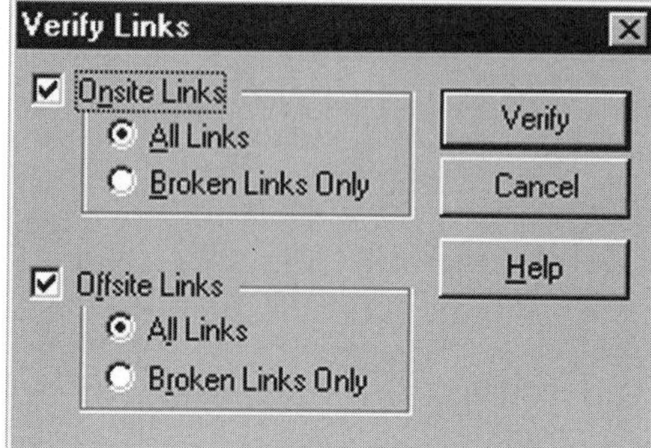

Figure 11-13 The Verify Links dialog box.

From the menu bar, select VIEW, PROGRAM OPTIONS to open the Program Options dialog box (Fig. 11-14). This dialog box can be used to configure default settings for Content Analyzer, including

- Which browser to use for opening objects (you can double-click on an object in the WebMap to open it in the browser)
- Proxy server settings, if you are using one
- Default Cyperbolic View options

Finally, in Cyperbolic View you can right-click on any label or icon to bring up a shortcut menu, with options including

- LAUNCH BROWSER, to open the page or file in Internet Explorer
- LINKS, to open the Link Info for dialog box for the selected object
- PROPERTIES, to open the Properties sheet for the object

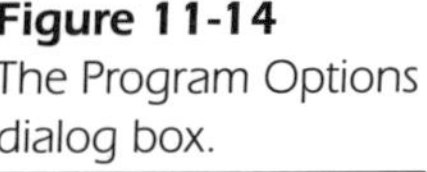

Figure 11-14
The Program Options dialog box.

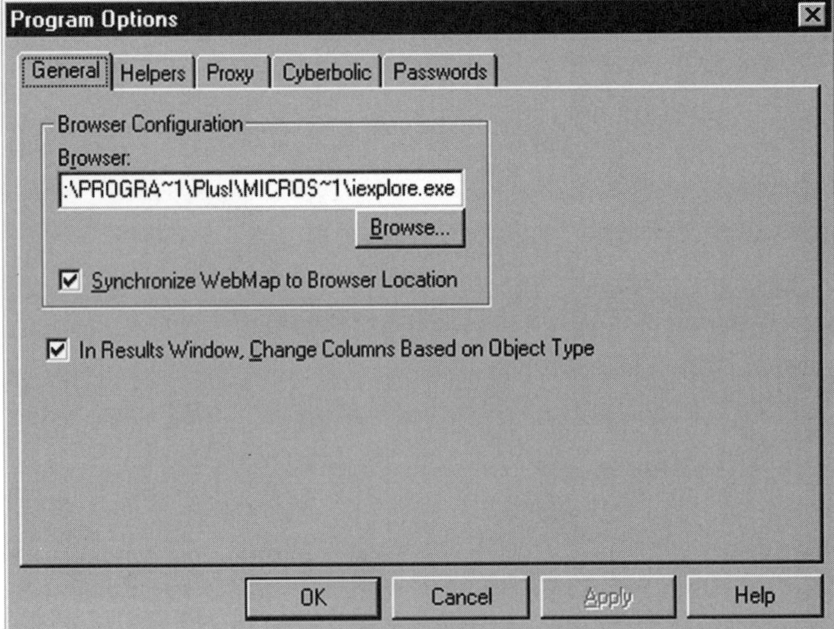

Performing Quick Searches Using Content Analyzer

Quick Searches are predefined search queries that can be run on a site with Content Analyzer. To perform a Quick Search, select TOOLS, QUICK SEARCH from the menu bar and select the search query you want to run. The predefined queries include finding

- Broken links
- Home site objects (in the same domain as the home page)
- Images without ALT attribute (important for text-only viewing)
- Load size over 32 kB (includes text and inline files such as images)
- Non-home-site objects (in a different domain from the home page)
- Not-found objects (status code 404) (did not exist when site was mapped)
- Unavailable objects (were not available when site was mapped)
- Unverified objects (linked to by other objects but not verified)

The result of running the Quick Search *Images Without ALT* on the default Web site map is shown in Fig. 11-15.

Generating Site Summary Reports Using Content Analyzer

Content Analyzer can be used to generate *Site Summary reports,* which include information on

- The number of levels in the site's structure (home page is level 1)
- The number and size of pages, images, and applications
- The number of onsite and offsite objects and links
- The number of missing objects or broken links
- The average number of hyperlinks per page

To create a Site Summary report for the currently open WebMap, either click the GENERATE SITE REPORTS button on the toolbar or select TOOLS, GENERATE SITE REPORTS from the menu bar. The Generate Site

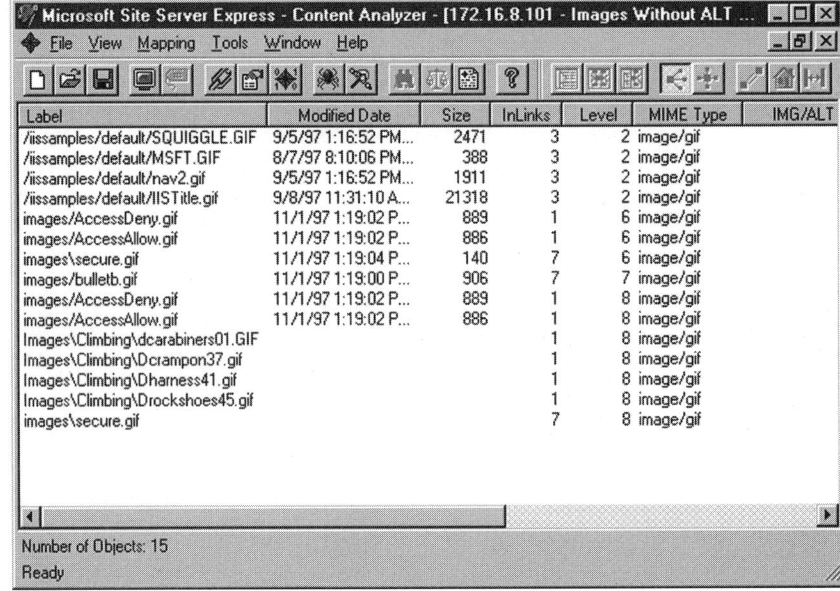

Label	Modified Date	Size	InLinks	Level	MIME Type	IMG/ALT
/iissamples/default/SQUIGGLE.GIF	9/5/97 1:16:52 PM...	2471	3	2	image/gif	
/iissamples/default/MSFT.GIF	8/7/97 8:10:06 PM...	388	3	2	image/gif	
/iissamples/default/nav2.gif	9/5/97 1:16:52 PM...	1911	3	2	image/gif	
/iissamples/default/IISTitle.gif	9/8/97 11:31:10 A...	21318	3	2	image/gif	
images/AccessDeny.gif	11/1/97 1:19:02 P...	889	1	6	image/gif	
images/AccessAllow.gif	11/1/97 1:19:02 P...	886	1	6	image/gif	
images\secure.gif	11/1/97 1:19:04 P...	140	7	6	image/gif	
images/bulletb.gif	11/1/97 1:19:00 P...	906	7	7	image/gif	
images/AccessDeny.gif	11/1/97 1:19:02 P...	889	1	8	image/gif	
images/AccessAllow.gif	11/1/97 1:19:02 P...	886	1	8	image/gif	
Images\Climbing\dcarabiners01.GIF			1	8	image/gif	
Images\Climbing\Dcrampon37.gif			1	8	image/gif	
Images\Climbing\Dharness41.gif			1	8	image/gif	
Images\Climbing\Drockshoes45.gif			1	8	image/gif	
images\secure.gif			7	8	image/gif	

Figure 11-15 Results of running the Images Without ALT Quick Search.

Reports dialog box appears (Fig. 11-16). Specify a location to save the report to (or accept the default location). Then specify a *Report Prefix* to identify the report (or accept the default one). For example, if the WebMap was created for the URL

```
http://server1
```

then the default report file will be

```
server1_summary.html
```

Generate Site Reports

Report Directory:

Files\Content Analyzer Express\Reports

Browse...

Report Prefix

172.16.8.101_

☑ Save Copy of Map to Report Directory

OK

Cancel

Help

Figure 11-16 The Generate Site Reports dialog box.

just as the default WebMap file was

```
server1.wmp
```

Click OK and Content Analyzer will generate a Site Summary report, launch Internet Explorer, and allow you to view the report (Fig. 11-17).

Using Site Server Express: Usage Import and Report Writer

Site Server Express has two tools that administrators can use to view and report on site traffic: the *Usage Import* module and the *Report Writer* module. Such reports would typically be used for

- Monitoring site usage to determine if upgrades are needed
- Calculating site traffic for billing customers
- Track the path clients typically take through your site to plan for customization

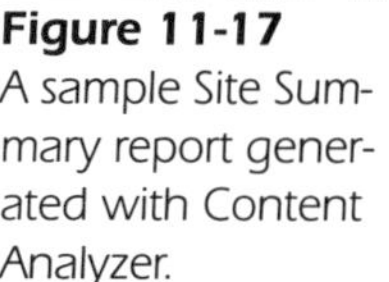

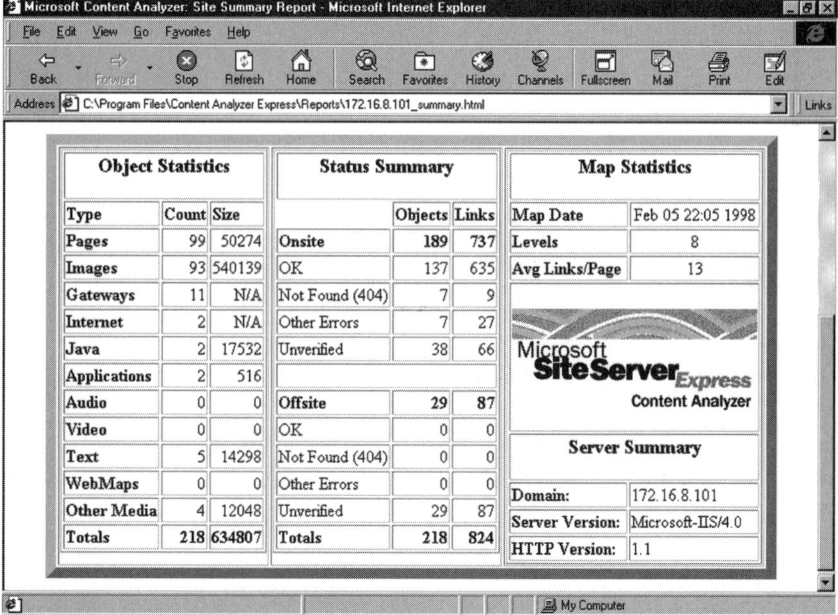

Object Statistics

Type	Count	Size
Pages	99	50274
Images	93	540139
Gateways	11	N/A
Internet	2	N/A
Java	2	17532
Applications	2	516
Audio	0	0
Video	0	0
Text	5	14298
WebMaps	0	0
Other Media	4	12048
Totals	218	634807

Status Summary

	Objects	Links
Onsite	189	737
OK	137	635
Not Found (404)	7	9
Other Errors	7	27
Unverified	38	66
Offsite	29	87
OK	0	0
Not Found (404)	0	0
Other Errors	0	0
Unverified	29	87
Totals	218	824

Map Statistics

Map Date	Feb 05 22:05 1998
Levels	8
Avg Links/Page	13

Server Summary

Domain:	172.16.8.101
Server Version:	Microsoft-IIS/4.0
HTTP Version:	1.1

Figure 11-17 A sample Site Summary report generated with Content Analyzer.

- Monitor certain audiences of your site to develop marketing strategies
- Showing management how good you are at paperwork (couldn't help mentioning this!)

Usage Import can import all log file formats generated by IIS 4.0, including

- Microsoft IIS Log File Format
- NCSA Common Log File Format
- ODBC Logging
- W3C Extended Log File Format

Report Writer can be used by administrators to design reports from scratch or using a series of 20 standard report formats, including both *summary* reports and *detail* reports of all aspects of site usage. These standard report formats can also be customized as desired. Reports include both tables and graphs and can be generated in several convenient output formats:

- HTML
- Microsoft Word
- Microsoft Excel

How Usage Import and Report Writer Work

Usage Import and Report Writer work together with the IIS logging facility as follows (see Fig. 11-18):

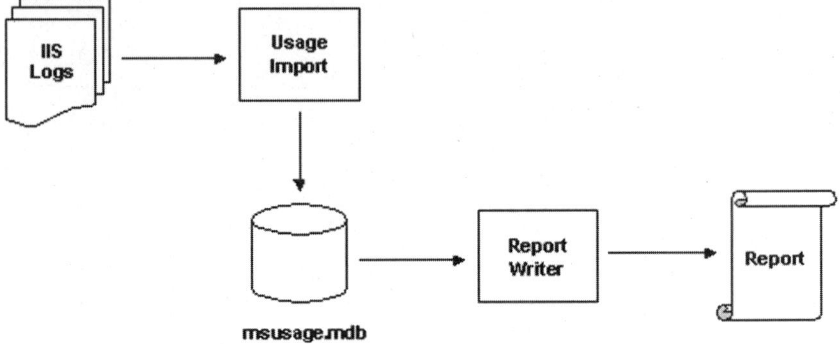

Figure 11-18 How to use Site Server Express to generate reports on site usage.

1. Log files are created using IIS 4.0 to log traffic to a Web site.
2. These log files are imported into the `msusage.mdb` database using Usage Import.
3. Report Writer is then used to generate site traffic reports from the data stored in the database.

Walkthrough: Importing IIS Log Files Using Usage Import

Before running Usage Import, you need to make sure that

- You have logging enabled on IIS.
- You have selected to log activity for a Web site on IIS.
- Log files have been generated that contain enough information to warrant importing them with Usage Import.

To enable logging on an IIS machine, start the Internet Service Manager, select an IIS machine, and click the PROPERTIES button on the rebar to open the server Properties sheet. Then, in the Master Properties dropdown box, select WWW SERVICE and click EDIT to open the WWW Service Master Properties sheet. Finally, on the Web Site tab of this sheet, make sure the ENABLE LOGGING checkbox is checked and that the desired log file format is selected (Fig. 11-19).

Next access the Home Directory tab on this property sheet, and make sure that the LOG ACCESS checkbox is selected. This ensures that access to the default Web site is being logged.

Finally, using Internet Explorer, browse the default Web site to generate some traffic for the log file.

Now we are ready to start Usage Import. Select START, PROGRAMS, WINDOWS NT 4.0 OPTION PACK, MICROSOFT SITE SERVER EXPRESS 2.0, USAGE IMPORT. If this is the first time you have started Usage Import, the program will walk you through the process of importing log files. First you will receive a message saying, "There are no Internet sites configured in this database. Please use the Server manager to configure your Internet sites now." Click OK to proceed.

The Log data source Properties dialog box appears. Select the log file format that matches your settings in IIS (Fig. 11-20).

The Server Properties sheet appears next (Fig. 11-21), asking you to specify

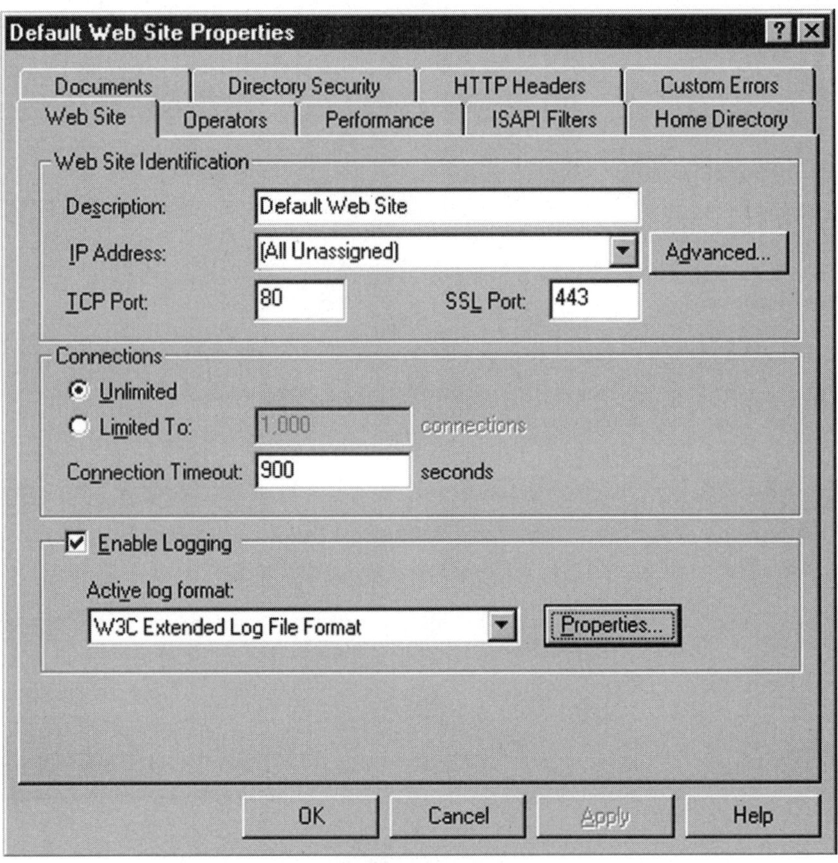

Figure 11-19
Enable logging on IIS.

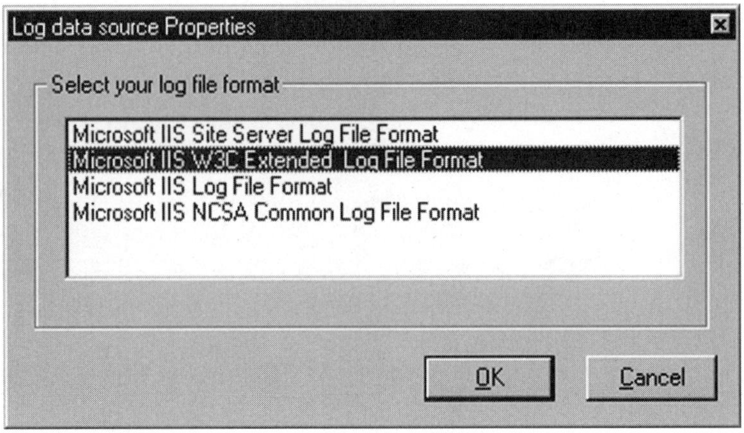

Log data source Properties

Select your log file format

Microsoft IIS Site Server Log File Format
Microsoft IIS W3C Extended Log File Format
Microsoft IIS Log File Format
Microsoft IIS NCSA Common Log File Format

OK Cancel

Figure 11-20
The Log data source Properties dialog box.

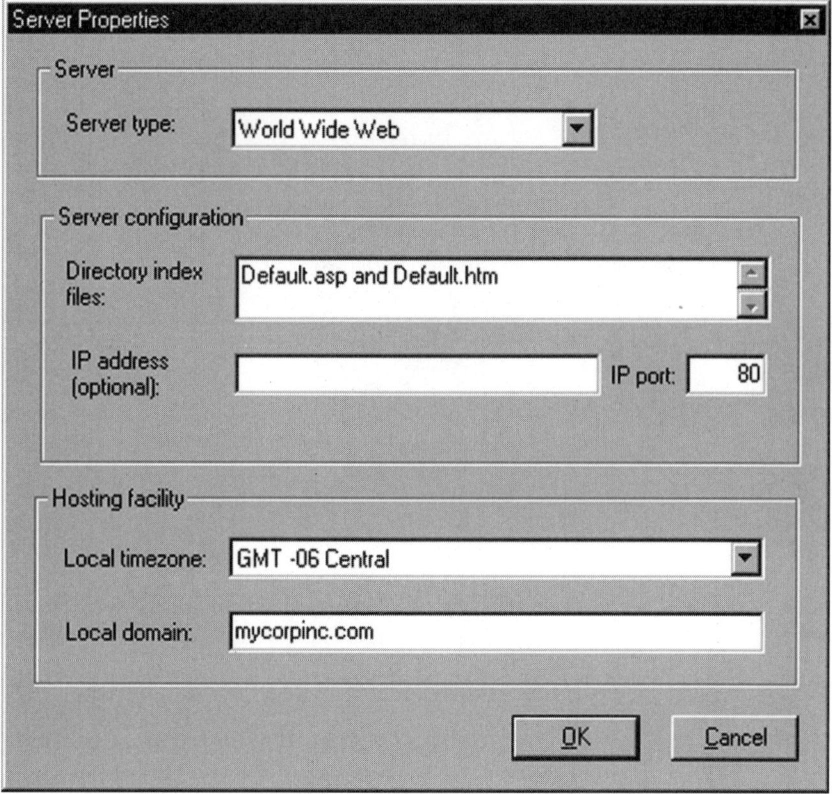

Figure 11-21 The Server Properties sheet.

- The server type (WWW, FTP, etc.)
- The default home page
- The IP address and port
- The local time zone relative to GMT
- The local domain (this is necessary to enable Site Server Express to distinguish between internal and external hits)

Enter or modify the data as desired, and click OK.

The Site Properties sheet appears next (Fig. 11-22). Specify the home page for your site, and modify any other data as desired.

Usage Import will now open up, showing two child windows (Fig. 11-23):

- *Log File Manager:* used to import IIS log files. Initially this window is empty, but after you import log files these will show up in the History scrollbox of the window.

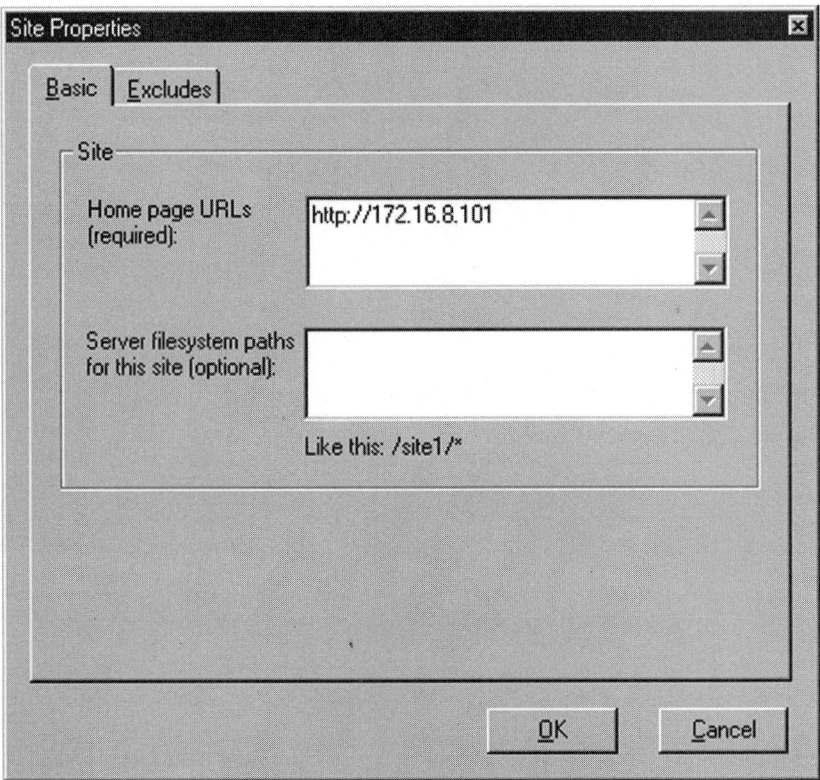

Figure 11-22 The Site Properties sheet.

- *Server Manager:* used to configure servers and sites within the database. This displays a hierarchical structure of
  - Log data sources (all log data sources)
  - Log data source (the log format chosen in Fig. 11-20)
  - Server (the settings selected in Fig. 11-21)
  - Site (the settings selected in Fig. 11-22)

To modify any of the settings in this hierarchy, right-click on the appropriate node and select EDIT from the shortcut menu. You can also use the shortcut menu to add new servers and sites to your database.

To import the IIS log files into Usage Import:

- Enter the full path and filename(s) of the file(s) to be imported in the Log location textbox.

or

- Click BROWSE and explore your file system until you find and select the file(s). Multiple files may be selected in the usual way for import into the database.

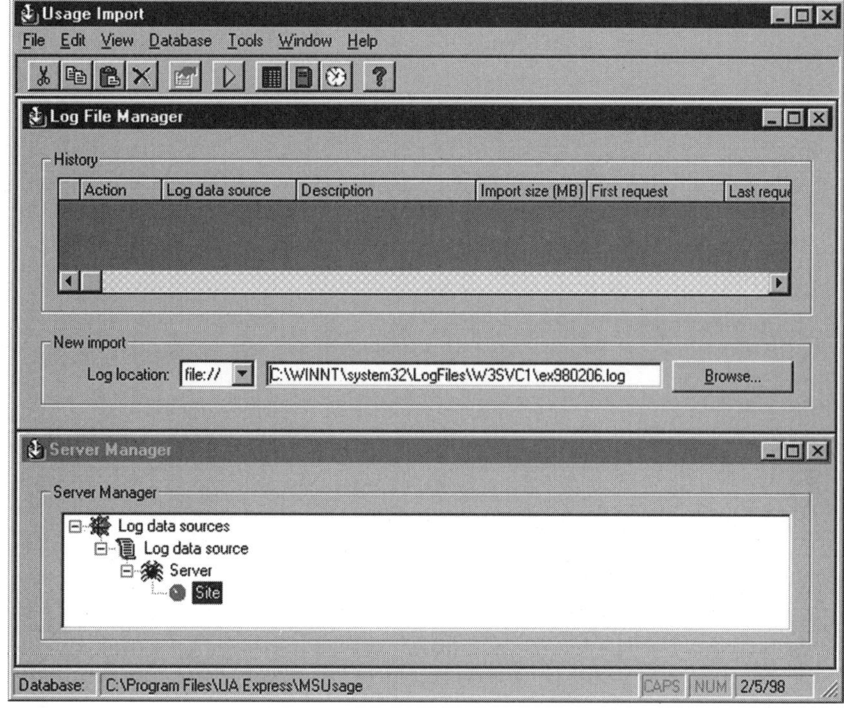

Figure 11-23 Usage Import showing the Log File Manager and Server Manager child windows.

By default, IIS log files are located in various subdirectories of:

```
C:\winnt\system32\log files\
```

Finally, click the green triangle button on the toolbar, or select FILES, START IMPORT from the menu bar. Usage Import will now begin importing and converting the selected log files to a format suitable for storage in the internal database. When Usage Import is done, the Usage Import Statistics dialog box will appear. Click CLOSE after you have read the contents of the box.

These files should show up as records in the Log File Manager window. Once the log files have been successfully imported, you can close Usage Import.

Walkthrough: Generating Site Usage Reports Using Report Writer

The final stage of analyzing site usage is the generation of reports using Report Writer. To start Report Writer, click START, PROGRAMS, WINDOWS NT

4.0 OPTION PACK, MICROSOFT SITE SERVER EXPRESS 2.0, REPORT WRITER. The Report Writer dialog box appears, asking you if you want to create a custom report or use one of the predefined ones (Fig. 11-24). Choose FROM THE REPORT WRITER CATALOG to choose from the predefined reporting formats.

Choose a *report definition file* of either the *summary* or *detail* style (Fig. 11-25). When you select a definition file, you can read a brief description of the report in the Report description box. These descriptions are listed later in this section for reference purposes. Select a report definition file and click NEXT.

The next screen in the wizard is shown in Fig. 11-26. Select whether you want to analyze

- Every request in the imported log files
- Only requests matching the date and time criteria specified

Make a selection here and click NEXT.

In the next screen of the wizard you can create Boolean expressions for custom filters that will include or exclude portions of your log file data from the analysis process.

Click FINISH when done, and Report Writer will begin generating the report as a database query. The result is soon displayed (Fig. 11-27).

Finally, to generate a formatted report, click the green arrow button on the toolbar (or select FILE, CREATE REPORT DOCUMENT from the menu bar). The Report document dialog box appears (Fig. 11-28), asking you to

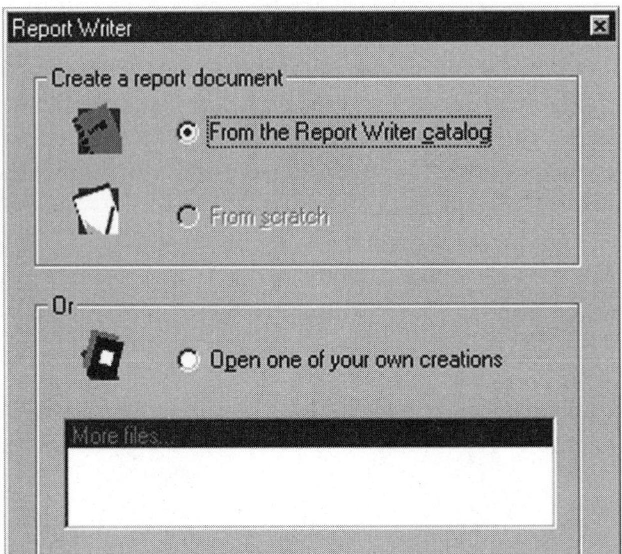

Figure 11-24 The Report Writer dialog box.

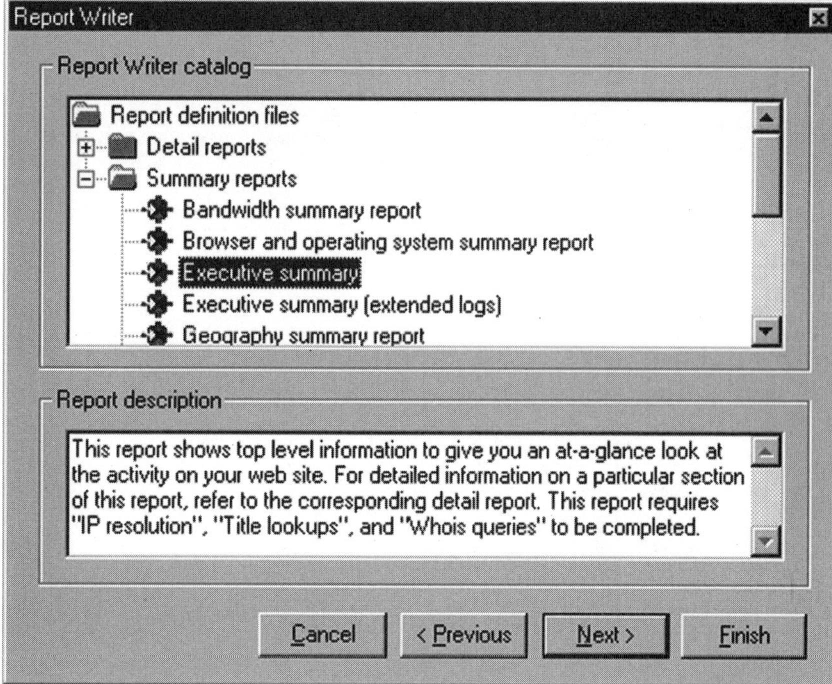

Figure 11-25 Report Writer report definition files.

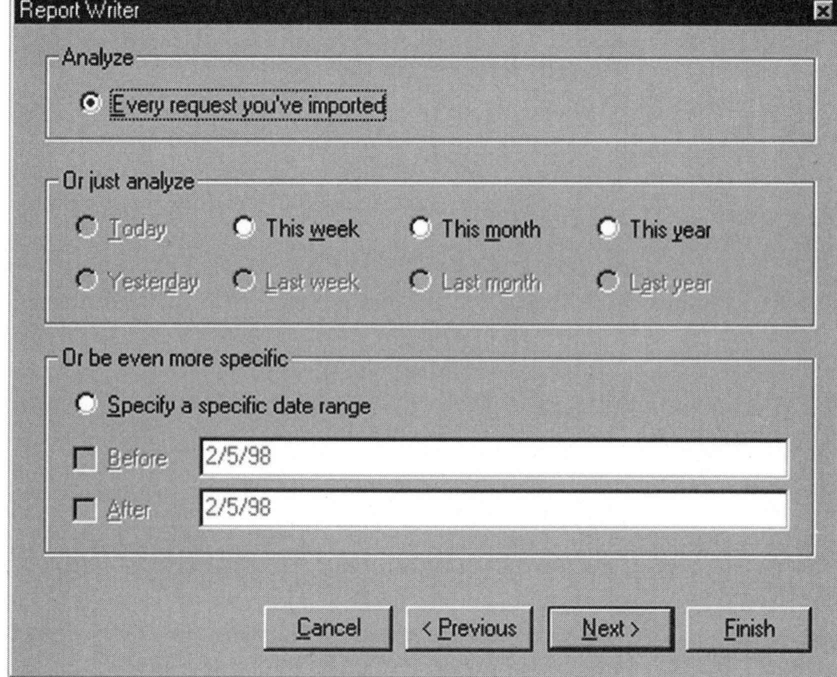

Figure 11-26 Specify which logged requests to analyze, based on the date and time the request was logged.

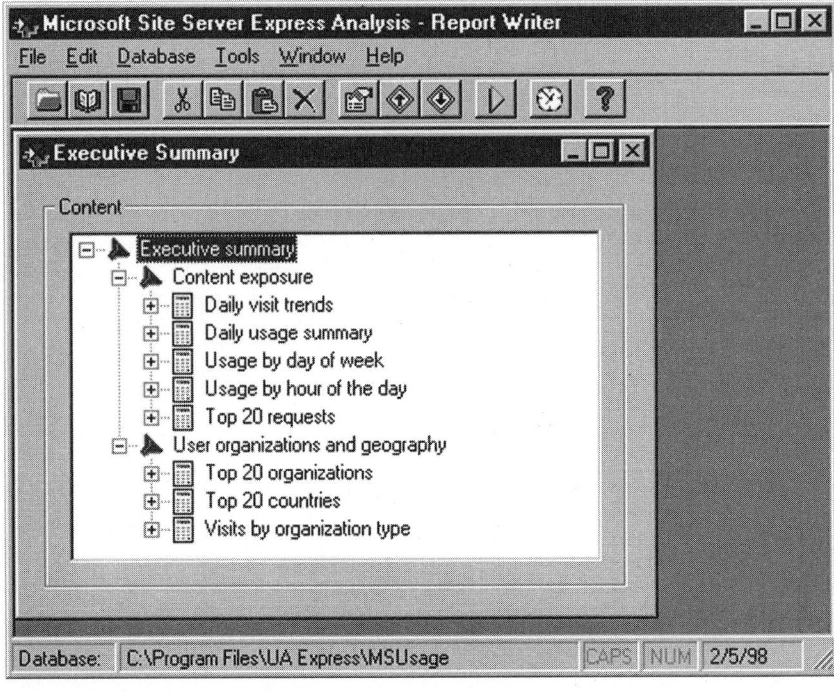

Figure 11-27 An Executive Summary report has been generated but not yet formatted.

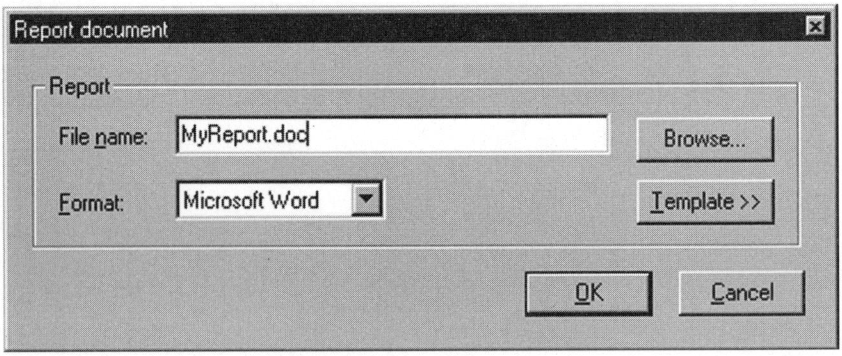

Report document
Report
File name: MyReport.doc
Browse...
Format: Microsoft Word
Template >>
OK
Cancel

Figure 11-28 The Report document dialog box.

name your report and select an output format, either HTML, Word, or Excel. The appropriate application (IE 4.01, Word, or Excel) will launch, and the report will be created. An example of a report in Word format is given in a later section of this chapter.

Report formats can be customized by selecting TOOLS, OPTIONS to open the Report Writer Options dialog box. Select or modify the options you desire and then generate a new report. Reports can also be customized by using a template (see Fig. 11-28).

Report Writer Predefined Report Definition Files

Summary Reports The following is a list of predefined summary reports from the Report Writer catalog with brief descriptions taken verbatim from the Report Writer dialog box. These reports can be used to generate instant reports of your site's activity. You can access the Report Writer catalog by selecting FILE, OPEN REPORT WRITER CATALOG.

Bandwidth summary report. This report shows byte transfers on an hourly and daily basis. Identify trends over time as well as averages per day of week and hour of day. Use this information to plan maintenance or upgrades or alert you to the need for additional capacity to maintain an optimal user experience on your site.

Browser and operating system summary report. This report shows browser market share and user operating systems. Use this information to design your site for proper user experience. This report requires "user-agent" data within your server log files.

Executive Summary. This report shows top level information to give you an at-a-glance look at the activity on your Web site. For detailed information on a particular section of this report, refer to the corresponding detail report. This report requires "IP resolution," "Title lookups," and "Whois queries" to be completed.

Executive Summary (extended logs). This report shows top level information to give you an at-a-glance look at the activity on your Web site. Included are browser market share and the top external organization names that users linked from to reach your site. For detailed information on a particular section of this report, refer to the corresponding detail report. This report requires "user-agent" and "referrer" data within your server log files, and "IP resolution," "Title lookups," and "Whois queries" to be completed before analysis.

Geography summary report. This report shows the top cities and states/provinces in the United States and Canada as well as the international countries visiting your site. Use this information to target your efforts towards the origin of your visitors, and to determine where to mirror your sites. This report requires "IP resolution" and "Whois queries" to be completed before analysis.

Hit summary detail. This report shows server "hits" on an hourly and daily basis. Learn about trends over time as well as averages per day of week and hour of day. Use this information to plan maintenance or upgrades or alert you to the need for additional capacity to maintain an optimal user experience on your site.

Organization summary report. This report shows the U.S., Canadian, and international organizations that visit your Web site. Use this information to monitor your target audience, identify new target customers, and generate leads from frequently visiting organizations. This report requires "IP resolution" and "Whois queries" to be completed before analysis.

Path summary report. This report shows the sequence of requests that users make when visiting your site. Use this information to assure proper location of key content and to optimize the navigation within your site. This report requires "Title lookups" to be completed before analysis.

Referrer summary report. This report shows the top external organization names and URLs that users linked from to reach your site. Use this information to evaluate the effectiveness of online advertising or promotions or to identify synergistic locations for such programs. This report requires "referrer" data within your server log files, and "IP resolution" to be completed before analysis.

Request summary report. This report shows the most requested documents. Learn about what elements in your site attract the most attention from users. This report requires "Title lookups" to be completed before analysis.

User summary report. This report shows trends in first time and total user visits and in unregistered and registered users. Frequent user visits signal that you have created a compelling site. This report requires registration on your site or "cookie" data within your server log files.

Visit summary report. This report shows when your users visit on an hourly and daily basis. Learn about trends over time as well as averages per day of week and hour of day. Use this information to understand the behavior of your customers.

Detail Reports The following is a list of predefined detail reports from the Report Writer catalog with brief descriptions taken verbatim from the Report Writer dialog box. You can access the Report Writer Catalog by selecting FILE, OPEN REPORT WRITER CATALOG.

Bandwidth detail report. This report shows byte transfers on an hourly, daily, and weekly basis. Identify trends over time as well as averages per day of week and hour of day. Use this information to plan maintenance or upgrades or alert you to the need for additional capacity to maintain an optimal user experience on your site.

Browser and operating system detail report. This report shows browser market share, trends in Netscape and Microsoft versions and security support, and user operating systems. Use this information to design your site for proper user experience. This report requires "user-agent" data within your server log files.

Geography detail report. This report shows the top cities, states/provinces, and regions in the United States and Canada as well as the international countries visiting your site. Use this information to target your efforts towards the origin of your visitors, and to determine where to mirror your sites. This report requires "IP resolution" and "Whois queries" to be completed before analysis.

Hit detail report. This report shows byte transfers on an hourly, daily, and weekly basis. Identify trends over time as well as averages per day of week and hour of day. Use this information to plan maintenance or upgrades or alert you to the need for additional capacity to maintain an optimal user experience on your site.

Organization detail report. This report shows the U.S., Canadian, and international organizations that visit your Web site. Use this information to monitor your target audience, identify new target customers, and generate leads from frequently visiting organizations. This report requires "IP resolution" and "Whois queries" to be completed before analysis.

Referrer detail report. This report shows the top external organization names and URLs that users linked from to reach your site. Use this information to evaluate the effectiveness of online advertising or promotions or to identify synergistic locations for such programs. This report requires "referrer" data within your server log files, and "IP resolution" to be completed before analysis.

Request detail report. This report shows the most and least requested documents over time and by directory. Learn about what elements in your site attract the most attention from users. This report requires "Title lookups" to be completed before analysis.

User detail report. This report shows trends in first time and total user visits, user visit frequency, and in unregistered and registered users.

Frequent user visits signal that you have created a compelling site. This report requires registration on your site or "cookie" data within your server log files.

Visit detail report. This report shows when your users visit on an hourly, daily, and weekly basis. Learn about trends over time as well as averages per day of week and hour of day. Use this information to understand the behavior of your customers.

Sample Report Generated by Report Writer

The following Executive Summary report was generated by Report Writer as an example of the kind of information and style of report formatting available with Report Writer. This report, generated as a Microsoft Word file, is based on log files generated on a stand-alone IIS machine by browsing the default Web site with sample WWW files installed over a period of several weeks. As a result, the information is not particularly interesting; the objective is just to illustrate the format of a Report Writer report. (See Fig. 11-29).

Figure 11-29 Sample Report Writer report.

Report document date: 2/6/98 1:09:28 AM

Internet sites analyzed: Site

First date analyzed: 1/13/98

Last date analyzed: 2/5/98

Analysis content

1. Content exposure
2. User organizations and geography
3. Definitions

Daily visit trends

Shows the number of visits for each day in the analysis period. Weekdays are shown as blue bars and weekends as red ones.

Figure 11-29
(Continued)

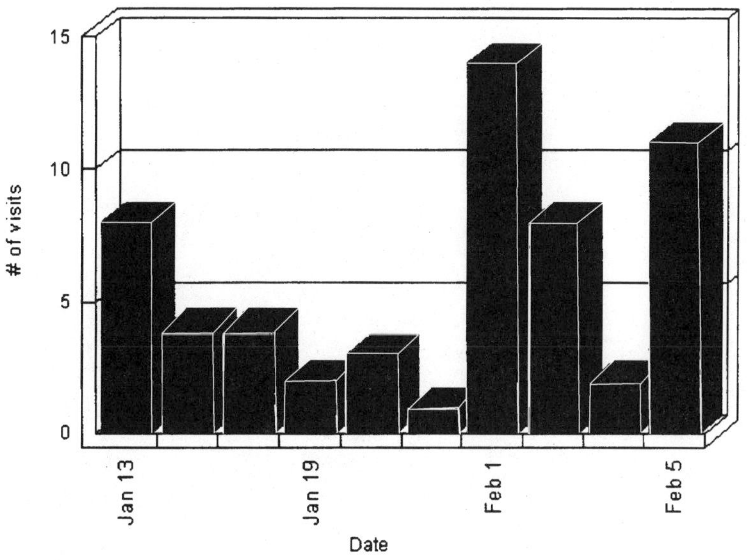

Daily usage summary

Date	Number of hits	Number of requests	Number of visits	Number of users	Average requests per visit
Jan 13	252	164	8	1	20.50
Jan 15	128	46	4	1	11.50
Jan 18	270	43	4	1	10.75
Jan 19	371	180	2	1	90.00
Jan 20	33	18	3	1	6.00
Jan 29	33	11	1	1	11.00
Feb 1	769	184	14	1	13.14
Feb 2	267	118	8	1	14.75
Feb 3	133	76	2	1	38.00
Feb 5	292	146	11	1	13.27
Total	**2,548**	**986**	**57**		**17.30**

Figure 11-29
(Continued)

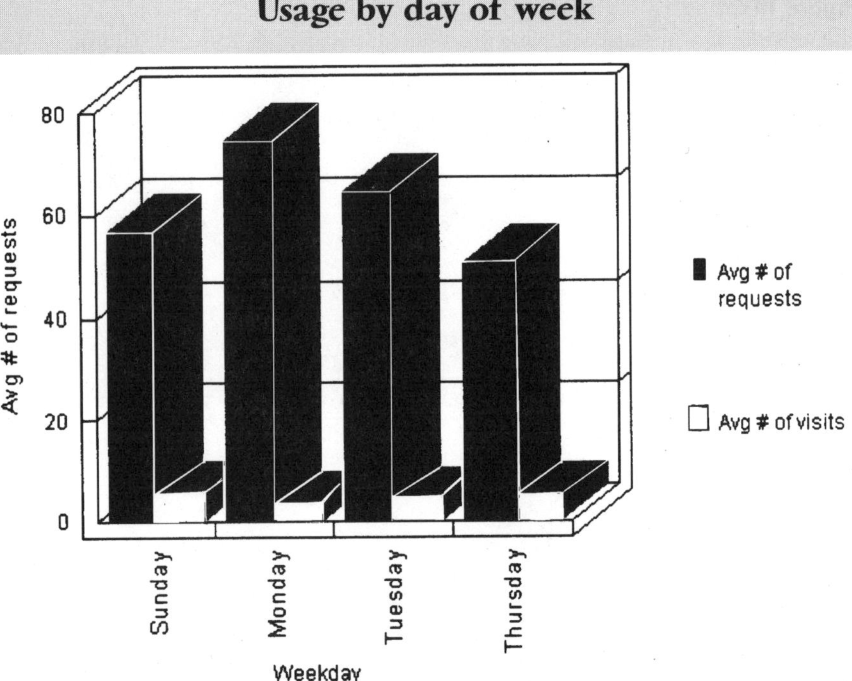

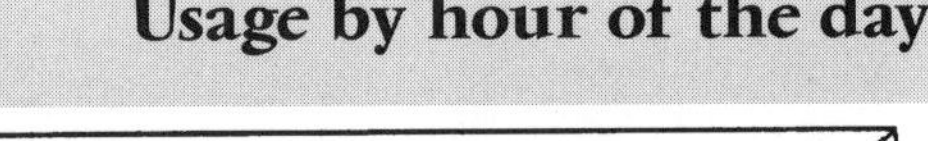

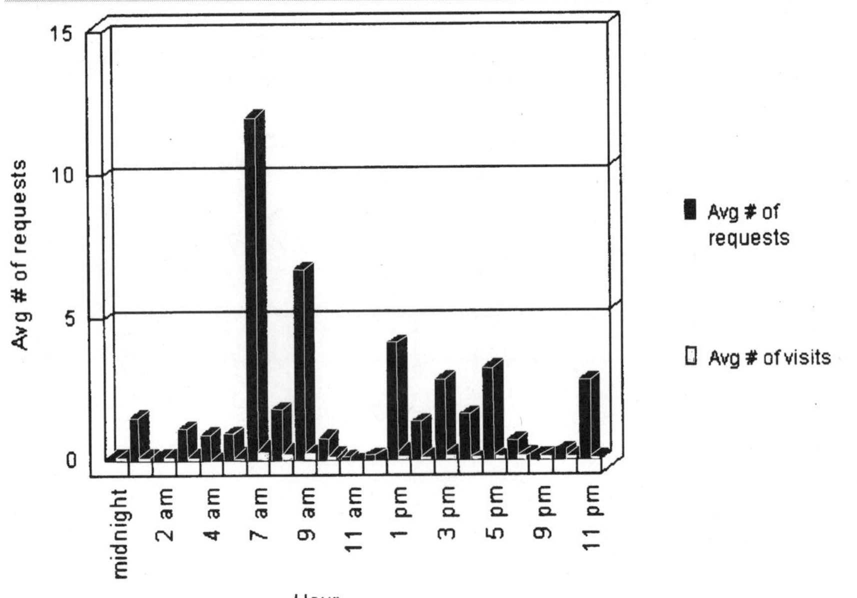

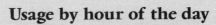

Figure 11-29
Continued)

Top 20 requests

Lists the 20 files that received the most requests.

Title	# of requests	% of requests
1. /iishelp/common/coua.css	59	5.98%
2. /iisHelp/iis/misc/contents.asp	42	4.26%
3. /iisHelp/iis/htm/core/opgstop.asp	31	3.14%
4. /iisHelp/iis/misc/	29	2.94%
5. /iisHelp/iis/htm/core/iiwltop.htm	27	2.74%
6. /iisHelp/iis/misc/cohhc.hhc	27	2.74%
7. /iisHelp/iis/misc/navbar.asp	27	2.74%
8. /CertAdm/wcalist.asp	22	2.23%
9. /iisHelp/iis/misc/Index.asp	22	2.23%
10. /certsrv/	21	2.13%
11. /	20	2.03%
12. /iisHelp/iis/misc/Search.asp	13	1.32%
13. /iisHelp/iis/misc/cohhk.hhk	13	1.32%
14. /iishelp/common/spidie4.css	12	1.22%
15. /CertSrv/CertEnroll/ceenroll.asp	12	1.22%
16. /CertQue/wcqlist.asp	12	1.22%
17. /iisHelp/iis/misc/iisrch.idq	12	1.22%
18. /CertSrv/CertEnroll/	11	1.12%
19. /iisadmin/isadmin/state.ida	9	0.91%
20. /CertSrv/CertEnroll/ceaccept.asp	8	0.81%
Total	**429**	**43.51%**

Figure 11-29 (Continued)

Top 20 organizations

Shows the 20 organizations that visited your site most frequently. Determine if your target customers are visiting as frequently as expected or learn about new organizations to target.

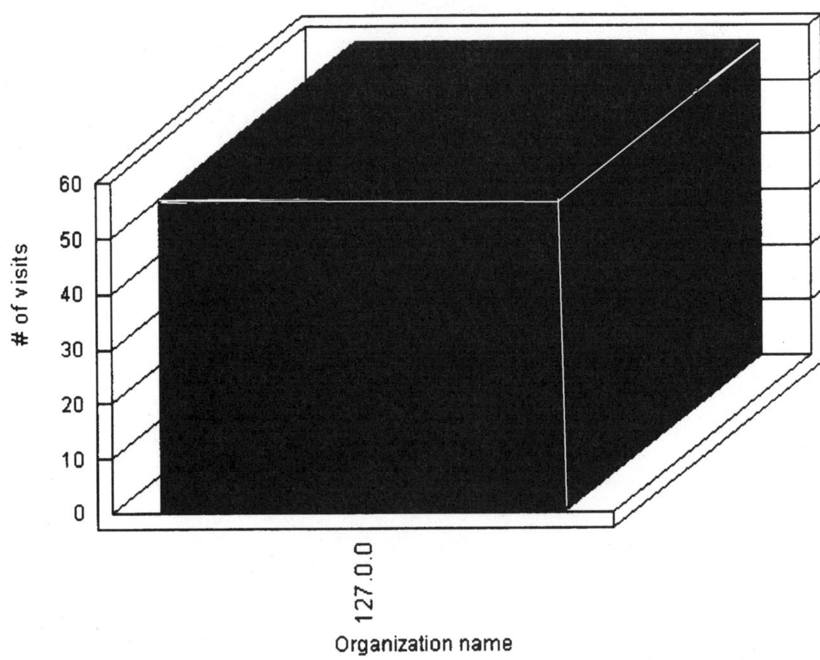

	Organization name	# of visits	% of visits
1.	127.0.0	57	100.00%
	Total	**57**	**100.00%**

Figure 11-29
(Continued)

Top 20 countries

Shows the top 20 countries from which users came to visit your site. This information can be valuable to determine if mirror sites are needed in other countries.

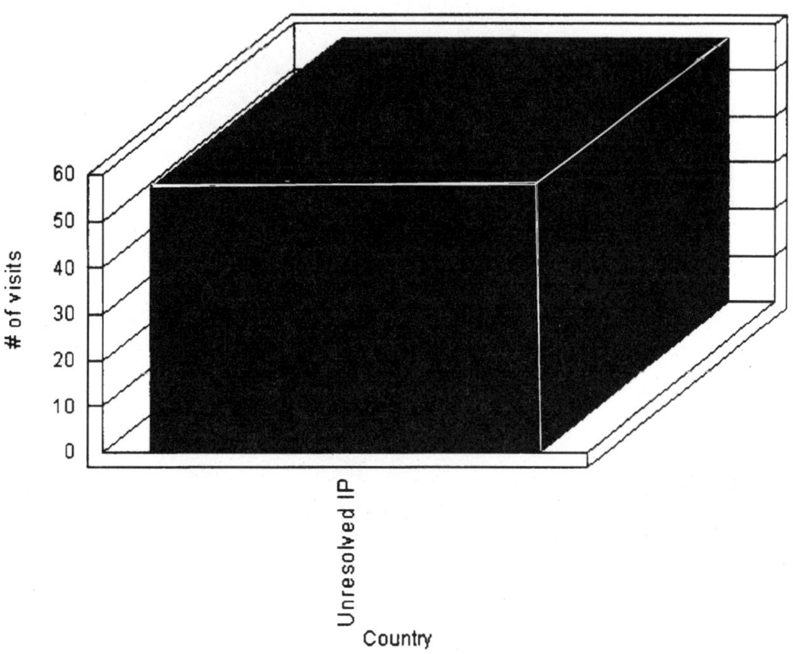

Organization type	# of visits	% of visits
Unresolved IP address	57	100.00%
Total	**57**	**100.00%**

Figure 11-29 (Continued)

Visits by organization type

Shows the percentage of visits from each organization type. This information can be used as another monitor for reaching target audience or identifying new organization types to target.

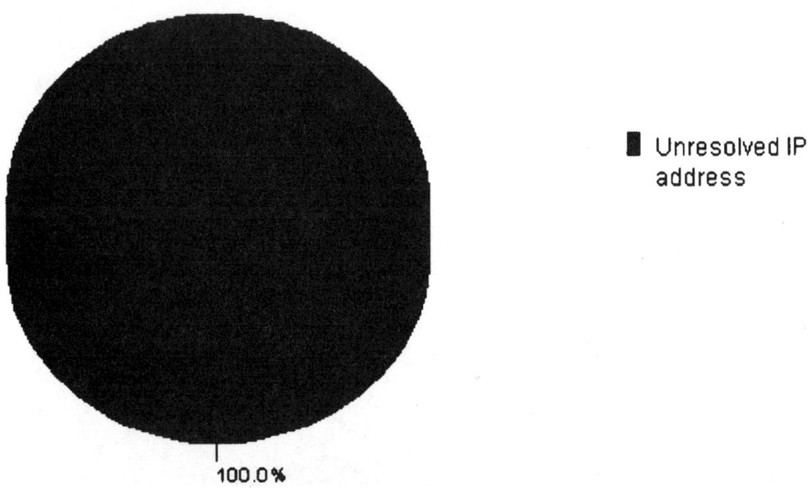

	Country	# of visits	% of visits
1.	Unresolved IP address	57	100.00%
	Total	**57**	**100.00%**

Hit Any connection to an Internet site, including inline image requests and errors.

Request A *hit* that successfully retrieves content. Requests don't include inline image, ad view, or ad click requests or errors. Request counts are conservative because browsers and many Internet gateways intercept some requests before reaching the server, and these cached requests are never logged.

Figure 11-29
(Continued)

Visit	A series of consecutive requests from a user to an Internet site. If your log data includes *referrer* data, then new visits begin with referring links external to your Internet site. Regardless of whether or not you have referrer data, if a user doesn't make a request for a certain period of time, the previous series of requests is considered a completed visit.
User	Anyone who visits the site at least once. If your log data contains *persistent cookie* data, the software uses this data to recognize unique users. If no cookie data is available, the software uses a registered *username* to recognize users. If no registration information is available, the software uses as a last resort, users' Internet *hostnames*. Many organizations use Internet gateways, which mask the real Internet hostnames, so user counts may be conservative for those users determined through their Internet hostnames.
Organization	A commercial, academic, nonprofit, government, or military entity that connects users to the Internet, identified by an entity's Internet domains. Microsoft Site Server Express Analysis groups together all domains registered to the same organization as one organization. If a domain is unavailable in the database, one Internet domain is used to identify one organization.
Request duration	The time between two consecutive requests within the same visit. Microsoft Site Server Express Analysis assigns the last request of a visit a request duration of 0 seconds because its actual duration can't be determined.
Visit duration	The time between the first and last request of a visit. This time doesn't include how long users viewed the last request of a visit.

Figure 11-29
(Continued)

Ad view	A hit that successfully retrieves advertiser content. Ad view counts are conservative because browser software and many Internet gateways intercept some requests before reaching the server, and these cached requests are never logged.
Ad click	The number of requests caused by the user "clicking" on advertising content. Typically, users are directed to the advertiser's site after the ad click.
Ad yield	The percentage of ad views that resulted in an ad click.
Geography	The continent, country, region, state, city, and Zip code are based on an organization's Internet domain registration. Only Internet domains found within the Analysis database are included within region, state, city, and Zip code report documents. Each Internet domain is associated with only one Zip code, so all users from a domain used in multiple locations are considered to be at one location.

Microsoft Site Server Express Analysis Report Writer produced this report document. Web to http://www.microsoft.com/SiteServer/.

Using Site Server Express: Posting Acceptor

Another component that is added when Site Server Express 2.0 is installed is *Microsoft Posting Acceptor.* Posting Acceptor is an add-on to IIS that allows content developers to upload their files to an IIS server using the HTTP Post protocol.

Posting Acceptor works with Internet Explorer 3.02 or later versions and Netscape Navigator 2.02 or later. The following walkthrough provides a brief demonstration of how to post content to a site using Posting Acceptor. Consult the online documentation for further information on how to customize this powerful tool.

Walkthrough: Posting Content to a Site Using Posting Acceptor

A user named Mitch is logged on to a Windows 95 workstation called SUPER2 that is part of a Windows NT 4.0 domain called MYSTUFF. The workstation has Internet Explorer 3.02 installed, and Mitch has created some Web content and saved it in the `C:\BIGCORP` folder on the workstation. Mitch wants to post the Web content to the default Web site on an IIS 4.0 server called SERVER1. Windows NT challenge/response authentication is enabled on SERVER1. Other users will need to post their content as well.

Here is one possible way to proceed. Begin by logging on to SERVER1 as *Administrator* and use Windows Explorer to create a `users` subdirectory under the default home directory

```
C:\InetPub\wwwroot\users\
```

Right-click on the `users` directory to access the Security tab on the `users` Property sheet. Click PERMISSIONS and remove the *Everyone* group from the users ACL. Add *Domain Users*, and give them *change* permission (Fig. 11-30). Click OK twice. We have now created a directory to which users' Web content will be posted, and we have assigned the directory appropriate permissions.

Log on as *Mitch* to the Windows 95 machine, select START, RUN, and type the following:

```
http://server1/scripts/upload.asp
```

Click OK, and Internet Explorer 3.02 opens up and begins loading the referenced page. A dialog box appears informing you that a Windows application is attempting to install a software component (Fig. 11-31). Click YES to install the component. Another, similar dialog box appears; click YES. Files are copied to the workstation, new Start menu shortcuts are created, and the Web page finishes loading (Fig. 11-32).

At this point, pause and examine your Start menu. You will discover that the *Microsoft Web Publishing Wizard* has been installed on your client machine. We will use this wizard in the next section.

To perform the post, open Windows Explorer and browse to locate the `default.htm` file in the working directory

```
C:\BigCorp\
```

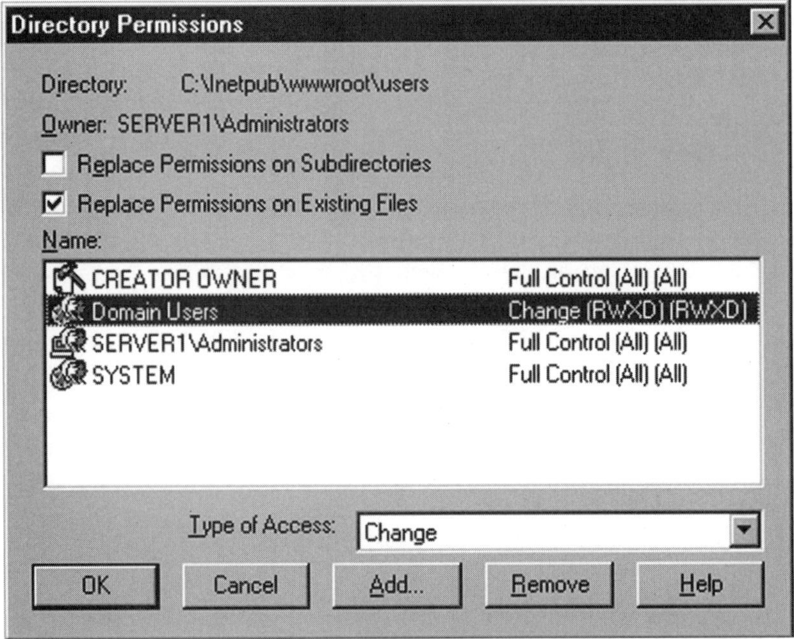

Figure 11-30 Configuring security on the `users` subdirectory.

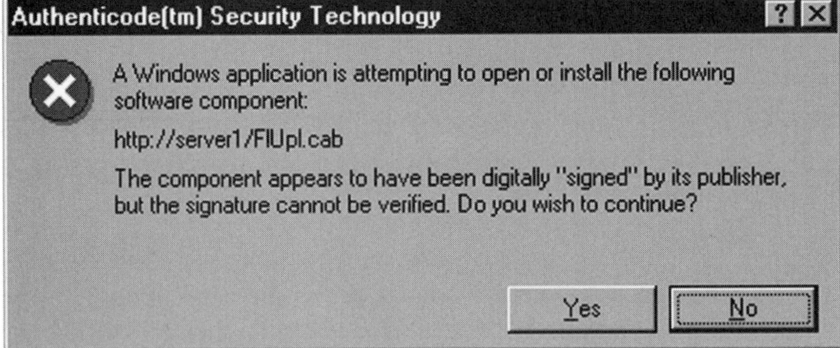

Figure 11-31 Installing a software component on the client.

Click and drag the `default.htm` file from the `BigCorp` folder in Windows Explorer onto the posting control (the computer image in Fig. 11-32) in Internet Explorer 3.02. A message appears, indicating that the page is being posted (Fig. 11-33).

Log on to SERVER1 as *Administrator* and start Windows Explorer. Check the contents of the previously created users folder, and you will see that a subfolder called `Mystuff` (the Windows NT domain name) has been created in it; within that is another subfolder called `Mitch`, and within that is the posted page `default.htm` (Fig. 11-34). Check the

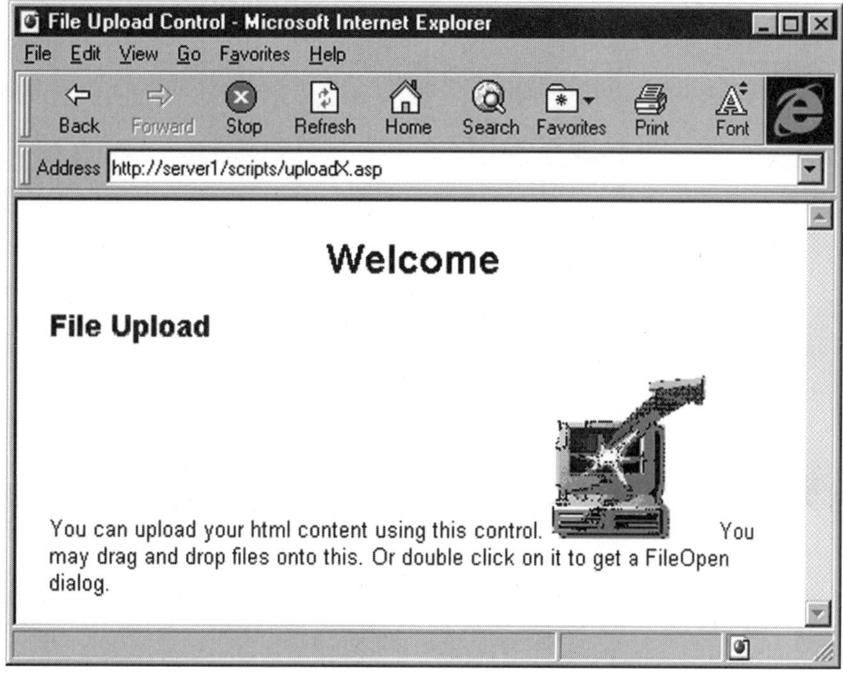

Figure 11-32 The Posting Acceptor upload page for Internet Explorer.

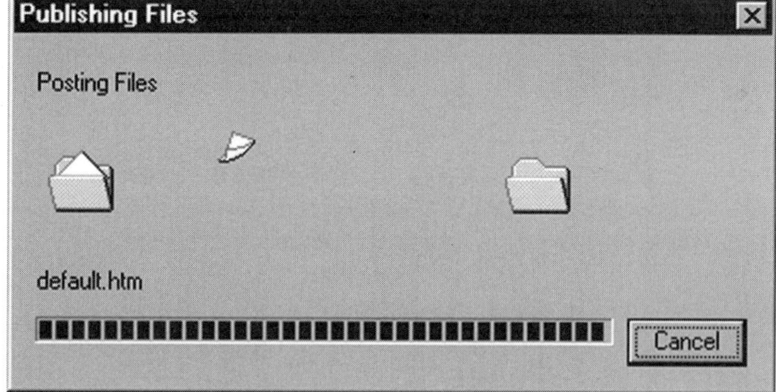

Figure 11-33 The file is being posted to the server.

ACL of the newly created `Mitch` folder and you will see that the user Mitch has been assigned *special access* (*full control*) to the new folder.

To test whether you can access the page, open the following URL from the client:

```
http://server1/users/mystuff/mitch/default.htm
```

The posted page should open up as expected.

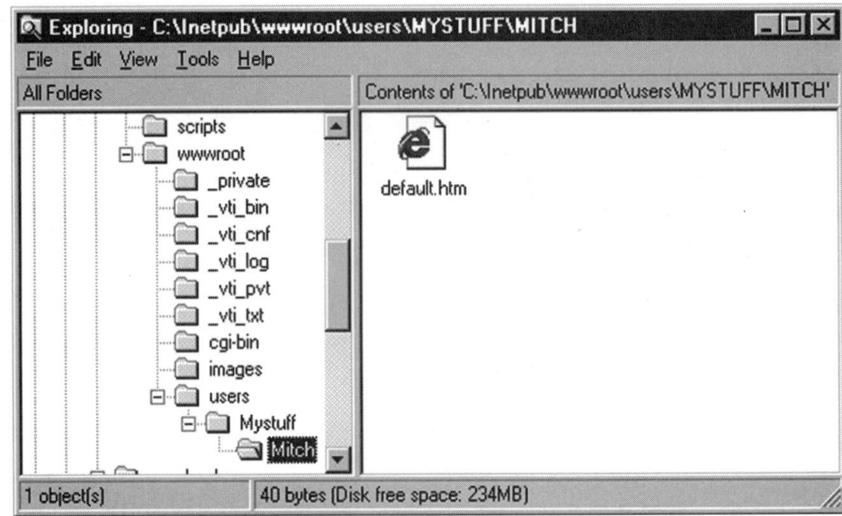

Figure 11-34 The file has been posted to a newly created directory structure.

Walkthrough: Publishing to a Site Using Web Publishing Wizard

Now that the Web Publishing Wizard has been installed on the client, we can use this tool to publish content to the server. But before we try this, let's configure a virtual directory for the newly created Web content posted by Mitch.

Log on to SERVER1 as *Administrator* and open the Internet Service Manager MMC window. Right-click on the SERVER1 icon and select NEW, VIRTUAL DIRECTORY. Create a virtual directory with the alias `mitch` mapped to the physical path

```
C:\InetPub\wwwroot\users\MyStuff\Mitch
```

Assign the virtual directory the following permissions:

- Read
- Script
- Write

Test your virtual directory by logging on to the client machine as *Mitch* and opening the URL

```
http://server1/mitch
```

Now start the Web Publishing Wizard on the client machine by selecting START, PROGRAMS, MICROSOFT WEB PUBLISHING, WEB PUBLISHING WIZARD. The welcome screen for the Wizard will open (Fig. 11-35). Click NEXT and browse to locate another Web page to publish (Fig. 11-36).

Click NEXT and the Select a Web Server screen appears. Click NEW and enter a friendly name for the Web site you are publishing to (for example, *The BigCorp Web Site*).

Click NEXT and specify the URL of the virtual directory you are publishing to—in this case,

```
http://server1/mitch
```

(see Fig. 11-37). Note that the next time you run the wizard, when you reach the Select a Web Server screen you will be able to choose the friendly name you defined earlier from a drop-down box.

Click NEXT and then FINISH to publish your files to SERVER1. Test your work by opening the following URL from the client machine:

```
http://server1/mitch/sale.htm
```

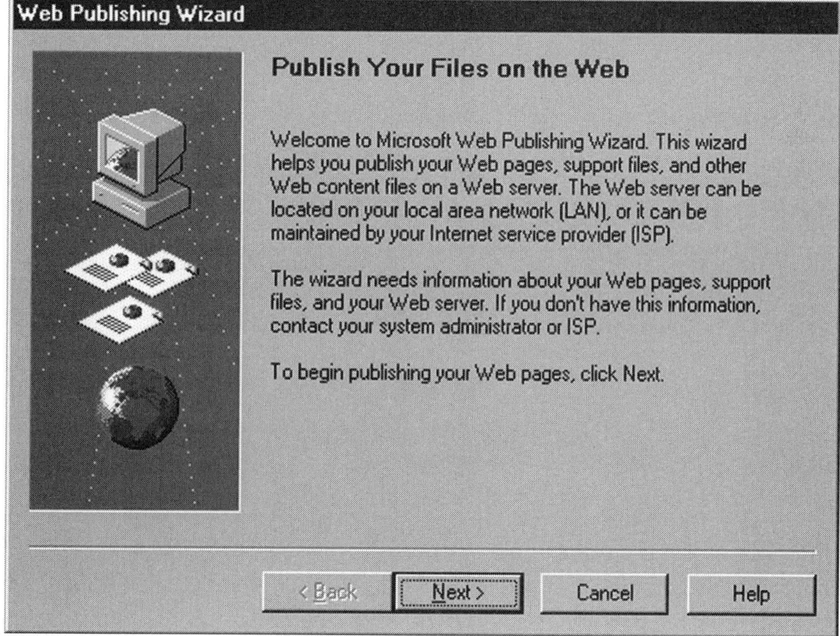

Figure 11-35 The Microsoft Web Publishing Wizard welcome screen.

Figure 11-36 Select a file or folder to publish.

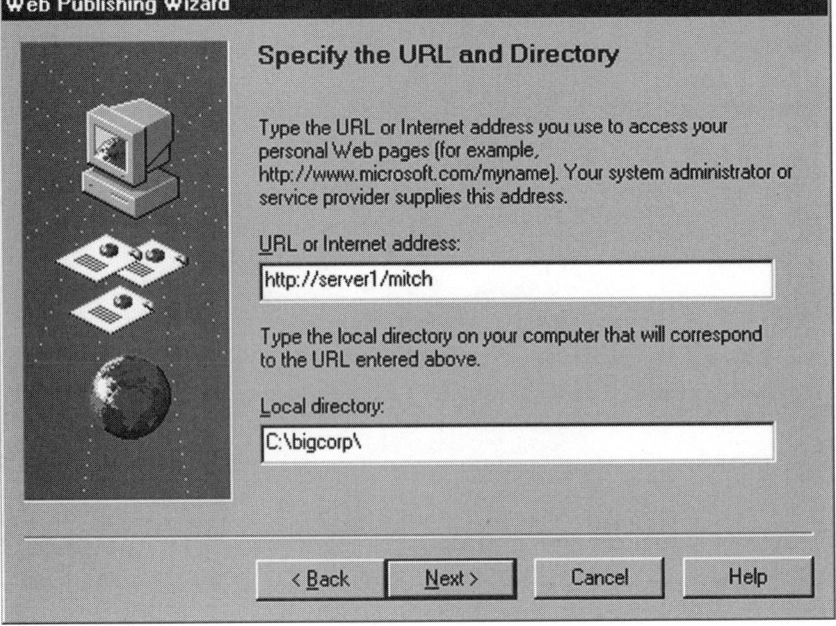

Figure 11-37 Specify the URL you are publishing to.

SUMMARY

Site Server Express 2.0 provides content management and usage reporting tools necessary for administrators to manage and maintain complex Web sites. Content Analyzer can create WebMaps and generate Site Summary reports. Usage Import and Report Writer can generate formatted site usage reports. Posting Acceptor and Web Publishing Wizard enable developers to post content to servers.

FOR MORE INFORMATION

Microsoft Web Site Site Server Express is a scaled-down version of *Microsoft Site Server* and *Microsoft Site Server Enterprise Edition.* Windows NT 4.0 Option Pack includes version 2.0 of Site Server Express. At the time of this writing, version 3.0 of Site Server is in beta form and is available for download from

```
www.microsoft.com/siteserver/default.asp
```

For information about Site Server Express and how it relates to IIS 4, visit

```
www.microsoft.com/iis/guide/ssx.asp
```

For information about Site Server Express and how it differs from Site Server, visit

```
backoffice.microsoft.com/products/siteserver/express/default.asp
```

Microsoft Public Newsgroups For newsgroups relating to Site Server, connect to the news server `msnews.microsoft.com` and subscribe to the following groups:

```
microsoft.public.site-server.commerce
microsoft.public.site-server.general
microsoft.public.site-server.postingacceptr
microsoft.public.site-server.publishing
microsoft.public.site-server.site-mgmt
microsoft.public.site-server.webpost
```

The following group relates to Usage Analyst:

```
microsoft.public.usageanalyst
```

Microsoft TechNet Another valuable resource is Microsoft TechNet, which contains a full copy of the MS Site Server Evaluation Guide under the category

Internet | Server | MS Site Server | Product Facts | Evaluation Guide

CHAPTER 12

Administering SSL with Certificate Server

Introduction

Administrators concerned about IIS security have an additional option to those described in Chap. 4. That option is to enable the Secure Sockets Layer (SSL) protocol for encrypted transfer of data between servers and clients. In order to simplify setting up and maintaining SSL, the Windows NT 4.0 Option Pack includes an additional tool called Certificate Server that provides administrators with the ability to issue, install, and revoke X.509 digital certificates. After completing this chapter you will be able to

- Understand how SSL enables secure transactions between Web servers and clients
- Install and configure Certificate Server for issuing X.509 digital certificates
- Use Certificate Server's HTML-based administration tools
- Generate a certificate request and public/private key pair
- Submit the certificate request to a Certificate Authority and install the received certificate on the server
- Enable SSL on virtual servers and virtual directories
- Install a Certificate Authority certificate on a browser's root store

Understanding Secure Sockets Layer

Secure Sockets Layer version 3.0 (SSL 3.0) is a protocol that enables encrypted sessions between browser clients and Web servers. SSL makes use of *public key cryptography,* a mechanism that uses two encryption keys to ensure that the session is secure:

- A *public key,* which can be given to any application or user that requests it
- A *private key,* which is only known to its owner

In addition to the public/private key pair, SSL makes use of *digital certificates,* which are files issued by Certificate Authorities that act as a kind of identity card for the application or user. Digital certificates are text files that contain information that identifies an application or user. The certificate also contains the public key of the application or user.

A *Certificate Authority* (*CA*) is a trusted agency that is responsible for confirming the identity of the application or user and issuing a digital certificate for identity purposes. An example of a third-party Certificate Authority is *VeriSign:*

```
www.verisign.com
```

Alternatively, Internet Information Server administrators can use Microsoft Certificate Server to act as their own Certificate Authority, issuing and revoking digital certificates within their organization as required.

Certificates installed on IIS servers to provide proof of identity for the servers are called *server certificates.* Those installed on client browsers are called *client certificates.* Both server and client certificates have to be signed (verified to be authentic) by a Certificate Authority. The certificate used to identify the Certificate Authority as being who it says it is is called a *site certificate,* or *CA certificate,* and is signed by the CA itself.

Certificates can expire and can also be *revoked* if necessary. The CA keeps a list of revoked certificates called the *Certificate Revocation List,* which may be used to check the identity of digital certificate holders.

How SSL Works

In SSL sessions all data passing between the client and the server is encrypted. An SSL session is established by a series of steps outlined in the following series of diagrams. In Fig. 12-1, a client establishes a connection to a server. After a connection is established, the server sends the browser its public key and server certificate (Fig. 12-2). At this point the server and client discuss and decide on the level of encryption to be used in encrypting the transmitted data (Fig. 12-3).

When an encryption strength has been decided on, the client creates a session key, which will be used to encrypt data during the current SSL

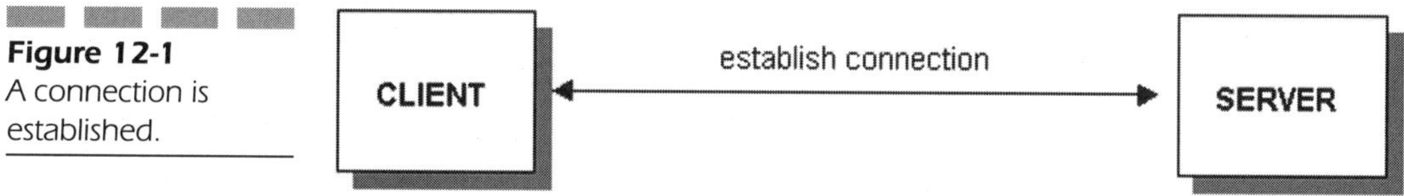

Figure 12-1 A connection is established.

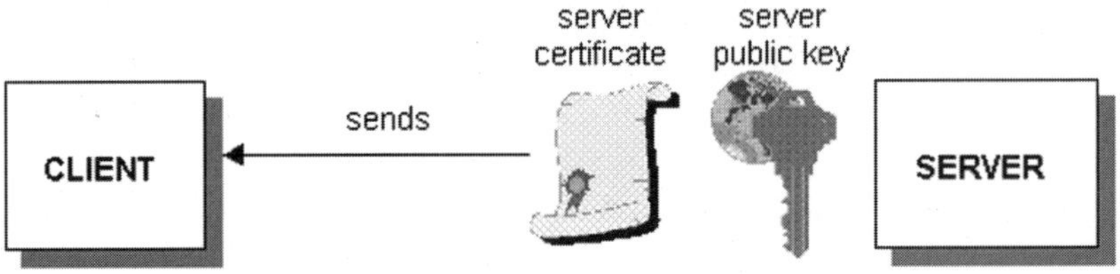

Figure 12-2
Server sends its server certificate and public key to client.

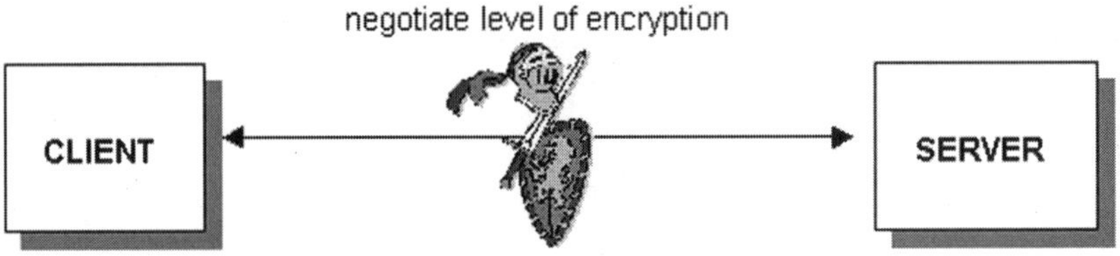

Figure 12-3
Client and server negotiate encryption strength.

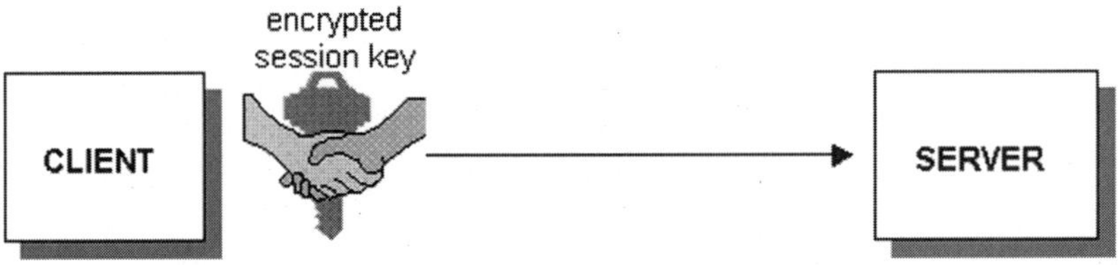

Figure 12-4
Client encrypts session key with server's public key.

session. The client takes the session key it created and encrypts it using the server's public key. The client then sends the encrypted session key to the server (Fig. 12-4). If anyone were to capture the session key at this stage, they would not be able to use it, because it can only be decrypted by the server's private key, which only the server possesses.

The server receives the encrypted session key and uses its private key to decrypt it. Both the client and the server now possess the session key, and they use this to establish a secure channel for sending data to one another (Fig. 12-5).

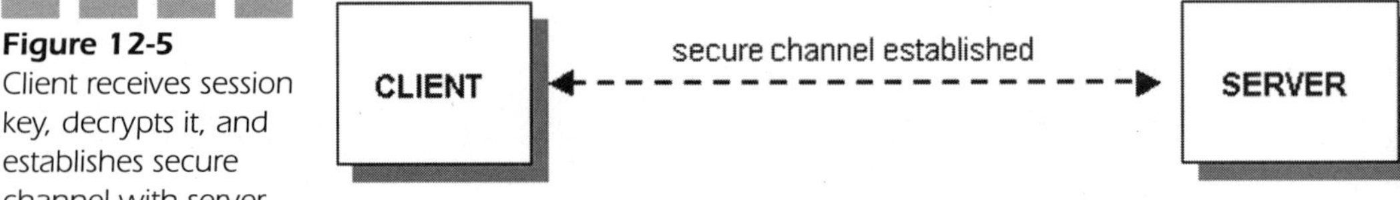

Figure 12-5
Client receives session key, decrypts it, and establishes secure channel with server.

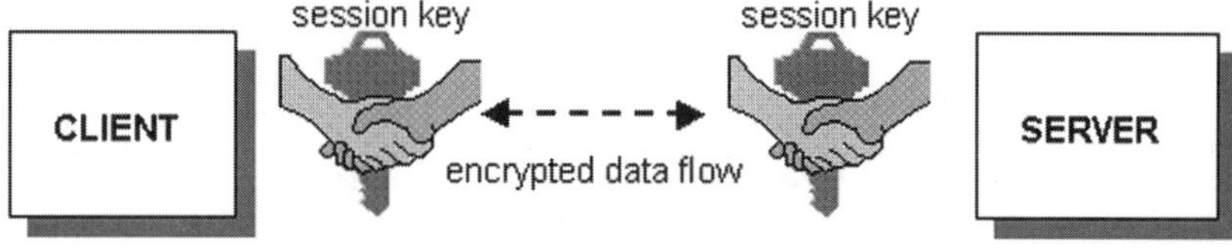

Figure 12-6 Secure channel for transmitting data is now established.

Finally, the client and server exchange data with each other, first encrypting then decrypting the data with their session keys (Fig. 12-6).

Implementing SSL on IIS 4.0

In order to enable an SSL session between a client browser and an IIS server, the following is required:

- The Web server requires a server certificate from a trusted CA.
- The server certificate must be installed on the server.
- SSL must be enabled on the selected virtual server (or virtual directory on the server) using the Directory Security tab on the virtual server's Property sheet.
- The client browser must add the CA certificate to its *root store* so that it can verify the authenticity of the server's certificate.
- The client must access the SSL-enabled server using a secure URL beginning with `https://`

This process will be illustrated in the walkthrough later on in this chapter.

Understanding Certificate Server

Microsoft Certificate Server provides administrators with the ability to issue, install, and revoke standard X.509 digital certificates. These certificates can be used to provide trusted verification of the identity of users of your corporate intranet, extranet, or Internet storefront.

Certificate Server can process standard Public-Key Cryptography Standards (PKCS) 10 certificate requests and issue standard X.509 certificates in response. Certificate Server is also extensible and can support other certificate formats by using third-party extensions.

Certificate Server includes tools for administering, logging, and revoking digital certificates for servers, clients, and other CAs. Clients supported include Internet Explorer 2.0 and higher, and Netscape Navigator 3.0 and higher. A server log (database) contains a record of all certificates requested, issued, and revoked by Certificate Server.

Certificate Server is a Windows NT service that runs continually in the background and takes full advantage of Windows NT's stability, security features, and reliability.

Installing Certificate Server

The hardware and software requirements for installing Microsoft Certificate Server are the same as those for installing IIS 4.0, namely:

- Windows NT 4.0 Server
- Service Pack 3
- Internet Explorer 4.01

Prior to installing Certificate Server, you need to create a shared folder for Certificate Server to use to store its Certificate Authority certificates and various configuration files (for example, `C:\CA` shared with read permission for everyone). It must be shared so that clients can access and install CA certificates from it. The shared folder must be stored on the local machine where Certificate Server is installed.

To install Certificate server, click START, PROGRAMS, WINDOWS NT OPTION PACK, WINDOWS NT OPTION PACK SETUP. When the welcome screen comes up, click NEXT and select ADD/REMOVE to open the Select Components screen (Fig. 12-7). Check the CERTIFICATE SERVER checkbox and click NEXT.

In the next screen, you need to specify the shared folder you created earlier as the Configuration Data Storage Location for Certificate Server (Fig. 12-8). You can also change the locations of the certificate store database and log locations, which by default are in

```
C:\winnt\System32\CertLog
```

The SHOW ADVANCED CONFIGURATION checkbox allows selection of hashing algorithms and cryptographic service providers, and configuration of Certificate Authority hierarchies, but these features are not functional in this release of Certificate Server.

Click NEXT and specify identification information for Certificate Server (Fig. 12-9).

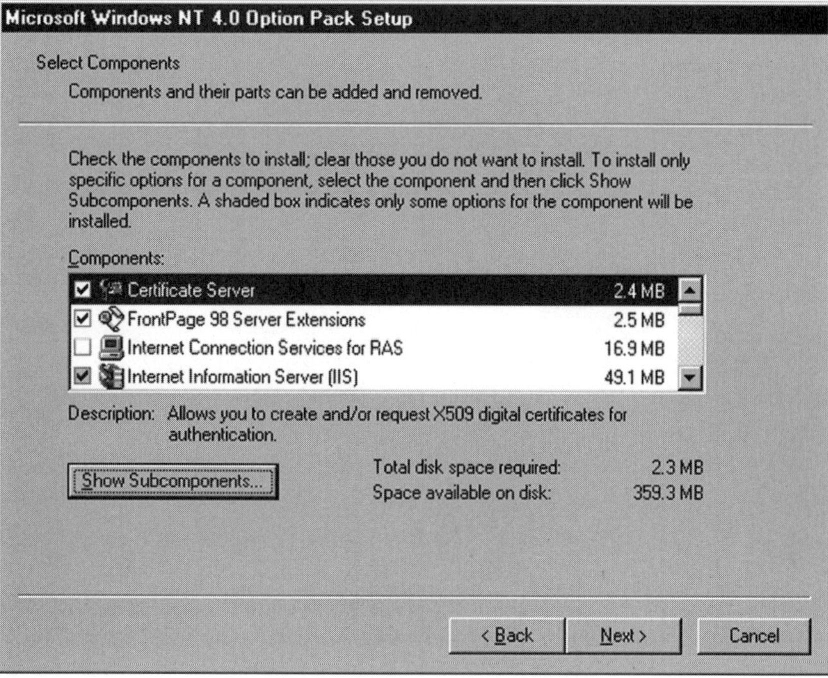

Figure 12-7 Selecting Certificate Server in the Select Components screen.

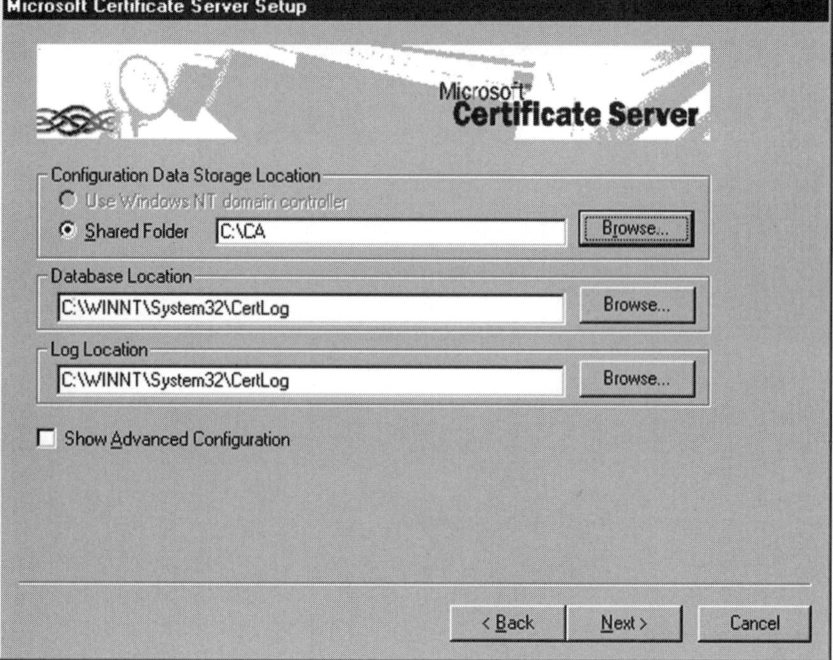

Figure 12-8 Specify a configuration data storage location for Certificate Server.

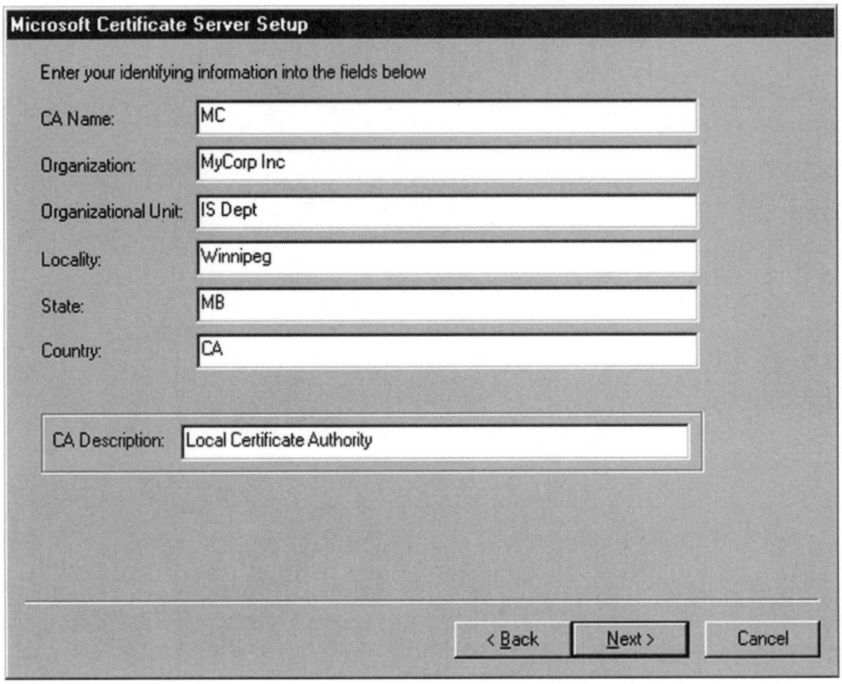

Figure 12-9 Specify identification information for Certificate Server.

Click NEXT and the Completing Installation screen will appear. Certificate server now installs on the local machine, and the following tasks are automatically performed:

- Certificate Server program files are installed in

  ```
  C:\winnt\System32
  ```

- HTML administration tools for managing Certificate Server are installed in

  ```
  C:\winnt\System32\CertSrv
  ```

  and this physical directory is mapped to a new virtual root:

  ```
  /CertSrv
  ```

- A self-signed root certificate is created and installed in the certificate storage location. A *root certificate* is one that identifies the Certificate Authority (CA) and is signed by the CA itself or by a root authority (also a CA) higher up in the CA hierarchy (this version of Certificate Server does not support CA hierarchies).

- A public/private key pair is created and saved in the key repository.
- Certificate Server is added to the Certificate Authority Certificate List Web page, stored in

```
C:\winnt\System32\CertSrv\CertEnroll\cacerts.htm
```

  and also in the shared folder.

- The following three files are saved in the shared location (`C:\CA`):

Certificate Server's configuration file
  `CertSrv.txt`
Certificate Server's signature certificate
  `<servername>_<CA_name>.crt`
Certificate Server's key exchange certificate

```
<servername>_<CA_name>_Exchange.crt
```

- The Certificate Authority service is installed in the list of system services. The Certificate Authority service is set to start automatically using the System account on NT startup.

Click FINISH and then reboot your machine, and the Certificate Service will start.

Certificate Server Tools

Microsoft Certificate Server is administered using the HTML administration tool launched by the URL

```
http://localhost/CertSrv/
```

The main administration screen is shown in Fig. 12-10 and has the following four options:

- *Certificate Administration Log Utility,* which is used to manage the server log, which contains copies of all certificates that have been issued by Certificate Server and are stored in Certificate Server's database. The default view is List View, with each certificate

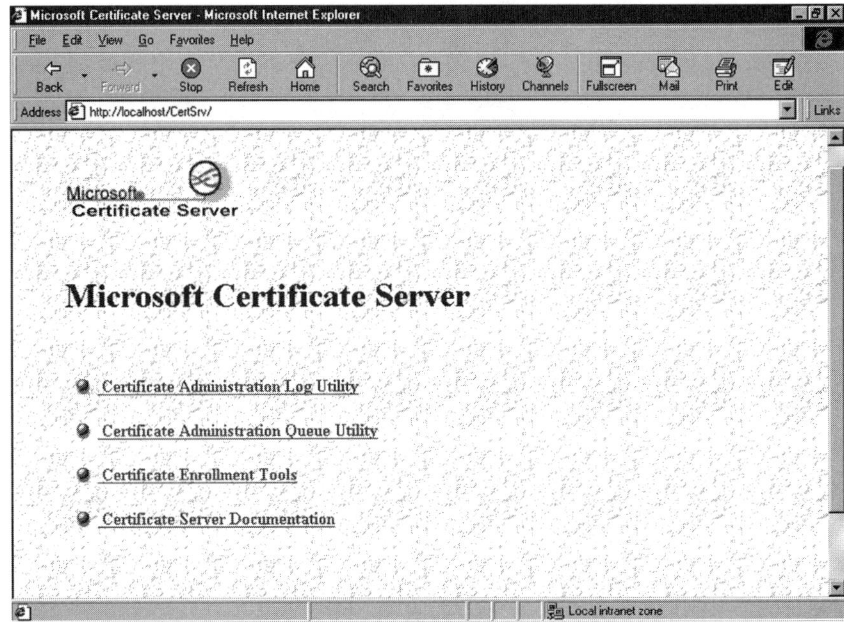

Figure 12-10 Microsoft Certificate Server HTML-based administration page.

issued occupying a record (row) and the certificates listed in the order they were issued. To view information about a particular certificate, select the certificate and click the Form View control.

This utility can also be used to revoke a certificate. Select the certificate you want to revoke and click REVOKE CERTIFICATE followed by REQUERY to refresh the display.

- *Certificate Administration Queue Utility,* which is used to manage the Server Queue, which contains a list of certificate requests in a format similar to the CA Log Utility above.
- *Certificate Enrollment Tools,* which has three links that are used to perform the following three tasks:
  - *Install Certificate Authority Certificates* takes you to the Certificate Authority Certificate List Web page, where client browsers can acquire and install a CA certificate. Client browsers must first install a CA certificate if they want to achieve an SSL connection with servers whose site certificates are issued by the same CA. This will be covered in the walk-through later in this chapter.
  - *Process a Certificate Request* takes you to the Web Server Enrollment page, where you can submit a site certificate request as

administrator to Certificate Server. You will need the PKCS 10 certificate request text file generated by Key Manager for the particular Web server you want to generate a site certificate for. This is covered later in the walkthrough.

- *Request a Client Authentication Certificate* takes you to the Microsoft Internet Explorer enrollment page, where clients can obtain and install client certificates (if needed for client authentication).

- *Certificate Server Documentation,* which allows access to online HTML documentation.

Walkthrough: Creating and Installing a Site Certificate

The following walkthrough takes us through the process of

- Generating a certificate request file for a server. A *certificate request file* is an ASCII text file that contains encrypted information used to obtain a digital certificate.
- Submitting the request file and generating a server certificate. A *server certificate* identifies the server (or virtual server) to browser clients and allows these clients to connect to the server through SSL.
- Installing the server certificate and enabling SSL on a Web site.
- Enabling the client to recognize the server's Certificate Authority so that SSL communication can take place.

The process illustrated below will work both with a local CA like Microsoft Certificate Server and a trusted third-party CA like VeriSign.

Begin by creating a new Web site on the IIS 4.0 server and placing some Web content in the site's home directory (we created the site SalesDept and assigned it the IP address 172.16.8.104). Open the Internet Service Manager (MMC), select the virtual root (here SalesDept), and click the KEY MANAGER button on the Rebar (Fig. 12-11).

When Key Manager opens up, select the WWW node in the left pane (Tree View) and choose KEY, CREATE NEW KEY from the menu bar (Fig. 12-12). Key Manager can be used to

- Create and administer public/private SSL key pairs

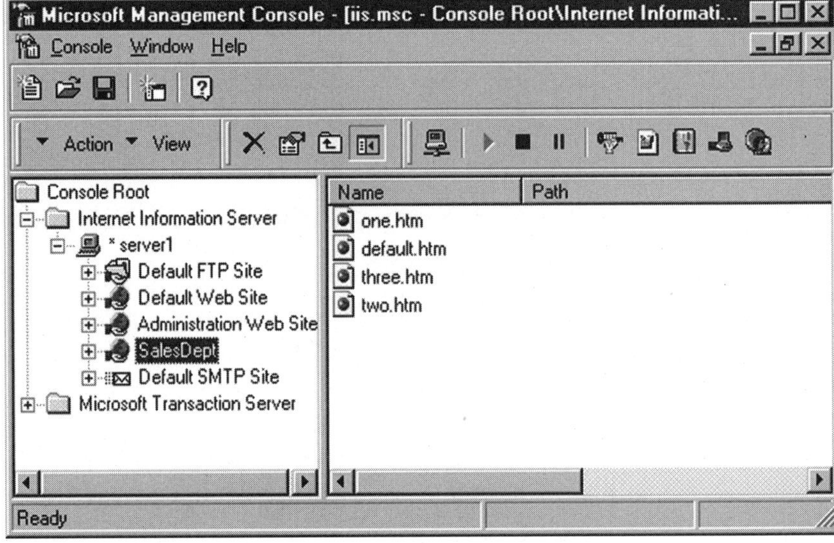

Figure 12-11 Beginning to create a site certificate for the SalesDept Web site.

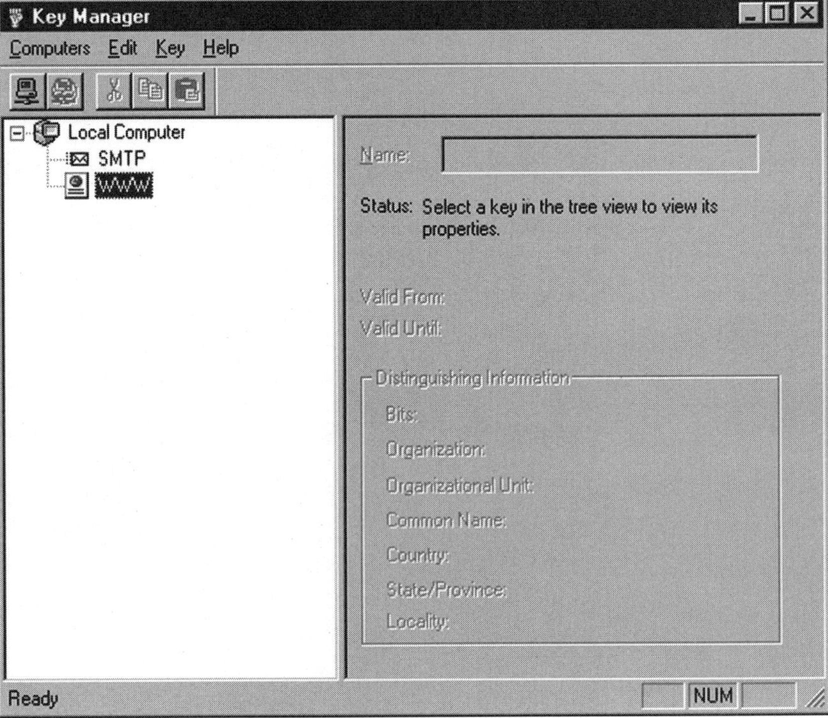

Figure 12-12 The Key Manager tool.

- Create a certificate request file in order to obtain a server certificate
- Install a server certificate on a server (or virtual server)
- Enable the virtual server for SSL
- Test accessing the virtual server with SSL

Creating a Key Pair and Certificate Request

Key Manager can also be started by accessing the Property sheet for a Web site, selecting the Directory Security tab, and clicking the KEY MANAGER button.

Selecting CREATE NEW KEY starts the Create New Key Wizard (Fig. 12-13). Administrators have a choice of two ways of creating keys:

- Select PUT THE REQUEST IN A FILE THAT YOU WILL SEND TO AN AUTHORITY if the Certificate Authority is a trusted third-party company like VeriSign.
- Select AUTOMATICALLY SEND THE REQUEST TO AN ONLINE AUTHORITY if you have Microsoft Certificate Server or some other CA server installed on your network.

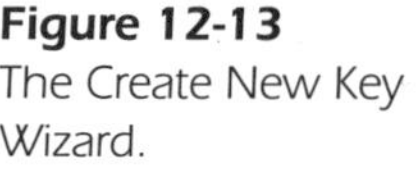

Figure 12-13
The Create New Key Wizard.

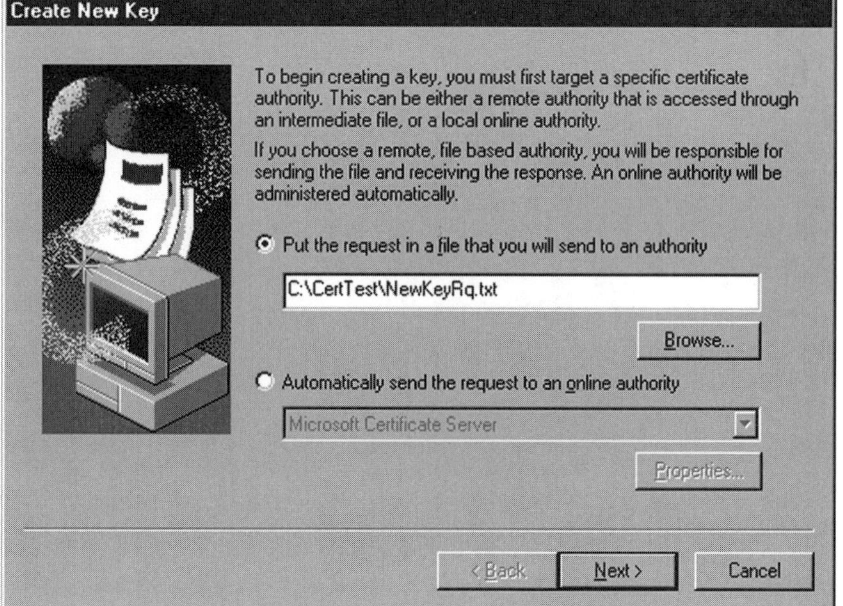

We will select the first option because it works in both cases and illustrates how to send a certificate request to a remote authority like VeriSign. A new directory called

```
C:\CertTest
```

was first created to hold the generated certificate request file. The default name

```
NewKeyRq.txt
```

is used for the certificate request file to be generated.

The next screen of the wizard (Fig. 12-14) requests you to

- Assign the key a name (here MyCorpKey)
- Assign the key a password (Don't lose it! You'll need it later!)
- Assign the key a bit length (Longer bit lengths are more secure but take longer to authenticate.)

The next few screens of the Wizard ask for the following information (in parentheses is what we submitted):

- *Organization:* The legal name of your company (MyCorp Inc).

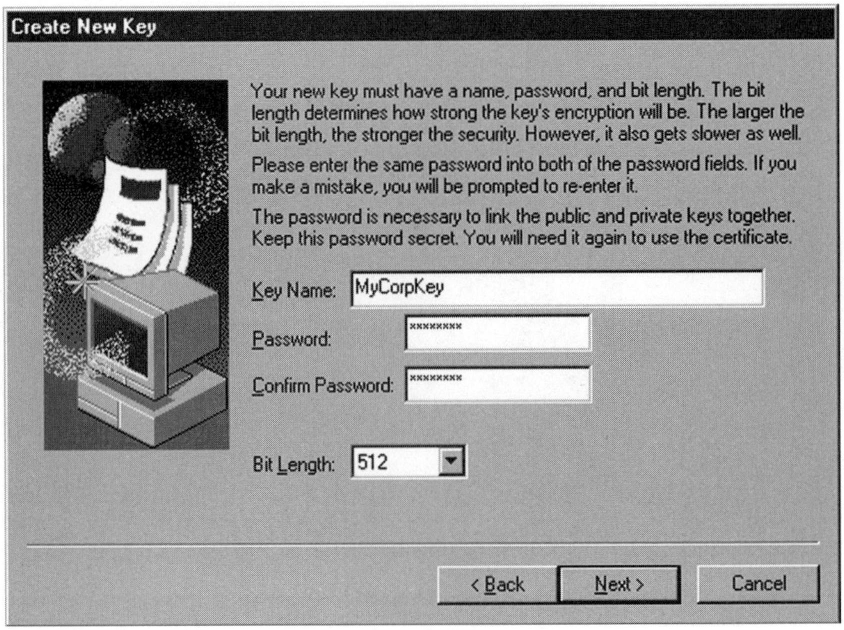

Figure 12-14 Assign the key a name, password, and bit length.

Create New Key

Your new key must have a name, password, and bit length. The bit length determines how strong the key's encryption will be. The larger the bit length, the stronger the security. However, it also gets slower as well.

Please enter the same password into both of the password fields. If you make a mistake, you will be prompted to re-enter it.

The password is necessary to link the public and private keys together. Keep this password secret. You will need it again to use the certificate.

Key Name: MyCorpKey

Password: xxxxxxxx

Confirm Password: xxxxxxxx

Bit Length: 512

< Back | Next > | Cancel

- *Organizational Unit:* The division in your company responsible for digital certificate security (IS Dept).
- *Common Name:* The fully qualified domain name (FQDN) for the server (here being `server1.mycorpinc.com`). Note that using the FQDN here for the Common Name implies that DNS is being used on your network for name resolution (see the Note later in this section on common names and FQDNs)
- *Country:* here Canada (CA).
- *State/Province:* here Manitoba (MB).
- *City* (Winnipeg).
- *Your Name:* name of Certificate Server administrator (Administrator).
- *Email address* (`admin@mycorpinc.com`)
- *Telephone Number* (204-555-1234)

Next you are informed that

- A certificate request will now be created.
- The key will be installed in Key Manager but requires a valid certificate to be activated.

Click FINISH to generate the key pair and request file. A dialog box will appear saying that the request file has been generated and is stored in the location you earlier specified (Fig. 12-15). Note that in Key Manager the new key has been created but is not activated because the certificate has not yet been received and installed (Fig. 12-16).

The newly created certificate request file

```
C:\CertTest\NewKeyRq.txt
```

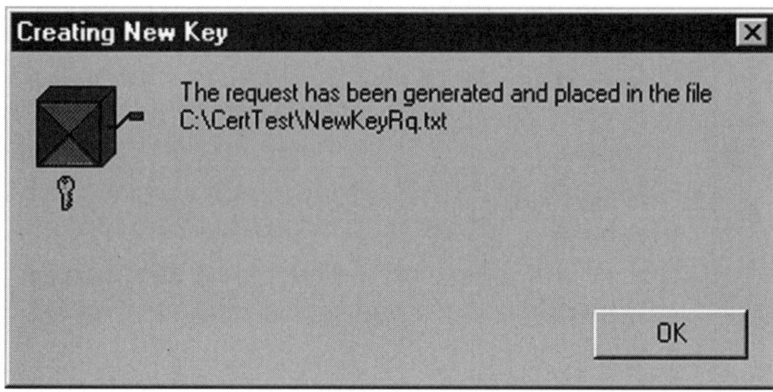

Figure 12-15 Dialog box confirming that a certificate request file has been created.

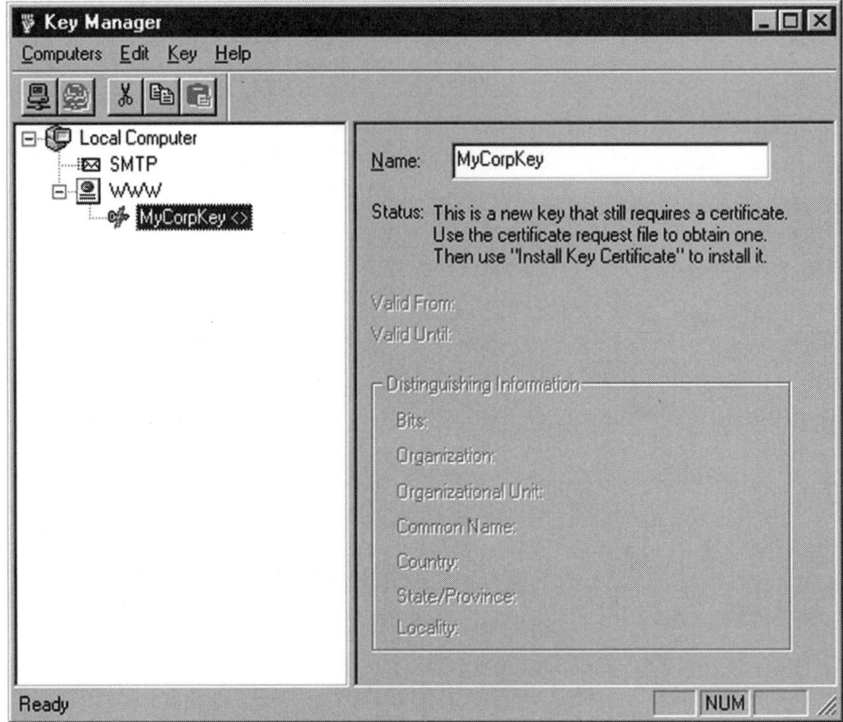

Figure 12-16 Status of newly created key is disabled until certificate is installed.

contains the information you entered into the wizard plus an encrypted new certificate request string (see Fig. 12-17). This file conforms to the standard PKCS 10 certificate request format. Open the certificate request file using Notepad, select the portion highlighted in Fig. 12-17, and choose EDIT, COPY to copy this highlighted text to the clipboard.

Submitting a Certificate Request File to a Certificate Authority

At this point, if we were going to request our server certificate from a trusted third-party organization like VeriSign, we would access a certificate request HTML form on a Web page, paste the clipboard text into the HTML form, and submit it. An alternative would be to email the clipboard text to the appropriate email address. See VeriSign's Web site:

```
www.verisign.com
```

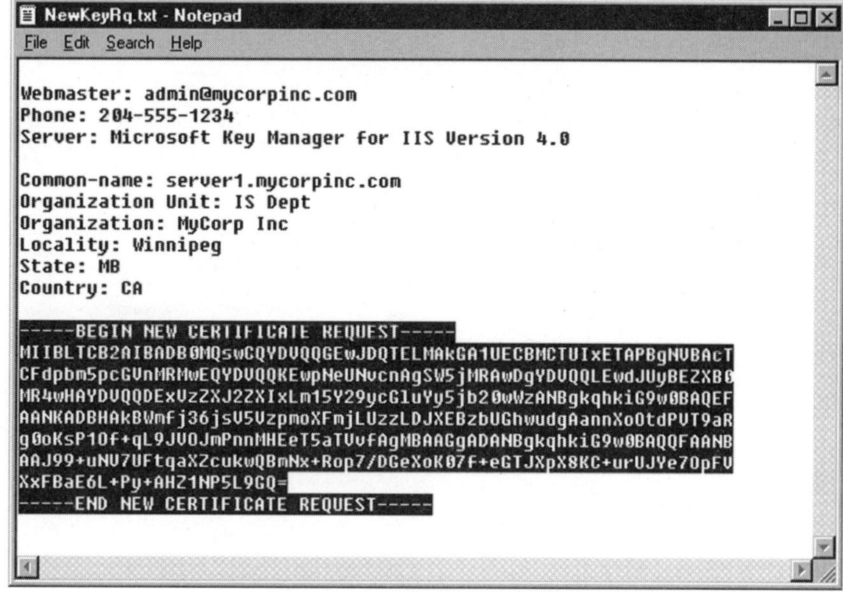

NewKeyRq.txt - Notepad
File Edit Search Help
Webmaster: admin@mycorpinc.com
Phone: 204-555-1234
Server: Microsoft Key Manager for IIS Version 4.0
Common-name: server1.mycorpinc.com
Organization Unit: IS Dept
Organization: MyCorp Inc
Locality: Winnipeg
State: MB
Country: CA
-----BEGIN NEW CERTIFICATE REQUEST-----
-----END NEW CERTIFICATE REQUEST-----

Figure 12-17 Selected portion of certificate request file will be used to request a certificate.

Instead, we will use our HTML-based Certificate Server administration Web site to submit the certificate request to our Certificate Server.

Open the Certificate Server HTML administration page using Internet Explorer on the machine where Certificate Server is installed by opening the URL

```
http://localhost/certsrv
```

Click the Certificate Enrollment Tools link, and then the Process a Certificate Request link to open the Web Server Enrollment Page. Click in the text area, paste the clipboard contents into the HTML form, and select SUBMIT REQUEST to submit your certificate request to Certificate Server (Fig. 12-18).

The Certificate Download page will appear, indicating that your request has been successfully processed and indicating that you should click the DOWNLOAD button to download your new server certificate. Click DOWNLOAD, and save the new server certificate

```
newcert.cer
```

to the same directory where the certificate request file is located:

```
C:\CertTest
```

Figure 12-18 Submitting a certificate request through the Web Server Enrollment Page.

See Fig. 12-19.

The new server certificate file is an ASCII text file similar to the certificate request file and can be viewed with Notepad (Fig. 12-20).

Installing a Server Certificate

We have now submitted our certificate request file to our Certificate Authority and received the server certificate file from them. The next step is to install the new server certificate on our virtual server so that we can enable SSL for accessing it.

If not still running, open Key Manager by selecting the virtual server node (here SalesDept) in the MMC and selecting the KEY MANAGER button on the Rebar. Select the inactive key under the WWW node in Tree View (here `MyCorpKey`) and select KEY, INSTALL KEY CERTIFICATE from the menu bar. In the Open box that appears, select the newly created certificate

```
C:\CertTest\newcert.cer
```

and click OPEN (Fig. 12-21). A Confirm Password box will appear asking you for the password you specified when you created the key pair (Fig. 12-22).

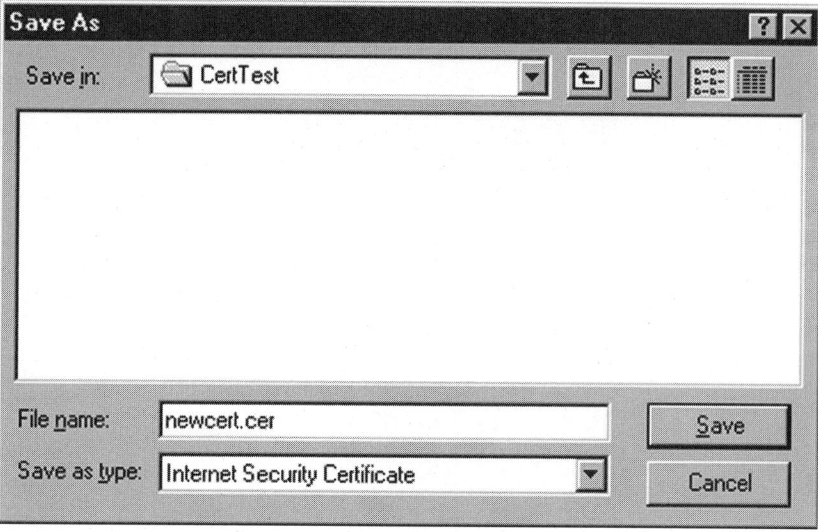

Figure 12-19 Saving the new certificate.

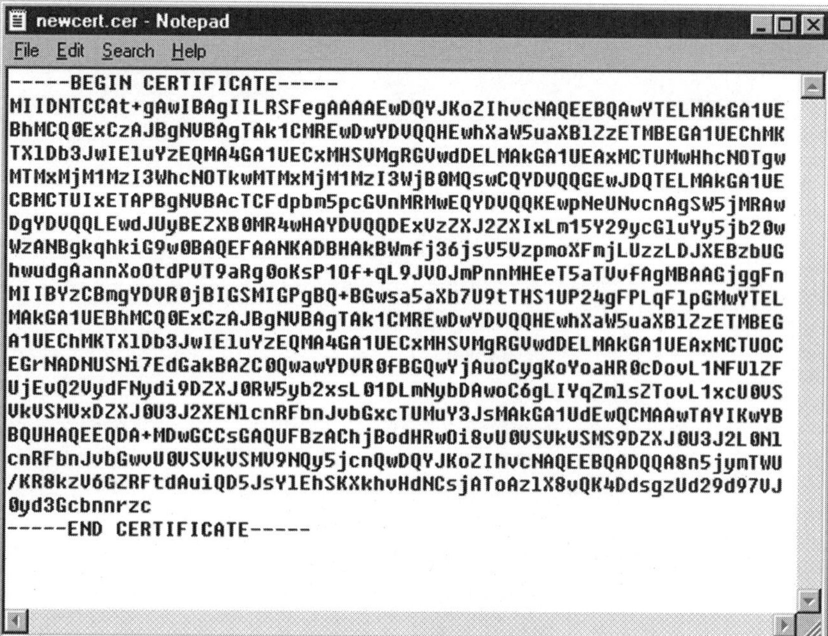

Figure 12-20 The new server certificate.

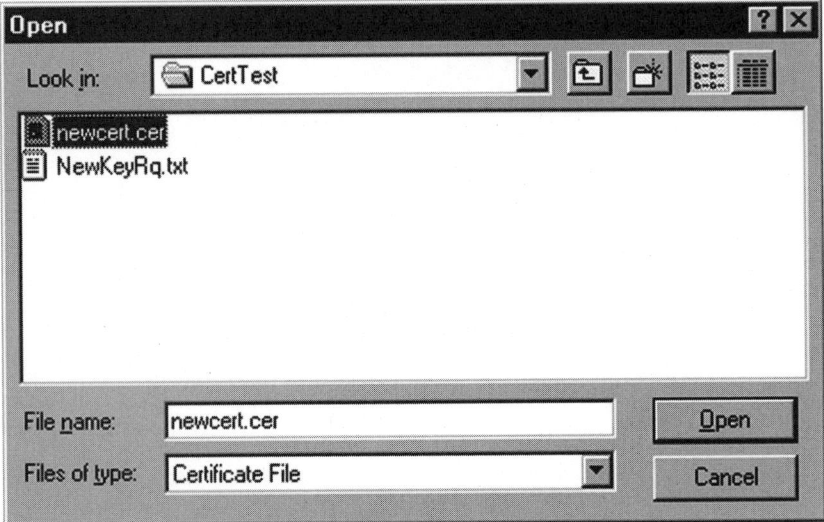

Figure 12-21 Installing a new server certificate.

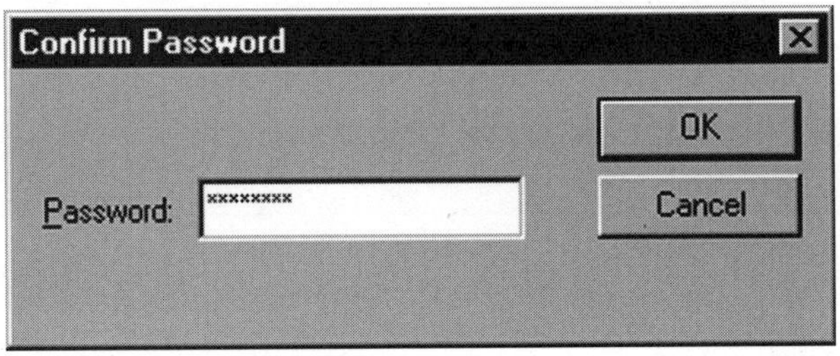

Confirm Password
OK
Password: ********
Cancel

Figure 12-22 Enter the key pair password to install the new certificate on the virtual root.

The Server Bindings dialog box appears next, asking you to specify which IP address binds to the virtual server you want to install the certificate on (Fig. 12-23). Edit the existing entry to enter in the IP address of the virtual server that you want to enable SSL on, and specify an SSL port if desired.

The server certificate is now installed and the public/private key pair is activated. Key Manager now shows the following:

- The status of the key pair is *complete and usable.*
- The key is valid until the date shown.
- The encryption length of the key (bits) and other key information is listed.

If you need to later modify the Server Bindings, select the key and choose KEY, PROPERTIES from the menu bar. See Fig. 12-24.

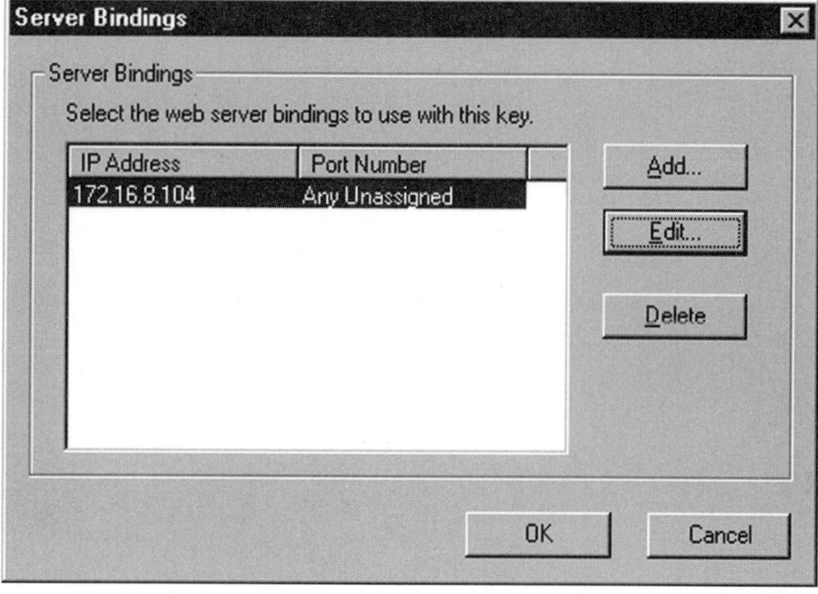

Figure 12-23 Specify the IP of the virtual server you want to enable for SSL.

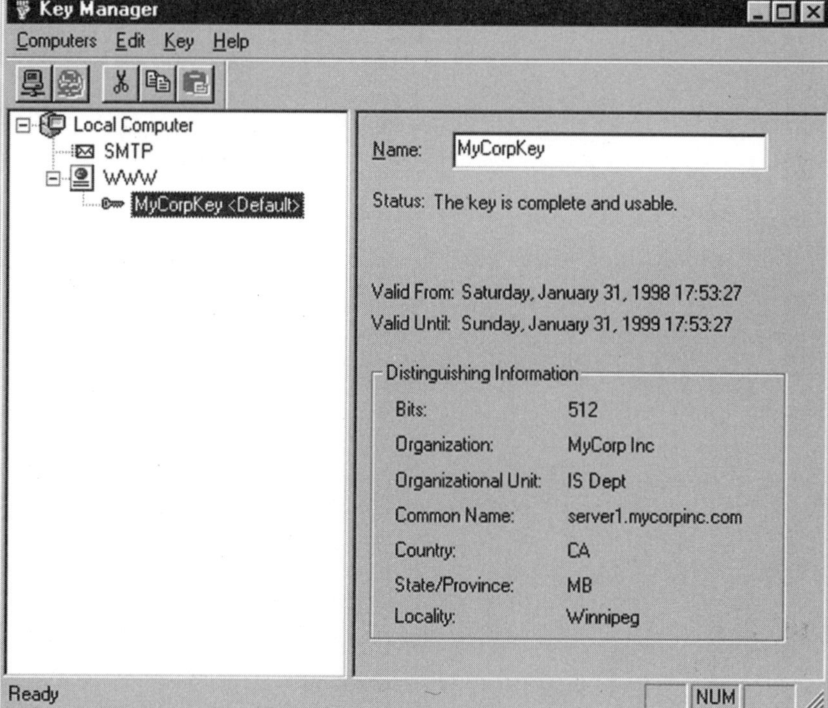

Figure 12-24 The key is complete and usable.

Close Key Manager by selecting COMPUTERS, EXIT from the menu bar. Agree to COMMIT ALL CHANGES NOW to finalize the server certificate installation. The virtual server SalesDept is now capable of being enabled for SSL.

If you now access the Certificate Server HTML administration page by opening the URL

```
http://localhost/certsrv
```

and on that page select the link Certificate Administration Log Utility, you will access the Certificate Log Administration page, where you will find the newly installed certificate listed (Fig. 12-25). On this page you can click the FORM VIEW control to view the certificate information in a more accessible layout (Fig. 12-26).

Details about the certificate issuance can be viewed by going back to the Certificate Server HTML administration page,

```
http://localhost/certsrv
```

and selecting the link Certificate Administration Queue Utility. This opens the Certificate Server Queue Administration page. In Form View, the information listed here for our certificate includes fields such as

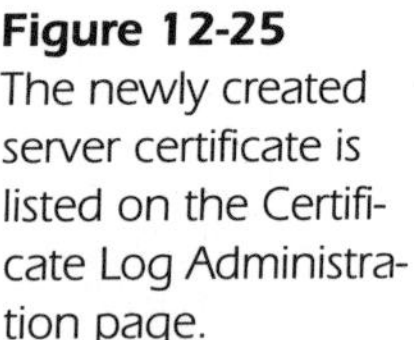

Figure 12-25 The newly created server certificate is listed on the Certificate Log Administration page.

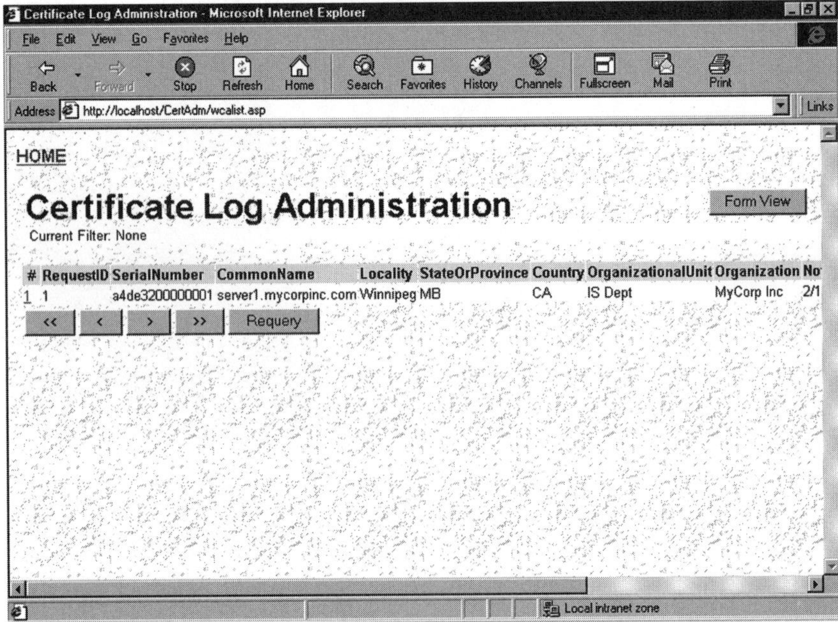

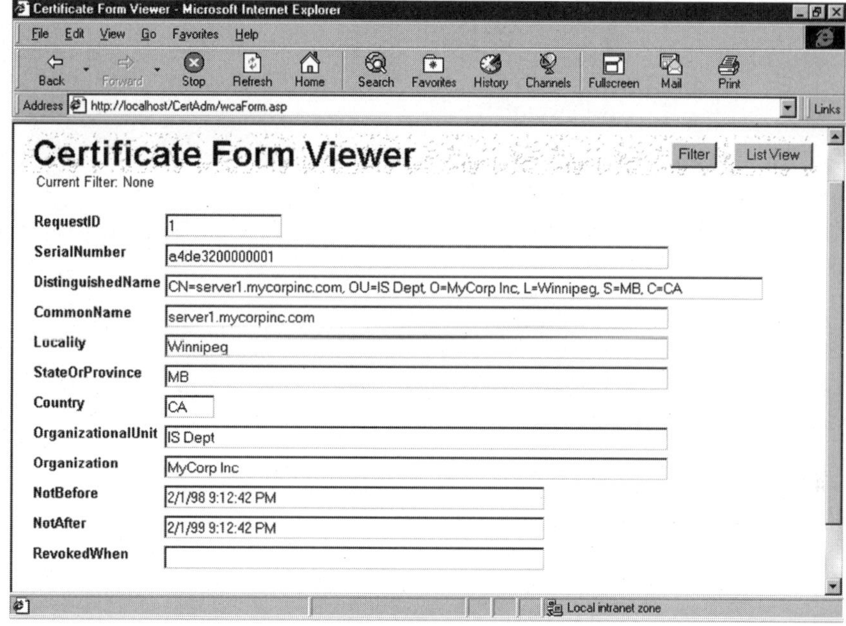

Figure 12-26 Viewing certificate information in Form View.

- *RequestID:* ordinal number of certificate request
- *SubmittedWhen:* date submitted
- *RequesterName:* NT user account of person submitting (here the anonymous user account)
- *DispositionMessage:* here *Issued*
- *RevokedWhen:* date revoked (not applicable here)

and so on. See Fig. 12-27.

Enabling SSL on a Virtual Server

Next we will enable SSL on the virtual server SalesDept. In the MMC, right-click on the SalesDept node and select PROPERTIES to open up the SalesDept Properties sheet. With the Web site tab selected, assign the number 443 as the SSL Port number. This is the default port for secure communications (Fig. 12-28).

Next select the Directory Security tab. Under Secure Communications select the EDIT button to open the Secure Communications dialog box. Place a checkmark in the checkbox labeled REQUIRE SECURE CHANNEL WHEN ACCESSING THIS RESOURCE. This action enables SSL for the selected

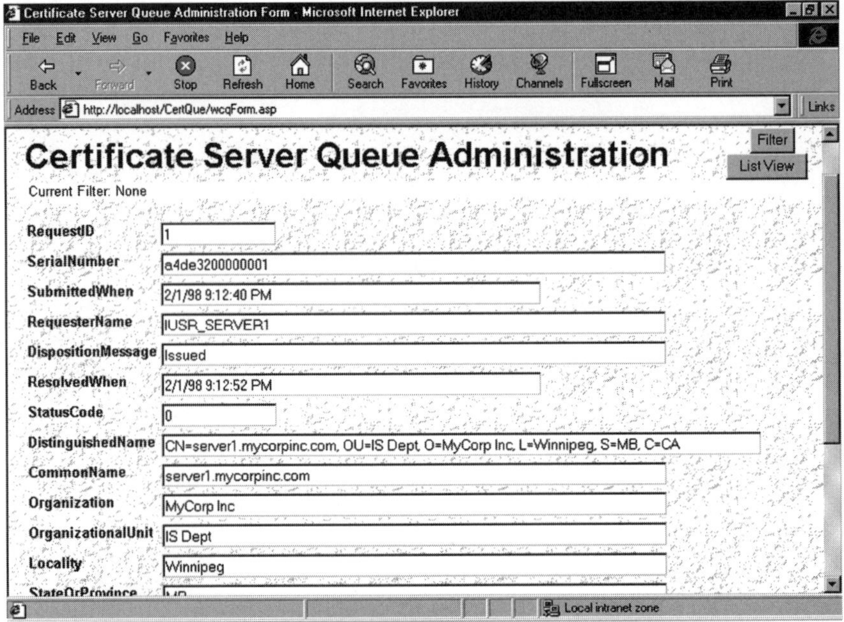

Figure 12-27 Details of certificate issuance on Certificate Server Queue Administration page.

virtual server (Fig. 12-29). This dialog box can also be used to determine what happens if the browser accessing the secure Web site has a client certificate installed. The three options are

- DO NOT ACCEPT CLIENT CERTIFICATES (default) If the client browser has a client certificate installed, an Access Denied message will be returned.
- ACCEPT CERTIFICATES. It makes no difference to the server whether the client browser has a client certificate installed or not; access is granted in either case.
- REQUIRE CLIENT CERTIFICATES. Unless a client has a valid certificate granted by the root CA (here Certificate Server), access will be denied.

This dialog box may also be used to map client certificates to users' NT accounts. Leave the default setting here and click OK twice.

Adding the CA Certificate to the Root Store of the Client Browser

Finally, before SSL communication can take place between the client browser and the Web site, the client must be able to recognize the

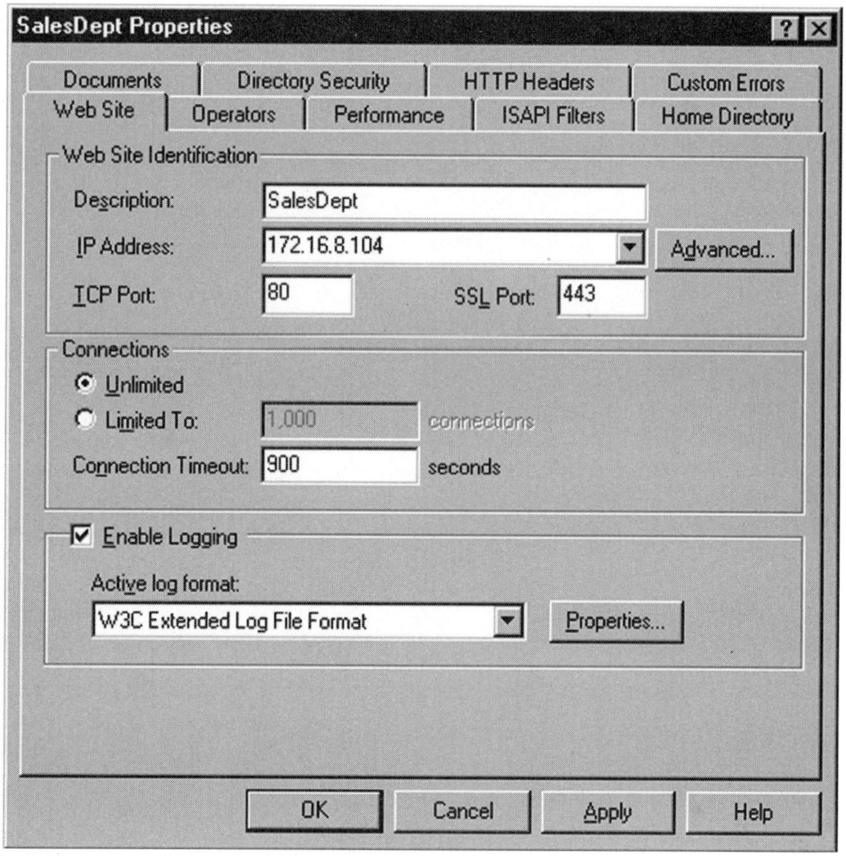

Figure 12-28 Assign the default port number 443 to SSL.

server's certificate as valid. To do this, the client must contact the server's Certificate Authority, which in this case is the local Certificate Server. In this example note that our client is Internet Explorer 4.01.

If you fail to perform the above step and instead try to connect directly to the SSL Web site using the secure HTTPS URL

```
https://server1.mycorpinc.com
```

you will first receive the normal and expected Security Alert message (Fig. 12-30). Click OK. A message saying that the certificate issuer is untrusted will appear (Fig. 12-31). This occurs because the client cannot verify the server's certificate because it does not yet recognize the CA's root certificate. If you click YES to proceed, another security alert box will inform you that a secure connection to the site cannot be verified

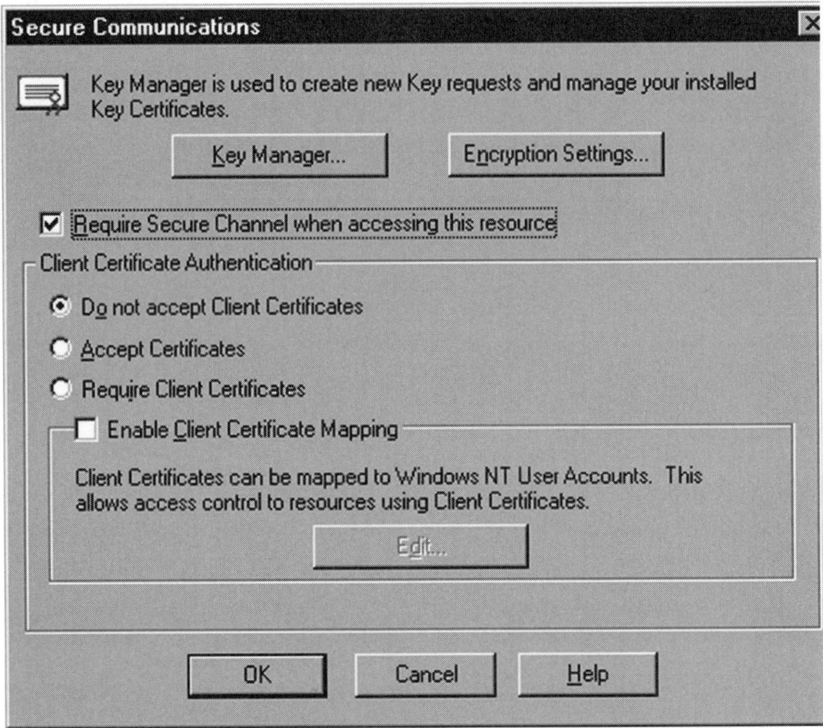

Figure 12-29 Check the checkbox to enable SSL on the virtual server.

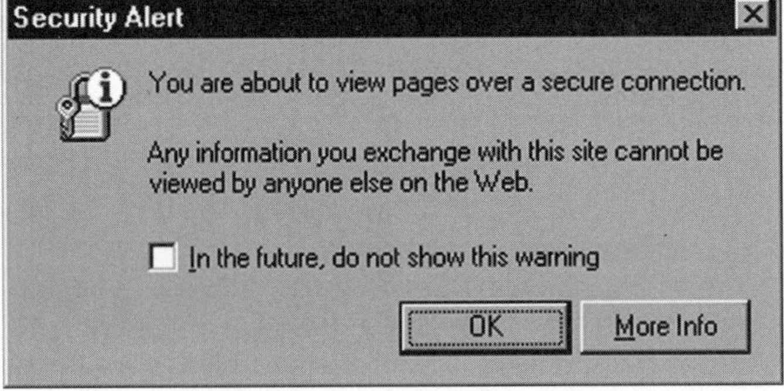

Figure 12-30 Security alert message seen when you are accessing a secure site.

(Fig. 12-32). Click YES a final time and the Web site will appear, but SSL will not be enabled for the connection.

To avoid this problem, the client browser needs to acquire and install the root CA certificate for the CA that issued a certificate to the server. Once this root CA certificate is loaded into the browser, the browser is able to verify the server's certificate and form an SSL connection to the server.

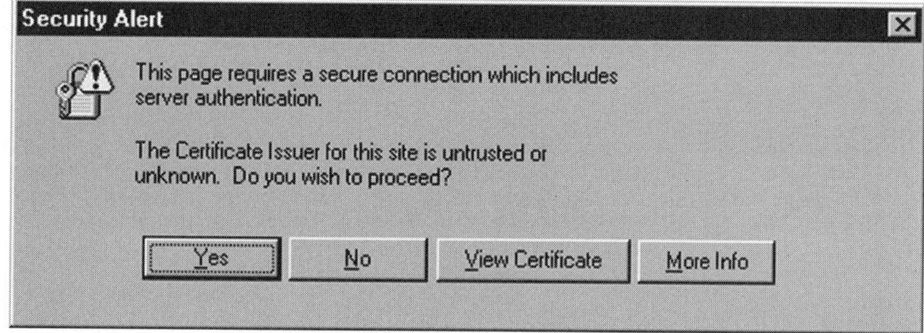

Figure 12-31 The certificate issuer is untrusted.

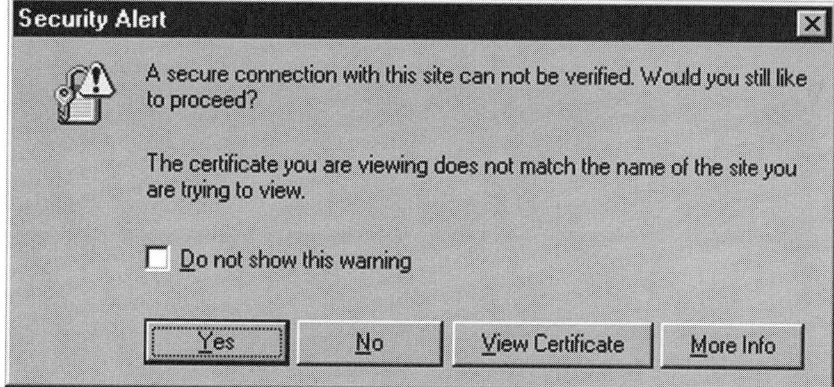

Figure 12-32 A secure connection cannot be verified.

NOTE: *Note that we are trying here to connect to the SSL-enabled virtual server using the fully qualified domain name (FQDN) of the virtual server. In other words, on the corporate DNS server there is a host record mapping the FQDN*

```
server1.mycorpinc.com
```

to the virtual server's IP address:

```
172.16.8.104
```

This is important *because when we used Key Manager at the beginning of this walkthrough to generate the key pair and certificate request, we defined the Common Name of the server (see page 417) as*

```
server1.mycorpinc.com
```

Entering this as the Common Name assumes that we are using DNS to resolve FQDNs in all URLs. Had we wanted to be able to access the secure site by its IP address alone, e.g.,

```
http://172.16.8.104
```

we would have had to define

```
172.16.8.104
```

as the common name when we created the key pair and certificate request.

To accomplish verification, the client browser needs to load the Certificate Authority Certificate List Web page, which is stored in the shared folder created when Certificate Server was installed. In this example, the client browser would be directed to load the page

```
C:\CA\cacerts.htm
```

Listed on this page is a link for the Local Certificate Authority. In this example the CA is called MC and resides on server1 (Fig. 12-33). The hyperlink points to the root certificate

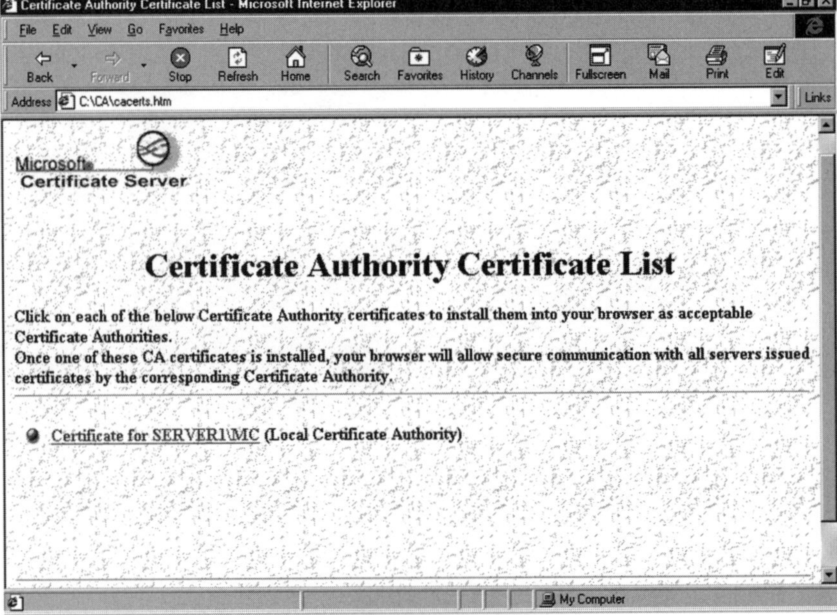

Figure 12-33 The Certificate Authority Certificate List Web page.

```
C:\CA\SERVER1_MC.crt
```

Click the link for the Local Certificate Authority to open the File Download dialog box. Select OPEN THIS FILE FROM ITS CURRENT LOCATION and click OK to open the New Site Certificate box (Fig. 12-34). Using this dialog box you can

- Accept and enable the CA certificate as one of your trusted certificate issuers
- Accept the CA certificate but leave it disabled
- Reject the CA certificate

In addition, you can view the certificate information and specify which uses the certificate can be used for.

Leave the defaults selected and click OK to open the Root Certificate Store dialog box (Fig. 12-35). Click YES to confirm that you want to add the CA certificate to your browser's root certificate store.

Shut down your browser and restart it to finish installing the new CA certificate in the root store. You can confirm that the certificate has been added to the root store by selecting VIEW, INTERNET OPTIONS (for IE 4.01), selecting the Content tab, and clicking the AUTHORITIES button. Note in Fig. 12-36 that the root CA name MC is listed and enabled in the Certificate Authorities box.

Figure 12-34
The New Site Certificate dialog box.

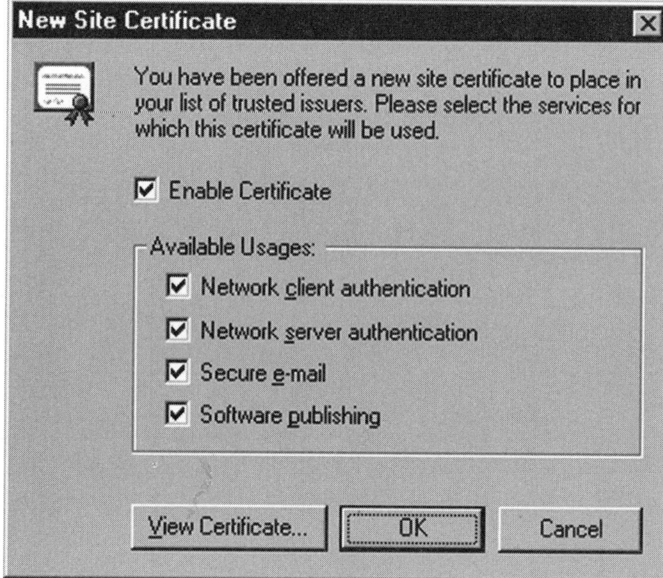

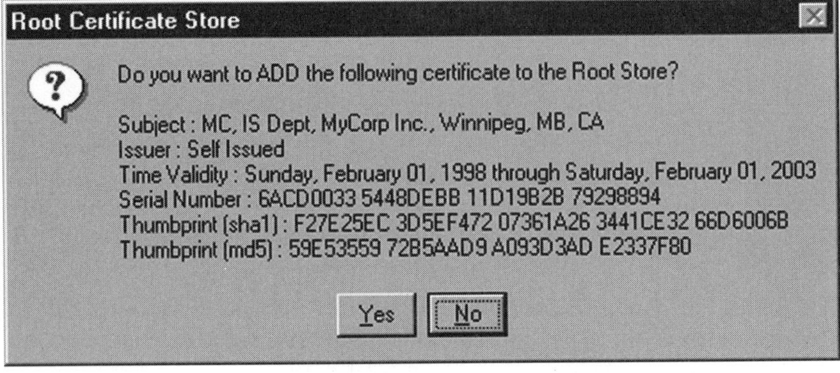

Root Certificate Store
Do you want to ADD the following certificate to the Root Store?
Subject : MC, IS Dept, MyCorp Inc., Winnipeg, MB, CA
Issuer : Self Issued
Time Validity : Sunday, February 01, 1998 through Saturday, February 01, 2003
Serial Number : 6ACD0033 5448DEBB 11D19B2B 79298894
Thumbprint (sha1) : F27E25EC 3D5EF472 07361A26 3441CE32 66D6006B
Thumbprint (md5) : 59E53559 72B5AAD9 A093D3AD E2337F80
Yes
No

Figure 12-35 Confirmation dialog box for adding CA certificate to browser's root store.

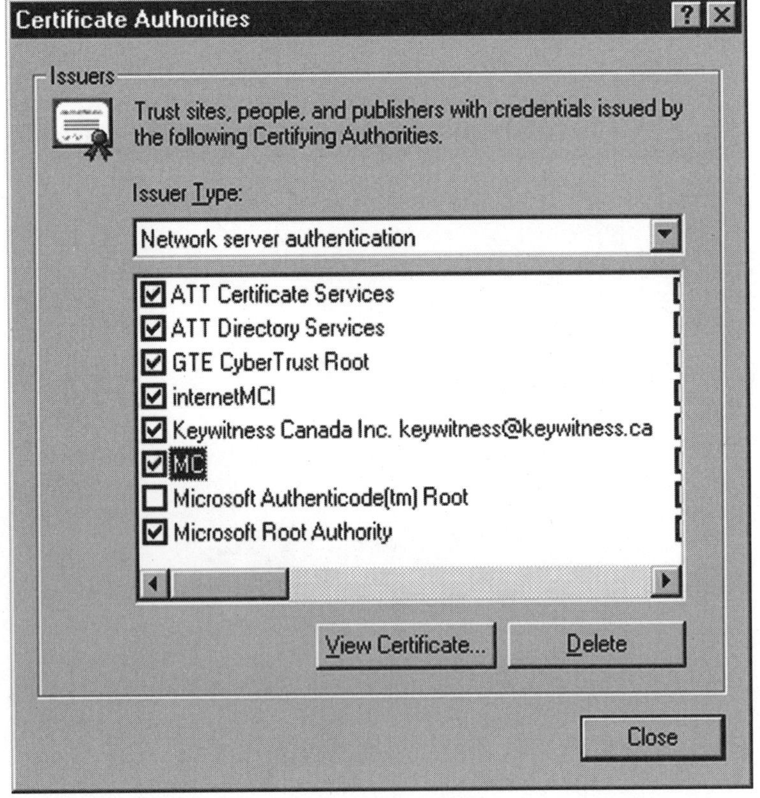

Figure 12-36 IE 4.0's Certificate Authorities box shows that the root CA certificate MC is installed.

Finally, test the SSL-enabled site SalesDept with the CA-enabled browser by opening the secure HTTPS URL

```
https://server1.mycorpinc.com
```

The home page of the SSL-enabled site should load without any security alerts.

NOTE: *To add the CA certificate to the root store of a remote IE 3.02 client, access the Certificate Authority Certificate List Web page, which is stored in the shared folder on the Certificate Server machine, e.g.,*

```
C:\CA\cacerts.htm
```

Click on the Local Certificate Authority link as above. When the File Download box appears, however, select SAVE (instead of OPEN) and save the CA certificate, which in this example is

```
SERVER1_MC.crt
```

to the client's hard drive. Then open the saved file with the browser and install the CA certificate in IE 3.02's root store as directed.

SUMMARY

By using Microsoft Certificate Server and IIS 4.0 SSL capabilities, clients and servers are able to establish secure channels to encrypt all data transmissions between them. This chapter has illustrated the steps involved in enabling an SSL session between clients and servers.

FOR MORE INFORMATION

Microsoft Web Site Search the Microsoft Web site

```
www.microsoft.com
```

for the topics "SSL" and "Certificate" for more information on these topics.

Microsoft Public Newsgroups The best group to post questions relating to SSL and Certificate Server is

```
microsoft.public.inetserver.iis
```

List Servers Try subscribing to the SSL-TALK mailing list by visiting the Web page

```
www.consensus.com/security/ssl-talk-faq.html
```

Other WWW Sites Be sure to visit VeriSign's site at

```
www.verisign.com
```

Netscape has a lot of information about SSL at its Web site. Start with the page

```
home.netscape.com/newsref/std/SSL.html
```

CHAPTER 13

Administering the SMTP Service

Introduction

The SMTP service running on Microsoft Internet Information Server 4.0 allows administrators to set up, maintain, and administer an SMTP service for sending and receiving messages over the Internet. After completing this chapter, you will be able to

- Understand how the SMTP service on IIS 4.0 works.
- Install the SMTP service on IIS 4.0.
- Administer the SMTP service using the MMC and remotely using a Web browser.
- Configure the various SMTP service properties.
- Create new local and remote SMTP domains.
- Create a message and send it using the SMTP service.
- Monitor and tune the performance of the SMTP service.

Understanding the SMTP Service

The Microsoft SMTP service on IIS 4.0 fully supports the *Simple Mail Transfer Protocol (SMTP)* and is compatible with most SMTP servers and clients. It is ideally suited for building Internet applications that use SMTP. For example, you could use it for an Active Server Pages application that mails a response to a user who submits a form. In general, its purpose in being included in the Windows NT 4.0 Option Pack is to provide an outbound mail service for applications that are designed to be mail-aware. It is *not* intended for use as a general-purpose Internet mail server for corporate or ISP use.

The SMTP service on IIS 4.0 can

- Support hundreds of simultaneous connections.
- Support multiple domains on one server.
- Receive mail from other applications or SMTP servers.
- Send mail to other SMTP servers.
- Support encrypted SSL security.
- Restrict unsolicited commercial email.

The SMTP service does *not* include

- Support for POP3 or IMAP
- Support for personal mailboxes for users

How the SMTP Service Works

When the SMTP service is installed as part of IIS, it creates a default folder structure that it uses to send and receive messages. This structure is shown in Fig. 13-1.

The folder located at

```
C:\Inetpub\Mail
```

contains the scripts to enable remote administration of the SMTP service using a Web browser. Do not modify any of these files.

The folder located at

```
C:\Inetpub\Mailroot
```

contains the various subfolders used by the SMTP service for sending and receiving messages. The `Mailroot` folder has five subfolders plus two undocumented subfolders. These subfolders are used by the SMTP service as follows:

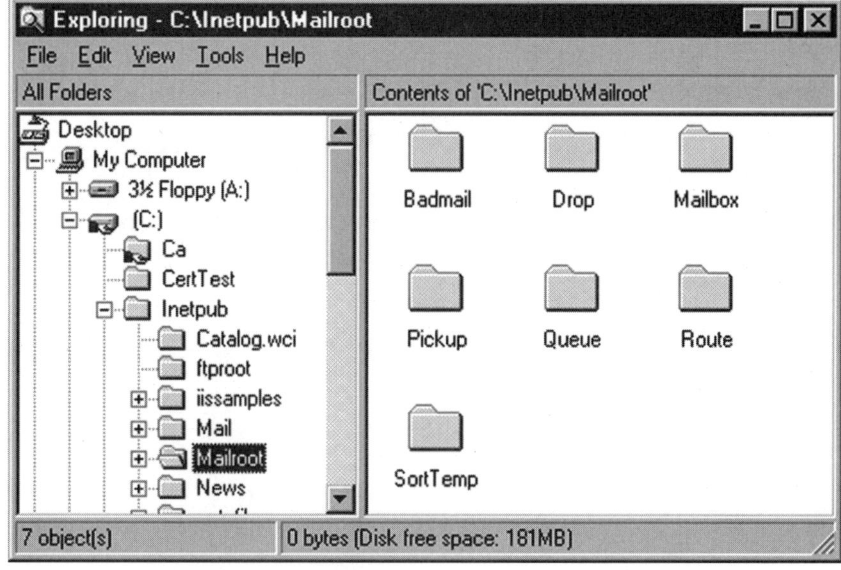

Figure 13-1 The default folder structure created when SMTP service is installed on IIS 4.0.

- `Badmail`: This folder is used to store messages that are undeliverable and cannot be returned to the sender.
- `Drop`: This folder is the drop box for all incoming messages to the SMTP service on IIS.
- `Pickup`: This folder is monitored continuously by the SMTP service, which will send any messages that are placed in it. If a message is placed here it is immediately moved to the `Queue` folder for further processing.
- `Queue`: This folder holds messages that SMTP is unable to send because of bad connections or busy servers. Messages held here are monitored at intervals until they can be sent, or else they are reported as undeliverable and moved to the `Badmail` folder.
- `SortTemp`: This folder is created during setup to hold temporary files.
- `Route`: This folder is not covered in the IIS 4.0 documentation but seems to be involved in the process of configuring a *route domain,* which is a specific delivery path for a selected domain.
- `Mailbox`: This folder is also undocumented, and it is not clear what it is used for, since in this release the SMTP service for IIS 4.0 does *not* support mailboxes! Its functionality will probably be enabled in a future release.

SMTP is a protocol for delivering mail from server to server. To understand how the SMTP service on IIS 4.0 works, we will separately examine what happens to incoming mail and outgoing mail.

How the SMTP Service Processes Mail

The following is a somewhat simplified presentation of how the SMTP service is used to deliver mail. Mail messages can originate from two sources (Fig. 13-2):

1. Messages can be manually created using a text editor and then copied to the directory

   ```
   C:\Mailroot\pickup
   ```

   When the SMTP service detects that a message has been placed in its `Pickup` directory, it forwards the message to the `Queue` directory, where it is automatically processed for delivery to its final destination, which may be either local or remote.

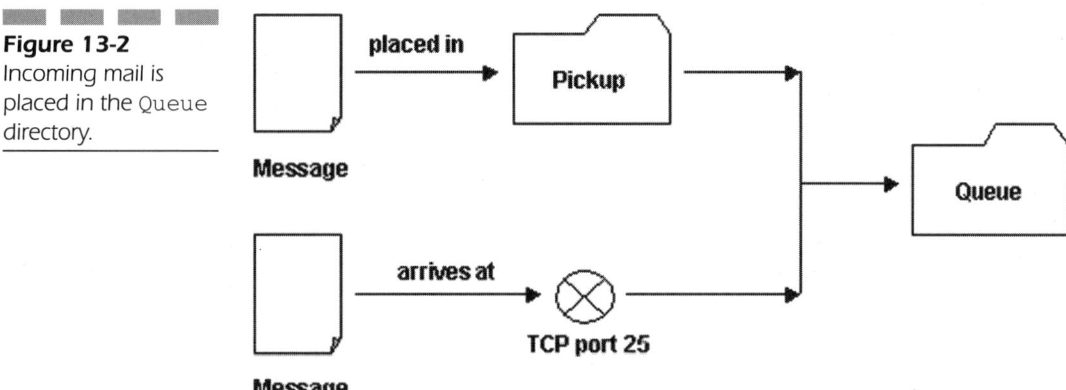

Figure 13-2 Incoming mail is placed in the `Queue` directory.

2. Messages may also enter the SMTP service using TCP port number 25 (the default port for SMTP) and be forwarded to the `Queue` directory, where they are processed and forwarded to another mail server along the route to the final destination.

What happens next to the mail depends on whether its destination is the local SMTP service running on IIS 4.0 or whether it needs to be relayed to another SMTP server to reach its remote destination (Fig. 13-3).

If the message's destination is *local,* the SMTP service moves the message from the `Queue` directory to the `Drop` directory. At that point the SMTP has finished the message delivery. There is no support in this release of Microsoft's SMTP service for delivering messages to personal mailboxes, or for creating and configuring such mailboxes.

If the message's destination is *remote,* the SMTP service sorts the message according to its destination domain. This is done so that the service can pipeline messages by sending multiple messages to a single destination domain using only one connection, which enhances the performance of the SMTP service.

After the message is sorted, the SMTP service tries to connect to the destination mail server. If the mail server fails to respond or indicates that it is not ready to receive the message, the message stays in the `Queue` folder and the SMTP service attempts to deliver the message at predefined intervals.

If after a predetermined number of tries the SMTP service fails to deliver the message, the service attempts to connect to the SMTP server that sent the message to return it to its sender. If it is successful in forming this connection, the message is returned to the sender along with a *non-delivery report (NDR)* outlining the reasons for the failure.

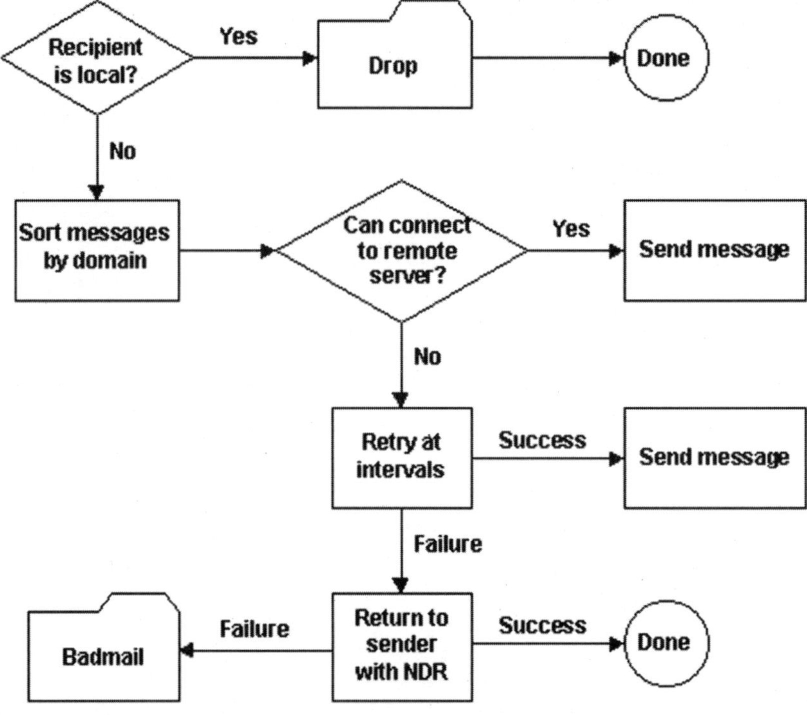

Figure 13-3 How the SMTP service delivers mail.

If the SMTP service can neither deliver the message nor return it to its sender, it moves the message to the `Badmail` directory. At that point the SMTP service has finished its job.

Installing the SMTP Service

The SMTP service is automatically installed on IIS 4.0 as part of a *typical* installation of the Windows NT 4.0 Option Pack. However, if you performed a *custom* installation of Option Pack and did not install the SMTP service, you can install it later by running setup in maintenance mode.

The hardware and software requirements for installing the Microsoft SMTP service are the same as those for installing IIS 4.0:

- Windows NT 4.0 Server
- Service Pack 3
- Internet Explorer 4.01

In addition, it is recommended that you install your `Mailroot` directory on an NTFS partition and make sure there is enough free space to hold your SMTP message queue.

To install the SMTP service by running setup in maintenance mode, click START, PROGRAMS, WINDOWS NT 4.0 OPTION PACK, WINDOWS NT 4.0 OPTION PACK SETUP. When the initial screen appears, click NEXT and select ADD/REMOVE to open the Select Components screen. Select INTERNET INFORMATION SERVER (IIS), and click the SHOW SUBCOMPONENTS button to open the Internet Information Server (IIS) component box (Fig. 13-4). Check the SMTP SERVICE checkbox, and click OK and then NEXT to continue with the setup.

The next screen (Fig. 13-5) asks you to confirm or change the SMTP `Mailroot` directory,

```
C:\InetPub\mailroot
```

Accept the default and proceed to completion of setup.

The result of installing the SMTP service is a new node under the server node in the Microsoft Management Console (MMC) (Fig. 13-6). This new node is called *Default SMTP Site* and has two subnodes:

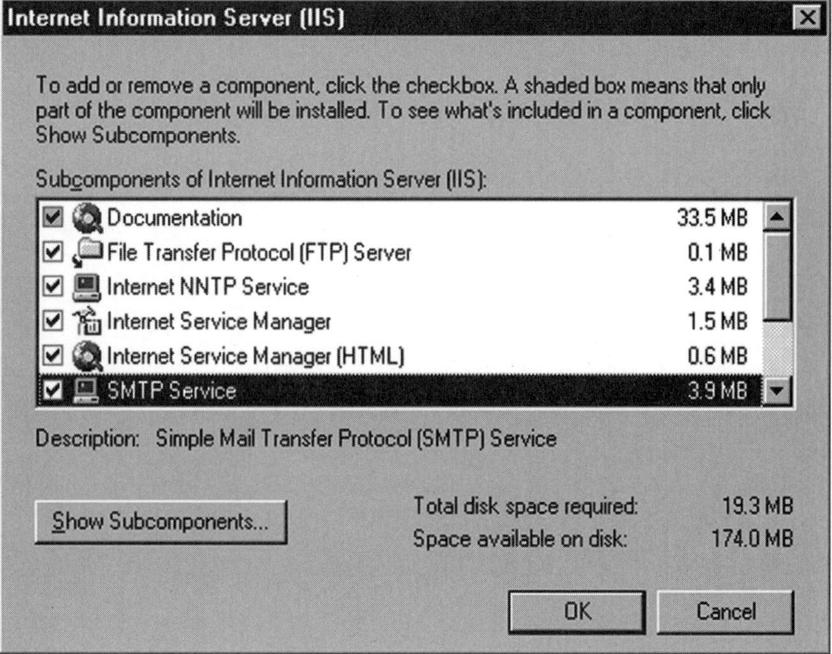

Figure 13-4
Select the SMTP SERVICE component for installation.

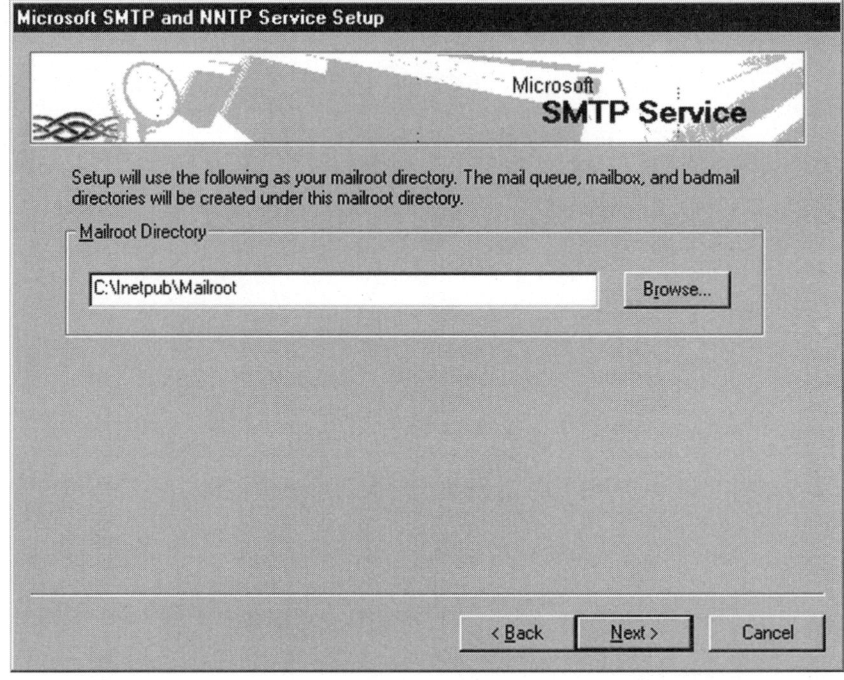

Figure 13-5 Select a mailroot directory to process messages.

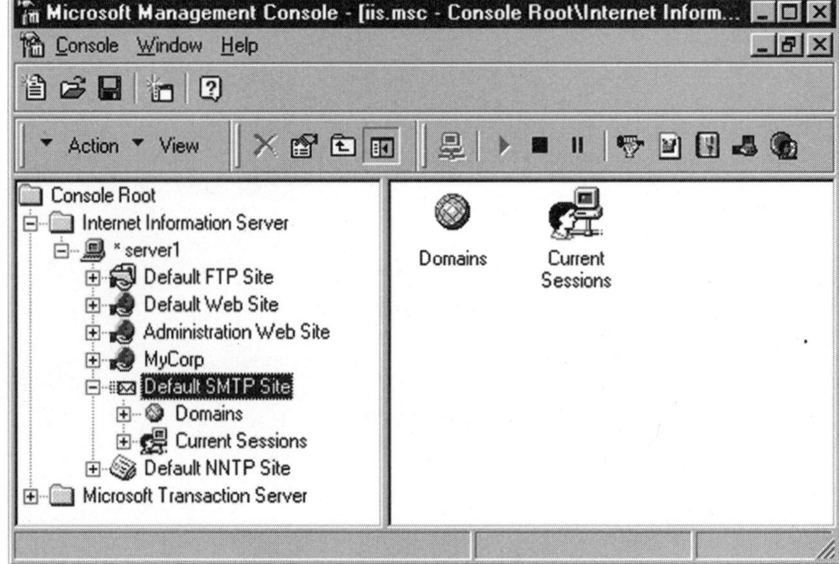

Figure 13-6 The MMC after the SMTP service has been installed.

- *Domains:* access property sheets for creating and configuring domains for the SMTP service
- *Current Sessions:* status information concerning current users, location of message source, and connection time since start of session

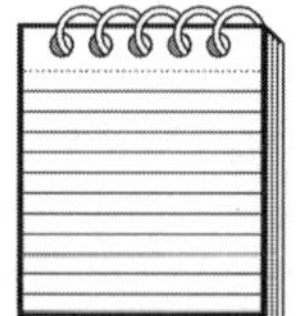

NOTE: Only one SMTP site may be installed on an IIS 4.0 server. You can rename the default SMTP site, but you cannot create other sites or delete the existing one (unless you uninstall the SMTP service on the IIS server).

Tools for Administering the SMTP Service

Windows NT 4.0 Option Pack provides three tools for administering and managing the SMTP service on IIS 4.0:

- *Internet Service Manager.* The SMTP snap-in extension in the MMC allows full administration of any SMTP server on the local LAN.
- *Internet Service Manager (HTML).* The Web-based administrative tool allows most administrative tasks to be performed using only a Web browser such as Internet Explorer 4.01, both on a local LAN and from a remote location over a WAN link.
- The *Windows Scripting Host (WSH).* This tool allows VBScript administration scripts to be run either from the graphical WSH utility (`Wscript.exe`) or from the command line (`Cscript.exe`).

This chapter deals only with use of the MMC version of Internet Service Manager to administer the SMTP service. The HTML version functions similarly to the MMC version. For information on administering SMTP through the WSH, refer to the Option Pack online documentation.

NOTE: Some administrative functions for the SMTP service cannot be performed using Internet Service Manager (HTML) and must be performed using the MMC instead. These functions include

- *Granting operator privileges*
- *Granting or denying access based on IP address or domain names*
- *Installing certificates with Key Manager*
- *Enabling transaction logging*
- *Configuring restrictions on relaying mail*

Various administrative tasks can be initiated and performed using the MMC version of the Internet Service Manager (see Fig. 13-6). Most of these actions can be performed by selecting the Default SMTP Site node in the scope pane (left pane) and then either using the rebar buttons, accessing the Action drop-down menu, or right-clicking on the node and using the context menu.

- The default SMTP site can be stopped, started, and paused.
  - *Stopping* the site disconnects all currently connected users and allows no new connections to be established.
  - *Pausing* the site allows no new connections to be established but does not disconnect current connections.
  - *Starting* the site allows new connections to be established with the server.
- Property sheets can be opened for the default SMTP site. These property sheets can be used to configure various aspects of the SMTP service and are described in the next section.
- Create a new domain. Domains in SMTP are different from Windows NT domains or DNS domains, and are administrative objects for organizing mail for delivery.
- View current connections and domain information.
- Terminate all current connections.
- Connect to and administer SMTP sites on other IIS 4.0 servers on the local LAN.

To verify that the SMTP service is running on an IIS 4.0 server, use the Services program in Control Panel.

NOTE: *Be careful when stopping the SMTP service, as it will close all connections, and mail being processed may fail to be delivered. If the SMTP service needs to be configured, it is better to pause the service, which doesn't affect current connections.*

Configuring the SMTP Service

The default SMTP site is configured through property sheets, similar to the WWW and FTP sites running on IIS 4.0. The Default STMP Site Properties sheet is opened by right-clicking on the Default SMTP Site node in the MMC and selecting PROPERTIES from the shortcut menu; it can also be opened using the PROPERTIES button on the rebar or the Action drop-down menu on the rebar.

The Default SMTP Site Properties sheet has five tabs that perform the following administrative functions:

- *SMTP Site.* Configure site identification, IP address, TCP ports, maximum connections, and connections timeout, and enable logging.
- *Operators.* Grant operator privileges.
- *Messages.* Limit message size and session size, limit number of messages per session and recipients per message, cc non-delivery report, specify `Badmail` directory.
- *Delivery.* Limit number of retries and retry interval for local and remote queue; limit maximum hop count; specify masquerade domain, fully qualified domain name, and smart host; perform reverse DNS lookup; configure authentication method for outgoing security.
- *Directory Security.* Specify authentication method, enable secure communications, set IP address restrictions, specify relay restrictions.

Configuring SMTP Site Identification

Using the SMTP Site tab, specify the following information (see Fig. 13-7):

- *Description.* This will appear beside the SMTP node in the MMC.
- *IP address.* Specify the IP address for the site. Click the ADVANCED button to open the Advanced Multiple SMTP Site Configuration dialog box, where you can specify additional IP addresses and TCP port numbers for the SMTP site. These IP addresses must have already been bound to the network adapter by using the Services program in Control Panel. You cannot use the same TCP port number for more than one IP address.

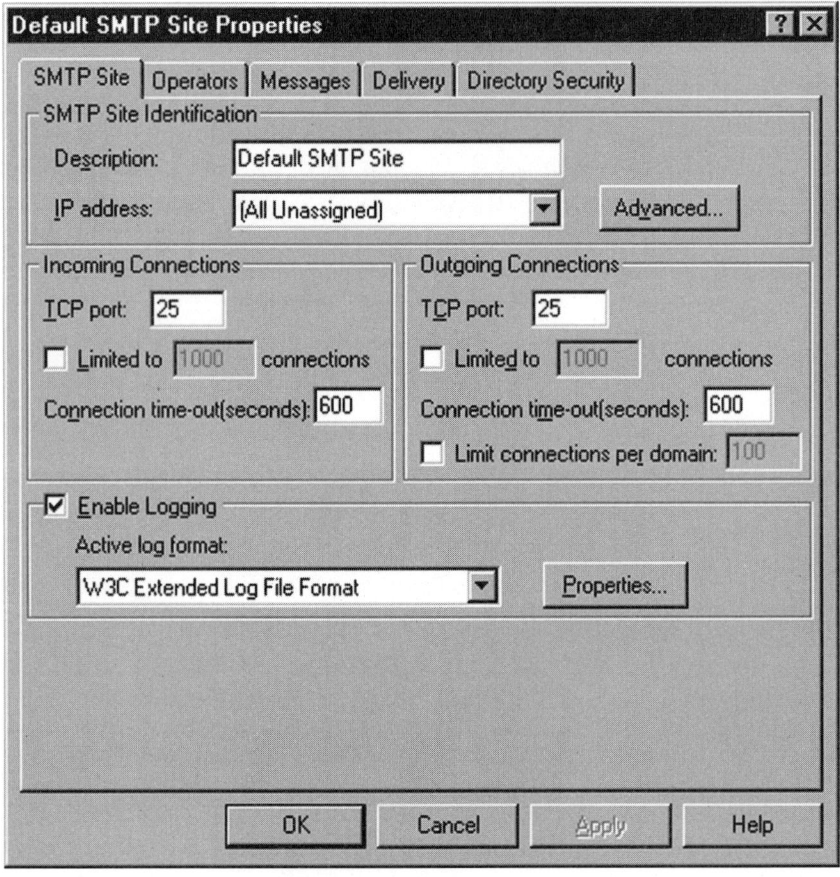

Figure 13-7 The SMTP Site tab on the Default SMTP Site Properties sheet.

NOTE: *In this release of the Microsoft SMTP service, you cannot bind multiple addresses to the SMTP site. For the IP Address setting on the SMTP Site tab, you must either select a single IP address or specify* ALL UNASSIGNED.

Configuring SMTP Incoming Connections

Incoming connections are made by remote SMTP servers connecting to the default SMTP site running on IIS in order to send mail. For these incoming connections you can specify (see Fig. 13-7)

- *TCP port number.* This is the TCP port that remote SMTP servers must connect to on the default SMTP site. The default SMTP port for incoming connections is TCP port 25.

- *Limited to (number).* Simultaneous incoming connections may be unlimited or may be limited to a specified number (1000 connections is suggested).
- *Connection time-out.* The time-out for inactive connections can be specified (the default is 600 seconds or 10 minutes).

Configuring SMTP Outgoing Connections

Outgoing connections are made by the default SMTP site running on IIS in order to connect and send mail to remote SMTP servers. For these outgoing connections you can specify (see Fig. 13-7)

- *TCP port number.* This is the TCP port that the default SMTP site uses to connect to remote SMTP servers. The default SMTP port for outgoing connections is TCP port 25.
- *Limited to (number).* Simultaneous outgoing connections can be unlimited or can be limited to a specific number (1000 connections is suggested).
- *Connection time-out.* The time-out for inactive connections can be specified (the default is 600 seconds or 10 minutes).
- *Limit connections per domain.* The number of simultaneous outgoing connections made to specific domain can be unlimited or can be limited to a specific number (100 connections is suggested). This number cannot be greater than the maximum number of simultaneous outgoing connections allowed.

Configuring SMTP Logging

Logging may be enabled or disabled for SMTP. Any of the four standard logging formats described in Chap. 3 may be selected and enabled here (see Fig. 13-7).

NOTE: *If you enable logging on SMTP and select the default settings, the SMTP events logged will be added to those of the WWW and other services running on IIS. You may want to configure a separate log file for each service running on IIS to keep separate and easily interpreted records. Do this by logging SMTP logs to a separate directory from the other service log files.*

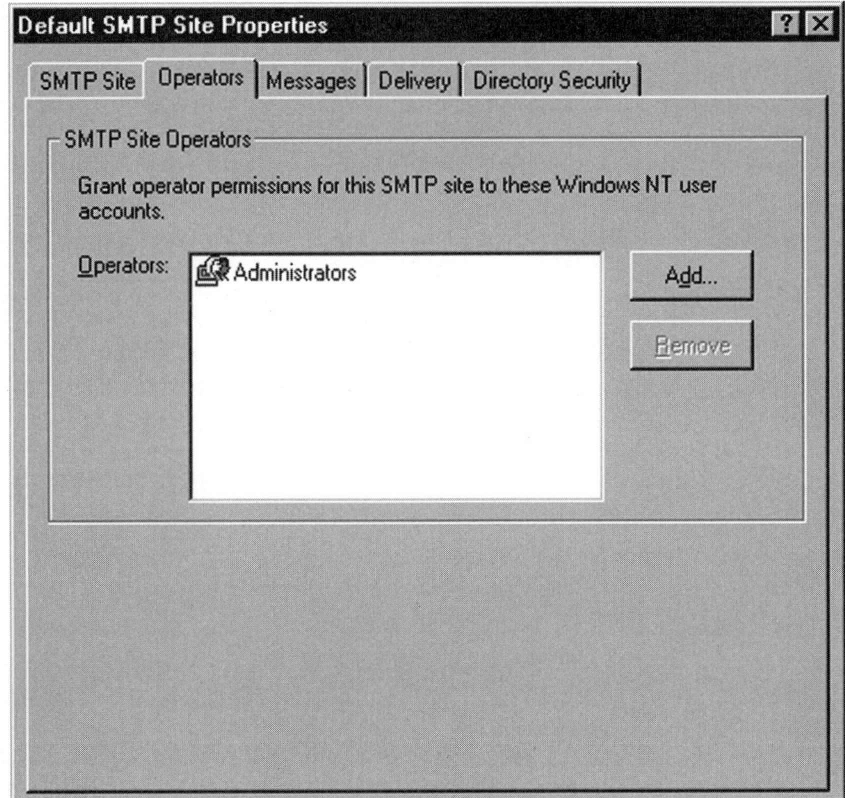

Figure 13-8 The Operators tab on the Default SMTP Site Properties sheet.

Configuring SMTP Site Operators

Grant and revoke operator privileges for administering the default SMTP site using the Operators tab of this property sheet (Fig. 13-8). By default, everyone in the Administrators local group on the IIS server is granted operator status for SMTP.

Configuring SMTP Message Limits

Using the Messages tab (Fig. 13-9), the maximum message size and maximum session size (bytes transferred per session) may be unlimited or limited to values specified. The default settings are

- *Maximum message size:* 2048 kB or 2 MB
- *Maximum session size:* 10240 kB or 10 MB

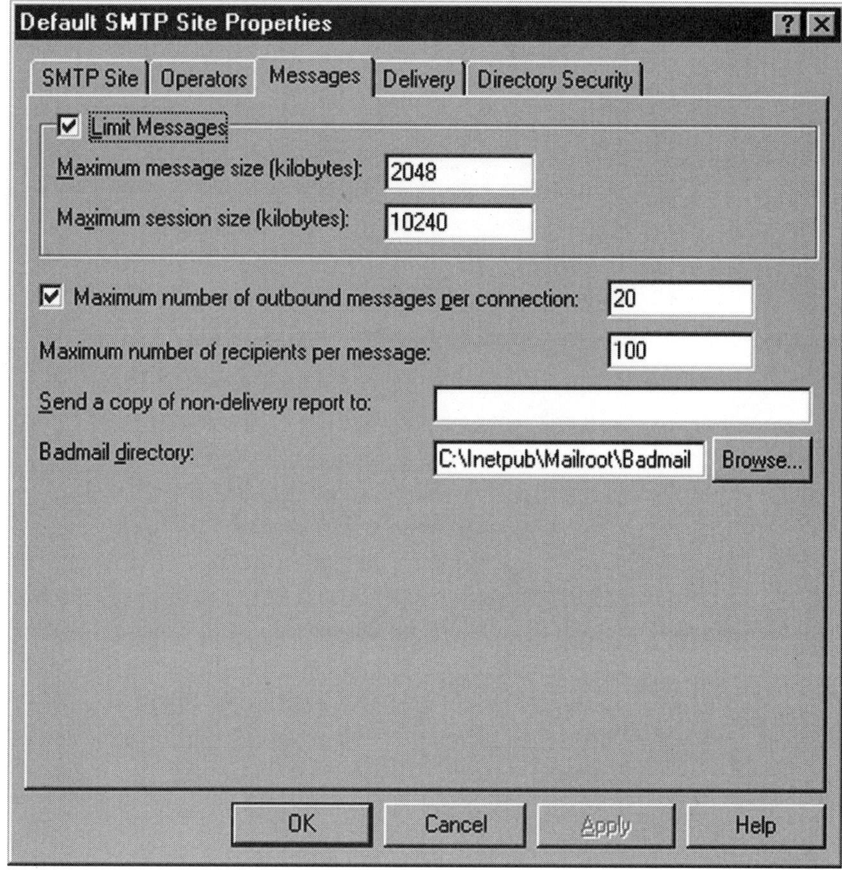

Figure 13-9
The Messages tab on the Default SMTP Site Properties sheet.

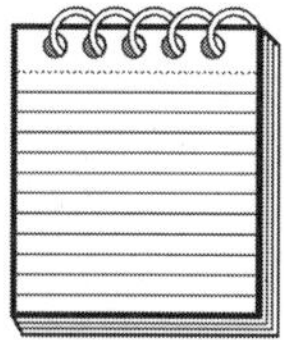

NOTE: *If a message is larger than the maximum message size, it will still be processed. But if an incoming message is larger than the maximum session size, the socket will close and the message will not be processed. In this case, the message transfer agent of the sending SMTP server will continue to resend the message until it times out, adding extra overhead on your server. To avoid this problem, do not set the maximum session size to too small a value.*

Configuring SMTP Messages per Connection Limits

The *maximum number of outgoing messages per connection* can be unlimited or limited to the value specified. The default setting is 20 messages per connection (see Fig. 13-9). Sending multiple messages using a single connection improves the performance of the SMTP service. Determining the best value for this setting is discussed later in this chapter.

The *maximum number of recipients per message* must be specified here. The default is 100 recipients per message.

You can also use this tab to specify that the SMTP service *send a copy of non-delivery reports to* a specified email address.

Finally, specify the location of the `Badmail` *directory*. This folder contains messages that can neither be delivered nor returned to sender (*dead letters*) and must be located on a local drive.

Configuring SMTP Retry Settings

Using the Delivery tab (Fig. 13-10), specify the *retry interval* (time between retries) for when the SMTP attempts to deliver a message and fails. The default value is 60 minutes. This setting can be configured separately for messages in the local and remote message queues.

Specify the *maximum retries* (maximum number of retries) before the SMTP will return the message to the sender together with a nondelivery report (NDR). The default value is 48 times. This setting can be configured separately for messages in the local and remote message queues. If a message cannot be delivered in

$$\text{retry interval} \times \text{maximum retries} = 60 \text{ min} \times 48 = 2 \text{ days}$$

then SMTP will attempt to return the message to its sender. If this also fails after two more days, the message will be moved to the `Badmail` directory.

Configuring SMTP Miscellaneous Delivery Settings

The *maximum hop count* (see Fig. 13-10) is the maximum number of SMTP servers to which the message may be routed along its delivery route. The default value is 15 hops. If this value is exceeded as the message travels along a route, the message is returned to sender with an NDR.

Specify a *masquerade domain* to replace the local domain name in the "From" field of messages sent from the default SMTP site. This replacement is only in effect on the first hop.

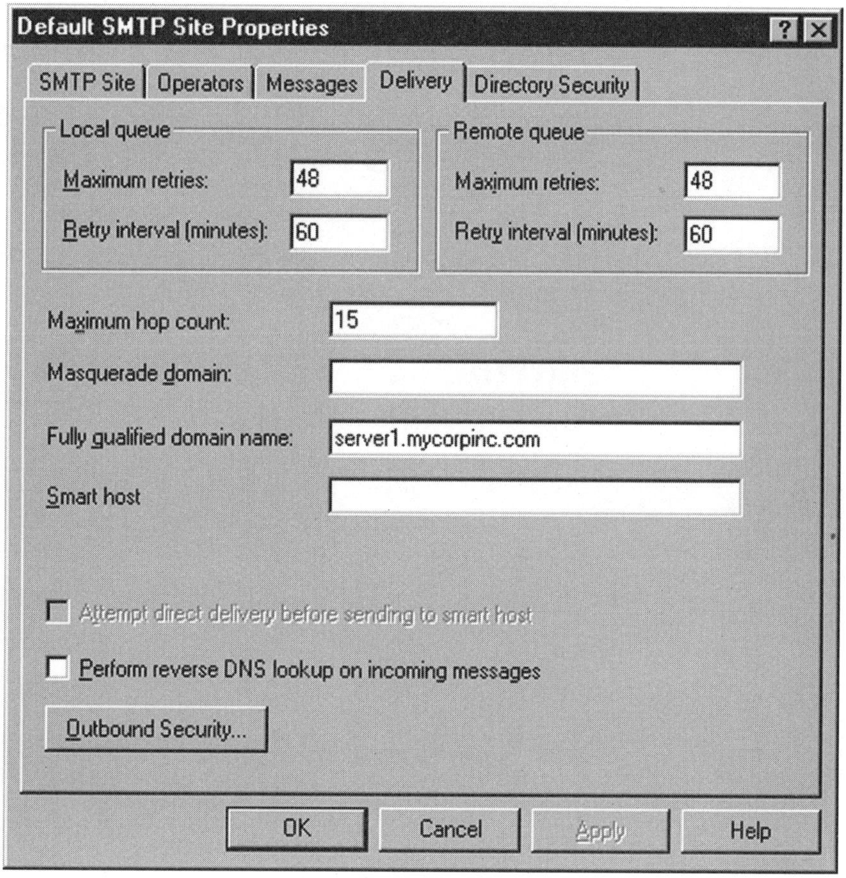

Figure 13-10
The Delivery tab on the Default SMTP Site Properties sheet.

Specify a *fully qualified domain name (FQDN)* for the default SMTP site.

- Use the domain name specified on the DNS tab of the TCP/IP Properties sheet.

or

- Specify a new, unique domain name.

By default, the name specified on the DNS tab of the TCP/IP Properties sheet is used. If you change the domain name, you must stop and restart the SMTP service before the new name will take effect.

Specify a *smart host,* which is an SMTP server to which all outgoing messages are routed. The name of the smart host can be

- The FQDN of the smart host
- The IP address of the smart host (enclose this value in parentheses)

You can choose to *attempt direct delivery before sending to smart host.* This will cause the SMTP service to try to deliver remote messages locally before sending them to the smart host. This option is available only if a smart host has been specified, and by default is disabled.

You can choose to *perform reverse DNS lookup on incoming messages* to configure the SMTP service to check that the IP address in the "From" field of the message matches the originating IP address in the message header. This option can slow performance if enabled, and is disabled by default.

Configuring SMTP Authentication Method for Outgoing Messages

For outgoing mail you can specify what authentication method will be required by the receiving SMTP server. To do this, click the OUTBOUND SECURITY button on the Delivery tab of the Default SMTP Site Properties sheet to open the Outbound Security dialog box (Fig. 13-11). The three options you can choose from are

- *No authentication.* This is the default setting, because choosing an authentication method for all receiving SMTP servers on a global level (i.e., for all remote domains) is unlikely to be required; most SMTP servers will accept connections without requiring any credentials. Therefore, you will probably want to leave this as the default setting.

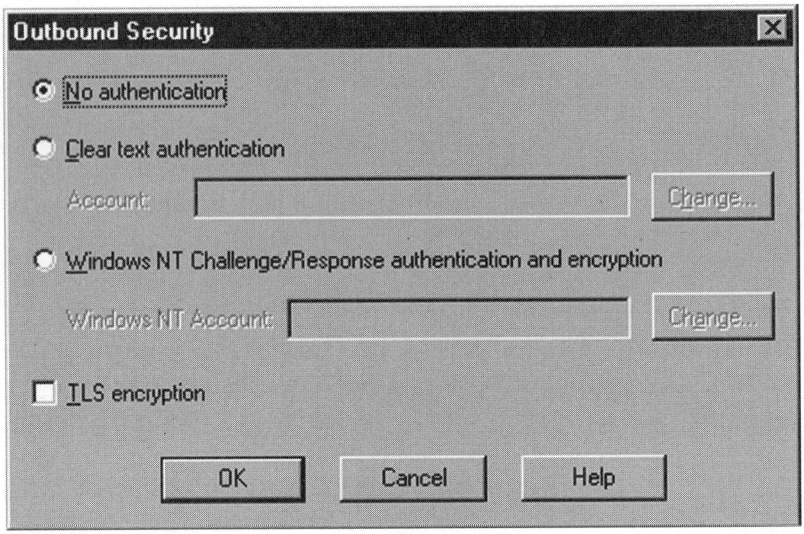

Figure 13-11 Specify the authentication method used by the receiving SMTP server.

- *Clear text authentication.* The account name and password recognized by the remote SMTP server are sent unencrypted.
- *Windows NT challenge/response authentication.* The Windows NT domain, account, and password recognized by the remote server are sent securely using Windows NT challenge/response, which encrypts the authentication exchange.

In addition, you can enable or disable *Transport Layer Security (TLS)* encryption globally for outgoing mail to all remote domains. In this case all receiving SMTP servers must support TLS.

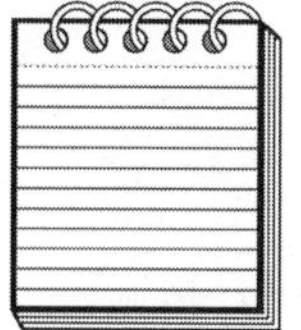

NOTE: *When you create remote domains, you can specify a different authentication method for delivering mail to these domains to override the one globally specified. Creating remote domains is explained later in this chapter.*

Configuring SMTP Authentication Method for Incoming Messages

For incoming mail you can specify what authentication method the sending SMTP server must use. To do this, click the EDIT button in the Anonymous Access and Authentication Control section of the Directory Security tab on the Default SMTP Site Properties (Fig. 13-12) sheet to open the Authentication Methods dialog box. Choose any or all of the three options specified:

- *Allow anonymous access.* Incoming messages are received by the SMTP service without being authenticated. This is enabled by default.
- *Basic authentication.* Incoming messages are received and authenticated using a valid Windows NT username and password for the Windows NT domain on which the default SMTP site resides, or on some other specified Windows NT domain. This is enabled by default. Note that basic authentication is not a secure means of authentication.
- *Windows NT challenge/response.* Incoming messages are received and authenticated using a valid Windows NT username and password for the Windows NT domain on which the default SMTP site resides. This is enabled by default. Windows NT challenge/response is a secure method of authentication and uses encrypted credentials.

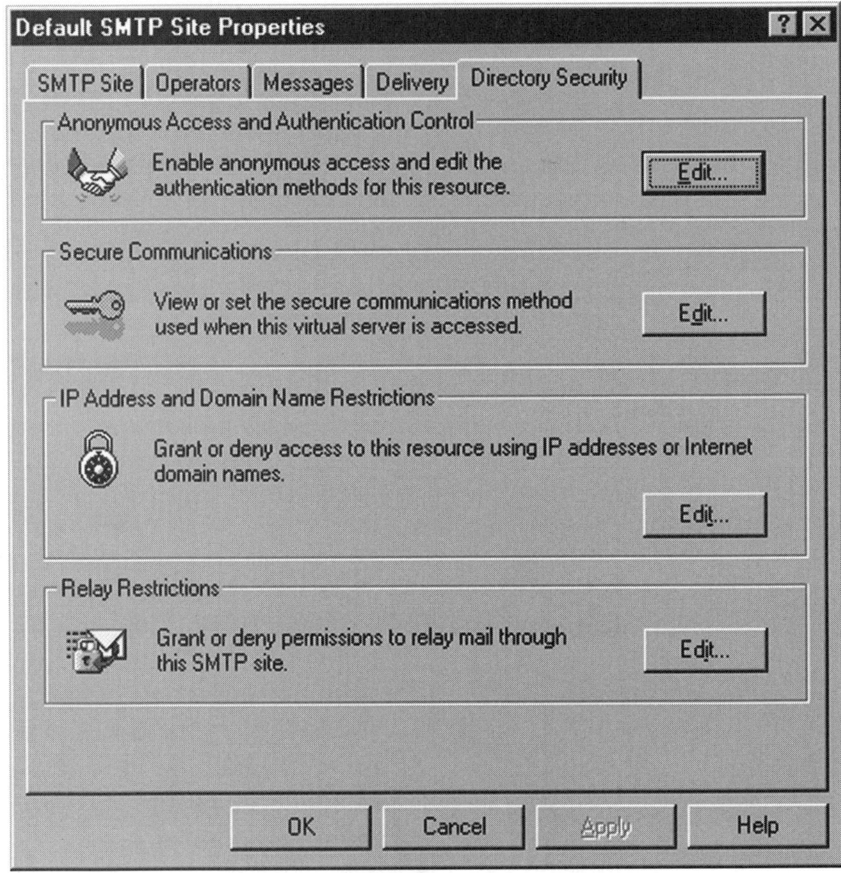

Figure 13-12 The Directory Security tab on the Default SMTP Site Properties sheet.

If you want to prevent the SMTP server from authenticating users, check the first checkbox and clear the other two.

Configuring SMTP Secure Communications for Incoming Messages with TLS

For incoming mail you can specify that *Transport Layer Security (TLS)* be used to encrypt incoming sessions from remote SMTP servers to the SMTP service on IIS. TLS is a form of SSL and must be enabled by creating a key pair and installing a server certificate. Click the EDIT button on the Secure Communications section of this property sheet (see Fig. 13-12) to access Key Manager (Fig. 13-13). (See Chap. 12 to find out more about how to use Key Manager.) Once the key pair has been generated

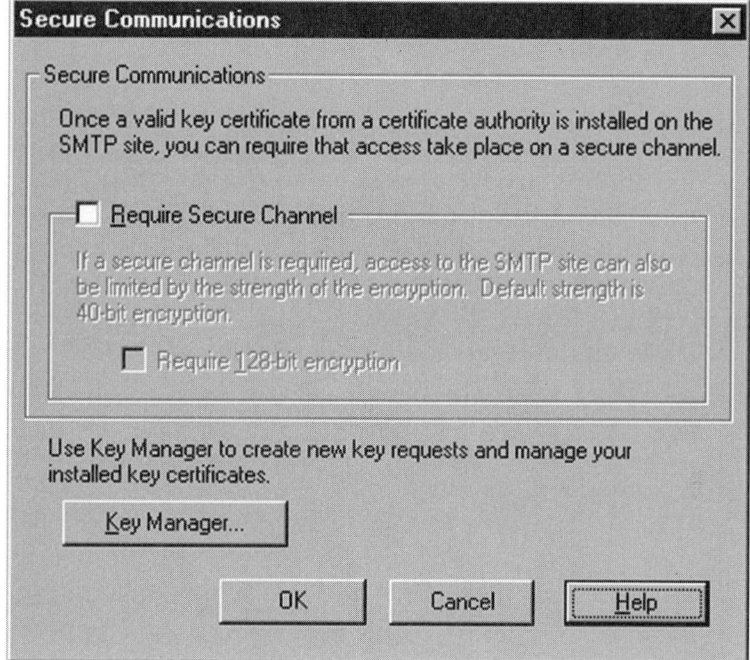

Figure 13-13 Enabling secure communications for incoming SMTP mail using TLS.

and the server certificate installed, check the REQUIRE SECURE CHANNEL checkbox to enable TLS for incoming mail.

The option of *128-bit encryption* is available to users of Windows NT Server in Canada and the United States. Standard encryption strength for international users is 40-bit.

NOTE: *When you create remote domains, you can override the allowed authentication methods globally specified by configuring different ones for receiving mail from these remote domains. Creating remote domains is explained later in this chapter. You can also override the global TLS settings for individual remote domains.*

Configuring SMTP IP Address and Domain Name Restrictions

You can grant or deny access to the default SMTP site based on the IP address or domain name of the remote SMTP server (see Fig. 13-12). This is done in the usual way, similar to the process for the WWW service described in Chap. 3.

Configuring SMTP Relay Restrictions

You can enable or disable relaying of incoming mail to remote addresses by clicking the EDIT button on the Relay Restrictions section of the Directory Security tab on the Default SMTP Site Properties sheet to open the Relay Restrictions dialog box (Fig. 13-14). The default setting is ALL COMPUTERS ARE NOT ALLOWED TO RELAY.

You can also ALLOW ANY COMPUTER THAT SUCCESSFULLY AUTHENTICATES TO RELAY by enabling this checkbox.

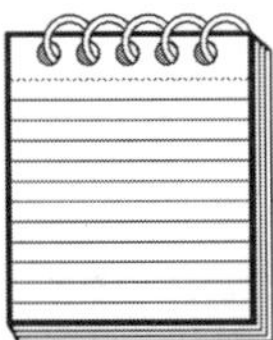

NOTE: *Be aware that if you are connected to the Internet and you enable relay restrictions without requiring authentication, you may be targeted by distributors of unsolicited commercial email, which can adversely affect the performance of your server.*

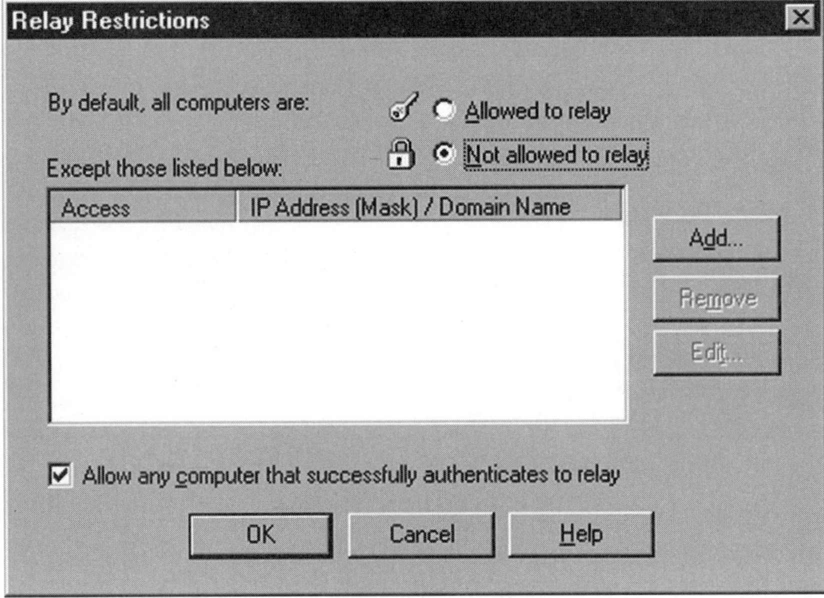

Figure 13-14 Enable or disable relaying for the SMTP service.

Understanding SMTP Service Domains

Domains in SMTP are not the same as domains in Windows NT. SMTP service domains can be either *local* or *remote.*

- *Local SMTP service domains* (also called *service domains* or *supported domains*) are DNS domains that are serviced by the SMTP service running on IIS. Arriving messages addressed to a local domain are delivered to the `Drop` directory. When SMTP is installed on IIS, it creates a *default domain,* which is usually the domain name specified in the DNS tab of the TCP/IP properties sheet for the server. Configuring the default SMTP site as described in the previous section configures the default domain. If you create a new local domain, it will be an *alias* of the default domain and will have the same properties as the default domain.
- *Remote SMTP service domains* (also called *remote domains* or *nonlocal domains*) are DNS domains of remote servers that are not local and that the SMTP must look up using DNS in order to deliver mail. Delivery settings can be configured individually for remote domains, and these settings override global settings configured using the Default SMTP Site Properties sheet.

Creating a New SMTP Service Domain

To create a new SMTP service domain using the MMC, right-click on the Default SMTP Site node and select NEW, DOMAIN from the shortcut menu to open the New Domain Wizard (Fig. 13-15). Select the type of domain you want to create:

- *Local:* an alias for the default domain and the end point for mail delivery
- *Remote:* for delivery to a remote SMTP server

If you choose the *remote* option, click NEXT and specify a name for the new domain (`mail.othercorp.com` has been used in Fig. 13-16, but you can also use wildcards, e.g., `*.othercorp.com`). The procedure is similar for creating a local (alias) domain. Figure 13-17 shows the MMC when two new domains have been created, one local and one remote.

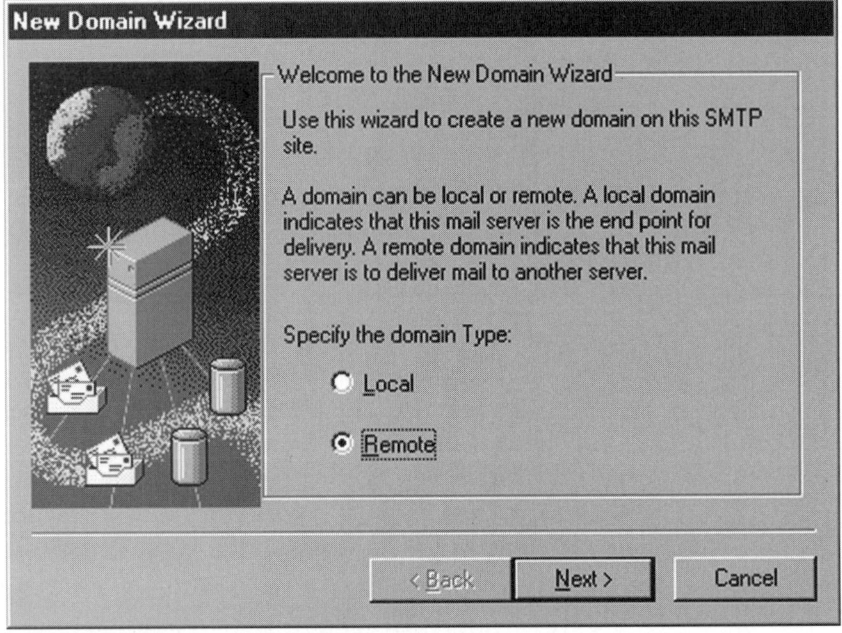

Figure 13-15 The New Domain Wizard for creating new SMTP domains.

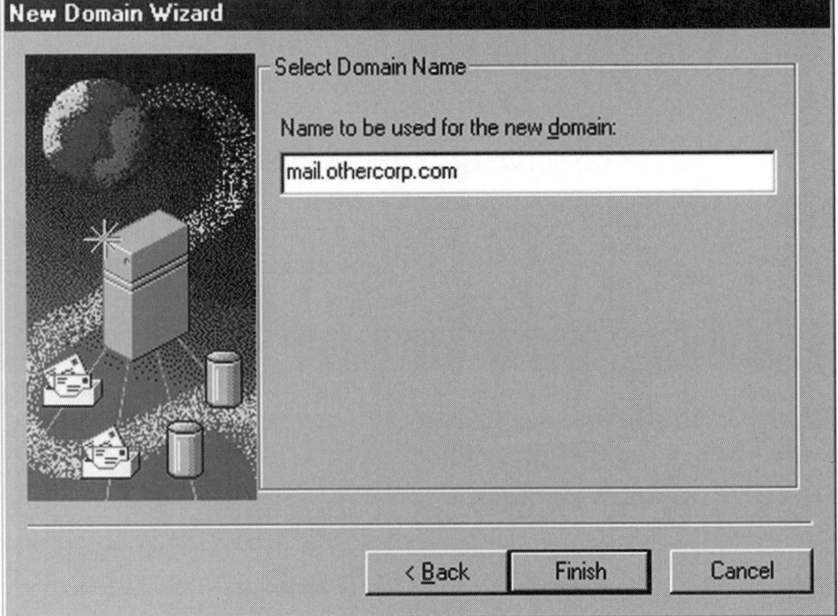

Figure 13-16 Specifying the name for a remote domain.

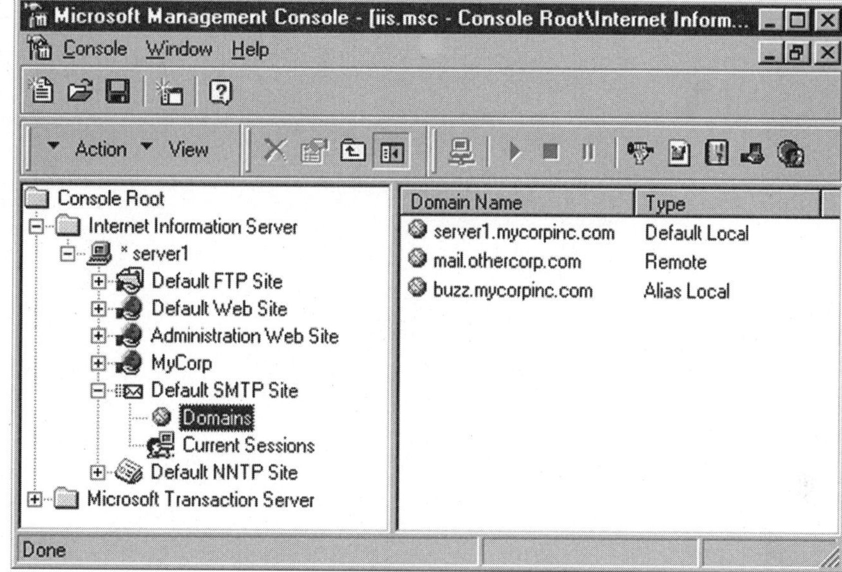

Figure 13-17 The default SMTP site with default, alias, and remote domains.

Configuring an SMTP Domain

To configure an SMTP domain, right-click on the domain node in the results pane of the MMC, and select PROPERTIES to open the <*domain*> Properties sheet. Figure 13-18 shows the property sheet for the `mail.othercorp.com` domain.

For the *default local domain,* you can specify the location of the `Drop` directory where incoming messages will be delivered. This directory must be on the local IIS server. The alias domains use the same `Drop` directory as the default domain.

For an *alias local domain,* there are no settings that can be configured.

For a *remote domain,* you can specify the following settings:

- Specify a *route domain* if there is a particular remote SMTP server to which you would like to route all mail addressed to the remote domain, if this route will get mail to its destination faster. Route settings override smart host settings configured on the Default SMTP Site Properties sheet.
- Enable ALLOW INCOMING MAIL TO BE RELAYED TO THIS DOMAIN to override relay restrictions on the Default SMTP Site Properties sheet.
- OUTBOUND SECURITY specifies which authentication method will be required by the receiving SMTP server.

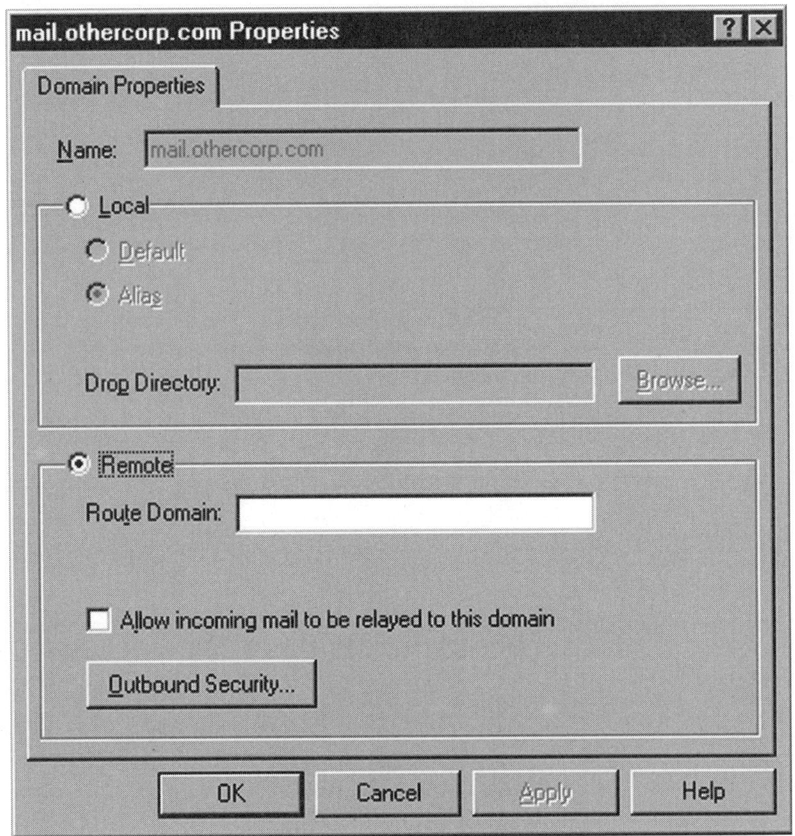

Figure 13-18 Properties sheet for the `mail.othercorp.com` remote domain.

Walkthrough: Sending a Message Using the Pickup Directory

To send a message using the SMTP service on IIS, use an ASCII text editor to create a simple text file similar to the one shown in Fig. 13-19. If you like, you can use a real email address for the recipient if you have a live Internet connection. We will use a nonexistent recipient domain so that we can observe the SMTP service at work on IIS 4.0.

Note the blank line (CR + LF) that must be included between the header and the message body. There is a similar blank line (CR + LF) at the end of the body of the message. Save the message as `message.txt` in the folder `C:\tempmail.`

Configure the settings on the Delivery tab of the Default SMTP Site Properties sheet as follows:

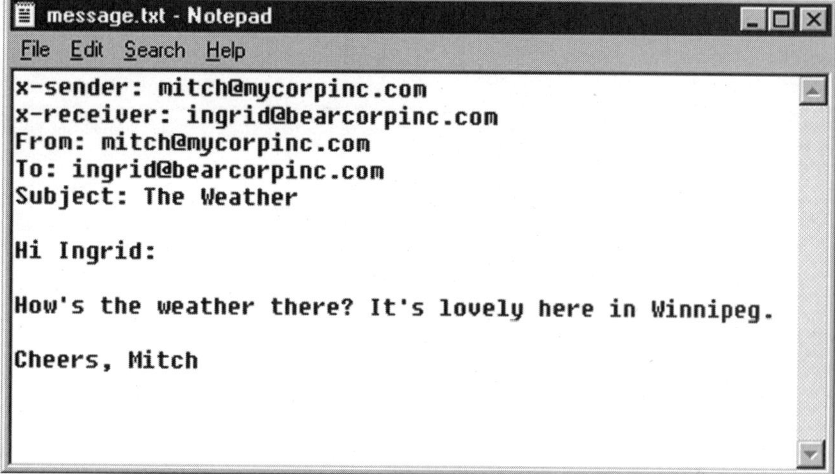

message.txt - Notepad
File Edit Search Help
x-sender: mitch@mycorpinc.com
x-receiver: ingrid@bearcorpinc.com
From: mitch@mycorpinc.com
To: ingrid@bearcorpinc.com
Subject: The Weather
Hi Ingrid:
How's the weather there? It's lovely here in Winnipeg.
Cheers, Mitch

Figure 13-19 An example of an SMTP message composed using Notepad.

- Remote queue maximum retries: 2 times
- Remote queue retry interval: 1 minute

Now use Windows Explorer to move the message from the `C:\tempmail` directory to the `C:\Mailroot\Pickup` directory. Click immediately on the `Pickup` directory to view its contents, and note that it is empty. The SMTP service continually monitors the `Pickup` directory for mail to deliver, and when it finds a message it moves it to the `Queue` directory.

Figure 13-20 shows the contents of the `Queue` directory immediately after the `message.txt` file has been moved into it. Note the mail message waiting to be delivered. Since the recipient's domain name is nonexistent, the mail cannot be delivered. Notice that the message has been renamed using a message ID number with the extension `*.eml`, which stands for "email." If you double-click on this message, it will open in Outlook Express. Figure 13-21 shows the `.eml` file opened in Notepad. Note the headers added by the SMTP service.

After one minute has expired (the retry interval), the contents of the `Queue` directory change; the directory now includes a `*.rtr` file, which indicates that SMTP service could not deliver the message and is attempting to return the message to the sender (see Fig. 13-22). The `.rtr` remote transcript file is a text file that explains why the message cannot be delivered. You can open and read this file if you like.

Finally, after 2 minutes the maximum retries value is exceeded, the `*.rtr` file is deleted, and the message `*.eml` file is moved to the `Badmail` directory. If you explore the `Badmail` directory and open the

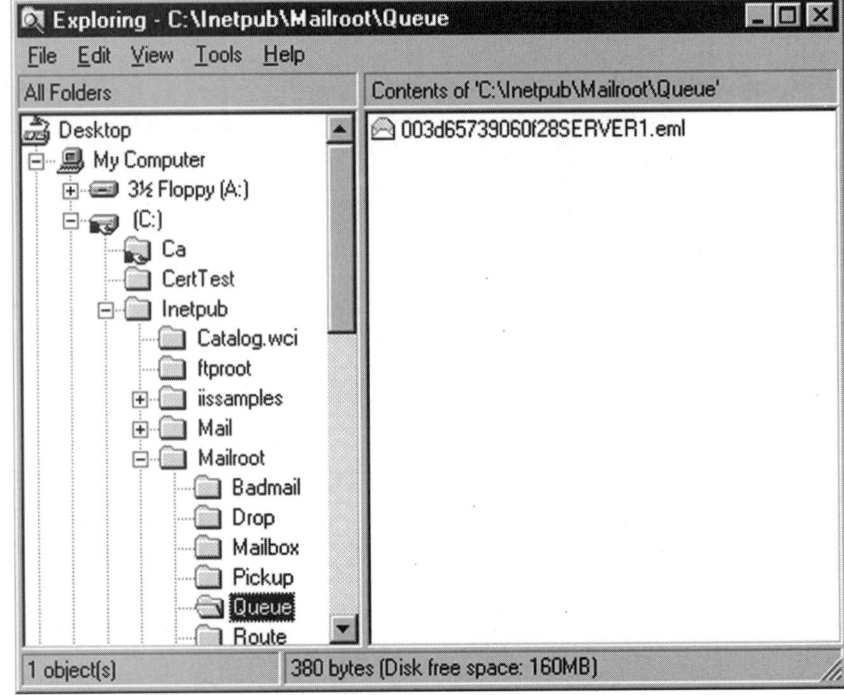

Figure 13-20 The message has been moved from the `Pickup` to the `Queue` directory.

`*.eml` file in it using Notepad, you can view the non-delivery report (NDR) (see Fig. 13-23).

As another exercise, try modifying the recipient headers to send the message to the destination address `ingrid@server1.mycorpinc.com` (or your equivalent), which will send the message to the local default SMTP domain. Move the message to the `Pickup` directory, and SMTP transfers it to the `Queue` directory and from there to the `Drop` directory, where incoming mail is stored.

Monitoring and Tuning SMTP Service Performance

The performance of the SMTP service on IIS 4.0 can be monitored using the following tools:

- *Event Viewer.* The SMTP service logs significant events to the Windows NT security log. Look for events whose source is `SMTPSVC`.

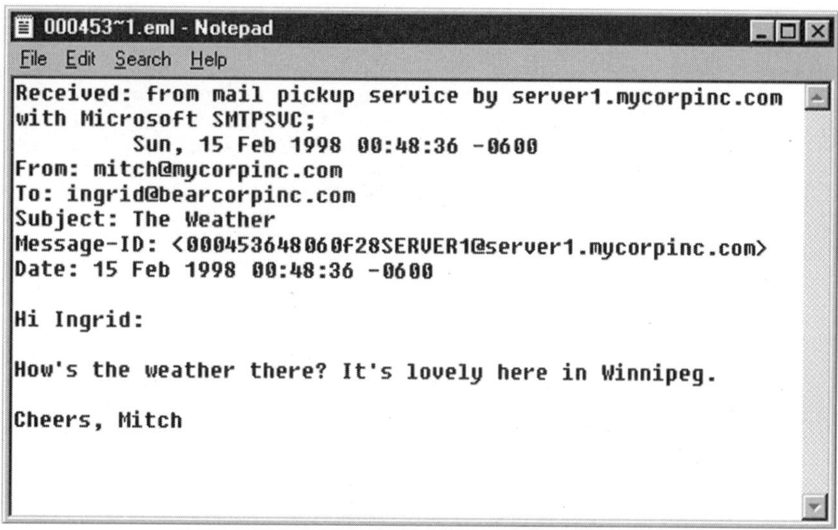

000453~1.eml - Notepad
File Edit Search Help
Received: from mail pickup service by server1.mycorpinc.com
with Microsoft SMTPSVC;
Sun, 15 Feb 1998 00:48:36 -0600
From: mitch@mycorpinc.com
To: ingrid@bearcorpinc.com
Subject: The Weather
Message-ID: <000453648060f28SERVER1@server1.mycorpinc.com>
Date: 15 Feb 1998 00:48:36 -0600
Hi Ingrid:
How's the weather there? It's lovely here in Winnipeg.
Cheers, Mitch

Figure 13-21
A formatted message in the `Queue` directory waiting to be delivered.

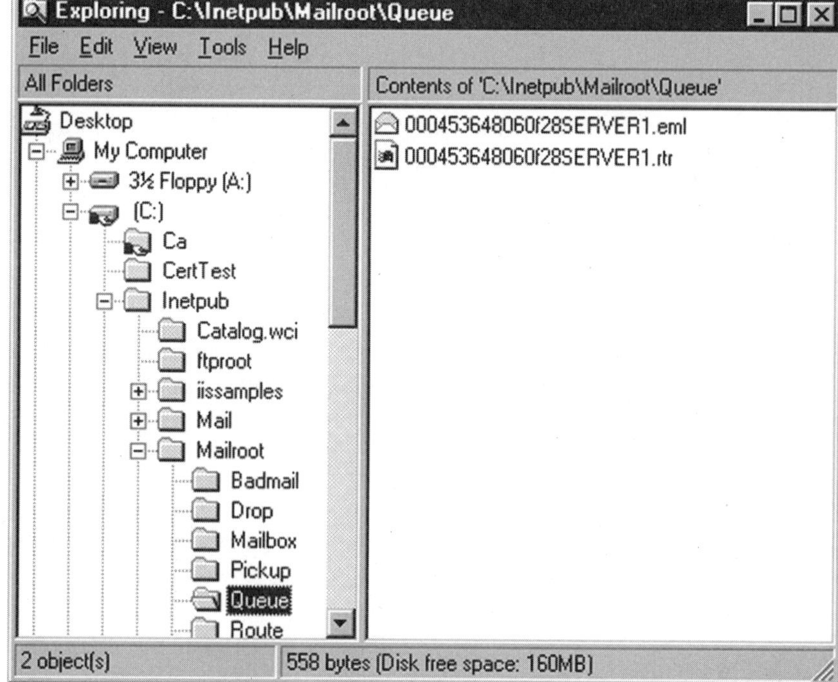

Figure 13-22
The message cannot be returned to the sender.

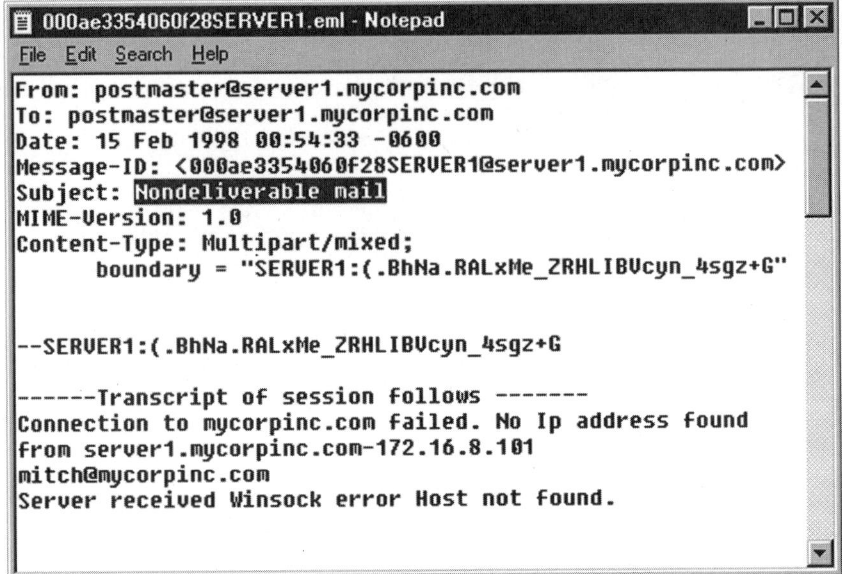

000ae3354060f28SERVER1.eml - Notepad

File Edit Search Help

```
From: postmaster@server1.mycorpinc.com
To: postmaster@server1.mycorpinc.com
Date: 15 Feb 1998 00:54:33 -0600
Message-ID: <000ae3354060f28SERVER1@server1.mycorpinc.com>
Subject: Nondeliverable mail
MIME-Version: 1.0
Content-Type: Multipart/mixed;
      boundary = "SERVER1:(.BhNa.RALxMe_ZRHLIBVcyn_4sgz+G"


--SERVER1:(.BhNa.RALxMe_ZRHLIBVcyn_4sgz+G

------Transcript of session follows -------
Connection to mycorpinc.com failed. No Ip address found
from server1.mycorpinc.com-172.16.8.101
mitch@mycorpinc.com
Server received Winsock error Host not found.
```

Figure 13-23 An NDR located in the `Badmail` directory.

- *IIS Logs.* View the IIS logs in a text editor or import them into Site Server Express to generate reports of SMTP site usage.
- *Performance Monitor.* The SMTP service includes the Performance Monitor SMTP Server object with a number of counters that may be monitored for that object.

You should monitor standard counters to detect memory, processor, disk, and network bottlenecks in addition to specific SMTP counters. In particular, you should set a Performance Monitor alert for low disk space on the volume where the `mailroot` directory is located, as low disk space conditions can lead to messages becoming corrupted.

Some of the more important SMTP Server Performance Monitor counters to watch are

Local Queue Length — Number of messages in the local queue. This should normally read zero. If it is greater than zero, the SMTP service may be receiving more messages than it can handle. If it steadily increases, something may be interfering with your SMTP process, causing a delay in message processing.

Remote Queue Length — Number of messages in the remote queue. The same concerns apply as for the Local Queue Length Counter.

Inbound Connections Current The total number of connections currently inbound. This should normally be greater than zero. If it remains zero for an extended period, you may have a network problem that is preventing mail from entering your server.

Following are some things you can do to enhance the performance of the SMTP service on IIS 4.0.

- Apply general enhancements, such as adding more memory, a faster processor, a stripe set, and a faster network connection to your server.
- Disable IIS logging for the SMTP service.
- Regularly clear the `Badmail` directory.
- Disable reverse DNS lookup.
- Optimally configure the *Maximum number of outbound messages per connection* setting on the Messages tab of the Default SMTP Site Properties sheet. Do this by monitoring the counter *SMTP Server: Messages Sent/sec,* and make sure that the setting on the property sheet is *less* than the average value of the Performance Monitor counter. This will ensure that the SMTP service opens simultaneous connections with remote servers to speed the processing of remotely destined mail.

SUMMARY

The Microsoft SMTP service is a fully functioning SMTP delivery service that can be configured to send mail to remote SMTP servers. The administration of the service is integrated into the MMC together with other IIS 4.0 services. Remote administration using a browser can also be performed.

FOR MORE INFORMATION

Microsoft Web Site Search the Microsoft Web site for the keyword "SMTP" to find more information about this service.

TechNet Search the TechNet knowledge base for articles relating to the SMTP service.

CHAPTER 14

Administering the NNTP Service

Introduction

Using the NNTP service running on Microsoft Internet Information Server 4.0, administrators can set up, maintain, and administer a news server for hosting USENET-style discussion groups on a corporate intranet/extranet. After completing this chapter, you will be able to

- Understand how the NNTP service works on IIS 4.0
- Install and configure the NNTP service on IIS 4.0
- Create and maintain newsgroups on IIS 4.0
- View and post to newsgroups using Outlook Express
- Set an expiration policy for a newsgroup
- Map a newsgroup directory to a virtual directory

Understanding the NNTP Service

The Microsoft NNTP service on IIS 4.0 fully supports the standard *Network News Transfer Protocol (NNTP)* and is compatible with most NNTP servers and clients. Some of its features include

- *Integration with standard Windows NT services such as Performance Monitor and Event Viewer.* The NNTP service installs a collection of performance counters for monitoring it with Performance Monitor. Error conditions are written to the Windows NT System Log viewable from Event Viewer.
- *Integration with Windows NT security, including access control lists (ACLs) on NTFS volumes.* Access to a particular newsgroup may be controlled by assigning NTFS permissions to the newsgroup's content directory.
- *Several forms of authentication.* Users may be authenticated through Basic authentication, NT Challenge/Response authentication, or as anonymous users.
- *Support for a variety of content formats.* In addition to plain ASCII text, other supported formats include MIME, HTML, GIF, and JPEG formats.
- *A variety of administration tools.* The NNTP service may be administered from the Microsoft Management Console, through a Web browser, and through the Windows Scripting Host.

- *Integration with Index Server.* Both text and properties of news messages can be fully indexed.
- *Integration with SSL.* Newsgroup sessions may be encrypted using the Secure Sockets Layer protocol version 3.0

How the Network News Transfer Protocol Works

NNTP is both a client/server protocol and a server/server protocol. In the client/server scenario, the following steps take place (see Fig. 14-1):

- An NNTP client connects to an NNTP server to receive a list of available newsgroups on the server. The default TCP port on the server for client connections is port 119 (the default TCP port for an SSL connection is 563).

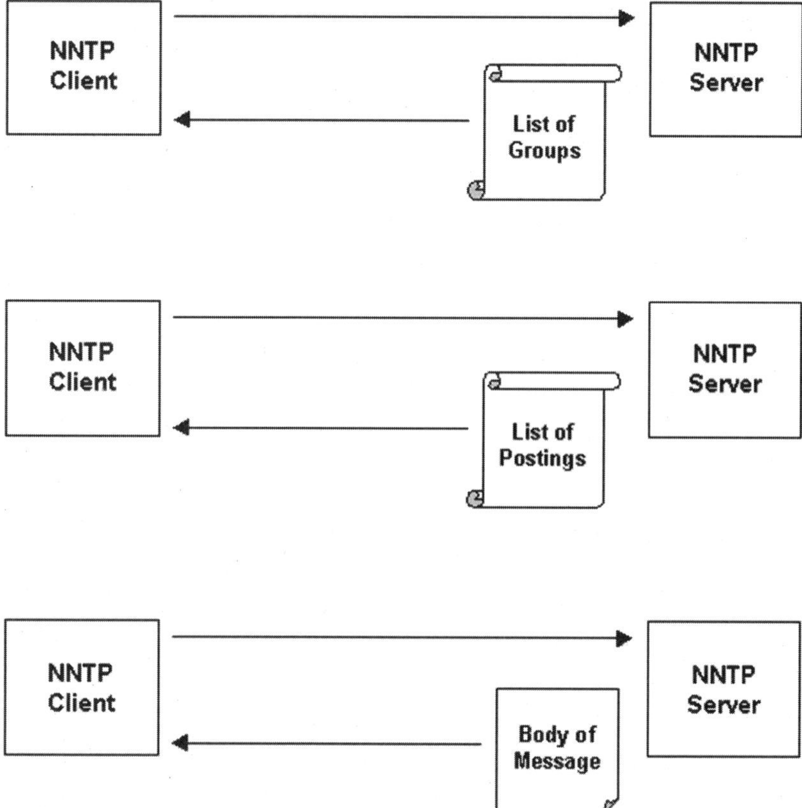

Figure 14-1 Interaction between NNTP clients and servers.

- The client selects an available newsgroup, and the server returns a list of headings of postings made to the newsgroup.
- The client selects a posting in the newsgroup, and the server returns the body of the message for the client to read.

In the server/server scenario, one NNTP server receives a news feed from another NNTP server to replicate newsgroup content between servers. This is the basis of the worldwide USENET news server network.

NOTE: *This release of the Microsoft NNTP service does not support receiving newsfeeds from USENET news servers.*

Installing the NNTP Service

The NNTP service is not installed during a Typical setup of Windows NT 4.0 Option Pack. Instead, it can be installed by doing a Custom setup or can be installed afterwards by running setup in maintenance mode.

The hardware and software requirements for installing Microsoft NNTP service are the same as those for installing IIS 4.0, namely:

- Windows NT 4.0 Server
- Service Pack 3
- Internet Explorer 4.01

To install the NNTP service on an IIS 4.0 server, click START, PROGRAMS, WINDOWS NT 4.0 OPTION PACK, WINDOWS NT 4.0 OPTION PACK SETUP. When the initial screen appears, click NEXT and select ADD/REMOVE to open the Select Components screen. Select INTERNET INFORMATION SERVER (IIS) and click the SHOW SUBCOMPONENTS button to open the Internet Information Server (IIS) component box (Fig. 14-2). Check the INTERNET NNTP SERVICE checkbox and click OK and then NEXT to continue with the setup.

The next screen (Fig. 14-3) asks you to confirm or change the NNTP content home directory, namely:

```
C:\InetPub\nntpfile\
```

Accept the default and proceed to completion of the setup.

The result of running the setup is a new node under the server node in the Microsoft Management Console (Fig. 14-4). This new node is called *Default NNTP Site* and has three subnodes under it:

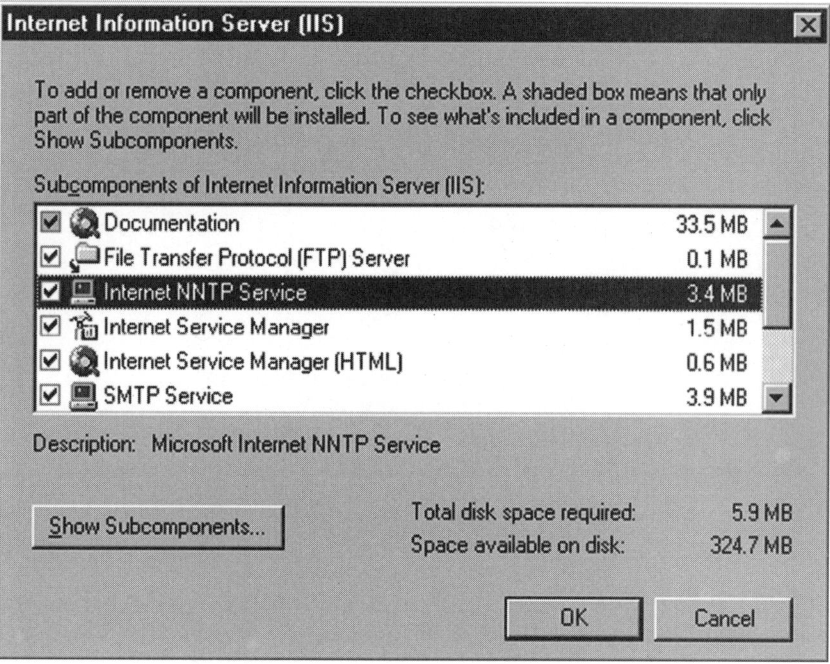

Figure 14-2 Select Internet NNTP Service component for installation.

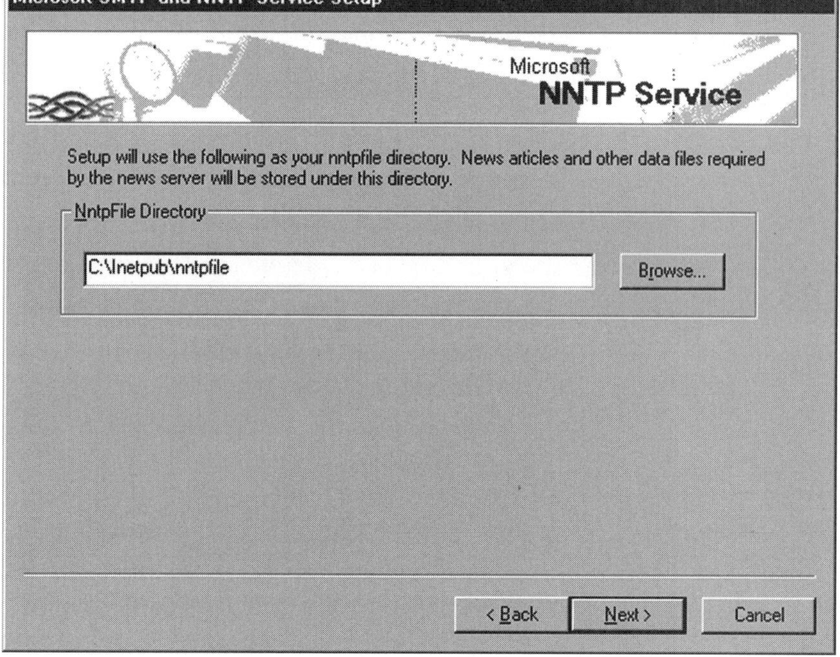

Figure 14-3 Select a root directory to store all news-group content.

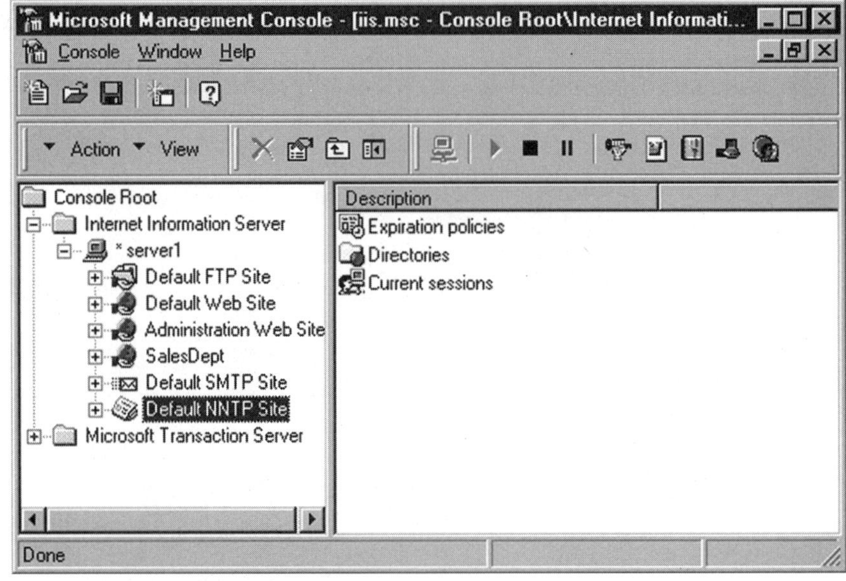

Figure 14-4 The Microsoft Management Console after the NNTP service has been installed.

- *Expiration policies.* Newsgroup articles can be configured to expire when a certain number of postings or a certain quantity in megabytes of postings occurs. Under this node any configured expiration policies are listed.
- *Directories.* Newsgroup content directories can be mapped to virtual directories, both local and remote. Under this node any configured virtual directories are listed.
- *Current sessions.* This shows the sessions still open, who is connected, and for how long.

The NNTP service installation process also creates the directory structure shown in Fig. 14-5. Included in this directory structure are

- `InetPub\News`, which contains Active Server Pages for the Web-based administration tool Internet Service Manager (HTML)
- `InetPub\nntpfile`, which contains all content directories, header files, hash files, and group list files
- `InetPub\nntpfile\root`, which contains all newsgroups created by administrator, plus demo and system groups

Individual newsgroups are stored as a series of nested folders under

```
InetPub\nntpfile\root
```

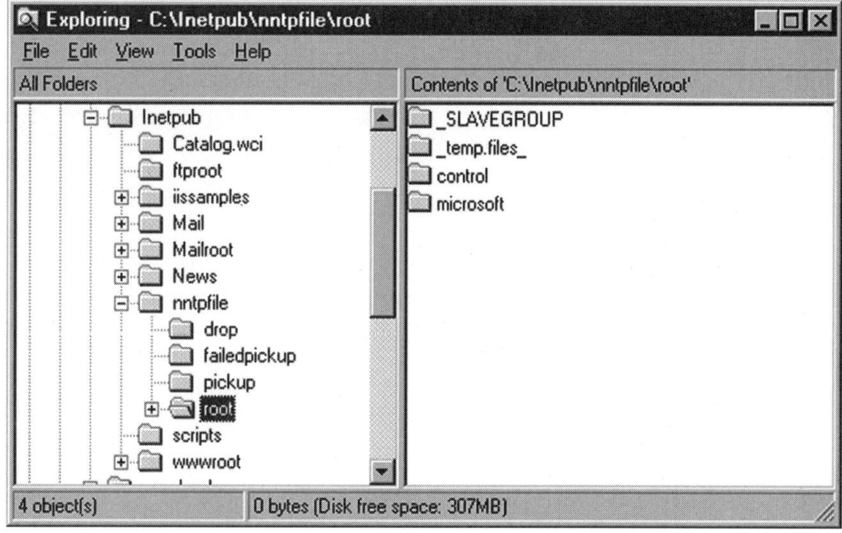

Figure 14-5
The directory structure created by the NNTP service installation process.

For example, creating the newsgroup `local.music.tribal` would create the following three folders to contain it:

- `InetPub\nntpfile\root\local`
- `InetPub\nntpfile\root\local\music`
- `InetPub\nntpfile\root\local\music\tribal`

The actual newsgroup content is stored in the last of the three folders listed above, and consists of the following files:

- A number of `.nws` files, each containing an individual newsgroup message. These files are plain ASCII files and can be viewed with Notepad.
- An `.xix` file, which contains a list of the `.nws` files contained in the folder. One `.xix` file can list up to 128 postings.

Tools for Administering the NNTP Service

Windows NT 4.0 Option Pack provides three tools for administering and managing the NNTP service:

- *Internet Service Manager.* The NNTP snap-in extension in the Microsoft Management Console (MMC) allows full administration of any NNTP server on the local LAN.

- *Internet Service Manager (HTML).* The Web-based administrative tool allows most administrative tasks to be performed using only a Web browser such as Internet Explorer 4.01 both on a local LAN and from a remote location over a WAN link.
- *Windows Scripting Host (WSH).* This allows VBScript administration scripts to be run either from the graphical WSH utility (`Wscript.exe`) or from the command line (`Cscript.exe`). Included in the Option Pack are several examples of VBScripts to perform common administrative tasks like modifying expiration policies, adding and deleting newsgroups and NNTP sites, and managing user sessions.

This chapter deals only with using the MMC version of Internet Service Manager to administer the NNTP service. The HTML version functions almost identically to the MMC version. For information on administering NNTP through the WSH, refer to the Option Pack online documentation.

A variety of administrative tasks can be initiated and performed using the MMC version of the Internet Service Manager (see Fig. 14-4). Most of these actions can be performed by selecting the Default NNTP Site node in the scope pane (left pane) and then either using the rebar buttons, accessing the Action drop-down menu, or right-clicking on the node and using the context menu.

- The Default NNTP Site can be stopped, started, and paused.
  - *Stopping* the site disconnects all currently connected users and allows no new connections to be established.
  - *Pausing* the site allows no new connections to be established but leaves currently connected users connected.
  - *Starting* the site allows new connections to be established with the server.
- Property sheets can be opened for the Default NNTP Site. These property sheets can be used to configure various aspects of the NNTP service and are described in the next section.
- A new expiration policy can be created. This will be demonstrated in the walkthrough later on in this chapter.
- Local and remote virtual directories for hosting newsgroup content can be created. This will also be demonstrated in the walkthrough.
- Current expiration policies, virtual directories, and connected user sessions can be viewed.

- NNTP sites on other IIS 4.0 servers on the local LAN can be connected to and administered.

NOTE: Stopping the Default NNTP Site does not stop the NNTP service but only prevents users from connecting to the news server. To actually stop the NNTP Service, open CONTROL PANEL, SERVICES *and stop the Microsoft NNTP Service. Once stopped like this, it cannot be restarted using the Internet Service Manager but instead must be restarted using the Services program in Control Panel.*

Configuring NNTP Properties

The Default NNTP Site is configured through property sheets, similar to the WWW and FTP sites running on IIS 4.0. The Default NNTP Site Properties sheet is opened by right-clicking on the Default NNTP Site node in the Microsoft Management Console, and selecting PROPERTIES from the shortcut menu (it can also be opened using the PROPERTIES button on the rebar or the Action drop-down menu on the rebar).

The Default NNTP Site Properties sheet has six tabs that perform the following administrative functions:

- *News Site.* Configure site identification, IP addresses, TCP ports, and maximum connections and enable logging.
- *Security Accounts.* Select anonymous user and grant operator privileges.
- *NNTP Settings.* Allow and disallow client posting, limit posting size, allow interaction with other servers, specify moderator.
- *Home Directory.* Specify location of content directory, restrict posting, index news content, control log access, and enable SSL.
- *Directory Security.* Specify authentication method and filter IP addresses.
- *Groups.* Create newsgroups and edit existing newsgroup properties.

Configuring NNTP News Site Identification

The News Site tab enables you to specify the following information (Fig. 14-6):

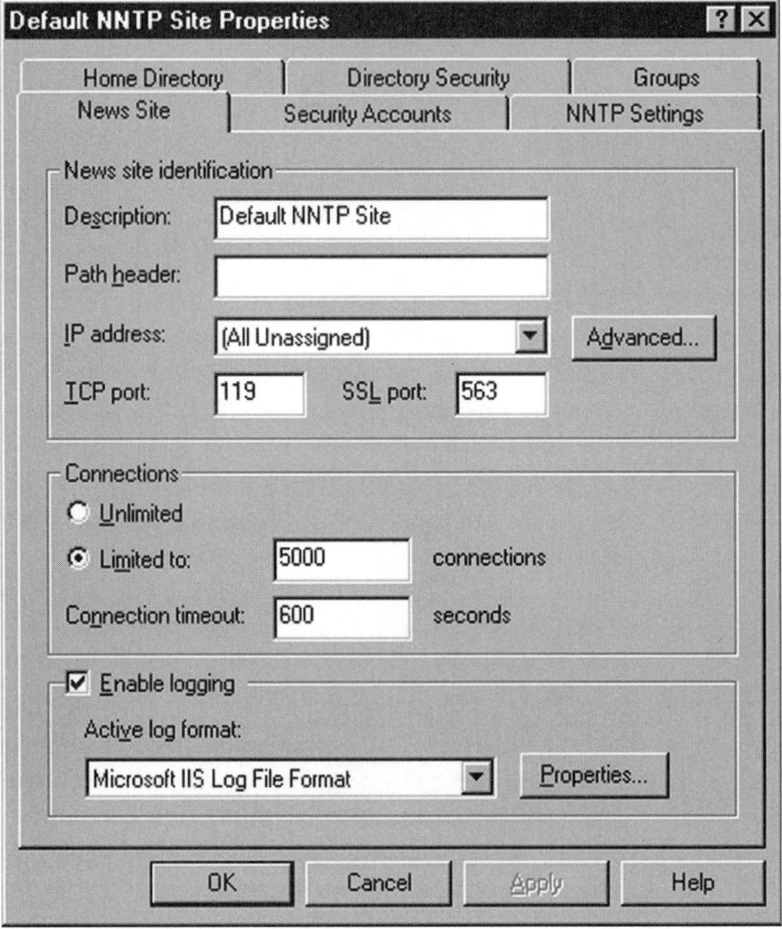

Figure 14-6 The News Site tab on the Default NNTP Site Properties sheet.

- *Description.* This will appear beside the NNTP node in the MMC.
- *Path Header.* The string specified here will be used for the Path heading in new postings (see Fig. 14-22 for an example).
- *IP Address.* Specify the IP address for the site. Click the ADVANCED button to open the Advanced Multiple News Site Configuration dialog box to specify additional IP addresses for the news server. These additional IP addresses must have already been bound to the network adapter by using the Control Panel, Network program.
- *TCP Port.* The default TCP port for NNTP is 119.

- *SSL Port.* The default TCP port for using SSL with NNTP is 563.

Configuring NNTP Connections

See Fig. 14-6. Client connections may be specified as either UNLIMITED or LIMITED TO a number the administrator may specify (the default setting is LIMITED to 5000 connections). *Connection timeout* specifies the period of inactivity after which a client's connection is terminated (the default is 600 seconds, or 10 minutes).

Configuring NNTP Logging

See Fig. 14-6. Logging may be enabled or disabled. Any of the four standard logging formats described in Chap. 3 may be selected and enabled here.

Configuring NNTP Anonymous User Account

In the Anonymous User section of the Security Accounts tab you specify the Windows NT user account used to allow Anonymous Access to the news site (Fig. 14-7). Refer to Chap. 4 for further information regarding configuring an Anonymous Access account and enabling or disabling automatic password synchronization between this property sheet and User Manager.

Configuring NNTP Site Operators

See Fig. 14-7. Grant and revoke operator privileges for administering the Default NNTP Site on the News Site Operators section of the Security Accounts tab. By default, everyone in the Administrators group on the IIS server is granted operator status for NNTP.

Configuring NNTP Posting Restrictions

See Fig. 14-8. Clearing the ALLOW CLIENT POSTING checkbox in the NNTP Settings tab prevents users from posting to the NNTP site. LIMIT POST SIZE specifies the maximum size of any individual posting submitted to the news server (the default limit is 1000 kB, or 1 MB, per posting). LIMIT

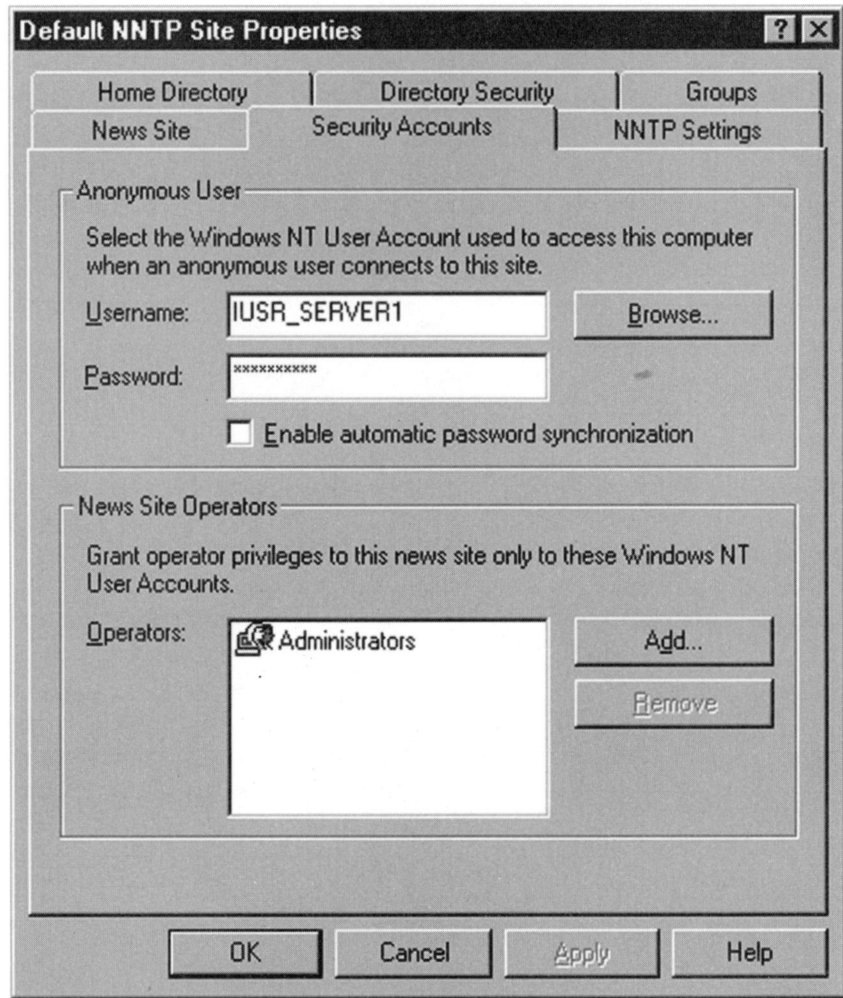

Figure 14-7 The Security Accounts tab on the Default NNTP Site Properties sheet.

CONNECTION SIZE specifies the maximum amount of posting a client may perform during a single connection (the default limit is 20 MB per connection).

Configuring NNTP Server Pulls and Control Messages

See Fig. 14-8. Checking ALLOW SERVERS TO PULL NEWS ARTICLES FROM THIS SERVER permits other news servers to pull news feeds from this server.

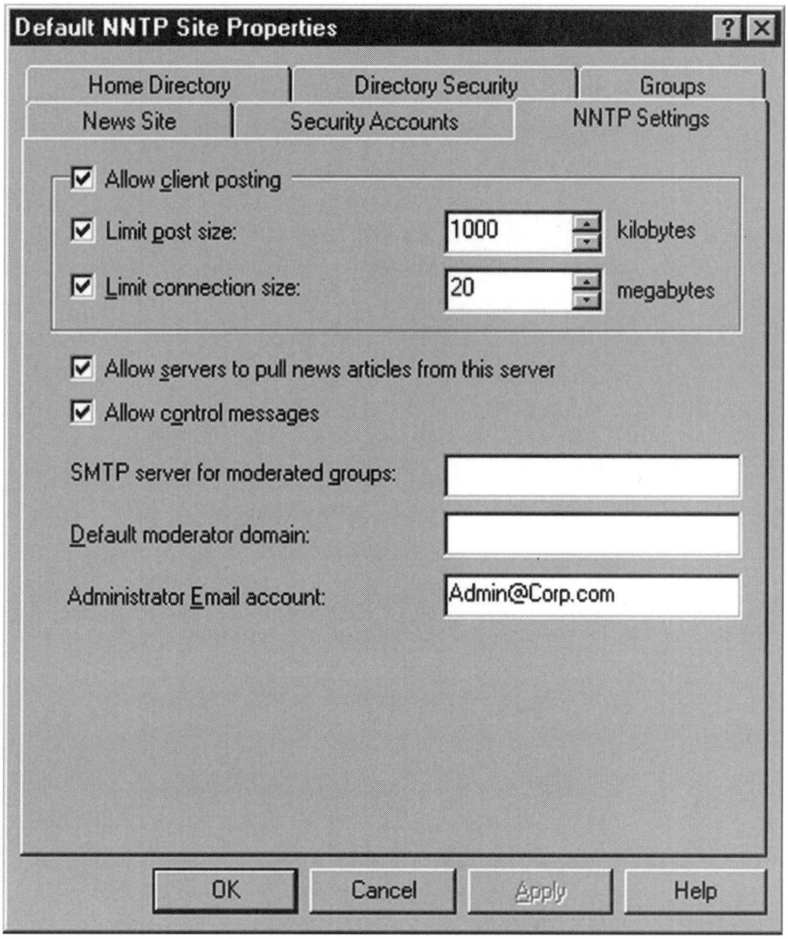

Figure 14-8
The NNTP Settings tab on the Default NNTP Site Properties sheet.

Checking ALLOW CONTROL MESSAGES permits both clients and servers to send control messages to the news server. *Control messages* direct the NNTP service to perform specific actions such as

- Deleting an article from a newsgroup
- Creating a new newsgroup
- Deleting an existing newsgroup

These messages are typically sent by other news servers but can also be used by hackers to target the news server. Refer to the Option Pack online documentation for further information about how to secure your news server against attack through use of control messages.

Configuring NNTP Moderated Newsgroups

Moderated newsgroups are groups where articles that are submitted are not posted immediately but are first sent to a newsgroup moderator, who either approves (and posts) them or rejects (and discards) them. Enabling moderated newsgroups requires an SMTP server for sending submitted articles directly to the moderator of the group. The *SMTP server for moderated groups* must be specified on this property sheet by using its DNS name, i.e., `mail.mycorpinc.com` (Fig. 14-8).

The *Default moderator domain* specifies the email address to which postings to a moderated news group are sent if there is no specific moderator assigned to the newsgroup. For example, if the name of the moderated newsgroup is

```
alt.talk.canola.moderated
```

and the default moderator domain is specified as

```
canolacorp.com
```

then submitted messages will be forwarded to the following email address:

```
alt.talk.canola.moderated@canolacorp.com
```

If for any reason a submission cannot be delivered to the moderator of the newsgroup, a *Non-Delivery Report (NDR)* will be sent to the Default NNTP Site administrator as specified by the *Administrator Email account* field.

Configuring NNTP Home Directory Properties

In the Home Directory Properties section of the Home Directory tab you specify the location of the home directory where newsgroup articles will be stored (Fig. 14-9). This directory must reside on an NTFS volume, but it can be either local or remote. The default home directory is specified by the local path

```
C:\InetPub\nntpfile\root\
```

Figure 14-9
The Home Directory tab on the Default NNTP Site Properties sheet.

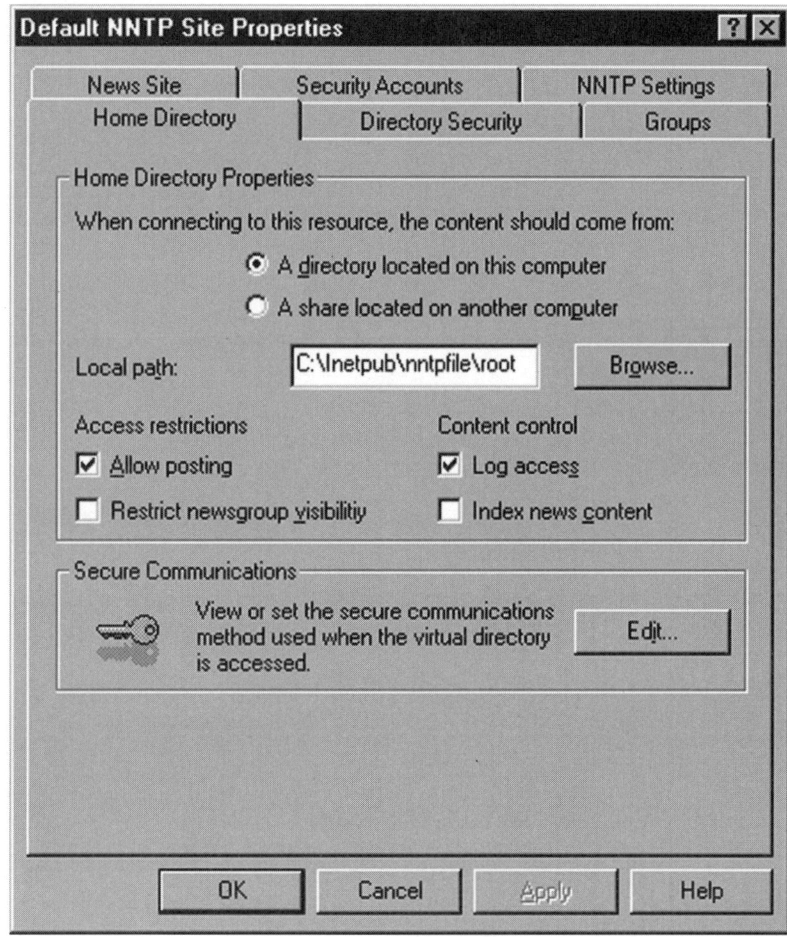

If a remote directory is selected, it must be specified as a valid UNC path. User credentials must also be specified to allow access to the share. Newsgroup content can also be mapped to virtual directories, as illustrated in the walkthrough later in this chapter.

The following *Access restrictions* may be specified regarding the NNTP home directory:

- ALLOW POSTING permits clients to post to newsgroups stored in this directory.
- RESTRICT NEWSGROUP VISIBILITY allows only users who have proper access permissions to view newsgroups located in this directory. This means that

If RESTRICT NEWSGROUP VISIBILITY is *checked* but the client does not have access permissions on the newsgroups, the client will *not* be able to retrieve the list of newsgroups from this server.

If RESTRICT NEWSGROUP VISIBILITY is *unchecked* and the client does not have access permissions on the newsgroups, the client *will* be able to retrieve the list of newsgroups from this server but will *not* be able to obtain any lists of articles for the newsgroups or read any of the articles.

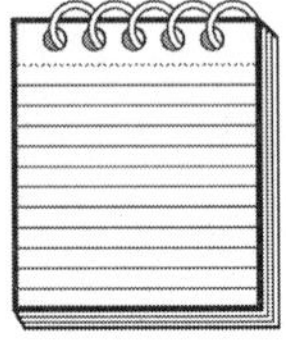

NOTE: *If the RESTRICT NEWSGROUP VISIBILITY option is checked, a performance drop will occur on the news server. This option should not be checked if anonymous access is allowed to your news server.*

In addition, the following *Content control* settings may be configured for this directory:

- LOG ACCESS enables the NNTP service to log access by individual clients to the newsgroups. ENABLE LOGGING must first be selected on the News Site tab.
- INDEX NEWS CONTENT allows message properties and content to be indexed by Index Server for full-text searching of newsgroup articles.

Configuring NNTP Secure Communications

See Fig. 14-9. To enable SSL on the Default NNTP Site, click the EDIT button to open the Secure Communications dialog box. Refer to Chap. 12 to find out more about how to set up SSL on IIS 4.0.

Configuring NNTP Password Authentication Method

See Fig. 14-10. To modify the password authentication method for the site, click the EDIT button to open the Password Authentication Method dialog box. Select any combination of the following options for authentication schemes:

- *Anonymous Access.* No username or password is required to access the news server.

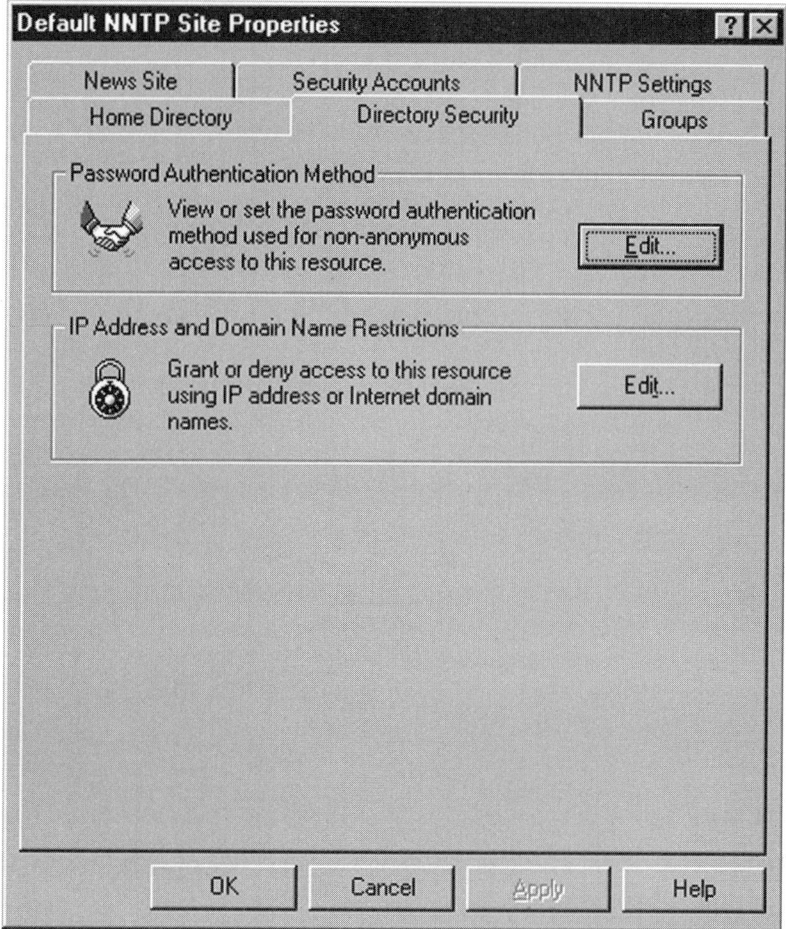

Figure 14-10 The Directory Security tab on the Default NNTP Site Properties sheet.

- *Basic Authentication.* Users must input a valid username and password to enter the site. These credentials are sent as clear text (actually unencoded text) over the network. This method makes use of the AUTHINFO standard NNTP extension.
- *Windows NT Challenge/Response.* Encrypted transmission of valid NT account credentials is used. This requires *Microsoft Mail and News (IE 3.02)* or *Microsoft Outlook Express (IE 4.01)* as the news client.
- *Enable SSL Client Authentication.* Refer to Chap. 12 for more information on enabling SSL. SSL is usually used together with Basic Authentication to provide secure encrypted authentication and data transmission.

Configuring NNTP IP Address and Domain Name Restrictions

Use the IP Address and Domain Name Restrictions option to grant or deny access to your Default NNTP Site by IP address or by domain name (Fig. 14-10). See Chap. 3 for more information on how to accomplish this.

Configuring NNTP Newsgroups

See Fig. 14-11. Select the CREATE NEW NEWSGROUP button in the Groups tab to create a new newsgroup. To edit an existing newsgroup, select the

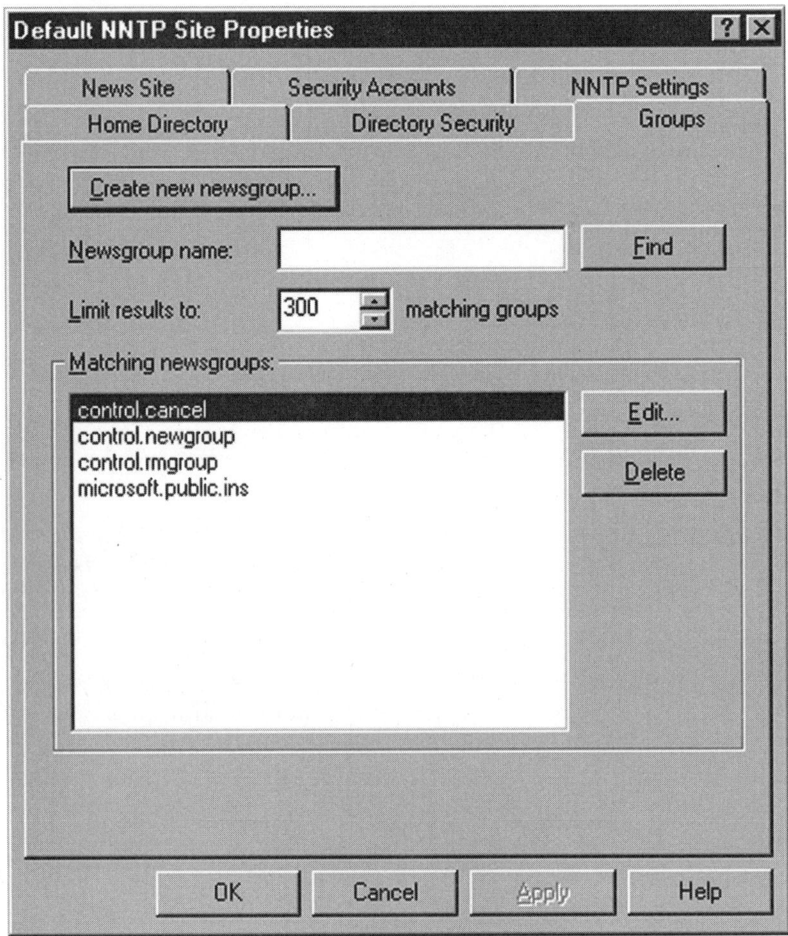

Figure 14-11 The Groups tab on the Default NNTP Site Properties sheet.

group in the *Matching newsgroups* listbox, or enter a portion of the group's name in the *Newsgroup name* field and click FIND to locate the group in the listbox. Select the group when you find it and click EDIT. Creating a new newsgroup will be demonstrated below.

Walkthrough: Creating and Administering a Newsgroup

The following walkthrough will take you through the creation, testing, and administration of a newsgroup. Modify settings as needed to match the particular configuration of your IIS setup.

Creating a New Newsgroup

Right-click on the Default NNTP Site node in the MMC and select PROPERTIES to open the Default NNTP Site Properties sheet. Select the Groups tab and click CREATE NEW NEWSGROUP to open the Newsgroup Properties dialog box (Fig. 14-12).

Specify a name for your new newsgroup. The name we have chosen is

```
local.buysell.computers
```

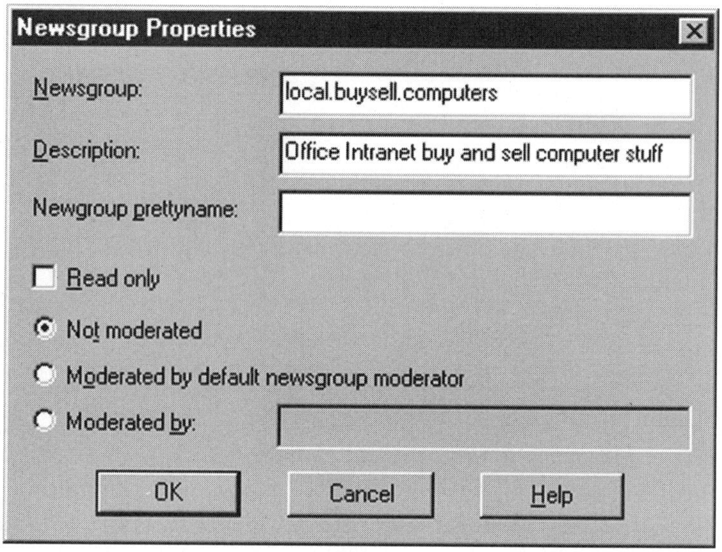

Figure 14-12 Specifying the properties of your new newsgroup.

since this will be a newsgroup on a local intranet news server. Leave the other settings unchanged.

Click OK to close the Newsgroup Properties dialog box. Notice that the new newsgroup is now listed in the listbox on the Groups tab of the Default NNTP Site Properties sheet (Fig. 14-13). Click OK to close the Default NNTP Site Properties sheet.

The NNTP service has now created the following directory structure to store messages posted to the new newsgroup (Fig. 14-14):

- `C:\InetPub\nntpfile\root\local\`
- `C:\InetPub\nntpfile\root\local\buysell\`
- `C:\InetPub\nntpfile\root\local\buysell\computers\`

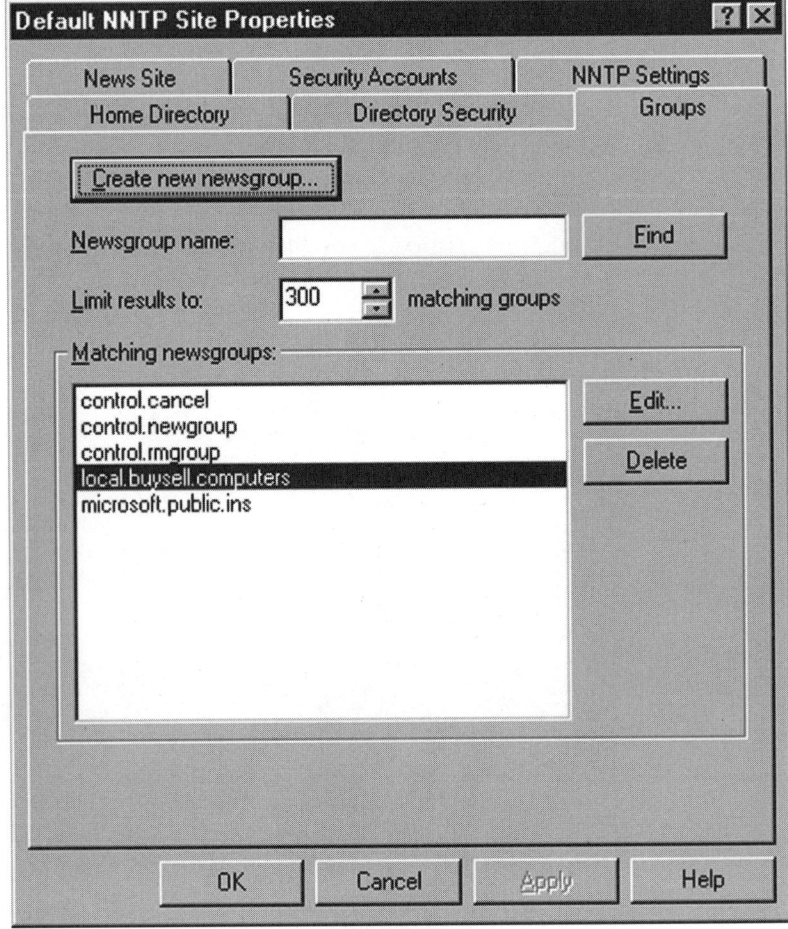

Figure 14-13 The newsgroup `local.buysell.computers` has been created.

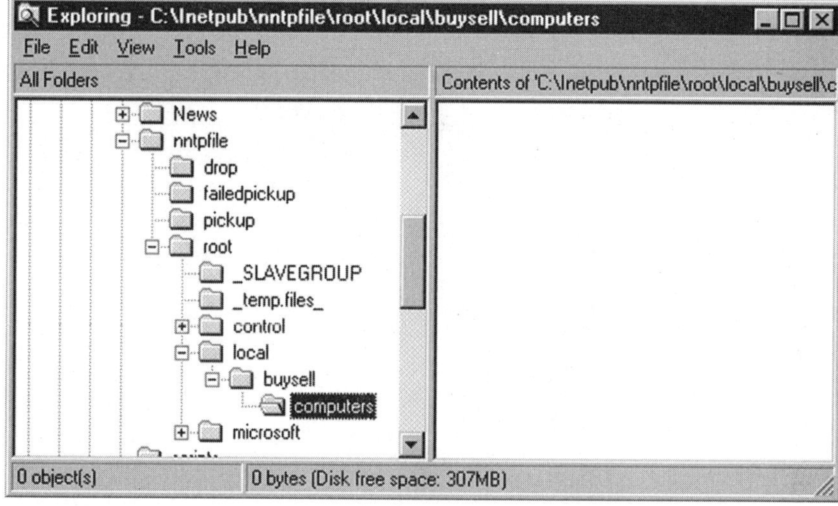

Figure 14-14 Folders created to store messages for the group `local.buy-sell.computers`.

Figure 14-14 shows us that there is no content yet in the newsgroup. Our next job will be to post a message to the group.

Posting to a Newsgroup Using Outlook Express

Outlook Express is the new Internet mail and news client that comes with Internet Explorer 4.01. We will assume that Outlook Express has already been configured for SMTP/POP3 mail and only needs to be configured for accessing newsgroups.

Open Outlook Express on the local machine (the news server) by double-clicking on its icon on your desktop. Select TOOLS, ACCOUNTS from the menu bar to open the Internet Accounts dialog box.

Select ADD, NEWS to open the Internet Connection Wizard (Fig. 14-15). This wizard will lead us through the steps of configuring our news client to connect to the Default NNTP Site on our local news server.

Begin by entering your name (we used Charlie Smith).

Click NEXT and enter in your email address (we used `charlie@mycorpinc.com`).

Click NEXT. The next screen is called Internet News Server Name. Enter your news server's name in the textbox (we entered server1).

Click NEXT and specify a friendly name for the news server account. We chose *News Server at MyCorp Inc.* as our friendly name.

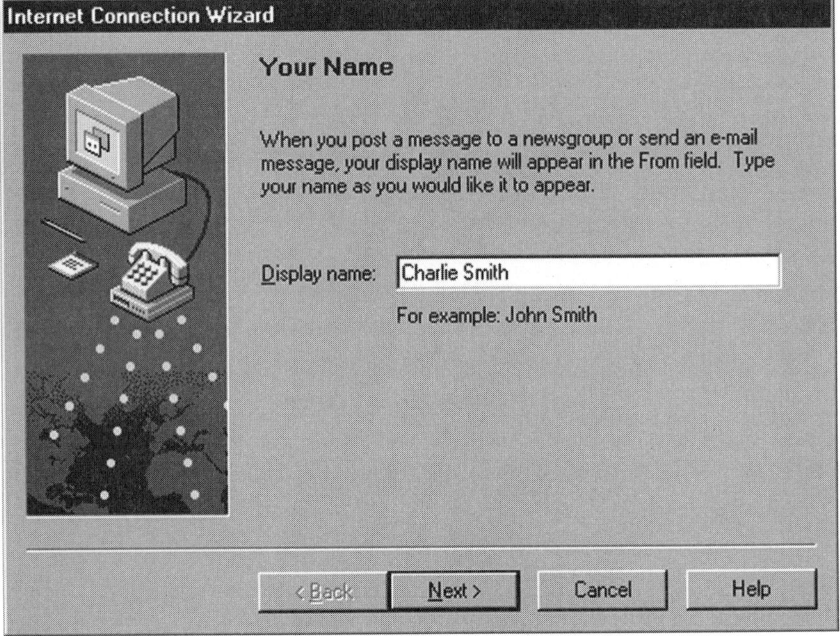

Figure 14-15
The Internet Connection Wizard.

Click NEXT and choose your type of connection (Fig. 14-16). As we are using our news server in a corporate LAN setting for this example, we chose CONNECT USING MY LOCAL AREA NETWORK (LAN).

Click FINISH on the Congratulations screen to close the wizard and finish configuring Outlook Express to connect to your news server.

Figure 14-17 shows the News tab on the Internet Accounts dialog box, showing that the new news server account has been created. To modify news server account settings, select NEWS SERVER AT MYCORP INC. and click EDIT to open the News Server at MyCorp Inc Properties sheet. Accessing the four tabs on this sheet allows us to modify settings selected through the wizard, plus additional settings on the Advanced tab such as

- Requiring SSL for logging onto the news server
- Modifying the SSL port number to match that of the server
- Configuring server timeouts
- Using newsgroup descriptions
- Breaking apart messages longer than a given length

Close the Internet Accounts dialog box. You are now prompted to download a list of newsgroups from the news server (Fig. 14-18). Click YES

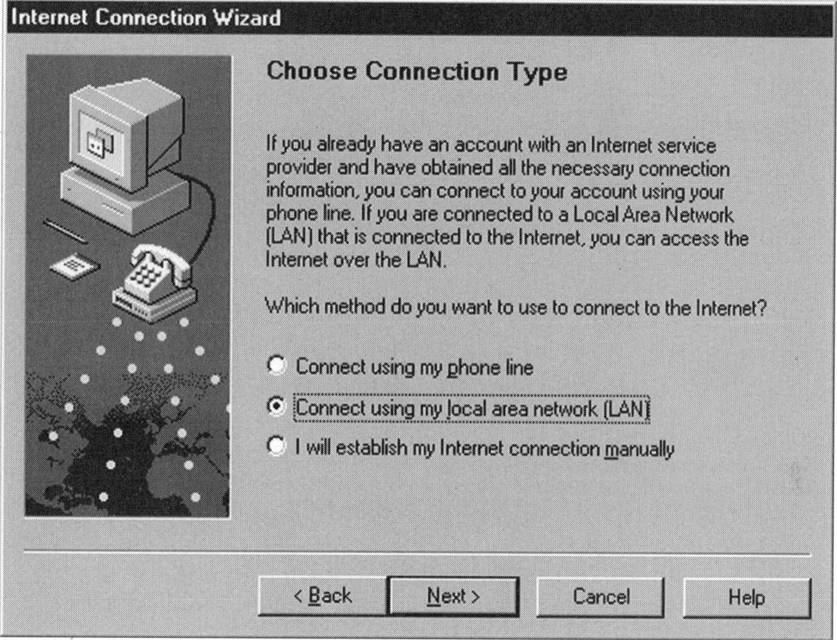

Figure 14-16 Choose connection type for connecting to your news server.

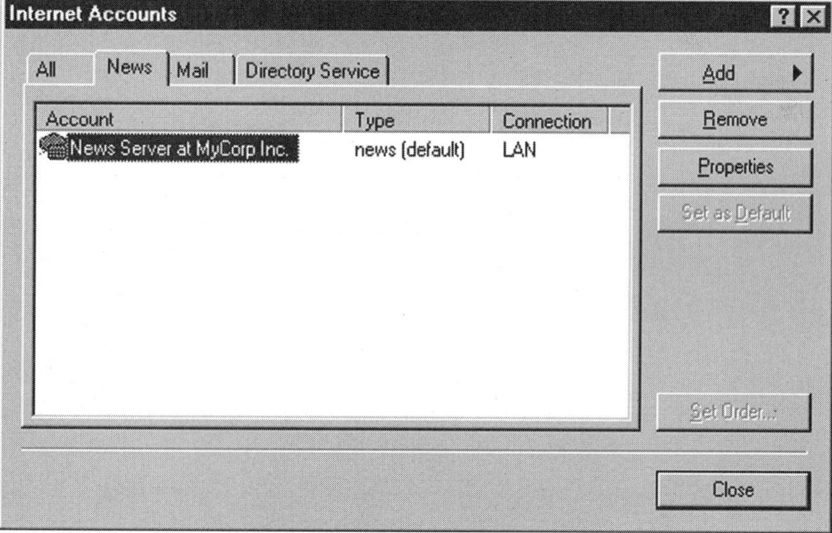

Figure 14-17 The new news server account has been created on the client.

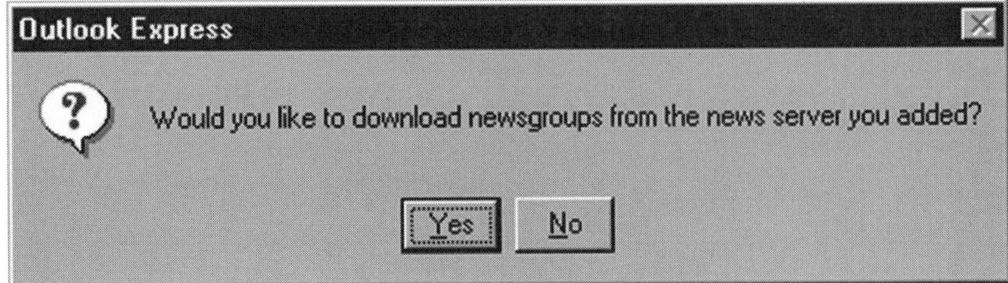

Figure 14-18 Downloading a list of newsgroups to your client newsreader.

and a message will appear indicating that a list of newsgroups from server1 is being downloaded.

A dialog box called Newsgroups will now appear, listing all the newsgroups on server1 that can be downloaded (Fig. 14-19). Double-click on the group

```
local.buysell.computers
```

to subscribe to the new group.

Note the other groups already there. The group

```
microsoft.public.ins
```

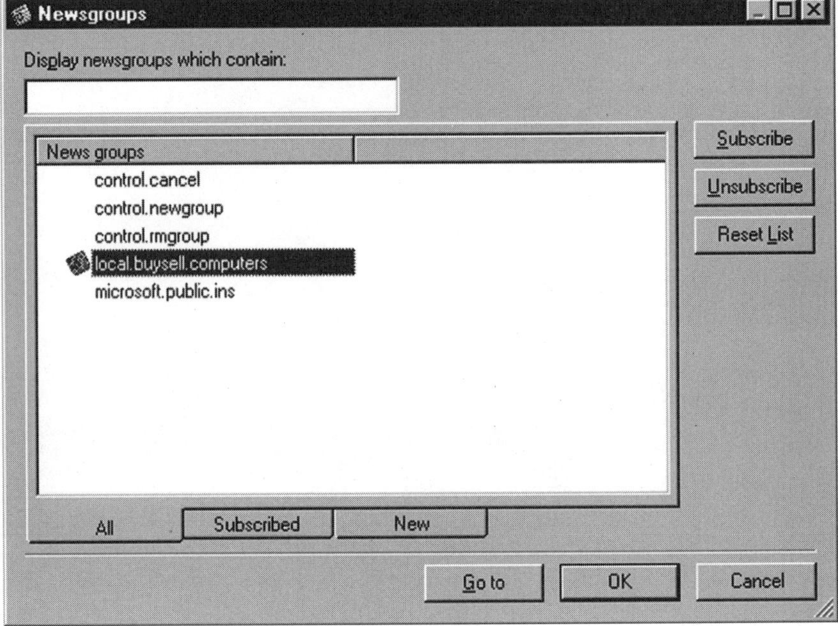

Figure 14-19 List of newsgroups available on the news server.

contains a welcome message. The other groups are `control` groups that handle control messages sent to the server by other news servers.

Select the newly created group and click GO TO in order to open the group in Outlook Express. Post a test message to your new newsgroup and then open it for reading in Outlook Express (Fig. 14-20). Continue making a few additional postings, replying to existing postings, or starting new threads.

Open Windows Explorer and view the folder containing the posted messages for the new newsgroup (Fig. 14-21). This folder is located at

```
C:InetPub\nntpfile\root\local\buysell\computers\
```

Notice the new files in this folder:

- `0.xix` is a file that lists the subjects of the posted messages.
- `1000000.nws` and similarly named files are individual messages posted to the news server.

These `.nws` files are plain ASCII text files that can be opened and examined using Notepad (see Fig. 14-22 for an example). The `.nws` files consist of a group of headers followed by the body of the message.

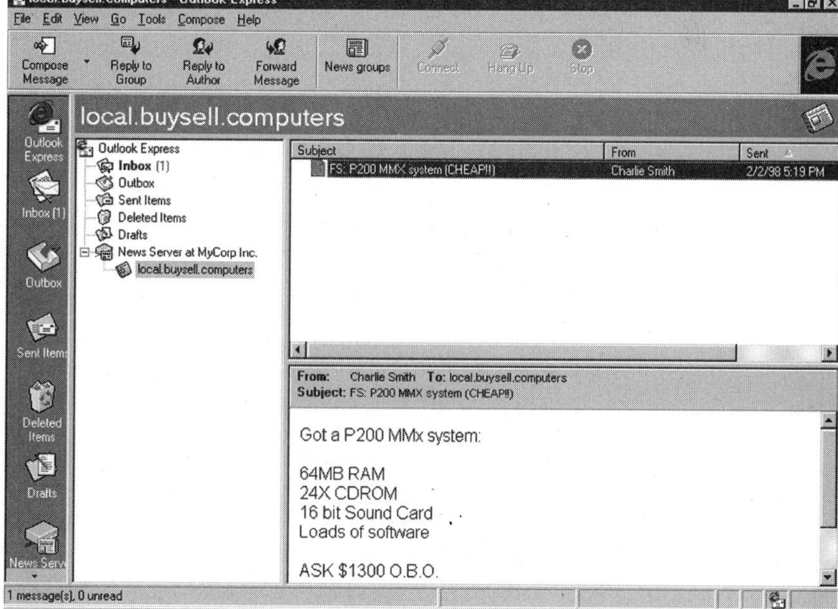

Figure 14-20
Reading a posted message in Outlook Express.

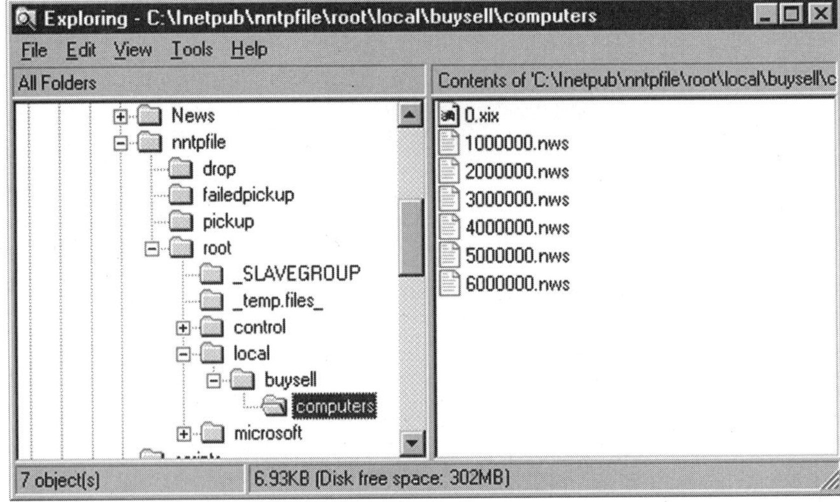

Figure 14-21 News files created in the content directory for `local.buy-sell.computers`.

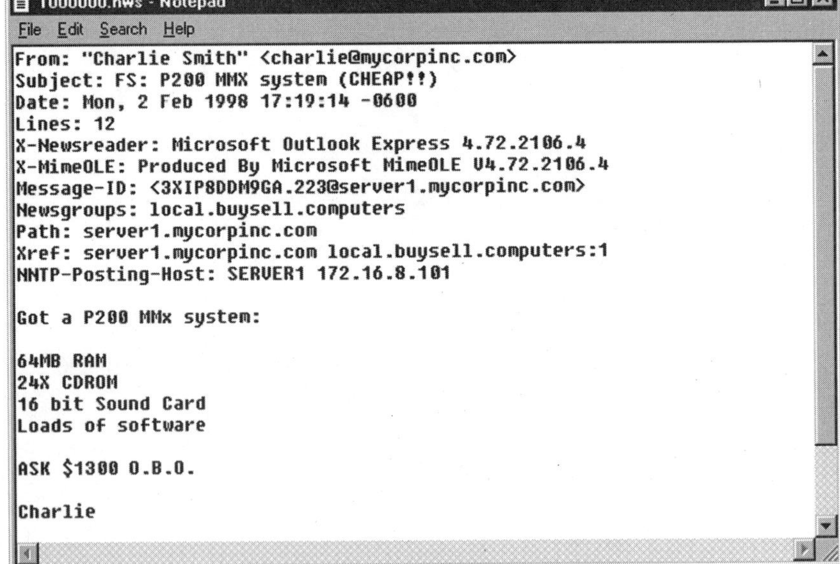

Figure 14-22 Inside a newsgroup posting `.nws` file.

Setting a Newsgroup Expiration Policy

We will next configure an expiration policy for the newly created newsgroup. Return to the Microsoft Management Console, expand the Default NNTP Site node in the scope pane, and select the Expiration Policies icon in the scope pane. Right-click on the Expiration Policies

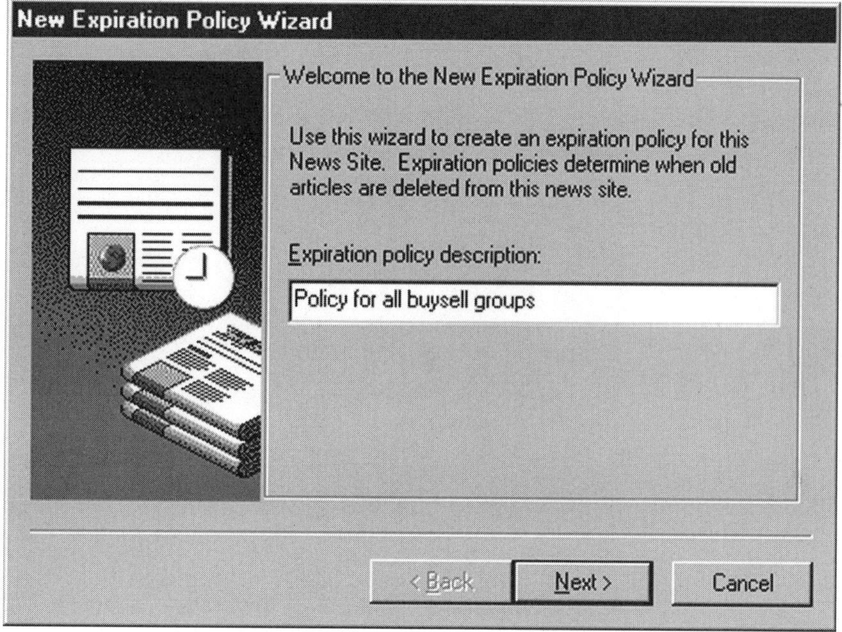

Figure 14-23 The New Expiration Policy Wizard.

node and select NEW, EXPIRATION POLICY. This will start the New Expiration Policy Wizard (Fig. 14-23).

Enter a description for the new expiration policy.

Click NEXT and enter a wildcard character string to find the name of the newsgroup(s) to which you want the expiration policy to apply.

Click NEXT and specify whether all newsgroups on this site are to be affected by the policy, or only selected newsgroups will be affected.

Click NEXT and configure when articles should be deleted (Fig. 14-24). Deletion criteria include

- *Age.* Articles older than a given setting are retired from the news server's store.
- *Size.* When the entire newsgroup reaches a specified size, older articles are expired in favor of new ones.

The result of creating this expiry policy is shown in the results pane of the MMC (Fig. 14-25). If we need to edit the properties of the expiration policy we have created, simply double-click on the *Policy for all buysell groups* node in the results pane, and the Policy for all buysell groups Properties sheet appears (Fig. 14-26). Use this property sheet to reconfigure settings entered during running of the wizard.

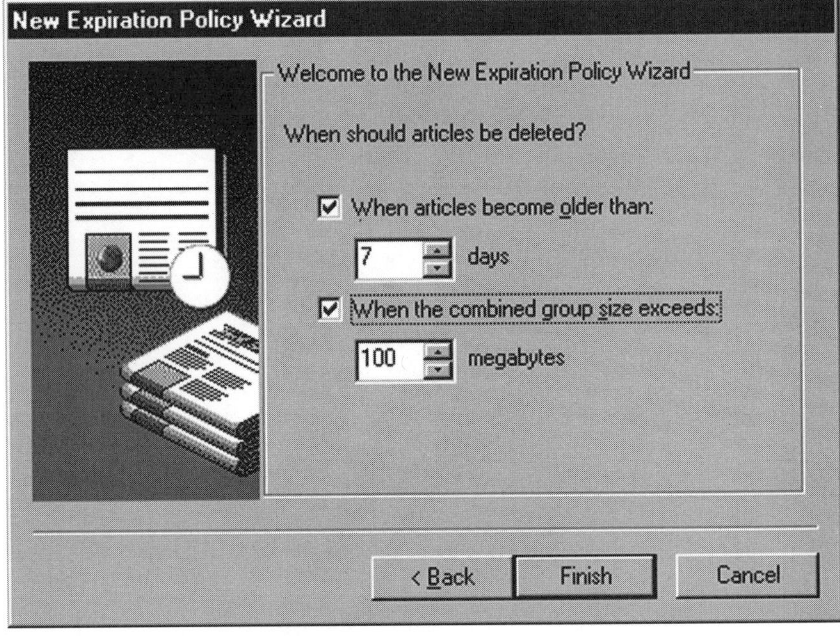

Figure 14-24 Configuring deletion time and size for a newsgroup.

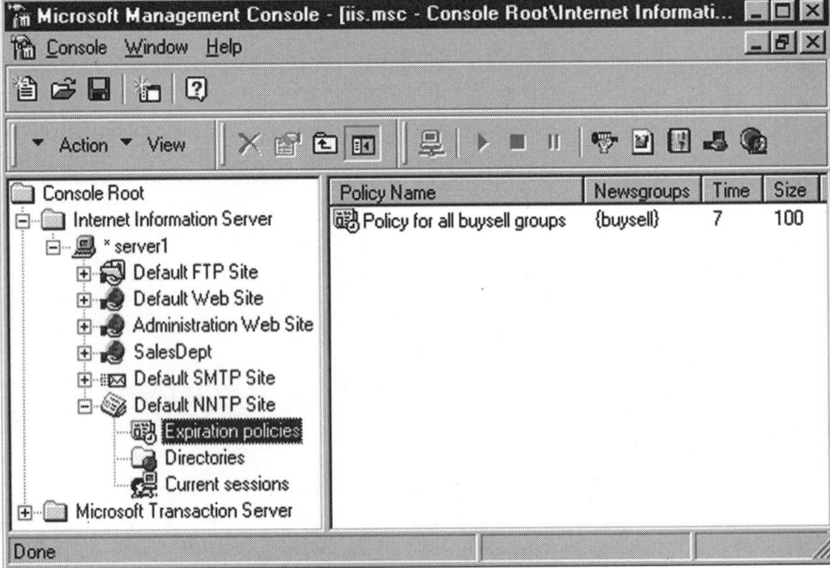

Figure 14-25 A new expiration policy has been created.

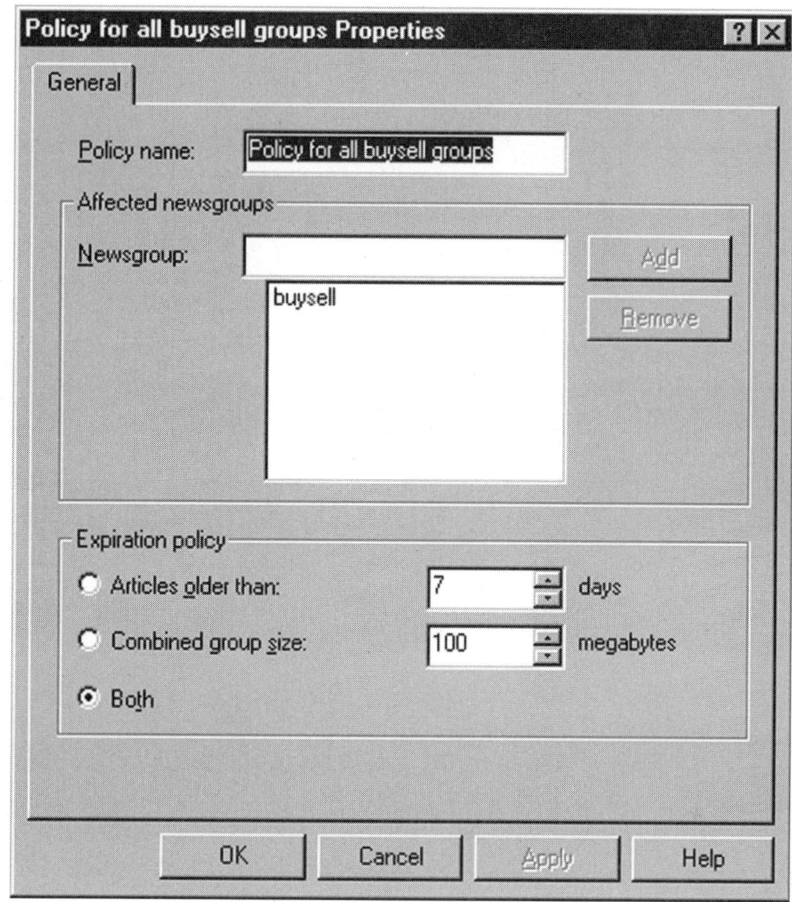

Figure 14-26 Expiration policy properties for the newly created expiration policy.

Mapping a Newsgroup's Home Directory to a Virtual Directory

Finally, we will conclude by creating a new newsgroup and mapping its home directory to the local path

```
D:\talkstuff
```

Begin by creating a new newsgroup called

```
local.talk.restaurants
```

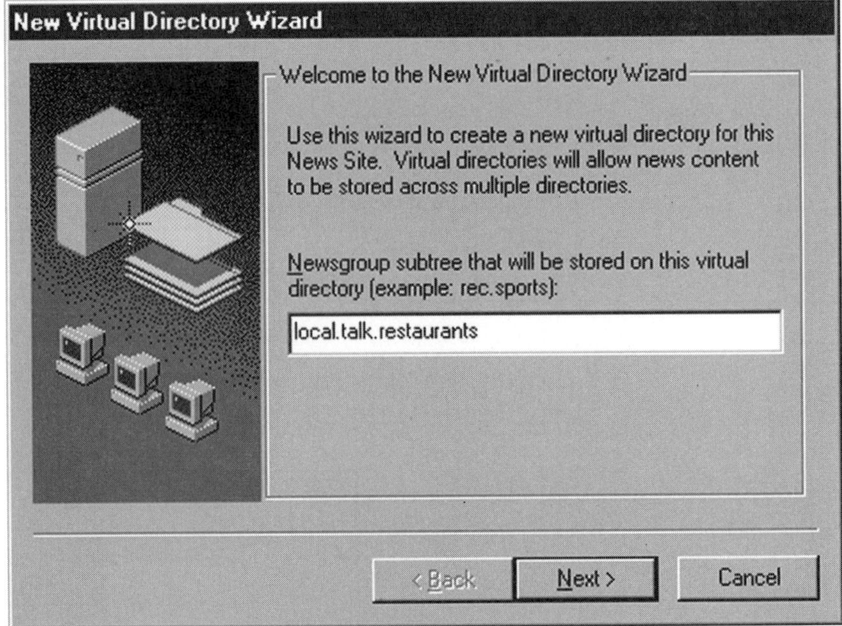

Figure 14-27 Creating a new virtual directory for newsgroup content.

Right-click on the Directories node under the Default NNTP Site node in the scope pane of the MMC and select NEW, VIRTUAL DIRECTORY to open the New Virtual Directory Wizard (Fig. 14-27).

Enter `local.talk.restaurants` in the text field.

Click NEXT and enter the physical path to the folder where the newsgroup content will be stored (Fig. 14-28). If this was to be a remote virtual directory (instead of a local one), you would enter the UNC path to the folder here. Then in the next screen you would be required to specify a Windows NT user account that can be used to grant access to the newsgroup's content. Because we are doing a local virtual directory, no user account is necessary.

Click FINISH to create the new virtual directory.

Select the Directories node under the Default NNTP Site node in the scope pane of the MMC, and you can view the new virtual directory in the results pane (Fig. 14-29). To make changes to the virtual directory settings, simply double-click the `local.talk` node in the results pane and the Local.talk Properties sheet will appear (Fig. 14-30). This property sheet allows us to modify the settings selected through the wizard.

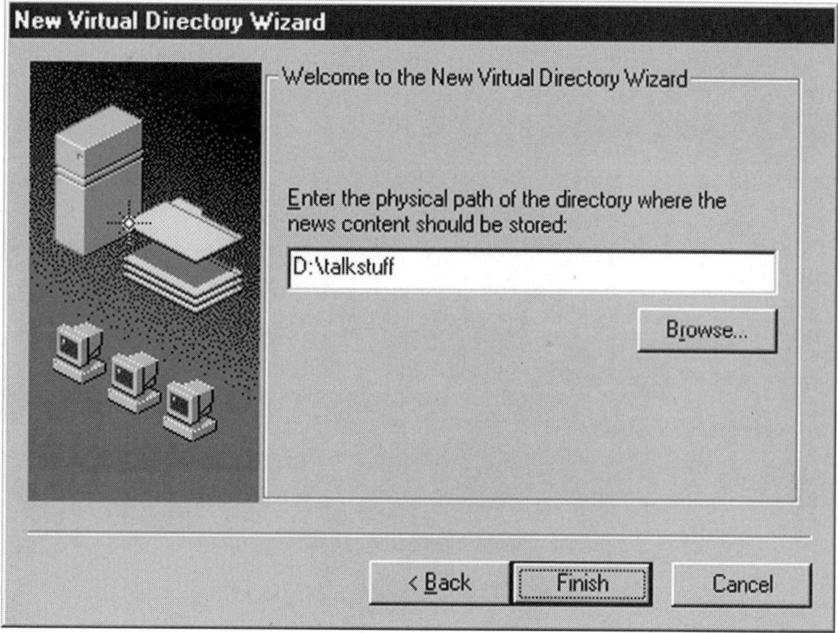

Figure 14-28 Specifying the physical path to be mapped to the virtual directory.

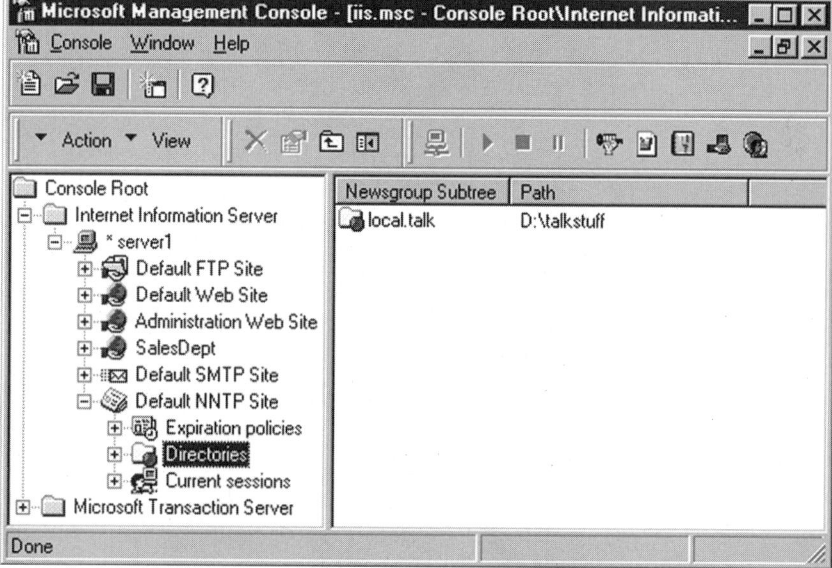

Figure 14-29 The new virtual directory is listed in the results pane.

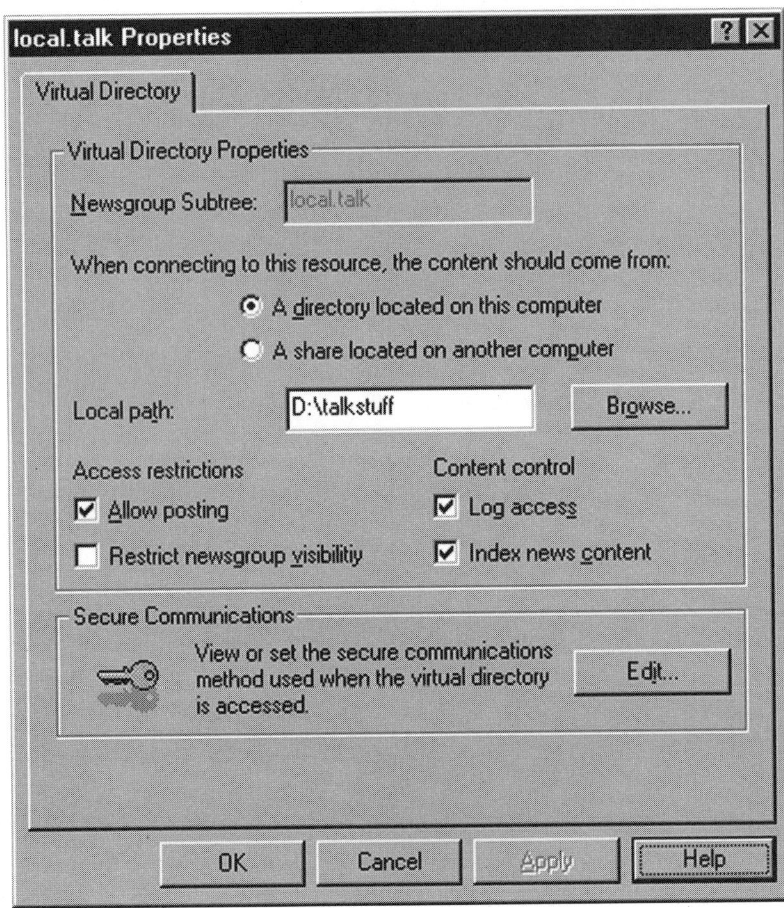

Figure 14-30 Editing the virtual directory properties.

Monitoring and Tuning NNTP Service Performance

The performance of the NNTP service on IIS 4.0 can be monitored using the following tools:

- *Event Viewer.* The NNTP service logs significant events to the Windows NT System Log. Look for events whose source is NNTPSVC.
- *IIS Logs.* View the IIS logs in a text editor or import them into Site Server Express to generate reports of NNTP site usage.

- *Performance Monitor.* The NNTP service includes the performance monitor *NNTP Server* and *NNTP Commands* objects with a number of counters that may be monitored for these objects.

You should monitor the standard counters for detecting memory, processor, disk, and network bottlenecks in addition to specific NNTP counters. In particular, you should set a performance monitor alert for low disk space on the volume where the `nntpfile` directory is located.

Some of the more important NNTP performance counters to watch are

NNTP Server: Bytes Total/sec, the total rate of bytes transferred by the NNTP service.

NNTP Server: Current Connections, the number of connections to the NNTP server.

NNTP Commands: Logon Failures/sec, the number of logons per second that have failed. If your server is connected to the Internet, a high value for this counter could indicate a possible attempt to hack into your system.

NNTP Server: Maximum Connections, the maximum number of simultaneous connections to the NNTP server. This counter should be *much less* than the setting for LIMITED TO on the News Site tab of the Default NNTP Site Properties sheet.

The NNTP service may require the maintenance action of *rebuilding the NNTP service* under the following circumstances:

- A disk failure causes a portion of the news files to be lost.
- You manually delete portions of the news files in order to free up resources.
- Access to messages in newsgroups becomes erratic.
- An error message is written to the System log indicating that you should rebuild the NNTP service.

Rebuilding the NNTP service reconstructs the index and hash files and can be accomplished by the following steps: STOP the Default NNTP Site using the MMC. Then right-click on the Default NNTP Site node and select TASK, REBUILD SERVER from the shortcut menu to open the Rebuild News Server dialog box (Fig. 14-31). Select the rebuild mode:

- *Standard* mode rebuilds only `group.lst`.
- *Medium* mode rebuilds files that are found to have errors.

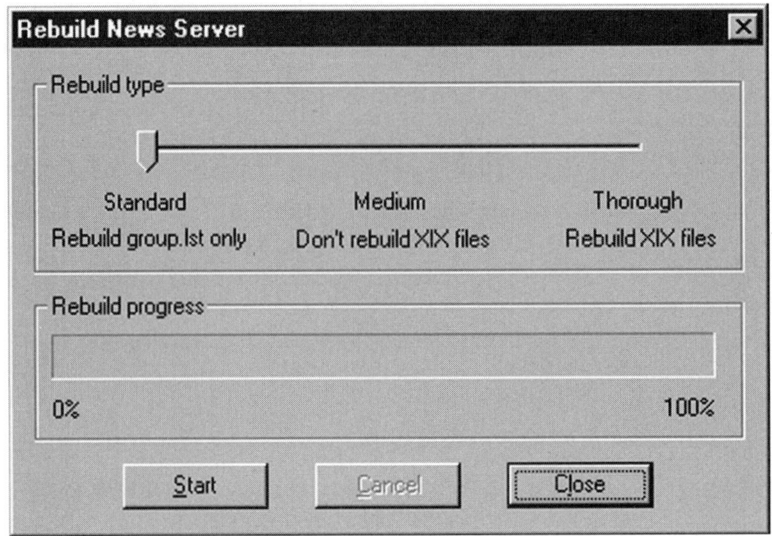

Figure 14-31 Rebuilding the Microsoft NNTP service.

- *Thorough* mode rebuilds all files including the `.xix` files.

When rebuilding is complete, START the Default NNTP Site again.

SUMMARY

Microsoft NNTP Service may be administered and configured using the Internet Service Manager, the Internet Service Manager (HTML), and the Windows Scripting Host. Simple wizards guide administrators through the process of creating and managing newsgroups, expiration policies, and virtual directories for storing newsgroup content.

FOR MORE INFORMATION

Microsoft Web Site Search the Microsoft Web site for the keyword "NNTP" to find more information about this service.

TechNet Search the TechNet knowledge base for articles relating to the NNTP service.

CHAPTER 15

Administering Active Server Pages with Transaction Server

Introduction

Using Active Server Pages (ASPs), developers can create dynamic Web applications incorporating HTML, scripts, and ActiveX components. Microsoft Transaction Server (MTS) adds transactional functionality to Active Server Pages, enabling developers to build transactional client-server Web applications that are reliable and scalable. After completing this chapter, administrators will be able to

- Understand the Active Server Pages model compared with CGI
- Create simple Active Server Pages using VBScript
- Understand the basic concept of a transaction
- Know the features of Microsoft Transaction Server 2.0
- Explain how Active Server Pages integrate with Transaction Server

This chapter provides only a brief introduction to Web application development using Active Server Pages and Microsoft Transaction Server. A full treatment of the subject would require a book of its own, and would be targeted more at a developer audience than network and system administrators.

Understanding Active Server Pages

Traditionally, the usual way of extending the functionality of Web servers has been to use the *Common Gateway Interface (CGI)*. CGI is a specification describing how a Web server communicates with gateway applications, which are server-side programs that can receive data from a client browser, process it, and return it to the client. Gateway programs can be written in high-level programming languages like C++ but are more often written in interpreted scripting languages like *Practical Extraction and Report Language (Perl)*. The CGI specification defines how data can be passed from the client browser to the Web server using URL query strings, extra URL path information, or HTTP POST method. Similarly, the CGI specification defines how data is passed from the server to the gateway application using command-line arguments, standard input, or environment variables.

CGI is widely implemented in the Web server community, primarily because Perl is a relatively easy scripting language to learn. Many webmasters earned their stripes by learning how to write Perl scripts to handle HTML forms, monitor hit counts, perform simple search functions, query databases, and so on. CGI suffers from an inherent defect, though: the gateway program must be started as a separate process every time it is referenced by the server. The result is that CGI tends to be slow and has high server overhead: every time a CGI form handler is invoked, the Perl interpreter has to be loaded into memory, the Perl script receives the data through the CGI and processes it, and the Perl interpreter is unloaded again.

A method that overcomes some of the weaknesses of CGI is to use custom gateway *application programming interfaces (APIs)* such as Microsoft's ISAPI and Netscape's NSAPI. Gateway applications written using these APIs tend to be much faster than CGI using Perl scripts, primarily because the processing is performed by compiled executables, or DLLs, written in C++ programming language. However, the negative side of using these APIs is that it requires the developer to know a high-level programming language like C++, and the binary executable is not portable across different server platforms but must be recompiled for each Web server.

To overcome these problems, Microsoft developed the Active Server Pages model, which incorporates the flexibility of scripts, the ease of Visual Basic, and the power of compiled ActiveX server components for the creation of powerful, dynamic Web-based applications.

What Are Active Server Pages?

Active Server Pages (ASPs) are a methodology for combining together HTML with the following three additional elements:

- *ASP scripts:* VBScript, JScript, and other scripts executed on the server
- *ASP objects,* built-in and installable server-side programming objects with methods and properties
- *ASP components,* written in any programming language to extend server functionality

Active Server Pages are ASCII text files saved with the extension `.asp` and stored on the Web server in a virtual directory that must have both read and script (or execute) access enabled.

The implementation of Active Server Pages on IIS 4.0 provide developers with tools for

- Creating dynamic Web content that responds to user input.
- Database connectivity for integrating an HTML front end with a back-end relational ODBC-compliant database.
- Building scalable Web applications using a component-based programming architecture.
- Optionally running Web applications in a separate address space, thus minimizing the impact on the server should the application fail.

Using Active Server Page Scripts

Active Server Page scripts are scripts written in any ActiveX scripting language and contained on an Active Server Page. The IIS 4.0 implementation of Active Server Pages includes a scripting engine that supports out of the box the following scripting languages:

- *Visual Basic Script (VBScript),* a subset of the Microsoft Visual Basic programming language. This is the default ASP scripting language.
- *Java Script (JScript),* supported by most browsers. JScript is not a subset of the Java programming language, but is a separate scripting language.

In addition, ActiveX scripting engines may be installed on IIS 4.0 for other scripting languages such as Perl and REXX.

ASP scripts run on the server, not the client. Typically, an ASP will be invoked as follows (Fig. 15-1):

- A client browser tries to access an ASP directly or accesses an HTML page that invokes the ASP as a form or event handler.
- The ASP is executed on the server and generates a plain HTML response page that is returned to the client.
- The client displays the HTML response page returned from the server.

The advantages of running scripts on the server include

1. Harnessing the processing power of the server
2. Making use of application libraries and DLLs on the server
3. Returning to the client a plain HTML file that is equally acceptable to all clients (hence no worries about client compatibility)

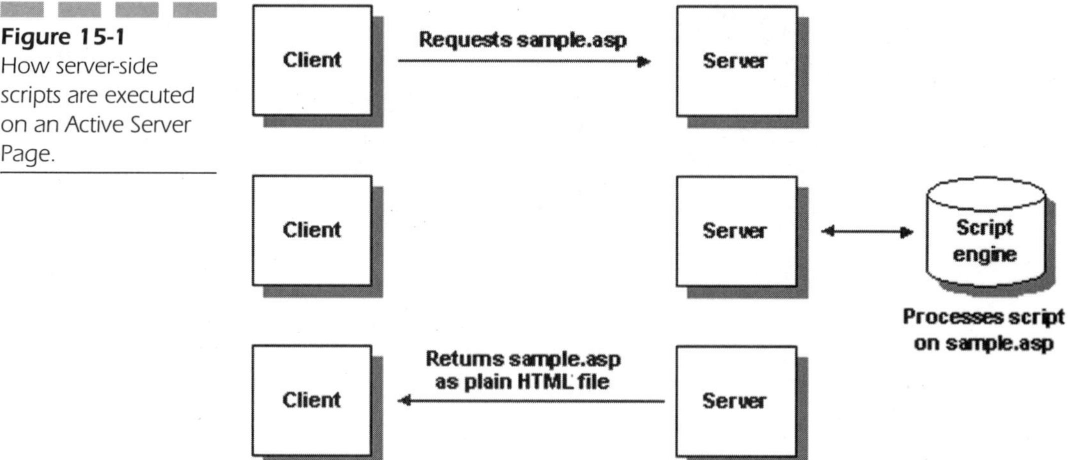

Figure 15-1 How server-side scripts are executed on an Active Server Page.

A few simple examples will illustrate the power and simplicity of the Active Server Pages methodology. For the following examples, a virtual directory `aspstuff` was created on the Default Web Site to contain the ASPs and corresponding HTML files.

EXAMPLE 1: A SIMPLE HTML FORM WITH AN ASP FORM HANDLER

The first example is a simple Web page, `one.htm`, that creates an HTML form asking the user to submit the user's name. When the user clicks the SUBMIT button on the page, the data submitted is passed to the Active Server Page `one.asp` that serves as a form handler for the HTML form. The script on `one.asp` is executed on the server, and the server returns the file `one.asp` as a plain HTML response, greeting the user.

Here is the code for `one.htm`:

```
<html>
<head><title>ASP Sample 1</title></head>
<body bgcolor = white>

<h1>ASP Sample 1</h1>
<hr>
Please enter your name and I will greet you!
<form method = post action = one.asp>
<input type = text name = "person">
<input type = submit>
</form>
```

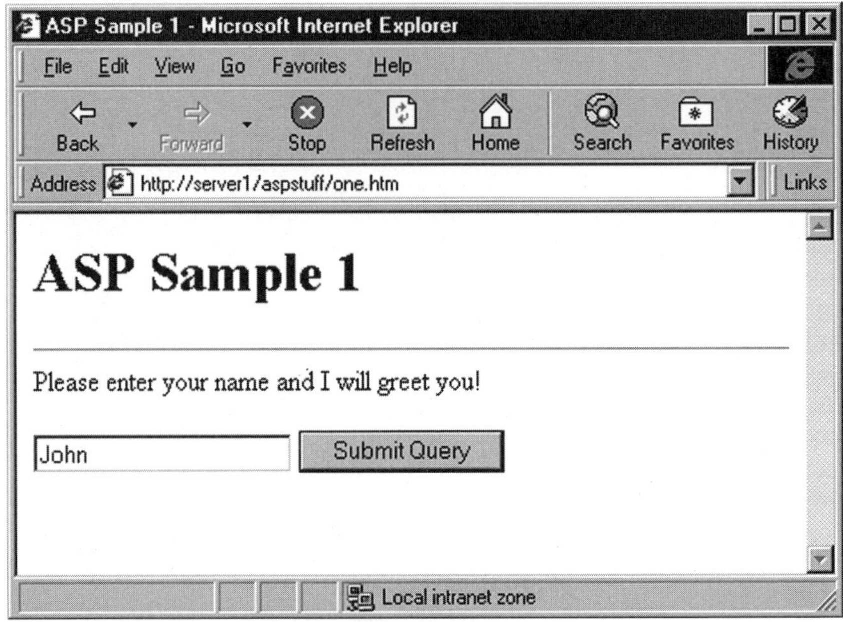

Figure 15-2 A simple HTML form with an ASP handler.

```
</body>
</html>
```

Figure 15-2 shows the client accessing the page `one.htm` in his browser and entering his name in the form. Here is the code for the ASP `one.asp` that acts as a form handler for `one.htm`:

```
<html>
<head><title>ASP Sample 1 Response</title></head>
<body bgcolor = white>
<p>Hello

<%
name = request.form("person")
response.write(name)
%>

</p>

<p>
Goodbye <%= name %>
</p>

</body>
</html>
```

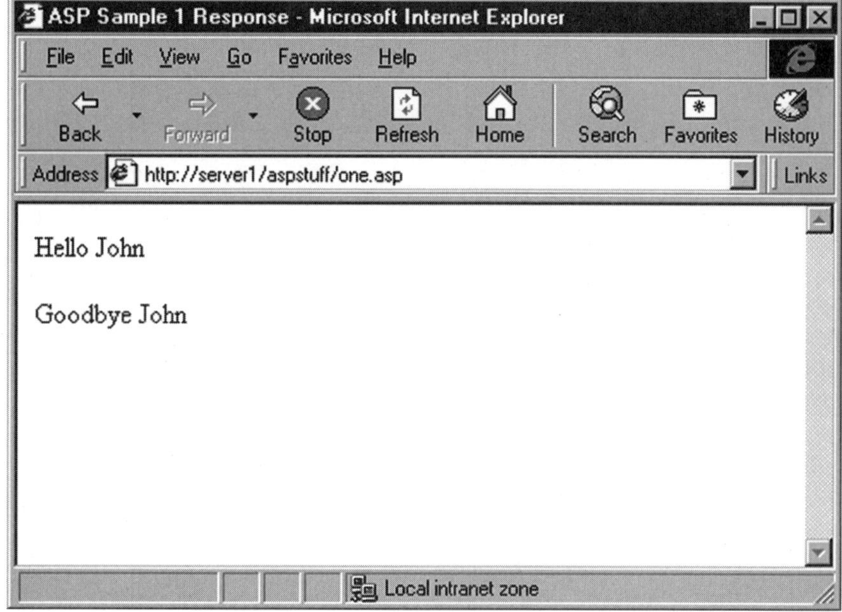

Figure 15-3 The response page returned by the ASP form handler.

Figure 15-3 shows the response page returned to the client's browser. Here is the actual HTML code returned to the browser, which can be viewed by selecting VIEW, SOURCE in Internet Explorer. Note that the page `one.asp` is returned to the browser, but the script on the page has been executed on the server and the resulting page has only plain HTML on it:

```
<html>
<head><title>ASP Sample 1 Response</title></head>
<body bgcolor = white>

<p>Hello
John

</p>

</p>Goodbye John</p>

</body>
</html>
```

Here's how it works:

1. The entire script on the `one.asp` ASP is enclosed in script delimiters <%...%>.

2. The form one.htm uses the HTTP POST method to invoke one.asp as its form handler.
3. The name that the client enters in the textbox in the form is passed to the server as the variable person.
4. The statement

```
name = request.form("person")
```

uses the form collection of the built-in object request to retrieve the contents of the variable person and assign it to the variable name. Built-in objects are discussed later in this chapter.
5. The statement

```
response.write(name)
```

uses the write method of the built-in object response to write the contents of the variable name to the HTTP output stream, displaying the name John on the browser.
6. The expression

```
<%= name %>
```

sends the contents of the variable name to the HTTP output stream, displaying the name John a second time on the browser. Note that this expression does not need to be part of the script on the ASP.

EXAMPLE 2: A SIMPLE ASP MILEAGE CONVERTER

The second example is a simple Web application for converting miles to kilometers. The page two.htm has an HTML form for the user to enter the number of miles. Pressing the CONVERT button sends the data to the ASP two.asp, which calculates the equivalent number of kilometers and returns the result to the user.

Here is the code for two.htm:

```
<html>
<Head><title>ASP Sample 2</title></head>
<body bgcolor = white>
```

```
<h1>ASP Sample 2</h1>
<hr>
<p>Conversion Utility</p>
<p>
<form method=post action=two.asp>
<input type=text name="miles"> miles=? kms
</p>
<p><input type=submit name=Convert value="Convert!"></p>
</form>

</body>
</html>
```

Figure 15-4 shows the client accessing the page `two.htm` in a browser and entering the number of miles in the textbox on the form.

Here is the code for the ASP `two.asp` that performs the calculation request by `one.htm`:

```
<html>
<head><title>ASP Sample 2 Response</title></head>
<body bgcolor=white>

<%
dim sMiles, sKms
const sConv=1.6
```

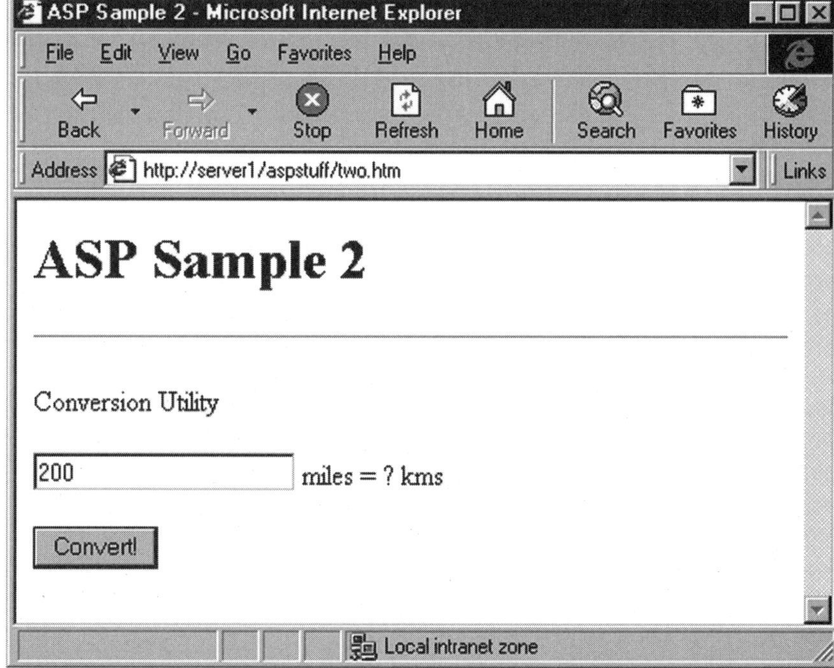

Figure 15-4 A simple Web application for converting mileage.

```
sMiles = request.form("miles")
sKms  = sConv * sMiles
response.write sMiles & " Miles = " & sKms & " kms"
%>

</body>
</html>
```

Figure 15-5 shows the resulting page returned to the client's browser. Here is the HTML code returned to the browser, which can be viewed by selecting VIEW, SOURCE in Internet Explorer:

```
<html>
<head><title>ASP Sample 2 Response</title></head>
<body bgcolor = white>

200 Miles = 320 kms

</body>
</html>
```

Explanatory notes:

1. If you are familiar with Visual Basic (or any other form of BASIC for that matter), you will recognize statements like

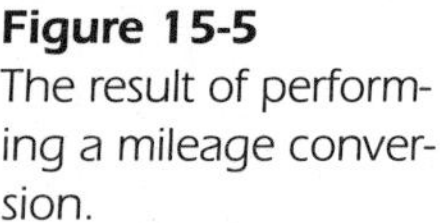

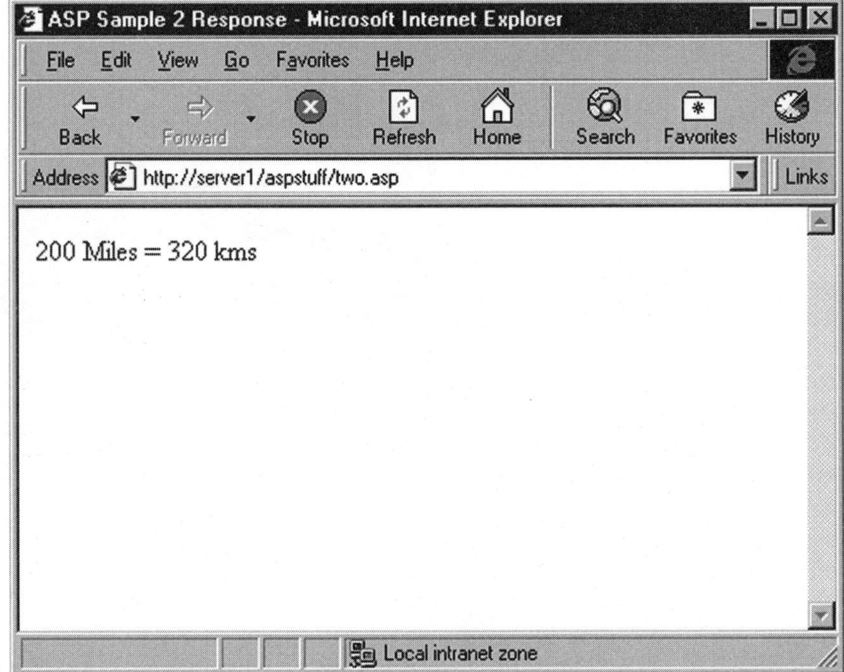

Figure 15-5
The result of performing a mileage conversion.

`dim sMiles, sKms` (declares two variables)
`const sConv = 1.6` (declares a constant and assigns it a value)
`sKms = sConv * sMiles` (an arithmetic expression converting miles to kilometers)

2. Active Server Page scripts use *Visual Basic script (VBScript)* by default, which is a subset of the Visual Basic programming language. So if you know any Visual Basic, you can leverage your knowledge for building Web applications on IIS 4.0.

EXAMPLE 3: ANOTHER ASP MILEAGE CONVERTER

The third example is a Web application that generates a conversion table for converting one unit of distance to another. The page `three.htm` has an HTML form for the user to select which unit to convert to which. Pressing the GENERATE! button causes the ASP `three.asp` to create and return a sample conversion table to the user.

Here is the code for `three.htm`:

```
<html>
<head><title>ASP Sample 3</title></head>
<body bgcolor = white>

<h1>ASP Sample 3</h1>
<p>Generate table to convert: </p>

<form method = post action = three.asp>
   <p>from <select name = "unit1" size = "1">
      <option selected value = 0>miles</option>
      <option value = 1>kilometers</option>
      <option value = 2>furlongs</option>
      </select> to <select name = "unit2" size = "1">
         <option value = 0>miles</option>
         <option selected value = 1>kilometers</option>
         <option value = 2>furlongs</option>
      </select></p>
      <p><input type = "submit" name = "Generate"
value = "Generate!"></p>
</form>

</body>
</html>
```

Figure 15-6 shows the client accessing the page `three.htm` in a browser and choosing to create a conversion table from kilometers into furlongs.

Here is the code for the ASP `three.asp` that generates the table:

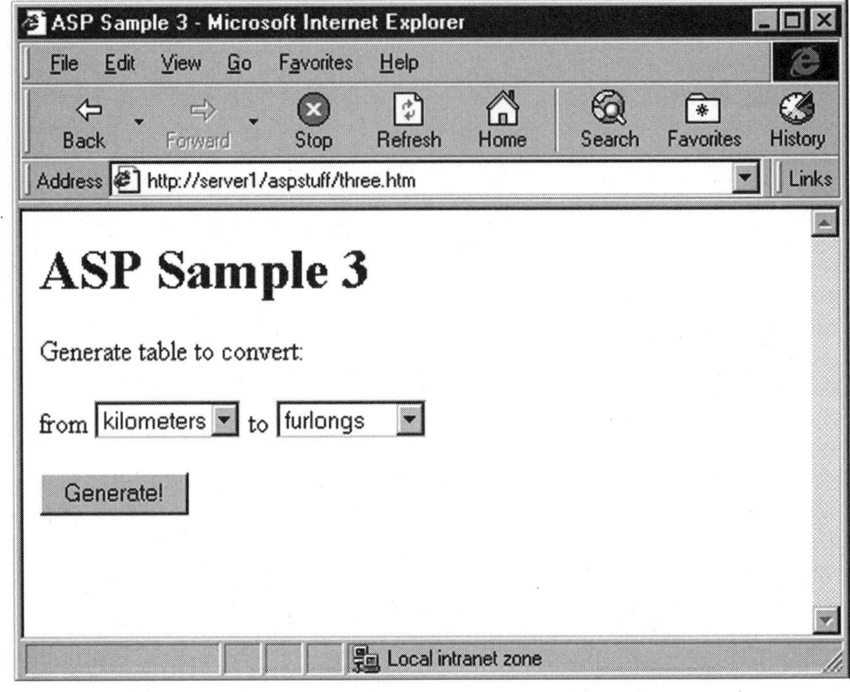

Figure 15-6
A Web application for generating a conversion table.

```
<html>
<head><title>ASP Sample 3 Response</title></head>
<body bgcolor = white>

<h1>Conversion Table</h1>
<hr>
<%
dim sConv(2,2), sLabel(2)
sConv(0,0) = 1
sConv(0,1) = 1.6
sConv(0,2) = 8
sConv(1,0) = .625
sConv(1,1) = 1
sConv(1,2) = 5
sConv(2,0) = .125
sConv(2,1) = 5
sConv(2,2) = 1
sLabel(0) = "miles"
sLabel(1) = "kms"
sLabel(2) = "furlongs"
sUnit1 = request.form("unit1")
sUnit2 = request.form("unit2")
response.write "<table border = 1 cellpadding = 5>"
for k =  1 to 5 step 1
var1 = k
var2 = var1 * sConv(sUnit1,sUnit2)
response.write "<tr>"
```

```
response.write "<td>" & var1 & " " & sLabel(sUnit1) & "</td>"
response.write "<td>" & var2 & " " & sLabel(sUnit2) & "</td>"
response.write "</tr>"
next
response.write "</table>"
%>

</body>
</html>
```

Figure 15-7 shows the resulting page returned to the client's browser. Explanatory notes:

1. A simple `for...next` loop is used to create the table.
2. The three-by-three matrix `sConv` holds the conversion factors, while the three-element vector `sLabel` holds the names of the units.

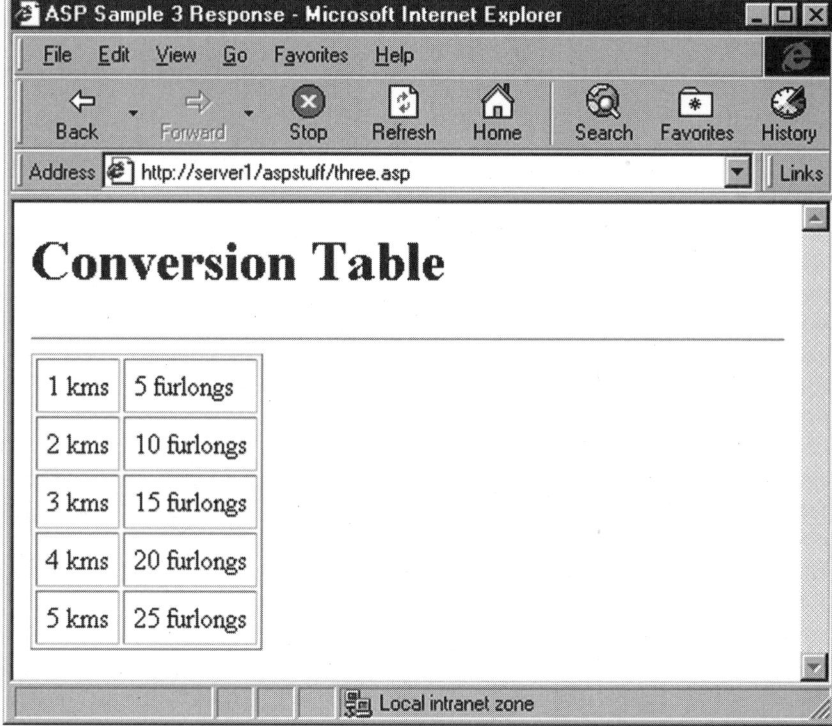

Figure 15-7
A conversion table generated by an Active Server Page.

EXAMPLE 4: USING ASP TO SEND EMAIL VIA THE SMTP SERVICE

The fourth example of using Active Server Pages is a simple Web application that allows users to send email from an HTML form, `four.htm`, by using the SMTP service on IIS 4.0. Refer to Chap. 13 to understand how to configure this service. Here the Active Server Page `four.asp` is the email form handler for the Web page `four.htm`.

Here is the code for `four.htm`:

```
<html>
<head><title>ASP Sample 4</title></head>
<body bgcolor = white>

<h1>ASP Sample 4</h1>
<hr>
<h2>Send email using the SMTP service</h2>
<form method = post action = four.asp>
<br>Sender's address:
<input type = text name = "sSender" size = 30>
<br>Receiver's address:
<input type = text name = "sReceiver" size = 30>
<br>Subject or message:
<input type = text name = "sSubject" size = 30>
<br>Body of message:<br>
<textarea cols = 40 rows = 4 name = "sBody"></textarea>
<br><input type = submit value = "Send mail now!">

</form>
</body>
</html>
```

Figure 15-8 shows the client accessing the page `four.htm` in his browser and using it to send mail.

Here is the code for the ASP `four.asp` that sends the email using the SMTP service on IIS 4.0:

```
<html>
<head><title>ASP Sample 4 Response</title></head>
<body bgcolor = white>
< %
Set fs = CreateObject("Scripting.FileSystemObject")
Set msg = fs.CreateTextFile("c:\InetPub\mailroot\
   pickup\message.txt", True)
msg.WriteLine("x-sender: " & Request.Form("sSender"))
msg.WriteLine("x-receiver: " & Request.Form("sReceiver"))
msg.WriteLine("From: " & Request.Form("sSender"))
msg.WriteLine("To: " & Request.Form("sReceiver"))
msg.WriteLine("Subject: " & Request.Form("sSubject"))
msg.WriteBlankLines(1)
msg.WriteLine(Request.Form("sBody"))
msg.Close
```

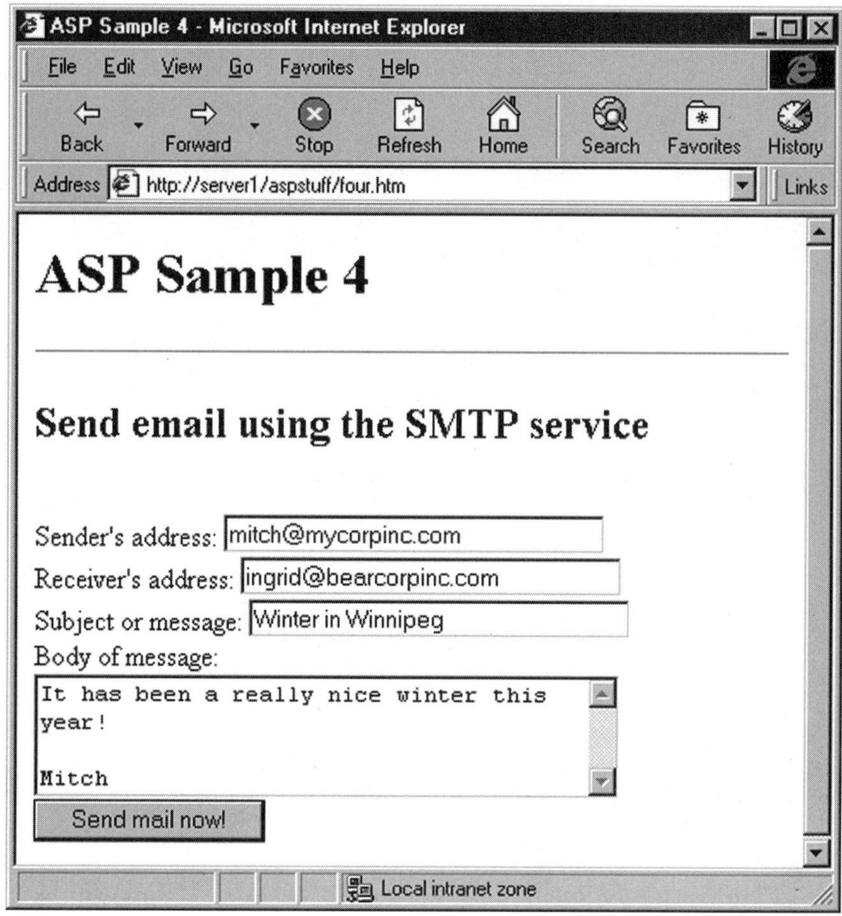

Figure 15-8 A simple form to send mail using an ASP form handler.

```
Response.Write("<html><body>")
Response.Write("<h1>Message sent!</h1>")
Response.Write("</html></body>")
%>

</body></html>
```

Here's how it works:

1. The user completes the form and passes the variables to the server using the HTTP POST method.
2. The statement

   ```
   Set fs = CreateObject("Scripting.FileSystemObject")
   ```

   creates a file system object and assigns it to the variable `fs`.

3. The statement

```
Set msg = fs.CreateTextFile("c:\InetPub\mailroot\
pickup\message.txt", True)
```

   creates a TextStream object and assigns it to the variable `msg`. In effect, it creates and opens the text file `message.txt` for writing.
4. The lines with `msg.WriteLine` use the `WriteLine` method of the TextStream object `msg` to write lines of text to the file `message.txt`.
5. The line `msg.Close` uses the `Close` method of the `msg` object to close the text file `message.txt`.
6. Since the file `message.txt` has been created in the `Pickup` subdirectory of the `Mailroot` directory, the SMTP service immediately moves it to the `Queue` subdirectory and processes it for delivery. See Chap. 13 for more information on various subdirectories of `Mailroot`.

We could continue creating more complex Active Server Page scripts and testing them, but the subject is so wide that it really demands a book of its own. For more information about writing Active Server Page scripts, consult the Windows NT 4.0 Option Pack online documentation item called the Scripter's Reference.

Using Active Server Page Objects

Another element of Active Server Pages is *ASP objects.* These programming objects come in two forms: *built-in* objects and *installable* objects. ASP objects can have forms, methods and collections just like VB objects.

Using Built-in ASP Objects

There are six *built-in objects* in the ASP methodology. These objects can be used in ASP scripts. They include the following:

- *Application.* This object can be used to share information between users of an application. In IIS 4.0, an application consists of all `.asp` files contained in a virtual directory and its subdirectories.

- *ObjectContext.* This object can be invoked to start or end a transaction.
- *Request.* This object retrieves the contents of variables passed from clients to servers during HTTP request messages. An example of using this object is the collection `request.form` used in Example 1 to pass a value from the HTML form to the ASP application.
- *Response.* This object is used to send a text stream to the requesting client. An example is the `response.write` method in Example 1.
- *Server.* This object can provide the developer with properties and methods on the IIS server.
- *Session.* This object stores values from page to page in an ASP application.

Using Installable ASP Objects

In addition to the above, the ASP framework is extensible and allows the installation of ActiveX components to generate useful objects. These five *installable objects* include

- *Browser capabilities,* which allow the server to determine the characteristics of the client browser connecting to it
- *Content linking,* which automatically generates a table of contents and navigational hyperlinks
- *Content rotator,* which can rotate a banner ad every time a page is viewed
- *Database connectivity,* by which a different ad is shown each time the client visits the site, depending on the state of the server
- *File access,* which allows you to use ASPs to interact with the local file system

For more information on the methods, properties, and collection of ASP objects, refer to the Windows NT 4.0 Option Pack documentation.

Using Active Server Page Components

ASP components are ActiveX server components conforming to the COM standard and written in any programming language that provide more speed and responsiveness than can be afforded by ActiveX scripts. The development language for ActiveX components can be

- C++
- Java
- Visual Basic

For more information on creating and using ASP components, refer to the Windows NT 4.0 Option Pack documentation.

Understanding Microsoft Transaction Server 2.0

Microsoft Transaction Server (MTS) is a developer tool for building three-tiered transaction-oriented Web applications using ActiveX components that integrate and manage the functions of clients, servers, and data sources. Transaction Server can be used to

- Package components into integrated applications
- Manage threads and processes in distributed applications
- Manage ODBC connections to provide high-performance database access
- Share data sources among users while managing states and synchronization
- Instantiate ActiveX objects when needed on a just-in-time basis
- Manage distributed transactions and provide recovery features in case of failure
- Isolate application processes to provide a robust fail-over environment
- Use DCOM for component integration and communications across the network

Understanding Transactions

The core of the Microsoft Transaction Server is the *Microsoft Distributed Transaction Coordinator (MS DTC),* which was first introduced with SQL

Server 6.5. The MS DTC manages *transactions,* which are collections of business processes that must either all succeed or all fail together as a group. The MS DTC runs as a Windows NT service and can be stopped and started using the Services program in Control Panel.

A good example of a transaction is a credit card purchase at a restaurant. The parties involved in the transaction are the client, the restaurant owner, and the credit agency. The following business processes must either all succeed or all fail in any given transaction:

- The client's credit account must be debited by the amount of the meal.
- The restaurant owner's merchant account must be credited by the amount of the meal minus the transaction fee.
- The credit agency's account must be credited by the amount of the transaction fee.

If any one portion of this transaction fails, the whole transaction must fail and any completed portions must be rolled back; otherwise, someone will lose money somewhere and will certainly complain.

Microsoft Transaction Server is designed to handle the underlying architecture to support such distributed transactions using ActiveX-based Web applications as the front-end interface.

Active Server Pages and Microsoft Transaction Server

In IIS 4.0, Active Server Pages are grouped together into applications. An *application* is a tree of directories and files (Active Server Pages), usually starting with a virtual server or virtual directory and extending downward into all subdirectories or until another application is defined.

Applications can be run in two different ways on IIS 4.0:

- They can be run *in-process* in the same address space as the main IIS process `inetinfo.exe` (this is the default method and was the only option in earlier versions of IIS).
- They can be run *out-of-process* as an isolated process in their own address space, being managed by the Microsoft Transaction Server process `mtx.exe`.

The second option above provides *process isolation,* which has the following advantages:

- The inetinfo.exe process and all other processes on the IIS server are protected against failure of the application.
- If the application does fail, the mtx.exe process can restart it automatically without requiring the server to be stopped and started again.
- ActiveX components can be loaded and unloaded without requiring that other processes and services be stopped first.

In effect, what has happened in IIS 4.0 is that the server code responsible for managing Active Server Pages and ISAPI applications has been moved from the main inetinfo.exe process to a new module, called the *Web Application Manager (WAM),* that is managed by the Microsoft Transaction Server. Applications are assigned *globally unique identifiers (GUIDs)* by the WAM and are registered by Microsoft Transaction Server as *packages.* Even the default IIS process inetinfo.exe is managed by Transaction Server as the *default in-process package.* Because of this management by MTS, each application can be started and stopped independently of other applications on IIS 4.0.

Walkthrough: Configuring an Application

To configure an application, we will use as an example the examples of Active Server Pages described earlier in this chapter. These ASPs were grouped together into a virtual directory called aspstuff that was part of the Default Web Site. Figure 15-9 shows the aspstuff virtual directory in the results pane of the MMC when the Default Web Site is selected in the scope pane.

Note that the icon representing the virtual directory aspstuff is a folder with a globe on it. This icon indicates that the virtual directory is not an application starting point but is instead somewhere in the hierarchy of folders and subdirectories beneath an application starting point. In other words, the Active Server Pages in the virtual directory aspstuff do not in themselves represent a separate application that could be run as an isolated process.

To define aspstuff as an application so that we can run it out-of-process, select the aspstuff icon in the results pane and click the PROPERTIES button on the rebar to open the aspstuff Properties sheet. Note that the name of the application that this virtual directory belongs to is the *Default Application,* and its starting point is the Default Web Site (Fig.

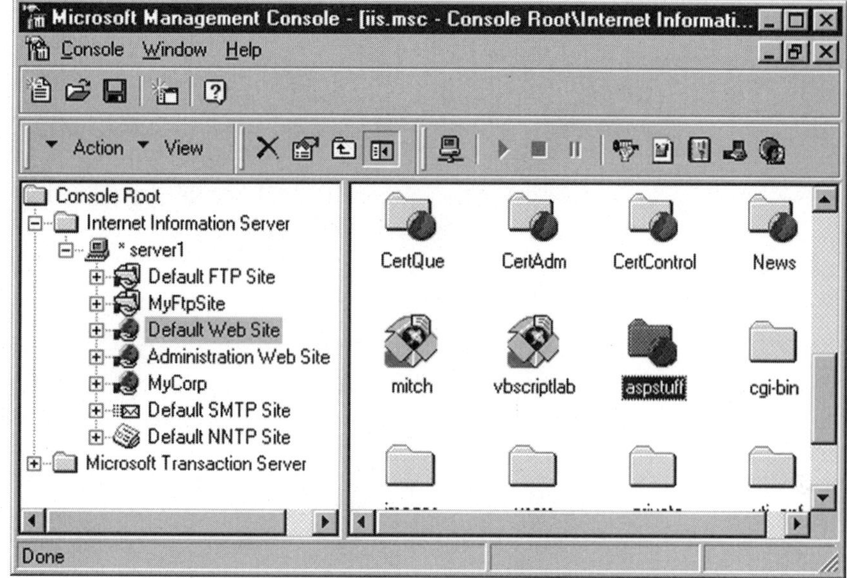

Figure 15-9 The virtual directory `aspstuff` contains ASPs but is not an application at this point.

15-10). Note also that the RUN IN A SEPARATE MEMORY SPACE checkbox is unavailable (grayed out) because the virtual directory `aspstuff` is not an *application starting point* (i.e., `aspstuff` is not an application).

To define the virtual directory `aspstuff` as an application starting point, click the CREATE button. A few moments later the Starting Point will change from Default Web Site to the `aspstuff` virtual directory. `Aspstuff` is now a new application. Note also that the RUN IN A SEPARATE MEMORY SPACE checkbox is now available. By checking this box, you can choose to run the new application out-of-process (as an isolated process). Type `aspstuff` as the name for the new application in the *Name* textbox (Fig. 15-11).

If you click APPLY and view the results pane of the Microsoft Management Console, you will see that the icon for the virtual directory `asp-stuff` has changed (Fig. 15-12). The new icon looks like a package and reflects the fact that Microsoft Transaction Server sees `aspstuff` as an application *package* that can be run either in-process or out-of-process by the Web Application Manager.

To configure the newly created application, return to the `aspstuff` Properties sheet (see Fig. 15-11) and click the CONFIGURATION button to open the Application Configuration dialog box. The settings on the three tabs in this dialog box were explained in Chap. 3. Refer back to this for information about configuring the new application.

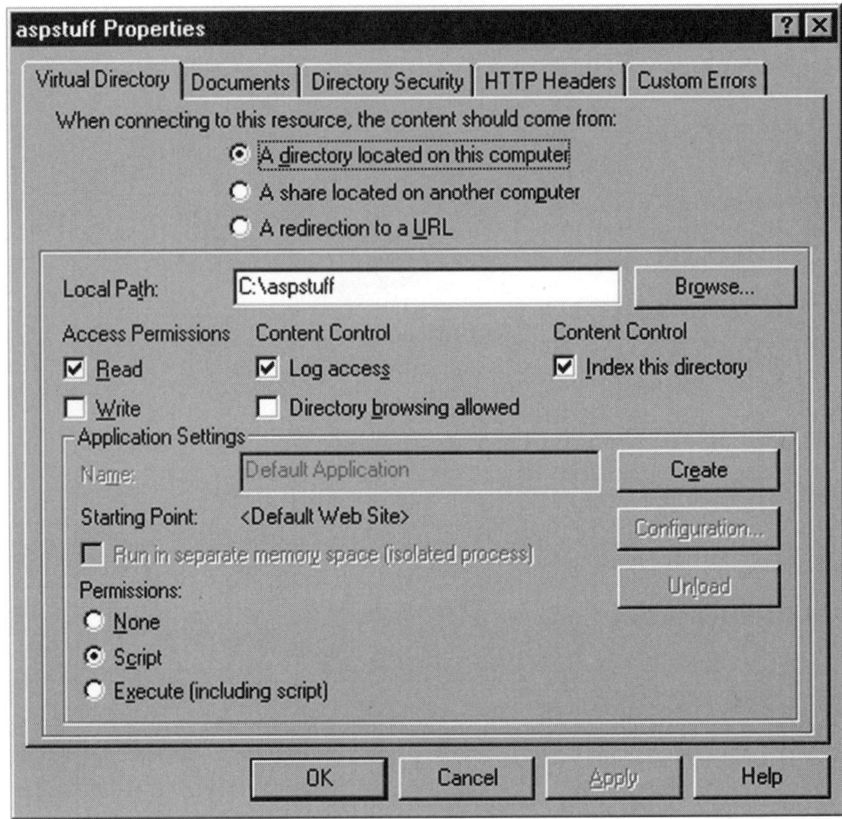

Figure 15-10 The `aspstuff` Properties sheet shows that `aspstuff` is part of the Default Application.

As a final test, we will observe how the Web Application Manager of Microsoft Transaction Server creates a new `mtx.exe` process when we run our new application out-of-process:

1. Open Task Manager and select the Processes tab. Note that one instance of `mtx.exe` is currently running. This is the default in-process package that runs the Default Application whose starting point is the root of the Default Web Site.
2. Access the `aspstuff` Properties sheet and enable the RUN IN A SEPARATE MEMORY SPACE checkbox and click APPLY. This enables `aspstuff` to run out-of-process (as an isolated process).
3. However, we have not yet started the new application, so in Internet Explorer open the URL

```
http://server1/aspstuff
```

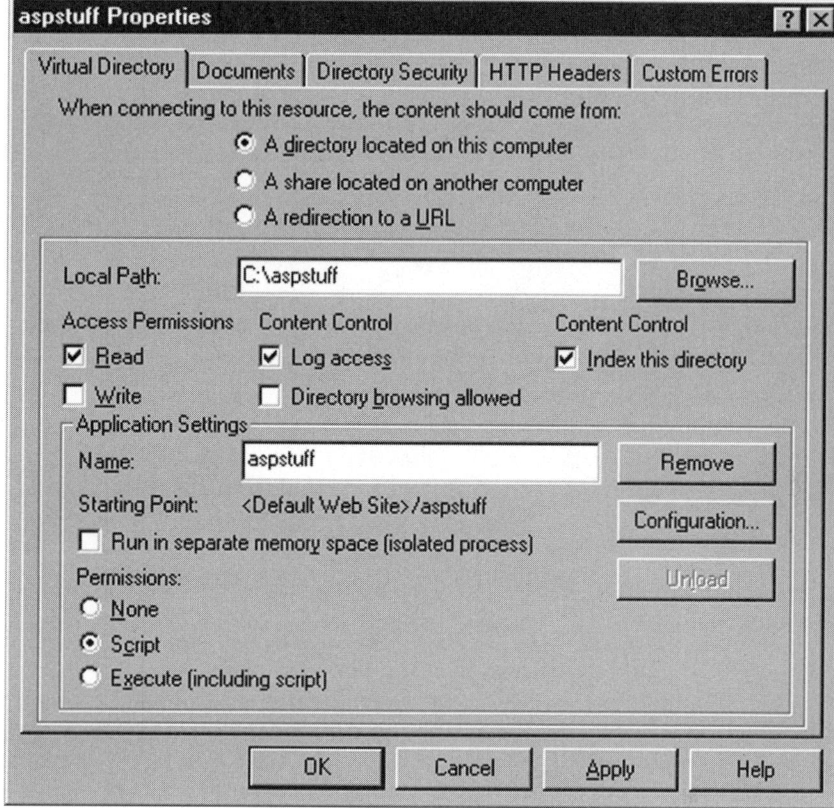

Figure 15-11 The new application `aspstuff` with starting point in the `aspstuff` virtual directory.

or your equivalent for your version of this walkthrough. Select one of the examples from earlier in this chapter—for example, open the Web page `one.htm` in your browser, enter your name, and click SUBMIT. This starts the application because we have accessed the Active Server Page `one.asp`, which is part of this application.

4. At this point if you examine Task Manager you will see that a second instance of the `mtx.exe` process has started. This second `mtx.exe` process is created by Microsoft Transaction Server to allow it to run `aspstuff` as an isolated process. In effect, each `mtx.exe` acts as a kind of "virtual machine" in which an application can run under Microsoft Transaction Server.
5. Finally, observe on the `aspstuff` Properties sheet that the UNLOAD button has now become available (no longer grayed out). This is because the application is running and is loaded into the

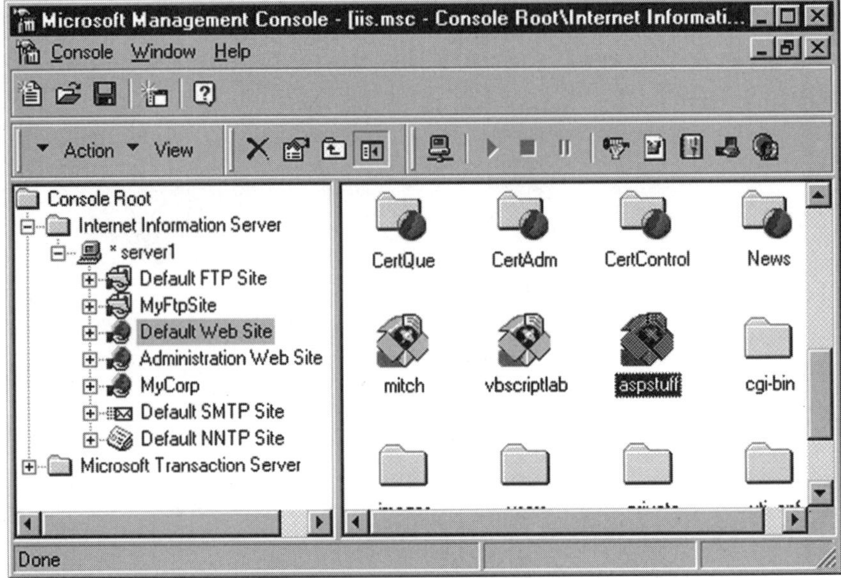

Figure 15-12 The new application package `aspstuff` has been created.

server's memory. Click the UNLOAD button and watch the second instance of `mtx.exe` disappear from Task Manager as the application unloads from memory and is no longer running.

Configuring Microsoft Transaction Server

Microsoft Transaction Server can be administered and configured by using the *MTS Explorer snap-in* for the Microsoft Management Console (Fig. 15-13). MTS Explorer can be used to create, deploy, and manage distributed transactional business solutions across a corporate network.

MTS Explorer includes a number of wizards for creating custom business solutions by assembling packages and components together. Using MTS Explorer requires extensive knowledge of technologies like ActiveX and DCOM, plus understanding of the methods and APIs of components created with high-level programming languages, all of which are beyond the scope of this book.

SUMMARY

Active Server Pages are a methodology that combines server-side scripts, ASP objects, and ActiveX server components to create Web applications

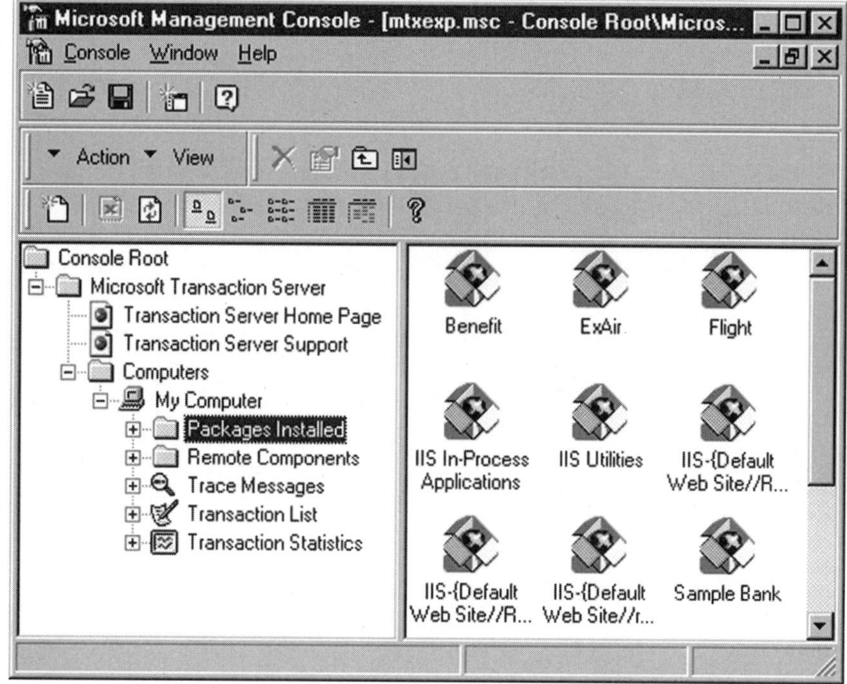

Figure 15-13 The Microsoft Management Console with the MTS Explorer snap-in installed.

that extend the functionality of a Web server. In IIS 4.0 Active Server Pages are managed by the Web Application Manager, a component of the Microsoft Transaction Server, which allows them to run either in-process or out-of-process depending on your needs for security and stability.

FOR MORE INFORMATION

Microsoft Web Site Read an Active Server Pages white paper at

`www.microsoft.com/iis/partners/aspwp.asp`

Microsoft has some tips and tricks for Active Server Pages located at

`www.microsoft.com/iis/partners/asp_tips.asp`

Read Transaction Server white papers at

`www.microsoft.com/ntserver/trans_whitepapers.asp`

For information on Microsoft's plan for using Transaction Server in the Enterprise, read

```
www.microsoft.com/enterprise/mtsblueprint.htm
```

Microsoft Public Newsgroups For discussing Active Server Pages, subscribe to the group

```
microsoft.public.inetserver.iis.activeserverpages
```

For discussing Microsoft Transaction Server, subscribe to

```
microsoft.public.microsofttransactionserver.programming
```

Other WWW Sites A really good site is

```
www.activeserverpages.com
```

CHAPTER 16

Troubleshooting

Introduction

Successful troubleshooting of a product is largely the result of three factors:

- Experience (you have seen something like this before)
- Training (you have read something about this before)
- Research (find someone else who has seen this before)

In addition, the following factors also help:

- Imagination (intuition)
- Methodical reasoning (the process of elimination)
- Risk-taking (try something new)
- Luck (you'll need it!)

This book has been designed to enhance your abilities to troubleshoot IIS 4.0 configurations by providing walkthroughs of basic tasks to allow you to gain experience, by clearly explaining configuration options to train you in the product and make you knowledgeable in it, and by listing additional resources you can consult for further research.

Nevertheless, from the author's own experience and that of many other administrators and webmasters, Internet Information Server 4.0 is a complex product that sometimes behaves in unexpected and highly frustrating ways. Despite rounds of vigorous beta-testing by Microsoft, the final release versions of IIS 4.0 and other Windows NT 4.0 Option Pack components still seem to have some bugs, and your contribution as an IIS 4.0 user can contribute toward making this product more stable and reliable.

The author has worked with the product extensively and has communicated with and listened to other administrators who have worked with it, and one result of this process is this final chapter called "Troubleshooting." Not simply a rehash of concepts from previous chapters, nor intended to replace a thorough study of the previous chapters and of the IIS online documentation, this chapter instead describes many problems from *real life* that administrators have wrestled with in their attempts to implement IIS 4.0 in their corporate and ISP environments, while other scenarios have been *contrived* to simulate known problems you might encounter as you implement IIS 4.0 in your network.

The result is not a cookbook of official solutions but rather a grab-bag of tips, tricks, workarounds, and warnings covering all of the areas dealt with in this book. Instead of telling you what the product should ideally be doing, we will look instead at what it really does in various situations and contexts, in combination with different hardware and software, and under different needs and demands.

In addition to reading this chapter, you can find additional information about troubleshooting IIS 4.0 in the following places:

- There are "Troubleshooting" chapters in the online documentation.
- The release notes for each component should be consulted.
- The IIS 4.0 Resource Kit should be available by the time you read this.
- You should browse the Microsoft public newsgroups.
- Consult Support Online on Microsoft's Web site to search the Knowledge Base.
- Search for mailing lists (list servers) dealing with IIS 4.
- Read current issues of *Windows NT Magazine* and other magazines.
- Visit other relevant Web sites like ntpro.org.
- Have a beer with colleagues from other companies using IIS (my favorite!).

I encourage you as you gain expertise with Internet Information Server 4.0 to take the time to document your stories of frustration and success and share them with the online community through your personal Web sites, online newsletters, mailing lists, and newsgroups. I also encourage you to be patient with and give clear advice to those who are still struggling with issues that now seem clear to you.

Finally, I ask you not to be frustrated or disappointed if your particular problem is not described here. Please remember that at the time of this writing, this product has only been in release version for two months, and that is barely time to become familiarized with its wealth of new features, let alone discover, document, and fix all of its bugs. This chapter is in no way intended to be the final word on troubleshooting IIS 4.0.

So let's look now at some examples of real problems and how administrators have tried to solve them, and contrived scenarios of problems you are likely to encounter as you work with IIS 4.0. All situations have been fictionalized to try to emphasize the key issues involved. The suggestions and workarounds are presented "as-is" by the author, who accepts no liability for the effects of implementing them but nevertheless presents them in good faith.

Good luck!

Installation Issues

Install or Upgrade?

"Hi. I've been reading the newsgroups on IIS 4.0 and I need to decide whether to upgrade my present IIS 3.0 system to IIS 4.0 or whether I should backup my content, reformat my system, re-install NT, and do a fresh install of IIS 4.0. What do you advise?"

This is not an official answer, but the consensus out there with administrators and webmasters seems to be that a fresh install is more likely to succeed than an upgrade. Having said that, there are those who have upgraded successfully and easily, while there are those who have done fresh installs and have come to grief. The bottom line seems to be that those administrators who really know their stuff (have MCSE designation, have taken Microsoft Official Curriculum courses, have years of experience with NT, etc.) are more likely to succeed than those who point, click, and don't read the release notes.

Error "Cannot detect OS Type"

You attempt to install IIS 4.0 from the Windows NT 4.0 Option Pack, but the installation fails with the message, "Cannot detect OS type."

Either the Netlogon or the Browser service is not running. Both of these services must be running in order for installation of IIS 4.0 to succeed.

Error "DCOM: an instance of this service is already running"

Installation succeeds, but Event Viewer afterwards shows the error, "DCOM: an instance of this service is already running."

This error is not an operational problem. It can be corrected by applying the post-SP3 hotfixes found at

```
ftp://ftp.microsoft.com/bussys/winnt/winnt-public/fixes/
usa/nt40/hotfixes-postSP3
```

or at the mirror site

```
ftp://198.105.232.37/fixes/usa/nt40/hotfixes-postSP3/
```

Upgrading IIS 4.0 Beta 2 Fails

"I had IIS 4.0 Beta 2 on a machine and tried to upgrade to IIS 4.0 release version. The upgrade failed."

IIS 4.0 release version does not upgrade IIS 4.0 Alpha, Beta 1, or Beta 2. Uninstall the previous versions and then install the release version.

Error "0x808005" during Installation

"I installed IE 4.01 on my IIS 3 machine and tried upgrading to IIS 4 but received this error. In Event Viewer I found a message that said, 'The IIS Admin service depends upon the following nonexistent service: ProtectedStorage.'"

When you install IE 4.01, you need to reboot your system *twice* before the ProtectedStorage service is properly configured. ProtectedStorage provides cryptoAPI services to IE.

Exchange Server and IIS 4.0

"I need to install both IIS 4.0 and Exchange Server on a single machine. What's the best order to proceed?"

Administrators who have tried this suggest the following installation order:

- NT 4.0 Server
- Service Pack 3
- Internet Explorer 4.01
- "Roll-up" post-SP3 hotfix
- Exchange Server 5.5

Note that Exchange 5.5 is needed, Exchange 5.0 seems to have some undetermined incompatibilities with IIS 4.0.

SQL Server and IIS 4.0

"I want to install IIS 4.0 on a machine with an SQL database on it as well. In what order should I install things?"

The following installation steps are recommended by some administrators:

- NT 4.0 Server
- NT Service Pack 3
- SQL Server 6.5
- SQL Service Pack 3
- IE 4.01
- IS 4.0

Perl on IIS 4.0

"I had Perl running perfectly on an IIS 3.0 machine that had custom CGI scripts. But when I upgraded to IIS 4.0, the Perl scripts wouldn't work."

Open your Web site Properties sheet for the site with the problem, select Home Directory tab, click CONFIGURATION to open the Application Configuration screen. If the path to Perl is there, select it and click EDIT. You will probably see something like

```
C:\bin\perl.exe %S %S
```

Edit this so that it appears

```
C:\bin\perl.exe %s %s
```

The capital letters were added during install.

One Hundred Percent CPU Usage

"I installed IIS 4.0 on a server with a huge number of documents to be scanned, filtered, and merged into a catalog. The problem is, I have just installed IIS 4.0 and for the last two hours my CPU usage has hovered close to 100 percent."

This is normal behavior on a fresh system when there is a great deal of preinstalled content (including the online documentation). When IIS boots, Index Server starts indexing the corpus, driving CPU usage high for a time of anywhere from a few minutes to many hours. Use Task Manager to observe the activity of the `cidaemon.exe` process.

Documentation Problems

Cannot Access Online Documentation from Any Machine Except the IIS Server

"I can access the online documentation from the IIS server console using the Start menu, but when I try to access it from any other machine by opening the URL

```
http://server1/iishelp
```

it doesn't work. I get a 403.6 Forbidden IP Address status message. Why?"

Using the MMC, open the Properties sheet for the IISHELP virtual directory under the server node. Select the Directory Security tab, click EDIT for IP Address and Domain Name Restrictions, and grant access to the IP address of the machine(s) you want to be able to access the documentation from.

Sections of Online Documentation Missing

"When I click on some of the links in my online documentation, I get 'File Not Found.' Why?"

You have performed a Typical install of NT 4.0 Option Pack, and the software component for the topic you want to study needs to be installed by performing a Custom installation or rerunning setup in maintenance mode (i.e., Add/Remove Components).

The Microsoft Management Console

Trouble Installing MMC on NT Workstation

From the Microsoft Web site at

```
www.microsoft.com/management
```

you can access a section dealing with the Microsoft Management Console. You can download the console and install it on Windows NT 4.0 Workstation or Windows 95. But when you try to use it to connect to an IIS 4.0 server and configure the server, it doesn't work.

You need the snap-ins on the machine on which the MMC executable is installed. Unfortunately, these snap-ins are at this time not available separately from Microsoft.

Remote Administration

Cannot Access Remote Administration Tools (HTML) Except on IIS Server

"I can open the Internet Service Manager (HTML) on the IIS server using the Start menu, but I can't open it from another computer using the URL

```
http://<server_ name>:<TCP_port>
```

What's wrong?"

The Administration Web Site in the MMC has IP address restrictions in place, granting access only to `127.0.0.1` and `localhost.` Access the Directory Security tab on the Administration Web Site Properties sheet, and EDIT the IP address restrictions to include the machine(s) you want to be able to access the site from.

If this is already set properly, check to see if the RPC Locator service is running in Control Panel, Services.

The WWW Service

No Logging Formats Available in WWW Properties Sheet

You try to enable logging on IIS by accessing the Web Site tab of the server Properties sheet, but there are no logging formats listed in the Active log format drop-down list.

Open a command prompt and type

```
cd \winnt\system32\inetsrv
```

```
regsvr32 iislog.dll
regsvr32 iscomlog.dll
regsvr32 logui.ocx
```

Exit the command prompt and enable logging. This will register the log files with IIS. Stop and start IIS after making these changes.
Also check out

```
premium.microsoft.com/support/kb/articles/q173/7/74.asp
```

Access and Authentication Issues

Users Cannot Access Web Site

You create a Web site for your corporate intranet, place content in the appropriate home directory, and access the site with your browser as Administrator. Users complain that they cannot access the Web site you have created. What should you do?

Try checking the following:

- Is IIS read permission is assigned to the home directory of the site? (Check the Home Directory tab of the WWW Properties sheet.)
- Is NTFS read permission assigned to the Users group?
- Are any applicable IP address restrictions in effect on this site? (Check the Directory Security tab of the WWW Properties sheet.)
- Is at least one authentication method (anonymous, basic, challenge/response) enabled for the site? (Check the Directory Security tab of the WWW Properties sheet.)

Anonymous Users Cannot Access Web Site

You create a Web site for an Internet server, place content in the appropriate home directory, and can access the site with your browser as Administrator. People complain that they cannot access the Web site you have created. What should you do?

Try checking the following:

- Is anonymous access enabled for your site? (Check the Directory Security tab of the WWW Properties sheet.)

- Is the anonymous user account IUSR_SERVERNAME synchronized with User Manager? (Check the Directory Security tab of the WWW Properties sheet.)
- Does the anonymous user account IUSR_SERVERNAME have the right to log on locally? (Select POLICIES, USER RIGHTS on the User Manager menu.)

Users Cannot Access Web Site Using Basic Authentication

You create a Web site, place content in the appropriate home directory, and can access the site with your browser as Administrator. Basic Authentication is enabled on the site, but users complain that they cannot access the Web site you have created. What should you do?

- Has a default domain been specified for Basic Authentication? (Check the Directory Security tab of the WWW Properties sheet.)
- Does the user have the right to log on locally? (Select POLICIES, USER RIGHTS on the User Manager menu.)

Netscape User on UNIX Workstation Cannot Access Web Site

"I'm using Netscape Navigator on a UNIX workstation, and I can't connect to a Web site on an IIS 4.0 server. I get a logon box, but when I enter a valid Windows NT account, logon fails."

Make sure Basic Authentication is enabled for the Web site. Netscape Navigator does not support Windows NT Challenge/Response authentication.

Third-Party Authentication Tools

If you want remote users to be authenticated, do not want to use Basic Authentication because it is insecure, and do not want to use NT Challenge/Response Authentication because some users are running Netscape Navigator or because you want to maintain a Web user database separate from your NT user database, you may want to consider installing a third-party ISAPI filter authentication tool. A number of administrators have recommended AuthentiX from Flicks Software, at

```
www.flicks.com/flicks/authx.htm
```

Virtual Directories and Servers

Cannot Create Virtual Servers with IIS 4.0 on NT 4.0 Workstation

"I have IIS 4.0 installed on Windows NT 4.0 Workstation with Service Pack 3 and Internet Explorer 4. I have a default Web site but I can't create any additional ones. What's wrong?"

Nothing is wrong. IIS 4.0 on NT 4.0 Workstation does not support virtual servers.

Making a Virtual Directory Available to All Virtual Servers

"On IIS 3.0 I could create a virtual directory called `images` *on the default Web site and leave its IP address as 'All unassigned.' This way the* `images` *virtual directory would be available on all virtual servers on the machine. How do I do this on IIS 4.0?"*

This feature is not supported on IIS 4.0.

Missing IP Addresses

"I have installed Windows NT on a machine and created 200 IP addresses for the Network Adapter Card in Control Panel, Network, TCP Properties. Then I went to the Web Site tab on my Web site Properties sheet and tried to select an IP address from the drop-down list. Unfortunately it is blank (or maybe incomplete)."

The workaround is to type the IP address directly into the IP Address box on this property sheet. Make sure you use one of the IP addresses you created using Control Panel's Network icon.

Content Development Issues

Cannot Enable a Site as a FrontPage Web

On the Home Directory tab of your Web site Properties sheet, the FRONTPAGE WEB checkbox is grayed out, preventing you from enabling your Web site as a FRONTPAGE Web.

Click START, PROGRAMS, WINDOWS NT 4.0 OPTION PACK, MICROSOFT INTERNET INFORMATION SERVER, FRONTPAGE SERVER ADMINISTRATOR. Uninstall and then re-install the FrontPage server extensions on your server.

Error "Server error: cannot access the server configuration files"

You have FrontPage extensions installed on your server, and you enable a site as a FrontPage Web using the Home Directory tab of your Web site Properties sheet. You start FrontPage and try to connect to the Web site but get the error, "Server error: cannot access the server configuration files."

Run the FrontPage Server Administrator and use the Check and Fix option.

Users Cannot Log On to IIS Using FrontPage

"As Administrator, I can connect to a Web running FrontPage on the local IIS server, but remote users cannot log on and connect to the Web using FrontPage. They have been given Authoring permission on the Web, and have the correct ACLs on the NTFS partition that contains the content. What's wrong?"

You need to give the user the right to log on locally to the IIS server as well.

Visual InterDev and IIS 4.0

"After upgrading my server from IIS 3.0 to 4.0, users who published to my server with Visual InterDev report that when they try to create a new project, a logon box appears that won't accept their credentials."

Many administrators have reported this problem. The temporary workaround seems to be to add these users to the Administrators group(!). When Microsoft releases an upgrade to the FrontPage server extensions, install them—Visual InterDev relies on FrontPage extensions to publish.

Problems with a Directory When You Installed FrontPage Server Extensions

FrontPage server extensions have been partially configured on a virtual server. Now the owner of the site has trouble connecting to the virtual server using FrontPage.

The best solution seems to be to manually delete the hidden FrontPage directories (e.g., `_vti`) and then install the extensions again on the directory.

Content Indexing

Documents to Filter Does Not Zero after Master Merge

"I forced a scan of all my virtual directories and forced a master merge, and I still have a few documents that are unfiltered. What's wrong?"

The documents are probably open or in use by an application that locks files in use, like Microsoft Word. The documents have been scheduled for filtering by the Content Indexing (CI) service and will be filtered at the first available opportunity.

Master Merge Halts before Completion

"I forced a Master Merge and was watching the CI statistics by selecting the Index Server node in the MMC, and I noticed that indexing was half completed and then stopped. I still have six persistent indexes, and nothing more is happening. What do I do?"

Check Event Viewer—your disk that holds the catalog is probably full. Free up disk space and stop and start the CI service.

Documents on Remote UNC Share Are Not Indexed

You create a new virtual directory mapped to a remote UNC share. You force a scan of the new virtual directory, but the documents are not filtered.

Check the domain\user and password you used to enable access to the UNC share.

Index Server Indexes Hidden FrontPage Directories

How do I stop Index Server from indexing the hidden `_vti` directories created by FrontPage?

Access the Properties sheets for these hidden directories in the MMC, and on the Directory tab clear the INDEX THIS DIRECTORY checkbox.

Query Does Not Return Expected Result

"I tried a query and several pages came up in the result set, but a page I know has the query keywords didn't come up. Why?"

Check out the following:

- Do you have NTFS permission to read the page?
- Has the page been filtered yet?
- Is the page in the same language as the query?

Message "Query too expensive"

"I have a large corpus indexed by Index Server, and I submitted a complex query on the corpus and got the message 'Query too expensive' instead of a result set."

Increase the value of the registry setting `MaxRestrictionNodes`.

Office 97 Corrupts Index Server Queries

"I installed Office 97 on a machine running Index Server, and now when I perform queries I get unusual results."

Office 97 overwrites some Index Server registry settings. Re-install Index Server.

The FTP Service

Cannot Upload to FTP Site When Anonymous Access is Disabled

"I have an FTP site that I want my users to access. The site does not have anonymous access enabled. Why can't my users log on and upload files?"

If anonymous access is disabled for an FTP site, a user has to enter a valid Windows NT user account and password to log on to the site. This account must be assigned the right to log on locally on the ISS server.

Performance Issues

Error "Winsock error: no bufferspace is supported"

"I have been adding more virtual servers to my server, and when I reached about 600 virtual servers I began to get intermittent error messages saying, 'Winsock error: no bufferspace is supported.' What do I do?"

Your server is reaching its capacity for hits. You will need to limit the number of hits per day to fewer than 10,000 for your busier sites, or offload some sites to another server. You can also try upgrading your server's hardware.

Limit hits per day by accessing the Performance tab of the Web site Properties sheet.

IIS 4.0 Runs Slowly on an Intel Pentium Machine with 256 MB of RAM

"I installed IIS 4.0 on an Intel Pentium machine with 64 MB of RAM. I increased the RAM to 256 MB and the machine actually runs slower. Why?"

Recent Intel chipsets for motherboards with Pentium processors do not support more than 64 MB of L2 cached RAM. For example, the older HX chipset supports more than 64 MB of L2 cached RAM, but the newer FX chipset doesn't. The result is that using more than 64 MB RAM on these newer motherboards actually decreases caching efficiency. The best solution is to upgrade to a motherboard with an Intel Pentium II processor with compatible motherboard. Pentium II systems support more than 64 MB of cached RAM.

High CPU Usage on IIS Server with Proxy Server 2 Installed

You have an IIS 4.0 server with Proxy Server 2 installed, and you find that at times the CPU usage goes to 100 percent for no apparent reason.

Remove the `webproxy.dll` from the IIS filters (ISAPI Filters tab of server Properties sheet) and stop and restart IIS.

MS Access ODBC Driver Memory Leak

Some administrators have reported that certain versions of the Microsoft Access ODBC driver have a memory leak. The result is that if you connect to an Access database on an IIS 4.0 site, you may gradually lose virtual memory until your server has to be rebooted.

The solution is to always use the most current Access ODBC driver.

`drwatson.exe` Slows Performance

Many administrators have reported seeing a `drwatson.exe` process start on their IIS 4.0 server from time to time. The `drwatson.exe` process then consumes most of the CPU resources. A Dr Watson dialog box never comes up.

Here are workarounds that have been suggested in the IS community:

- Reboot when this occurs.
- End the `drwatson.exe` process using Task Manager.
- Remove the `drwatson.exe` executable from your system.
- Disable Dr Watson by setting the following registry key to zero:

```
Hkey_software
    Microsoft
        Windows NT
            CurrentVersion
                AeDebug
```

 Site Server Express

Database Errors Occur When Content Analyzer Is Run on a Web Site

"I have a Web site that is connected to an ODBC-compliant database. I ran Content Analyzer to get a webmap for my site, and there have been some unexpected changes to some records in my database."

Content Analyzer analyzes and tests every link in a Web site, including links to server-side gateway scripts. When it was testing the links to your database, it must have created or modified some records unexpectedly by invoking the gateway program.

Imported Log Has Wrong Times for Hits

"I imported a log file into Usage Import and generated a report using Report Writer. The times when the hits occurred are wrong. What happened?"

When you import a log into Usage Import, make sure that the regional settings on the IIS server on which the log was created match the regional settings of the machine on which you are running Site Server Express.

Scheduled Import of Logs from Remote Share Fails

"I tried to set up Site Server Express to perform a scheduled import of IIS log files from a remote network share, but it doesn't work. Why?"

Make sure the scheduler starts with a user who has permissions on the share.

Error Using Internet Explorer on a Machine with Posting Acceptor Installed

"When I try to use Internet Explorer on a machine that has Posting Acceptor installed on it, I get an error, 'Error initializing the cache.'"

This is a known issue. See the Microsoft Knowledge Base article Q106387.

SSL and Certificate Server

Cannot Use Host Header Names with SSL Enabled

You have SSL enabled for the default Web site on an IIS 4.0 server, and you create a virtual server on the same IP address using Host Header Names. You try to access the virtual server and get the default Web site instead.

Host Header Names cannot be used with SSL.

Cannot Install Certificate Server on a BDC

"I have IIS 4.0 running on a BDC and want to install Certificate Server, but when I tried I got errors."

This release of Certificate Server cannot be installed on a BDC.

Certificate Server Shared Folder Must Be Local

"I installed Certificate Server and specified the shared folder in the Configuration Wizard as a network share, and now I can't get Certificate Server to work properly."

In this release of Certificate Server the shared folder must be on the local machine.

Cannot Create Certificate Authority Hierarchies

"I want to install several Certificate Servers in my enterprise and create a hierarchy of Certificate Authorities. How do I do this?"

This feature is not supported in the current release of Certificate Server.

The SMTP Service

Messages Are Corrupted

"I've noticed that lately some of my SMTP messages are corrupted. What do I do?"

You have low disk space on the volume where the `mailroot` directory is located. Free more space.

Queue Directory Filling Up

"My `queue` directory is gradually filling up, and users complain that some of their messages are not getting through to their intended recipients."

A remote SMTP server may be down, or some other problem may be occurring. Use Notepad to view the `.rtr` and `.ltr` transcript files in the `queue` directory to try to determine why the messages are not remaining in the queue.

Also check that the route domain path to the remote host is correct.

.bad Files in the Queue Directory

"I noticed there are some `.bad` files in the queue. What are these?"

Your `badmail` directory is full. Clear it.

The NNTP Service

Configuring the NNTP Service to Pull USENET Newsfeeds

"I want to configure my Default NNTP Site to pull newsfeeds from a USENET server. How do I configure this?"

This release of Microsoft NNTP Service cannot pull newsfeeds from other NNTP servers.

Allowing Other NNTP Servers to Pull Newsfeeds from Your Server

"I want to allow a third-party news server to pull news feeds off my Default NNTP Site on my IIS 4.0 server. In Default NNTP Site Properties, NNTP Settings tab, I check the ALLOW SERVERS TO PULL NEWS ARTICLES FROM THIS SERVER *checkbox, but nothing happens. What's wrong?"*

This setting is not implemented in the current release of Microsoft NNTP Service.

Using Telnet to Verify That NNTP Service Is Accepting Connections

"I can't post messages to my NNTP service on IIS from Outlook Express on a client machine. I'm not sure if the problem is with the server or with the client."

Start Telnet on the client machine, set the preferences for local echo, and open the remote system

```
<news_server>:119
```

- If the result is "200 NNTP Service," then the NNTP service is accepting client connections.
- If the result is "502 Connection refused," then the NNTP service may be paused or may have reached its connection limit.
- If the result is "Connect Failed," then the service may be stopped. If it is not stopped, then it is not accepting connections. Try rebuilding the NNTP service.

If you can connect to the service, enter the command

```
List
```

- If the result is a list of newsgroups, then the NNTP service is running well and the problem must be with the client.
- If the result is the message "480 Logon required," then anonymous access is not enabled on the Default NNTP Site.

Active Server Pages

Changes to ASPs Are Not Displayed in Browser

"I uploaded new versions of some Active Server Pages to my Web site, but when I try to access them using my browser, I still see the old versions. I have emptied my browser cache, but it still doesn't work."

The workaround is that the virtual directory you are accessing must be marked as an Application Starting Point on the Virtual Directory tab of the directory Properties sheet. Otherwise ASP does not process the file change notifications. This issue is being looked at by Microsoft.

ASPs and FrontPage Server Extensions

There have been some reports of administrators installing FrontPage extensions on IIS 4.0 servers already hosting ASPs, and finding that the FrontPage extensions caused some of the HTML on their ASPs to be rewritten in various ways. Beware!

Service Packs

Service Pack 4 for Windows NT 4.0

Just prior to this book going to press, Microsoft released a beta version of Service Pack 4.0 for Windows NT. In addition to many upgrades and bug files, this Service Pack will address a number of known issues with all the components of the Windows NT 4.0 Option Pack. Be sure to obtain and install this service pack when it becomes available..

APPENDIX A

ESSENTIAL TCP/IP

Introduction

The TCP/IP protocol suite is the core protocol underlying the Internet, so installing and configuring WWW, FTP, and other IIS services requires a good understanding of TCP/IP. This appendix is a brief overview of some of the more essential aspects of TCP/IP as implemented in the Microsoft Windows NT 4.0 operating system, and includes information on

- The history, nature, and purpose of TCP/IP
- The underlying architecture of Microsoft TCP/IP
- Installing and configuring TCP/IP on Windows NT 4.0
- TCP/IP addressing and subnetting
- Microsoft Dynamic Host Configuration protocol (DHCP)
- Troubleshooting TCP/IP networks

What Is TCP/IP?

TCP/IP is not a single protocol but a *suite*, or collection, of protocols developed as an industry standard for wide-area networking (WAN) connectivity. Of the three standard networking protocols included with Microsoft Windows NT 4.0 operating system (NetBEUI Protocol, NWLink IPX/SPX Compatible Transport, and TCP/IP Protocol), TCP/IP is the widest in scope of implementation and the most complex to configure and maintain.

TCP/IP is generally used for

- Connectivity to the Internet, a worldwide network based on TCP/IP
- Heterogeneous networks, which combine Microsoft, UNIX, and other operating systems

- Enterprise-scale networks where a standard, reliable, routable protocol is needed

History of TCP/IP

TCP/IP originated with the U.S. Department of Defense Advanced Research Projects Agency (DARPA) in the late 1960s, and it has continued being refined and extended by various agencies and governing bodies until the present. The standards for the TCP/IP protocol suite are established though a process of submitting and approving documents called *Request for Comments (RFCs).* The development of TCP/IP involves the interworking of a number of agencies, including the Internet Architecture Board (IAB), the Internet Engineering Task Force (IETF), the Internet Research Task Force (IRTF), the Internet Assigned Numbers Authority (IANA), and the Internet Society (ISOC).

Some of the milestones in the development of TCP/IP have included

- Telnet (1972)
- File Transfer Protocol (FTP) (1973)
- Transmission Control Protocol (1974)
- Internet Protocol (1981)
- TCP/IP Protocol Suite (1983)
- Domain Name System (1984)

Requests for Comments go through a series of stages before becoming accepted standards:

- Proposed Standard
- Draft Standard
- Internet Standard

When an RFC is published, it receives a number. For example, the original FTP protocol was defined in RFC 454. Often a later RFC will supercede an earlier one due to revisions and extensions in the protocol. For more information on RFCs and to download or view RFCs, visit

```
http://www.isi.edu/rfc-editor/rfc.html
```

For an index of all RFCs, go to:

```
ftp://ftp.isi.edu/in-notes/rfc-index.txt
```

Comparison with Other Protocols

The other protocol used for enterprise-level networks, NWLink IPX/SPX, is generally similar to TCP/IP in the number of Ethernet frames generated to accomplish basic networking processes like transferring files, logging on, and so on. Where NWLink and TCP/IP differ is that TCP/IP is the native protocol of the Internet, and with the surge of interest in corporate connectivity to the Internet, it has become the default to install TCP/IP as the networking protocol, while reserving NWLink only for backward compatibility with NetWare systems.

NetBEUI is not suitable for enterprise-level computing since it is not routable and is hence unsuited for large internetworks.

Architecture of the TCP/IP Protocol Suite

The basis for developing networking protocols to link together dissimilar systems is the *Open Systems Interconnection (OSI) model,* developed in 1978 by the International Standards Organization (ISO). The OSI model serves as a starting point from which vendors can develop commercial networking protocols and software.

The OSI model utilizes a seven-layer model in which each layer on one machine communicates logically with the same layer on another machine, regardless of whether the two machines come from the same vendor or run the same networking operating systems. The OSI model is outlined in Fig. A-1.

The TCP/IP protocol suite is based on a simplified version of the OSI model that has only four layers:

- Application Layer
- Transport Layer
- Internet Layer
- Network Layer

The correspondence between the OSI and TCP/IP models is shown in Fig. A-2.

Within the four layers of the TCP/IP architecture model, a number of protocols have been defined (Fig. A-3):

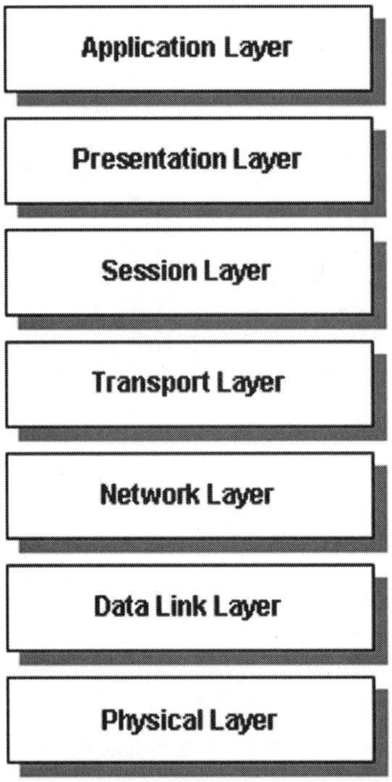

Figure A-1
The seven-layer OSI networking model.

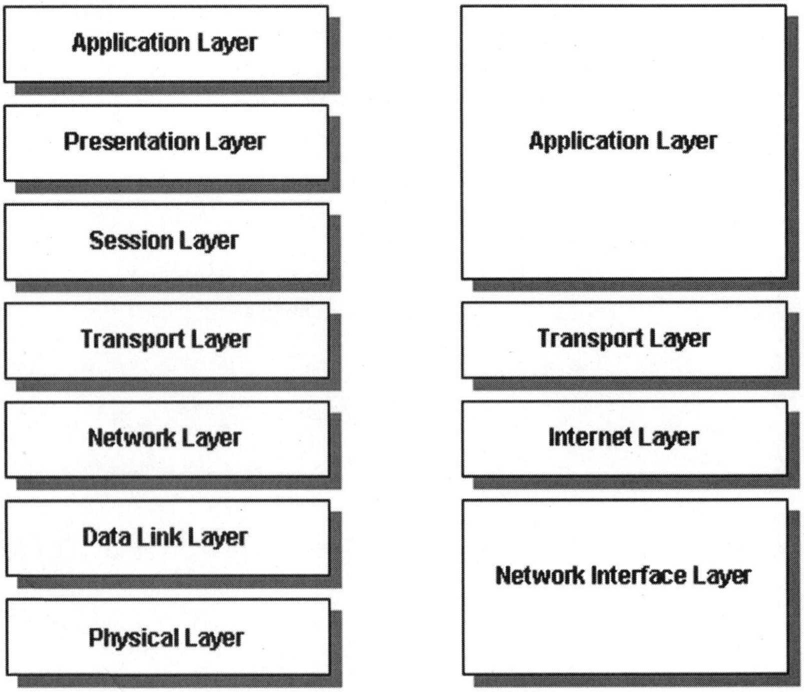

Figure A-2
Comparison between the OSI model (left) and the TCP/IP model (right).

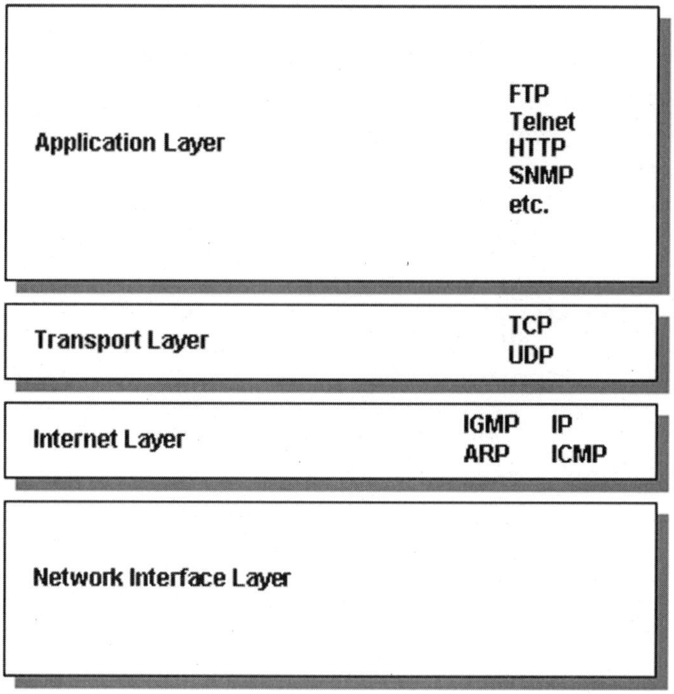

Figure A-3
The various protocols in the TCP/IP protocol suite.

Application Layer — FTP, Telnet, HTTP, SNMP, etc.

Transport Layer — TCP, UDP

Internet Layer — IGMP, IP, ARP, ICMP

Network Interface Layer

Application Layer protocols are protocols used by user applications to access Internet technologies. Of the many protocols here, some examples are

- *FTP (File Transfer Protocol),* used for transferring files from one machine to another
- *Telnet,* which enables terminal emulation for running remote applications
- *HTTP (HyperText Transfer Protocol),* which enables transfer of HTML Web pages
- *SNMP (Simple Network Management Protocol),* for monitoring network data

Application Layer protocols interface with the Transport Layer protocols through one of two methods in Microsoft TCP/IP:

- *Windows Sockets (WinSock),* an interface between socket-based applications and TCP/IP
- *NetBIOS over TCP/IP (NetBT),* which enables NetBIOS sessions and naming functions

Transport Layer protocols enable sessions between hosts so that communication is possible. The two defined protocols are

- *TCP (Transmission Control Protocol),* for one-to-one, connection-oriented, guaranteed-delivery, reliable sessions for transfer of large quantities of data
- *UDP (User Datagram Protocol),* for one-to-many, connectionless, no-guarantee sessions for transfer of small quantities of data

Internet Layer protocols enable routing of packets according to IP address, plus other protocol management functions. The four protocols here are

- *IP (Internet Protocol),* for addressing and routing of packets on an internetwork
- *ICMP (Internet Control Message Protocol),* for reporting delivery errors
- *IGMP (Internet Group Message Protocol),* used for multicasting
- *ARP (Address Resolution Protocol),* for resolving IP addresses into physical-layer network interface card addresses

Network Interface Layer protocols deal with actually moving the data onto and off of the network wiring. No TCP/IP protocols are defined at this layer; instead, topology-dependent network interface card *drivers* are used to provide networking services here.

Structure of a TCP/IP Frame

Here is an example to illustrate how a typical TCP/IP frame is formed and transported over a network (Fig. A-4):

An application like Internet Explorer running in the Application Layer formulates an *instruction* like HTTP GET and passes this instruction down to the next layer, the Transport Layer.

The Transport Layer segments the information sent down to it from the Application Layer into data packets no greater than 1460 bytes in size, and adds a TCP header of 20 bytes that specifies the source and destination ports, sequence number, and other information. The *TCP packet* thus constructed is then passed down to the Internet Layer.

The Internet Layer adds a header of 20 bytes to the TCP packet sent down to it from the Transport Layer. The IP layer includes information concerning the source and destination IP addresses, the packet Time to

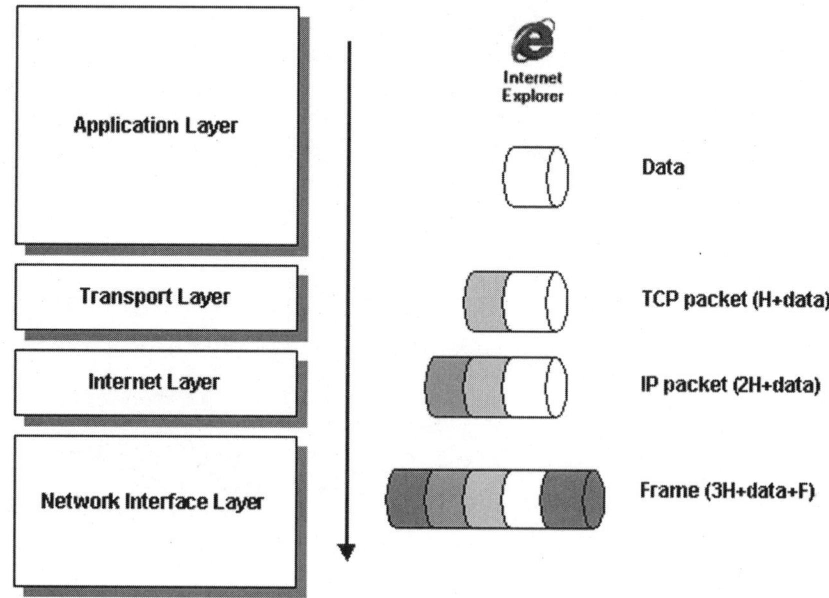

Figure A-4 Formation of a TCP/IP frame by protocol encapsulation.

Live (TTL), and other information relating to routing functions. The *IP packet* thus constructed is then passed down to the Network Interface layer.

The Network Interface Layer formats the packet passed down from the Internet Layer in an appropriate fashion for the networking method (Ethernet, Token Ring, FDDI, etc.) that will be used. For example, if the IP packet is destined to travel on an Ethernet network, it is formatted into an 802.3 Ethernet frame by adding a 22-byte header containing the source and destination physical addresses, and a four-byte footer containing checksum information. The result is an *Ethernet frame* of length up to 1514 bytes.

We can view the structure of TCP/IP frames in detail using the tool *Microsoft Network Monitor.* A limited version of this tool is included with Windows NT 4.0 under the Administrative Tools Start menu item. Figure A-5 shows a Network Monitor capture with detailed information on the various encapsulated protocols for an `HTTP GET` request on an Ethernet network.

Here is the detailed packet information from the *detail pane* (middle pane) of Network Monitor's display window in Fig. A-5. Note the encapsulation of the various protocols, the source and destination ports and addresses, and various other details. Note also the complexity of the TCP/IP protocol!

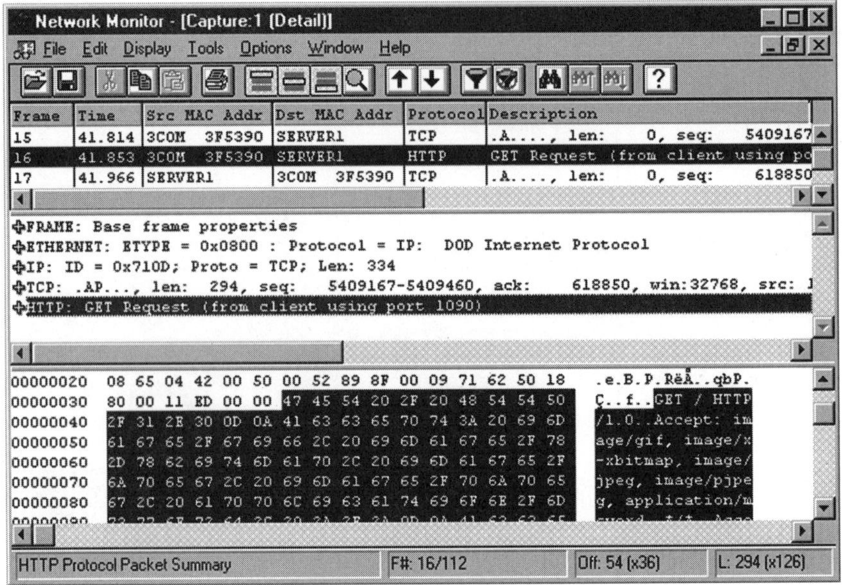

Figure A-5
A Network Monitor capture showing an `HTTP GET` request frame.

```
FRAME: Base frame properties
    FRAME: Time of capture = Feb 21, 1998 22:10:39.862
    FRAME: Time delta from previous physical frame: 39 milliseconds
    FRAME: Frame number: 16
    FRAME: Total frame length: 348 bytes
    FRAME: Capture frame length: 348 bytes
    FRAME: Frame data: Number of data bytes remaining = 348 (0x015C)
ETHERNET: ETYPE = 0x0800 : Protocol = IP: DOD Internet Protocol
    ETHERNET: Destination address : 48543300CD6A
        ETHERNET: .......0 = Individual address
        ETHERNET: ......0. = Universally administered address
    ETHERNET: Source address : 02608C3F5390
        ETHERNET: .......0 = No routing information present
        ETHERNET: ......1. = Locally administered address
    ETHERNET: Frame Length : 348 (0x015C)
    ETHERNET: Ethernet Type : 0x0800 (IP: DOD Internet Protocol)
    ETHERNET: Ethernet Data: Number of data bytes remaining = 334
(0x014E)
IP: ID = 0x710D; Proto = TCP; Len: 334
    IP: Version = 4 (0x4)
    IP: Header Length = 20 (0x14)
    IP: Service Type = 0 (0x0)
        IP: Precedence = Routine
        IP: ...0.... = Normal Delay
        IP: ....0... = Normal Throughput
        IP: .....0.. = Normal Reliability
    IP: Total Length = 334 (0x14E)
    IP: Identification = 28941 (0x710D)
    IP: Flags Summary = 2 (0x2)
        IP: .......0 = Last fragment in datagram
        IP: ......1. = Cannot fragment datagram
    IP: Fragment Offset = 0 (0x0) bytes
    IP: Time to Live = 32 (0x20)
```

```
    IP: Protocol = TCP - Transmission Control
    IP: Checksum = 0x8003
    IP: Source Address = 172.16.8.20
    IP: Destination Address = 172.16.8.101
    IP: Data: Number of data bytes remaining = 314 (0x013A)
TCP: .AP..., len: 294, seq: 5409167-5409460, ack: 618850,
win:32768, src: 1090 dst: 80
    TCP: Source Port = 0x0442
    TCP: Destination Port = Hypertext Transfer Protocol
    TCP: Sequence Number = 5409167 (0x52898F)
    TCP: Acknowledgement Number = 618850 (0x97162)
    TCP: Data Offset = 20 (0x14)
    TCP: Reserved = 0 (0x0000)
    TCP: Flags = 0x18 : .AP...
        TCP: ..0..... = No urgent data
        TCP: ...1.... = Acknowledgement field significant
        TCP: ....1... = Push function
        TCP: .....0.. = No Reset
        TCP: ......0. = No Synchronize
        TCP: .......0 = No Fin
    TCP: Window = 32768 (0x8000)
    TCP: Checksum = 0x11ED
    TCP: Urgent Pointer = 0 (0x0)
    TCP: Data: Number of data bytes remaining = 294 (0x0126)
HTTP: GET Request (from client using port 1090)
    HTTP: Request Method = GET
    HTTP: Uniform Resource Identifier = /
    HTTP: Protocol Version = HTTP/1.0
    HTTP: Accept = image/gif, image/x-xbitmap, image/jpeg,
image/pjpeg, application/mswo
    HTTP: Accept-Language = en
    HTTP: Undocumented Header = UA-pixels: 800x600
        HTTP: Undocumented Header Fieldname = UA-pixels
        HTTP: Undocumented Header Value = 800x600
    HTTP: Undocumented Header = UA-color: color8
        HTTP: Undocumented Header Fieldname = UA-color
        HTTP: Undocumented Header Value = color8
    HTTP: Undocumented Header = UA-OS: Windows 95
        HTTP: Undocumented Header Fieldname = UA-OS
        HTTP: Undocumented Header Value = Windows 95
    HTTP: Undocumented Header = UA-CPU: x86
        HTTP: Undocumented Header Fieldname = UA-CPU
        HTTP: Undocumented Header Value = x86
    HTTP: User-Agent = Mozilla/2.0 (compatible; MSIE 3.0; Windows
95)
        HTTP: Host = server1
        HTTP: Connection = Keep-Alive
```

Installing TCP/IP on Windows NT 4.0

The first step in configuring TCP/IP is installing it. Click START, SETTINGS, CONTROL PANEL, NETWORK to open the Network dialog box. Select the

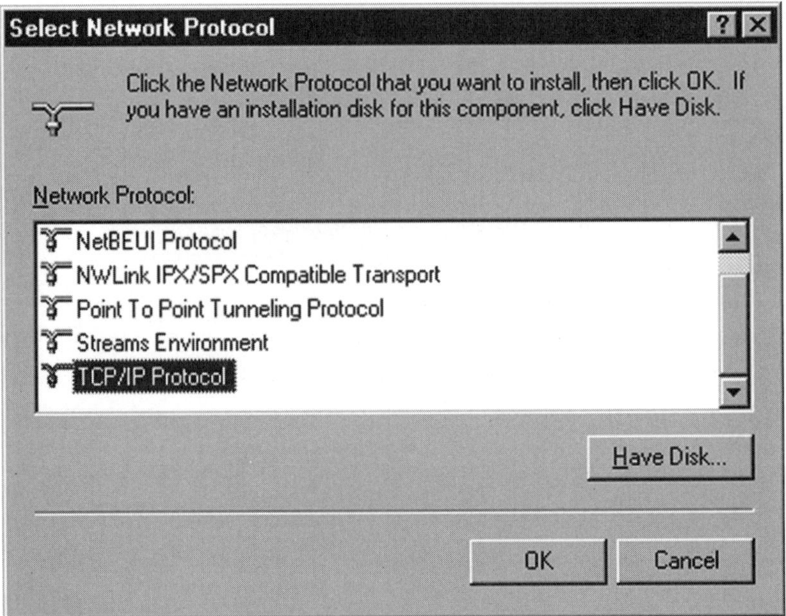

Figure A-6 Installing TCP/IP on Windows NT 4.0

Protocols tab and click ADD to open the Select Network Protocol dialog box (Fig. A-6).

Select TCP/IP and click OK. Enter the path to the Windows NT source files in the Windows NT Setup box and click CONTINUE to install the files for the protocol. When this is finished, click CLOSE, and the Microsoft TCP/IP Properties box appears (Fig. A-7).

If you are installing TCP/IP on a server, specify an IP address, subnet mask, and default gateway address. Click OK, and when prompted to restart the computer, do this. When the machine boots up again, TCP/IP should be properly installed and initialized. Before rebooting the machine (or afterward) you can configure additional settings for TCP/IP as described in the next section.

Configuring TCP/IP on Windows NT 4.0

Configuring TCP/IP is performed by using the TCP/IP Properties box illustrated in Fig. A-7. This dialog box has five tabs, each containing controls for configuring various TCP/IP settings.

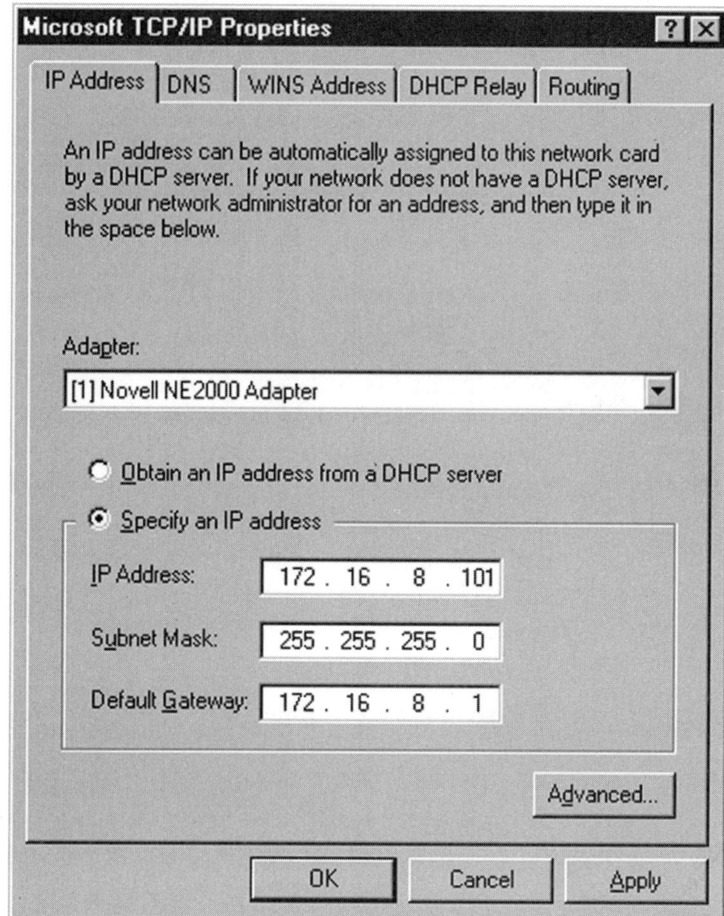

Figure A-7
The TCP/IP Properties box appears after you install the files for TCP/IP.

The IP Address Tab of the TCP/IP Properties Sheet

The IP Address tab (Fig. A-7) is used to configure the following TCP/IP settings:

Select the *Network Adapter* (Network Interface Card) that you wish to configure TCP/IP on. Windows NT 4.0 allows computers to be *multi-homed,* i.e., to have multiple network cards installed, each of which can be configured separately as far as protocols and services bindings are concerned.

Choose whether to manually SPECIFY AN IP ADDRESS or to automatically OBTAIN AN IP ADDRESS FROM A DHCP SERVER. A *DHCP server* can be either a

Microsoft Windows NT server running the DHCP Server service, or some other DHCP server. IP addresses can be obtained either over local network or through a PPP dialup router (e.g., when you connect to an ISP through Dial-up Networking, the DHCP server at the ISP will lease your machine an IP address over the serial PPP line).

If your machine is a server, it should have either a manually assigned IP address or a DHCP reservation so that it always receives the same IP address from the DHCP server. If your machine is a client, it is easiest to have it obtain its IP address from a DHCP server.

If you configure your settings manually, you should enter three settings:

- *IP Address:* the unique 32-bit identifier for the machine on the TCP/IP network.
- *Subnet Mask:* a 32-bit number that divides the IP address into two numbers, a host number and a network number. The subnet mask is used during TCP/IP communications to determine whether the destination machine is on the local subnet or a remote one, in order to route it appropriately.
- *Default Gateway:* the default gateway is a 32-bit number specifying where IP frames should be sent if there is no specified route to the destination machine. Note: Specifying a default gateway is optional, but if one is not specified then access may be restricted to the local subnet only.

Click the ADVANCED button to open the *Advanced IP Addressing* dialog box (Fig. A-8). The Advanced IP Addressing dialog box is used to configure the following:

Additional IP addresses for the network adapter selected: The *What's this?* help says that you can add up to five additional IP addresses per adapter (giving a maximum total of six IP addresses per adapter), but this is actually older information relating to Windows NT 3.51. With Windows NT 4.0 you can continue adding as many additional IP addresses as you wish.

Additional gateways for the Network Adapter selected: These gateways can be reordered using the UP and DOWN buttons. TCP/IP on Windows NT 4.0 includes dead gateway detection. If a machine needs to send a packet to a gateway and the gateway will not respond, the next gateway on the list will be tried.

Enable PPTP filtering: This is used to set up a Virtual Private Network (VPN) and is beyond the scope of this appendix.

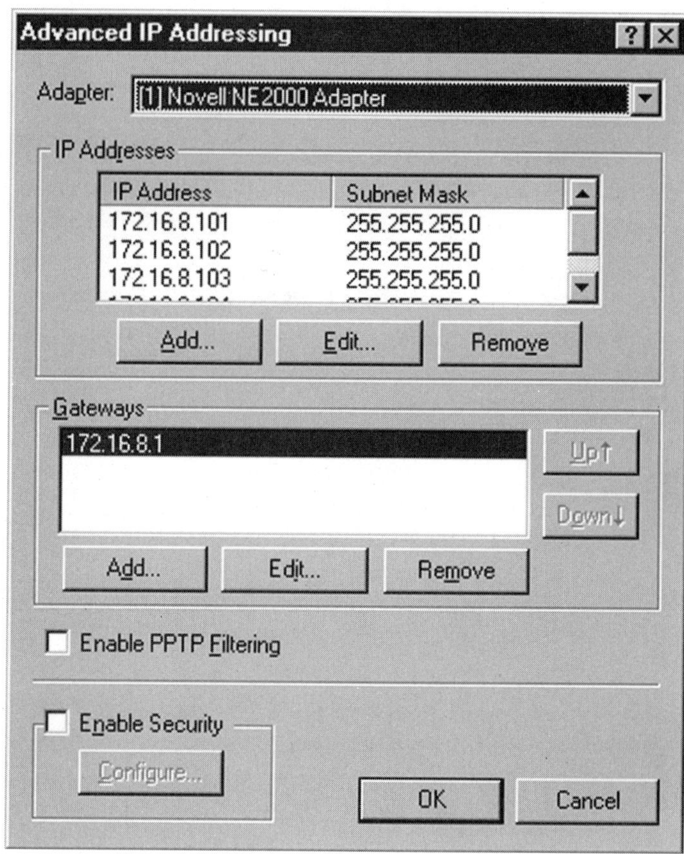

Figure A-8 The Advanced IP Addressing dialog box.

Enable Security: This is used to grant or deny access based on IP address or port number. These settings should not be used; instead, use the Security tab on the Web site properties sheet in Internet Service Manager.

The DNS Tab of the TCP/IP Properties Sheet

The DNS tab (Fig. A-9) is used to configure the following TCP/IP settings:

Host Name: By default, this is the same as the *NetBIOS name* for your computer, which is assigned using the Identification tab of the Network dialog box, which is opened using CONTROL PANEL, NETWORK. Administrators may choose, however, to assign a different host name to the Windows NT computer. The host name is the first half of the *Fully Qualified Domain Name (FQDN)* of the machine.

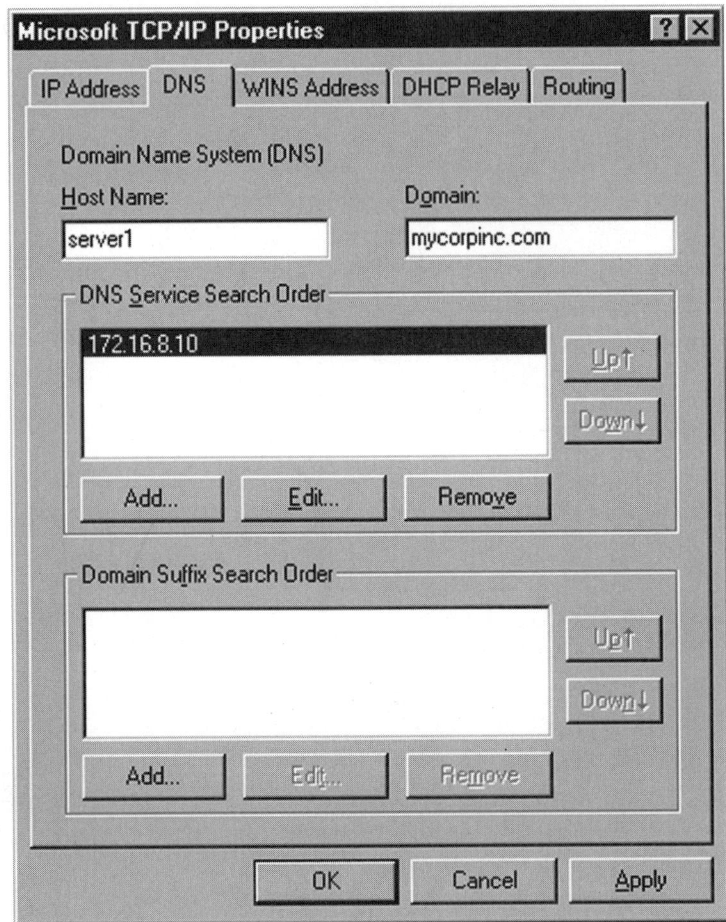

Figure A-9
The DNS tab on the Microsoft TCP/IP Properties sheet.

Domain Name: This is the Internet domain to which the host belongs. The domain name is the last half of the Fully Qualified Domain Name of the machine. In this example the FQDN of the machine is

```
server1.mycorpinc.com
```

DNS Service Search Order: This list shows the various Domain Name System (DNS) servers that are used by your machine to resolve the FQDN queries for destination or target machines into IP addresses. This list may contain any number of DNS servers, but they will be used in the order listed.

Domain Suffix Search Order: Specify additional DNS suffixes that should be appended to host names for DNS name resolution.

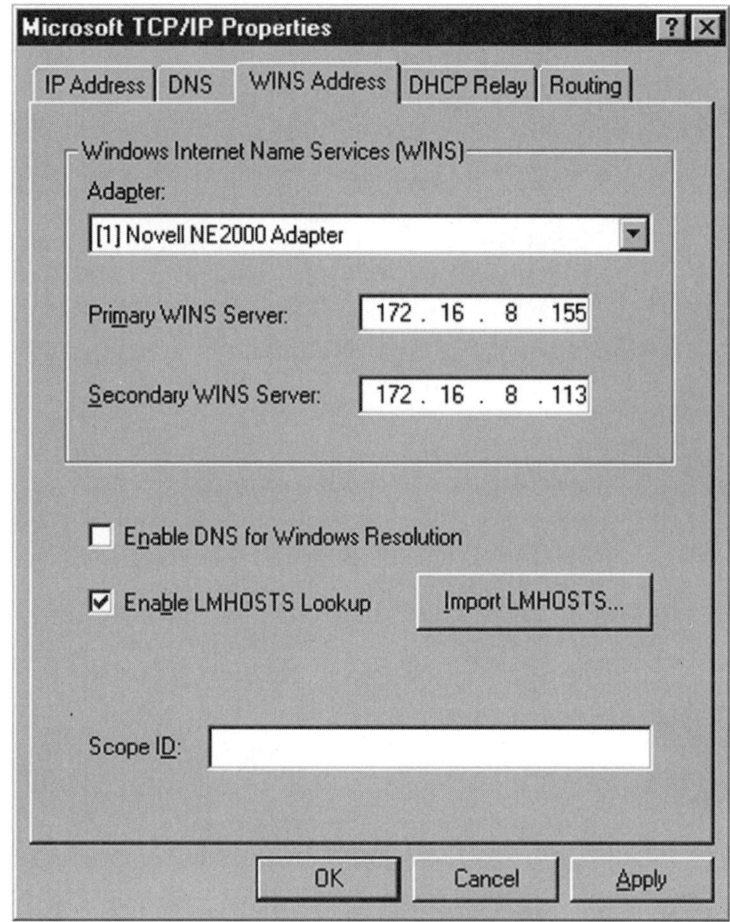

Figure A-10 The WINS Address tab on the Microsoft TCP/IP Properties sheet.

The WINS Address Tab of the TCP/IP Properties Sheet

The WINS Address tab (Fig. A-10) is used to configure the following TCP/IP settings:

Primary and secondary WINS servers. These are the IP addresses of the WINS servers that should be used by the selected network adapter. WINS stands for Windows Internet Naming Service, and represents a Microsoft alternative to the Domain Name System suitable for small to medium-sized networks. If using TCP/IP however, DNS is preferred to WINS. Even though WINS supports a dynamic name database and thus has lower administrative overhead than DNS, nevertheless DNS is preferred on medium- to large-sized networks because of its compatibility with standard Internet functionality.

Enable DNS for Windows Resolution. This ensures that DNS servers are used for name resolution, if specified on the DNS tab.

Enable LMHOSTS Lookup. This enables the use of a local LMHOSTS file for NetBIOS name resolution. LMHOSTS files contain mappings of NetBIOS names to IP addresses and can provide a backup to or an alternative to WINS resolution of NetBIOS names. A sample LMHOSTS file is located in

```
C:\winnt\system32\drivers\etc\
```

Scope ID. This is a character string that is appended to the NetBIOS name that can be used to segregate the machines on the network into groups that can only communicate using NetBIOS with machines in the same group (i.e., having the same scope ID). Usually this is left blank and subnetting is used instead.

The DHCP Relay Tab of the TCP/IP Properties Sheet

DHCP uses broadcast frames, so it is usual to have one DHCP server on each subnet since routers are generally configured to block broadcasts. An alternative to this, however, is to use a single DHCP server in the main administrative subnet of the enterprise network and configure one computer in each of the other subnets to be a *DHCP Relay Agent.* When a machine in one of these subnets needs an IP address, it broadcasts its request for an address, and the DHCP Relay Agent hears the request and forwards it directly to the DHCP server on the main subnet, which returns the IP address directly to the requesting client.

Use the DHCP Relay tab (Fig. A-11) to enter the IP address of the DHCP Relay Agent in your subnet, if there is one.

The Routing Tab of the TCP/IP Properties Sheet

The Routing tab (Fig. A-12) is used to enable *static routing* on the Windows NT machine. Use this on multihomed computers to enable them to route packets from one network adapter to another.

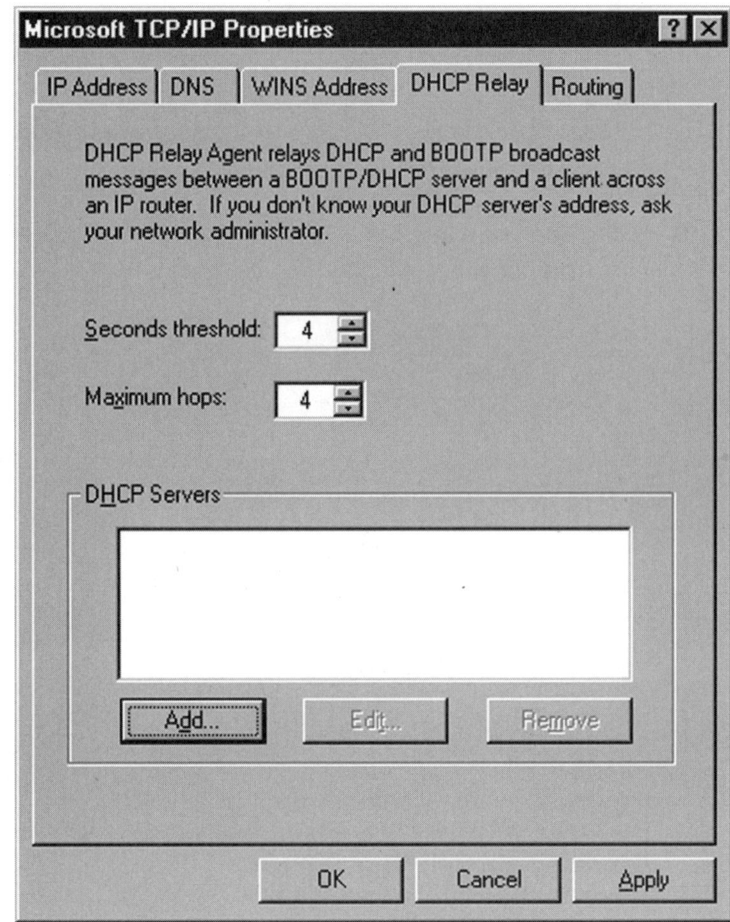

Figure A-11
The DHCP Relay tab of the Microsoft TCP/IP Properties sheet.

An alternative is to install the *Routing Information Protocol (RIP)* service by entering the Control Panel, choosing Network, clicking on the Services tab, and clicking ADD. RIP supports dynamic routing on NT and eliminates the need to manually set up routing tables on multihomed machines.

Understanding IP Addressing and Subnetting

IP addresses are 32-bit binary numbers that are represented in decimal form as *w.x.y.z*, where *w*, *x*, *y*, and *z* may range from 0 to 255. IP addresses

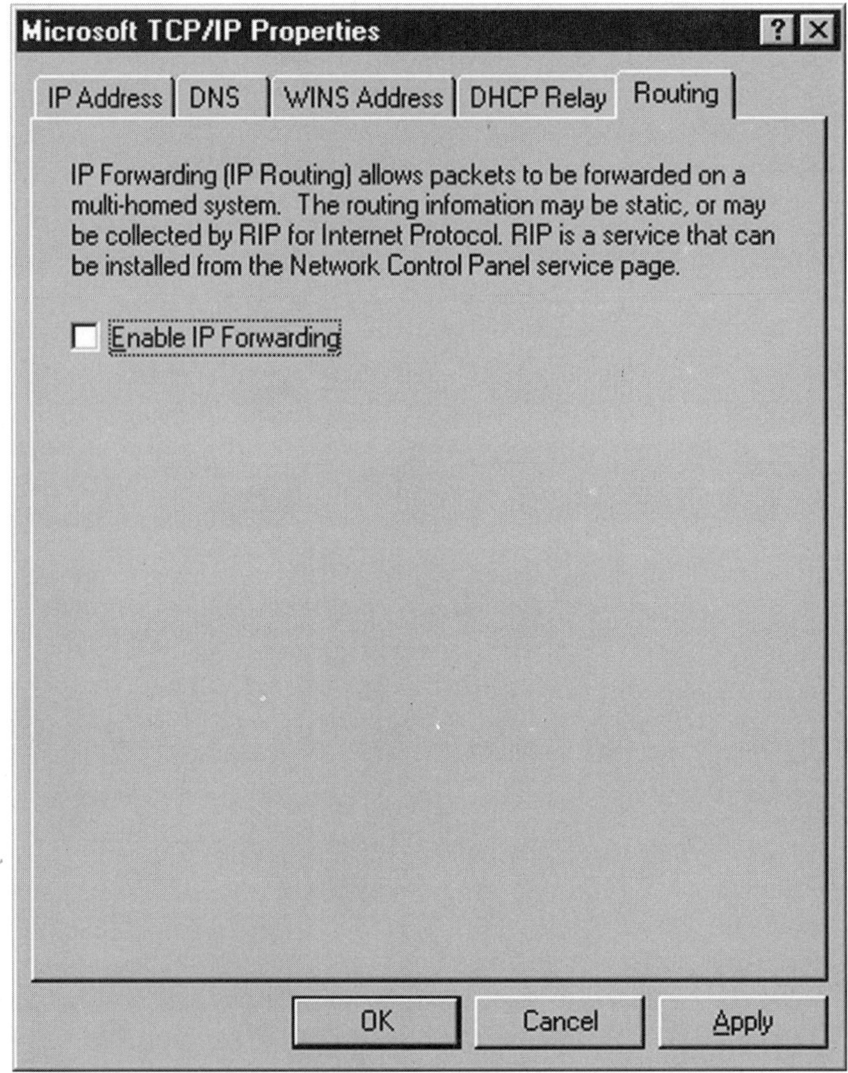

Figure A-12
The Routing tab on the Microsoft TCP/IP Properties sheet.

provide a unique way of identifying machines, routers, and other active networking hardware on a TCP/IP internetwork. A unique IP address is required by each machine on a TCP/IP internetwork. If two or more machines have the same IP address, communications on the internetwork may not work properly.

IP addresses can be split into two sections:

- *Network ID:* the portion of the address that identifies the subnetwork the computer is on. Computers on the same network can talk to each other using TCP/IP; computers on different networks must have their messages routed to each other by a dedicated router or multihomed Windows NT computer.

- *Host ID:* the portion of the address that identifies the host on the subnetwork. This must be unique to the subnetwork defined by the network number above.

IP Address Classes

Five classes of IP addresses are defined, of which you only need to be familiar with three: classes A, B, and C. Table A-1 outlines some information concerning these three classes. Note the following:

- 127.*x.y.z* is reserved for `loopback` functions.
- Network and host IDs cannot be either all zeros or all ones.
- The host ID must be unique on the locally defined network ID.

If your network is not connected to the Internet, or if you are using a firewall/proxy server combination to shield your network from the Internet, you can use any of the following IP address blocks, which are reserved for *private* TCP/IP networks:

Class A (one network): 10.*x.y.z*

Class B (16 networks): 172.16.*y.z* to 172.31.*y.z*

Class C (255 networks): 192.168.*y.z*

Table A-1 IP Address Classes

Class	IP Address	Network Number	Host Number	Start of First Octet	End of First Octet	Number of Hosts per Network
A	*w.x.y.z*	*w*	*x.y.z*	1.*x.y.z*	126.*x.y.z*	16,777,214
B	*w.x.y.z*	*w.x*	*y.z*	128.*x.y.z*	191.*x.y.z*	65,534
C	*w.x.y.z*	*w.x.y*	*z*	192.*x.y.z*	223.*x.y.z*	254

Subnet Masks

IP addresses are split into network and host IDs by applying a subnet mask. The *default subnet masks* for the three classes of addresses described above are

Class A: 255.0.0.0

Class B: 255.255.0.0

Class C: 255.255.255.0

The way it works is that the IP address and the subnet are ANDed together in binary notation to determine the network number belonging to the IP address. For example:

192.168.12.45 = 11000000 10101000 00001100 00101101

255.255.255.0 = 11111111 11111111 11111111 00000000

ANDing the IP address with the subnet mask gives the network number:

192.168.12.0 = 11000000 10101000 00001100 00000000

The host number is the remaining portion:

45 = 00000000 00000000 00000000 00101101

When TCP/IP wants to contact a host, it has to first determine if the host is local or remote. The host is determined to be *remote* if

(Source IP) AND (source subnet mask)

does NOT equal

(destination IP) AND (source subnet mask)

If a route to the remote host is found in the local routing table, the route is used; if no route is found, the IP frame is sent to the default gateway.

Subnetting IP Networks

To make better use of the limited number of available IP addresses, *custom subnet masks* can be constructed to further subdivide the network. The process of creating custom subnet masks is called *subnetting*.

As a simple example, consider the following class B IP address and default subnet mask:

172.16.119.5 = 10101100 00010000 01110111 00000101

255.255.0.0 = 11111111 11111111 00000000 00000000

Since 16 bits (the number of ones in the default subnet mask) are used for the network ID, the remaining 16 bits (the number of zeros in the default subnet mask) can be used for host IDs. What that means is that the network 172.16.0.0 can have a maximum of $2^{16}-2 = 65{,}534$ hosts, since there are 16 bits in the host number and the cases "all zeros" and "all ones" are disallowed (hence subtract 2).

With subnetting we can "borrow" bits from the host ID and use them for the network ID. For example, consider the same IP address, this time used with the custom subnet mask `255.255.240.0`, as shown below:

172.16.119.5 = 10101100 00010000 01110111 00000101

255.255.240.0 = 11111111 11111111 11110000 00000000

This arrangement gives more bits for network IDs (20 bits) and hence more subnetworks, but fewer bits for host IDs (12 bits) and hence fewer possible hosts per subnetwork. In fact, the number of possible hosts per subnetwork is now reduced to $2^{12}-2 = 4{,}094$ hosts.

In general, subnetting is somewhat complicated mathematically to perform, but Table A-2 provides a practical tool that can be used to perform simple subnetting calculations for class B networks. Similar tables can be constructed for class A and class C networks.

The table item called *network ID increment* is important to understand. Building on the previous example, if the IP address and subnet mask for a host are configured as

IP address: 172.16.119.5

Subnet mask: 255.255.240.0

then which range of IP addresses represents hosts on the *same subnet* as this host? The answer lies in using the network ID increment. For a third octet of 240 the increment is given in the table as 16. There are 14 networks, each differing in the third octet by 16 from the previous one; the 14 possible networks are given in Table A-3.

From the bold entry in Table A-3 we can see that the network ID for the host in our example is 172.16.112.0 and that our host will be able to

Table A-2 Subnetting Calculation Aid for Class B Networks

N, Number of Bits Borrowed from Host ID for Network ID	2^N-2, Number of Possible Subnets	Third Octet = $256-2^{(8-N)}$, Custom Subnet Mask	$2^{(8-N)}$, Network ID Increment	$2^{(16-N)}-2$, Number of Hosts per Subnet
1	Invalid	Invalid	Invalid	Invalid
2	2	255.255.192.0	64	16,382
3	6	255.255.224.0	32	8,190
4	14	255.255.240.0	16	4,094
5	30	255.255.248.0	8	2,046
6	62	255.255.252.0	4	1,022
7	126	255.255.254.0	2	510
8	254	255.255.255.0	1	254

communicate directly (i.e., without the need of a router) with all other hosts whose IP addresses range from 172.16.112.1 to 172.16.127.254.

An application of using network IDs and custom subnet masks would be for granting or denying access to a Web site on IIS according to IP number. See Chap. 3 for information on where to configure these settings.

Installing Microsoft DHCP Server Service

If you want to use DHCP to automatically configure TCP/IP for machines on your network, you will have to make at least one of your servers a DHCP server.

To configure your Windows NT 4.0 Server as a DHCP Server for automatically assigning IP address, subnet mask, default gateway, and other TCP/IP information to client machines on your network, you must first install the Microsoft DHCP Server service on your server. Note that the machine you want to install DHCP Server service on must have a manually configured (static) IP address

Table A-3

Possible Networks for the Example

Network ID	Starting IP Address	Ending IP Address
172.16.0.0	Invalid (borrowed bits all 0s)	Invalid
172.16.16.0	172.16.16.1	172.16.31.254
172.16.32.0	172.16.32.1	172.16.47.254
172.16.48.0	172.16.48.1	172.16.63.254
172.16.64.0	172.16.64.1	172.16.79.254
172.16.80.0	172.16.80.1	172.16.95.254
172.16.96.0	172.16.96.1	172.16.111.254
172.16.112.0	**172.16.112.1**	**172.16.127.254**
172.16.128.0	172.16.128.1	172.16.143.254
172.16.144.0	172.16.144.1	172.16.159.254
172.16.160.0	172.16.160.1	172.16.175.254
172.16.176.0	172.16.176.1	172.16.191.254
172.16.192.0	172.16.192.1	172.16.207.254
172.16.208.0	172.16.208.1	172.16.223.254
172.16.224.0	172.16.224.1	172.16.239.254
172.16.240.0	Invalid (borrowed bits all 1s)	Invalid

Click START, SETTINGS, CONTROL PANEL, NETWORK to open the Network dialog box. Select the Services tab and click ADD to open the Select Network Services dialog box. Select Microsoft DHCP Server and click OK to install the files from the NT source files. You will need to restart your system to complete the installation.

Configuring Microsoft DHCP Server Service

To configure your Microsoft DHCP Server service, click START, PROGRAMS, ADMINISTRATIVE TOOLS, DHCP MANAGER. The DHCP Manager (Local) window opens up (Fig. A-13).

The next step is to create a scope on the DHCP server. A *scope* is a pool of IP addresses that are available to be leased by DHCP clients from the DHCP server. To create a scope, double-click on the Local Machine

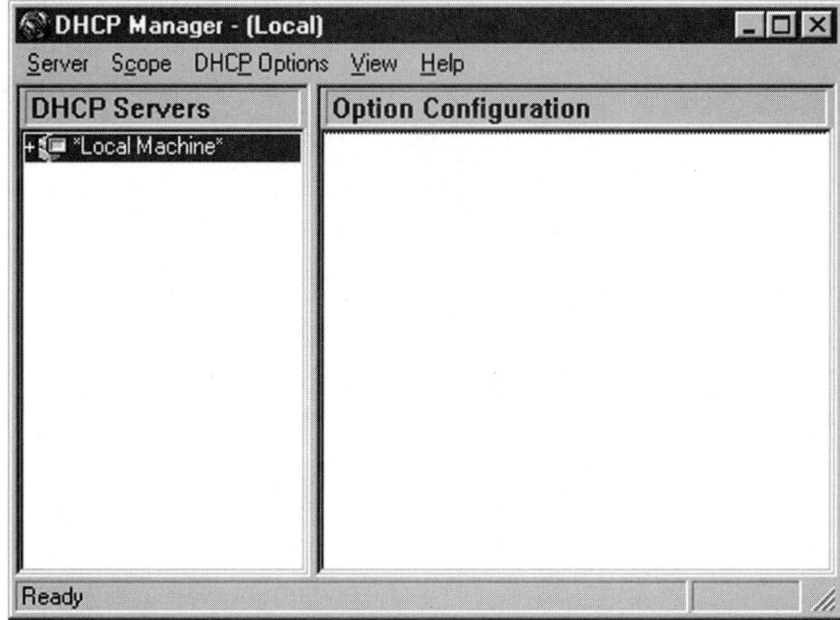

Figure A-13 The DHCP Manager (Local) window.

icon in the DHCP Manager (Local) window. Then select SCOPE, CREATE from the menu bar. This opens the Create Scope dialog box (Fig. A-14). In Fig. A-14, note that

- The available IP addresses range from 172.16.8.125 to 172.16.8.149.
- The subnet mask handed out to clients is 255.255.255.0.
- The range of addresses 172.16.8.130 to 172.16.8.133 is excluded from the pool.
- The individual address 172.16.8.140 is excluded from the pool.
- The duration of the DHCP lease is 3 days (this is the default value).
- The scope has been named *MyCorp Inc LAN*.

Click OK. You are asked if you want to activate the new scope. Click YES. Now in the DHCP Manager window, double-click again on the Local Machine icon, and you should see an active scope (yellow light bulb).

So far we have configured our DHCP server to automatically hand out IP addresses and a subnet mask. But how about configuring it to hand out other information like default gateway, IP addresses of WINS and DNS servers, and so on? To do this, select the active scope in the DHCP Manager window and select DHCP OPTIONS, SCOPE from the menu bar. This opens the DHCP Options: Scope dialog box.

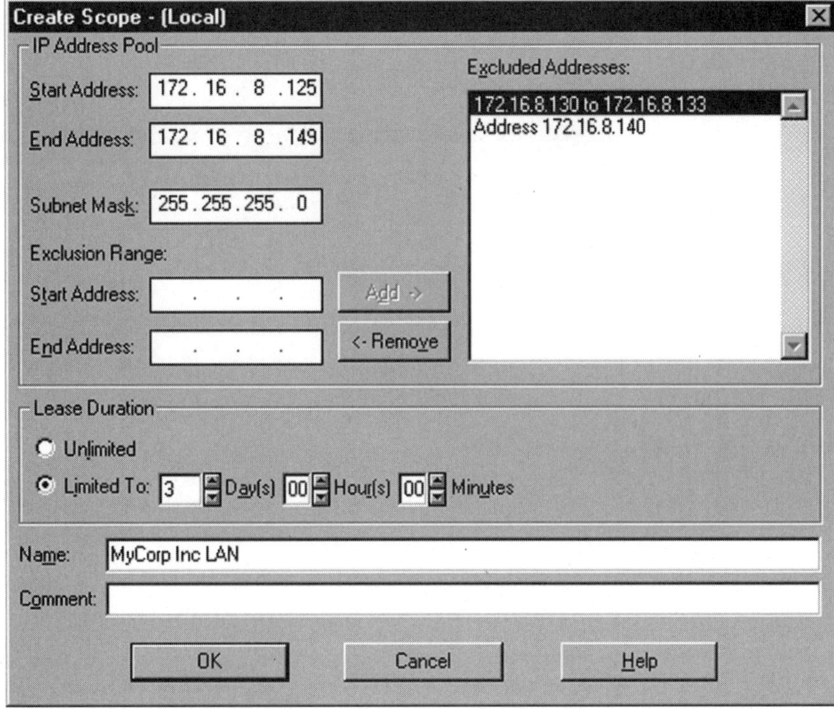

Figure A-14 Creating a scope in DHCP Manager.

To enable DHCP to assign a default gateway address to DHCP clients on your network, select the 003 ROUTER Unused Option and click ADD to make it an Active Option. Click VALUE to expand the dialog box, click EDIT ARRAY, enter the IP address of the default gateway, and click ADD and then OK (see Fig. A-15).

Other scope options you can define are

- *006 DNS Servers:* IP address of DNS servers
- *046 WINS/NBT node type:* type of NetBIOS over TCP/IP (NBT) name resolution used by client (usually you will choose 8 = H node)
- *044 WINS/NBNS servers:* IP address of WINS servers
- *047 NetBIOS Scope ID:* local NetBIOS scope ID

Once you have defined all your scope options, click OK to close the DHCP Options: Scope dialog box and return to the DHCP Manager (Local) window. If you close and then reopen this window, you will see your new scope options listed (Fig. A-16).

To view the currently leased IP addresses, double-click on the active scope (yellow bulb) to open the Active Leases dialog box.

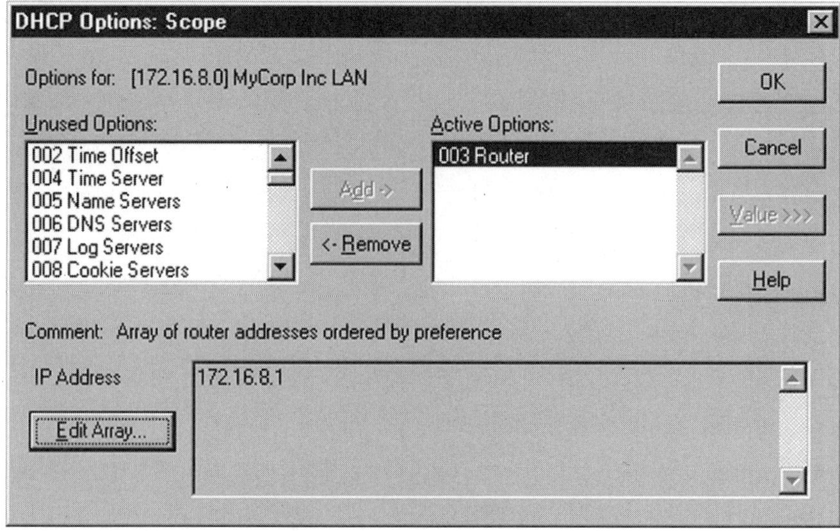

Figure A-15 Configuring the 003 Router scope option to assign a default gateway to DHCP clients.

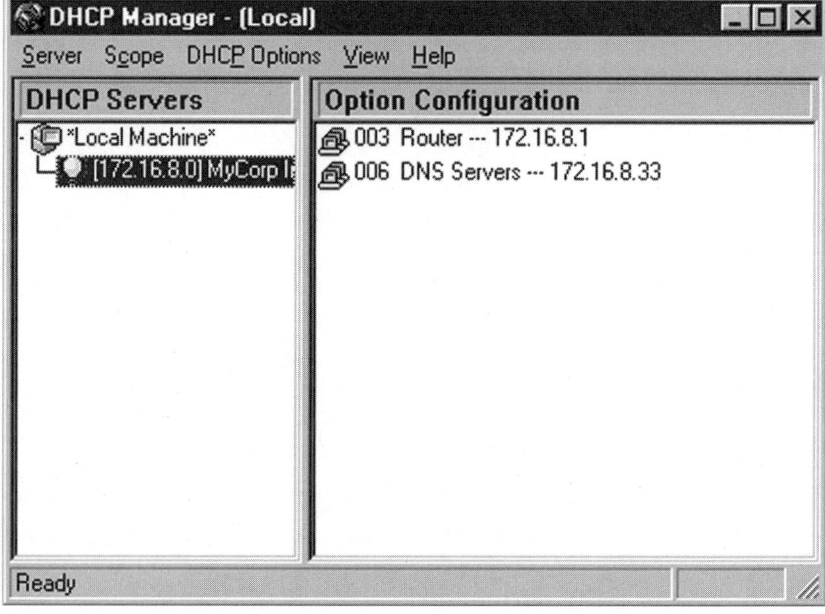

Figure A-16 DHCP scope options configured using the DHCP Manager.

Troubleshooting TCP/IP

Finally, Microsoft TCP/IP includes a number of standard command-line tools for troubleshooting TCP/IP. This section will briefly examine three of them.

Using the `ipconfig` Utility

The `ipconfig` tool can be used to list the currently assigned TCP/IP settings for the host. Command-line options include

- `ipconfig`: shows basic TCP/IP settings
- `ipconfig /all`: shows all TCP/IP settings
- `ipconfig /release`: releases leased IP address (DHCP clients only)
- `ipconfig /renew`: requests new IP address lease (DHCP clients only)

Here is a typical output from the command `ipconfig /all`:

```
Windows NT IP Configuration
    Host Name . . . . . . . . . . : server1.mycorpinc.com
    DNS Servers . . . . . . . . . : 172.16.8.10
    Node Type . . . . . . . . . . : Broadcast
    NetBIOS Scope ID. . . . . . . :
    IP Routing Enabled. . . . . . : No
    WINS Proxy Enabled. . . . . . : No
    NetBIOS Resolution Uses DNS : No

Ethernet adapter NE20001:

    Description . . . . . . . . . : 3Com Fast EtherLink XL Adapter
                                    (3C509).
    Physical Address. . . . . . . : 48-54-33-00-CD-6A
    DHCP Enabled. . . . . . . . . : No
    IP Address. . . . . . . . . . : 172.16.8.110
    Subnet Mask . . . . . . . . . : 255.255.255.0
    Default Gateway . . . . . . . : 172.16.8.1
```

Using the `ping` Utility

Another useful utility for testing and troubleshooting TCP/IP is `ping`. The following sequence of commands uses `ping` to progressively test TCP/IP on an internetwork:

`ping 127.0.0.1`: Ping loopback address to test if TCP/IP is properly installed and initialized.

`ping 172.16.8.110`: Ping your own IP address to verify it is correctly configured.

`ping 172.16.8.1`: Ping the default gateway to see if it is functioning correctly.

`ping 172.16.23.95`: Ping a remote host to see if it is reachable.

Here is a typical output from the first command above:

```
Pinging 127.0.0.1 with 32 bytes of data:
Reply from 127.0.0.1: bytes = 32 time<10ms TTL = 128
Reply from 127.0.0.1: bytes = 32 time<10ms TTL = 128
Reply from 127.0.0.1: bytes = 32 time<10ms TTL = 128
Reply from 127.0.0.1: bytes = 32 time<10ms TTL = 128
```

The time is the time from sending the packet until a response packet is received. The TTL is the remaining Time to Live of the packet. TTL is decremented for each hop across a router, and may be decremented further if router congestion causes the packet to be delayed.

Using the `tracert` Utility

The `tracert` utility can be used to trace the route (i.e., the hops through routers) from your machine to a destination host on the Internet. It is useful for troubleshooting WAN connections to determine if routers are functioning correctly.

The following example shows the result of typing the command `tracert ntt.co.jp`:

```
Tracing route to www.ntt.co.jp [210.130.164.102] over a maximum of
30 hops:

1   227 ms  185 ms  185 ms  tnt01.escape.ca [204.112.225.50]
2   196 ms  208 ms  211 ms  bb.escape.ca [204.112.225.4]
3   241 ms  209 ms  221 ms  escape.mbnet.mb.ca [204.112.54.194]
4   210 ms  252 ms  198 ms  e0.manitoba.mbnet.mb.ca [204.112.54.193]
5   207 ms  217 ms  199 ms  psp.mb.canet.ca [192.68.64.5]
6   240 ms  241 ms  254 ms  border1-atm1-0.quebec.canet.ca
                            [205.207.238.45]
7   252 ms  258 ms  240 ms  psp.ny.canet.ca [205.207.238.154]
8   245 ms  239 ms  257 ms  borderx2-hssi2-0.Boston.mci.net
                            [204.70.179.117]
9   817 ms  666 ms  245 ms  core2-fddi1-0.Boston.mci.net
                            [204.70.179.65]
10  363 ms  325 ms  342 ms  core7.SanFrancisco.mci.net [204.70.4.93]
```

```
11  327 ms  323 ms  320 ms  mae-west3.SanFrancisco.mci.net
                            [204.70.10.246]
12  328 ms  341 ms  320 ms  mae-west.iij.net [198.32.136.47]
13  337 ms  339 ms  334 ms  PaloAlto0.iij.net [202.232.0.109]
14  488 ms  478 ms  489 ms  iijgate.iij.net [202.232.0.245]
15  517 ms  678 ms  502 ms  otemachi00.iij.net [202.232.1.129]
16  498 ms  495 ms  493 ms  www-nttgw.iij.net [202.232.10.134]
17  550 ms  794 ms  539 ms  www.ntt.co.jp [210.130.164.102]

Trace complete.
```

APPENDIX B

ESSENTIAL DNS

Introduction

The *Domain Name System (DNS)* is a distributed hierarchical naming system used for naming hosts on the Internet and on enterprise-scale TCP/IP networks. It is therefore essential to be able to understand DNS if you plan to use IIS as an Internet server or for large-scale corporate intranets/extranets. This appendix is a brief overview of some of the more essential aspects of DNS as implemented in the Microsoft Windows NT 4.0 operating system, and includes information on

- The history, nature, and purpose of DNS
- Host names and how to resolve them on Microsoft networks
- Installing and configuring Microsoft DNS Server service on Windows NT 4.0 Server

Understanding DNS

DNS is a system for managing the naming of hosts primarily on the Internet and also on enterprise-scale TCP/IP networks. DNS is a client/server system, where DNS clients (called *resolvers*) send name resolution requests to DNS servers (called *name servers*). No single DNS server can handle all name resolution requests; instead, various DNS servers around the world are each responsible for administering a subset of DNS namespace called a *zone of authority*, and together all the DNS servers around the world on the Internet form a distributed database for resolving host names anywhere in the world.

Name resolution is the process whereby a client (resolver) sends a request to a server (name server) requesting that the host name of a third computer (destination or target machine) be resolved into an IP address. For example, suppose you are connected to the Internet and type the command

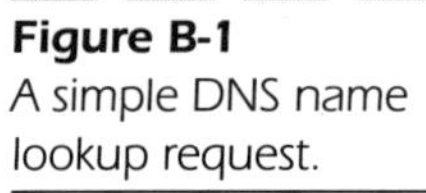

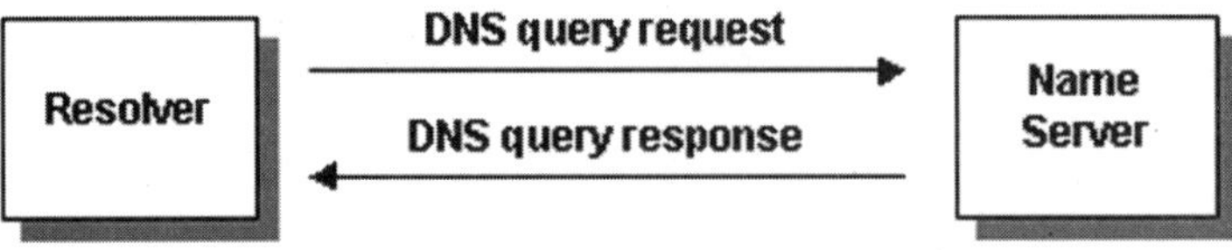

Figure B-1 A simple DNS name lookup request.

```
ping www.yahoo.ca
```

Your machine will first have to resolve the *Fully Qualified Domain Name (FQDN)* `www.yahoo.ca` into its IP address (Fig. B-1). To do this, a DNS *name lookup* request (e.g., "Who the heck is `www.yahoo.ca`?") is sent to a DNS server, and the DNS server returns a *name resolution* response ("`www.yahoo.ca` is 147.75.116.3") with the IP address of the target machine. At this point, `ping` is able to execute (actually `arp` must be used next to resolve the IP address of the target machine into a physical layer network interface card address). If the name server is unable to resolve the request, it may forward the request to another DNS server to do so.

History of DNS

The history of DNS is tightly bound to the history of TCP/IP, discussed in App. A. The original ARPANET (DARPA's precursor to the modern-day Internet) only had a few hundred hosts in the 1970s, so name resolution was performed by copying a simple text file called HOSTS to every machine on the ARPANET. This *HOSTS file* had a static table of mappings between host names (or FQDNs) and their associated IP addresses.

As the ARPANET evolved into the Internet and the number of hosts grew tremendously, a new system for managing the namespace had to be devised, since HOSTS files were growing so large that they took too long to process name resolution requests. This system was called the *Domain Name System (DNS)*, and its new feature was that it divided the namespace of the Internet into a hierarchical structure with machines called name servers each being responsible for administering a small portion of this space. The most widely implemented version of DNS for many years was the *Berkeley Internet Name Daemon (BIND)* server running on Unix. Windows NT 4.0 has its own implementation called *Microsoft DNS Server service*, which is the main focus of this appendix.

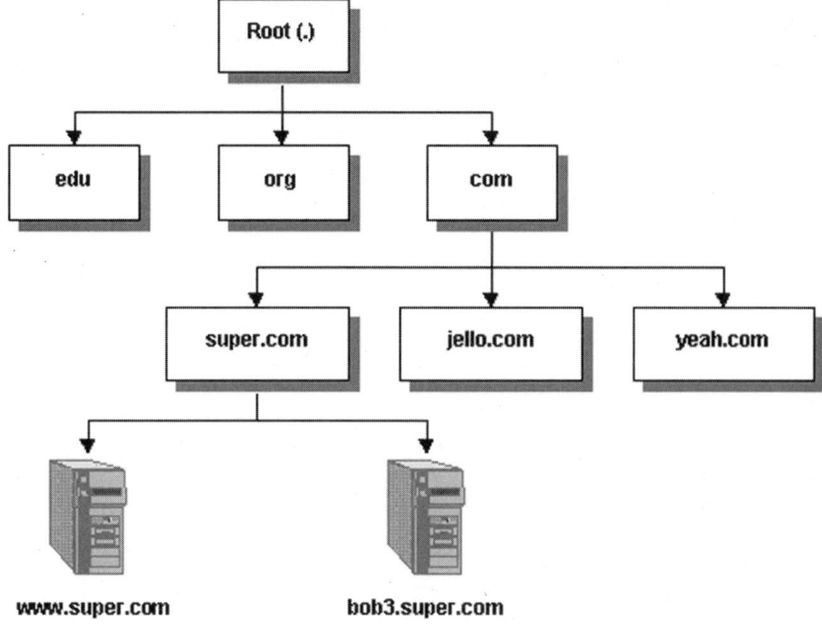

Figure B-2 Hierarchical structure of the DNS namespace.

Understanding the DNS Namespace

The namespace of all Internet hosts around the world is organized in a hierarchical structure (Fig. B-2). At the top of the namespace is the *root domain,* which is symbolized by a period (.), though usually this is omitted and a null label is used instead.

Beneath the root domain are the *top-level domains.* These include domains like the following:

com	Commercial companies anywhere in the world
edu	Universities, mostly in the United States
org	Not-for-profit organizations
net	Networking companies
gov	U.S. government
mil	U.S. military

Other top-level domains include two-letter country codes, such as these:

ca	Canada
uk	United Kingdom
fr	France

Beneath the top-level domains, individual companies and organizations can apply for and register their own *second-level domains,* such as

- microsoft.com
- yahoo.ca
- canola-council.org
- manitobanow.com

and so on. If your company wants to register a domain name and will be connected to the Internet, contact *Internic* at

```
www.internic.com
```

to find out how to register a domain name for your company.

Beneath the second-level domains, you can either register *subdomains* or, more usually, register names of individual TCP/IP host computers, such as

- ftp.supercorpinc.com
- www.supercorpinc.com
- charlie.supercorpinc.com

and so on. These last expressions are examples of *Fully Qualified Domain Names,* or *FQDNs.* Thus for example, in the FQDN `charlie.supercorpinc.com` we have

- The host `charlie`
- The second-level domain `supercorpinc.com`
- The top-level domain `com`

To configure host names on a Microsoft Windows NT 4.0 machine, open the Network program in Control Panel, select the Protocols tab, select TCP/IP, and click PROPERTIES to open the Microsoft TCP/IP Properties dialog box. Select the DNS tab and enter your desired Host Name in the textbox.

By default on Windows NT, the host name is the same as the NetBIOS name entered in the Computer Name textbox on the Identification tab of the Network program in Control Panel. But the host name doesn't have to be the same as the NetBIOS name.

Host names should be composed only of letters, numbers, and hyphens. Do not use the underscore or other special characters, even though these are allowed for the NetBIOS name. If you don't follow this rule, your host name resolution will fail. To determine the hostname of your computer from the command line, type

```
hostname
```

How the DNS Namespace Is Administered

Ideally, each domain in the DNS space would have its own DNS server. For example, if the company SuperCorp Inc. has 20,000 computers, then it would most likely have its own DNS server (or probably several) for resolving name lookup requests for anything in the `supercorpinc.com` domain. The administrators of SuperCorp Inc. would be responsible for setting up and administering their own name servers for local name resolution within the company. The local name servers would be responsible for a *zone of authority* that includes all hosts (or portions of hosts if there are multiple name servers) within the `supercorpinc.com` domain.

In practice, however, many domain names either are used by small companies or apply only to a single Web server and at an Internet service provider (ISP) that houses the Web site for the company owning that domain. In this case, names in the domain would be resolved using the DNS server belonging to and administered by the ISP.

A *zone of authority* is the section of the DNS namespace that a particular DNS server is responsible for. DNS servers can have authority over

- One or more domains
- Some, all, or none of the subdomains for any domain

Regarding how they relate to other name servers and are configured, DNS servers can be configured as follows:

- *Primary name servers* store their *zone data* (hostname to IP mapping files) as local files.
- *Secondary name servers* receive their zone data from a *master name server* across the network by means of a process called a *zone transfer*. Secondary name servers provide redundancy and load balancing, but zone transfers can increase network traffic.
- *Master name servers* are a source of zone data for secondary name servers, and may be either primary or secondary name servers themselves.

- *Caching-only name servers* are not authoritative for any domain, but merely cache name lookup queries and their results (the other kinds of name servers above also cache name lookups, but caching-only name servers *only* cache name lookups and do not have any zone information).

How DNS Queries Are Performed

Two types of queries can be sent by a resolver to a name server:

- *Recursive queries* basically mean, "Please give me the IP address corresponding to this host name, and if you can't then please return an error indicating that the data does not exist."
- *Iterative queries* basically mean, "Please give me the IP address corresponding to this host name, and if you can't then give me the IP address of another name server that might be able to help me."

There is also a third type of query that is a bit different. These are called *inverse queries*, and basically mean, "Please give me the host name corresponding to this IP address." Inverse queries make use of a special domain called `in-addr-arpa` that is used for inverse name lookups. We won't be considering this type of query any further, though.

Here is a scenario to illustrate how name resolution might work in a large company that has its own DNS server and is also connected to the Internet (Fig. B-3). Let's say that someone in the company tries to browse the site `www.yahoo.com` using Internet Explorer. Before an HTTP GET request can be sent to the Web server hosting this site, the host `www.yahoo.com` must be resolved to an IP address. Here are the steps in Fig. B-3, which are typical:

1. A *recursive* query is sent by the resolver (client) to the company local name server, which basically says, "Either resolve the host name `www.yahoo.com` or give me an error telling me it doesn't exist." This places the burden of the further work on the company local name server.
2. The local name server looks in its zone database and realizes it can't answer the query. Since it has to give an answer one way or another, it sends an *iterative* query to a root name server, saying, "Who the heck is `www.yahoo.com`?" There are fewer than a dozen root name servers in the world, and their responsibility is to keep track of who the top-level domain name servers are.

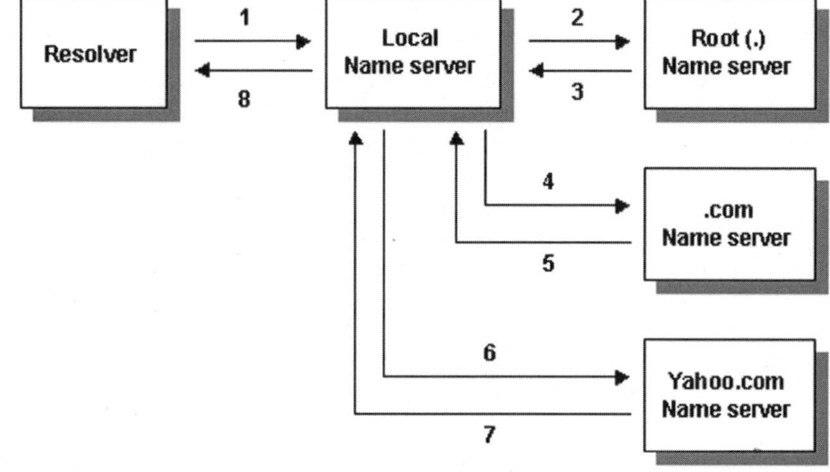

Figure B-3 Example of a DNS name query being executed.

3. The root name server receives the query and sends an answer to the local name server, saying, "I'm sorry, I don't know who `www.yahoo.com` is, but here is the IP of a `.com` name server who can probably help you."
4. The local name server then sends an iterative query to the `.com` name server saying, "Who the heck is `www.yahoo.com`?"
5. The `.com` name server replies to the local name server, saying, "I'm sorry, I don't know who `www.yahoo.com` is, but here is the IP address of the name server that is authoritative over the `yahoo.com` second-level domain." There are a number of `.com` name servers in the world, and they are responsible for resolving second-level domains under the `.com` top-level domain.
6. The local name server then sends an iterative query to the name server that is authoritative over the `yahoo.com` domain, saying, "Who the heck is `www.yahoo.com`?"
7. The name server that is authoritative over the `yahoo.com` domain replies to the local name server saying, "Oh yeah! I know just whom you're talking about. The IP address for the host `www.yahoo.com` is etc."
8. The local name server *caches* the results of the whole series of queries and responses (in case something similar is requested soon), and returns the IP address for `www.yahoo.com` to the resolver (client) that requested it.

Microsoft Methods for Name Resolution

With Windows NT, there are two basic kinds of name resolution when using TCP/IP:

- Resolve NetBIOS names (computer names) into IP addresses (*NetBIOS name resolution*).
- Resolve host names into IP addresses (*host name resolution*).

These two methods of name resolution use different procedures for resolving the requested name into an IP address.

An example of when NetBIOS name resolution would be used with Microsoft platforms would be if you tried to map a drive to a network share at the command line using the NetBIOS command `net use`:

```
net use m: \\<server_name>\<share_name>
```

where <server_name> is the NetBIOS name of the server you are mapping to. Other examples of when NetBIOS name resolution would occur include

- Accessing a network resource using Windows Explorer
- Browsing Network Neighborhood for a network resource
- Mapping a drive to a network share by right-clicking on My Computer and selecting Map Network Drive from the shortcut menu

An example of when host name resolution would be used with Microsoft platforms would be if you used any TCP/IP utility from the command line, for example the utility `ping`.

```
ping daisy.mycorpinc.com
```

or simply

```
ping daisy
```

where the host name is `daisy` and the FQDN is `daisy.mycorpinc.com`. Other examples of when host name resolution would occur include

- Browsing an Internet site using Internet Explorer
- Using other TCP/IP utilities like `Telnet`, `tracert`, and so on
- Accessing a database or mail server that uses a Windows Sockets (Winsock) programming interface

We will not look any further at the process for resolving NetBIOS names on the network. Instead, Fig. B-4 illustrates the process by which host names (or FQDNs) are resolved on a TCP/IP network by Microsoft platforms. The process may or may not go through all seven steps, depending on how TCP/IP is configured on the computers and whether

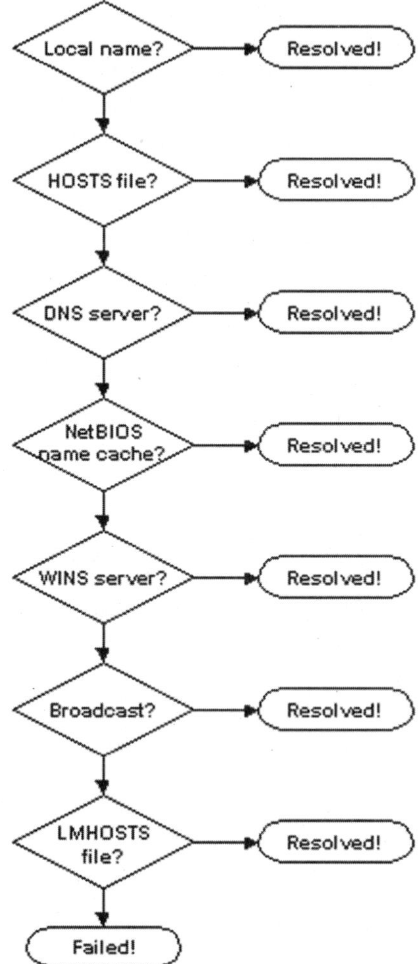

Figure B-4 Microsoft methods for resolving host names or FQDNs.

an earlier step succeeds or not. A step will be skipped if it is not configured in the TCP/IP settings of the client that is trying to resolve the host name.

Here is a brief explanation of each step, assuming for this scenario that the user typed

```
ping hal.mycorpinc.com
```

at the command line of the user's local machine:

1. The user's local machine first checks to see whether its *own* host name is `hal`. If it is, it returns its own IP address and `ping` then executes.
2. If that fails, the local machine parses its HOSTS file (if there is one). The HOSTS file contains static host name to IP mappings and can be used as an alternative to DNS servers for small TCP/IP networks. On a Windows NT system the HOSTS file is located in

   ```
   C:\winnt\system32\drivers\etc\HOSTS
   ```

   The sample HOSTS file that installed here when TCP/IP is installed on your Windows NT system initially contains instructions on how to construct a HOSTS file, plus one mapping: `127.0.0.1 = localhost.`
3. If that fails, the local machine sends a name lookup query to the DNS server specified in its TCP/IP properties (or by the DHCP server scope options). If the DNS server does not respond after 5 seconds, the query is resent after 10, 20, 40, 5, 10, and 20 seconds more.

If these three methods fail, then the local host may attempt to perform the following steps, if TCP/IP is configured to allow these. These steps are actually NetBIOS name resolution steps; that is, if host name resolution fails, the Microsoft platform will attempt to use NetBIOS name resolution to resolve the host name to an IP address.

4. The local machine checks its local NetBIOS name cache to see if the mapping is present there.
5. If that fails, the local machine tries three times to contact a WINS server (if one has been specified in the TCP/IP settings for the local machine).

6. If that fails, the local machine sends out three broadcast NetBIOS name requests to the local network.
7. If that fails, the local machine parses its LMHOSTS file (if there is one). The LMHOSTS file contains static NetBIOS name to IP mappings, and can be used as an alternative to WINS servers for small networks. On a Windows NT system the LMHOSTS file is located in

   ```
   C:\winnt\system32\drivers\etc\LMHOSTS
   ```

   The sample LMHOSTS.SAM file that is installed here when TCP/IP is installed on your Windows NT system initially contains no mappings but only instructions on how to construct a valid LMHOSTS file.
8. If that fails, then an error is returned indicating that the host name cannot be resolved.

Looking at the above process, it is quite possible that it could take as long as several minutes to successfully resolve a host name to an IP address, and that doesn't even include iterative queries to other DNS servers!

Installing DNS Server Service

Before you install Microsoft DNS Server service on a Windows NT 4.0 Server, you must ensure that TCP/IP is properly installed on the machine, and that the host name and domain name are properly specified on the DNS tab of the Microsoft TCP/IP Properties sheet, and that the IP address of the DNS server is specified in the DNS Service Search Order on the DNS tab also. See App. A for instructions on how to perform these steps.

Once this is done, install the Microsoft DNS Server service by performing the following steps: Click START, SETTINGS, CONTROL PANEL, NETWORK to open the Network dialog box. Select the Services tab and click ADD to open the Select Network Service dialog box (Fig. B-5). Select Microsoft DNS Server and click OK. Enter the path to the Windows NT source files in the Windows NT Setup box and click CONTINUE to install the files for the service. When this is finished, click CLOSE and then click YES when prompted to restart the computer. When the machine boots

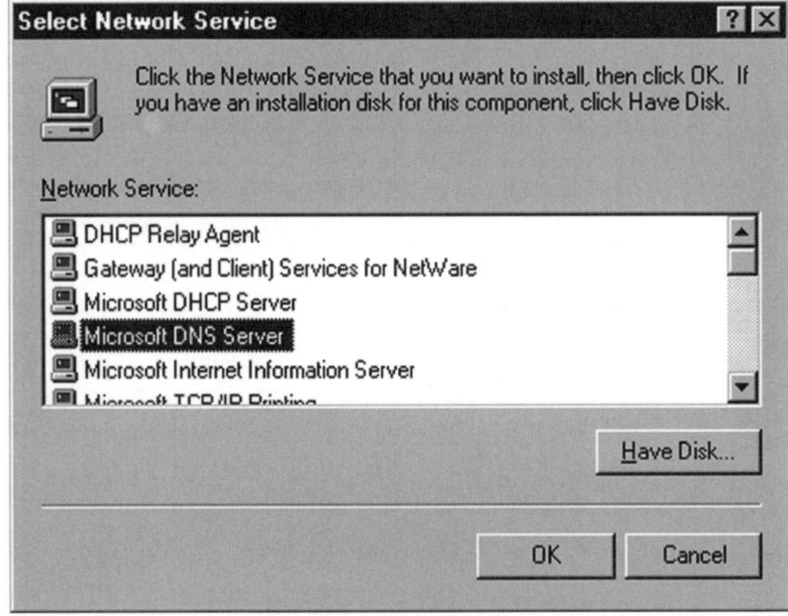

Figure B-5 Installing the Microsoft DNS Server service.

up again, the DNS service will be installed and will start automatically on startup.

Walkthrough: Configuring Microsoft DNS Server

A full treatment of configuring Microsoft DNS Server is beyond the scope of this appendix, since it depends greatly on the portion of the DNS namespace over which the server will be authoritative, and on how the server will be configured for iterative queries and zone transfers with other DNS servers. This walkthrough will be limited to creating a primary zone and adding a new host record to the server.

Click START, PROGRAM FILES ADMINISTRATIVE TOOLS, DNS MANAGER to open the Domain Name Service Manager window (Fig. B-6). The *Domain Name Service Manager* is a GUI-based utility for configuring the DNS database files and other associated DNS files. These files are ASCII text files and are located in

```
C:\winnt\system32\dns\
```

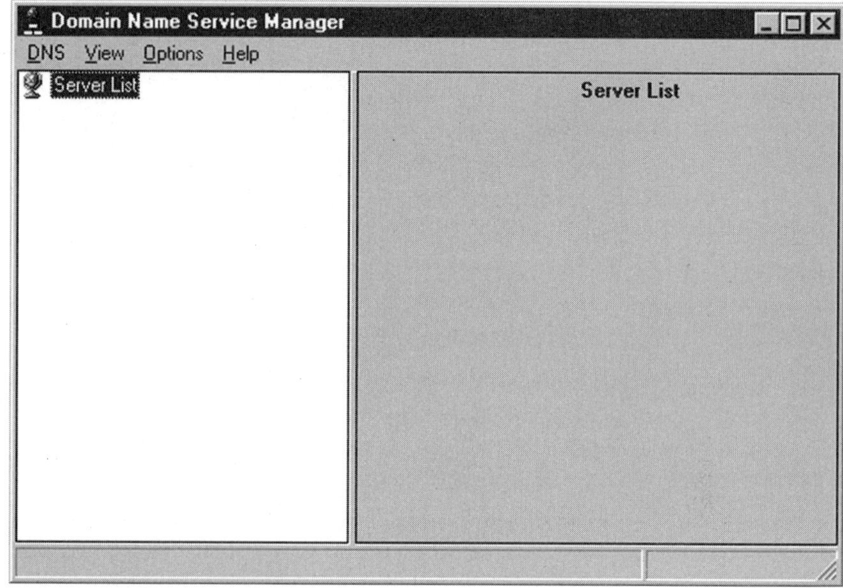

Figure B-6 The Domain Name Service Manager window.

Included are the following text files:

- `<zone>.dns` files contain resource records for a given zone (an example of such a file would be `mycorpinc.com.dns`).
- `z.y.x.w.in-addr.arpa` contains the reverse lookup records.
- `cache.dns` contains the FQDNs and IP addresses of root name servers on the Internet.
- `boot` is not RFC-compliant and is not needed, but it can be used to control how the DNS server behaves upon startup.

Included in the above path are also sample files for each of the above, and instructions on how you can create DNS files manually using a text editor like Notepad.

In the Domain Name Service Manager window, select DNS, NEW SERVER from the menu to open the Add DNS Server box (Fig. B-7). Enter the IP address of your DNS server and click OK to return to the Domain Name Service Manager window.

Double-click on the node for the new server, and you will see an icon for *Cache* underneath it. Your DNS Server is now functioning as a *caching-only DNS server* at this point, and has no authority over any portion of the DNS namespace (Fig. B-8).

Select the icon for the DNS server and select DNS, NEW ZONE from the menu bar to open the Creating new zone for <IP_address> wizard (Fig.

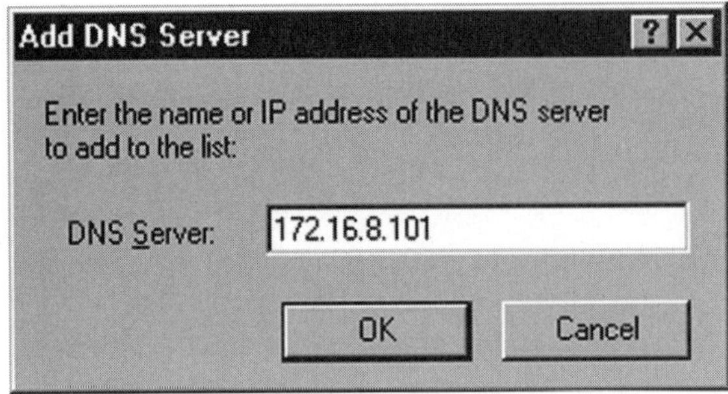

Figure B-7 Adding a new DNS server to the Domain Name Service Manager.

B-9). Select PRIMARY to create a *primary zone* (one in which the resource records are stored on the local machine) and click NEXT.

In the next step of the wizard, enter the domain name `mycorpinc.com` in the Zone Name textbox (or any other domain name you want to use) and press the tab key to automatically suggest the Zone File as `mycorpinc.com.dns`. This zone file will contain the host records for hosts on the `mycorpinc.com` domain that will be resolved using this DNS server (Fig. B-10). Click NEXT and then FINISH.

The Domain Name Service Manager uses the TCP/IP settings of the server to create a set of default host records for the server itself (Fig. B-11). The records created in this instance include

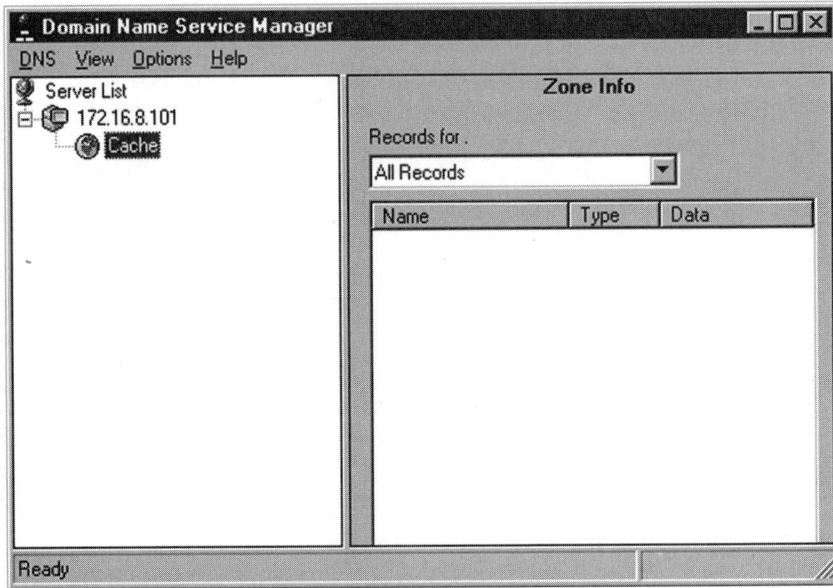

Figure B-8 The new DNS server is a caching-only server at this point.

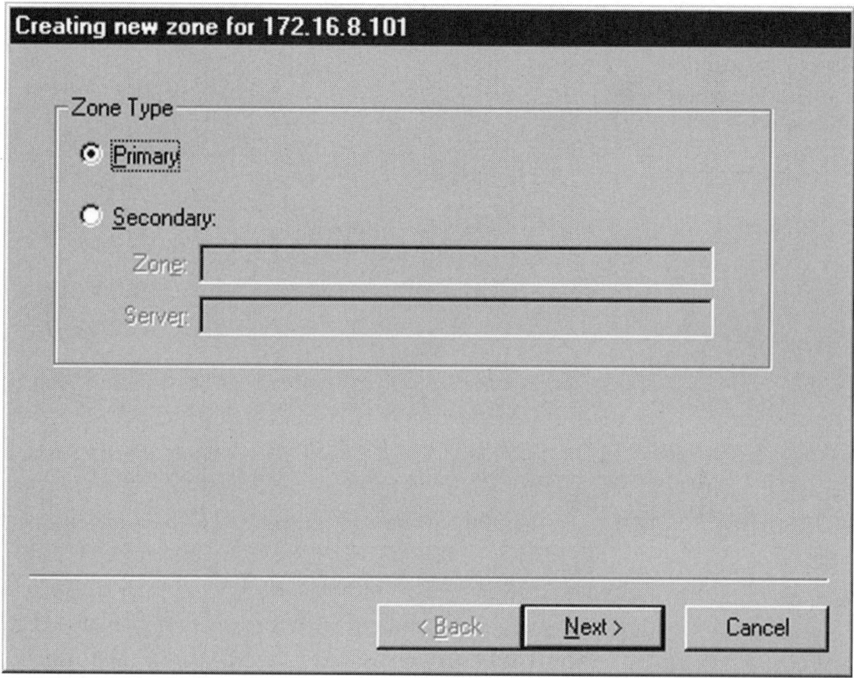

Figure B-9
The wizard for creating a new zone.

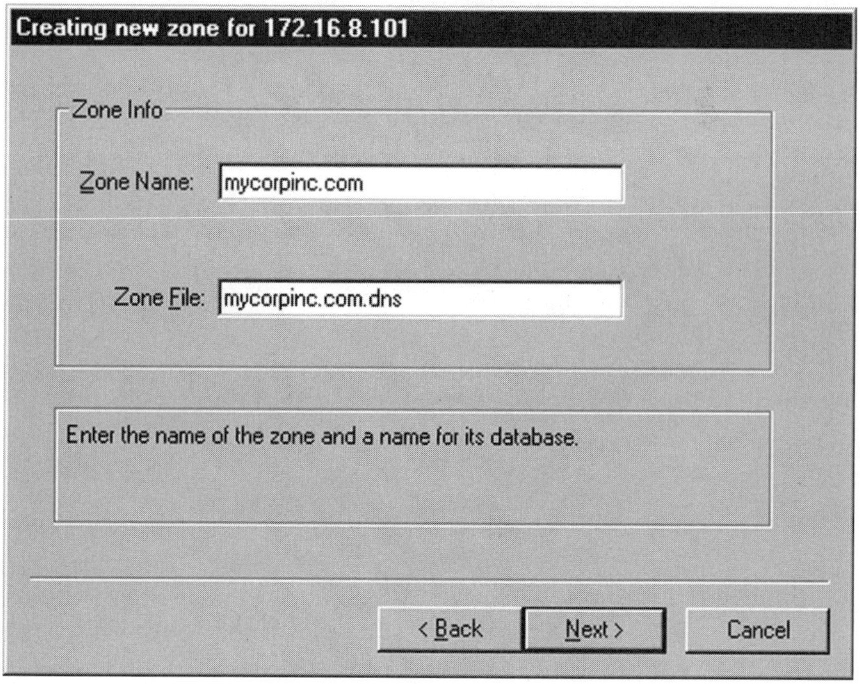

Creating new zone for 172.16.8.101

Zone Info

Zone Name: mycorpinc.com

Zone File: mycorpinc.com.dns

Enter the name of the zone and a name for its database.

< Back | Next > | Cancel

Figure B-10
Specifying a zone name and zone file.

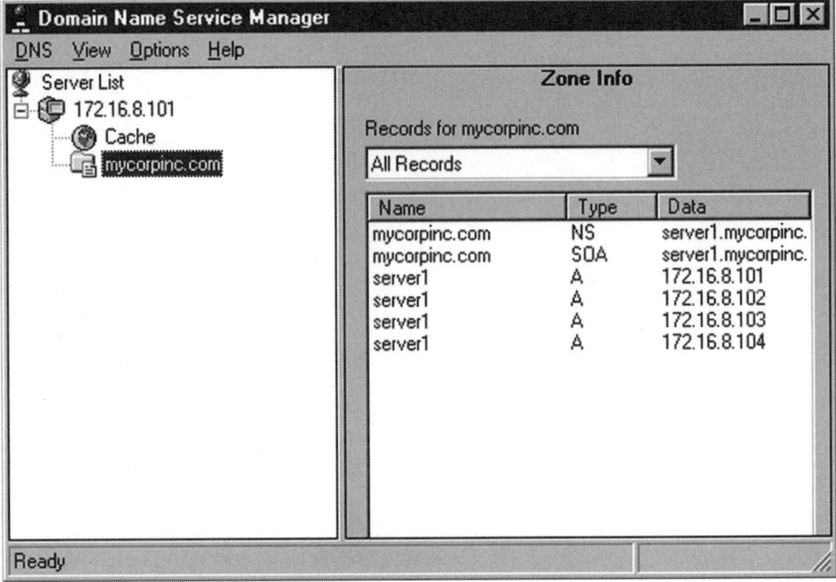

Figure B-11 The new primary zone with its default host records.

- *SOA (Start of Authority) record,* which defines the basic parameters of the DNS zone
- *NS (Name Server) record,* which lists the server as a name server
- *A (host) record,* which maps the server's IP address to its host name (in this case the server is multihomed, so there are four A records)

Select the `mycorpinc.com` zone icon and select DNS, NEW HOST from the menu bar to open the New Host dialog box (Fig. B-12). This is where you can create new mappings for the DNS database. Enter in a Host Name (we chose super2) and enter the Host IP Address for the host.

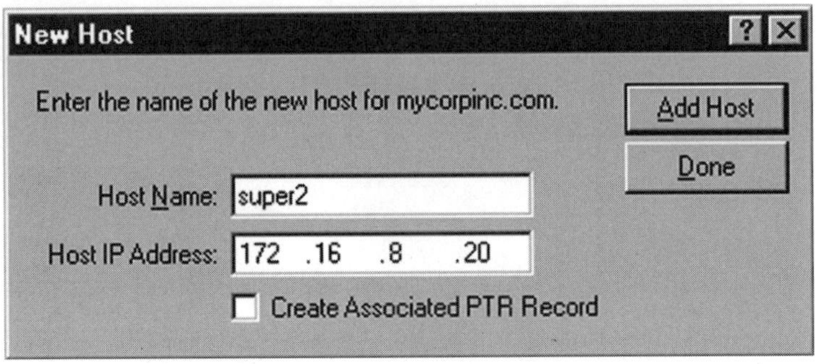

Figure B-12 Adding a new record for a host.

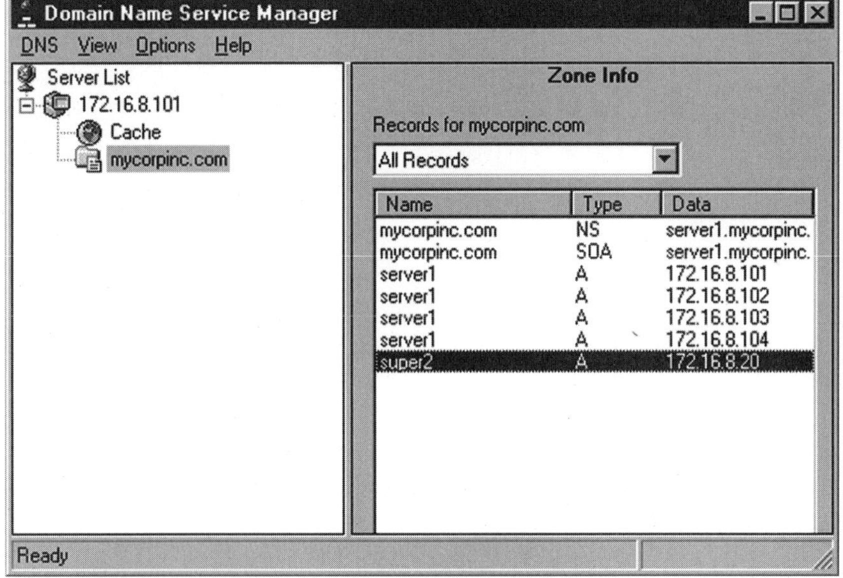

Figure B-13 The new record is visible in the Domain Name Service Manager.

Click the checkbox if you want to create a *PTR record* for inverse name resolution through the `in-addr-arpa` zone. Click ADD HOST and then DONE. The new record has been created in the zone (Fig. B-13). To view the record details, double-click on the record.

There is a *lot* more to configuring DNS, but this is all we can cover in this brief appendix. Refer to the *Windows NT 4.0 Server Resource Kit* for more information on configuring DNS.

INDEX

J

K

L

M

N

Z

ABOUT THE AUTHOR

Mitch Tulloch is a trainer and consultant with Productivity Point, a leading Microsoft products training firm, and is a Microsoft Certified Trainer as well as a Microsoft Certified Systems Engineer.